THE TRADE POLICY REVIEW MECHANISM

INTERNATIONAL ECONOMIC LAW

Andrew D. Mitchell is Professor at Melbourne Law School, The University of Melbourne
Tania Voon is Professor at Melbourne Law School, The University of Melbourne

The *International Economic Law* series, established by the late Professor John H. Jackson, addresses a range of issues in international economic law, which includes international trade law, international investment law, and the global financial order. The Series aims to encourage interest in the broad contours of international economic law, heightening awareness of its significance across the globe as well as its continuous interactions with other areas. The Series Editors encourage quality submissions from a wide range of perspectives, including doctrinal, theoretical, empirical, and interdisciplinary. Novel and cutting edge research is particularly welcome, as are contributions from both emerging and established scholars from around the world.

ALSO PUBLISHED IN THIS SERIES

Mega-Regional Trade Agreements: CETA, TTIP, and TiSA
New Orientations for EU External Economic Relations
Edited by Stefan Griller, Walter Obwexer, and Erich Vranes

Small and Medium-Sized Enterprises in International Economic Law
Edited by Thilo Rensmann

Domestic Law in International Investment Arbitration
Jarrod Hepburn

Treaty Shopping in International Investment Law
Jorun Baumgartner

Good Faith and International Economic Law
Edited by Andrew D. Mitchell, M Sornarajah, and Tania Voon

Development at the WTO
Sonia E. Rolland

The BRIC States and Outward Foreign Direct Investment
David Collins

The Trade Policy Review Mechanism

A Critical Analysis

MATHIAS KENDE

OXFORD
UNIVERSITY PRESS

OXFORD
UNIVERSITY PRESS

Great Clarendon Street, Oxford, OX2 6DP,
United Kingdom

Oxford University Press is a department of the University of Oxford. It furthers the University's objective of excellence in research, scholarship, and education by publishing worldwide. Oxford is a registered trade mark of Oxford University Press in the UK and in certain other countries

First Edition published in 2018

Published in the United States of America by Oxford University Press
198 Madison Avenue, New York, NY 10016, United States of America

British Library Cataloguing in Publication Data
Data available

Library of Congress Control Number: 2017958193

ISBN 978–0–19–881761–1

Foreword

The Trade Policy Review Mechanism (TPRM) is the second mainstay of institutional reform, next to binding dispute settlement, within the new World Trade Organization (WTO) established in 1995. Periodical reporting on trade policy of WTO Members and periodic peer review and discussion of the state of play all seek to bring about greater transparency and induce, where necessary, domestic reform by exerting peer pressure via naming and shaming policies which exert negative effects. Other than in dispute settlement the lawfulness of measures is not foregrounded; instead, political considerations and feasibility of reform and adjustments recommended take centre stage. While the dispute settlement system attracts greatest attention in the literature, the TPRM is granted less attention, beyond comments on individual country reports, both in terms of their negotiating history and development. Little was known in detail about the gradual development of TPRM, which took place via a process of trial and error. Vast amounts of materials needed to be analysed and discussed which would help explore the scope of review, its potential effects, and its relationship to judicial dispute settlement.

The present book undertakes just this task. It presents a thorough history of TPRM organized in three stages, from the early days in 1999 to the sixth appraisal completed in 2016. These periods are analysed in parallel using the same criteria, focusing on individual reports, their periodicity, and informational value, and on participation by governments and the role of the Secretariat. In using these criteria, the author depicts the evolution of the system, leading to an assessment of strengths and weaknesses, and he submits proposals for further reform. He concludes that TPRM has worked reasonably well but concludes that the system could and should do better than it currently does.

This book amounts to the most comprehensive and authoritative work on the subject. Mathias Kende combines experience as a trade diplomat and academic curiosity, both of which strongly contribute to the importance of the work. It is based upon his PhD, researched and written within the Graduate School of Economic Globalization and Integration (EGI) of the World Trade Institute (WTI) at the University of Bern. The doctoral thesis was written under my supervision and benefited from the advice by Professor Michael Hahn, was submitted to the Faculty of Law of the University of Berne, and was adopted *summa cum laude* 26 May 2016.

Working with Mathias Kende was truly enriching. In doctoral seminars, he introduced professors and fellow students to a subject which is of increasing practical relevance and importance to other fields of international law, beyond the World Trade Organization.

Thomas Cottier
Former Managing Director of the World Trade Institute,
Professor Emeritus of European and International Economic Law
at the University of Bern

The Trade Policy Review Mechanism (TPRM) is at the heart of the World Trade Organization (WTO), the guardian of the multilateral trading system. Its work is undertaken in the Trade Policy Review Body (TPRB), which together with the WTO's General Council and its Dispute Settlement Body (DSB), is the trinity that forms the structure of the WTO. There is good reason for this. The fundamental objective of the TPRM is transparency, a transparency that will inform all Members of the WTO, and the world at large, about the trade policies and measures of their fellow Members, facilitate a critical discussion of a Member's policy stance, and, in so doing, encourage a greater adherence to the disciplines of the WTO, thus improving the ability of all Members to benefit from the gains from trade, the ultimate objective of the WTO.

None of this is obvious. Not all Members are always aware of the effects of their own policies, either internally or externally. It is not immediately clear to many, for example, that an import restriction is a de facto export tax which may work against a development strategy, nor that a self-sufficiency policy in agriculture may harm food security, in that it could constrain the gross domestic product (GDP) and thus the purchasing power for food. In addition, an instrument of one Member may frustrate the economic goals of another: think only of distorting domestic support in some of the larger economies that limits the ability of others to take advantage of their comparative advantage in the area, to the detriment of their growth. It is the task of the TPRM to shed light on these matters, to ensure that Members do not trade with each other in the dark where vested interests can gather huge, unearned rents, to ensure that when Members negotiate with each other on improving the WTO they do so in full knowledge of the policies and instruments of their partners. This is particularly important for smaller Members who often lack the resources for gathering information about others and would thus be placed at an unfair disadvantage. The same applies to traders—the documents produced by the TPRM are in the public domain, informing the trading community of opportunities and constraints. In short, the TPRM is a vital instrument.

This volume does an excellent job of explaining and analysing the TPRM. As Dr Kende notes, it is producing good work but it can be improved. By and large, its transparency function is up to par—it is at the root of the reason why the WTO has a superb database—but its 'naming and shaming' could be strengthened, as could its analytics. Both will require the co-operation of the Members, the former for a greater willingness to accept not only praise but also criticism and the latter to provide more resources: neither will obviously happen. Yet, in an environment of significant change in trading conditions (creeping protectionism) and products (value chains and electronic commerce), Members would benefit enormously from an improved TPRM. In this context, Mathias Kende has presented us with an essential piece of work.

Dr Clemens Boonekamp
Former Director of the Trade Policy Review Division (TPRD) (1989–2009)
and the Agriculture and Commodities Divisions (AGCD) (2009–12)
at the World Trade Organization, and partner at the IDEAS Centre

Series Editors' Preface

International economic law faces challenging times, exemplified as much by the United States' withdrawal from the signed *Trans-Pacific Partnership* agreement as by continuing difficulties in multilateral negotiations at the World Trade Organization (WTO). And while delays are nothing new in international trade negotiations, political problems in the reappointment of WTO Appellate Body Members now pose a major potential stumbling block to the WTO dispute settlement system as well. This situation threatens a second major pillar of the WTO—a pillar that has typically in the past represented stability and faith in the multilateral trading system notwithstanding slow progress in negotiations.

At such a time, a third and often overlooked pillar of the WTO—the Trade Policy Review Mechanism (TPRM)—increases in significance. The express purpose of the TPRM is 'to contribute to improved adherence by all Members' to the WTO agreements 'and hence to the smoother functioning of the multilateral trading system, by achieving greater transparency in, and understanding of, the trade policies and practices of Members'.[1] Yet the TPRM is also 'not ... intended to serve as a basis for the enforcement of specific obligations under the Agreements or for dispute settlement procedures';[2] nor is the TPRM one of the agreements covered by WTO dispute settlement. The non-binding nature of the TPRM process and its separation from the WTO dispute settlement system may paradoxically enhance its utility when the dispute settlement system is struggling and the core foundations of international trade law are under threat. In one sense, the non-binding nature of the TPRM harkens back to the more power-based system of the *General Agreement on Tariffs and Trade 1947*, whereas the WTO dispute settlement system represents a step change towards a more rule-based system. At the same time, the less rigid TPRM framework offers the possibility of enhanced transparency and understanding of the WTO while capitalising on the strengths of diplomacy through the function of 'naming and shaming' in a relatively collegial environment, as a means towards increasing WTO compliance.

Mathias Kende's book is a timely contribution to the under-researched TPRM by an expert in WTO law with an insider's understanding of not only the legal nuances but also the practical implications and day to day operations of this unusual system, thanks to his previous academic pursuits in addition to his roles in private legal practice and as a government representative of Belgium. Yet Kende is not content to write to a WTO audience in investigating WTO matters. Instead, his critical analysis includes historical, theoretical and comparative elements, placing the TPRM in the context of other forms of peer review, including in other international organisations such as the International Monetary Fund (IMF), the Organisation

[1] *Marrakesh Agreement Establishing the WTO*, Annex 3 (Trade Policy Review Mechanism), [A(i)].
[2] Ibid.

for Economic Co-operation and Development (OECD), and the United Nations Framework Convention on Climate Change (UNFCCC). By analysing the TPRM within this broader context, Kende is able to identify weaknesses in current TPRM approaches that could be remedied by recourse to strategies adopted in other peer review mechanisms.

Kende undertakes a detailed examination of the five formal appraisals of the TPRM's operations between 1989 (when it was temporarily established during the Uruguay Round negotiations that led to the creation of the WTO in 1995, formalising the TPRM) and 2013. He agrees with these appraisals' generally positive conclusions about the TPRM. But he delves further, assessing the TPRM with respect to the three elements he identifies as core to an international peer review mechanism of this kind: the simultaneous objectives of transparency and encouraging compliance; a legal or institutional structure that enables peer surveillance, which may include an investigative process; and active participation by the party under review and its peers, often in addition to the relevant Secretariat or other entities.

Kende rejects a strict dichotomy between the TPRM and WTO dispute settlement, instead incorporating a fascinating study of the interaction between these two systems, including by tracking the invocation of trade policy reviews in disputes and investigating the implications of trade policy reviews of respondent WTO Members before and after particular disputes. These kinds of connections are rarely made and are of particular interest to those outside the WTO's intergovernmental community, since delegates' references to particular disputes or trade policy reviews in various WTO meetings may otherwise go undisclosed or unnoticed.

Kende concludes that the primary objective of the TPRM is rightly understood as transparency, but its corrective function deserves greater institutional attention. Both of these objectives could be promoted by structural modifications he proposes, including increased attention to processes for following up TPRM recommendations after reviews of individual Members. Moreover, processes for reviewing the TPRM itself could be improved. Kende highlights the surprising absence of a comprehensive empirical analysis of the impact of trade policy reviews on WTO Members' trade policy; instead, the impact is generally assumed to be positive. In other contexts, such studies have sometimes led to significant institutional reforms to international peer review mechanisms. In relation to participation in the TPRM, he proposes greater provision for input by external stakeholders in individual trade policy reviews and in reviews of the TPRM itself. More fundamentally, Kende questions whether current levels of participation by WTO Members and the Secretariat in trade policy reviews are sufficient to achieve the twin objectives of transparency and compliance.

Some of Kende's proposals would require budget increases within the WTO and within WTO Members. He acknowledges that these may not be likely. But others would not necessarily require greater financial resources. For example, he suggests that the Secretariat's reporting style has become more deferential to Members under review, while the contribution of discussants to TPRM debates has diminished. Changes to both these elements could allow for a more interactive or even intrusive engagement within each trade policy review, increasing both transparency and the possibility of effective naming and shaming of WTO Members. If the WTO pillars of negotiation and dispute settlement continue to waver, these softer forms of persuasion may become all the more crucial.

Andrew D Mitchell
Tania Voon
January 2018

Acknowledgements

> As our circle of knowledge expands, so does the circumference of darkness surrounding it.
>
> Albert Einstein

This book, which is based on a review of my doctoral thesis, would not have been possible without the invaluable encouragement, continuous inspiration, and never-ending support of my PhD supervisor and thesis promoter, Professor Thomas Cottier. Few people have such an enormous grasp of international economic law. Even fewer have managed to translate it into a truly academic powerhouse which continuously shapes the contours of the global WTO debate. Yet this is exactly what Professor Cottier achieved over the years with the World Trade Institute (WTI). As one of his last PhD students, I owe this book to him. In addition, I am also extremely indebted to Dr Clemens Boonekamp, whose experience and insight as the longest serving director of the Trade Policy Review Division (TPRD) (1998–2009) remains unmatched.

As a former PhD student, I have benefited tremendously from the WTI's doctoral programme (efficiently run by Dr Shaheeza Lalani) and from its seminars (often in the presence of distinguished former Trade Policy Review Mechanism (TPRM) practitioners such as Malcolm Bosworth). In addition, the lectures which I had the privilege to deliver to the students of the 2013 and 2014 intakes of the Master of International Law and Economics (MILE) programme of the WTI proved to be extremely valuable in testing some of the arguments elaborated in this book.

My gratitude also goes to numerous experts—within and beyond the WTO—who have contributed their thoughts and views to my thinking. As a career diplomat formerly posted to the trade section of the Belgian Permanent Representation to the UN, the WTO, and other international institutions in Geneva (2011–15), I was lucky to have privileged access to both.[1]

Within the WTO, these specialists include, first and foremost, the five successive directors of the Trade Policy Review Division. As well as Dr Boonekamp (1998–2009), these are Frank Wolter (1989–91), Peter Tulloch (1991–98), Dr Richard Eglin (2009–14), and Willy Alfaro (2014–present). They have all been very generous in sharing their wisdom and experience. I also want to thank Sergios Stamnas, who never struggled to meet my requests for yet another TPRM-related working

[1] This book expresses the strictly personal views of the author and does not necessarily represent the official and/or informal views of the Belgian Ministry of Foreign Affairs, Foreign Trade and Development Co-operation, nor of any of its staff. While this book is based upon the input of many experts, none except the author bears any responsibility for any error or omission in this book. The author can be reached at mathiaskende@hotmail.com.

lunch. In the context of legal affairs, I am also grateful to Professor Peter Van den Bossche (Member and subsequent Chair of the Appellate Body) and to Professor Gabrielle Marceau (who was in the Cabinet of Director-General Lamy and the Legal Affairs Division). In the framework of economic affairs, I am indebted to Dr Robert Teh (Economic Research Division).

Beyond the WTO, I treasure my multiple conversations with the Belgian Permanent Representative, François Roux, and the head of our economic section, Serge Dickschen. In addition, I was obliged to benefit from various interesting discussions with Professor Carolyne Deere (Oxford University, Global Economic Governance Programme), Professor Armin von Bogdandy (Max Planck Institute for Comparative Public Law and International Law), Professor Jan Wouters (Catholic University of Leuven, Institute for International Law), Professor Joost Pauwelyn (Graduate Institute in Geneva) and Dr Gustavo Luengo (European Commission). As a Belgian diplomat, I was also greatly inspired by discussions with colleagues from other WTO delegations, including but not limited to those of Argentina, Australia, Brazil, Canada, China, Chile, Colombia, Egypt, the European Union, India, Indonesia, Israel, Japan, Korea, Nigeria, Norway, Panama, Peru, Russia, Singapore, South Africa, Switzerland, Thailand, Tunisia, and the United States.

Finally, above all, I wish to thank my family, especially my wife and children for supporting their often absent (-minded) husband and father. It is to them that this book is dedicated.

Summary Contents

Contents

Table of Cases

EUROPEAN COURT OF JUSTICE

UNITED STATES

Table of Legislation

Table of International Instruments

List of Abbreviations

APRM	African Peer Review Mechanism
DAC	Development Assistance Committee
DSB	Dispute Settlement Body
EC	European Communities
EU	European Union
FOGS	Functioning of the GATT System
FSB	Financial Stability Board
GATT	General Agreement on Tariffs and Trade
GI	Geographical Indications
HRC	Human Rights Council
IMF	International Monetary Fund
LDC	Least-Developed Country
NEPAD	New Partnership for Africa's Development
OECD	Organisation for Economic Co-operation and Development
OHCHR	Office of the United Nations High Commissioner for Human Rights
SPS	Sanitary and Phyto-sanitary
TBT	Technical Barriers to Trade
TPR	Trade Policy Review
TPRB	Trade Policy Review Body
TPRD	Trade Policy Review Division
TPRM	Trade Policy Review Mechanism
TRIMS	Trade-Related Investment Measures
TRIPS	Agreement on Trade-Related Aspects of Intellectual Property Rights
TSR	Triennial Surveillance Review
UN	United Nations
UNCTAD	United Nations Conference on Trade and Development
UNFCCC	United Nations Framework Convention for Climate Change
UPR	Universal Periodic Review
WTO	World Trade Organization

I
Introduction

A. Executive Summary

In order to enhance the transparency of Members' trade policies and thus facilitate the smooth functioning of the multilateral trading system, the World Trade Organization (WTO) Membership established the Trade Policy Review Mechanism (TPRM), the function of which is to review the trade policies of each WTO Member at regular intervals.[1] Annex 3 of the Marrakesh Agreement therefore establishes that the four Members with the largest shares of world trade be reviewed every two years, that the next sixteen be reviewed every four years, and that others be reviewed every six years. A longer period may be fixed for Least-Developed Country (LDC) Members. Reviews are conducted by the Trade Policy Review Body (TPRB) on the basis of a policy statement by the Member under review and a report prepared by the staff of the Secretariat's Trade Policy Review Division (TPRD). In preparing the reports, the Secretariat seeks the co-operation of the relevant Members but has the sole responsibility for the facts presented and the views expressed.[2]

This book demonstrates that the narrative according to which the TPRM has been functioning relatively well as the WTO's mechanism for peer review is correct. A descriptive review of a series of other internationally recognized mechanisms for peer review (in the respective contexts of the International Monetary Fund (IMF), the Organisation for Economic Co-operation and Development (OECD), the Financial Stability Board (FSB), the United Nations Framework Convention for Climate Change (UNFCCC) and its Kyoto Protocol, the African Peer Review Mechanism (APRM), and the Human Rights Council's (HRC) Universal Periodic Review (UPR)) shows that these mechanisms have certain elements in common which are related to their objectives, structure, and participation. The historic development of these elements has also gradually transformed the TPRM into the WTO's (fully fledged) mechanism for peer review. Moreover, the TPRB participants agree with the finding that the TPRM has been performing reasonably well. First, they

[1] Marrakesh Agreement Establishing the World Trade Organization (15 April 1994) <https://www.wto.org/english/docs_e/legal_e/29-tprm_e.htm> accessed 20 May 2017 (hereafter Marrakesh Agreement Establishing the World Trade Organization).

[2] WTO, *Exploring the Links between Subsidies, Trade and the WTO* (WTO 2006) 109.

recognize that the TPRM's pursuit of increased transparency has been functioning rather well. Second, the consecutive appraisals of the TPRM have confirmed that the mechanism's enabling institutional structure has allowed for periodic reviews, a more or less standardized form of reporting, and well-structured TPRB meetings. Third, in terms of participation, the TPRB Members acknowledge the efficiency of the Secretariat's reporting, recognize a relatively good governmental participation, and seem to value the participation of discussants in order to make Trade Policy Reviews (TPRs) more interactive.

Nonetheless, this book demonstrates that too much complacency with the overly positive assessment of the TPRM as a result of the consecutive appraisals is not in order. This is partly due to the lack of critical comparative studies with regard to mechanisms for peer review and their impact on the (national or international) context, to the rather repetitive and sometimes almost ritualistic character of the TPRM's appraisal process and yearly TPRB documentation,[3] and to the (often overly) diplomatic courtesy with which the appraisal processes and reviews tend to be handled.[4]

This raises the question as to how far the TPRM has been able to function successfully as the WTO's mechanism for peer review. This book attempts to answer this question on the basis of the following perspectives: (a) *ratione temporis*, the book is based on an analysis of all reviews which have taken place since the establishment of the mechanism in 1989 up until the TPR of Costa Rica of 24–26 September 2013; (b) *ratione materiae*, this book examines the TPRM's gradual development from Article X of the General Agreements on Tariffs and Trade (GATT, 1947) to the modifications to the mechanism as a result of its fifth appraisal (2013). This book's conclusions dwell substantially upon the latest modifications proposed as a result of the sixth appraisal which preceded the Eleventh Ministerial Conference of the WTO in Buenos Aires (scheduled for December 2017); and (c) *ratione personae*, this book is based on an analysis of the capabilities and the performance of the main entities (ie staff of the TPRD Secretariat, governments under review, and their peers and the discussants) which participate in the reviews.

Based upon these elements, this book is not to diminish the TPRM's actual value but comes to the conclusion that the TPRM *should* and *could* do better.

The TPRM *should* do better. The TPRM will need to prove that it can do more and better with less. In organizational terms, its relatively constant human resources and possibly diminishing budgetary means will need to match the requirements of a growing WTO Membership. In terms of substance, the TPRM will need to prove that it still has the analytical/political capacity to remain the WTO's foremost transparency forum. In addition, the mechanism

[3] Very often, the structure and content of consecutive TPRM appraisals and yearly TPRB reports are based on somewhat minimalistic modifications to their (respective) previous versions.

[4] As a Belgian career diplomat, the author took active part in the 2011 and 2013 appraisals of the TPRM.

could do better. In terms of objectives, increased attention should be paid to the TPRM's secondary goal of naming and shaming. This book does not argue for an amendment of the TPRM which would transform it into some appendix of the WTO's Dispute Settlement Body (DSB). Nevertheless, it aims to draw attention to the fact that the naming and shaming function of the TPRM—though of a secondary nature—should be fully recognized. This is not only in line with academia's persistent questioning of the scope of the TPRM's (current) objectives and with Members' continuing attempts to bring some of the TPRM's findings into DSB proceedings but it may also result in increased attention to and participation in the TPRM. With regard to some of the TPRM's structural elements (ie periodicity, reporting, and the structure of the meetings), this book proposes several institutional modifications. These are based on empirical analysis which proves (a) that the current periodicity requirements for individual reviews seldom work; (b) that the informational added value which is claimed to derive from the TPRM's double reporting structures (ie individual reviews and yearly overviews) is positive but sometimes overrated, whereas the reporting structures' added value in terms of naming and shaming is clearly present but underrated; and (c) that the current structure of individual review meetings is still sub-optimally geared towards the provision of increased transparency and naming and shaming, especially in comparison with similar structures for peer review which are proper to other international organizations. Increased transparency and peer pressure derive from a higher attendance and an increased participation. This book therefore advocates primarily for a funding which is better articulated, for a higher governmental attendance and participation in reviews, and for a bigger institutional role of discussants. Currently, these elements function below their potential.

In order to achieve these objectives, this book argues that the TPRB should start by drastically modifying the current procedures of its appraisal mechanism and thereby find inspiration in the more elaborate procedures of other appraisal mechanisms which are part and parcel of other (international) mechanisms for peer review. After all, the WTO is a Member-driven organization. If the Membership is not fully appraised of the TPRM's actual challenges and future potential, chances for change are minimal.

B. Motivation

The motivation behind this book is based on three elements. Each provides sufficient ground for further academic analysis of the TPRM. Taken together, these arguments overwhelmingly militate for extensive further research of the topic.

First of all, academic output with regard to the TPRM has been relatively limited. Despite the fact that the TPRM celebrated its twentieth anniversary in 2009, the number of books and articles with regard to the TPRM is somewhat small in comparison with those covering the DSB, and minuscule in proportion to those with regard to the WTO.[5] Although a variety of writings has analysed specific Trade Policy Reviews[6] and although some articles have covered the functioning of the

[5] This anniversary resulted in an electronic compilation of all 305 TPRs undertaken in the period 1989–2009. These covered 136 of the then 153 WTO Members <http://www.amazon.in/Years-Trade-Policy-Reviews-1989-2009/dp/928703821X> accessed 20 May 2017.

[6] Anne O Krueger, 'US Trade Policy and the GATT Review' [1995] The World Economy: Global Trade Policy 65; VN Balasubramanyam, 'India's Trade Policy Review' [1995] The World Economy: Global Trade Policy 79; Kym Anderson, 'The GATT's Review of Australian Trade Policy' [1995] The World Economy: Global Trade Policy 91; Sübidey Togan, 'Trade Policy Review of the Republic of Turkey' [1995] The World Economy: Global Trade Policy 107; Merle Holden, 'GATT Trade Policy Review—South Africa: 1993' [1995] The World Economy: Global Trade Policy 121; Timothy J Kehoe, 'A Review of Mexico's Trade Policy from 1982 to 1994' [1995] The World Economy: Global Trade Policy 135; Mathias Kende, 'Monetary affairs in the WTO Trade Policy Review Mechanism' in Thomas Cottier, Rosa M Lastra, Christian Tietje, and Lucia Satragno (eds), *The Rule of Law in Monetary Affairs* (Cambridge University Press 2014) 384; Ronald J Wonnacott, 'Canadian Trade Policy: The GATT's 1995 Review' [1996] The World Economy: Global Trade Policy 67; Jacques Pelkmans and Antonia Giulia Carzaniga, 'The Trade Policy Review of the European Union' [1996] The World Economy: Global Trade Policy 81; George Fane, 'The Trade Policy Review of Indonesia' [1996] The World Economy: Global Trade Policy 101; Mordechai E Kreinin, 'Israel's Trade Policy Review' [1996] The World Economy: Global Trade Policy 119; Robert M Stern, 'The Trade Policy Review of Japan' [1996] The World Economy: Global Trade Policy 133; Jan Willemn Gunning, 'The Trade Policy Review of Zimbabwe' [1996] The World Economy: Global Trade Policy 157; Renato G Flores, 'Brazilian Trade Policy and the WTO' [1997] The World Economy: Global Trade Policy 615; AG (Sandy) Cuthbertson, 'The Trade Policy Review of Sri Lanka' [1997] The World Economy: Global Trade Policy 633; Paul Collier, 'The Trade Policy Review of Uganda' [1997] The World Economy: Global Trade Policy 649; Heinz Hauser and Robert Straw, 'Swiss Trade Policy and the 1996 WTO Review' [1997] The World Economy: Global Trade Policy 665; Robert M Stern, 'The WTO Trade Policy Review of the United States' [1998] The World Economy: Global Trade Policy 483; Sarath Rajapatirana, 'Columbian Trade Policies and the 1996 WTO Trade Policy Review' [1998] The World Economy: Global Trade Policy 515; Martin Richardson, 'New Zealand Trade Policy and the 1996 WTO Review' [1998] The World Economy: Global Trade Policy 529; Arvind Panagariya, 'The WTO Trade Policy Review of India, 1998' [1999] The World Economy: Global Trade Policy 799; PKM Tharakan, 'Beyond Transparency: An Analysis of the Trade Policy Review of the European Union' [1999] The World Economy: Global Trade Policy 825; Julio Berlinski, 'The WTO Trade Policy Review of Argentina' [2000] The World Economy: Global Trade Policy 1195; Peter G Warr, 'Thailand's Post-crisis Trade Policies: The 1999 WTO Review' [2000] The World Economy: Global Trade Policy 1215; Paul G Hare, 'Trade Policy Review of Poland, 2000' [2001] The World Economy: Global Trade Policy 1179; Kumar Ratnesh, *WTO (World Trade Organization): Structure, Functions, Tasks and Challenges* (New Delhi 2002); Prema-chandra Athukorala, 'Malaysian Trade Policy and the 2001 WTO Trade Policy Review' [2002] The World Economy: Global Trade Policy 1297; Francis Teal, 'Export Growth and Trade Policy in Ghana in the Twentieth Century' [2002] The World Economy: Global Trade Policy 1319; VN Balasubramanyam, 'India: Trade Policy Review' [2002] The World Economy: Global Trade Policy 1357; Joze P Damijan and Boris Majcen, 'Trade Policy in a Small Advanced Transition Economy: Trade Policy Review of Slovenia, 2002' [2002] The World Economy: Global Trade Policy 1369; Chris Milner, 'Trade Policy in Burundi: Reform Without Political Stability' [2004] The World Economy: Global Trade Policy 1363; Keith Head and John Ries, 'Regionalism Within Multilateralism: The WTO Trade Policy Review of Canada' [2004] The World Economy: Global Trade Policy 1377; Prema-chandra Athukorala, 'Trade Policy Making in a Small Island Economy: The WTO Review of the Maldives' [2004] The World Economy: Global Trade Policy 1401; Andrew McKay, 'Trade Policy Issues in a Small African Economy: The Trade Policy Review of The Gambia 2004' [2005] The World Economy: Global Trade Policy 1197; SM Thangavelu and Mun-Heng Toh, 'Bilateral WTO-Plus Free Trade Agreements: The WTO Trade Policy Review of Singapore 2004' [2005] The World Economy: Global Trade Policy 1211; Sübidey Togan, 'Turkey: Trade Policy Review' [2005] The World Economy: Global Trade Policy 1229; Thomas J Prusa, '2004 Trade Policy Review—The United States' [2005] The World Economy: Global Trade Policy 1263; PKM Tharakan, 'Storm Signals: An Analysis of the Trade Policy Review of the European Communities' [2006] The World Economy: Global Trade

TPRM from a more systemic perspective,[7] very few of them have analysed the functioning of the TPRM from a detailed historical, institutionally systemic, and exclusively TPRM-related angle. Notable exceptions are Donald Kessings' book, *Improving Trade Policy Reviews in the World Trade Organization*,[8] Axel Borrmann and Georg Koopmann's study, *Adapting the WTO Trade Policy Reviews to the Needs of Developing Countries: Starting Points and Options*,[9] Arunabha Ghosh's unpublished PhD thesis, '*Hear no evil, see no evil, do no evil*',[10] and three books by Chinese

Policy 1301; Jong-Eun Lee, 'Identifying Trade Structure and Macroeconomic Caveats: The Post-crisis of Korea' [2006] The World Economy: Global Trade Policy 1311; Arne Melchior, 'The Most and Least Favoured Nations: Norway's Trade Policy in Perspective' [2006] The World Economy: Global Trade Policy 1329; Bala Ramasamy and Matthew Yeung, 'Malaysia—Trade Policy Review 2006' [2007] The World Economy: Global Trade Policy 1193; Rodney D Ludema, 'Allies and Friends: The Trade Policy Review of the United States, 2006' [2007] The World Economy: Global Trade Policy 1209; Michael Henry, 'Formulating Trade Policy in a Small Hydrocarbon-dependent Economy: The Case of Trinidad and Tobago' [2007] The World Economy: Global Trade Policy 1222.

[7] Richard Blackhurst, 'Strengthening GATT Surveillance of Trade-Related Policies' in Meinhard Hilf and Ernst-Ulrich Petersman (eds), *The New GATT Round of Multilateral Trade Negotiations: Legal and Economic Aspects* (Kluwer Law and Taxation Publishers 1988); HJ Bourgeois, 'GATT Surveillance of Trade Related Policies: A Comment' in Meinhard Hilf and Ernst-Ulrich Petersman (eds), *The New GATT Round of Multilateral Trade Negotiations: Legal and Economic Aspects* (Kluwer Law and Taxation Publishers 1988); Asif H Qureshi, 'The New GATT Trade Policy Review Mechanism: An Exercise in Transparency or "Enforcement"' (1990) June, Journal of World Trade 149; Victoria Curzon Price, 'GATT's New Trade Policy Review Mechanism' (1991) 14(2) The World Economy 27; Victoria Curzon Price, 'New Institutional Developments in GATT' (1992) 1(1) Minnesota Journal of Global Trade 227; Petros Mavroidis, 'Surveillance Schemes: The GATT's New Trade Policy Review Mechanism' (1992) 13(2) Michigan Journal of International Law 399; Asif H Quereshi, 'Some Reflections on the GATT TPRM, in the Light of the Trade Policy Review of the European Communities—A Legal Perspective' (1992) 26(6) Journal of World Trade 103; Roderick Abbot, 'GATT and the Trade Policy Review Mechanism: Further Reflections on Earlier Reflections' (1993) 27(3) Journal of World Trade 117; Asif H Qureshi, 'Some Lessons from "Developing Countries" Trade Policy Reviews in the GATT Framework: An Enforcement Perspective' (1995) 18(3) The World Economy 489; Asif H Quereshi Asif, *The World Trade Organization: Implementing Trade Norms* (Manchester University Press 1996); Sam Laird, 'The WTO's Trade Policy Review Mechanism—From Through the Looking Glass' (1999) 22(6) The World Economy 741 (hereafter Laird, 'The WTO's Trade Policy Review Mechanism—From Through the Looking Glass'); Joseph F Francois, 'Maximizing the Benefits of the Trade Policy Review Mechanism for Developing Countries' [1999] Tinbergen Institute and CEPR < https://www.iatp.org/sites/default/files/Maximizing_the_Benefits_of_the_Trade_Policy_5.htm> accessed 6 May 2017; Joseph F Francois, 'Trade Policy Transparency and Investor Confidence: Some Implications for an Effective Trade Policy Review Mechanism' (2001) 9(2) Review of International Economics, 303; Valentin Zahrnt, 'The WTO's Trade Policy Review Mechanism: How to Create Political Will for Liberalization' (2009) 11 ECIPE Working Paper <http://www.ecipe.org/app/uploads/2014/12/the-wto2019s-trade-policy-review-mechanism-how-to-create-political-will-for-liberalization-1.pdf> accessed 6 May 2017; Sam Laird and Raymundo Valdés, 'The Trade Policy Review Mechanism', in A Narlikar, M Daunton, and RM Stern (eds), *The Oxford Handbook on The World Trade Organization* (Oxford University Press 2012); Craig VanGrasstek, *The History and Future of the World Trade Organization* (WTO 2013); Julien Chaisse and Mitsuo Matsuhita, 'Maintaining the WTO's Supremacy in the International Trade Order: A Proposal to Refine and Revise the Role of the Trade Policy Review Mechanism' (2013) 16(1) Journal of International Economic Law 9.

[8] Donald Kessing, *Improving Trade Policy Reviews in the World Trade Organization* (Institute for International Economics 1998) (hereafter Kessing, *Improving Trade Policy Reviews in the World Trade Organization*).

[9] Axel Borrmann and Georg Koopmann, *Adapting the WTO Trade Policy Reviews to the Needs of Developing Countries: Starting Points and Options* (Hamburg Institute of International Economics 2002), (hereafter Borrmann and Koopmann, *Adapting the WTO Trade Policy Reviews to the Needs of Developing Countries: Starting Points and Options*).

[10] Arunabha Ghosh, 'See No Evil, Speak No Evil, The WTO, The Trade Policy Review Mechanism, and Developing Countries' (DPhil thesis, University of Oxford 2008). Some of these findings were

scholars on the TPRM (including works published in 1991 and 2012).[11] Moreover, even these academic contributions to today's understanding of the TPRM could profitably be further updated or completed. Kessing's book was published more than a decade ago and was therefore only able to cover the TPRM's first ten years of existence. Borrmann and Koopmann's study took a very specific angle of analysis. Their study, conducted at the request of the German Federal Ministry for Economic Co-operation and Development, was explicitly tasked with analysing how the TPRM could be further adapted to the needs of developing countries and LDCs.[12] A similar (pro-) development angle seems to be present in Ghosh's unpublished PhD thesis. Moreover, this thesis dates back to 2008 and was essentially based on an analysis of TPRs which took place between 1995 and 2007. Finally, the Chinese publications on the TPRM of 1991 and 2012 remain untranslated. This book therefore aims to enrich the existing academic literature by providing a long-term historical narrative, a systemic institutional analysis, and a neutral (ie non-development-oriented) focus.

Second, the need for further analysis of the TPRM remains high. The TPRM is one of the few WTO entities that triggers a unique theoretical osmosis between trade diplomacy, political naming and shaming, and the Membership's interpretation of the WTO rulebook. It should therefore also claim its rightful place as one of the (two) '*crown-jewels*' of the WTO,[13] more so since the TPRM is one of the oldest WTO entities which is considered to have run smoothly to the benefit of all WTO Members.[14] In addition, the TPRD has almost consistently been described as one of the substantial recipients of the GATT and WTO budgets.[15] However, in spite of an ever-increasing WTO Membership and a correlated increase in the TPRD's workload, the public's general understanding of the TPRD's activities is rarely backed by accurate knowledge of its underpinning financial resources. It is therefore essential not only to analyse past and current financial data in order to ascertain the TPRD's efficacy but also to forecast what this might mean in terms of future performance.

tabled in two separate articles: Arunabha Ghosh, 'Developing Countries in the WTO Trade Policy Review Mechanism' (2010) 9(3) World Trade Review 419; and Arunabha Ghosh, 'Strengthening WTO Surveillance: Making Transparency Work for Developing Countries', in Carolyn Deere Birbeck (ed), *Making Global Trade Governance Work for Development: Perspectives and Priorities from Developing Countries* (Cambridge University Press 2011).

[11] Chen Yong Mei, *WTO Trade Policy Review Mechanism, Legal Issues* (1991); Qu Yan Ying, *WTO Trade Policy Review Mechanism* (2009); Qu Yan Ying, *The Principles and Functions of WTO Trade Policy Review Mechanism* (2012).

[12] Borrmann and Koopmann, *Adapting the WTO Trade Policy Reviews to the Needs of Developing Countries: Starting Points and Options* 11.

[13] The Dispute Settlement Body is often said to be the (only) crown jewel of the WTO.

[14] *Appraisal of the Operation of the Trade Policy Review Mechanism—Draft Report to Ministers* (30 September 1999) WT/TPR/W/24; *Second Appraisal of the Operation of the Trade Policy Review Mechanism—Draft Report to Ministers* (12 August 2005) WT/TPR/W/33; *Draft—Third Appraisal of the Operation of the Trade Policy Review Mechanism* (15 October 2008) WT/TPR/W/38; *Fourth Appraisal of the Operation of the Trade Policy Review Mechanism* (17 November 2011) WT/TPR/W/44; *Fifth Appraisal of the Trade Policy Review Mechanism, Ministerial Conference, Ninth Session, Bali, 3–6 December 2013* (28 October 2013) WT/MIN(13)/5.

[15] Interview with a diplomat of the Delegation of the Russian Federation (Geneva, 20 January 2014); Interview with a diplomat of the Delegation of Canada (Geneva, 20 January 2014); Interview with a diplomat of the Delegation of the European Union (Geneva, 27 January 2014); Interview with

This would not only enable the TPRD to do more and better with less in the short term but also potentially enable the mechanism to transform itself (again) into '*The show in town*' in the longer term.[16] In this regard, it should be noted that theoretical and budgetary understanding and knowledge—in[17] and beyond the WTO[18]—about the TPRM and its activities seem to have been starkly reduced.

Finally, the TPRM can be analysed as a mechanism for peer review. Interestingly, academic literature with regard to the concept of peer review is growing but still remains relatively scarce in view of the enormous use which is made of the concept. Given the remarkable epistemological and symbolic burden placed on peer review, observers have sometimes lamented that '*it is surprising that so little research has analysed the concept either empirically (in its actual daily applications) or philosophically (as one of the conditions for the possibility of (academic) knowledge)*'[19] and underlined the fact that '*the jury, in general, is still out on their effectiveness*'.[20] After all, peer review remains a tool which not only helps shape our general understanding but also delineates the borders of our (scientific) knowledge. This book aims to fill part of this lacuna by analysing the institutional development and functioning of the TPRM as the WTO's mechanism for peer review.

C. Methodology

The second chapter of this book analyses whether the TPRM has institutionally evolved into the WTO's mechanism for peer review. A threefold methodology is applied. First, some international mechanisms for peer review are identified, both through the historical development of the concept of peer review and through the identification of some of the concept's actual embodiments. The next section then attempts to distil a peer review mechanism's theoretical core elements in terms of objectives, structure, and participants. The remainder of the first part of Chapter II analyses whether the gradual establishment of the TPRM has displayed the evolving institutional characteristics of a nascent ideal mechanism for peer review. In order to do so, it examines

a diplomat of the Delegation of the Republic of Argentina (Geneva, 6 August 2014); Interview with a diplomat of the Delegation of the Republic of Peru (Geneva, 6 May 2015); Interview with a diplomat of the Delegation of the Republic of Israel (Geneva, 7 September 2015).

[16] Answers from Frank Wolter (first director of the Trade Policy Review Division, 1989–91) to a questionnaire of the author (2 April 2014).

[17] Meetings of the Trade Policy Review Body (TPRB) have consistently been less well-attended than the regular meetings of the General Council or than sessions whereby the General Council was convened to discharge the responsibilities of the Dispute Settlement Body (DSB). Nevertheless, paragraphs 2 to 4 of Article IV of the Marrakesh Agreement imply that the latter two have a similar institutional standing and Membership as the TPRB; WTO, 'WTO Organization Chart', <https://www.wto.org/english/thewto_e/whatis_e/tif_e/org2_e.htm> accessed 13 May 2017.

[18] International Monetary Fund—Independent Evaluation Office, *Involvement in International Trade Policy Issues, Evaluation Report* (IMF 2009) 5; According to a survey of IMF staff, most had never read or were unsure whether they had read a WTO TPR on their country.

[19] Mario Biagioli, 'From Book Censorship to Academic Peer Review' (2002) 12 (1) Emergences: Journal for the Study of Media & Composite Cultures 11.

[20] Edward McMahon and Marta Ascherio, 'A Step Ahead in Promoting Human Rights? The Universal Periodic Review of the UN Human Rights Council' (2012) 18 Global Governance 234.

whether/how the TPRM's core elements (ie objectives, structure, and participants) have gradually appeared throughout the five defining institutional phases of the TPRM. These include: (1) Article X of the GATT (1947),[21] (2) the Tokyo Round negotiations resulting in the Understanding Regarding Notification, Consultation, Dispute Settlement and Surveillance (1979),[22] (3) the (so-called) Wise Men's report, '*Trade Policies for a Better Future: Proposals for Action*' (1985),[23] (4) the Functioning of the GATT System (FOGS) negotiations (1986),[24] and (5) the provisional adoption of the TPRM during the Montreal mid-term review of the Uruguay Round (December 1988),[25] followed by the decision taken by the Trade Negotiations Committee of 12 April 1989 to immediately start with the implementation of the TPRM.

Chapter II will then measure whether the TPRM has been performing well as the WTO's mechanism for peer review, and to what extent. In order to do so, the second part of the chapter (Part B: The TPRM's Performance as the WTO's Mechanism for Peer Review) closely follows the sequence of the first five institutionally mandated appraisals of the TPRM (ie those of 1999, 2005, 2008, 2011, and 2013). For each of the periods covered by these consecutive appraisals, the second part of Chapter II will assess the objectives, structure and participants to the TPRM.

In terms of objectives, Part B will follow a twofold approach. First, academia's (evolving) interpretation of the scope of the TPRM's stated double objectives is contrasted with that of the Membership as expressed in the consecutive appraisals. Second, this part will examine whether and/or to which degree the Members themselves have adhered to the (original) idea of institutionally separating the TPRM from the DSB. Paragraph A of Annex 3 to the Marrakesh Agreement is very clear in stating that the TPRM '*is not, however, intended to serve as a basis for the enforcement of specific obligations under the Agreements or for dispute settlement procedures, or to impose new policy commitments on Members*'.[26] In addition, Annex 3 to the Marrakesh Agreement is not a covered agreement under Appendix I to Annex II to the Marrakesh Agreement which embodies the Understanding on Rules and Procedures Governing the Settlement of Disputes.[27] This part therefore analyses

[21] Article X GATT (1947), Marrakesh Agreement Establishing the World Trade Organization (15 April 1994) <https://www.wto.org/english/docs_e/legal_e/gatt47_01_e.htm> accessed 20 May 2017; Sylvia Ostry traces transparency even further down to the 'vaguely defined yet non-controversial principle' of Article 38 of the Havana Charter of the International Trade Organization; Sylvia Ostry, 'China and the WTO: Transparency Issue' (1998) 3(1) UCLA Journal of International Law and Foreign Affairs 4.

[22] Understanding Regarding Notification, Consultation, Dispute Settlement and Surveillance (28 November 1979) BISD L/4907.

[23] *Trade Policies for a Better Future, Proposals for Action*, Geneva (GATT 1985). This report was also inspired by the 1982 Conference on Trade Policy organized by the Institute of International Economics in Washington, USA; see also Wiliam R Cline (ed), *Trade Policy in the 1980s* (The Institute for International Economics 1983).

[24] Draft Ministerial Declaration on the Uruguay Round (20 September 1986) BISD Min (86)/W/19, 15–16.

[25] Mid-term Review Agreements, News of the Uruguay Round of Multilateral Trade Negotiations, NUR 027, 24 April 1989, 33–36.

[26] Marrakesh Agreement Establishing the World Trade Organization (n 2).

[27] Marrakesh Agreement Establishing the World Trade Organization (15 April 1994) <https://www.wto.org/english/docs_e/legal_e/28-dsu_e.htm#appendix1> accessed 20 May 2017.

whether the TPRM and its findings have nevertheless been invoked within the proceedings of the Dispute Settlement Body.

With regard to structure, Part B of Chapter II will attempt to analyse the strengths and weaknesses of individual TPRs and yearly Overviews of Developments in the International Trading Environment from the dual perspectives of increased transparency and improved naming and shaming.

- First, it analyses whether the institutional periodicity requirements of individual TPRs have functioned well. This part will therefore contrast the recommendations and predictions of the annual TPRB reports with the consecutive implementation of individual reviews.
- It will then attempt to measure how well the TPRM's transparency and naming and shaming objectives have been implemented throughout the TPRM's double reporting structures (ie the individual reviews and the yearly Overviews).

  In this context, this part of the chapter will analyse (available) academic views with regard to individual TPRs' added value in terms of transparency. In order to do so, it attempts to rank these views on the TPRs' added informational value into three categories: (a) TPRs with missing information; (b) TPRs which, according to academia, contain a too positive or a too negative assessment; and (c) TPRs with incorrect information. For each of these three categories, this part contrasts the views of the academics—where possible—with the anonymous perspectives of WTO staff. This part of the chapter will also focus on some twenty trade disputes within the context of the Sanitary and Phytosanitary (SPS) and Technical Barriers to Trade (TBT), examining individual TPRs' structural added value—not only in terms of increased transparency but also in terms of naming and shaming. In this context, the underlying Secretariat reports, government reports, minutes of the meeting, and written questions and answers are studied.

  At the same time, this part of the chapter will pay specific attention to the second structural leg of reporting—the yearly Overviews of Developments in the International Trading Environment. In this regard, it focuses (again) on SPS and TBT measures and examines their structural and substantive coverage. In this regard, this part will assess: (a) whether the Overviews contain a standardized form of reporting on the TPRM's yearly activities; (b) whether and why certain individual TPRs received more attention than others (resulting in a (merited or unwarranted) higher degree of transparency and naming and shaming); and (c) whether the yearly Overview's coverage of SPS and TBT measures was coherent and comprehensive. In this respect, it aims to assess whether the yearly Overviews reported on the identified measures' consecutive coverage—first by the committee(s) concerned, and potentially followed by the TPRM's and the DSB's.
- Third, this part of the chapter will analyse the consecutive modifications to the structure of individual TPR meetings. In this regard, it contrasts the proposals with regard to the procedures of the review meetings which were derived from

the yearly TPRB reports with those structural changes which have resulted from the appraisal process. This part will also analyse whether and/or to which degree these proposed structural changes—*senso lato*—have managed to contribute to increased transparency and naming and shaming, and will examine which proposals were specifically made in order to reinforce the institutional position of the discussant.

In terms of participation, the second part of Chapter II will examine the capabilities and performances of the main participants to the review (ie the government under review and its peers, the Secretariat, and the discussant(s)).[28] The TPRM can only offer added value in terms of increased transparency and effective naming and shaming if it is based on a substantive level of attendance and on a high quality of participation. The Secretariat's participation in the review process will therefore be analysed through the lens of its changing staffing levels, its evolving budgets, and through the Secretariat's internal and external interactions with other divisions of the WTO and the Members. In a similar vein, this part will examine governments' participation in the individual review processes through an analysis of the evolving governmental attendance and participation rates. Finally, the institutionally changing role of the discussant(s) will be analysed through the institutional modifications with regard to the required number of discussants, the degree of discussants' deferral to the Secretariat's and governmental reporting with regard to discussants' propensity to criticize both reports, their willingness to draw upon additional external studies, and with regard to the discussants' evolving positions with regard to issues of compliance and dispute settlement.

Finally, Chapter III draws some conclusions with regard to each of the TPRM's three main building blocks (ie its objectives, structure, and participants). These conclusions are derived from the TPRM's historical and actual performance as analysed throughout this book and tested in the light of the recommendations of the mechanism's most recent sixth appraisal.

[28] The Chair of the TPRB is another prominent participant in the reviews. Nevertheless, in general, his/her interventions are carefully choreographed by the Secretariat; Laird, 'The WTO's Trade Policy Review Mechanism—From Through the Looking Glass' (n 8) 749.

II

Critical Analysis of the TPRM

> The peer review system is satisfactory during quiescent times, but not during a revolution in a discipline such as astrophysics, when the establishment seeks to preserve the status quo.
>
> Hannes Alfvén (Swedish Nobel Laureate for physics)

A. The TPRM as the WTO's Mechanism for Peer Review

1. Mechanisms for peer review: historical conceptual development and actual settings

Before the seventeenth century, the limited literature on peer review makes it almost impossible to trace the gradual evolution of the theoretical concept or its practical applications.[1] Nevertheless, academic observers seem to concur that the conceptual origins of peer review can be found in medical and academic practices in ancient times. Ishaq ibn Ali al-Ruhawi's (854–931 AC) *Ethics of the Physician* recommended that a visiting physician duplicate notes of a patient's condition on every visit. If the patient's condition altered, the notes of the physician would be examined by a medical council composed of the physician's peers. This council would then decide whether the treatment conformed to the required standards of medical care. If the review by the physician's peers was negative, a lawsuit would follow.[2]

The establishment of academies for sciences in the second half of the seventeenth century resulted in a substantial increase in and usage of the concept of peer review. This development had found its origins in Francis Bacon's (1561–1626 AC) *Novum Organum* (1620 AC) which enunciated a universal method for the generation and assessment of new sciences and which consequently inspired many scholars to

[1] Mario Biagioli, 'From Book Censorship to Academic Peer Review' (2002) 12(1) Emergences: Journal for the Study of Media & Composite Cultures 14 (hereafter Biagioli, 'From Book Censorship to Academic Peer Review').

[2] Marcelo Marotti, '*Primum non nocere*: Authors or Reviewers' (2011) 57(5) Revista Da Associacao Medica Brasileira 487; Ray Spier, 'The History of the Peer-Review Process' (2002) 20(8) Trends in Biotechnology 357 (hereafter Spier, 'The History of the Peer-Review Process').

engage in series of meetings to discuss and exchange their views on the unfolding sciences.[3] These meetings were initially informal but became structured via the formal creation of fully fledged academies, first in the United Kingdom with the establishment of the Royal Society of London (1662), then in France with the creation of the Académie Royale des Sciences (1699). These inevitably led to the gradual erosion of (state and religious) monopolies on licensing and censorship. They also resulted in increased scientific output and a corresponding growth in the requirement and demand for mechanisms for formal peer review.[4]

Since the second half of the seventeenth century, a wide variety of scientific disciplines including physical science, psychology, sociology, and medical research has resulted in an enormous literature on and application of peer review.[5] Likewise, the realm of finance, economics, and political affairs has witnessed an exponential increase in the number of mechanisms for peer review. In the context of international monetary affairs, the International Monetary Fund (IMF) has undertaken Article IV consultations from 1978 in order to exercise surveillance on exchange rate policies.[6] In a similar vein, the Development Assistance Committee (DAC)

[3] Spier, 'The History of the Peer-Review Process' (n 2) 357.

[4] Biagioli, 'From Book Censorship to Academic Peer Review' (n 1) 14–35.

[5] Tracey Brown, '*Peer Review and the Acceptance of New Scientific Ideas*' (Sense About Science, Discussion paper from a Working Party on equipping the public with an understanding of peer review, November 2004–May 2004) 49 <http://archive.senseaboutscience.org/data/files/resources/17/peer-Review.pdf> accessed 13 May 2017; Some of this literature is obviously less critical of the concept of peer review than others, cf 'Trouble at the lab—Scientists like to think of science as self-correcting. To an alarming degree, it is not', *The Economist* (London, 19 October 2013) 21–24.

[6] IMF, 'Surveillance' <https://www.imf.org/external/about/econsurv.htm> accessed 13 May 2017; International Monetary Fund—Independent Evaluation Office, *The Historical Development of IMF Governance* (IMF 2008) 11; Petros Mavroidis, 'Surveillance Schemes: The GATT's New Trade Policy Review Mechanism' (1992) 13(2) Michigan Journal of International Law 399–414 (hereafter Mavroidis, 'Surveillance Schemes: The GATT's New Trade Policy Review Mechanism'); A Chayes and AH Chayes, *The New Sovereignty—Compliance with International Regulatory Agreements* (Harvard University Press 1995) 234–42 (hereafter Chayes and Chayes, *The New Sovereignty—Compliance with International Regulatory Agreements*); Michael Mussa, 'IMF Surveillance' (1997) 87(2) The American Economic Review 28 (hereafter Mussa, 'IMF Surveillance'); Armin Schäfer, 'A new form of governance? Comparing the open method of coordination to multilateral surveillance by the IMF and the OECD' (2004), No 04/5, MPIFG working paper <https://www.econstor.eu/bitstream/10419/41651/1/639580173.pdf> accessed 6 May 2017 (hereafter Schäfer, 'A new form of governance? Comparing the open method of coordination to multilateral surveillance by the IMF and the OECD'); The review criterion is whether a Member's economic developments and policies are consistent with the achievement of sustainable growth and domestic and external stability. The consultations thus primarily concern macro-economic and financial sector policies but they also cover structural policies and governance issues to the extent that they are relevant to macro-economic stability; see WTO, Communication from the Working Group on the Interaction between Trade and Competition Policy, WT/WGTCP/W/243, 28 July 2003, 25–27 (hereafter WTO, Communication from the Working Group on the Interaction between Trade and Competition Policy (WT/WGTCP/W/243)); Bessma Momani, 'Assessing the Utility of, and Measuring Learning from, Canada's IMF Article IV Consultations' (2006) 39(2) Canadian Journal of Political Science 249 (hereafter Momani, 'Assessing the Utility of, and Measuring Learning from, Canada's IMF Article IV Consultations'); Domenico Lombardi and Ngaire Woods, 'The Politics of Influence: An Analysis of IMF Surveillance' (2008) 15(5) Review of International Political Economy 711 (hereafter Lombardi and Woods, 'The Politics of Influence: An Analysis of IMF Surveillance'); Adarsh Kishore and Deepak Mohanty, 'How Effective Will the IMF's New Surveillance Framework Be?' (2008) 43 (18) Economic and Political Weekly 31 (hereafter Kishore and Mohanty, 'How Effective Will the IMF's New Surveillance Framework Be?'); Manuela Moschella, 'IMF Surveillance in Crisis: The

of the Organisation for Economic Co-operation and Development (OECD) has been undertaking peer reviews since 1962 with the aim of improving the individual and collective co-operation efforts of its Members.[7] A more recent embodiment of a fully fledged mechanism for peer review can be found in the peer reviews organized by the Financial Stability Board (FSB), the successor to the Financial Stability Forum (FSF) which was established by the G7 Finance Ministers and Central Bank Governors in 1999 in the aftermath of the Asian financial crisis. Since 2010, FSB reviews have resulted in surveillance of the implementation and effectiveness of international financial standards developed by Standard-Setting Bodies (SSBs) and of policies agreed within the FSB.[8] In a similar vein, the United Nations Framework Convention on Climate Change (UNFCCC) and the Kyoto Protocol (which came into force in 2005) both feature elements of peer review. The Framework aims to increase transparency by securing the accurate measurement, reporting, and verification of greenhouse gas emissions under the Protocol and the effective functioning of its carbon-market mechanism. In addition, the Protocol's structures seek to foster compliance with its emission targets.[9] Similarly, the realm of political affairs is

Past, Present and Future of the Reform Process' (2012) 26(1) Global Society 43 (hereafter Moschella, 'IMF Surveillance in Crisis: The Past, Present and Future of the Reform Process').

[7] Fabrizio Pagani, 'Peer Review, A Tool for Global Co-operation and Change' (2002)No 235The OECD Observer <http://oecdobserver.org/news/archivestory.php/aid/881/Peer_review.html> accessed 13 May 2017; Guido Ashoff, '50 Years of Peer Reviews by the OECD's Development Assistance Committee: an Instrument of Quality Assurance and Mutual Learning' (2013) 12 German Development Institute, Briefing Paper <https://www.die-gdi.de/en/briefing-paper/article/50-years-of-peer-reviews-by-the-oecds-development-assistance-committee-an-instrument-of-quality-assurance-and-mutual-learning/> accessed 6 May 2017 (hereafter Ashoff, '50 Years of Peer Reviews by the OECD's Development Assistance Committee: an Instrument of Quality Assurance and Mutual Learning'); The OECD also engages in other kinds of peer review. These include the two-yearly economic surveys undertaken by the OECD Economic and Development Review Committee (EDRC); cf Organisation for Economic Co-operation and Development, About Economic Surveys and the EDRC; <http://www.oecd.org/eco/surveys/abouteconomicsurveysandtheedrc.htm> accessed 13 May 2017.

[8] Financial Stability Board, 'Peer Reviews' <http://www.financialstabilityboard.org/what-we-do/implementation-monitoring/peer_reviews/> accessed 13 May 2017; Financial Stability Board—Standing Committee on Standards Implementation, 'Handbook for FSB Peer Reviews' (FSB 7 January 2014) <http://www.fsb.org/wp-content/uploads/r_140106.pdf> accessed 13 May 2017 (hereafter Financial Stability Board—Standing Committee on Standards Implementation, Handbook for FSB Peer Reviews (FSB 7 January 2014)); Financial Stability Board, 'FSB Framework for Strengthening Adherence to International Standards' (FSB 9 January 2010) <http://www.fsb.org/wp-content/uploads/r_100109a.pdf> accessed 13 May 2017 (hereafter Financial Stability Board, FSB Framework for Strengthening Adherence to International Standards (FSB 9 January 2010)); Larry Cata Backer, 'Private Actors and Public Governance Beyond the State: The Multinational Corporation, the Financial Stability Board, and the Global Governance Order' (2011) 18(2) Indiana Journal of Global Legal Studies 75 (hereafter Backer, 'Private Actors and Public Governance Beyond the State: The Multinational Corporation, the Financial Stability Board, and the Global Governance Order'); Stavros Gadinis, 'The Financial Stability Board: The New Politics of International Financial Regulation' (2013) 48(2) Texas International Law Journal 157 (hereafter Gadinis, 'The Financial Stability Board: The New Politics of International Financial Regulation'); Jan Wouters and Jed Odermatt, 'Comparing the 'Four Pillars' of Global Economic Governance: A Critical Analysis of the Institutional Design of the FSB, IMF, World Bank, and WTO' (2014) 17 Journal of International Economic Law 49 (hereafter Wouters and Odermatt, 'Comparing the 'Four Pillars' of Global Economic Governance: A Critical Analysis of the Institutional Design of the FSB, IMF, World Bank, and WTO').

[9] Farhana Yamin and Joanna Depledge, *The International Climate Change Regime, A Guide to Rules, Institutions and Procedures* (Cambridge University Press 2004) (hereafter Yamin and Depledge, *The*

replete with mechanisms for peer review. These structures can have a regional focus, like the African Peer Review Mechanism (APRM) which was adopted in 2002 by the African Heads of State and Government as a key component of the New Partnership for Africa's Development (NEPAD), designed to promote African good governance and development as contained in NEPAD's Declaration on Democracy, Political, Economic and Corporate Governance.[10] They can also have a universal perspective, like the Universal Periodic Review (UPR) of the United Nations Human Rights Council (UNHRC) which was mandated in 2006 by the UN General Assemblies' Resolution 60/251 to promote and deepen respect for human rights through the provision of feedback to Member states on their human rights performance.[11]

International Climate Change Regime, A Guide to Rules, Institutions and Procedures) 327–97; Jutta Brunneé, Meinhard Doelle, and Lavanya Rajamani (eds), *Promoting Compliance in an Evolving Climate Regime* (Cambridge University Press 2012) (hereafter Brunnée, Doelle, and Rajamani, *Promoting Compliance in an Evolving Climate Regime*) 77–78.

[10] African Union (Assembly of Heads of State and Government) 'Declaration on Democracy, Political, Economic and Corporate Governance' (8 July 2002) AHG/235 (XXXVIII) Annex I (hereafter African Union, Declaration on Democracy, Political, Economic and Corporate Governance); New Partnership for Africa's Development (6th Summit of the NEPAD Heads of State and Government Implementation Committee), 'African Peer Review Mechanism (APRM): Base Document' (9 March 2003) NEPAD/HSGIC/03-2003/APRM/MOU/Annex II (hereafter New Partnership for Africa's Development, African Peer Review Mechanism (APRM), Base Document); New Partnership for Africa's Development (6th Summit of the NEPAD Heads of State and Government Implementation Committee), 'African Peer Review Mechanism Organisation and Process' (9 March 2003) NEPAD/HSGIC/03-2003/APRM/Guideline/O&P (hereafter New Partnership for Africa's Development, African Peer Review Mechanism Organisation and Process); Jinmi Adisa, 'Making the Mechanism Work' (2002) 11(4) African Security Review 110 (hereafter Adisa, 'Making the Mechanism Work'); Ross Herbert, 'The Survival of NEPAD and the African Peer Review Mechanism: A Critical Analysis' (2004) 11(1) South African Journal of International Affairs 21 (hereafter Herbert, 'The Survival of NEPAD and the African Peer Review Mechanism: A Critical Analysis'); Ravi Kanbur, 'The African Peer Review Mechanism—An Assessment of Concept and Design' (2004), January, Cornell University, Working Paper <http://www.arts.cornell.edu/poverty/kanbur/APRM.pdf> accessed 6 May 2017 (hereafter Kanbur, 'The African Peer Review Mechanism—An Assessment of Concept and Design'); Okezie Chukwumerije, 'Peer Review and the Promotion of Good Governance in Africa' [2006–07] North Carolina Journal of International Law and Commercial Regulation 49–114 (hereafter Chukwumerije, 'Peer Review and the Promotion of Good Governance in Africa'); Magnus Killander, 'The African Peer Review Mechanism and Human Rights: The First Reviews and the Way Forward' (2008) 30(1) Human Rights Quarterly 41 (hereafter Killander, 'The African Peer Review Mechanism and Human Rights: The First Reviews and the Way Forward'); Steven Gruzd, 'The African Peer Review Mechanism: Assessing Origins, Institutional Relations and Achievements' (2009) No 29, Governance and APRM Programme, Occasional Paper <http://dspace.africaportal.org/jspui/bitstream/123456789/29715/1/SAIIA%20Occasional%20Paper%20no%2029.pdf?1> accessed 6 May 2017 (hereafter Gruzd, 'The African Peer Review Mechanism: Assessing Origins, Institutional Relations and Achievements'); André Mbata Mangu, 'The African Union and the Promotion of Democracy and Good Political Governance under the African Peer-Review Mechanism: 10 Years On' (2014) 6(1) Africa Review 59 (hereafter Mangu, 'The African Union and the Promotion of Democracy and Good Political Governance under the African Peer-Review Mechanism: 10 Years On').

[11] UNGA Res 60/251 UN Doc A/RES/60/251 (hereafter UNGA Res 60/251); M Cherif Bassiouni and William A Schabas (eds), *New Challenges for the UN Human Rights Machinery—What Future for the UN Treaty Body System and the Human Rights Council Procedures* (Intersentia Publishing 2011) (hereafter Bassiouni and Schabas, *New Challenges for the UN Human Rights Machinery*); Edward McMahon and Marta Ascherio, 'A Step Ahead in Promoting Human Rights? The Universal Periodic Review of the UN Human Rights Council' (2012) 18 Global Governance 231 (hereafter McMahon and Ascherio, 'A Step Ahead in Promoting Human Rights? The Universal Periodic Review of the UN Human Rights Council'); Elvira Dominguez Redondo, 'The Universal Periodic Review: Is there Life Beyond Naming and Shaming in Human Rights Implementation' (2012) 4 New Zealand Law Review 673 (hereafter

Mechanisms for peer review appear to have a bright future. At the European and the international level, political will exists to promote the concept in the widest context of international relations. In addition, there is growing academic interest to study the functioning of peer review from the perspective of political science.

At the European level, former WTO Director-General (DG) Lamy has emphasized that he '*believed that the European experience of... peer review offers interesting avenues for the global level*'. Peer review appeared to him '*an efficient "Westphalian" tool of governance. It leverages the pride and self-esteem of sovereign nations. Within the European Union it is used frequently, with the European Commission monitoring the actions of individual states in a number of policy areas, including the application of the rules of the single market, state aid to industries and environmental questions, to name just three.*'[12] At the global level, discussions are being held regarding developing mechanisms for peer review in the context of the Convention on the Development, Production and Stockpiling of Bacteriological (Biological) and Toxin Weapons and on their Destruction.[13] In this context, the discussions are based '*on the need to improve national implementation and build confidence in compliance, in the absence of a developed treaty organization and a compliance regime*'.[14] In addition, the United Nations Conference on Trade and Development's (UNCTAD) voluntary peer reviews of competition policy recently celebrated their tenth anniversary. UNCTAD seized this occasion to draw up a number of best practices and lessons

Redondo, 'The Universal Periodic Review: Is there Life Beyond Naming and Shaming in Human Rights Implementation'); Edward R McMahon, Koja Busia, and Marta Ascherio, 'Comparing Peer Reviews: The Universal Periodic Review of the UN Human Rights Council and the African Peer Review Mechanism' (2013) 12 African and Asian Studies 266 (hereafter McMahon, Busia, and Ascherio, 'Comparing Peer Reviews: The Universal Periodic Review of the UN Human Rights Council and the African Peer Review Mechanism'); Rosa Freedman, *The United Nations Human Rights Council—A Critique and Early Assessment* (Routledge 2013) 253 (hereafter Freedman, *The United Nations Human Rights Council—A Critique and Early Assessment*); Nathalie Lihuvud Svensson, 'The Universal Periodic Review—A study on the effectiveness of the United Nations Human Rights Council's monitoring mechanism' (2015) 9(5) Vienna Journal on International Constitutional Law <https://www.icl-journal>; Nathalie Lihuvud Svensson, The Universal Periodic Review—A study on the effectiveness of the United Nations Human Rights Council's monitoring mechanism (Stockholm University, Faculty of Law, 2014) 87 <http://www.diva-portal.se/smash/get/diva2:798622/FULLTEXT01.pdf> accessed 13 May 2017 (hereafter Svensson, 'The Universal Periodic Review—A study on the effectiveness of the United Nations Human Rights Council's monitoring mechanism'); Humberto Cantu Rivera (ed), *The Special Procedures of the Human Rights Council—A Brief Look from the Inside and Perspectives from Outside* (Intersentia Publishing 2015) 16 (hereafter Rivera, *The Special Procedures of the Human Rights Council—A Brief Look from the Inside and Perspectives from Outside*); Jane K Cowan and Julie Billaud, 'Between Learning and Schooling: The Politics of Human Rights Monitoring at the Universal Periodic Review' (2015) 36(6) Third World Quarterly 1175 (hereafter Cowan and Billaud, 'Between Learning and Schooling: The Politics of Human Rights Monitoring at the Universal Periodic Review').

[12] Pascal Lamy, *The Geneva Consensus, Making Trade Work for All* (Cambridge University Press 2013).

[13] James Revill, 'A Peer-Review Mechanism for the Biological and Toxin Weapons Convention' (UNIDIR, 2013) <http://sro.sussex.ac.uk/43353/9/UNPeer_Review.pdf> accessed 13 May 2017 (hereafter Revill, 'A Peer-Review Mechanism for the Biological and Toxin Weapons Convention').

[14] The Kingdom of Belgium took the lead in developing a mechanism for peer review within the context of the BTWC; Benelux BTWC peer review 2014–15, Concept Paper (30 September 2014) (Document on file with the author); Revill, 'A Peer-Review Mechanism for the Biological and Toxin Weapons Convention' (n 13).

learned in order to reinforce the need for the mechanism's continued application in the future.[15]

Although in the humanities, academic analysis of the (theoretical) concept of peer review has been rather limited, the formal establishment of a so-called Peer Review Observatory, attached to the University of Maastricht, attests to a growing academic interest in the subject beyond its standard usage across the sciences.[16]

The main reason behind this increased recourse to mechanisms for peer review (at least within the realm of international law) seems to stem from their '*potential to achieve state compliance in a collegial, and sovereign-respecting way*'. These mechanisms are said to substitute '*command with acceptability, sanctions with peer pressure, and enforcement with learning*'.[17] Simply put, the increased recourse to mechanisms for peer review appears to be prompted by their capacity to produce soft rather than hard law.[18] Moreover, the characteristics of soft law accommodate the ongoing (increased and inevitable) trend in international economic law and policy towards more decentralization perfectly.[19]

2. Mechanisms for peer review: theoretical core elements

It is difficult to distil the theoretical core elements of an ideal mechanism for peer review. This difficulty mainly derives from two facts. On the one hand, there is an ever-increasing variety of mechanisms for peer review. Some of these are mechanisms for political peer review. In these instances, the mechanism has generally been designed in order to exert some degree of (political, legal, economic, or financial) control on the subject under review. Others constitute mechanisms for scientific peer review. These mechanisms focus on a rather higher degree of (scientific) control, often of a binary nature, classifying the eventual results of the peer review exercise in terms of their correct or incorrectness. Each of these mechanisms stands to be characterized by some specific institutional features, leading to the difficulty found in attempting to distil their lowest common. On the other hand, in spite of a recent

[15] United Nations Conference on Trade and Development, *Feed for improving the efficiency of the application of UNCTAD voluntary peer reviews* (TD/RBP/CONF.8/10, UNCTAD, 27 April 2015).

[16] David Shatz, *Peer Review—A Critical Inquiry* (Rowman & Littlefield Publishers 2004) 4 (hereafter Shatz, *Peer Review—A Critical Inquiry*).

[17] Georgios Dimitropoulos, 'Compliance Through Collegiality—Peer Review in International Law' (Max Planck Institute Luxembourg, Working paper 3, 2014) 72 pp. <http://www.mpi.lu/fileadmin/mpi/medien/research/Dimitropoulos_Compliance_through_Collegiality_2014_8_18_WPS.pdf> accessed 6 May 2017 (hereafter Dimitropoulos, 'Compliance Through Collegiality—Peer Review in International Law').

[18] Schafer Armin, 'A New Form of Governance? Comparing the Open Method of Coordination to Multilateral Surveillance by the IMF and the OECD' (2006) 13(1) Journal of European Public Policy 70 (hereafter Armin, 'A New Form of Governance? Comparing the Open Method of Coordination to Multilateral Surveillance by the IMF and the OECD').

[19] Mitsuo Matsushita, 'A View on Future Roles of the WTO: Should There be More Soft Law in The WTO' (2014) 17 Journal of International Economic Law 714 (hereafter Matsushita, 'A View on Future Roles of the WTO: Should There be More Soft Law in The WTO').

increase in academic writing, expert analysis of the theoretical concept of peer review remains relatively scarce,[20] hence the difficulty in orienting the analysis.

A limited number of theoretical definitions of peer review have been advanced. In the context of a study by the OECD, peer review has been defined as '*the systematic examination and assessment of the performance of a State by other States, with the ultimate goal of helping the reviewed State improve its policy making, adopt best practices, and comply with established standards and principles*'. Moreover, this OECD study has emphasized that '*[w]hen peer review is undertaken in the framework of an international organization—as is usually the case—the Secretariat of the organization also plays an important role in supporting and simulating the process*'.[21] Peer review has also been defined within the context of the WTO Working Group on the Interaction between Trade and Competition Policy.[22] In this context, peer review was described as '*a method by which countries can assess the quality and effectiveness of their policies, legislation, policy environments and key institutions. It provides a forum where policies can be explained and discussed, where information be sought and concerns expressed, on a non-confrontational and non-adversarial basis. The feedback provides the reviewee with a yardstick for measuring its system against those of other peers while also informing the reviewing countries.*'[23]

Mechanisms for peer review—such as those embodied within the respective frameworks of the IMF, the OECD, the FSB, the APRM, the UPR, and the structures for the mitigation of international climate change as embodied in the UNFCCC and the Kyoto Protocol—therefore seem to have several theoretical core elements in common. The OECD study and the discussions within the WTO Working Group on the Interaction between Trade and Competition Policy seem to point to at least three core elements. These are: (1) the mechanisms' pursuit of at least two simultaneous *objectives*—transparency and naming and shaming; (2) the presence of a *structure* which legally/institutionally enables peer surveillance (by means of increased transparency and naming and shaming) and which may encompass a process (ie the assessment of a Member against specified review criteria, beginning with an investigation stage, followed by an examination, and ending with a dissemination stage) based on one or several product(s) (normally including but not necessarily limited to an investigation and a final report); and (3) an active *participation*

[20] George W Downs, David M Rocke, and Peter N Barsoom, 'Is the Good News about Compliance Good News about Co-operation?' (1996) 50(3) International Organization 379 (hereafter Downs, Rocke, and Barsoom, 'Is the Good News about Compliance Good News about Co-operation?'); H Ruiz Fabri, LA Sicilianos, and JM Sorel, *L'effectivité des Organisations Internationales, Mécanismes de suivi et de contrôle* (Paris 2000) (hereafter Fabri, Sicilianos, and Sorel, *L'effectivité des Organisations Internationales, Mécanismes de suivi et de contrôle*).

[21] Fabrizio Pagani, 'Peer Review: A Tool for Co-operation and Change—An Analysis of an OECD Working Method' (OECD 2002) 4–5 (hereafter Pagani, 'Peer Review: A Tool for Co-operation and Change').

[22] WTO, Communication from the Working Group on the Interaction between Trade and Competition Policy, WT/WGTCP/W/244, 28 July 2003 (hereafter WTO, Communication from the Working Group on the Interaction between Trade and Competition Policy (WT/WGTCP/W/244)).

[23] WTO, Communication from the Working Group on the Interaction between Trade and Competition Policy (WT/WGTCP/W/244) (n 22) 1.

by several entities—at least by the Member under review and its peers, often also by the peer review-enabling Secretariat and/or by other entities.[24] In practice, each of these three abstract building blocks may vary to a great extent from an institutional perspective.

a) *Objectives*

Although all mechanisms pursue at least two simultaneous objectives (ie transparency and naming and shaming), they may differ in the degree (ie stricter or more lenient) to which they aim or are able to achieve their goals. By way of illustration, marked differences exist between Article IV consultations of the IMF, the Universal Periodic Review of the Human Rights Council, and the structures for mitigation of international climate change as contained in the UNFCCC and the Kyoto Protocol on the one hand (as mechanisms that aim for and are able to achieve a rather strict and specific degree of transparency and naming and shaming) vis-à-vis the peer review mechanisms of the OECD's DAC and the APRM on the other hand (which seem to strive towards or are only able to work towards the achievement of a more general and less stringent level of transparency and naming and shaming).[25] Both types of mechanisms can—but do not necessarily need to—work in a non-confrontational way.[26] In addition to these two types, peer reviews of the FSB embody a third type of mechanism since these explicitly provide for some flexibility in their goal-setting.

Article IV of the IMF seeks to ensure that IMF Members do not disrupt orderly world economic growth by manipulating their exchange rate systems or the international monetary system. As a result, Article IV consultations put a heavy focus on specific information and strict respect with regard to exchange rate systems. Section 3 of Article IV provides in this respect that *'(a) The Fund shall oversee the international monetary system in order to ensure its effective operation, and shall oversee the compliance of each Member with its obligations under Section 1 of this Article, (b) In order to fulfil its functions under (a) above, the Fund shall exercise firm surveillance over the exchange rate policies of Members and shall adopt specific principles for the guidance of all Members with respect to those policies. Each Member shall provide the Fund with the information necessary for such surveillance, and, when requested by the Fund, shall consult with*

[24] WTO, Communication from the Working Group on the Interaction between Trade and Competition Policy (WT/WGTCP/W/243) (n 6) 1–2.

[25] Mavroidis also makes a distinction between the surveillance schemes of the IMF and the OECD whereby the IMF is performing its review function in a stricter way than the OECD (and the GATT); Mavroidis, 'Surveillance Schemes: The GATT's New Trade Policy Review Mechanism' (n 6) 408; Herbert laments the too general and broad focus of the APRM; Herbert, 'The Survival of NEPAD and the African Peer Review Mechanism: A Critical Analysis' (n 10) 37; For an analysis of the NEPAD's and the APRM's broad set of objectives, see Mangu, 'The African Union and the Promotion of Democracy and Good Political Governance under the African Peer-Review Mechanism: 10 Years On' (n 10) 59–72.

[26] Redondo, 'The Universal Periodic Review: Is there Life Beyond Naming and Shaming in Human Rights Implementation' (n 40) 673–706; Cowan and Billaud, 'Between Learning and Schooling: The Politics of Human Rights Monitoring at the Universal Periodic Review' (n 11) 1175–90.

it on the Member's exchange rate policies.'[27] Similarly, the Universal Periodic Review of the Human Rights Council aims to achieve an increased degree of transparency and naming and shaming with regard to some specific rights through the pursuit of several objectives. These include: '*(1) the improvement of the human rights situation on the ground, (2) the fulfilment of the State's human rights obligations and commitments and assessment of positive developments and challenges faced by the State, (3) the enhancement of the State's capacity and of technical assistance, in consultation with, and with the consent of, the State concerned, (4) the sharing of best practice among States and other stakeholders, (5) support for co-operation in the promotion and protection of human rights and (6) the encouragement of full co-operation and engagement with the Council, other human rights bodies and the Office of the UN High Commissioner for Human Rights.*'[28] In a similar vein, the respective structures for the mitigation of climate change as contained in the UNFCCC and its Kyoto Protocol aim for a strict and specific degree of transparency, naming and shaming, and even enforcement. The UNFCCC contains the basis for reporting and review since it requires all Parties to make emissions inventories available to the Conference of the Parties and to submit regular communications. These encompass a required inventory of national greenhouse gas (GHG) emissions and removals, and a general description of the steps Parties are taking or envisaging to take in order to implement the Convention, along with other information relevant to achieving the Convention's transparency objective. The international regime's compliance features are mainly contained within the two branches of the Kyoto Protocol's Compliance Committee, its facilitative and enforcement branch. Whereas the former mainly functions as an early-warning mechanism with respect to questions of implementation regarding emission targets, the latter focuses on addressing potential cases of non-compliance.[29]

The peer review mechanisms of the OECD's DAC and the APRM strive towards the achievement of a more general level of transparency and a more lenient naming and shaming protocol. Due to the lower degree of specificity of DAC and APRM obligations (including voluntary commitments and good practices for the DAC and values, codes, and standards for the APRM), the level to which these mechanisms for peer review contribute to increased transparency and naming and shaming is less stringent and more general. The OECD's peer review of the DAC explains in rather general terms that it continuously aims to improve Member efforts in all areas of development co-operation through the exchange of good practices and the

[27] Section 3 of Article IV of the Articles of Agreement of the International Monetary Fund; International Monetary Fund, 'Articles of Agreement' <http://www.imf.org/external/pubs/ft/aa/#a4s3> accessed 13 May 2017.

[28] UNHRC Res 5/1 UN Doc A/HRC/RES/5/1, 6–7 (hereafter UNHRC Res 5/1).

[29] Yamin and Depledge, *The International Climate Change Regime, A Guide to Rules, Institutions and Procedures* (n 9) 327; Brunnée, Doelle, and Rajamani, *Promoting Compliance in an Evolving Climate Regime* (n 9) 78–82; Malgosia Fitzmaurice, David M Ong, and Panos Merkouris (eds), *Research Handbook on International Environmental Law* (Edward Elgar 2001) 429 (hereafter Fitzmaurice, Ong, and Merkouris, *Research Handbook on International Environmental Law*).

promotion of coordination and collaboration. Paragraph 3 of the Information Note of the DAC Peer Review Process specifies in this regard that '*The objectives of DAC peer reviews are to improve the quality and effectiveness of development co-operation policies and systems, and to promote good development partnerships for better impact on poverty reduction and sustainable development in developing countries. DAC peer reviews therefore promote individual and collective behaviour change of DAC Members to ensure their development co-operation policy framework and systems are fit for purpose. This is achieved through: (I) holding DAC Members accountable for the commitments they have made, and reviewing their performance against key dimensions of development co-operation and other domestic policies with an impact on developing countries; and (II) learning and sharing good practice.*'[30] In a similar vein, the APRM aims to foster a more general increase of transparency and some 'soft' naming and shaming. The mandate of the APRM, a mutually agreed instrument for self-monitoring by the participating Member governments, states in this regard that it is to ensure '*that the policies and practices of participating States conform to the agreed political, economic and corporate governance values, codes and standards contained in the Declaration on Democracy, Political, Economic and Corporate Governance*'.[31] The primary objectives of the APRM as contained in paragraph 3 of its Base Document are therefore general enough '*to foster the adoption of policies, standards and practices that lead to political stability, high economic growth, sustainable development and accelerated sub-regional and continental economic integration through sharing of experiences and reinforcement of successful and best practice, including identifying deficiencies and assessing the needs for capacity building*'.[32]

FSB (thematic and country) peer reviews steer a third way in regard of the specificity and strictness with which their objectives are pursued. Within the overall goals of the FSB—as set out in Article 1 of the FSB Charter—FSB (thematic and country) peer reviews pursue several distinct objectives.[33] These include the goals to '*(I) exchange information on regulatory, supervisory and other financial sector policies, and receive feedback from peers about the effective implementation of these policies, (II) to evaluate the adherence of FSB Member jurisdictions to their commitment... to (a) pursue the maintenance of financial stability, (b) maintain the openness and transparency of the financial sector and (c) implement international financial standards, (III) to foster a race to the top with regard to the implementation of effective regulatory supervisory and other financial sector policies and (IV) to assess the effectiveness of international financial standards, and of policies agreed within the FSB in*

[30] Organisation for Economic Co-operation and Development, 'Information Note on the DAC Peer Review Process' (DCD(2013)6, OECD 27 October 2014), paragraph 3 (hereafter Organisation for Economic Co-operation and Development, Information Note on the DAC Peer Review Process).

[31] New Partnership for Africa's Development, African Peer Review Mechanism (APRM), Base Document (n 10) paragraph 2.

[32] New Partnership for Africa's Development, African Peer Review Mechanism (APRM), Base Document (n 10) paragraph 3.

[33] Wouters and Odermatt, 'Comparing the 'Four Pillars' of Global Economic Governance: A Critical Analysis of the Institutional Design of the FSB, IMF, World Bank, and WTO' (n 8) 56.

realising their intended results'.[34] Nevertheless, the FSB Handbook also explicitly emphasizes the fact that '*the extent to which this fourth objective can be achieved will depend on the topic and degree of intensity of the peer review as well as on the time period elapsed since the relevant policy or standard has been implemented*'.[35] Moreover, the FSB Handbook specifically comments that its peer reviews should focus on areas where the FSB can add value and that it should adapt a flexible approach in setting the objectives for these peer reviews.[36]

The mechanisms for peer review mentioned earlier illustrate the fact that their objectives oscillate between a maximalist stance (ie to increase convergence, to encourage policy coordination and co-operation, to improve transparency, to share information and experience, to improve domestic policy-making, to provide policy advice, to examine policy, to provide technical assistance, capacity building, and aid, to gather and disseminate information and best practice models, to ensure risk and/or quality control, to boost policy stability and investor confidence)[37] and a minimalist position which would reduce these goals to the two (core) objectives of transparency and naming and shaming. Whatever perspective is applied, the fact remains that the relationship between the transparency and the naming and shaming objective is complex. On one hand, transparency is a *conditio sine qua non* to naming and shaming.[38] If there is a lack of transparency, intentional or unintentional, it will be difficult to pursue the goal of naming and shaming effectively. On the other hand, if too much emphasis is put on this aim, participants may be less inclined to offer themselves up, full transparency being a risky business. Mechanisms for peer review should therefore be able to simultaneously pursue both objectives.

[34] Financial Stability Board—Standing Committee on Standards Implementation, 'Handbook for FSB Peer Reviews' (FSB 12 March 2015) 3–4 <http://www.fsb.org/wp-content/uploads/FSB-Peer-Review-Handbook-12-March-2015.pdf> accessed 13 May 2017 (hereafter Financial Stability Board—Standing Committee on Standards Implementation, Handbook for FSB Peer Reviews (FSB 12 March 2015)).

[35] Financial Stability Board—Standing Committee on Standards Implementation, Handbook for FSB Peer Reviews (FSB 12 March 2015) (n 34) 3.

[36] Financial Stability Board—Standing Committee on Standards Implementation, Handbook for FSB Peer Reviews (FSB 12 March 2015) (n 34) 3.

[37] WTO, Communication from the Working Group on the Interaction between Trade and Competition Policy (WT/WGTCP/W/243) (n 6) 1; WTO, Communication from the Working Group on the Interaction between Trade and Competition Policy (WT/WGTCP/W/244) (n 22) 2–8; Joseph F Francois, 'Maximizing the Benefits of the Trade Policy Review Mechanism for Developing Countries' (1999), Tinbergen Institute and CEPR <https://www.iatp.org/sites/default/files/Maximizing_the_Benefits_of_the_Trade_Policy_5.htm> accessed 6 May 2017 (hereafter Francois, 'Maximizing the Benefits of the Trade Policy Review Mechanism for Developing Countries'); Joseph F Francois, 'Trade Policy Transparency and Investor Confidence: Some Implications for an Effective Trade Policy Review Mechanism' (2001) 9(2) Review of International Economics 303–16 (hereafter Francois, 'Trade Policy Transparency and Investor Confidence: Some Implications for an Effective Trade Policy Review Mechanism').

[38] Asif H Qureshi, 'The New GATT Trade Policy Review Mechanism: An Exercise in Transparency or "Enforcement"' (1990) June, Journal of World Trade 149–60 (hereafter Qureshi, 'The New GATT Trade Policy Review Mechanism: An Exercise in Transparency or "Enforcement"').

b) *Structure*

The structure of a mechanism for peer review should at least enable it to effectively pursue the (minimalistic) objectives of transparency and naming and shaming. This structure should therefore logically consist of: (1) a mechanism which enables the formal selection of entities which are to be reviewed (hereafter, the first structural element); (2) a procedure to obtain the information needed for the review (ie the investigative stage, hereafter the second structural element); and (3) elements which guide and regulate the transmission and use of information *within* the review process *itself* (hereafter, the third structural element).[39] This third element concerns several process- and product-related sub-features. These include: (a) the reporting requirements to provide for a standardized degree of transparency; (b) requirements which determine the actual structure of the review meeting in order to foster a standardized rate of naming and shaming; and (c) elements, equal to all participants, which guide the potential follow-up to the conclusions of the review. These three sub-elements form part and parcel of the examination and dissemination stages. In addition, mechanisms for peer review are generally based on a fourth structural element. This fourth feature consists of a procedure which provides for the possibility of a formal review of the peer review process itself. Although these four structural elements seem clear at first sight, the respective mechanisms for peer review of the IMF, the OECD's DAC, the FSB, the APRM, the UPR, and the structures for the mitigation of international climate change (as contained in the UNFCCC and its Kyoto Protocol) again attest to the bewildering variety of their specific institutional features.

i) **First structural element: a formal selection mechanism**

Mechanisms which select the entities to be reviewed function either on a quasi-automatic basis (ie based on a certain predetermined periodicity cycle potentially mitigated if the entity which is to be reviewed is (temporarily) unable to undergo the exercise), foresee some flexibility (ie are based on some political decision-making), or are based on a combination of the aforementioned elements.

Most mechanisms for peer review—especially the older ones such as the Article IV consultations of the IMF and the DAC peer review of the OECD, but also some newer ones such as the UPR of the Human Rights Council—have a selection mechanism that functions in a quasi-automatic (periodic) way.

In principle, Article IV consultations of the IMF are planned on an annual basis with each of the IMF's 188 countries.[40] Nevertheless, the initial periodicity cycle

[39] According to Blackhurst, who advised as early as 1988 on institutional structures for surveillance, it appears that a procedure which is built on the collection and dissemination of information on policies (ie on a structural investigation) as well as on the evaluation and discussion of these policies (ie on a structured treatment of this information) enhances the likelihood of effective surveillance of these policies, see Richard Blackhurst, 'Strengthening GATT Surveillance of Trade-Related Policies' in Meinhard Hilf and Ernst-Ulrich Petersman (eds), *The New GATT Round of Multilateral Trade Negotiations: Legal and Economic Aspects* (Kluwer Law and Taxation Publishers 1988) 143 (hereafter Blackhurst, 'Strengthening GATT Surveillance of Trade-Related Policies').

[40] International Monetary Fund, 'Bilateral Surveillance Over Members' Policies, Executive Board Decision' (15 June 2007) <https://www.imf.org/external/np/sec/pn/2007/pn0769.htm#decision>

has been amended in certain circumstances. Consultations for countries without a Fund arrangement are normally still to be reviewed annually. On the other hand, Members which were granted a Flexible Credit Line (FCL) or a Precautionary Liquidity Line (PLL) are also automatically placed on the twelve-month consultation cycle, while those with other Fund arrangements or a Policy Support Instrument (PSI) are automatically placed on a twenty-four-month cycle. Moreover, with some exceptions, the Executive Board may decide to put Members without an arrangement on a longer cycle of up to twenty-four months, but only with the Member's consent and only after consulting with its Executive Director.[41] As a result, the IMF was able to undertake 123 Article IV consultations in 2014.[42] These increased to 131 in 2015.[43] A similar (quasi) automaticity is present within the OECD's peer review of the DAC. In this context, reviews of the development co-operation efforts of each of the twenty-nine DAC Members are scheduled every four to five years.[44] As a result, the Committee handled reviews of New Zealand, Belgium, Germany, and Portugal in 2015 and planned to handle those of Spain, Denmark, the Czech Republic, the United States, and Poland in 2016.[45] In a similar vein, the UPR aspires to a certain (quasi-) automatic regularity of review of all its Member and Observer states. Indeed, the UPR was conceived as '*the banner that would distance the Human Rights Council from the politicization, subjectivity and selectivity*' which had characterized its predecessor, the Commission on Human Rights, during its last years.[46] The automatic selection mechanism of the UPR was therefore one of its main assets. Under this new mechanism, the period for the first UPR cycle (2008–11) was determined to be four years (implying the consideration of forty-eight States per year).[47] According to Resolution 16/21, the period of review for the second (2012–16) and

accessed 13 May 2017 (hereafter International Monetary Fund, Bilateral Surveillance Over Members' Policies, Executive Board Decision (15 June 2007)); International Monetary Fund, 'IMF Proposed Decision on Article IV Consultation Cycles' (21 September 2010) <https://www.imf.org/external/np/pp/eng/2010/092110a.pdf> accessed 13 May 2017; International Monetary Fund, 'Preliminary Consideration of Options to Address Excessive Delays in the Completion of Article IV Consultations' (28 April 2011) <http://www.imf.org/external/np/pp/eng/2011/042811.pdf> accessed 13 May 2017.

41 International Monetary Fund, 'Guidance Note for Surveillance Under Article IV Consultations' (May 2015), 45 <http://www.imf.org/external/np/pp/eng/2015/031915.pdf> accessed 13 May 2017 (hereafter International Monetary Fund, Guidance Note for Surveillance Under Article IV Consultations).

42 International Monetary Fund, *From Stabilization to Sustainable Growth—Annual Report 2014* (IMF 2014) 21.

43 International Monetary Fund, *Tackling Challenges Together—Annual Report 2015* (IMF 2015) 25.

44 Organisation for Economic Co-operation and Development, 'DAC Peer Review Reference Guide' (DCD/DAC(2014)52, OECD 2014) 2 (hereafter Organisation for Economic Co-operation and Development, DAC Peer Review Reference Guide (2014)).

45 Organisation for Economic Co-operation and Development, 'Peer Reviews of DAC Members' <http://www.oecd.org/dac/peer-reviews/peerreviewsofdacmembers.htm> accessed 13 May 2017.

46 Rivera, *The Special Procedures of the Human Rights Council—A Brief Look from the Inside and Perspectives from Outside* (n 40) 16; Freedman, *The United Nations Human Rights Council—A Critique and Early Assessment* (n 11) 253 and 255; Elvira Dominguez Redondo, 'The Universal Periodic Review of the UN Human Rights Council: An Assessment of the First Session' (2008) 7(3) Chinese Journal of International Law 722

47 UNHRC Res 5/1 (n 28) 7.

subsequent cycles became four-and-a-half years (resulting in an annual consideration of forty-two States).[48]

At the other end of the spectrum, the FSB maintains a (highly) flexible selection mechanism for its (country and thematic) peer reviews. In this regard, the Handbook for FSB Peer Reviews simply states that '*The Standing Committee on Standards Implementation (SCSI) will agree on the prioritisation of countries and themes on a rolling basis, based on the recommendation of the Chair of the SCSI. When deciding both in terms of the number of country and thematic reviews as well as in the mix between the two types of reviews, the SCSI will consider FSB Member and Secretariat resource constraints as well as inputs from other FSB committees and relevant Organizations as appropriate. Proposed priorities will be submitted to the Plenary (as part of the SCSI work plan) for endorsement on an annual basis. The schedule may be further revised during the year to ensure that it remains appropriate in light of international market and policy developments.*'[49] Nevertheless, Articles 3.1 and 3.2 of the FSB Handbook for Peer Reviews provide some (limited) selection criteria for thematic and country reviews.[50] As a result, in 2014 the FSB organized country peer reviews of Indonesia, Germany, and The Netherlands and a thematic peer review of the FSB principles for reducing reliance on Credit Rating Agency (CRA) ratings.[51] In 2015, it organized country peer reviews of Russia, China, Saudi Arabia, and Turkey as well as thematic peer reviews of resolution regimes, supervisory frameworks and approaches for Systemically Important Banks (SIBs), the FSB Policy Framework for Shadow Banking Entities and Over The Counter (OTC) derivatives trade reporting.[52]

The selection mechanism of the APRM steers a third way since it is based on a combination of quasi-automaticity and flexible decision-making. In this regard, the mechanism provides for four types of review: (1) the base review which is the country's first review to be carried out within eighteen months of the country's accession to the APRM process; (2) the periodic review which is due to take place every two to four years after the first review; (3) reviews at the request of Member states; and (4) crisis reviews provoked by early signs of impending political or economic crisis. The Base Document of the APRM stipulates in addition that participating Heads of State and Government can also call for such a review in a spirit of helpfulness to the country concerned.[53] Nonetheless, in spite of the flexibility of the review

[48] UNHRC Res 16/21 UN Doc A/HRC/RES/16/21, 3 (hereafter UNHRC Res 16/21); United Nations Human Rights Office of the High Commissioner, 'UPR sessions' <http://www.ohchr.org/EN/HRBodies/UPR/Pages/UPRSessions.aspx> accessed 13 May 2017.

[49] Financial Stability Board—Standing Committee on Standards Implementation, Handbook for FSB Peer Reviews (FSB 12 March 2015) (n 34) 4–5.

[50] Financial Stability Board—Standing Committee on Standards Implementation, Handbook for FSB Peer Reviews (FSB 12 March 2015) (n 34) 4–5.

[51] Financial Stability Board, 'Peer Review Reports' <http://www.fsb.org/2014/?content_type=peer-review-reports> accessed 13 May 2017.

[52] Financial Stability Board, 'Peer Review Reports' <www.fsb.org/2015/?content_type=peer-review-reports> accessed 13 May 2017.

[53] New Partnership for Africa's Development, African Peer Review Mechanism (APRM), Base Document (n 10) paragraph 14; Zein Kebonang and Charles Manga Fombad, 'The African Peer Review Mechanism: Challenges and Prospects', in Henning Melber (ed), *AU, NEPAD and the*

mechanism which had been established in 2003, its performance seemed to be a mixed success. In March 2015, out of all fifty-four African countries, only thirty-five had become formal Members of the APRM. Moreover, only seventeen had completed the base review and no country had produced a second review.[54] In a similar vein, the international structures for the mitigation of climate change contain a variety of trigger mechanisms. With regard to the transparency objective, these depend on the specific quality of the Parties (ie Annex I versus non-Annex I Parties) which are subject to the review. This distinctive triggering is absent in the compliance system as contained in the Kyoto Protocol, however. The selection mechanism can be triggered in several ways, according to the Protocol. It may be activated by questions stemming (1) from an expert review team; (2) by a party with respect to itself; and (3) by a party with respect to another party. Nevertheless, triggering is not fully automatic since minimal procedural standards for submissions of questions of implementation have to be respected.[55]

ii) Second structural element: investigative procedure(s)

There is great institutional variety between the procedures that are applied in order to obtain the information required for the review. The investigative procedures (generally undertaken by means of (a) questionnaire(s) and/or (b) specific mission(s)) can be analysed in two different categories. Either the reviewing entity is assuming the primary responsibility for the collection of information (such as the examples of Article IV consultations of the IMF and OECD DAC reviews demonstrate)[56] or the entities under review have a more equally shared responsibility for the provision of information together with the reviewing entity (as the examples of the APRM and the FSB show). Interestingly, in some settings, such as the UPR, civil society has an important reinforced role to play as a third independent provider of information to the review.[57]

If the institutional structures for reporting and review also allow for a (later potential) pursuit of compliance (as the UNFCCC and its Kyoto Protocol do), these

APRM—Democratisation Efforts Explored (2006) 32 Current African Issues 46 <http://www.diva-portal.org/smash/get/diva2:240536/FULLTEXT02.pdf> accessed 13 May 2017 (hereafter Kebonang and Fombad, 'The African Peer Review Mechanism: Challenges and Prospects').

[54] Terence Corrigan, 'Why the African Peer Review Mechanism Must Remain Voluntary, Policy Briefing No. 130' (SAIIA, March 2015) <http://www.saiia.org.za/policy-briefings/why-the-african-peer-review-mechanism-must-remain-voluntary> accessed 6 May 2017.

[55] Yamin and Depledge, *The International Climate Change Regime, A Guide to Rules, Institutions and Procedures* (n 9) 328; Brunnée, Doelle, and Rajamani, *Promoting Compliance in an Evolving Climate Regime* (n 9) 86.

[56] Craig VanGrasstek, *The History and Future of the World Trade Organization* (WTO 2013) 284 (hereafter VanGrasstek, *The History and Future of the World Trade Organization*).

[57] Interestingly, the WTO Working Group on the Interaction between Trade and Competition Policy applies a different categorization: either the Member under review conducts its own investigation without the Secretariat's involvement, or the Secretariat conducts its own investigation, or the member under review and the Secretariat conduct separate investigations and issues separate investigation reports which are then submitted for peer review separately or as a consolidated document; see WTO, Communication from the Working Group on the Interaction between Trade and Competition Policy (WT/WGTCP/W/243) (n 6) 11.

sometimes also foresee an additional preliminary examination in order to smoothen the pursuit of their enforcement objective. The Compliance Committee of the Protocol is a case in point. Since it features two branches, the Committee's bureau first allocates the question of implementation to the appropriate branch in accordance with its respective mandate. The responsible branch will then conduct a preliminary examination of the question.[58]

In the context of Article IV consultations, missions are initiated after the elaboration of a mission brief by the respective IMF departments which may also involve the IMF senior management. IMF missions then involve a country visit by at least four or five staff members. These visits involve meetings with concerned ministries and representatives of civil society and conclude with the presentation of a statement which summarizes the staff's view on the economy, the current policy stance, and any recommendations for changes.[59] In a similar vein, the OECD's DAC reviews are highly driven by its Secretariat. Nevertheless, the country under review and the Secretariat have an almost equal responsibility for the collection and provision of information for the review. In this regard, the OECD Secretariat generally agrees on a plan with the reviewed Member and the examiners (including the provision of documentation by the reviewed Member and the timing and parameters of all Secretariat's missions).[60] The OECD Secretariat moreover consults a wide variety of sources but nevertheless requires some technical and financial input from the country under review. In this context, it is noteworthy that the country under review not only needs to submit a country memorandum and an annual statistical report but is also required to make funds available in the form of a voluntary contribution to cover the cost of field missions. Interestingly, participants who intervened in IMF and OECD investigative processes therefore felt that OECD missions were more useful '*because of the greater emphasis on dialogue and exchange*'.[61] This is due to the OECD's investigative procedures' higher level of procedural interactivity, joint ownership, and budgetary dependence on the country under review.[62]

The APRM and the FSB are iconic for investigative review processes where the entities under review have a more equally shared responsibility for the provision of information but where the country under review carries preponderant weight in the process. In the context of the APRM, country review visits comprise the second (institutional) stage of the APRM process.[63]

[58] Brunnée, Doelle, and Rajamani, *Promoting Compliance in an Evolving Climate Regime* (n 9) 87.

[59] International Monetary Fund, *Report by a Group of Independent Experts, External Evaluation of IMF Surveillance* (IMF 1999) 24–26 (hereafter International Monetary Fund, *Report by a Group of Independent Experts, External Evaluation of IMF Surveillance*).

[60] Organisation for Economic Co-operation and Development, Information Note on the DAC Peer Review Process (n 30) paragraphs 10–14.

[61] Lombardi and Woods, 'The Politics of Influence: An Analysis of IMF Surveillance' (n 6) 723; Momani, 'Assessing the Utility of, and Measuring Learning from, Canada's IMF Article IV Consultations' (n 6) 262.

[62] Lombardi and Woods, 'The Politics of Influence: An Analysis of IMF Surveillance' (n 6) 723.

[63] Kebonang and Fombad, 'The African Peer Review Mechanism: Challenges and Prospects' (n 53) 46–47.

This stage is initiated after the conclusion of the APRM's first stage. The latter encompasses the provision of a draft country programme of action by the country under review and the elaboration of a background document and paper on the country by the Secretariat. In the second stage, the review team will visit the country concerned and carry out the widest possible range of consultations—including with civil society.[64] Although the APRM process could lead to greater accountability on the African continent, civil societies' participation in these consultations de facto greatly depends on the different political contexts in each country.[65] The second stage concludes with the elaboration of a final draft country programme of action which includes recommendations on required improvements.[66] In the framework of thematic and country reviews by the FSB, the countries under review also carry a preponderant weight in the procedures which are followed in the investigation stage. This concerns both the preparatory and consultation sub-stages. Countries under review therefore have a wide discretion in the topic selection (for country reviews only), in the preparation of the terms of reference of the review, in the collection of information (primary through a questionnaire), and in the determination of the parameters of the brief onsite visit in the reviewed jurisdiction (where the possibility of meeting with relevant market participants is subject to the explicit agreement of the reviewed jurisdiction).[67]

In the context of the UPR, civil society constitutes a third independent provider of information. This is the case as the documentation which is used in the UPR review is not only based on a national report and a compilation of UN information but also on a required summary of other stakeholder information.[68] Nevertheless, the latter is prepared by the Office of the High Commissioner for Human Rights and is explicitly limited to a maximum of ten pages.[69] Moreover, the UPR process involves in principle no missions which is a significant difference with the investigative procedures of the IMF, the OECD, and the APRM.[70]

iii) Third structural element: elements which guide and regulate the transmission and use of information within the review process itself

Peer review is based on the principle of equality. The reviewed entity submits itself to the review (mainly) in the assumption (a) that its peers will do the same at a later stage and (b) that they will receive a similar treatment on this occasion. Comparability (or

[64] New Partnership for Africa's Development, African Peer Review Mechanism (APRM), Base Document (n 10) paragraph 19.

[65] Gruzd, 'The African Peer Review Mechanism: Assessing Origins, Institutional Relations and Achievements' (n 10) 13; McMahon, Busia, and Ascherio, 'Comparing Peer Reviews: The Universal Periodic Review of the UN Human Rights Council and the African Peer Review Mechanism (n 11) 277.

[66] Kebonang and Fombad, 'The African Peer Review Mechanism: Challenges and Prospects' (n 53) 47.

[67] Financial Stability Board—Standing Committee on Standards Implementation, Handbook for FSB Peer Reviews (FSB 12 March 2015) (n 34) 5–10.

[68] UNHRC Res 5/1 (n 28) 7–8.

[69] Svensson, 'The Universal Periodic Review—A study on the effectiveness of the United Nations Human Rights Council's monitoring mechanism' (n 11) 22.

[70] McMahon and Ascherio, 'A Step Ahead in Promoting Human Rights? The Universal Periodic Review of the UN Human Rights Council' (n 11) 234.

equality of legal arms) is therefore crucial, not only from a transparency angle (the reporting requirements need to be similar) but also from the perspective of naming and shaming (the structure of the peer review meeting needs to be equal in order to ensure a 'blind' regarding peer pressure—ie equal to all) and its further follow-up (conclusions should be equally (un)binding to all actual and future participants in the review process). These elements which guide and regulate the transmission and use of information within the examination and dissemination stages of the process therefore constitute a third structural core element inherent in most mechanisms for peer review.

Reporting requirements

Reporting requirements render a standardized structure—not only to the data which feed into the actual peer reviews but sometimes also to their structural follow-up. In addition, they can constitute a filter mechanism against the misuse of the review or compliance mechanism (as the preliminary examination in the context of the compliance system of the UNFCCC's Kyoto Protocol demonstrates).[71] Nevertheless, the question of standardization receives different answers throughout the aforementioned mechanisms for peer review. Some review mechanisms (such as Human Rights Council's UPR, the IMF's Article IV consultations, the FSB's peer reviews, and the APRM) seem to frown on too much flexibility whereas others (such as the OECD's DAC) explicitly foresee the possibility of a more flexible reporting format. Furthermore, some mechanisms such as the FSB peer reviews and the APRM entail highly detailed guidance with regard to the possible formulation of structural follow-up recommendations.

In the context of the Human Rights Council's UPR, reporting requirements vis-à-vis the States under review and vis-à-vis the Office of the High Commissioner for Human Rights are highly standardized. They are codified in the UN General Assemblies' Resolution 60/251 on the Human Rights Council,[72] in the Human Rights Council's Resolution 5/1 containing the institution-building package,[73] in its Decision 6/102 containing follow-up to Human Rights Council resolution 5/1,[74] in its Decision 16/21 on the review of the work and functioning of the Human Rights Council,[75] and in its Decision 17/119 with regard to Human Rights Council resolution 16/21 with regard to the Universal Periodic Review.[76] Moreover, Decision 16/21 on the review of the work and functioning of the Human Rights Council also aims to standardize the UPR's structural follow-up while stressing that '*the second and subsequent cycles of review should focus on, inter*

[71] Brunnée, Doelle, and Rajamani, *Promoting Compliance in an Evolving Climate Regime* (n 9) 87; This preliminary investigation aims to ensure that the question of implementation: (1) is supported by sufficient information; (2) is not *de minimis* or ill founded; (3) is based on the requirements of the Protocol; and (4) meets the standards of the Rules of Procedure (unless the case is a self-trigger).

[72] UNGA Res 60/251 (n 11).

[73] UNHRC Res 5/1 (n 28).

[74] UNHRC Decision 6/102 UN Doc A/HRC/DEC/6/102 (hereafter UNHRC Decision 6/102).

[75] UNHRC Res 16/21 (n 48).

[76] UNHRC Decision 17/119 UN Doc A/HRC/DEC/17/119, 1–2 (hereafter UNHRC Decision 17/119).

alia, the implementation of the accepted recommendations and the developments of the human rights situation in the States under review'.[77] In a similar vein, reporting requirements for Article IV consultations of the IMF are highly standardized. Missions in pursuit of these consultations result in a 'back-to-office' report to the IMF senior management (summarizing the most important information about the visit) and in a Staff report for the Fund's Executive Board. Before its final submission to the Executive Board, the latter is circulated for comments to other functional departments and for approval by the Policy Development and Review Department and by IMF senior management.[78] As a result, Staff reports generally include a rather standardized description of the macro-economic environment (including monetary policy, fiscal policy, exchange rate policy, capital mobility and capital account convertibility, financial systems, interrelations, and early warning indicators and standards), the main economic policy issues that face the country, the staff's forecast, an account of the discussions between the staff and the authorities, and a staff appraisal containing its own views and recommendations. Nevertheless, in spite of this standardized way of reporting, the IMF Executive Board's Decision of 15 June 2007 on Bilateral Surveillance sought to update its earlier degree of surveillance and render it even more standardized. However, in spite of this further streamlining of traditional issues and their coverage, staff reporting has (again) started to develop a tendency to cover micro-economic and supply-side matters (such as trade liberalization, labour markets, offshore banking, supervision, tax reforms, expenditure streamlining, income distribution, poverty, land reform, and environment), which seems to detract (again) from the effectiveness of IMF surveillance.[79] In a similar vein, the FSB mechanism for peer review attempts to reduce flexibility to a minimum. Its reporting structure for and structural follow-up to thematic and country peer reviews is therefore carefully circumscribed. On the one hand, the preparatory stage of the FSB peer review process comprises both topic selection (for country reviews) as well as the requirement to reach agreement on the terms of reference for the review, thereby leaving an element of flexibility.[80] On the other, the FSB Handbook for Peer Review provides some clear guidelines for the drafting of preliminary (thematic and country) peer review reports.[81] According to the Handbook, these reports should encompass an executive summary and analytical sections which describe recent accomplishments and evaluate areas where progress is lagging as well as a concluding section with recommendations. In addition, the FSB Handbook

[77] UNHRC Res 16/21 (n 48) 3.

[78] International Monetary Fund, *Report by a Group of Independent Experts, External Evaluation of IMF Surveillance* (n 59) 25 and 37–40.

[79] International Monetary Fund, *Report by a Group of Independent Experts, External Evaluation of IMF Surveillance* (n 59) 25 and 37–41; Kishore and Mohanty, 'How Effective Will the IMF's New Surveillance Framework Be?' (n 6) 31–36; International Monetary Fund, Guidance Note for Surveillance Under Article IV Consultations (n 41) 8–11.

[80] Financial Stability Board—Standing Committee on Standards Implementation, Handbook for FSB Peer Reviews (FSB 12 March 2015) (n 34) 5–6.

[81] Financial Stability Board—Standing Committee on Standards Implementation, Handbook for FSB Peer Reviews (FSB 12 March 2015) (n 34) 10–11.

specifically requires that '*the analytical sections of these reports will distinguish, where appropriate, weak compliance or performance caused by capacity or legislative constraints from that caused by unwillingness or other factors*'. Moreover, according to the Handbook '*recommended actions, as well as the elements upon which they are based, will be clearly articulated and prioritised in the concluding section, with timelines where possible*'. However, '*where the report will include an evaluation, the review will not conduct assessments or assign assessment grades*'.[82] The APRM can be analysed as a last example of a mechanism which features highly standardized structural reporting requirements—both for the report itself as for the report's further follow-up. APRM reports contain information based on the findings resulting from the country review visit as well as data from other sources. Nonetheless, these reports also contain recommendations with regard to possible improvements to the programme of action of the country under review. Both elements are discussed with the country under review before the report is finally submitted to peer review. Moreover, the reactions of the country under review with regard to the reports' findings and recommendations are included in the report. Interestingly, the APRM Base Document explicitly emphasizes that '*the Team's report will need to be clear on a number of points in instances where problems are identified. Is there the will on the part of the Government to take the necessary decisions and measures to put right what is identified to be amiss? What resources are necessary to take corrective measures? How much of these can the Government itself provide and how much is to come from external sources? Given the necessary resources, how long will the process of rectification take?*'[83]

Other mechanisms for peer review such as the OECD's DAC explicitly foresee the possibility of a more flexible structure and style of reporting. The Secretariat report which feeds into the DAC's peer review consists of two parts. The report's Main Findings and Recommendations (Part 1) are elaborated together with the future examiners of the review meeting. The country under review only receives Part 1 once it has been made publicly available. Part 2 of the report, which contains the report's factual analysis, is shared with the examiners for comments and subsequently sent to the reviewed Members for factual checks on the text.[84] Although this structure is specifically based on the recommendations of the DAC's Peer Review Reference Guide, the Guide also emphasizes that while it '*provides benchmarks and conditions that define a good and effective development co-operation actor, there is no "one size fits all" model. Therefore, each peer review is situated in its own context – which is presented at the beginning of the peer review report, and the reference guide applies in a flexible manner. Recommendations are adjusted to each specific situation with the view*

[82] Financial Stability Board—Standing Committee on Standards Implementation, Handbook for FSB Peer Reviews (FSB 12 March 2015) (n 34) 10.

[83] Kebonang and Fombad, 'The African Peer Review Mechanism: Challenges and Prospects' (n 23) 47; New Partnership for Africa's Development, African Peer Review Mechanism (APRM), Base Document (n 10) paragraphs 20–22.

[84] Organisation for Economic Co-operation and Development, Information Note on the DAC Peer Review Process (n 30) paragraph 18.

to support efforts made by the reviewed Member to build quality development co-operation and humanitarian assistance policies and systems'.[85]

The institutional forum for peer review

The structure of the institutional forum for peer review tends to be standardized in order to ensure that all participants in the process will sooner or later be subject to a similar degree of informational intrusiveness and peer pressure. Nevertheless, here again, no one-size-fits-all approach exists. In some instances, such as the Article 4 consultations of the IMF, the OECD DAC reviews, the UPR, and the FSB, the report is discussed and adapted by just one institutional entity (be it sometimes in changed settings or by different branches). In other mechanisms, such as the APRM or the structures for the mitigation of international climate change (as contained in the UNFCCC and its Kyoto Protocol), the report's discussion and adaption are split over several entities.

In the context of Article IV consultations of the IMF, after approval by the senior management, the staff submits its report to the Fund's Executive Board for discussion. Interestingly, IMF Executive Board Discussions of Article IV consultations tend to be limited in time and tend to lack interaction between Executive Directors, who may need to rely on prior comments received from the Members they represent.[86] At the end of the discussion, the Chair of the Board will summarize the views of the Board. This summary—which represents the official collective view of the Fund—generally begins with the expression of broad agreement with the staff appraisal. It forms the basis for a Public Information Notice (PIN) which also contains a factual background section.[87] In a similar vein, the OECD's DAC review process culminates in the report's discussion and adoption by the Committee itself. This discussion is led by the DAC Chair. It includes the presentation by the examiners of the review team's findings and recommendations and thematic discussions on key aspects of the reviewed Member's development co-operation. The reviewed country is also given an opportunity to present its response to the report and to engage in a debate with the DAC. Ultimately, the DAC agrees recommendations to the Member under review.[88] Likewise, in the context of the UPR, reviews take place in the framework of its Working Group (which consists of forty-seven Members of the Council chaired by the President of the Council) and entail a discussion between the State under review and other UN Member states. During the discussion, any UN Member State can pose questions, comments, and table recommendations to the State under review. The Troika (a group of three rapporteurs selected by the

[85] Organisation for Economic Co-operation and Development, DAC Peer Review Reference Guide (2014) (n 44) 2.

[86] However, this may partly reflect a compromise between the depth of discussion in the examination stage and the number of reviews undertaken, see WTO, Communication from the Working Group on the Interaction between Trade and Competition Policy (WT/WGTCP/W/243) (n 6) 26.

[87] International Monetary Fund, *Report by a Group of Independent Experts, External Evaluation of IMF Surveillance* (n 59) 26.

[88] Organisation for Economic Co-operation and Development, Information Note on the DAC Peer Review Process (n 30) 5.

drawing of lots amongst the Members of the Council and from different Regional Groups) may group issues or questions to be shared with the State under review and facilitate each review (including the preparation of the report of the Working Group).[89] Following these discussions, a report with a summary of exchanges and a list of recommendations is issued.[90] After potential further editing and adoption of the report by the UPR Working Group, the report is considered and adopted at the next Council Session together with possible further observations by the State under review, other Members, and civil society.[91] Within the context of the FSB, the peer's discussion of the report represents a key element of the review. This substantive discussion will take place in the Standing Committee on Standards Implementation (SCSI) under the direction of its Chair. The draft report will first be presented by the team leader which was selected for the drafting of the report. In the case of country reviews, the reviewed jurisdiction will be invited to the discussion, whether or not it is an SCSI Member. The reviewed jurisdiction will also be invited to take the floor prior to the discussion in order to comment on the peer review report and to explain how it intends to respond to the peer review recommendations. The Secretariat, with support from the review team as needed, will then revise the report based on feedback received during the discussion so as to reflect the consensus views of the SCSI. The report, including any comments and responses by the relevant jurisdiction(s), will be recirculated to SCSI Members for approval before being submitted to the Plenary.[92]

At the other end of the spectrum, the APRM is based on an enclosed review process. After its receipt of the APR Team reports, the APRM Panel is responsible for ensuring the credibility and integrity of the review process.[93] As a result, the APRM Base Document sets high thresholds on the selection of Panel Members while academic literature has also expressed caution on the appointment of persons who are still active in partisan politics in their own home countries.[94] The APR Panel then meets to review the report in accordance with its mandate and submits its recommendations on the report to the APR Forum for consideration and decision on what actions to take.[95] In a similar vein, peer review in the context of international climate change mitigation (as embodied by the structures of the UNFCCC and its Kyoto Protocol) is undertaken by several entities (the Conference of Parties, the Meeting of Parties, expert review teams, and the Subsidiary Body for Implementation), depending on the specific nature of the Parties (ie Annex I Parties versus non-Annex I Parties).[96]

[89] UNHRC Res 5/1 (n 28).

[90] Bassiouni and Schabas, *New Challenges for the UN Human Rights Machinery* (n 11) 47.

[91] Freedman, *The United Nations Human Rights Council—A Critique and Early Assessment* (n 11) 264.

[92] Financial Stability Board—Standing Committee on Standards Implementation, Handbook for FSB Peer Reviews (FSB 12 March 2015) (n 34) 12.

[93] Chukwumerije, 'Peer Review and the Promotion of Good Governance in Africa' (n 10) 80.

[94] New Partnership for Africa's Development, African Peer Review Mechanism Organisation and Process (n 10) paragraphs 3.3–3.6; Kebonang and Fombad, 'The African Peer Review Mechanism: Challenges and Prospects' (n 53) 51.

[95] New Partnership for Africa's Development, African Peer Review Mechanism Organisation and Process (n 10) paragraph 7.15.

[96] Yamin and Depledge, *The International Climate Change Regime, A Guide to Rules, Institutions and Procedures* (n 10) 338–39, 353, and 367.

Follow-up to peer review

Follow-up to peer review should be equally accessible and available to all participants in order to foster a similar degree of transparency and naming and shaming. Nevertheless, (political) peer review is different from traditional (legal) enforcement which is triggered by the formal judgment terminating the judiciary process. On the other hand, peer reviews are similarly contingent upon some concluding act which formally legitimizes the outcome of the review process or its potential conclusions (especially since the outcomes or conclusions of the review process are often not legally binding). This can be done by unanimity (such as in the OECD peer reviews of the DAC), consensus (as the peer reviews of the FSB or the Human Rights Council's UPR demonstrate), or more flexibly (such as in the Article 4 consultations of the IMF and in the context of the APRM). Moreover, the act which concludes the peer review process may sometimes lead to elaborate further processes for follow-up (such as the FSB peer reviews or the UPRs showcase) or enforcement (as is the case for the compliance regime as contained in the UNFCCC's Kyoto Protocol).

In the framework of the OECD, DAC delegates must approve the final report. Nonetheless, this final approval is preceded by an editorial session that may cover Parts 1 (the Main Findings and Recommendations) and 2 (the Secretariat Report) of the report. Once approved, the report, a press advisory and—subject to the country's approval—its memorandum, are published. Moreover, eighteen to twenty-four months after the peer review meeting, implementation of the recommendations made by the DAC may be discussed. In this case, a new (mid-term) report is submitted to the Committee. Nonetheless, Members may opt out of mid-term reviews if circumstances dictate them so to do.[97]

In the context of FSB peer reviews, reports need to be approved by the Plenary, as the decision-making body of the FSB. These reports will normally be discussed by the Plenary so that all FSB Members have the opportunity to express their views and agree on revisions if needed. However, in exceptional circumstances, Plenary approval by written procedure will also be possible. Furthermore, Plenary decisions are taken by consensus. This is not synonymous with unanimity. Rather, for the purpose of peer reviews, consensus is understood to mean that the views of all Members are considered and compromises are sought, but that no single jurisdiction can block a decision supported by a clear majority. Moreover, the report provides the opportunity for the jurisdiction(s) being assessed to (separately) express their views. The final report will therefore reflect the views of both the peers and the reviewed jurisdiction(s), including any differences that may arise on a specific topic.[98] Moreover, it should be emphasized that the FSB has no capacity to take legally binding decisions. It therefore has to rely on highly elaborate mechanisms such as

[97] Organisation for Economic Co-operation and Development, Information Note on the DAC Peer Review Process (n 30) 5.

[98] Financial Stability Board—Standing Committee on Standards Implementation, Handbook for FSB Peer Reviews (FSB 12 March 2015) (n 34) 12.

those of its peer review and supervision to ensure compliance.[99] This institutional need is thus also reflected in the complexity of the settings of the FSB's structure for further follow-up. Following approval by the Plenary, the peer review reports and a press release will be published and shared. Nevertheless, the FSB review process also provides for an extremely elaborate further follow-up process. This consists on the one hand of monitoring and reporting of agreed implementation actions, and on the other hand of sharing insights and lessons learned with other stakeholders. With regard to the former, a distinction needs to be made between country reviews and thematic reviews. For country reviews, the reviewed jurisdiction will update the Standing Committee on Standards Implementation (SCSI) on an informal basis after about one year on progress made in addressing the recommendations. The FSB Secretariat will also explore, if requested by the reviewed jurisdiction, ways to support the implementation of those recommendations by leveraging the capacity-building and technical assistance programs of FSB Members. In addition, a natural opportunity for follow-up will be subsequent Financial Sector Assessment Programs (FSAPs) or Reports on the Observance of Standards and Codes (ROSCs). Country review reports can potentially flag issues for analysis in a subsequent FSAP, while FSB Member jurisdictions could request coverage in the FSAP or ROSC of particular areas found in the country review to require follow-up. Monitoring of thematic peer review recommendations and agreed implementation actions will take place on a case-by-case basis as determined by the SCSI; in certain cases, existing monitoring mechanisms by the FSB (such as the Implementation Monitoring Network) or its Members may be used for this purpose. If implementation in a particular jurisdiction is lagging, then the SCSI should be ready to propose exceptional measures for the Plenary's approval, which would be employed on a graduated basis in order to incentivize actions. These could include a letter from the FSB Chair to the relevant Member outlining the Plenary's concerns, a discussion by the Plenary with the reviewed jurisdiction, or the publication of the Plenary's concerns on the FSB website. The timeframe and conditions that necessitate peer pressure measures would be defined and agreed by the SCSI beforehand in order to ensure consistency and transparency of treatment.[100] In addition, follow-up also involves bringing to the attention of other FSB Committees and international bodies any gaps in standards or recurring weaknesses that impede their effectiveness in achieving the desired outcomes and thereby merit being addressed through adjustments to the standards themselves or in best practices for their implementation. The SCSI will highlight any such gaps or weaknesses identified in peer review reports and bring them to the attention of other FSB Committees or to the Plenary for approval to communicate to other bodies, as appropriate. With support from the Secretariat, the SCSI may submit periodically to the Plenary a report outlining trends or common shortcomings

[99] Gadinis, 'The Financial Stability Board: The New Politics of International Financial Regulation' (n 8) 164; Wouters and Odermatt, 'Comparing the 'Four Pillars' of Global Economic Governance: A Critical Analysis of the Institutional Design of the FSB, IMF, World Bank, and WTO' (n 8) 64.

[100] Financial Stability Board—Standing Committee on Standards Implementation, Handbook for FSB Peer Reviews (FSB 12 March 2015) (n 34) 13–14.

identified during peer reviews and proposing actions to address them. The report could include suggestions for improving the peer review process itself, based on the experience with FSB peer reviews.[101] In the framework of the UPR, outcome reports for the States reviewed during the session need to be adopted by consensus by the Plenary.[102] These reports will contain a summary of the proceedings of the review process, the conclusions and/or recommendations, and the voluntary commitments and pledges of the concerned State. Furthermore, the reviewed State should have an opportunity to make preliminary comments on the recommendations, choosing either to accept or to note them. As a result, the outcome report may contain both kinds of recommendations. Moreover, similar to the FSB—the UPR provides for an elaborate follow-up process. In this regard, Resolution 60/251 establishing the Human Rights Council explicitly adds that UPR outcomes '*should be implemented primarily by the State concerned and, as appropriate by other relevant stakeholders*' and underlines that a '*subsequent review should focus, inter alia, on the implementation of the preceding outcome*'.[103] During the second review, the States under review are therefore expected to provide information on what they have been doing to implement the recommendations made during the first review as well as on any other developments in the field of human rights. Furthermore, States are encouraged to provide the Council, on a voluntary basis, with a mid-term update on their follow-up to accepted recommendations. Moreover, the international community is required to provide assistance—in consultation with the country concerned—in implementing the recommendations and conclusions regarding capacity-building and technical assistance. Furthermore, the Resolution stipulates that the Council will address, as appropriate, cases of persistent non-co-operation with the mechanism.[104] Nonetheless, the '*lack of punitive sanctions attached to the process was very likely a sine-qua-non for the support of many G-77 states, which feared that the UPR could turn into a one-sided mechanism for OECD Member states to criticize their human rights record, warranted or not*'.[105]

In the context of the IMF's Article IV consultations, the result of the Board's discussions is simply transmitted to the country.[106] Since there is no need to come to an agreement and since discussants sometimes disagree, discussions can be frank.[107] The transmission of recommendations of the APR Forum to the reviewed country is not subject to the reviewed government's approval. Moreover, the APRM explicitly

[101] Financial Stability Board—Standing Committee on Standards Implementation, Handbook for FSB Peer Reviews (FSB 12 March 2015) (n 34) 14.

[102] Freedman, *The United Nations Human Rights Council—A Critique and Early Assessment* (n 11) 264.

[103] UNGA Res 60/251 (n 11).

[104] UNHRC Res 16/21 (n 48) 4.

[105] McMahon, Busia, and Ascherio, 'Comparing Peer Reviews: The Universal Periodic Review of the UN Human Rights Council and the African Peer Review Mechanism' (n 11) 272; McMahon and Ascherio, 'A Step Ahead in Promoting Human Rights? The Universal Periodic Review of the UN Human Rights Council' (n 11) 234.

[106] International Monetary Fund, *Report by a Group of Independent Experts, External Evaluation of IMF* Surveillance (n 88) 28.

[107] Armin, 'A New Form of Governance? Comparing the Open Method of Coordination to Multilateral Surveillance by the IMF and the OECD' (n 18) 70–88.

foresees that the Final APRM Report be tabled formally and publicly in key regional and sub-regional structures such as the Summit of the African Union, the Pan-African Parliament, the African Commission on Human and Peoples' Rights, the Peace and Security Council, and the Economic, Social and Cultural Council (ECOSOC) of the African Union, as well as the Regional Economic Community of the region of which the country reviewed is a Member.[108] In this regard, the Forum is '*expected to use peer dialogue and persuasion, including the offer of assistance and the use of other appropriate measures, to encourage the reviewed country to implement the suggested changes*'.[109] Moreover, the Base Document of the APRM emphasizes that where a country shows a willingness to rectify the shortcomings identified, other countries and agencies are expected to provide help. However, the Base Document also provides for the fact that where a State wilfully fails to take appropriate measures to implement the recommendations of the review, it may be subjected to collective adverse action.[110] However, the Base Document of the APRM is not clear on what these 'appropriate measures' entail.[111]

iv) Fourth structural element: formal review of peer review

The institutional structure and practical functioning of mechanisms for peer review can generally be improved. The enabling structure of mechanisms for peer review therefore generally contains a procedure which provides for the possibility of formal review of the peer review mechanism itself. This procedure may be elaborate (such as the one foreseen in the context of the IMF or contained in the UNFCCC or its Kyoto Protocol) or simple (such as the modalities foreseen for review of peer review within the context of the FSB or the UPR).

The IMF engages in regular reviews of its surveillance activities such as those under its Article IV consultations by means of its Triennial Surveillance Reviews (TSRs). The mandate for the TSR's is contained in paragraph 21 of the IMF's Executive Board's Decision of 15 June 2007 on Bilateral Surveillance over Member's Policies. It stipulates that '*the Executive Board shall review this Decision and the general implementation of bilateral surveillance at intervals of three years, and at such other times as consideration of such matters may be placed on the agenda of the Executive Board*'.[112] Moreover, in order to make the TSR's self-assessment more independent, the IMF's Executive Board has followed the suggestion to include elements of independent evaluation in its consecutive TSRs.[113] Whereas the 2008

[108] New Partnership for Africa's Development, African Peer Review Mechanism Organisation and Process (n 10) paragraphs 7.17 and 7.18.

[109] Chukwumerije, 'Peer Review and the Promotion of Good Governance in Africa' (n 10) 79.

[110] New Partnership for Africa's Development, African Peer Review Mechanism (APRM), Base Document (n 10) paragraph 24.

[111] Kebonang and Fombad, 'The African Peer Review Mechanism: Challenges and Prospects' (n 53) 51.

[112] International Monetary Fund, Bilateral Surveillance Over Members' Policies, Executive Board Decision (15 June 2007) (n 42).

[113] Robert Lavigne and Lawrence Schembri, 'Strengthening IMF Surveillance: An Assessment of Recent Reforms' (2009–10), Bank of Canada, Discussion Paper <https://www.econstor.eu/handle/10419/66936> accessed 6 May 2017 (hereafter Lavigne and Schembri, 'Strengthening IMF Surveillance: An Assessment of Recent Reforms'); International Monetary Fund—Independent

TSR contained only one paper written by an external consultant on the Article IV process in Europe,[114] the 2011 TSR encompassed four studies written by external consultants, commentaries by two external advisors, and a review of the entire package by the external advisory group.[115] The 2014 TSR continued this trend and even contained surveys with stakeholders and civil society.[116] The consecutive TSR's have thereby attempted and succeeded in keeping the IMF's surveillance function relevant. The 2011 TSR diagnosed IMF surveillance '*as too fragmented, with risk assessments lacking depth and insufficient focus on interconnections and transmission of shocks*'.[117] The TSR therefore recommended improvements with regard to interconnectedness, risk assessments, financial stability, external stability, legal framework, traction, and resource requirements.[118] In a similar vein, the 2014 TSR aimed to ensure that '*IMF surveillance continues to best support sustainable growth in a deeply interconnected post-crisis world*'.[119] It thus identified several operational priorities which were to integrate and deepen risk and spill-over analysis, make more mainstream any macro-financial surveillance, pay more attention to tailored, cohesive, and expert policy advice in order to achieve greater impact, and be more even-handed.[120] Likewise, the UNFCCC and its Kyoto Protocol contain several elaborate review procedures. These include Article 7.2 of the UNFCCC which allows the Convention of Parties to examine the institutional arrangements under the Convention, in the light of Article 2 and experience gained in its implementation and the evolution of scientific and technical knowledge. Nonetheless, there is no periodic review requirement for the examination of the UNFCCC's institutional machinery. In a similar vein, Article 9 of the Kyoto Protocol mandates the Convention of Parties/Meeting of Parties to review the Protocol as a whole. However, contrary to the UNFCCC, the Kyoto Protocol foresees some periodicity since its Article 9.2 states that its first review is to take place at the second session of the Convention of Parties/Meeting of Parties. Moreover, although the Convention

Evaluation Office, *The Role of the IMF as Trusted Advisor* (IMF 2013), 30–31 <http://www.ieo-imf.org/ieo/files/completedevaluations/RITA_-_Main_Report.pdf> accessed 20 May 2017 (hereafter International Monetary Fund, The Role of the IMF as Trusted Advisor).

[114] International Monetary Fund, '2008 Triennial Surveillance Review—Overview Paper' <http://www.imf.org/external/pp/longres.aspx?id=4295> assessed 13 May 2017.

[115] International Monetary Fund, '2011 Triennial Surveillance Review' <http://www.imf.org/external/np/spr/triennial/2011/> assessed 13 May 2017 (hereafter International Monetary Fund, 2011 Triennial Surveillance Review).

[116] International Monetary Fund, '2014 Triennial Surveillance Review' <http://www.imf.org/external/np/spr/triennial/2014/> assessed 13 May 2017 (hereafter International Monetary Fund, 2014 Triennial Surveillance Review).

[117] International Monetary Fund, 2011 Triennial Surveillance Review (n 115).

[118] International Monetary Fund, 'Managing Director's Statement on Strengthening Surveillance - 2011 Triennial Surveillance Review' (27 October 2011), 6 <http://www.imf.org/en/Publications/Policy-Papers/Issues/2016/12/31/Managing-Director-s-Statement-on-Strengthening-Surveillance-2011-Triennial-Surveillance-PP4607> assessed 13 May 2017.

[119] International Monetary Fund, 2014 Triennial Surveillance Review (n 116).

[120] International Monetary Fund, 'Managing Director's Action Plan for Strengthening Surveillance—2014 Triennial Surveillance Review' (December 2014) <https://www.imf.org/external/np/pp/eng/2014/112114.pdf> accessed 26 May 2017.

of Parties/Meeting of Parties may determine the timing for further reviews, the Protocol requires that these take place at regular intervals and in a timely manner.[121]

The review procedures of the FSB and the UPR are less elaborate. Within the context of the FSB, the Handbook for FSB Peer Reviews only foresees that '*the design of FSB peer reviews will be further refined and the Handbook will be accordingly revised—to take account of changes in the assessment mechanisms of other international bodies as well as the experience with FSB peer reviews*'.[122] In the same way, Resolution 60/251 states that '*the UPR is an evolving process. Therefore, the Council, after the conclusion of the first review cycle, may review the modalities and the periodicity of this mechanism, based on best practices and lessons learned*'.[123] The review of the UPR process has consequently resulted in Resolution 16/21 on the Review of the work and functioning of the Human Rights Council.[124]

c) *Participants*

Mechanisms for peer review are based on the active involvement of several participants. At minimum, these consist of the entity under review and its peers.[125] At maximum, the enabling structure may also entail the presence of additional participants in order to increase or guarantee the effectiveness and/or the legitimacy of the review. These additional participants can be tasked with the drafting of the review report(s), the general facilitation of the review process, and/or its examination. Moreover, observers or other external relevant stakeholders are often allowed to attend the review meetings. Furthermore, mechanisms for peer review may even involve a wider public (especially if they result in some other follow-up process).

In the context of Article IV consultations, the IMF's Executive Board will discuss most Staff reports in some detail. Nonetheless, these meetings have almost no influence on the outcome of the appraisals made by its staff.[126] During the Executive Board's meeting, most or all Executive Directors will participate whereupon the Managing Director or a Deputy Managing Director will sum up the views of the Board.[127] As a result, '*the only influence the Executive Board has over bilateral surveillance is to place different degrees of emphasis on the various elements raised in the staff appraisal and to voice that emphasis in a summing up, an initial draft of which is prepared by staff prior to the Board meetings*'.[128] Moreover, the

[121] Yamin and Depledge, *The International Climate Change Regime, A Guide to Rules, Institutions and Procedures* (n 9) 552–54.

[122] Financial Stability Board—Standing Committee on Standards Implementation, Handbook for FSB Peer Reviews (FSB 12 March 2015) (n 34) 1.

[123] UNGA Res 60/251 (n 11).

[124] UNHRC Res 16/21 (n 48).

[125] Interestingly, the set-up for the IMF's final discussions within the framework of its Article IV consultations is even more limited. In this context, the Executive Director representing the Member presents the final report at the meeting of the Executive Board; Chayes and Chayes, *The New Sovereignty—Compliance with International Regulatory Agreements* (n 6) 235.

[126] Lombardi and Woods, 'The Politics of Influence: An Analysis of IMF Surveillance' (n 6) 723.

[127] International Monetary Fund, *Report by a Group of Independent Experts, External Evaluation of IMF Surveillance* (n 59) 25.

[128] Lombardi and Woods, 'The Politics of Influence: An Analysis of IMF Surveillance' (n 6) 723.

external evaluation of IMF surveillance of 1999 stressed that the Executive Board's Membership (of twenty-four Members) was '*extremely large for useful exchanges of views, discussion, and group decision making*'. It therefore suggested that Article IV Staff reports in the first instance be discussed in a committee rather than by the full Board.[129] The IMF's peer review can also not be described as very rigorous since there are '*no pre-appointed reviews and no government delegation participates*'.[130] The IMF has therefore consistently sought to increase the efficiency of its Executive Board, including reflection on possible best practices and lessons learned from similar structures in other international organizations. Nonetheless, in this regard it has so far not looked to the WTO for inspiration since the latter was basically considered '*a Member-driven organization in which little authority is delegated to the Secretary General and the Secretariat*'.[131] Moreover, in spite of the existence of some (academic and political) criticism which has described the IMF's organizational culture as '*hierarchical, technocratic, officious and conformist*', the IMF has so far not adequately managed to look into the possibility of making organizational change at staff level.[132]

Most mechanisms for peer review (such as those of the OECD's DAC, the FSB, the Human Rights Council's UPR, the APRM, and the structures for international climate change mitigation as contained in the UNFCCC and its Kyoto Protocol) function with a larger range of participants. These organizations therefore seem to trade the principle of efficiency (which is often derived from a limitation to the set of participants) for increased legitimacy. In these instances, increased legitimacy is often not only derived from a more diverse participation but also (a) from a close interaction between the expert entities which are in charge of the initial stages of the review (such as the examiners in the OECD DAC peer reviews, the team leader for FSB reviews, or the UPRs' rapporteurs) and those which participate as fully fledged political peers in the (final) review, and/or (b) from the adversarial nature of the review process (which explicitly allows the country under review to intervene).

Peer reviews undertaken within the framework of the OECD's DAC are based on the active participation of five entities.[133] These include: (a) the DAC Chair who leads the meeting; (b) the Secretariat which presents its findings as a result of the field visit(s); (c) the two examiners (who are selected from a country with a programme of similar size and complexity to the programme being examined; language and geography are other factors which are taken into account) who present the review's team

[129] International Monetary Fund, *Report by a Group of Independent Experts, External Evaluation of IMF Surveillance* (n 59) 74–75.

[130] Armin, 'A New Form of Governance? Comparing the Open Method of Coordination to Multilateral Surveillance by the IMF and the OECD' (n 18) 70–88.

[131] International Monetary Fund—Independent Evaluation Office, *Studies of IMF Governance—A compendium* (IMF 2009), 82–126 (particularly at 104) <http://www.ieo-imf.org/ieo/files/books/16956_IEO_Gov_Compend_WEB.pdf> accessed 13 May 2017.

[132] Bessma Momani, 'IMF Staff: Missing Link in Fund Reform Proposals' (2007) 2 Review of International Organizations 39 (hereafter Momani, 'IMF Staff: Missing Link in Fund Reform Proposals').

[133] Organisation for Economic Co-operation and Development, Information Note on the DAC Peer Review Process (n 30) 5–6.

findings and lead discussions based on Part 1 issues; (d) the country under review which presents its responses to issues and questions raised by the examiners and the DAC; and (e) other DAC Members.

In the context of FSB peer reviews, at least three entities will provide input: (a) the team leader (assisted as need be by other team members) who will present a draft report; (b) the reviewed jurisdiction (which will be invited to the discussion whether or not it is a Member of the Standing Committee on Standards Implementation) which will comment on the report and explain how it intends to respond to its recommendations; and (c) other Members of the Standing Committee on Standards Implementation who will provide comments and approve the report in the Plenary.[134] The latter include not only the other Member jurisdictions but also international financial institutions and international standard-setting, regulatory, supervisory, and central bank bodies.[135] Moreover, this list is not-exhaustive since Article 5 of the FSB Charter explicitly provides that '*the eligibility of Members will be reviewed periodically by the Plenary in the light of the FSB objectives*'.[136]

Peer reviews which are undertaken within the framework of the UPR are based on the active participation of at least five entities. In this regard, it is interesting to note that the term 'peer review', which was explicitly contained in several initial proposals for the creation of the new mechanism, was (conspicuously) absent from UN Resolution 60/251 which finally established the Universal Periodic Review.[137] The ultimately crystallized term (ie Universal Periodic Review) semantically allowed other stakeholders to participate alongside the peers in the review process.[138] Overall participants to the UPR therefore encompass: (a) the Office of the High Commissioner for Human Rights which compiles a report with information contained in official UN documents and a summary of other stakeholder information; (b) the President of the Council who will oversee the review meeting in the framework of a Working Group; (c) a group of three rapporteurs (ie the so-called Troikas which are selected by drawing of lots among the different regional groups of the Council—interestingly, the country under review may request that one of the rapporteurs be from its own regional group and/or may ask to substitute a rapporteur on only one occasion) which will facilitate each review and prepare the report of the Working Group; (d) the country under review and its national human

[134] Financial Stability Board, FSB Framework for Strengthening Adherence to International Standards (FSB 9 January 2010) (n 8) 2; Financial Stability Board—Standing Committee on Standards Implementation, Handbook for FSB Peer Reviews (FSB 12 March 2015) (n 34) 12.

[135] Wouters and Odermatt, 'Comparing the 'Four Pillars' of Global Economic Governance: A Critical Analysis of the Institutional Design of the FSB, IMF, World Bank, and WTO' (n 8) 59.

[136] Wouters and Odermatt, 'Comparing the 'Four Pillars' of Global Economic Governance: A Critical Analysis of the Institutional Design of the FSB, IMF, World Bank, and WTO' (n 8) 60.

[137] UNGA Res 60/251 (n 11); Freedman, *The United Nations Human Rights Council—A Critique and Early Assessment* (n 11) 255–56; Redondo, 'The Universal Periodic Review of the UN Human Rights Council: An Assessment of the First Session' (n 46) 725–26.

[138] Freedman, *The United Nations Human Rights Council—A Critique and Early Assessment* (n 11) 256; Redondo, 'The Universal Periodic Review of the UN Human Rights Council: An Assessment of the First Session' (n 46) 725.

rights institution; and (e) the forty-seven Member states of the Council which may participate in the debates.[139]

In the context of the APRM, the final peer review starts with the submission of the APR team's report to the participating Heads of State and Government through the APRM Secretariat. Consequently, presentations to the Forum are made by the eminent person responsible for the country review and by the president of the country under review. However, in certain instances, countries under review have been provided with some time to study the final reports before these were discussed.[140] Moreover, it should be noted that States are not required to participate in the APRM. In addition, the APRM's Membership is only open to African States. This contrasts with UPRs which subject all UN Member States to reviews.[141] The consideration and adoption of the final report by the participating Heads of State and Government, including their decision in this regard, marks the end of this stage.[142]

Peer review undertaken in the context of international climate change mitigation (as embodied by the structures of the UNFCCC and its Kyoto Protocol) is based on the involvement of several participants (the Conference of Parties, the Meeting of Parties, expert review teams, and the Subsidiary Body for Implementation), depending on the specific nature of the Parties (ie Annex I parties versus non-Annex I Parties).[143] The set-up of the Compliance Committee of the UNFCCC's Kyoto Protocol is even more restricted than the IMF's Executive Board since it is limited to twenty members as well as their alternates.[144] Interestingly, this Committee provides for individuals to be elected in their personal capacity. Such a set-up supposedly enhances the objectivity of the Compliance Committee's proceedings, contrary to a situation of party membership which could have the effect of furthering the common interest of the parties.[145]

The presence of the aforementioned theoretical core elements (in terms of objectives, enabling structure, and participants) and their specific practical biases (in terms of transparency and naming and shaming (objective), typical institutional features (enabling structure), and involvement by the reviewed country, the peers, and other entities (participation)) may be used to distinguish mechanisms for peer review from other procedures such as judicial proceedings, fact-finding missions, or reporting and data collection.

[139] UNGA Res 60/251 (n 11); UNHRC Res 5/1 (n 28) 7–8; UNHRC Res 16/21 (n 48) 4.

[140] Killander, 'The African Peer Review Mechanism and Human Rights: The First Reviews and the Way Forward' (n 10) 52–53.

[141] McMahon, Busia, and Ascherio, 'Comparing Peer Reviews: The Universal Periodic Review of the UN Human Rights Council and the African Peer Review Mechanism (n 11) 288; Kebonang and Fombad, 'The African Peer Review Mechanism: Challenges and Prospects' (n 53) 52–53.

[142] New Partnership for Africa's Development, African Peer Review Mechanism (APRM), Base Document (n 10) paragraph 23, and New Partnership for Africa's Development, African Peer Review Mechanism Organisation and Process (n 10) paragraph 7.16.

[143] Yamin and Depledge, *The International Climate Change Regime, A Guide to Rules, Institutions and Procedures* (n 9) 338–39, 353, and 367.

[144] Brunnée, Doelle, and Rajamani, *Promoting Compliance in an Evolving Climate Regime*) (n 9) 82.

[145] Fitzmaurice, Ong, and Merkouris, *Research Handbook on International Environmental Law* (n 29) 430.

Although these other procedures are also used to monitor and to ensure compliance with internationally agreed policies and norms, several differences exist.[146] With regard to the latter two it should be noted that peer review is only partly based on fact-finding processes and activities which encompass reporting and data collection. These two elements are indeed encapsulated in peer review's transparency objective. Nonetheless, the concept of peer review is broader in scope since it also encompasses a second objective of naming and shaming. Moreover, the concept of peer review is different from judicial proceedings. Peer review is essentially managerial and therefore based on the dynamics of dialogue and accountability.[147] As a consequence, it cannot guarantee that its practical outcomes or formal conclusions should or will be implemented. In other words, the naming and shaming objective is different from the goal of legal enforcement. Likewise, the structural features and participants in judicial proceedings differ markedly from those that typically form/take part in a mechanism for peer review. Moreover, peer review is essentially future-oriented whereas traditional dispute settlement mainly focuses on the determination of a causal link between a wrongful act and its (actual or potential) damage.[148]

3. The advent of the Trade Policy Review Mechanism: a nascent mechanism for peer review?

The TPRM has generally been equated with a mechanism for peer review. Nevertheless, academic output with regard to the history of the TPRM is extremely limited.[149] Moreover, expert literature analysing the concept of peer review (especially) in international law has been equally scarce.[150] This section will therefore analyse the history of the TPRM and examine whether the mechanism's institutional evolution matches that of a nascent ideal mechanism for peer review.

Throughout the functioning of the GATT and the WTO, the final establishment of the TPRM in Annex 3 of the Marrakesh Agreement establishing the World Trade Organization (1995)[151] was preceded by mainly five historical steps. These

[146] Pagani, 'Peer Review: A Tool for Co-operation and Change' (n 21) 5.

[147] Chayes and Chayes, *The New Sovereignty—Compliance with International Regulatory Agreements* (n 6) 230.

[148] Fitzmaurice, Ong, and Merkouris, *Research Handbook on International Environmental Law* (n 29) 439.

[149] Asif H Qureshi, *The World Trade Organization: Implementing Trade Norms* (Manchester University Press 1996) 108–09 (hereafter Qureshi, *The World Trade Organization: Implementing Trade Norms*); Sam Laird and Raymundo Valdés, 'The Trade Policy Review Mechanism', in A Narlikar, M Daunton, and RM Stern (eds), *The Oxford Handbook on The World Trade Organization* (Oxford University Press 2012) 464–65 (hereafter Laird and Valdés, 'The Trade Policy Review Mechanism'); VanGrasstek, *The History and Future of the World Trade Organization* (n 56) 298–87.

[150] Chayes and Chayes, *The New Sovereignty—Compliance with International Regulatory Agreements* (n 6).

[151] Trade Policy Review Mechanism—Arrangements for the Continued Operation of the Mechanism, Decision of 10 May 1994 (11 May 1994) BISD L/7458 (hereafter Trade Policy Review Mechanism—Arrangements for the Continued Operation of the Mechanism, Decision of 10 May 1994); WTO, 'Trade Policy Review Mechanism' <https://www.wto.org/english/docs_e/legal_e/29-tprm_e.htm> accessed 20 May 2017 (hereafter, the Trade Policy Review Mechanism).

include: (1) Article X of the GATT (1947),[152] (2) the Tokyo Round negotiations resulting in the Understanding Regarding Notification, Consultation, Dispute Settlement and Surveillance (1979),[153] (3) the (so-called) Wise Men's report '*Trade Policies for a Better Future: Proposals for Action*' (1985),[154] (4) the Functioning of the GATT System (FOGS) negotiations (1986),[155] and (5) the provisional adoption of the TPRM during the Montreal mid-term review of the Uruguay Round (December 1988)[156] followed by the decision taken by the Trade Negotiations Committee of 12 April 1989 to start with the implementation of the TPRM immediately.

During each of these steps, the Contracting Parties of the GATT (later evolving into the Members of the WTO) decided to modify some institutional elements which either related to (1) the objectives; (2) the (enabling) structure; or (3) their (participatory) involvement in the nascent TPRM. As a result, there is a wide institutional difference between the original simplicity of Article X and the final complexity of Annex 3 of the Marrakesh Agreement.

a) Article X of the GATT (1947): nascent transparency

The translation and proliferation of the general transparency objective into various articles and mechanisms of the GATT and the WTO seems to stem originally from Article X of the GATT (1947).[157] This Article provides the requirement for Contracting Parties/Members to notify their trade policy and practices in order to enhance their transparency. As a result, the Article may be considered as the earliest precursor to the TPRM.

Nevertheless, during the early years of the GATT, the transparency objective and requirement almost never stood centre stage, formally or substantially. From a formal point of view, there was no mention of Article X (GATT 1947) in any adopted

[152] WTO, 'The General Agreement on Tariffs and Trade (GATT 1947)' <https://www.wto.org/english/docs_e/legal_e/gatt47_01_e.htm> accessed 20 May 2017; Sylvia Ostry traces transparency even further down to the '*vaguely defined yet non-controversial principle*' of Article 38 of the Havana Charter of the International Trade Organization; Sylvia Ostry, 'China and the WTO: Transparency Issue' (1998) UCLA Journal of International Law and Foreign Affairs 3(1) 4–5 (hereafter Ostry, 'China and the WTO: Transparency Issue').

[153] Understanding Regarding Notification, Consultation, Dispute Settlement and Surveillance (28 November 1979) BISD L/4907 (hereafter Understanding Regarding Notification, Consultation, Dispute Settlement and Surveillance).

[154] *Trade Policies for a Better Future, Proposals for Action*, Geneva (GATT 1985) (hereafter *Trade Policies for a Better Future, Proposals for Action*). This report was also inspired by the 1982 Conference on Trade Policy organized by the Institute of International Economics in Washington DC. See also Wiliam R Cline (ed), *Trade Policy in the 1980s* (The Institute for International Economics 1983) (hereafter Cline, *Trade Policy in the 1980s*).

[155] Draft Ministerial Declaration on the Uruguay Round (20 September 1986) BISD Min (86)/W/19, 15–16 (hereafter Draft Ministerial Declaration on the Uruguay Round).

[156] Mid-term Review Agreements, News of the Uruguay Round of Multilateral Trade Negotiations, NUR 027, 24 April 1989, 33–36 (hereafter Mid-term Review Agreements, News of the Uruguay Round of Multilateral Trade Negotiations).

[157] Organisation for Economic Co-operation and Development, *Export Restrictions: Benefits of Transparency and Good Practices* (TAD/TC/WP(2012)22/FINAL, OECD 20 March 2013), 11.

GATT (1947) decision from 1947 to 1984.[158] Moreover, only nine GATT cases featured Article X of the GATT (1947) between 1984 and 1994.[159] The same was true from a substantial point of view since GATT Panels and Contracting Parties seemed to marginalize the content and meaning of this mainly procedural Article. According to GATT Panels and Contracting Parties, if a measure was inconsistent with the '*substantive*' obligations of the GATT, '*the publication of the measure or whether it had been applied in an "impartial, uniform and reasonable" manner became irrelevant*'.[160] Nonetheless, the transparency objective grew in importance over the years. This was due to several reasons: GATT-systemic grounds and the overall rise in the number of GATT Contracting Parties. The GATT gradually moved away from a tariff-based reciprocal bargaining structure to a system of rule creation and enforcement. Both of which require transparency.[161] Moreover, the continuous increase of the GATT Membership inevitably resulted in a higher demand for transparency.[162] In the words of the Appellate Body in *United States—Restrictions on Imports of Cotton and Man-made Fibre Underwear* (1997): '*from a due process point of view Members and other persons affected, or likely to be affected, by governmental measures imposing restraints, requirements and other burdens, should have a reasonable opportunity to acquire authentic information about such measures and accordingly to protect and adjust their activities or alternatively seek modification of such measures*'.[163]

Article X of the GATT (1947) features almost none of the structural elements that are typical for a mechanism for peer review.[164] However, Article X of the GATT (1947) gradually gave rise to several other specific articles and wider surveillance structures which aimed to foster the transparency objective. The need for further transparency thus inspired the Ninth session of the GATT (1954–55) which also doubled as a review session. During the Eighth session, parties had observed that

[158] Padideh Ala'I, 'From the Periphery to the Center? The Evolving Jurisprudence on Transparency and Good Governance', (4th Global Administrative Law Seminar: from Fragmentation to Unity? Viterbo, 2008) <https://prd-idrc.azureedge.net/sites/default/files/openebooks/455-0/index.html#page_165> accessed 6 May 2017 (hereafter Ala'I, 'From the Periphery to the Center? The Evolving Jurisprudence on Transparency and Good Governance').

[159] Ala'I, 'From the Periphery to the Center? The Evolving Jurisprudence on Transparency and Good Governance', (n 158) 7.

[160] Padideh Ala'I, 'Transparency and the Expansion of the WTO Mandate' (2011) 26(4) American University International Law Review 1013 (hereafter Ala'I, 'Transparency and the Expansion of the WTO Mandate').

[161] Ala'I, 'From the Periphery to the Center? The Evolving Jurisprudence on Transparency and Good Governance' (n 187) 4.

[162] World Trade Organization, 'Members and Observers' <https://www.wto.org/english/thewto_e/whatis_e/tif_e/org6_e.htm> accessed 20 May 2017.

[163] Steve Charnovitz, 'Transparency and Participation in the World Trade Organization' (2004) Rutgers Law Review 8 (hereafter Charnovitz, 'Transparency and Participation in the World Trade Organization'); WTO, *United States—Restrictions on Imports of Cotton and Man-made Fibre Underwear—Appellate Body Report* (10 February 1997) WT/DS24/AB/R, 21.

[164] See section 2 of this chapter: 'Mechanisms for peer review—theoretical core elements'; Article X(3) (b) of the GATT 1947 required each Contracting Party to maintain, or to institute as soon as practicable, judicial, arbitral, or administrative tribunals or procedures for the purpose, *inter alia*, of the prompt review and correction of administrative action relating to customs matters. As a result, Article X laid the groundwork for more (internal) transparency-related structures.

international trade continued to be hampered by tariff barriers and other restrictions.[165] The need for further information gathering—by means of structured review sessions—was therefore recognized. Although the working party reports had resulted in regular consultations in order to review quantitative restrictions maintained for balance-of-payment purposes, the Contracting Parties decided not to extend additional authority to the GATT Secretariat to conduct reviews on other trade issues.[166] The drive for transparency—chaperoned by Article X of the GATT (1947)—also led to the so-called Haberler report (1958). Developing countries had complained that their mainly agricultural interests were being infringed upon and that they had capacity constraints in undertaking independent surveillance of the developed countries' trade policies. The Haberler report thus lead to further surveillance of agricultural policies of developed and developing countries and indirectly also to the later establishment of a new Committee for agricultural trade.[167] The need for increased transparency resulted furthermore in the creation of a series of mechanisms between 1960 and 1970. These included the Committee on Balance-of-Payments Restrictions, the Textile Surveillance Body, and a variety of codes under the Multilateral Trade Negotiations which were also subject to notification requirements for Contracting Parties that had signed the codes.[168]

In terms of participation, Article X of the GATT (1947) only affected the Contracting Parties to the GATT (and later Members of the WTO). These had to notify their trade policy and practices in order to enhance their transparency. Nonetheless, during the initial years, GATT Membership grew exponentially (reaching seventy-five Contracting Parties by the end of the 1960s with developing countries constituting roughly half of these).[169]The GATT Secretariat's involvement in the notification procedures under Article X or its role in any other transparency-related articles or surveillance-structures was, however, rather limited. Coherent reporting and follow-up was quite easy to achieve in view of the (still) limited membership of the GATT. Moreover, as observers noted, '*in the case of pronouncements on the legality of specific actions, it is essential to keep in mind that only the Contracting Parties are empowered to interpret the General Agreement*'.[170] In other words, there was simply no need for a strong mandate of the Secretariat.

[165] Multilateral Trade Negotiations, The Uruguay Round, Negotiating Group on Functioning of the GATT System, the 1954/55 Review Session, Note by the Secretariat, MTN.GNG/NG14/W/12, 14 August 1987, 1.

[166] Arunabha Ghosh, 'Developing Countries in the WTO Trade Policy Review Mechanism' (2010) 9(3) World Trade Review 428 (hereafter Ghosh, 'Developing Countries in the WTO Trade Policy Review Mechanism').

[167] *Trends in International Trade: Contracting Parties to the General Agreement on Tariffs and Trade, a report by a panel of experts* (Geneva 1958); Ghosh, *See No Evil, Speak No Evil, The WTO, The Trade Policy Review Mechanism, And Developing Countries* (DPhil thesis, University of Oxford 2008).

[168] Blackhurst, 'Strengthening GATT Surveillance of Trade-Related Policies' (n 39) 133; Ghosh, 'Developing Countries in the WTO Trade Policy Review Mechanism' (n 166) 429.

[169] World Trade Organization, 'Members and Observers' <https://www.wto.org/english/thewto_e/whatis_e/tif_e/org6_e.htm> assessed 13 May 2017.

[170] Blackhurst, 'Strengthening GATT Surveillance of Trade-Related Policies' (n 39) 128.

b) *The Tokyo Round negotiations resulting in the Understanding Regarding Notification, Consultation, Dispute Settlement and Surveillance (November 1979): a first step towards institutionalizing peer review?*

The initial machinery which was in place at the outset of the negotiations of the Tokyo Round (1973–79) consisted solely of the Trade Negotiations Committee (which was composed of all countries that took part in the Round). Nonetheless, in February 1975 the Trade Negotiations Committee established six groups which were to concern themselves with the six subjects set out in paragraph 3 of the Tokyo Declaration (ie tropical products, tariffs, non-tariff measures, agriculture, sector approach, and safeguards) and several sub-groups (quantitative restrictions, technical barriers to trade, customs matters, subsidies and countervailing duties, government procurement, grains, meat, and dairy products) to deal with the Round's substantive negotiations. Moreover, in November 1976 Brazil proposed the setting up a seventh group, the so-called Framework Group.[171] In view of the rather outdated (ie thirty-year-old) GATT rules, the far-reaching developments which that had taken place in international trading relationships and the increased GATT membership, this group was tasked '*with the consideration of improvements in the international framework for the conduct of world trade which might be desirable in the light of progress in the negotiations*'.[172] Until February 1978, the Framework Group was therefore responsible for work on several topics including discussions on consultations, dispute settlement, and surveillance procedures under Articles XXII (providing for consultations on any matter affecting the operations of the GATT) and XXIII (relating to GATT complaints).[173] In this regard, it should be noted that the discussions on (annual) surveillance were initially limited to the safeguards area[174] but also that they had gradually morphed into other thematic fields due to a rising interest by other negotiating groups.[175] By the middle of July 1978, the Secretariat proposed draft texts (either under its own auspices or as a reflection of the views of delegations) which lead to an intensifying of the negotiations in early 1979. By April 1979, all texts were agreed for submission to the Trade Negotiations Committee.[176] The ensuing Understanding Regarding Notification, Consultation, Dispute Settlement and Surveillance therefore became a first stepping-stone towards

[171] The Tokyo Round of Multilateral Trade Negotiations, Report by the Director-General of GATT, Geneva April 1979, 95–96.

[172] The Tokyo Round of Multilateral Trade Negotiations, Report by the Director-General of GATT, Geneva April 1979, 96.

[173] The Tokyo Round of Multilateral Trade Negotiations, Report by the Director-General of GATT, Geneva April 1979, 97.

[174] Statement by the representative of Canada on 28 June 1977—Notification, Consultation, Surveillance and Dispute Settlement, Multilateral Trade Negotiations, Group 'Safeguards', MTN/SG/W/36, 6 June 1977, 3.

[175] Outline Regarding Institutions, Consultations, Dispute Settlement and Surveillance in Code for Preventing Technical Barriers to Trade, Multilateral Trade Negotiations, Group 'Non-Tariff Measures', Sub-Group 'Technical Barriers to Trade', MTN/NTN/W/144, 13 March 1978.

[176] The Tokyo Round of Multilateral Trade Negotiations, Report by the Director-General of GATT, Geneva April 1979, 97.

institutionalized peer review within the GATT/WTO.[177] Its structural novelties included '*the requirement for governments—in addition to their existing GATT obligations regarding publication and notification—to notify to the maximum extent possible the adoption of trade measures that affect the operation of GATT*', and '*the introduction of a regular and systemic review of developments in the trading system by the GATT Contracting Parties*'.[178] Several Contracting Parties explicitly welcomed the further elaboration of the Understanding.[179]

In terms of its objective-setting, the Understanding remains rather undeveloped. The text of the Understanding with regard to the goal of surveillance is relatively limited. Nevertheless, for the first time, the transparency objective ('*the Contracting Parties agree to conduct a regular and systemic review of developments in the trading system*') was linked with an element of naming and shaming—albeit in a relatively light version ('*particular attention would be paid to developments which affect rights and obligations under the GATT ... and to measures which have been subject to consultation, conciliation or dispute settlement procedures laid down in this Understanding*').[180]

Furthermore, the Understanding only prescribes that '*the Contracting Parties agree to a regular and systemic review of developments in the trading system*'.[181] The GATT Council was therefore asked to elaborate appropriate procedures at an early meeting.[182] This resulted in special GATT Council meetings which were to take place twice a year to review general developments in the trading system. Documents (prepared by the GATT Secretariat) for these meetings were based on '*a combination of official trade policy notifications and on what the Secretariat itself was able to glean from the press and unofficial sources. After discussion through the GATT Council, they were made available to the general public.*'[183] Since the Council had explicitly recognized that its arrangements would be necessarily experimental and would unavoidably lead to some overlap, it also suggested that the arrangements should be kept as simple as possible and would be reviewed in the light of experience.[184] The Understanding and its practical elaboration therefore—for the first time—contain some of the typical structural features of a mechanism for peer

[177] Understanding Regarding Notification, Consultation, Dispute Settlement and Surveillance (n 153) 200–08.

[178] The Tokyo Round of Multilateral Trade Negotiations, Report by the Director-General of GATT, Geneva April 1979, 151.

[179] Summary Record of Fourth Meeting, Held in the Palais des Nations, Geneva on Wednesday, 28 November 1979, Contracting Parties, Thirty-Fifth Session, SR. 35/4, 18 December 1979.

[180] Understanding Regarding Notification, Consultation, Dispute Settlement and Surveillance (n 153) 204.

[181] Understanding Regarding Notification, Consultation, Dispute Settlement and Surveillance (n 153) 204.

[182] GATT Annual Sessions Acts on Tokyo Round Results and Sets Future Work Programme, Press Release of 30 November 1979, GATT/1253, 30 November 1979, 8.

[183] Notification and Surveillance, Proposal by the Director-General (26 March 1980) BISD C/111, 2–3 (hereafter Notification and Surveillance, Proposal by the Director-General); Victoria Curzon Price, 'New Institutional Developments in GATT' (1992) 1(1) Minnesota Journal of Global Trade 97 (hereafter Price, 'New Institutional Developments in GATT').

[184] Notification and Surveillance, Proposal by the Director-General (n 183) 2.

review.[185] The structure of the Secretariat reports and the institutional setting of the special GATT Council meetings thus started to guide and regulate the transmission and use of information within the review process in order to achieve an increased but standardized degree of transparency and naming and shaming.

Participation in the surveillance activities of the special GATT Council meetings was open to all Contracting Parties. Furthermore, neither the Understanding itself nor its procedures as elaborated by the GATT Council foresaw an increased role for the Secretariat.[186]

c) *'Trade Policies for a Better Future: Proposals for Action' (March 1985)—further reflection towards a fully fledged mechanism for peer review*

After the Ministerial Meeting of 1982 had declared that '*the multilateral trading system, of which GATT is the legal foundation, is seriously endangered*', the GATT Council, in conformity with the Understanding Regarding Notification, Consultation, Dispute Settlement and Surveillance and its further structural elaboration, started to held special meetings between 1983 and 1985.[187] These meetings repeatedly came to the conclusion that many Contracting Parties were not adhering to the commitments contained in the 1982 Ministerial Declaration.[188] The period between the end of the Tokyo Round in 1979 and the launch of the Uruguay Round in 1986 was indeed marred '*by an increased use of safeguards, anti-dumping and other trade-remedy laws, balance-of-payments restrictions, voluntary exports restraints and other grey-area measures*'.[189] GATT Director-General Dunkel therefore decided to invite an independent panel of seven eminent persons (headed by Dr Fitz Leutwiler) '*to identify the fundamental causes of the problems afflicting the international trading system and to consider how these may be overcome during the remainder of the 1980s*'. In November 1983, the so-called Wise Men's group started its work. All members of the group contributed working papers to one or more meetings of the group. In March 1985, the group came up with its final report '*Trade Policies for a Better Future: Proposals for Action*'.[190] The report was written against the background of the first fragile signs of an economic recovery (in 1973) which were, however, not echoed in the realm of international trade. Instead, the report characterized the latest developments in this context as '*choked by a growing accumulation of restrictive measures*'.[191] The report therefore critically analysed the role of international trade in the world economy (Chapter I), looked into the pros and

[185] See section 2 of this chapter, 'Mechanisms for peer review—theoretical core elements'.

[186] Understanding Regarding Notification, Consultation, Dispute Settlement and Surveillance (n 153) 204.

[187] Ministerial Declaration (1982) BISD L/5424, 1.

[188] Terence P Steward, *The GATT Uruguay Round: A Negotiating History (1986–1992)* (Kluwer Law International 1993–99) vol II, 1901–11 (hereafter Steward, *The GATT Uruguay Round: A Negotiating History (1986–1992)*).

[189] VanGrasstek, *The History and Future of the World Trade Organization* (n 56) 280.

[190] *Trade Policies for a Better Future, Proposals for Action* (n 154).

[191] *Trade Policies for a Better Future, Proposals for Action* (n 154) 5.

cons of liberal trading policies (Chapter II), and proposed fifteen recommendations for specific, immediate action to meet the crisis in the trading system (Chapter III).[192]

Several of these recommendations had a clear bearing on the nascent TPRM.[193] These include: (1) Recommendation No 1 which advocated that '*[i]n each country, the making of trade policy should be brought into the open. The costs and benefits of trade policy actions, existing and prospective, should be analysed through a "protection balance sheet". Private and public companies should be required to reveal in their financial statements any subsidies received. Public support for open trade policies should be fostered*'; (2) Recommendation No 8 which argued that '*[a]t the international level, trade policy and the functioning of the trading system should be made more open. Countries should be subject to regular oversight or surveillance of their policies and actions, about which the GATT Secretariat should collect and publish information*'; and (3) Recommendation No 13 which emphasized that the group supported '*the launching of a new round of GATT negotiations, provided they are directed toward the primary goal of strengthening the multilateral trading system and further opening of world markets*'.

Recommendations Nos 1 and 8 were almost entirely inspired by the double needs for increased transparency and (stronger) naming and shaming. Recommendation No 1 was based on analysis contained in Chapter II of the report '*Why open trade is better trade*'.[194] This chapter argued (convincingly) not only that protectionism inevitably harms an economy but also that the harmful (informational, political, social, or agricultural) costs of protectionism seldom appear in an immediate and clear way.[195] The report consequently proposed that '*any proposal for protective action should be systematically analysed. This could be done by what might be called a "protection balance sheet". Such statements, similar in aim to the "environmental impact" statements now required for construction projects in some countries, would allow periodic appraisal of existing measures and informed judgements on proposed new measures. They would set out the benefits and costs to the national economy of protectionist measures, as compared with withholding protection and/or with providing adjustment assistance.*' The recommendation also suggested '*that each country introduce a statutory requirement that annual financial statements of private and public firms give details of any subsidies (including tax subsidies) received from governments. Governments themselves should also provide clear and full information on subsidies granted and on preferential treatment provided in their own procurement of goods and services.*' The first recommendation was therefore clearly convinced that '*the dangers of secrecy and administrative discretion are greater than those of more open procedures*'.[196] If increased transparency was the objective, stronger naming and shaming constituted one of its means. In other words, the mechanism '*would not only review Members' trade policies but*

192 *Trade Policies for a Better Future, Proposals for Action* (n 154) 9–10.
193 *Trade Policies for a Better Future, Proposals for Action* (n 154) 9–10.
194 *Trade Policies for a Better Future, Proposals for Action* (n 154) 23–31.
195 *Trade Policies for a Better Future, Proposals for Action* (n 154) 23–31.
196 *Trade Policies for a Better Future, Proposals for Action* (n 154) 36.

would also raise the alarm when non-compliance affected other Members' rights in the system'.[197] The underlying ideas behind recommendations Nos 1 and 8 were therefore largely similar. Recommendation No 1 foresaw a greater role for the (general) public (universities and schools, strengthened consumer and advisory groups) with the argument that '*an open approach, exposing conflicting interests and helping to resolve them shields politicians against protectionist pressures*',[198] whereas Recommendation No 8 assumed that a similar (positive) influence could be derived from an institutionalized form of pressure by politicians' peers.[199]

At the same time, recommendations Nos 8 and 13 were intrinsically related to the structural development of the TPRM as the WTO's mechanism for peer review. According to Recommendation No 8, '*[a]t the international level, trade policy and the functioning of the trading system should be made more open. Countries should be subject to regular oversight of surveillance of their policies and actions, about which the GATT Secretariat should collect and publish information.*'[200] Nonetheless, the recommendation foresaw two alternative proposals. Each of these implied a more active role by the Secretariat. The first proposal consisted of the establishment of a panel (representing three to five governments) to review the GATT Secretariat report on the trade policies of the country under review, to subject the countries' representatives to questioning, and to make recommendations.[201] The recommendation furthermore emphasized that this procedure would be similar to the examination of national economic policies by the OECD. Under the second proposal, an independent Trade Policy Committee (serviced by the GATT Secretariat) would publish periodic reports on policy developments.[202] This second proposal resembled an earlier proposal made by a study group chaired by former GATT Director-General Long '*who was the first to draw a—tentative—link between a review mechanism and GATT*'. It also argued for the establishment of national independent bodies to prepare annual reports to their governments on public assistance to industries. These reports would in addition be available to the Contracting Parties of the GATT and could assist them in understanding and evaluating the policies of governments as presented in international negotiations.[203] Further structural developments of the TPRM as the WTO's mechanism for peer review were also fuelled by the arguments which had led to Recommendation No 13. This recommendation was based on a critical assessment of the trading system which it described as outdated, inadequate to deal with pressures from special interests, and abused by its Contracting Parties.[204] Recommendation No 13 therefore advocated the launch of a new round of GATT negotiations.[205] In this regard, it

[197] Ghosh, 'Developing Countries in the WTO Trade Policy Review Mechanism' (n 166) 431.
[198] *Trade Policies for a Better Future, Proposals for Action* (n 154) 37.
[199] *Trade Policies for a Better Future, Proposals for Action* (n 154) 42.
[200] *Trade Policies for a Better Future, Proposals for Action* (n 154) 42.
[201] *Trade Policies for a Better Future, Proposals for Action* (n 154) 42.
[202] *Trade Policies for a Better Future, Proposals for Action* (n 154) 42.
[203] VanGrasstek, *The History and Future of the World Trade Organization* (n 56) 282.
[204] *Trade Policies for a Better Future, Proposals for Action* (n 154), 17–22.
[205] *Trade Policies for a Better Future, Proposals for Action* (n 154), 47.

should be noted that the Leutwiler report formed the second attempt (after the failure of the 1982 Ministerial Meeting) to relaunch a new round.[206]

Participation in the proposed oversight and surveillance exercise was open to all governments. However, Recommendation No 8 already encompassed some institutional elements for the selection of the Contracting Parties to be reviewed. The first of the two proposals had indeed proposed a periodic annual examination of the major trading countries and a lesser frequency for others.[207] Moreover, both options which were contained in Recommendation No 8 substantially increased the role of the Secretariat. Under the first option, the Secretariat even had the option to question governments and/or to make recommendations. Under the second option, the Secretariat had the power to initiate studies of national trade policies. The Secretariat was thus mandated to act '*as a watchdog (though not judge) on behalf of the trading system as a whole*' and '*was supposed to defend the trade interests—especially those of the smaller and developing countries—and to provide them with the necessary technical assistance*'.[208] Nevertheless, academic literature at the time of the Leutwiler report warned that the probable opposition of governments against a strengthened Secretariat should not be underestimated: '*It is one thing to have periodic examinations of national economic policies in the Organisation for Economic Co-operation and Development where there are no international legal obligations and rights. It is quite another to have an examination and assessment of a country's trade policies in the GATT where such an exercise would be against the background of formal legal undertakings.*'[209] The proposal was therefore considered as a possible 'litmus test' of whether the GATT Contracting Parties were serious about refining and strengthening the system.

d) The Functioning of the GATT System (FOGS) negotiations (1986)

After the failed Ministerial of 1982, the Punta del Este Ministerial of 1986 refocused attention on the development of a framework for a new trade round. This culminated in the Punta del Este Declaration which contained the mandate of the future Uruguay Round.[210] In the aftermath of the Ministerial, the Contracting Parties established fifteen negotiating groups and agreed on a schedule for their discussions. The mandates of these groups generally followed the list of subjects included in the Punta del Este Declaration.[211] At that time, GATT's overall

[206] John H Jackson, *The World Trade Organization, Constitution and Jurisprudence* (The Royal Institute of International Affairs 1998), 24 (hereafter Jackson, *The World Trade Organization, Constitution and Jurisprudence*).

[207] *Trade Policies for a Better Future, Proposals for Action* (n 154) 42.

[208] *Trade Policies for a Better Future, Proposals for Action* (n 154) 42.

[209] Gardner Patterson and Eliza Patterson, 'Importance of a GATT Review in the New Negotiations' (1986) 9(2) The World Economy 167 (hereafter Gardner and Patterson, 'Importance of a GATT Review in the New Negotiations').

[210] Draft Ministerial Declaration on the Uruguay Round (n 155); Jackson, *The World Trade Organization, Constitution and Jurisprudence* (n 206) 25.

[211] The Uruguay Round—Decisions of 28 January 1987, GATT Information, GATT/1405, 5 February 1987; Jackson, *The World Trade Organization, Constitution and Jurisprudence* (n 206) 25.

institutional structure was the result of the failed wish to establish the International Trade Organization (ITO) and some further gradual evolution. At the outset of the Functioning of the GATT System (FOGS) negotiations, GATT's institutional structure therefore consisted of six different types of institutional entities: '*(1) the Contracting Parties, (2) the Council of representatives, (3) the Director-General, (4) the GATT Secretariat, (5) numerous (specific and more general) Committees or (temporary) Working Parties that were generally open to all parties and (6) the Consultative Group of Eighteen*'.[212] According to the Contracting Parties and the Leutwiler group, this institutional set-up was generally perceived as neither effective nor well-functioning: Membership to the GATT had grown, the Secretariat was not able to properly discharge its new functions within its still limited mandate, and international trading patterns had changed.[213] The activities undertaken by one of these fifteen negotiating groups, the FOGS group, literally and figuratively '*transformed the GATT—as it stood at the end of the Tokyo Round—into a formal international organization*'.[214] This was so since the FOGS group was tasked with the pursuit of three different negotiating objectives: '*(1) to enhance the surveillance in the GATT to enable regular monitoring of trade policies and practices of Contracting Parties and their impact on the functioning of the multilateral trading system, (2) to improve the overall effectiveness and decision-making of the GATT as an institution, including, inter-alia, through involvement of Ministers and (3) to increase the contribution of the GATT to achieving greater coherence in global economic policy-making through strengthening its relationship with other international organizations responsible for monetary and financial matters*'.[215] Mr Julius L Katz (United States) and Ambassador Julio Lacarte-Murto (Uruguay) were jointly appointed as Chairmen for the initial phase of the negotiations of the FOGS group and the group Dispute Settlement. Nevertheless, Mr Katz would have the primary responsibility for the FOGS negotiations.[216] At the start of the FOGS negotiations, surveillance within GATT encompassed a bewildering variety of activities which were undertaken (1) in the context of the periodic reviews of waivers and protocols of accession; (2) in the special meetings of the GATT Council (which were to review the extent of compliance with existing notification requirements, analyse general developments in the trading system, and review compliance of paragraph 7(i) of the November 1982 Ministerial declaration); (3) in the Committee on Trade and Development, (which mainly reviewed the operation of part IV of the General Agreement and the implementation of the Enabling Clause); (4) in the Committee on Balance-of-Payments Restrictions; (5) in the framework of various surveillance procedures under different Codes (which varied from Code to Code but which all

[212] Steward, *The GATT Uruguay Round: A Negotiating History (1986–1992)* (n 188) 1901–11.

[213] 'After Kennedy and Tokyo, the Leutwiler Round', *The Economist* (London, 30 March 1985), 73–74.

[214] Steward, *The GATT Uruguay Round: A Negotiating History (1986–1992)* (n 188) 1894

[215] Draft Ministerial Declaration on the Uruguay Round (n 155) 16.

[216] Multilateral Trade Negotiations, The Uruguay Round, Negotiating Group on Functioning of the GATT System, Meeting of 7 April 1987, Note by the Secretariat, MTN.GNG/NG14/1, 10 April 1987, 1.

contained a provision for annual review); (6) in the Textiles Surveillance Body or in its Sub-Committee on Adjustment (which respectively reviewed the Member countries' non-tariff trade measures affecting textiles and clothing in order to ensure their conformity to the Multi-fibre Arrangement and the extent to which these quantitative restrictions were imposed to promote structural adjustment in the textile and clothing industry); and (7) in the Uruguay Round Surveillance Body (which was to review the stand-still and roll-back commitments of the Punta del Este Ministerial Declaration).[217] The establishment of a unified forum for overall surveillance was therefore clearly sought. Moreover, the creation of such a structure also managed to fill an institutional gap which was (still) left by GATT's emerging structure for dispute settlement. Since '*there was no director of public prosecutions and because people in glass houses don't throw stones, the GATT system risked decay from neglect*'.[218] In other words, the nascent mechanism for peer review '*intended to do "more" than the Dispute Settlement Body in the sense of covering not only single cases but also "less" than the Dispute Settlement Body in the sense of not delegating the judgment on compliance or non-compliance to a third party*' for enforcement.[219]

As a result, the Contracting Parties set out on what would turn out to be the most important set of negotiations in the lead up to the TPRM's formal establishment. In this respect, a couple of elements should be emphasized. First, negotiations often stand to be characterized by their relatively unstructured approach. In despite of the excellent Chairmanship of Mr Katz, the FOGS negotiations were no exception. This heading's subsequent analysis is therefore (again) based on a chronological review of the discussions with regard to each of the three traditional building blocks which are inherent in a mechanism for peer review (ie objectives, structure, and participation). Second, the amount of diplomatic attention which was spent on these blocks and especially on their sub-elements was rather unevenly divided. Most discussions were (logically) spent on the fine-tuning of the structure of the nascent TPRM. However, in this regard, some structural sub-elements such as the selection mechanism (ie the first structural element) or the reporting requirements (ie a feature of the third structural element), received a relatively substantial degree of attention whereas the group's negotiations of other structural features such as the investigative stage (ie the second structural element) or the structural follow-up to peer review (ie another feature of the third structural element), had a less protracted nature.[220]

In terms of objectives, the proposals which were tabled during the first, second, fourth, fifth, and ninth meeting of the FOGS group, all advanced the general

[217] Multilateral Trade Negotiations, The Uruguay Round, Negotiating Group on Functioning of the GATT System, Existing Surveillance Functions in the GATT, Note by the Secretariat, MTN/GNG/NG14/W/3, 9 June 1987; Blackhurst, 'Strengthening GATT Surveillance of Trade-Related Policies' (n 39) 131–35.

[218] Price, 'New Institutional Developments in GATT' (n 183) 96.

[219] Thomas Conzelmann, 'Beyond the Carrot and the Stick—(How) Do State Reporting Procedures Matter?' (ECPR Uppsala Joint Sessions, 2004) <https://ecpr.eu/Filestore/PaperProposal/8e9b4d5a-1ba2-4933-af69-c2c59f40f368.pdf> accessed 6 May 2017 (hereafter Conzelmann, 'Beyond the Carrot and the Stick—(How) Do State Reporting Procedures Matter?').

[220] See 'Mechanisms for peer review—theoretical core elements'.

concept of surveillance (as contained in the Punta del Este Ministerial Declaration). This notion covers the transparency objective and the goal of naming and shaming (even though the term 'compliance' was sometimes explicitly used).[221] Nonetheless, whereas some developed countries (such as the European Union, Japan, and the United States) were mainly interested in surveillance activities which would not only serve as an early warning system but also in order to ensure compliance with contractual obligations, most developing countries (such as India and Jamaica) were primarily interested in strengthening the existing surveillance procedures with a view to regular monitor the trade policies of major trading powers so as to ensure a certain symmetry in surveillance in the GATT without creating any new obligations.[222] The general debates thus mirrored advocates in favour of a strict approach to peer review with proponents of a softer stance.[223]

The discussions on the objectives of the nascent mechanism for peer review started with an Australian Communication of April 1987 which argued for an increased surveillance role.[224] In this regard, the Communication emphasized that '*given the nature of the GATT, as an Agreement setting out specific rights and obligations, the focus of the surveillance role should be on achieving a proper evaluation of Contracting Parties' adherence to GATT (provisions) and agreements reached in multilateral rounds), and through this process to exert influence on domestic protection policies*'. The Australian Communication therefore proposed as options regular reporting by all Contracting Parties (an approach with emphasis on the transparency objective) and the organization of trade policy reviews of selected Contracting Parties (an option which would provide increased scope for naming and shaming).[225] The Communication furthermore stated that '*an enhanced surveillance role for the GATT . . . would represent an evolution of the institution's role consistent with its tradition and be responsive to the greater expectations which Contracting Parties have from the GATT system as highlighted by the Punta del Este Ministerial Declaration*'.[226]

The debate then focused on the specific roles the concept of surveillance should assume (during the first meeting of the FOGS) and on how these roles should be practically achieved and institutionally determined (during the second, fourth, fifth,

[221] Multilateral Trade Negotiations, The Uruguay Round, Negotiating Group on Functioning of the GATT System, Communication from Australia, MTN.GNG/NG14/W/1, 3 April 1987; Multilateral Trade Negotiations, The Uruguay Round, Negotiating Group on Functioning of the GATT System, Meeting of 7 April 1987, Note by the Secretariat, MTN.GNG/NG14/1, 10 April 1987, 2.

[222] Ghosh, 'Developing Countries in the WTO Trade Policy Review Mechanism' (n 166) 432; VanGrasstek, *The History and Future of the World Trade Organization* (n 56) 283.

[223] See section 2 of this chapter, 'Mechanisms for peer review—theoretical core elements'.

[224] Multilateral Trade Negotiations, The Uruguay Round, Negotiating Group on Functioning of the GATT System, Communication from Australia, MTN.GNG/NG14/W/1, 3 April 1987, 1–3.

[225] Multilateral Trade Negotiations, The Uruguay Round, Negotiating Group on Functioning of the GATT System, Communication from Australia, MTN.GNG/NG14/W/1, 3 April 1987, 4–6; This annex specifically emphasizes that 'as is the case with present notification obligations, it would be understood that information in the reports would of itself be without prejudice to views on the consistency of the measures, with, or their relevance to rights and obligations under the General Agreement'.

[226] Multilateral Trade Negotiations, The Uruguay Round, Negotiating Group on Functioning of the GATT System, Communication from Australia, MTN.GNG/NG14/W/1, 3 April 1987, 3.

and ninth meeting of the group). During the first meeting of the FOGS, there was '*widespread agreement that there was room for the expansion and improvement of surveillance activities in the GATT*'.[227] In this regard, '*it was suggested that an adequate system of surveillance should be preventive in the sense of operating as an "early warning system", but that surveillance should also be used to ensure compliance with contractual obligations on a continuing and systematic basis*'. Furthermore, Contracting Parties stated that '*multilateral surveillance activities should also provide a counter-weight to pressures from domestic special interest lobbies*'. Although the term 'compliance' was used, some delegations expressed the view that '*to be effective (surveillance) must be seen in terms of evaluation and not judgement*'.[228] This view was also reiterated in a US Communication of June 1987 which confirmed that '*enhanced surveillance should not be the basis for judgements on the relationship between trade measures maintained by Contracting Parties and GATT obligations, which properly belong in the dispute settlement process*'.[229]

Between the second and the ninth meeting of the FOGS, the Contracting Parties attempted to determine the exact scope of surveillance. Whereas all Parties agreed that surveillance was distinct from dispute settlement, differences persisted as to the weight of the transparency objective versus that of naming and shaming. These differences crystallized in recurrent questioning with regard to the appropriate form of surveillance (individual versus collective) or regarding the scope for follow-up activities to (potentially negative) surveillance outcomes. During the second meeting of the FOGS, '*it was widely agreed that effective surveillance was an important means of ensuring transparency and predictability in policy-making, but views differed on how far the essential role of surveillance was to monitor and ensure compliance with GATT obligations, as opposed to providing a more general overview of trends in policy-making among trading partners*'. Contracting Parties seemed to agree, however, '*that surveillance should be quite distinct from the dispute settlement procedures of the GATT in that it should not involve judgements on the GATT-consistency of measures; it should be seen as a shared endeavour supportive of an open trading system*'. Views differed nevertheless on whether surveillance should be carried out on a country-by-country basis, which would be effective in ensuring fuller adherence to GATT obligations, or in terms of a collective assessment, which would avoid creating the impression that countries were being placed 'in the dock'.[230] According to a Canadian Communication of July 1987, '*the issue of surveillance of trade policies was quite possibly the fundamental*

[227] Multilateral Trade Negotiations, The Uruguay Round, Negotiating Group on Functioning of the GATT System, Meeting of 7 April 1987, Note by the Secretariat, MTN.GNG/NG14/1, 10 April 1987, 2.

[228] Multilateral Trade Negotiations, The Uruguay Round, Negotiating Group on Functioning of the GATT System, Meeting of 7 April 1987, Note by the Secretariat, MTN.GNG/NG14/1, 10 April 1987, 2.

[229] Multilateral Trade Negotiations, The Uruguay Round, Negotiating Group on Functioning of the GATT System, Communication from the United States, MTN.GNG/NG14/W/9, 23 June 1987, 3.

[230] Multilateral Trade Negotiations, The Uruguay Round, Negotiating Group on Functioning of the GATT System, Negotiating Group on Functioning of the GATT System, Note by the Secretariat, MTN.GNG/NG14/2, 26 June 1987, 2.

question before the Negotiating Group'.[231] According to Canada, '*the consideration of trade policy surveillance would require the group to assess what the follow-up to such surveillance ought to be: to draw conclusions for future GATT work or to make recommendations to the government under review*'. According to the Communication, '*this question would also require an examination of the relationship of trade policy surveillance and any obligations in this respect with the rights and obligations of Contracting Parties under the GATT and the role of the dispute settlement system*'. Moreover, it was interested in the further (international/domestic) follow-up to the proposed surveillance activities. According to Canada, the extent of the political or legal intrusiveness of these follow-up actions needed to be reflected upon. On the other hand, Jamaica doubted the effectiveness of the surveillance proposals. According to a Jamaican Communication of July 1987, '*improved surveillance in the GATT might increase respect for GATT rules but to improve surveillance without Contracting Parties having additional means to influence removal of the restrictive or distorting practices of Contracting Parties, is to build up unrealizable expectations*'.[232] Nevertheless, New Zealand persisted. According to its proposal of September 1987, the objectives of enhanced surveillance were '*(1) to ensure that the existing or additional GATT commitments are maintained and (2) to improve trade policies by increasing their transparency, not only internationally but also domestically*'.[233] Although New Zealand recognized the practical limitations of the GATT to achieve these objectives, it proposed several criteria that could be considered in the negotiating group in order to establish domestic surveillance bodies.[234]

At the fourth meeting of the FOGS negotiating group, many Contracting Parties reiterated that the objective of the proposed review process '*should be clearly distinguished from the surveillance or enforcement of individual GATT obligations or for dispute settlement procedures, which should continue to be dealt with in the appropriate fora*'. Nevertheless, it was recognized that '*the extra transparency resulting from the review process should lead to a strengthening of the observation of GATT provisions by all Contracting Parties*'.[235] In the same vein, Contracting Parties emphasized that although the proposed review process '*would not be related to specific GATT obligations, it was not intended purely to serve purposes of information, but to enable Contracting Parties collectively to survey the course of trade policies and to assess what should be done, as well as to assist government administrators*

[231] Multilateral Trade Negotiations, The Uruguay Round, Negotiating Group on Functioning of the GATT System, Communication from Canada, MTN.GNG/NG14/W/10, 2 July 1987, 2.

[232] Multilateral Trade Negotiations, The Uruguay Round, Negotiating Group on Functioning of the GATT System, Communication from Jamaica, MTN.GNG/NG14/W/11, 8 July 1987, 2.

[233] Multilateral Trade Negotiations, The Uruguay Round, Negotiating Group on Functioning of the GATT System, Communication by New Zealand, MTN.GNG/NG14/W/13, 25 September 1987, 1.

[234] Multilateral Trade Negotiations, The Uruguay Round, Negotiating Group on Functioning of the GATT System, Communication by New Zealand, MTN.GNG/NG14/W/13, 25 September 1987, 3–4.

[235] Multilateral Trade Negotiations, The Uruguay Round, Negotiating Group on Functioning of the GATT System, Meeting of 3 and 4 November 1987, Note by the Secretariat, MTN.GNG/NG14/4, 30 November 1987, 1–2.

in taking stock of how national policies should evolve'.[236] As a result, the fourth meeting emphasized both the transparency and the naming and shaming objectives.

During its fifth meeting, the FOGS group had before it a revised draft of the Chairman's informal discussion paper on the nascent trade policy review mechanism. At this occasion, most Contracting Parties emphasized that '*the objective of the review mechanism was not to examine the conformity of particular measures with GATT obligations but to provide for greater transparency in and understanding of the trade policies of all Contracting Parties*'. Nonetheless, the Parties also indicated that '*the exercise of collective appreciation of trade policies should lead to greater adherence to the principles and objectives of the General Agreement*'.[237] A Communication from the Nordic countries of the end of January 1988 attempted to add further flesh to the bone of this statement. It re-emphasized the naming and shaming component but also explicitly highlighted the potential use of surveillance outcomes—at a later stage—for purposes of dispute settlement.[238] Although the Nordic countries agreed that the aim of enhanced surveillance was to increase transparency, the Communication also emphasized that '*it must not, however, be left out of sight that an important aim of the new surveillance mechanism is to improve the adherence to agreed rules, even if it is understood that the review exercise is not to serve as a basis for an enforcement mechanism for specific GATT obligations*'. It reiterated its opinion that '*all Contracting Parties have the same legal obligation to observe the rules and provisions they have subscribed to. At the same time, it is clear that violations by major trading parties have a more harmful effect on the multilateral trading system than the measures taken by small countries.*' The Communication therefore indicated that '*the surveillance mechanism should from a legal point of view be distinct from all existing legal GATT mechanisms, e.g. existing surveillance, dispute settlement procedures, notification requirements*' but emphasized that '*if the review reveals anything which other Contracting Parties want to complain about, the normal consultation and panel procedures could be followed*'.[239] As a result, the nascent mechanism's output's potential for (later) litigation purposes was clearly highlighted. Nevertheless, in March 1988 once again the European Community formally distinguished the proposed surveillance mechanism from (formal) procedures for dispute settlement: '*reviews are not considered as a form of passing judgement on countries or a mechanism for the enforcement of rights and*

[236] Multilateral Trade Negotiations, The Uruguay Round, Negotiating Group on Functioning of the GATT System, Meeting of 3 and 4 November 1987, Note by the Secretariat, MTN.GNG/NG14/4, 30 November 1987, 4.

[237] Multilateral Trade Negotiations, The Uruguay Round, Negotiating Group on Functioning of the GATT System, Meeting of 25–28 January 1988, Note by the Secretariat, MTN.GNG/NG14/5, 16 February 1988, 3.

[238] Multilateral Trade Negotiations, The Uruguay Round, Negotiating Group on Functioning of the GATT System, Communication from the Nordic Countries, MTN.GNG/NG14/W/17, 28 January 1988, 1.

[239] Multilateral Trade Negotiations, The Uruguay Round, Negotiating Group on Functioning of the GATT System, Communication from the Nordic Countries, MTN.GNG/NG14/W/17, 28 January 1988, 2.

obligations'.[240] This view was also reconfirmed by a Jamaican Communication of May 1988[241] and by an Indian statement of June 1988 on behalf of the developing countries.[242] Moreover, in the latter Communication, India explicitly added that the proposed process of review was '*not intended to lead to conclusions or recommendations which may be of a binding nature*'. Furthermore, India stated that '*for the developing countries "enhanced surveillance" contained a stronger connotation of moral suasion than did "trade policy review".*'[243]

During the ninth meeting of the FOGS, Contracting Parties summed up their views and reiterated that '*the mechanism should not be a basis for the enforcement of specific obligations under GATT or for the institution of dispute settlement procedures. Rather, the surveillance of trade policies and practices should contribute to better adherence by Contracting Parties to GATT commitments, through regular collective appreciation of individual Contracting Parties' trade policies and practices and their impact on the functioning of the multilateral trading system*'.[244] In October 1988, a Communication from a number of Contracting Parties translated these objectives into a document which established the (semantic) basis for the actual objectives of the TPRM.[245]

The main discussions of the FOGS negotiations did not focus on the objectives of the nascent surveillance mechanism but rather on its structural modalities. Interestingly, these discussions concentrated first on the structure for the peer reviews meetings, the applicable reporting requirements, and their follow-up (ie elements of the third structural element) before they started paying attention to the investigation stage which would lead to the review meetings (ie the second structural element) and to the selection criteria for countries which were to be reviewed (ie the first structural element).[246] Moreover, the proposals which were specifically floated with regard to the structure for review meetings oscillated between (1) individual countries' reporting on their measures (a structure which hence constituted a sort of expanded notification procedure); (2) a small group of Contracting Parties being tasked with surveillance (thus acting like a panel or a working party); and (3) the establishment of a fully fledged surveillance mechanism which was (partly or

240 Multilateral Trade Negotiations, The Uruguay Round, Negotiating Group on Functioning of the GATT System, Communication from the European Community, MTN.GNG/NG14/W/20, 22 March 1988, 2.

241 Multilateral Trade Negotiations, The Uruguay Round, Negotiating Group on Functioning of the GATT System, Communication from Jamaica, MTN.GNG/NG14/W/22, 16 May 1988, 3.

242 Multilateral Trade Negotiations, The Uruguay Round, Negotiating Group on Functioning of the GATT System, Communication from the Delegation of India, MTN.GNG/NG14/W/23, 22 June 1988, 2.

243 Multilateral Trade Negotiations, The Uruguay Round, Negotiating Group on Functioning of the GATT System, Meeting of 20 and 22 June 1988, Note by the Secretariat, MTN.GNG/NG14/8, 13 July 1988, 13.

244 Multilateral Trade Negotiations, The Uruguay Round, Negotiating Group on Functioning of the GATT System, Meeting of 26–30 September 1988, Note by the Secretariat, MTN.GNG/NG14/9, 18 October 1988.

245 Multilateral Trade Negotiations, The Uruguay Round, Negotiating Group on Functioning of the GATT System, Communication from a number of Contracting Parties, MTN.GNG/NG14/W/30, 24 October 1988, 3.

246 See section 2 of this chapter, 'Mechanisms for peer review—theoretical core elements'.

mainly) driven by the Secretariat.[247] Furthermore, the FOGS discussions witnessed only a limited interest in the elaboration of a review structure for the review mechanism itself (ie the fourth structural element).[248]

The structural proposals started to emerge with an Australian Communication of April 1987. This Communication had set forward two parallel approaches for an improved surveillance mechanism.[249] The first would consist of annual reporting by all Contracting Parties to be reviewed by the annual Special Council Session. The second approach would encompass more extensive reviews on a rotational basis by a small group of Contracting Parties (on behalf of the Council) of the trade policies of larger Contracting Parties. Both approaches entailed some (limited) form of reporting.[250] The first meeting of the FOGS saw some partial backtracking vis-à-vis the Australian proposals since '*it was suggested that a proper system of notifications and full transparency would partly obviate, the need for surveillance*'. Nevertheless, another view '*was that notification procedures and transparency could not by themselves provide the accountability inherent in appropriate surveillance arrangements*'.[251] The meeting therefore requested the Secretariat to provide an overview of (existing) institutional mechanisms for surveillance within the GATT.[252] The Australian idea for nascent trade policy reviews (ie the second track of its proposal) was however supported by a Swiss, a Japanese, and a US Communication of June 1987.[253] The Swiss Communication advocated the formal establishment of a Trade Policy Committee. In addition to monitoring trade policies of the Contracting Parties (as proposed by Australia), this Communication also proposed that this Committee would '*conduct a general exchange of views at least once a year on trade policy trends in the global economic context*'. The Japanese and the US Communications of June 1987 added further institutional flesh to the bones.[254] In particular, the Japanese Communication was rich in detail

[247] VanGrasstek, *The History and Future of the World Trade Organization* (n 56) 283–4

[248] Multilateral Trade Negotiations, the Uruguay Round, Negotiating Group on Functioning of the GATT System, Communication from Japan, MTN.GNG/NG14/W/8, 23 June 1987.

[249] Multilateral Trade Negotiations, The Uruguay Round, Negotiating Group on Functioning of the GATT System, Communication from Australia, MTN.GNG/NG14/W/1, 3 April 1987.

[250] Multilateral Trade Negotiations, The Uruguay Round, Negotiating Group on Functioning of the GATT System, Communication from Australia, MTN.GNG/NG14/W/1, 3 April 1987, 2.

[251] Multilateral Trade Negotiations, The Uruguay Round, Negotiating Group on Functioning of the GATT System, Meeting of 7 April 1987, Note by the Secretariat, MTN.GNG/NG14/1, 10 April 1987, 2.

[252] Multilateral Trade Negotiations, The Uruguay Round, Negotiating Group on Functioning of the GATT System, Existing Surveillance Functions in the GATT, Note by the Secretariat, MTN/GNG/NG14/W/3, 9 June 1987.

[253] Multilateral Trade Negotiations, The Uruguay Round, Negotiating Group on Functioning of the GATT System, Communication from the United States, MTN.GNG/NG14/W/7, 18 June 1987, 1; Multilateral Trade Negotiations, the Uruguay Round, Negotiating Group on Functioning of the GATT System, Communication from Japan, MTN.GNG/NG14/W/8, 23 June 1987; Multilateral Trade Negotiations, The Uruguay Round, Negotiating Group on Functioning of the GATT System, Communication from the United States, MTN.GNG/NG14/W/9, 23 June 1987.

[254] Multilateral Trade Negotiations, the Uruguay Round, Negotiating Group on Functioning of the GATT System, Communication from Japan, MTN.GNG/NG14/W/8, 23 June 1987; Multilateral Trade Negotiations, The Uruguay Round, Negotiating Group on Functioning of the GATT System, Communication from the United States, MTN.GNG/NG14/W/9, 23 June 1987.

since it covered almost all structural core elements.[255] It provided specific guidance with regard to the Contracting Parties which would be subject to the review, the measures subject to the review, the entity to conduct the reviews (no formal Trade Policy Committee as proposed by Switzerland but the Contracting Parties on a rotational basis), the frequency of the reviews, the implementation of the reviews, the compilation of reports and their publication, the timing for the implementation of the Agreement on Trade Policy Reviews (ie in a balanced manner, taking account of the progress of other negotiating items), and, for the first time the system for reassessment of the review system (ie the fourth structural element). The US Communication of 1987 supported the two parallel approaches as advocated by Australia (ie reporting, which should be rigorous and tough, with a bigger role for the Secretariat, and increased surveillance) but in addition advocated for a central repository of notifications relevant to GATT surveillance and for the enhancement of economic analysis and research.

In view of the wide range of options proposed for the structural set up of the surveillance mechanism and its modalities, it was not unsurprising that the second FOGS meeting was rather inconclusive. There was '*some discussion as to whether it was desirable to create a standing surveillance body*'. In this regard, differing views were voiced. Some Contracting Parties favoured the idea whereas others preferred to consider the improvement of existing arrangements before a decision was taken. Moreover, the Contracting Parties also disagreed on the method of reporting with some Parties arguing in favour of public reporting while other preferred a more confidential procedure.[256] Furthermore, Jamaica had no political appetite at all for the creation of (yet) another institutional setting for surveillance. Jamaica's Communication of July 1987 therefore unambiguously stated that '*the temptation to seek to solve problems by creating new mechanisms within the GATT should be avoided*'.[257] This was not only based on its weak level of confidence in the capacities of a new surveillance mechanism that had no actual teeth[258] but also on Jamaica's wish to avoid duplication of efforts and strive towards the rationalization of the functioning of the fifty existing GATT mechanisms that already engaged in some form of surveillance.[259] Nevertheless, New Zealand's proposal of September 1987 voiced further support for all previous proposals to enhance international surveillance by the establishment of country reviews (in line with the Australian proposal) and the improvement of notifications (as proposed by the US Communication). It also lent support to the creation of one or more surveillance bodies (in line with the Swiss, US, Australian, and Canadian proposals). Moreover, New Zealand's proposal even came up with

[255] See section 2 of this chapter, 'Mechanisms for peer review—theoretical core elements'.

[256] Multilateral Trade Negotiations, The Uruguay Round, Negotiating Group on Functioning of the GATT System, Negotiating Group on Functioning of the GATT System, Note by the Secretariat, MTN.GNG/NG14/2, 26 June 1987, 3.

[257] Multilateral Trade Negotiations, The Uruguay Round, Negotiating Group on Functioning of the GATT System, Communication from Jamaica, MTN.GNG/NG14/W/11, 8 July 1987, 2

[258] See coverage with regard to the objectives of the Functioning of the GATT System (FOGS) negotiations (1986).

[259] Multilateral Trade Negotiations, The Uruguay Round, Negotiating Group on Functioning of the GATT System, Communication from Jamaica, MTN.GNG/NG14/W/11, 8 July 1987, 3.

some innovative criteria for the establishment of independent domestic surveillance bodies.[260] Further to a request which the Negotiating Group tabled at its third meeting, the Secretariat compiled a summary tabulation encompassing the main proposals of the respective delegations.[261] Interestingly, the Secretariat structured its overview according to four general building blocks: '*(1) notification requirements and nature of surveillance, (2) institutional arrangements for surveillance, (3) further arrangements and (4) review of arrangements*'. These four building blocks are less detailed than the structural elements which are inherent in mechanisms for peer review, mentioned earlier.[262] Nevertheless, there seems to be some substantial overlap. The Secretariat's first building block—'notification requirements and nature of surveillance'—includes some elements that are more intrinsically related to the general objectives of surveillance (ie transparency and naming and shaming). Moreover, the Secretariat's second category—'institutional arrangements for surveillance'—encompasses three out of the proposed four structural elements which are inherent in mechanisms for peer review (ie reporting requirements, requirements that determine the actual structure of the review meeting, and elements which guide the potential follow-up to the review's conclusions). Furthermore, Secretariat's fourth building block—'review of arrangements'—matches entirely with the fourth structural element (ie the structural modalities for the review of the review mechanism itself).[263]

The fourth meeting of the FOGS resulted in some substantial debate with regard to several points. These included first and foremost the continued discussions with regard to the (formal) forum where reviews should take place (ie either among a small group of reviewers or among an open-ended type of committee). On the other hand, the meeting also started to pay an (increased) attention (1) to the reporting modalities (ie to the structural and thematic borders of reporting and to the nature of reports) and (2) to the structure which would enable the selection of the countries to be reviewed (ie the first structural element).[264] In this regard, the view was expressed that the frequency for reviews should take account of several factors such as countries' importance in international trade and countries' potentially overlapping review engagements in other fora.[265] A Communication from the Nordic countries of January 1988 provided further impetus to the results of the fourth

[260] Multilateral Trade Negotiations, The Uruguay Round, Negotiating Group on Functioning of the GATT System, Communication by New Zealand, MTN.GNG/NG14/W/13, 25 September 1987.

[261] Multilateral Trade Negotiations, the Uruguay Round, Negotiating Group on Functioning of the GATT System, Summary of points made in the Group concerning 'Surveillance', Note by the Secretariat, MTN.GNG/NG14/W/14, 21 October 1987.

[262] See section 2 of this chapter, 'Mechanisms for peer review—theoretical core elements'.

[263] See section 2 of this chapter, 'Mechanisms for peer review—theoretical core elements'.

[264] See section 2 of this chapter, 'Mechanisms for peer review—theoretical core elements'. The Contracting Parties were therefore quick in realizing the benefits of a well-delineated and clearly mandated form of reporting; see also the early academic conclusions in this regard at Blackhurst, 'Strengthening GATT Surveillance of Trade-Related Policies' (n 39) 143.

[265] Multilateral Trade Negotiations, The Uruguay Round, Negotiating Group on Functioning of the GATT System, Meeting of 3 and 4 November 1987, Note by the Secretariat, MTN.GNG/NG14/4, 30 November 1987, 2–4.

meeting. It contained proposals with regard to the nature of the reports, the forum which would receive them (the Council would not in any formal sense adopt or endorse the reports), and with regard to the structural selection element (in this regard, a core group of thirty trading partners was to be reviewed more often than others whereas a small number of major trading entities was to be reviewed at least every eighteen months).[266]

During the fifth meeting of the FOGS, the concept of a '*core group*' was generally accepted. The Secretariat was therefore requested to provide information on the share of world trade accounted for by a core group of twenty or thirty contrasting Parties and to provide estimates of the staff requirements and costs which would be implied by the operation of the proposed review mechanism. Moreover, the meeting agreed that '*consultations should be held concerning a common format for country reports*'.[267] Throughout its Communication of March 1988, the European Community tabled its perspectives on the nascent structure for peer review in a holistic way. This Communication thereby aimed to refine the proposed reporting methodology (reports should be policy oriented with the inclusion of significant proposals or pending measures), the frequency of the reviews (which should be based on time, trade, policy, and organizational criteria), the proposed review of general developments (on the basis of all reports, the Secretariat could be requested to prepare an analysis of trade policy developments which could serve as a basis for a better focused discussion in a single special session of the Council replacing the biannual review sessions), and the conduct of reviews (whereby the European Community aimed to avoid the creation of a Permanent Surveillance Body and suggested its replacement by the scheduling of special Council sessions).[268]

The discussions at the sixth meeting of the FOGS were partly inspired by a note by the Secretariat on multilateral surveillance activities in other international organizations (covering the OECD, the IMF, and the World Bank).[269] During the meeting, there was widespread support for the idea that reviews should be conducted by an open-ended body (with a special preference for the special sessions of the GATT Council). However, Contracting Parties still disagreed on the extent of coverage to be undertaken by the new surveillance structure (with some Contracting Parties arguing that the clear yardstick of reporting should be GATT obligations whereas other parties indicated that the reporting should also extend to general macroeconomic policies). The Contracting Parties therefore continued their informal

[266] Multilateral Trade Negotiations, The Uruguay Round, Negotiating Group on Functioning of the GATT System, Communication from the Nordic Countries, MTN.GNG/NG14/W/17, 28 January 1988.

[267] Multilateral Trade Negotiations, The Uruguay Round, Negotiating Group on Functioning of the GATT System, Meeting of 25–28 January 1988, Note by the Secretariat, MTN.GNG/NG14/5, 16 February 1988, 4.

[268] Multilateral Trade Negotiations, The Uruguay Round, Negotiating Group on Functioning of the GATT System, Communication from the European Community, MTN.GNG/NG14/W/20, 22 March 1988, 3–5.

[269] Multilateral Trade Negotiations, The Uruguay Round, Negotiating Group on Functioning of the GATT System, Multilateral Surveillance Activities in Other International Organizations, Note by the Secretariat, MTN.GNG/NG14/W/19, 18 March 1988.

exchange of views on the Chairman's discussion paper on the nascent trade policy review mechanism.[270] The Secretariat was moreover requested to refine its outline format for country reports still further.[271]

At the eighth meeting of the FOGS negotiations, India's Communication on behalf of the developing countries triggered several comments although it was presented as '*a contribution to the Group's work and was not intended to supplant or substitute for the Chairman's discussion paper*'.[272] In terms of the reporting format, Contracting Parties still disagreed on the extent to which the wider financial and monetary environment should also be taken into account. The Secretariat was nevertheless able to report that two informal consultations had led to a broad consensus on what should go into reports (the only remaining difference of views essentially derived from the proposal that countries with a smaller share of world trade should only be required to report on a more limited scale). Moreover, Contracting Parties agreed that the frequency of reviews and the criteria for the selection of countries should be directly related to their impact on the functioning of the multilateral trading system. Nevertheless, some argued that the definition of the 'core' and the 'non-core' group—as reflected in the Chairman's informal discussion paper—should still be kept open, that the Indian Communication on behalf of the developing countries focused too heavily on the concept of the 'principal trading countries', and that further discussion was therefore still needed in order to fine-tune the exact periodicity of the review cycles and their exceptions. Interestingly, the idea of enabling a regular review of the mechanism itself (ie the fourth structural element) also resurfaced.[273] The period between the ninth and the tenth meeting of the FOGS negotiating group focused essentially on the further determination of (1) the structural element which enabled the selection of the countries under review (ie the first structural element); (2) of the mechanism's reporting requirements and structure (ie both part of its third structural element); and (3) of its appraisal (ie the fourth structural element).[274] The negotiating group largely neglected to elaborate formalized (investigative) procedures to obtain the information needed for the review (ie the second structural element).

At the ninth meeting, in terms of frequency, most participants agreed in principle that '*the major trading countries should be subject to review every two years,*

[270] Multilateral Trade Negotiations, The Uruguay Round, Negotiating Group on Functioning of the GATT System, Meeting of 21–23 March 1988, Note by the Secretariat, MTN.GNG/NG14/6, 15 April 1988, 1–2; Multilateral Trade Negotiations, The Uruguay Round, Negotiating Group on Functioning of the GATT System, Meeting of 2–3 May 1988, Note by the Secretariat, MTN.GNG/NG14/7, 26 May 1988, 5.

[271] Multilateral Trade Negotiations, The Uruguay Round, Negotiating Group on Functioning of the GATT System, Communication from Jamaica, MTN.GNG/NG14/W/22, 16 May 1988, 3.

[272] Multilateral Trade Negotiations, The Uruguay Round, Negotiating Group on Functioning of the GATT System, Meeting of 20 and 22 June 1988, Note by the Secretariat, MTN.GNG/NG14/8, 13 July 1988, 12–16; Multilateral Trade Negotiations, The Uruguay Round, Negotiating Group on Functioning of the GATT System, Communication from the Delegation of India, MTN.GNG/NG14/W/23, 22 June 1988.

[273] See section 2 of this chapter, 'Mechanisms for peer review—theoretical core elements'.

[274] See section 2 of this chapter, 'Mechanisms for peer review—theoretical core elements'.

with other core countries every four years and remaining Contracting Parties every six years'. Nevertheless, some Parties still argued that more frequent reviews would be desirable.[275] A Communication on behalf of a number of Contracting Parties in October 1988 therefore formally reproposed two-, four-, and six-year cycles of review coupled with the possibility of exceptions.[276]

In this regard, Parties agreed during the tenth meeting of the FOGS that LDCs could be granted a longer than six-year time lapse between reviews.[277] In terms of the reporting requirements and structure, Jamaica—supported by many other countries—seized the occasion of the ninth meeting of the FOGS group to argue for a holistic interpretation of surveillance. According to Jamaica, '*the surveillance of macro-economic policies carried out by the IMF under its Article IV, while not involving any binding commitments, could provide a degree of moral suasion on all Members, while by contrast, the surveillance carried out by the World Bank, limited to the policies of borrowing countries, did not cover the macro-economic or trade policies of developed economies. These would be covered by the proposed GATT review mechanism*'. Nevertheless, a number of participants cautioned against such '*background*' considerations becoming themselves a subject for review. In this connection, the suggestion was made that the country under review should decide on aspects of the '*background*' which should be considered relevant. Moreover, for purposes of transparency, there was also agreement that the reports by the consulting country and Secretariat, together with a record of the points made during the reviews should be made public. Nonetheless, further discussions were necessary with regard to the nature of the reports.[278] The Communication on behalf of a number of Contracting Parties in October 1988 therefore spelled out some further institutional suggestions for the methodology of reporting (including the importance of taking into account the external trading, monetary, and financial environment). It also contained a draft outline format for country reports (allowing for the temporary introduction of the TPRM on a provisional basis as of 1 January 1989).[279]

Nevertheless, during the tenth meeting of the FOGS group, the participants still '*expressed differing views concerning the nature of the report to be drawn up by the Secretariat as part of the review process*' (ie independent assessment versus purely

[275] Multilateral Trade Negotiations, The Uruguay Round, Negotiating Group on Functioning of the GATT System, Meeting of 26–30 September 1988, Note by the Secretariat, MTN.GNG/NG14/9, 18 October 1988.

[276] Multilateral Trade Negotiations, The Uruguay Round, Negotiating Group on Functioning of the GATT System, Communication from a number of Contracting Parties, MTN.GNG/NG14/W/30, 24 October 1988.

[277] Multilateral Trade Negotiations, The Uruguay Round, Negotiating Group on Functioning of the GATT System, Meeting of 24–28 October 1988, Note by the Secretariat, MTN.GNG/NG14/10, 14 November 1988.

[278] Multilateral Trade Negotiations, The Uruguay Round, Negotiating Group on Functioning of the GATT System, Meeting of 26–30 September 1988, Note by the Secretariat, MTN.GNG/NG14/9, 18 October 1988.

[279] Multilateral Trade Negotiations, The Uruguay Round, Negotiating Group on Functioning of the GATT System, Communication from a number of Contracting Parties, MTN.GNG/NG14/W/30, 24 October 1988.

factual and/or notification-based reports).[280] With regard to the structure of the review body, at the ninth meeting of the FOGS group, most—though not all—Contracting Parties reiterated their wish that the GATT Council in special meetings be tasked with this function.[281] The Communication on behalf of a number of Contracting Parties in October 1988 formalized this proposal. It also included a provision on the future appraisal structure of the mechanism.[282] As a result, the Contracting Parties formally agreed during the tenth meeting of the FOGS that trade policy reviews would be carried out by the GATT Council at periodic special meetings. In addition, there was consensus to complete the enhanced surveillance process by a more general (overall) assessment by the Council of developments significantly affecting the trading system.[283]

Mechanisms for peer review are logically based on the participation of at least two entities.[284] These are the entity under review (the reviewee) and the reviewing peers. Nevertheless, the enabling structure for peer review may also entail the presence of additional participants to increase or guarantee the effectiveness and/or the legitimacy of the review. These additional participants may be tasked with the drafting of the review report(s), the general facilitation of the review process, and/or its examination. During the FOGS negotiations, various proposals were tabled with regard to the participating entities and their exact role.

The Australian Communication of April 1987 had proposed two alternative approaches with regard to the reviewees and the role of the Secretariat. Under both proposals, the Contracting Parties were invited to be assessed. Nevertheless, the first approach focused on all Contracting Parties whereas the second stated that '*the group of countries invited to submit (itself to) such reviews would include all developed country Contracting Parties as well as the more important developing country traders*'. Furthermore, the role of the Secretariat under both approaches was different. Under the first proposal, the GATT Secretariat would provide guidance on measurement methods and would review measurements to ensure consistency among Contracting Parties' reports. Moreover, it would compile the reports in a document to be submitted to an annual special Council session devoted to a review of developments in the trading system. Under the second approach, the Secretariat would have a more limited role and compile a report based on the material submitted by the Contracting Parties and other available material. This

[280] See section 2 of this chapter, 'Mechanisms for peer review—theoretical core elements'; Multilateral Trade Negotiations, The Uruguay Round, Negotiating Group on Functioning of the GATT System, Meeting of 24–28 October 1988, Note by the Secretariat, MTN.GNG/NG14/10, 14 November 1988.

[281] Multilateral Trade Negotiations, The Uruguay Round, Negotiating Group on Functioning of the GATT System, Meeting of 26–30 September 1988, Note by the Secretariat, MTN.GNG/NG14/9, 18 October 1988; See section 2 of this chapter, 'Mechanisms for peer review—theoretical core elements'.

[282] Multilateral Trade Negotiations, The Uruguay Round, Negotiating Group on Functioning of the GATT System, Communication from a number of Contracting Parties, MTN.GNG/NG14/W/30, 24 October 1988.

[283] See section 2 of this chapter, 'Mechanisms for peer review—theoretical core elements'; Multilateral Trade Negotiations, The Uruguay Round, Negotiating Group on Functioning of the GATT System, Meeting of 24–28 October 1988, Note by the Secretariat, MTN.GNG/NG14/10, 14 November 1988.

[284] See section 2 of this chapter, 'Mechanisms for peer review—theoretical core elements'.

report would form the basis for the reviews.[285] Under a Swiss Communication of June 1987, the Secretariat would similarly be tasked with the preparation of a background document on trade policy trends in the global economic context.[286] A Japanese Communication of June 1987 led to extensive further debates with regard to the identity of the Contracting Parties to the review, the reviewers, and the role of the Secretariat.[287] According to this Japanese Communication, about thirty Contracting Parties should be selected amongst those registering the highest trade performance (all developed Contracting Parties, the European Union, and major developing countries). These would be subject to the review, in addition to other Contracting Parties, as necessary and on an ad hoc basis. Nevertheless, during the second meeting of the FOGS negotiating group, differing views were expressed regarding the countries which would be subject to review (ie review of all the major trading countries (the approach of the Australian Communication) or of the approximately thirty Contracting Parties plus other Contracting Parties as necessary and on an ad hoc basis (the Japanese proposal)).[288] A proposal from New Zealand of September 1987 therefore attempted to provide a constructive solution. It was the first proposal which explicitly linked the participation in the mechanism to its structural feature for selection.[289] As a result, New Zealand proposed different cycles for the periodicity of the review. According to its proposal, '*reviews might be concentrated on those Contracting Parties with a dominant share of world trade and should be conducted on the basis of a regular reporting cycle. Other Contracting Parties would also be reviewed but this could be on the basis of a longer reporting cycle.*'[290] The idea gained traction and during the fourth meeting of the FOGS negotiating group, Contracting Parties concurred on the need to review all Parties on a different periodicity (although one Party suggested that LDCs should be excluded completely from the reviews).[291] Moreover, the Japanese Communication of June 1987 proposed that the '*two or three Contracting Parties in charge of the review would be selected on a rotational basis from those subject to the review*' and that '*note should be taken in selecting the reviewer countries of the necessity to ensure impartial review by, for example, avoiding combination of Contracting*

[285] Multilateral Trade Negotiations, The Uruguay Round, Negotiating Group on Functioning of the GATT System, Communication from Australia, MTN.GNG/NG14/W/1, 3 April 1987.

[286] Multilateral Trade Negotiations, The Uruguay Round, Negotiating Group on Functioning of the GATT System, Communication from Switzerland, MTN.GNG/NG14/W/7, 18 June 1987.

[287] Multilateral Trade Negotiations, the Uruguay Round, Negotiating Group on Functioning of the GATT System, Communication from Japan, MTN.GNG/NG14/W/8, 23 June 1987, 1.

[288] Multilateral Trade Negotiations, The Uruguay Round, Negotiating Group on Functioning of the GATT System, Negotiating Group on Functioning of the GATT System, Note by the Secretariat, MTN.GNG/NG14/2, 26 June 1987.

[289] See section 2 of this chapter, 'Mechanisms for peer review—theoretical core elements'.

[290] Multilateral Trade Negotiations, The Uruguay Round, Negotiating Group on Functioning of the GATT System, Communication by New Zealand, MTN.GNG/NG14/W/13, 25 September 1987, 2–3.

[291] Multilateral Trade Negotiations, The Uruguay Round, Negotiating Group on Functioning of the GATT System, Meeting of 3 and 4 November 1987, Note by the Secretariat, MTN.GNG/NG14/4, 30 November 1987, 2.

Parties which share interests, or have large developed economies, or belong to the same region'.[292] Nevertheless, no consensus was found. During the fourth meeting of the FOGS negotiating group, Parties (again) adhered to different views with regard to the reviewing entity (ie a small group of reviewers appointed from among government representatives, as suggested in the informal Chairman's paper, an open-ended committee potentially replacing the special Council meetings, or a combination of the two).[293] Furthermore, the Japanese Communication aimed to strengthen the role of the Secretariat and explicitly stated that '*substantial assistance and involvement of the GATT Secretariat is indispensable in the implementation of the trade policy review, especially in the drafting of reports and other relevant work*'.[294] A Communication of the United States of June 1987, foresaw a (similar) increased role for the Secretariat, either as the central repository of notifications, the (main) drafter of country reviews, in its normal operations with regard to surveillance or by an enhancement of the Secretariat's economic analysis and research.[295] In a similar vein, Canada stated in July 1987 that the Secretariat's ability to monitor and analyse the impact of trade policies and practices and structural adjustment processes is currently relatively weak compared to other international economic institutions in their respective areas. It therefore argued for an expansion and improvement in the GATT responsibilities which even entailed the Secretariat-initiated reviews.[296] Nevertheless, during the second meeting of the FOGS negotiating group, differing views were expressed on the role of the respective participants. (In this regard, marked differences also existed with regard to the budgetary implications resulting from a more active Secretariat.)[297] Nonetheless, the proposal from New Zealand of September 1987 fully subscribed to a greater role for the Secretariat and advocated consequently for additional resources to this effect.[298] However, in spite of all arguments in favour of an increased role and clout for the Secretariat, several delegations present at the third meeting of the FOGS negotiating Group stressed the difference in nature between GATT and the international financial organizations. The contractual nature of GATT rights and obligations and the role of the Contracting Parties implied a different role for the Secretariat from those of

[292] Multilateral Trade Negotiations, the Uruguay Round, Negotiating Group on Functioning of the GATT System, Communication from Japan, MTN.GNG/NG14/W/8, 23 June 1987, 1.

[293] Multilateral Trade Negotiations, The Uruguay Round, Negotiating Group on Functioning of the GATT System, Meeting of 3 and 4 November 1987, Note by the Secretariat, MTN.GNG/NG14/4, 30 November 1987, 2.

[294] Multilateral Trade Negotiations, the Uruguay Round, Negotiating Group on Functioning of the GATT System, Communication from Japan, MTN.GNG/NG14/W/8, 23 June 1987, 1.

[295] Multilateral Trade Negotiations, The Uruguay Round, Negotiating Group on Functioning of the GATT System, Communication from the United States, MTN.GNG/NG14/W/9, 23 June 1987.

[296] Multilateral Trade Negotiations, The Uruguay Round, Negotiating Group on Functioning of the GATT System, Communication from Canada, MTN.GNG/NG14/W/10, 2 July 1987, 2.

[297] Multilateral Trade Negotiations, The Uruguay Round, Negotiating Group on Functioning of the GATT System, Negotiating Group on Functioning of the GATT System, Note by the Secretariat, MTN.GNG/NG14/2, 26 June 1987.

[298] Multilateral Trade Negotiations, The Uruguay Round, Negotiating Group on Functioning of the GATT System, Communication by New Zealand, MTN.GNG/NG14/W/13, 25 September 1987, 2–3.

the IMF and the World Bank: the aims of the General Agreement was to regulate trade rules and not trade itself. The Contracting Parties therefore' *emphasized the need to keep a clear distinction between the surveillance functions exercised by the international financial organizations, particularly the IMF (and its closer surveillance exercised over debtor countries' policies and the looser monitoring of others) and the development of monitoring of trade policies by GATT. GATT surveillance of trade policies should be applied to all Contracting Parties and should therefore not become a means of strengthening pressures on developing countries in relation to their trade policies*'.[299] As a result, Contracting Parties concluded the fourth meeting of the FOGS negotiating group with the opinion that '*the part to be played by the Secretariat would need to be examined more closely and the staffing implications of the review process would also have to be worked out*'. Some Contracting Parties indeed sensed the need for a combination of basic country documents with factual Secretariat background papers.[300]

A Communication from the Nordic countries of January 1988 broadened the group of entities which participated in the review process (ie the countries under review, the reviewers, and the Secretariat) with the new concept of 'examiners'.[301] In this regard, the Communication thought it practicable to designate some three to five Contracting Parties as examiners, who together with the review team, could prepare a draft of appropriate questions to be submitted in advance to the country under review. A Communication by the Nordic countries (August 1988) provided further modalities for the participation of these examiners which the proposal now described as 'discussants'.[302] The Nordics proposed this new term since it would seem less intrusive than the previously suggested designation of 'examiners'. Moreover, in order to be efficient, the proposal suggested that the best method to select the examiners/discussants would be to entrust the Secretariat with the selection from a roster of governmental representatives proposed by the Contracting Parties. With regard to the countries to be reviewed, the Nordics favoured the (already existing) idea to let a core group of thirty trading entities (to be determined by their proportion of world trade) be reviewed more often than others. With regard to the Secretariat's involvement, the Communication stated that '*the report constituting the basis for the review should be written by a team of experts with experience in trade policy matters chosen from a roster of outside experts and/or GATT staff Members*'.[303]

299 Multilateral Trade Negotiations, the Uruguay Round, Negotiating Group on Functioning of the GATT System, Meeting of 28 September 1987, Note by the Secretariat, MTN.GNG/NG14/3, 8 October 1987, 2.

300 Multilateral Trade Negotiations, The Uruguay Round, Negotiating Group on Functioning of the GATT System, Meeting of 3 and 4 November 1987, Note by the Secretariat, MTN.GNG/NG14/4, 30 November 1987, 2.

301 Multilateral Trade Negotiations, The Uruguay Round, Negotiating Group on Functioning of the GATT System, Communication from the Nordic Countries, MTN.GNG/NG14/W/17, 28 January 1988, 2.

302 Multilateral Trade Negotiations, The Uruguay Round, Negotiating Group on Functioning of the GATT System, Proposal by the Nordic Countries, MTN.GNG/NG14/W/25, 11 August 1988.

303 Multilateral Trade Negotiations, The Uruguay Round, Negotiating Group on Functioning of the GATT System, Communication from the Nordic Countries, MTN.GNG/NG14/W/17, 28 January 1988.

During the fifth meeting of the FOGS negotiating group, disagreement existed on the specific manner in which the European Communities would participate in the reporting and review process and on whether reviews should be carried out by a small group or in an open-ended forum (the latter being the preference of the European Community).[304] Nevertheless, the concept of a core group was agreed.[305]

Between the sixth and the tenth meeting of the FOGS negotiating group, Contracting Parties focused mainly (1) on the determination of the countries to be reviewed; (2) on the role of the Secretariat; and (3) on the role of the discussants. During the sixth meeting of the FOGS, there was clear agreement that Contracting Parties or entities whose policies have a significant impact on the trading system should be reviewed more frequently than others. However, there was (still) no consensus on the criteria guiding the exact frequency (ie a direct relation to the share of world trade or a more flexible approach possibly implying the formal selection of a core group). There was also a widely held view that the four major trading entities (out of a core group of twenty trading nations) should be reviewed on a more regular base than others. In this regard, the European Communities would be counted as one entity although one Contracting Party reiterated concerns about the way in which the policies pursued by individual Member states of the European Communities would be reviewed.[306] At the eighth meeting of the FOGS negotiating group, India speaking on behalf of the developed countries stated that it was necessary to establish procedures for enhanced surveillance through regular monitoring of the trade policies and practices of the major trading countries with a predominant impact on the multilateral trading system, so as to ensure symmetry surveillance in the GATT. According to India's view, all Contracting Parties would be subject to periodic reviews. However, less-developed countries and in particular least-developed countries should be surveyed on a less frequent basis.[307] During the sixth meeting of the FOGS, several participants also continued to plead for a strengthened role of the Secretariat.[308] Nevertheless, during the tenth meeting, the Contracting Parties disagreed on the nature of the reports and the exact role of the Secretariat. Some argued in favour of independent assessments, others for a merely

[304] Multilateral Trade Negotiations, The Uruguay Round, Negotiating Group on Functioning of the GATT System, Communication from the European Community, MTN.GNG/NG14/W/20, 22 March 1988, 4.

[305] Multilateral Trade Negotiations, The Uruguay Round, Negotiating Group on Functioning of the GATT System, Meeting of 25–28 January 1988, Note by the Secretariat, MTN.GNG/NG14/5, 16 February 1988, 3–4.

[306] Multilateral Trade Negotiations, The Uruguay Round, Negotiating Group on Functioning of the GATT System, Meeting of 21–23 March 1988, Note by the Secretariat, MTN.GNG/NG14/6, 15 April 1988, 2.

[307] Multilateral Trade Negotiations, The Uruguay Round, Negotiating Group on Functioning of the GATT System, Meeting of 20 and 22 June 1988, Note by the Secretariat, MTN.GNG/NG14/8, 13 July 1988, 12–14; Multilateral Trade Negotiations, The Uruguay Round, Negotiating Group on Functioning of the GATT System, Communication from the Delegation of India, MTN.GNG/NG14/W/23, 22 June 1988.

[308] Multilateral Trade Negotiations, The Uruguay Round, Negotiating Group on Functioning of the GATT System, Meeting of 21–23 March 1988, Note by the Secretariat, MTN.GNG/NG14/6, 15 April 1988, 2.

factual compilation of notifications. Some Contracting Parties came out in favour of a required national assistance to the Secretariat's reporting whereas others saw no need at all for it. Likewise, disagreement existed with regard to the frequency and nature (ie voluntary, obligatory for all or for some) of the Secretariat's investigative visits to capitals (ie the second structural element).[309] At the eighth meeting of the FOGS negotiating group, the debate on the role of discussants resurfaced. Some Contracting Parties proposed that 'a small group of discussants, selected from all Contracting Parties, should lead the discussion in the review body. These discussants, who should act on a personal basis, should not take part in the preparation of the documentation and should be selected from a list of interested persons by the Secretariat.'[310] Nevertheless, during the tenth meeting, the proposal to appoint discussants for each review triggered discussion. Some delegations believed that it would be useful to have discussants, appointed by the Chairman of the Council, acting in their personal capacity to assist the Chairman in opening the review's discussions. Other Contracting Parties disagreed.[311]

e) *The provisional adoption of the TPRM during the Montreal mid-term review of the Uruguay Round (December 1988) and the Trade Negotiation Council Meeting (April 1989): finalizing the institutional framework*

The Contracting Parties decided to organize a mid-term Ministerial review meeting towards the end of 1989. This meeting would survey the progress of the Uruguay Round and establish directions for the remainder of its negotiations.[312] A report of the FOGS negotiating group to the Trade Negotiations Committee at Ministerial level therefore set out the basis for the provisional adoption of the TPRM.[313] At the mid-term review meeting (5 to 9 December 1988), Ministers reached agreement on decisions affecting the future conduct of work in eleven of the fifteen Uruguay Round negotiating areas.[314] With regard to the TPRM, Ministers specifically

[309] Multilateral Trade Negotiations, The Uruguay Round, Negotiating Group on Functioning of the GATT System, Meeting of 24–28 October 1988, Note by the Secretariat, MTN.GNG/NG14/10, 14 November 1988, 1–4.

[310] Multilateral Trade Negotiations, The Uruguay Round, Negotiating Group on Functioning of the GATT System, Meeting of 20 and 22 June 1988, Note by the Secretariat, MTN.GNG/NG14/8, 13 July 1988, 12–14; Multilateral Trade Negotiations, The Uruguay Round, Negotiating Group on Functioning of the GATT System, Communication from the Delegation of India, MTN.GNG/NG14/W/23, 22 June 1988.

[311] Multilateral Trade Negotiations, The Uruguay Round, Negotiating Group on Functioning of the GATT System, Meeting of 24–28 October 1988, Note by the Secretariat, MTN.GNG/NG14/10, 14 November 1988, 1–4.

[312] Jackson, *The World Trade Organization, Constitution and Jurisprudence* (n 206) 25.

[313] Multilateral Trade Negotiations, The Uruguay Round, Report to the Trade Negotiations Committee meeting at Ministerial level, Montreal, December 1988, Group of Negotiations on Goods, MTN.GNG/13, 22 November 1988, 1 and 32; Reports finalized for Montreal TNC Meeting, News of the Uruguay Round of Multilateral Trade Negotiations, NUR 022, 30 November 1988.

[314] Multilateral Trade Negotiations, The Uruguay Round, Trade Negotiations Committee Meeting at Ministerial level, Montreal, December 1988, MTN.TNC/7(Min), 9 December 1988; Montreal Meeting of the Trade Negotiations Committee, News of the Uruguay Round of Multilateral Trade Negotiations, NUR 023, 14 December 1988; Consultations continue in Geneva in effort to free Montreal Package, News of the Uruguay Round of Multilateral Trade Negotiations, NUR 024, 23

recommended its establishment and provisional implementation from the date of the adoption of the Ministerial decision.[315] Nevertheless, since no overall consensus could be reached, all results would remain on hold until a Trade Negotiations Committee meeting in the first week of April 1989. In the meantime, GATT Director-General Dunkel conducted further high-level consultations on the four remaining items (ie textiles and clothing, safeguards, agriculture, and trade-related aspects of intellectual property) on which the Montreal Ministerial had been unable to agree.[316] Following final agreement on these four issues, the meeting of the Trade Negotiation Council of 12 April 1989 was due to ensure immediate implementation of the TPRM.[317] After the Council's decision, the TPRM became almost operational.[318] Moreover, at the Council's meeting Australia and Sweden volunteered to undergo a review as soon as possible.[319] At the same meeting, the Committee on Budget, Finance and Administration was also instructed '*to take appropriate action on the financial aspects of the decision relating to the Trade Policy Review Mechanism*'.[320] Nevertheless, a number of practical and procedural details still had to be worked out before the first TPR was able to take place (December 1989). These included the elaboration of '*(a) the initial program of reviews, (b) some standardized agenda for the conduct of the reviews by the TPRB, (c) timelines for the documents used in the process, (d) the procedures and (e) the program for TPR-related visits to capitals*'.[321] The so-called Brussels draft of December 1990 therefore called on the Council to establish guidelines for reviews by June 1991.[322] The final Dunkel draft of December 1991 consequently stated that Ministers recommend that the Contracting Parties confirm the establishment of the TPRM as established by the Decision of the Contracting Parties of 12 April 1989.[323] Moreover, in May 1994, the Contracting Parties decided explicitly to continue the operation of the

February 1989 (hereafter Consultations continue in Geneva in effort to free Montreal Package, News of the Uruguay Round of Multilateral Trade Negotiations).

315 Multilateral Trade Negotiations, The Uruguay Round, Trade Negotiations Committee Meeting at Ministerial level, Montreal, December 1988, MTN.TNC/7(Min), 9 December 1988, 35–38.

316 Consultations continue in Geneva in effort to free Montreal Package, News of the Uruguay Round of Multilateral Trade (n 313).

317 GATT/AIR/2746, 31 March 1989; General Agreement on Tariffs and Trade, 12 April 1989 Council, Matters Arising from the December 1988 and April 1989 Meetings of the Trade Negotiations Committee, Communication from the Council Chairman, C/W/585, 31 March 1989, 10–13; Multilateral Trade Negotiations, The Uruguay Round, Trade Negotiations Committee Meeting at level of High Officials, Geneva, 5–8 April 1989, MTN.TNC/9, 11 April 1989; Mid-term Review Agreements, News of the Uruguay Round of Multilateral Trade Negotiations (n 156).

318 Decisions of 12 April 1989 (13 April 1989) BISD L/6490 (hereafter Decisions of 12 April 1989); Mid-Term Meeting, Trade Negotiations Committee, MTN.TNC/11, 21 April 1989.

319 General Agreement on Tariffs and Trade, Council, Minutes of Meeting, Held in Centre William Rappard on 12 April 1989, C/M/231, 2 May 1989, 2.

320 General Agreement on Tariffs and Trade, Council, Minutes of Meeting, Held in Centre William Rappard on 12 April 1989, C/M/231, 2 May 1989, 2.

321 Answers from Mr Frank Wolter (first director of the Trade Policy Review Division, 1989–1991) to a questionnaire of the author (2 April 2014).

322 Draft Final Act Embodying the Results of the Uruguay Round of Multilateral Trade Negotiations, Revision, MTN.TNC/W/35/Rev.1, 3 December 1990, 321.

323 Draft Final Act Embodying the Results of the Uruguay Round of Multilateral Trade Negotiations, MTN.TNC/W/FA, 20 December 1991, p Y.1.

mechanism until its successor as established by Annex 3 of the WTO Marrakesh Agreement came into effect.[324]

The mid-term review Ministerial of December 1988 and the Council Decision of April 1989 both reconfirm the central objective of transparency of the TPRM. Nonetheless, they also explicitly foresee the mechanism's secondary goal of naming and shaming. Moreover, the twin objectives of the WTO's nascent mechanism for peer review were identical in the two texts.[325] This consistency attested to the maturity of these objectives and the broad political acceptance by all Contracting Parties of them.

Some questions remained with regard to the TPRM's broader structural set-up. These concerned both the institutional set-up of its mechanism for individual peer reviews (including its periodicity, reporting requirements, and structure for the review meeting) but also the framework for the TPRB's annual Overview of Developments of the International Trading Environment.

In terms of periodicity, both the mid-term review Ministerial of December 1988 and the Council's Decision of April 1989 agreed—in identical terms—on the structural element determining the periodic selection of the entities that are to be reviewed (ie the first structural element).[326] This frequency of review depends

[324] Trade Policy Review Mechanism—Arrangements for the continued operation of the Mechanism, Decision of 10 May 1994 (n 151).

[325]

> The purpose of the mechanism is to contribute to improved adherence by all contracting parties to GATT rules, disciplines and commitments, and hence to the smoother functioning of the multilateral trading system, by achieving greater transparency in, and understanding of, the trade policies and practices of contracting parties. Accordingly, the review mechanism will enable the regular collective appreciation and evaluation by the contracting parties of the full range of individual contracting parties trade policies and practices and their impact on the functioning of the multilateral trading system. It is not, however, intended to serve as a basis for the enforcement of specific GATT obligations or for dispute settlement procedures, or to impose new policy commitments on contracting parties.

and

> The assessment to be carried out under the review mechanism will, to the extent relevant, take place against the background of the wider economic and developmental needs, policies and objectives of the contracting party concerned, as well as of its external environment. However, the function of the review mechanism is to examine the impact of a Contracting Party's trade policies and practices on the multilateral trading system.

Multilateral Trade Negotiations, The Uruguay Round, Trade Negotiations Committee Meeting at Ministerial level, Montreal, December 1988, MTN.TNC/7(Min), 9 December 1988, 35; General Agreement on Tariffs and Trade, Functioning of the GATT System, Decisions of 12 April 1989 (n 317) 1.

[326]

> The trade policies and practices of all contracting parties will be subject to periodic review. Their impact on the functioning of the multilateral trading system, defined in terms of share of world trade in a recent representative period, will be the determining factor in deciding on the frequency of the reviews. The first four trading entities so identified (counting the European Communities as one) will be subject to review every two years. The next sixteen will be reviewed every four years. Other contracting parties will be reviewed every six years, except that a longer period may be fixed for least-developed countries. It is understood that the review of entities having a common external policy covering more than one contracting party shall cover all components of policy affecting trade including relevant policies and practices of the individual contracting parties. Exceptionally, in the event of change in a contracting party's trade policies or practices which may have a significant impact on its

on the designated Parties' share of world trade in a recent representative period. Interestingly, this share has so far been based on the average value of Parties' trade in goods and services over a reference period of three years.[327] Nevertheless, academic literature has voiced mixed feelings about this criterion. On one hand, several positive arguments were advanced in that (a) the criterion is dynamic and therefore constantly updated and (b) it avoids countries automatically designating themselves as developing or developed countries.[328] On the other hand, some critical thoughts were shared. In this respect, it has been argued that a country's share of world trade could be unusually small precisely because of the country's protectionist instincts, in which case the country might need to be examined more frequently than might be otherwise expected (ie as prescribed by the low frequency of its reviews).[329]

With regard to reporting, the mid-term review Ministerial of December 1988 and the Council's Decision of April 1989 both agreed, again in identical language, up the formal contours of reporting (ie part of the third structural element).[330]

> trading partners, the contracting party may be requested by the Council after consultations to bring forward its next review

and

> contracting parties recognize the need to minimize the burden for governments also subject to full consultations under the GATT balance-of-payments provisions. To this end, the Chairman of the Council shall, in consultation with the contracting party or parties concerned, and with the Chairman of the Committee on Balance-of-Payments Restrictions, devise administrative arrangements which would harmonize the normal rhythm of the trade policy reviews with the timetable for balance-of-payments consultations but would not postpone the trade policy review by more than 12 months.

Multilateral Trade Negotiations, The Uruguay Round, Trade Negotiations Committee Meeting at Ministerial level, Montreal, December 1988, MTN.TNC/7(Min), 9 December 1988, 36; Decisions of 12 April 1989 (n 317) 1; See section 2 of this chapter, 'Mechanisms for peer review—theoretical core elements'.

[327] Laird and Valdés, 'The Trade Policy Review Mechanism' (n 149) 470.

[328] Mavroidis, 'Surveillance Schemes: The GATT's New Trade Policy Review Mechanism' (n 6) 379.

[329] Qureshi, *The World Trade Organization: Implementing Trade Norms* (n 149) 113.

[330]

> In order to achieve the fullest possible degree of transparency, each contracting party shall report regularly to the contracting parties. Initial full reports shall be submitted in the year when the contracting party is first subject to the review: however, in no case shall the initial report be submitted later than four years after the introduction of the mechanism. Subsequently, full reports shall be provided in years when the contracting party is due for review. Full reports will describe the trade policies and practices pursued by the contracting party or parties concerned, based on an agreed format to be decided on by the Council. This format may be revised by the Council in the light of experience. Between reviews, contracting parties will provide brief reports when there are any significant changes in their trade policies; an annual update of statistical information will be provided according to the agreed format. Particular account will be taken of difficulties presented to least-developed contracting parties in compiling their reports. The secretariat shall make available technical assistance on request to less-developed contracting parties, and in particular to the least-developed contracting parties. Information contained in country reports should to the greatest extent possible be coordinated with notifications made under GATT provisions

and

> The Council will base its work on the following documentation: (a) The full report (as referred above) supplied by the contracting party or parties under review, (b) A report, to be drawn up by the Secretariat on its own responsibility, based on the information available to it and that provided by the contracting party or parties concerned. The secretariat should

Nonetheless, further discussions and proposals followed later in April[331] (containing an indicative list of the type of measures that should be included in countries' reports), May,[332] and June 1989.[333] The June meeting led to the adoption of the text containing the format for country reports. Nonetheless, several Parties remained critical. They either advocated more critical reporting (regretting that the draft format did not include a specific reference to domestic policy measures directly affecting trade or highlighting the need for analytical and probing Secretariat reports that could play a catalytic role) or for less intrusion (construing the draft format as purely indicative, not setting the parameters for the collective assessments that were to be carried out by the Council, and explicitly excluding reporting on labour standards).[334] The June meeting also decided to schedule further discussions to develop a simplified format for reports by the least-developed countries.[335] These issues resurfaced in November 1989 with the chairman of the FOGS still noting unresolved consultations.[336] The first TPRs which were organized as of December 1989 therefore took place while negotiations still unfolded with regard to the format of country reports which needed to be respected by the least-developed countries.[337] In April 1990, the FOGS negotiating group adopted the format for country reports by least-developed countries.[338] In this regard, the option was explicitly provided not to submit data which either concerned only a small proportion of total trade or which could not be collected without disproportionate effort.

> seek clarification from the contracting party or parties concerned of their trade policies and practices

and

> '[t]he reports by the contracting party under review and by the secretariat, together with the minutes of the respective meeting of the Council, will be published promptly after the review'. Multilateral Trade Negotiations, The Uruguay Round, Trade Negotiations Committee Meeting at Ministerial level, Montreal, December 1988, MTN.TNC/7(Min), 9 December 1988, 35–37; Decisions of 12 April 1989 (n 317) 1–3; See section 2 of this chapter, 'Mechanisms for peer review—theoretical core elements'.

331 Multilateral Trade Negotiations, The Uruguay Round, Negotiating Group on Functioning of the GATT System, Communication from Canada, MTN.GNG/NG14/W/33, 24 April 1989, 4.

332 Multilateral Trade Negotiations, The Uruguay Round, Negotiating Group on Functioning of the GATT System, Meeting of 1 and 3 May 1989, Note by the Secretariat, MTN.GNG/NG14/11, 23 May 1989.

333 Multilateral Trade Negotiations, The Uruguay Round, Negotiating Group on Functioning of the GATT System, Meeting of 19–20 June 1989, Note by the Secretariat, MTN.GNG/NG14/12, 30 June 1989.

334 Multilateral Trade Negotiations, The Uruguay Round, Negotiating Group on Functioning of the GATT System, Meeting of 19–20 June 1989, Note by the Secretariat, MTN.GNG/NG14/12, 30 June 1989, 2–3.

335 Multilateral Trade Negotiations, The Uruguay Round, Negotiating Group on Functioning of the GATT System, Meeting of 19–20 June 1989, Note by the Secretariat, MTN.GNG/NG14/12, 30 June 1989, 6.

336 Multilateral Trade Negotiations, The Uruguay Round, Negotiating Group on Functioning of the GATT System, Meeting of 6 and 9 November 1989, Note by the Secretariat, MTN.GNG/NG14/13, 12 December 1989, 1.

337 Multilateral Trade Negotiations, The Uruguay Round, Negotiating Group on the Functioning of the GATT System, Meeting of 15 December 1989, Note by the Secretariat, MTN.GNG/NG14/14, 12 February 1990.

338 Multilateral Trade Negotiations, The Uruguay Round, Negotiating Group on the Functioning of the GATT System, Meeting of 2 April 1990, Note by the Secretariat, MTN.GNG/NG14/16, 9 May 1990, 5 and 16.

In terms of the structure of the review meeting, the mid-term review Ministerial of December 1988 and the Council's Decision of April 1989 also agreed in identical terms on the formal establishment of the forum where the peer review process was to take place.[339] Successful negotiations between the mid-term review Ministerial and the Council's Decision also led to stating the final competency of the Chairman of the Council: '*In consultation with the Contracting Party or Parties under review, the Chairman will choose discussants who, in their personal capacity will introduce the discussions in the review body*.'[340]

As a result of the successful FOGS negotiations, the mid-term review Ministerial of December 1988 and the Council's Decision of April 1989 also agreed—again in unchanged language—to schedule a yearly Overview of Developments in the International Trading Environment.[341] The first

[339] '(i) Trade policy reviews will be carried out by the GATT Council at periodic special meetings'; and '(ii) The Council will establish a basic plan for the conduct of the reviews. It may also discuss and take note of update reports from contracting parties. The Council will establish a program of reviews for each year in consultation with the contracting parties directly concerned.' Both texts also foresaw a special role for the Council in the framework of its yearly overview of developments in the International Trading Environment (see coverage with regard to Overview of developments in the International Trading Environment under The provisional adoption of the TPRM during the Montreal mid-term review of the Uruguay Round (December 1988) and the Trade Negotiations Council Meeting (April 1989)):

> Such an overview should also be undertaken by the Council. It should be assisted by an annual report by the Director-General setting out major GATT activities and highlighting significant policy issues affecting the trading system. The enhanced surveillance thus provided would also strengthen the existing 'early warning' aspect of the special meetings of the Council. It is understood that this overview by the Council, together with the trade policy review mechanism, would replace the existing reviews in special Council meetings established under paragraph 24 of the 1979 Understanding Regarding Notification, Consultation, Dispute Settlement and Surveillance.

Multilateral Trade Negotiations, The Uruguay Round, Trade Negotiations Committee Meeting at Ministerial level, Montreal, December 1988, MTN.TNC/7(Min), 9 December 1988, 38 and 71–72; Decisions of 12 April 1989 (n 317) 1–4; See section 2 of this chapter, 'Mechanisms for peer review—theoretical core elements'.

[340] Multilateral Trade Negotiations, The Uruguay Round, Trade Negotiations Committee Meeting at Ministerial level, Montreal, December 1988, MTN.TNC/7(Min), 9 December 1988, 38 and 71–72; Decisions of 12 April 1989 (n 317) 1–4; See section 2 of this chapter, 'Mechanisms for peer review—theoretical core elements'.

[341]

> Enhanced surveillance requires, in addition, an overview of developments in the international trading environment which are having an impact on the multilateral trading system. Such an overview should also be undertaken by the Council. It should be assisted by an annual report by the Director-General setting out major GATT activities and highlighting significant policy issues affecting the trading system. The enhanced surveillance thus provided would also strengthen the existing 'early warning' aspect of the special meetings of the Council. It is understood that this overview by the Council, together with the trade policy review mechanism, would replace the existing reviews in special Council meetings established under paragraph 24 of the 1979 Understanding Regarding Notification, Consultation, Dispute Settlement and Surveillance.

Overview was discussed during a special meeting of the Council of 11 December 1989.[342]

The mid-term review Ministerial of December 1988 and the Council's Decision of April 1989 came up with an identical identification and description of the countries to be reviewed, of the reviewing countries, and of the role of the Secretariat. In addition, they contained a limited description of the role of discussants. In this regard, both stated that '*[i]n consultation with the contracting party or parties under review, the Chairman may choose discussants who, in their personal capacity, will introduce the discussions in the review body*'.[343]

The countries to be reviewed were to be identified by means of the TPRM's cyclical periodicity whereas the reviewing countries were assembled in the Trade Policy Review Body which was to be open to all. The application of the review was therefore blind. Nevertheless, certain reviewees such as the European Communities (to be counted as one) or the category of least-developing countries (which could avail themselves with longer review cycles, flexible reporting, and technical assistance) were provided with some special and differential form of treatment.

The Secretariat was tasked with the analysis of and reporting on national trade policies and practices. Its first budgetary estimates to cover these goals (drawn up in accordance with the Council's Decision of 12 April 1989) were based on an allocation of CHF 474.000 for 1989 and at a cost of CHF 2.354.000 for 1990, the TPRM's first full year of functioning.[344] These overall budgets were used for the functioning of the TPRM, including salary payments for six TPRD officials in 1989 and for nine officials in 1990.[345] Nevertheless, several factors led to a quick increase in the budgetary allocation for the TPRD. These included the (inevitable) growth in the GATT/WTO Membership but also the increased complexities of global trade policy. With regard to the latter, ongoing debates with regard to the so-called Coherence (mandate) between trade, monetary, and financial policies played an important role.[346] The participants to this debate generally agreed on the need for closer contacts, collaboration, and technical assistance between the respective staff of the WTO, the IMF, and the World Bank. A Swiss Communication of May 1990 therefore proposed to strengthen the capacity of the Secretariat. In this context,

Multilateral Trade Negotiations, The Uruguay Round, Trade Negotiations Committee Meeting at Ministerial level, Montreal, December 1988, MTN.TNC/7(Min), 9 December 1988, p. 38; Decisions of 12 April 1989 (n 317) 4.

[342] General Agreement on Tariffs and Trade, Council, 11 December 1989, Council Overview of Developments in the International Trading Environment, Annual Report by the Director-General, C/171, 5 December 1989.

[343] Mid-term Review Agreements, News of the Uruguay Round of Multilateral Trade Negotiations (n 156); Decisions of 12 April 1989 (n 317) 3.

[344] Budget Estimate for the Trade Policy Review Mechanism, Note by the Secretariat, Spec(89)20, 21 April 1989, 5.

[345] Answers from the Human Resources Department of the WTO to questions of the author (4 December 2015).

[346] Multilateral Trade Negotiations, The Uruguay Round, Negotiating Group Functioning of the GATT System, Communication from the European Community, MTN.GNG/NG14/W/40, 13 March 1990, 6.

it explicitly asked the Secretariat '*to analyse its manpower requirement to play an active role in trade policy dialogue and make a comparison with the means invested by the IMF for Article IV consultations or by the World Bank for structural adjustment programs*'.[347] Nevertheless, some Members took issue with the proposed additional analytical capacities of the TPRD. They questioned the necessity of setting up another system, stated that the newly proposed independent and analytical role of the Secretariat went beyond the role given to the Secretariat when the TPRM had been adopted, and affirmed that the WTO's role in national monetary and financial policies was carefully circumscribed under Article XV of the GATT.[348] Switzerland counterargued that it had not intended to construct a new TPRM but merely wanted to provide the GATT with similar resources as those available to the IMF and the World Bank in order to entrust it with its new role as embodied in the TPRM.[349] In an attempt to overcome the differences, Switzerland consequently drafted a non-paper.[350] Nonetheless, several participants considered the non-paper similar to Switzerland's earlier proposals. They reiterated their views, which left no space for a more active role of the Secretariat. According to these views, there was no need to change the GATT Secretariat from an institution which provided support to the deliberations to one which had independent status and participated as such in the trade policy dialogue. Furthermore, the Swiss proposal to extend the scope of the TPRM to services, TRIPS (Agreement on Trade-Related Aspects of Intellectual Property Rights), and TRIMS (Agreement on Trade-Related Investment Measures) was considered to be confusing.[351]

B. The TPRM's Performance as the WTO's Mechanism for Peer Review

The first part of this chapter has demonstrated that the TPRM has gradually acquired all institutional trappings of a typical mechanism for peer review. We now analyse whether and/or to what degree the TPRM has performed well as the WTO's mechanism for peer review.

[347] Multilateral Trade Negotiations, The Uruguay Round, Negotiating Group Functioning of the GATT System, Communication from Switzerland, MTN.GNG/NG14/W/41, 17 May 1990, 4.

[348] Multilateral Trade Negotiations, The Uruguay Round, Negotiating Group Functioning of the GATT System, Meeting of 22–23 May 1990, Note by the Secretariat, MTN.GNG/NG14/17, 19 June 1990, 5–8.

[349] Multilateral Trade Negotiations, The Uruguay Round, Negotiating Group Functioning of the GATT System, Meeting of 22–23 May 1990, Note by the Secretariat, MTN.GNG/NG14/17, 19 June 1990, 10.

[350] Multilateral Trade Negotiations, The Uruguay Round, Negotiating Group Functioning of the GATT System, Meeting of 25–26 June 1990, Note by the Secretariat, MTN.GNG/NG14/18, 9 July 1990, 3.

[351] Multilateral Trade Negotiations, The Uruguay Round, Negotiating Group Functioning of the GATT System, Meeting of 25–26 June 1990, Note by the Secretariat, MTN.GNG/NG14/18, 9 July 1990, 3–4.

Annex 3 to the Marrakesh Agreement establishing the TPRM, states that '*the TPRB shall undertake an appraisal of the operation of the TPRM not more than five years after the entry into force of the Agreement Establishing the WTO. The results of the appraisal will be presented to the Ministerial Conference. It may subsequently undertake appraisals of the TPRM at intervals to be determined by it or as requested by the Ministerial Conference*'.[352] In accordance with the requirements of this provision, formal appraisals were undertaken in 1999, 2005, 2008, 2011, and 2013.[353]

For each of these institutionally mandated appraisals, the second part of this chapter assesses (1) the TPRM's practical pursuit of its double objectives (degree to which the transparency and naming and shaming objectives have been met); (2) the structure of the review mechanism (degree to which the structure enabled increased transparency and naming and shaming); and (3) the degree of active participation in the reviews.

In terms of objectives, the evolving interpretation of academic literature vis-à-vis the WTO Membership's own interpretation of the TPRM's stated double objectives are assessed. Where possible, academic findings with regard to the TPRM's objectives in the successive periods are contrasted with those of the Membership as expressed in the consecutive appraisals. Moreover, the question is asked whether and/or to what degree the Members themselves have adhered to the (original) idea of institutionally separating the TPRM from the DSB. Paragraph A of Annex 3 to the Marrakesh Agreement is very clear in stating that the TPRM '*is not . . . intended to serve as a basis for the enforcement of specific obligations under the Agreements or for dispute settlement procedures, or to impose new policy commitments on Members*'.[354] In addition, Annex 3 to the Marrakesh Agreement is not a covered agreement under Appendix I to Annex II to the Marrakesh Agreement which embodies the Understanding on Rules and Procedures Governing the Settlement of Disputes.[355] Therefore analysis will be undertaken in order to examine whether the TPRM and its findings have nevertheless been invoked within the proceedings of the Dispute Settlement Body.

With regard to structure, the strengths and weaknesses of individual TPRs and yearly Overviews of Developments in the International Trading Environment will be analysed from the twin perspectives of increased transparency and better naming and shaming. The focus will thereby lie on the periodicity requirements for

[352] The Trade Policy Review Mechanism (n 151).

[353] *Appraisal of the Operation of the Trade Policy Review Mechanism—Draft Report to Ministers* (30 September 1999) WT/TPR/W/24; *Second Appraisal of the Operation of the Trade Policy Review Mechanism—Draft Report to Ministers* (12 August 2005) WT/TPR/W/33; *Draft—Third Appraisal of the Operation of the Trade Policy Review Mechanism* (15 October 2008) WT/TPR/W/38; *Fourth Appraisal of the Operation of the Trade Policy Review Mechanism* (17 November 2011) WT/TPR/W/44; *Fifth Appraisal of the Trade Policy Review Mechanism, Ministerial Conference, Ninth Session, Bali, 3–6 December 2013* (28 October 2013) WT/MIN(13)/5; The results of the last appraisal (2016) are analysed in the Conclusions.

[354] The Trade Policy Review Mechanism (n 151).

[355] Marrakesh Agreement Establishing the World Trade Organization (15 April 1994) <https://www.wto.org/english/docs_e/legal_e/28-dsu_e.htm#appendix1> accessed 20 May 2017 (hereafter the Marrakesh Agreement).

individual TPRs, on the reporting structure and requirements of individual reviews and yearly Overviews, and on the evolving structure of review meetings.

This part focuses on several institutional features of individual TPRs. In this regard, it will first analyse whether the institutional periodicity requirements for individual TPRs have functioned well. It thus contrasts the recommendations and predictions of the annual TPRB reports with their consecutive implementation and appraisals. It will then attempt to measure how well the TPRM's reporting requirements have performed in practice, both from a transparency angle as well as from the perspective of naming and shaming. In order to do so, this part analyses academic writing with regard to individual TPRs' added value in terms of transparency. It will rank the (available) academic views on the TPRs' added informational value into three categories: (a) TPRs with missing information; (b) TPRs which, according to academia, contain a too positive or a too negative assessment; and (c) TPRs with incorrect information. Moreover, for each of these three categories, this part of the chapter attempts to contrast the views of the (external) academics where possible with some (anonymous) views of current and former WTO staff with regard to the same point. This part also examines twenty trade disputes within the context of Sanitary and Phytosanitary (SPS) and Technical Barriers to Trade (TBT), for which it examines individual TPRs' structural added value not only in terms of increased transparency but also in terms of naming and shaming. In this context, the underlying Secretariat report, government report, minutes of the meeting, and written questions and answers are examined in an attempt to assess the individual TPRs' added value. This part's analysis of the institutional features of TPRs will finally focus on the evolving structure of the review meeting. It contrasts the proposals with regard to the procedures of the review meetings which were derived from the yearly TPRB reports with those structural changes which resulted from the appraisal process. It also analyses whether and/or to what degree these proposed structural changes—*sensu lato*—have managed to contribute to increased transparency and naming and shaming, and examines which proposals were made with regard to the specific institutional position of the discussant.

At the same time, it will pay specific attention to the second structural leg of the WTO's peer review mechanism, the yearly Overviews of Developments in the International Trading Environment. In this regard, its focus will be again on SPS and TBT measures and their structural and substantive coverage by the Overviews in order to assess the Overviews' added value in terms of transparency and naming and shaming. This part thereby specifically assesses: (a) whether the Overviews contain a standardized form of reporting on the TPRM's yearly activities; (b) whether and why certain individual TPRs received more attention than others (resulting in a (merited or unwarranted) higher degree of transparency and naming and shaming); and (c) whether the yearly Overview's coverage of SPS and TBT measures was coherent and comprehensive. In this respect, it assesses whether the yearly Overviews reported on the identified measures' consecutive coverage first by the committee(s) concerned, potentially also followed by the TPRM's and the DSB's coverage.

In terms of participation, the main participants to the review (ie the government under review and its peers, the Secretariat, and the discussant(s)) will be examined for each of the periods covered by the five consecutive appraisals. The TPRM can only have an added value in terms of increased transparency and effective naming and shaming if it is based on a substantive level of attendance and on a high degree of interaction. The Secretariat's participation in the process is therefore analysed through the lens of its changing staffing levels, its evolving budgets, and its internal and external interactions with other divisions of the WTO and the Members. Government participation in the review process is analysed through changing attendance and participation rates of those nations involved. Finally, the institutionally evolving role of the discussants is examined and contrasted with the discussants' practical functioning in the process. In this regard, this part analyses several elements including institutional modifications with regard to the required number of discussants, discussants' deferral to the Secretariat's and governmental reporting, their propensity to criticize both reports, discussants' willingness to draw on additional external studies, and their (changing) position with regard to issues of compliance and dispute settlement.

1. First appraisal of the operation of the Trade Policy Review Mechanism (January–September 1999): review of the TPRM's functioning between 1989 and September 1999

On 27 January 1999, the TPRB agreed on a procedure for the first appraisal of the operation of the TPRM.[356] Subsequently the TPRB held twelve informal meetings in the period between January and September 1999. This review started with the elaboration of an informal questionnaire (the so-called non-paper) which structured the review and gradually resulted in the draft[357] and formal appraisal report to Ministers on 8 October 1999.[358]

a) Objectives

Mechanisms for peer review—and, as the first part of this chapter has demonstrated, the TPRM gradually crystallized into one of them—are useful. They are distinct from procedures for legal enforcement and from fact finding and/or data collection and reporting.[359] In other words, '*there is a middle ground between the legal assessment of doubtful trade measures on the one hand, and mere factual representation of such measures on the other*'.[360] Theoretically, the achievement of this

[356] WTO, TPRB, Trade Policy Review Mechanism, Draft Report of the Trade Policy Review Body for 1999, WT/TPR/W/23, 30 September 1999, 2.

[357] Informal draft questionnaire, 11 January 1999 (Document on file with the author); WTO, TPRB, Appraisal of the operation of the Trade Policy Review Mechanism, Draft Report to Ministers, WT/TPR/W/24, 30 September 1999.

[358] WTO, Ministerial Conference, Third Session, Seattle 30 November–3 December 1999, Appraisal of the operation of the Trade Policy Review Mechanism, WT/MIN(99)/2, 8 October 1999.

[359] Pagani, 'Peer Review: A Tool for Co-operation and Change' (n 21) 5; See section 2 of this chapter, 'Mechanisms for peer review—theoretical core elements'.

[360] Victoria Curzon Price, 'GATT's New Trade Policy Review Mechanism' (1991) 14(2) The World Economy 23 (hereafter Price, 'GATT's New Trade Policy Review Mechanism').

middle ground—which is based on direct naming and shaming and the promotion of increased transparency—is exactly what the mandate of the TPRM enables Members and the Secretariat to do. In the words of public choice theory, the introduction of the TPRM (supposedly) solves the free-rider problem by increasing transparency and compliance.[361]

Nonetheless, some academic literature—be it specifically with regard to the nascent TPRM—begged to disagree and pointed out that '*these reviews are not likely to have a significant impact on the implementation or effectiveness of the legal obligations contained in the variety of GATT treaties and protocol, including those that will come into effect at the end of the Uruguay Round. Indeed, there are (even) some risks that this review mechanism will divert attention from the legal norms in such a way as to actually decrease the pressure on Contracting Parties to observe these norms.*'[362] Others were more positive, adopted a longer perspective, and stated that '*the TPRM will serve only as a means of enhanced transparency because GATT's dispute settlement procedures are currently the only way to legally determine compatibility of national policies with GATT rules. Still, in the words of GATT Director-General Arthur Dunkel, "the TPRM is a long-term enterprise". As such, if the TPRM progresses to become a more integrated scheme, the boundary between transparency and legal assessment will become more indistinguishable and, ultimately, the latter will replace the former*'.[363]

The question, therefore, '*really boils down to an assessment of whether the peer pressure and increased transparency generated by the TPRM will have more than a marginal effect on the trade system and whether the TPRM is complementary to, rather than in competition with, the dispute settlement regime*'.[364]

In answering this question it is important not to underestimate the TPRM's corrective goal of naming and shaming (not all WTO-conforming behaviour derives from the threat of (legal) enforcement) nor to overestimate the mechanism's informative objective in terms of transparency (not all transparency within the WTO is derived from and/or linked to the TPRM).[365] First, the TPRM's corrective goal in terms of naming and shaming should not be underestimated. In this regard, academic literature has pointed to two reasons for this corrective component: '*the TPRM invites Contracting Parties to evaluate and appreciate the respective Contracting Party's trade policies*'. Alternatively, '*the transparency that results may well be drawn upon by Contracting Parties subsequent to the review for further bilateral consultations with the Contracting Party under review or, alternatively, prior pressure might*

[361] Price, 'New Institutional Developments in GATT' (n 183) 101.

[362] John H Jackson, *Restructuring the GATT System* (The Royal Institute of International Affairs 1990) 80 (hereafter Jackson, *Restructuring The GATT System*).

[363] Mavroidis, 'Surveillance Schemes: The GATT's New Trade Policy Review Mechanism' (n 6) 413.

[364] Price, 'New Institutional Developments in GATT' (n 183) 101.

[365] Some recent academic literature on transparency and international law even does not refer at all to the TPRM: Panagiotis Delimatsis, 'Institutional Transparency in the WTO', in Andrea Bianchi and Anne Peters (eds), *Transparency in International Law* (Cambridge University Press 2014) 112–42, versus G Marceau and M Hurley, 'Transparency and Public Participation in the WTO: A Report Card on WTO Transparency Mechanisms' (2012) 4(1) Trade Law and Development 19–44; Pascal Lamy, *The Geneva Consensus—Making Trade Work For All* (Cambridge University Press 2013) 158.

conceivably be brought, that is prior to the actual reviews, to induce the Contracting Party under review into giving unilateral commitments or undertakings in the TPRM exercise'.[366] Furthermore, academic literature has clearly stated that '*legal appraisal is not precluded under the TPRM—nor is it inconsistent with the broad appraisal of policy and practice*'.[367] Second, the TPRM's objective in terms of transparency should not be overestimated. Nevertheless, academic literature has precisely emphasized or (sometimes) overemphasized the priority of the TPRM's transparency objective. According to Dr Abbott (director in the EC Commission—part of one of the first entities to be subject to the TPR process), the above-mentioned academic stance flies '*in the face of the expressed intention of the exercise, which was precisely to avoid a debate that was too focused on issues of GATT conformity—there are other occasions for that—and to favour a more general and wide-ranging debate of trade policies in the broad context of world trade developments together with the specific historic and other features relevant to each country's policies, and how these factors influence policy-making*'.[368] Any reference '*to the efficacy of the TPRM as an instrument of "compliance"*' was therefore perceived as '*certainly misconceived*'.[369]

What followed was a sometimes acrimonious debate whereby the advocates of the TPRM as a mechanism for naming and shaming (and compliance) further equated the TPRM with an instrument of enforcement. This view was based on the TPRM's compulsory character, its normative framework, and the fact that '*it could lead to, or form a basis for, the enforcement of specific GATT obligations, or for dispute settlement, or impose new commitments on Contracting Parties*'.[370] This view was furthermore supported with the argument that '*Information that is revealed in a TPRM exercise may be used by Members as a basis for enforcement trough the WTO dispute settlement procedures. The TPRM cannot have been intended to function as a process whereby, upon revelation of a "misdemeanour", the Member becomes immune from enforcement in respect of it. The TPRM does not accord absolution from trade sins. Indeed, Members in actual reviews may state on record that they reserve the right to, or intend to take up, as the case may be, the matter further through the dispute settlement*

[366] Qureshi, 'The New GATT Trade Policy Review Mechanism: An Exercise in Transparency or "Enforcement"' (n 38) 153.

[367] Asif H Qureshi, 'Some Reflections on the GATT TPRM, in the Light of the Trade Policy Review of the European Communities—A Legal Perspective' (1992) 26(6) Journal of World Trade 104 (hereafter Qureshi, 'Some Reflections on the GATT TPRM, in the Light of the Trade Policy Review of the European Communities—A Legal Perspective'); This position is very much line with the view of the Nordics during the FOGS negotiations; Multilateral Trade Negotiations, The Uruguay Round, Negotiating Group on Functioning of the GATT System, Communication from the Nordic Countries, MTN.GNG/NG14/W/17, 28 January 1988, 1.

[368] Roderick Abbot, 'GATT and the Trade Policy Review Mechanism: Further Reflections on Earlier Reflections' (1993) 27(3) Journal of World Trade 117 (hereafter Abbot, 'GATT and the Trade Policy Review Mechanism: Further Reflections on Earlier Reflections').

[369] Abbot, 'GATT and the Trade Policy Review Mechanism: Further Reflections on Earlier Reflections' (n 366) 118.

[370] Asif H Qureshi, 'Some Lessons from "Developing Countries" Trade Policy Reviews in the GATT Framework: An Enforcement Perspective' (1995) 18(3) The World Economy 493–96 (hereafter Qureshi, 'Some Lessons from "Developing Countries" Trade Policy Reviews in the GATT Framework: An Enforcement Perspective').

procedure. Furthermore, there is nothing to preclude a Member from subsequently invoking statements made in a review in relation to the state which made the representation. In addition, there is nothing to prevent the Member under review itself from unilaterally undertaking a binding commitment'.[371]

This academic debate between advocates of the TPRM as an enforcement structure for the GATT's and/or the WTO's legal obligations (ie Qureshi and India) and those emphasizing the TPRM's primary transparency objective (ie Abbott, Blackhurst, Curzon Price, and the United States) was noted by Laird.[372] The author attempts to explain this dichotomy by emphasizing that '*one can understand how a jurist might take a narrower, enforcement interpretation, while economists with a background in the public policy debate would focus on the economic issues, seeing no fundamental dichotomy between good domestic policies and good international citizenship*'.[373] Other writings of this period have a (similar) balanced view. Francois initially analyses the TPRM's naming and shaming as part of its transparency objective. In this regard, the author emphasizes that '*the stated purpose of the TPRM is the enhancement of the transparency and understanding of WTO Members' trade policies*' and that '*the TPRM is at its heart a vehicle for providing information. It was not meant to be used for policy recommendations.*' Nevertheless, Francois also acknowledges the TPRM's secondary objective—its goal of naming and shaming. In this regard, the author indicates that*the TPRM, by subjecting the largest OECD markets to periodic review, shifts the balance of power in the WTO, ever so slightly, in favour of the developing countries. It ensures that the trade policy practices of the industrial countries are subject to periodic, public peer review. While the TPRM is not charged with passing judgement on the compliance of Members with WTO obligations, its pays an important transparency role*'.[374]

Nonetheless, the academic tension between the proponents of the TPRM as a pure transparency mechanism and those who also saw a prime or partial naming and shaming/compliance/enforcement role for the TPRM was largely absent from the discussions leading to the Singapore Ministerial (1996) or from those resulting in the TPRM's first appraisal (1999).

The TPRB's report to the Singapore Ministerial—which provided a first interim assessment of the TPRM—emphasized that the TPRM occupied a unique place within the WTO in promoting non-confrontational discussions of key trade policy issues. The report therefore emphasized that the TPRM's '*specific de-linkage from dispute settlement procedures is an essential feature which must be safeguarded*'. Nevertheless, the report also explicitly emphasized that '*further opportunities might*

[371] Qureshi, 'Some Lessons from "Developing Countries" Trade Policy Reviews in the GATT Framework: An Enforcement Perspective' (n 368) 493–96.

[372] Sam Laird, 'The WTO's Trade Policy Review Mechanism—From Through the Looking Glass' (1999) 22(6) The World Economy 742–44 (hereafter Laird, 'The WTO's Trade Policy Review Mechanism—From Through the Looking Glass').

[373] Laird, 'The WTO's Trade Policy Review Mechanism—From Through the Looking Glass' (n 370) 743.

[374] Francois, 'Maximizing the Benefits of the Trade Policy Review Mechanism for Developing Countries' (n 37) 1, 4, and 6.

be sought for encouraging greater cross-fertilization between TPRB discussions and those undertaken in other WTO bodies'.[375]

During the informal meeting of 12 May 1999, the discussions of the appraisal were structured around the theme '*What is the mission of the TPRM?*'. A first sub-theme which was analysed in this context was built on the question of how far the TPR should be linked to legal provisions of the WTO agreement. More concretely, the question of what kind of relationship should exist between the work of the TPRB and the activities of regular WTO committees was tabled. Argentina, Brazil, Brunei on behalf of ASEAN, Canada, Cuba, Hungary, India, Japan, Korea, Mexico, Morocco, Norway, Poland, Switzerland, the United States, and Uruguay all answered that '*it was not pertinent to examine how far the TPRM should be linked to legal WTO provisions because the TPRM had been conceived as a political rather than a legal exercise and/or because Annex 3 explicitly required the TPRM not to serve as a basis for the enforcement of WTO obligations: the TPR's were a political-economy, not a legal exercise*'. Moreover, the European Union noted that '*although TPRM did not imply verifying compliance with WTO commitments, it did not preclude comparing policies with WTO principles and identifying implementation problems*'. Furthermore, Mexico and India commented that '*there should be a strengthened two-way flow of information between TPRB and WTO Committees provided it did not affect Member's rights and obligations*'.[376] The final Ministerial report of the first appraisal therefore repeats that the '*TPRM had been conceived as a policy exercise*' and that '*it was not intended to serve as a basis for the enforcement of specific WTO obligations or for dispute settlement procedures, or to impose new policy commitments on Members*'. The report therefore urged that the mechanism continue to pursue its objectives, as enunciated in paragraphs A and B of Annex 3 to the Marrakesh Agreement.[377]

Although the first appraisal of the TPRM was largely self-congratulatory (especially with regard to the assessment of its objectives), two critical points stand out. First of all, the appraisal urged for a review of all Members. By the end of 1999, reviews had covered seventy-one Members which represented only 84 per cent of world trade and just 63 per cent of the total WTO Membership.[378] The appraisal also required the TPRM to maintain its own capacity for analysis with the WTO '*being the only multilateral mechanism undertaking comprehensive evaluation of trade policies and their coherence within a given economic setting*'.[379] Under the Marrakesh Ministerial Declaration on the Contribution of the World Trade Organization to

[375] WTO, TPRB, Trade Policy Review Mechanism, Report to the Singapore Ministerial Conference, WT/TPR/27, 28 October 1996, 3.

[376] Appraisal of the operation of the TPRM, Informal meeting of 12 May 1999, Checklist of main points, 20 May 1999, No 2933, 1–2 (Document on file with the author).

[377] WTO, Ministerial Conference, Third Session, Seattle 30 November–3 December 1999, Appraisal of the operation of the Trade Policy Review Mechanism, WT/MIN(99)/2, 8 October 1999, 1.

[378] WTO, TPRB, Draft Report of the Trade Policy Review Body for 1999, Trade Policy Review Mechanism, WT/TPR/W/23, 30 September 1999, 1.

[379] WTO, Ministerial Conference, Third Session, Seattle 30 November–3 December 1999, Appraisal of the operation of the Trade Policy Review Mechanism, WT/MIN(99)/2, 8 October 1999, 1–2.

Achieving Greater Coherence in Global Economic Policymaking, the WTO had been enabled to use macro-economic information and co-operation from other intergovernmental organizations such as the IMF and the World Bank. Nevertheless, the lead-up to the first appraisal had witnessed Members' concern about these external inputs and collaboration replacing the WTO TPRD's own nascent technical capacities.[380] Clearly, even the TPRM's achievement of its transparency objective was still incomplete.

The TPRM and the DSB were conceived as two separately functioning entities. Paragraph A of Annex 3 to the Marrakesh Agreement is very clear in stating that the TPRM '*is not ... intended to serve as a basis for the enforcement of specific obligations under the Agreements or for dispute settlement procedures, or to impose new policy commitments on Members*'.[381] In addition, Annex 3 to the Marrakesh Agreement is not a covered agreement under Appendix I to Annex II to the Marrakesh Agreement which embodies the Understanding on Rules and Procedures Governing the Settlement of Disputes.[382] As a result, the TPRM and its findings should in principle not be invoked within the proceedings of the Dispute Settlement Body. Nevertheless, in the period between the establishment of the WTO and the end of the period which was covered by the first appraisal, findings of the TPRM had been invoked in five Panel proceedings (covering 2.7 per cent of all disputes covered in this period).[383] In some of these, the adversaries explicitly emphasized that TPRs have no relevance whatsoever for the purposes of dispute settlement.[384]

b) Structure

i) Individual trade policy reviews

Periodicity

The first appraisal of the TPRM covered ten years (ie the period between December 1989 and September 1999). Nonetheless, in most of these years, the TPRM's periodicity functioned in a sub-optimal way.

In three of these years (1989, 1994, and 1999), the Secretariat was correct in forecasting the number of TPRs which it would be implementing in the coming year.[385]

[380] Appraisal of the operation of the TPRM, Informal Meeting of 12 May 1999, Checklist of Main Points, No 2933, 20 May 1999, 3–4 (Document on file with the author).

[381] The Trade Policy Review Mechanism (n 151).

[382] The Marrakesh Agreement (n 353).

[383] WTO, *Turkey—Restrictions on Imports of Textile and Clothing Products—Report of the Panel* (31 May 1999) WT/DS34/R; WTO, *Canada—Measures Affecting the Export of Civilian Aircraft—Report of the Panel* (14 April 1999), WT/DS/70/R, 104–05; WTO, *India—Quantitative Restrictions on Imports of Agricultural, Textile and Industrial Products—Report of the Panel* (6 April 1999) WT/DS90/R, 189; WTO, *India—Measures Affecting the Automotive Sector—Report of the Panel* (21 December 2001), WT/DS146 and DS175/R.

[384] WTO, *Canada—Measures Affecting the Export of Civilian Aircraft—Report of the Panel* (14 April 1999), WT/DS/70/R, 104–05.

[385] For 1989: GATT, Council, Trade Policy Review Mechanism, Program of Reviews, Communication from the Chairman, Council, C/W/603, 7 July 1989; Data of the author. For 1994 see: GATT, Council, Trade Policy Review Mechanism, Programme of Reviews for 1994, L/7285,

Nevertheless, in six years (1990, 1991, 1993, 1995, 1997, and 1998), the number of implemented TPRs fell below the Secretariat's initial estimates[386] whereas the number of TPRs which were implemented in 1992 exceeded the Secretariat's initial forecast.[387] Moreover, until 1998, the Secretariat's annual reporting on the TPRM did not include a categorization of the countries under review as ranked by their cyclical periodicity. Furthermore, between 1990 and 1999, there were substantial differences between the countries which were scheduled for review in the coming year and the countries which were effectively examined during that year.

It should also be remembered that the Secretariat based its determination of a country's review cycle on that country's representative share of world trade of finalized goods and services over a fixed period of three years. Nevertheless, global trading relations had started to evolve from the 1970s. International trade in intermediate goods gradually increased.[388] Moreover, '*starting in the mid-1980s and accelerating sharply in the 1990s, nations signed agreements with new disciplines to underpin the trade–investment–services–IP nexus*'.[389] As a result of these two developments, intermediate goods and intellectual property became increasingly important in international trade.

Nonetheless, in spite of the increased importance of intermediate goods and intellectual property and although all Quad Members (bar the United States) supported a changed frequency of review, the final Ministerial report of the appraisal deemed the existing periodicity of the TPRB to be generally balanced.[390] The existing frequency was therefore maintained, but it was suggested that all Members—including

22 July 1993; Data of the author. For 1999: WTO, TPRB, Draft Report of the Trade Policy Review Body for 1999, Trade Policy Review Mechanism, WT/TPR/W/23, 30 September 1999, 1 and 5; Data of the author. There are no publicly available data for the estimated number of reviews in 1996. According to the author's own data, fifteen reviews were undertaken in this year.

[386] For 1990: GATT, Council, Trade Policy Review Mechanism, Program of Reviews, Communication from the Chairman, Council, C/W/603, 7 July 1989, 2; GATT, Trade Policy Review Mechanism, Programme of Reviews—1989 and 1990, Decision of 19 July 1989, Addendum, L/6554/Add. 1, 28 July 1989, 1; Data of the author. For 1991: GATT, Council, Trade Policy Review Mechanism, Programme of Reviews, Communication from the Chairman, C/W/642, 4 July 1990, 2; Data of the author. For 1993: GATT, Council, Trade Policy Review Mechanism, Programme of reviews for 1993, L/7040, 24 June 1992, 1; Data of the author. For 1995: GATT, Trade Policy Review Mechanism, Programme of Reviews for 1995, L/7494, 22 July 1994, 1; Data of the author. For 1997: WTO, TPRB, Report on the meeting held on 10 March 1997, Trade Policy Review Body, WT/TPR/R/1, 20 March 1997, 4; Data of the author; For 1998: WTO, TPRB, Trade Policy Review Mechanism, Report of the Trade Policy Review Body for 1997, Trade Policy Review Body, WT/TPR/41, 28 November 1997, 7; WTO, TPRB, Draft Report of the Trade Policy Review Body for 1998, Trade Policy Review Mechanism, WT/TPR/W/21, 11 November 1998, 6; WTO, TPRB, Trade Policy Review Mechanism, Report of the Trade Policy Review Body for 1998, Trade Policy Review Body, WT/TPR/59, 27 November 1998, 6.

[387] GATT, Council, Trade Policy Review Mechanism, Programme of Reviews, Communication from the Chairman, C/W/642, 4 July 1990, 1; GATT, Council, Trade Policy Review Mechanism, Programme of Reviews for 1992, L/6887, 17 July 1991, 1.

[388] Organisation for Economic Co-operation and Development, *Mapping Global Value Chains, Policy Dialogue on Aid for Trade* (TAD/TC/WP/RD(2012)9, OECD, 3 December 2012), 8.

[389] Deborah K Elms and Patrick Low (eds), *Global Value Chains in a Changing World* (Fung Global Institute (FGI), Nayang Technological University (NTU) and WTO 2013) 26 (hereafter Elms and Low, *Global Value Chains in a Changing World*).

[390] WTO, Ministerial Conference, Third Session, Seattle 30 November–3 December 1999, Appraisal of the operation of the Trade Policy Review Mechanism, WT/MIN(99)/2, 8 October 1999, 3.

LDCs—should be reviewed at least once as soon as possible.[391] Moreover, the concept of interim reviews and groups reviews was briefly mentioned but was not further elaborated in the final report.[392]

Reporting

The coverage of TPRs undertaken prior to the conclusion of the Uruguay Round was restricted to the review of trade in goods.[393] Nevertheless, over time their coverage gradually extended to all areas formally treated by the WTO (including a noted increase of regional agreements, services, and intellectual property (IP)—which only became an integral part of the TPRs' discussions as of 2005)[394] but also to several 'newer' topics such as investment and competition which were only identified in the framework of certain WTO Ministerial Meetings.[395] As a result, it has become impossible to determine the desired standard of reporting. Within each of the successive periods covered by the consecutive appraisals, the standard for reporting by the government and the Secretariat has continuously evolved.

During the informal meeting of 12 May 1999, Members were asked '*(a) how far reviews should be able to take up issues beyond the strict scope of the WTO and (b) which weight should be given to the "economic context" discussion (as opposed to the strict exposition of trade policies)*'.[396] Interestingly, several Members (including Argentina, Brazil, Brunei, Chile, China, Cuba, Hong Kong, Hungary, India, Mexico, Korea, and Poland) explicitly emphasized that labour and environmental issues (though not other issues such as those with regard to the macro-economic environment) had no place in the TPRM's normal scope of reporting.[397]

As a consequence, the first appraisal was rather relaxed about governmental reporting but relatively strict in its requirements for reporting by the Secretariat. Under the first appraisal, governments are not only (completely) free to determine the structure and coverage of their report but even encouraged to keep these short.[398] Nevertheless, in line with the encouragement contained in paragraph B of Annex 3 of the Marrakesh Agreement, Members have supported the call for

[391] Appraisal of the operation of the TPRM, Informal Meeting of 21 May 1999, Checklist of Main Points, No 3274, 3 June 1999, 2 (Document on file with the author).

[392] Appraisal of the operation of the TPRM, Informal Meeting of 21 May 1999, Checklist of Main Points, No 3274, 3 June 1999, 2 (Document on file with the author).

[393] Donald Kessing, *Improving Trade Policy Reviews in the World Trade Organization* (Institute for International Economics 1998) 5 (hereafter Kessing, *Improving Trade Policy Reviews in the World Trade Organization*).

[394] Answers from Mr Frank Wolter (first director of the Trade Policy Review Division, 1989–91) to a questionnaire of the author (2 April 2014); Kessing, *Improving Trade Policy Reviews in the World Trade Organization* (n 391) 5.

[395] Points for Review of the TPRM, Draft, 11 January 1999, 2 (Document on file with the author).

[396] Appraisal of the operation of the TPRM, Informal meeting of 12 May 1999, Checklist of main points, 20 May 1999, No 2933, 2 (Document on file with the author).

[397] Appraisal of the operation of the TPRM, Informal meeting of 12 May 1999, Checklist of main points, 20 May 1999, No 2933, 2 (Document on file with the author).

[398] WTO, Ministerial Conference, Third Session, Seattle 30 November–3 December 1999, Appraisal of the operation of the Trade Policy Review Mechanism, WT/MIN(99)/2, 8 October 1999, 2.

greater domestic transparency in trade policy matters.[399] With the arrival of Dr Boonekamp (as the third TPRD director in the second half of 1998), Members were moreover '*persuaded to move from a system in which their own reports were given equal consideration to one in which the government and Secretariat reports had different aims*'.[400] Dr Boonekamp thereby built on a Canadian precedent of 1996 whereby the country '*had kept its own report down to a concise statement regarding the aims and priorities of its trade policies*'. Since then, government reports '*have been brief policy declarations that help to set the tone of the TPRB meeting rather than factual reviews that used the Secretariat's report as a template for their own submitting a parallel document that differed only in its spin*'.[401] However, the requirements for Secretariat's reporting were more detailed. Their structure—which Dr Boonekamp reduced from six to four chapters—was generally deemed to be satisfactory.[402] Nevertheless, in terms of coverage, several critical elements were raised. These include: the need to find an appropriate balance between traditional and relatively new areas of the WTO (ie investment and competition but also privatization and possibly environment),[403] the need for more readable summary observations, and the suggestion to report subsequent developments on issues raised at previous reviews.[404]

TPR's informational value – The period which was covered by the first appraisal (ie December 1989 to September 1999) resulted in a prolific academic literature which analysed the information contained in the Secretariat's (and sometimes governmental) reporting in the context of individual TPRs.

The remainder of this section will analyse those views. In order to do so, it ranks the academic views on the TPRs' added informational value into three categories: (a) TPRs with missing information; (b) TPRs which according to academia contain a too positive or a too negative assessment; and (c) TPRs with incorrect information. Moreover, for each of these three categories, this section will contrast the views of the external academics where possible with (anonymous) perspectives of existing and former WTO staff with regard to the same point.

At the outset, it should be emphasized that all academics of this period were positive or even enthusiastic about the successive TPRs' overall added value in terms of fostering increased transparency. Nevertheless, a clear majority of experts also complained about missing information. Academic complaints about TPR assessments which were perceived as too positive or too negative were also often heard. However, there were no complaints at all during this period about TPRs which contained incorrect information.

[399] WTO, Ministerial Conference, Third Session, Seattle 30 November–3 December 1999, Appraisal of the operation of the Trade Policy Review Mechanism, WT/MIN(99)/2, 8 October 1999, 1.

[400] VanGrasstek, *The History and Future of the World Trade Organization* (n 56) 290.

[401] VanGrasstek, *The History and Future of the World Trade Organization* (n 56) 290.

[402] VanGrasstek, *The History and Future of the World Trade Organization* (n 56) 290.

[403] Appraisal of the operation of the TPRM, Informal meeting of 12 May 1999, Checklist of main points, 20 May 1999, No 2933, 2 (Document on file with the author).

[404] WTO, Ministerial Conference, Third Session, Seattle 30 November–3 December 1999, Appraisal of the operation of the Trade Policy Review Mechanism, WT/MIN(99)/2, 8 October 1999, 1.

Most academic literature complained about TPRs' lack of certain specific information.

- In his overview of India's TPR of 1993, Professor Nalasubramanyam made the point that the TPR did not provide any estimates of the effective rates of Indian tariff protection although the TPR provided some comments on the likely levels. Furthermore, the author commented on the danger of policies being reversed and the TPR's failure to question the sustainability of Indian reforms.[405]
- In her analysis of the US TPR of 1994, Professor Krueger argued that American attention in trade policy matters focused more on regional arrangements than on the implementation of the results of the Uruguay Round and the (subsequent) strengthening of the WTO. The author therefore partly bemoaned that the lack of US leadership was not highlighted in the Secretariat's report. Moreover, Professor Krueger expressed regret that the GATT report did not contain any analysis of the issue of labour standards and their relevance to the international trading system.[406] Her reading of the same TPR found insufficient attention to a worrying US tendency towards unilateral demands for market openings, increased reliance on anti-dumping actions and countervailing duties, and a variety of other departures from open, multilaterally sanctioned practices.[407]
- In his overview of South Africa's TPR of 1993, Professor Holden observed that '*if there is a weakness in the GATT Trade Review, it is the failure to address the thorny issue of the phasing in of trade reform in a country that will experience problems with transition while at the same time emerging from a prolonged recession and deeply engrained distortions in the economy.*'[408] WTO experts agreed with this criticism but made the point that the outgoing South African government's hand was tied and that it did not want to engage in politics.[409] Moreover, Professor Holden noted several other interesting omissions in the reporting. These included: (a) the lack of analysis of the real exchange rate in the development of the South African economy (especially since it had been demonstrated that movements in the nominal exchange rate had largely been driven by changes in the price of gold and capital flows)[410] and (b) the lack of analysis with regard to the treatment of sanctions by the GATT dispute mechanism during the 1980s.[411] Furthermore, Professor Holden expressed

[405] VN Balasubramanyam, 'India's Trade Policy Review' [1995] The World Economy: Global Trade Policy 87 (hereafter Balasubramanyam, 'India's Trade Policy Reviews').

[406] Anne O Krueger, 'US Trade Policy and the GATT Review' [1995] The World Economy: Global Trade Policy 73–74 (hereafter Krueger, 'US Trade Policy and the GATT Review').

[407] Kessing, *Improving Trade Policy Reviews in the World Trade Organization* (n 391) 32.

[408] Merle Holden, 'GATT Trade Policy Review—South Africa: 1993' [1995] The World Economy: Global Trade Policy 121 (hereafter Holden, 'GATT Trade Policy Review—South Africa: 1993').

[409] Interview with a former WTO expert, April 2015, 1 (Document on file with the author).

[410] WTO experts make the point that this kind should rather be made by the IMF than by the WTO, Interview with a former WTO expert, April 2015, 1 (Document on file with the author).

[411] Holden, 'GATT Trade Policy Review—South Africa: 1993' (n 406) 123 and 127.

regret that '*the degree of the anti-export bias inherent in the regime (for import substitution) is not addressed in the review*', while indicating that this lack may have stemmed from the difficulty of obtaining the necessary data and the reviewing team's claim that providing any estimates was impossible.[412]

- In his analysis of Mexico's TPR of 1993, Professor Kehoe confirmed the difficulty of the TPR to foresee the Mexican crisis of 1994–95. This difficulty has been attributed to a lack of appropriate data with regard to Mexico's financial position (especially its foreign reserves and the composition of its debt)[413] and to the inadequate periodicity of the TPR.[414]
- In his overview of Canada's TPR of 1995, Professor Wonnacott described the review as '*an extremely important source of information that deserves high praise as a reference work*'. Nevertheless, he also urged that one 'shouldn't expect amusement, let alone penetrating analysis of what often goes wrong with trade policy'.[415] This argument is based on the remark that although the TPR provided detail on recent US pressure to induce Canada to 'voluntarily' restrict its exports of softwood lumber, the Secretariat report lacked analysis of the remarkable and perverse welfare effects of this policy.[416] As in earlier critical academic literature, Professor Wonnacott expressed regret about the lack of substantial analysis of Canada's policies in terms of promoting various and overlapping bilateral and plurilateral FTAs.[417] Furthermore, in commenting on the same TPR, Kessing bemoaned the fact that the WTO did not consider devoting full reviews to certain regional groupings such as the North American Free Trade Agreement (but also Mercosur, the Andean Common Market, or the Asia Pacific Economic Co-operation) as they extend and consolidate themselves over time.[418]
- In their analysis of the European Union's TPR of 1995, Dr Pelkmans and Mrs Carzaniga seemed to complain that the '*TPR fails to provide information concerning the sectorial and country incidence of anti-dumping actions*'.[419] Moreover, the authors observed that '*the GATT Secretariat has gone through a learning process in understanding the Community and its trade policy*' but

[412] Holden, 'GATT Trade Policy Review—South Africa: 1993' (n 406) 123 and 130.

[413] Timothy J Kehoe, 'A Review of Mexico's Trade Policy from 1982 to 1994' [1995] The World Economy: Global Trade Policy 135–51 (hereafter Kehoe, 'A Review of Mexico's Trade Policy from 1982 to 1994'); Kessing, *Improving Trade Policy Reviews in the World Trade Organization* (n 391) 28–29.

[414] Mathias Kende, 'Monetary affairs in the WTO Trade Policy Review Mechanism' in Thomas Cottier, Rosa M Lastra, Christian Tietje, and Lucia Satragno (eds), *The Rule of Law in Monetary Affairs* (Cambridge University Press 2014) 384–408 (hereafter Kende, 'Monetary affairs in the WTO Trade Policy Review Mechanism').

[415] Ronald J Wonnacott, 'Canadian Trade Policy: The GATT's 1995 Review' [1996] The World Economy: Global Trade Policy 67 (hereafter Wonnacott, 'Canadian Trade Policy: The GATT's 1995 Review').

[416] Wonnacott, 'Canadian Trade Policy: The GATT's 1995 Review' (n 413) 67–69.

[417] Wonnacott, 'Canadian Trade Policy: The GATT's 1995 Review' (n 413) 78.

[418] Kessing, *Improving Trade Policy Reviews in the World Trade Organization* (n 391) 35.

[419] Jacques Pelkmans and Antonia Giulia Carzaniga, 'The Trade Policy Review of the European Union' [1996] The World Economy: Global Trade Policy 88–99 (hereafter Pelkmans and Carzaniga 'The Trade Policy Review of the European Union').

recognized at the same time that '*the 1995 TPR is authoritative and unbiased*'.[420] In his reading of the same TPR, Kessing noticed that the review said very little about the remaining divergent policy measures of the EU Member countries or about the problems associated with administering and coordinating trade and trade-related policies from Brussels.[421]

- In his analysis of Indonesia's TPR of 1994, Professor Fane expressed regret that the Report's summary of the commitments which Indonesia made in the Uruguay Round Agreement on Agriculture was seemingly written for experts on the subject.[422] '*The description took for granted the distinction between "ceiling bindings" and "tariffication" and did not explain that a loophole could be used to justify the pretence that even a policy such as Indonesia's banning of rice import is not an NTM, if it was imposed by granting an import monopoly to a state trading company.*'[423] Moreover, Professor Fane bemoaned the short time focus of TPR reviews. According to the author, the report's central finding, namely that Indonesia made considerable progress in trade liberalization, would have been much stronger if the report had taken into account the initiatives undertaken by Indonesia in the 1980s. Furthermore, Indonesia's TPR (and others') did not point to the bias towards high tariffs inherent in the 'tariffication' procedure and the choice of base years.[424]
- In his overview of Israel's TPR of 1994, Professor Kreinin noted that the Secretariat report did not address any issues with regard to potential trade diversion that could stem from Israel's Free Trade Agreements with Europe, the United States, and the Palestinian authority.[425]
- In his analysis of the Japanese TPR of 1995, Professor Stern noted that the past reduction of Japan's current account surplus (which was not discussed in the Secretariat's report) could lead to defuse US accusations of neo-mercantilism.[426] Nevertheless, WTO experts pointed to the fact that the TPR covered Japan, not the United States.[427]
- In his overview of Zimbabwe's TPR of 1994, Professor Gunning raised several critical points. These include: (a) the lack of a (detailed) examination of Zimbabwe's various regional and bilateral trade agreements, including Zimbabwe's bilateral textile agreement with South Africa[428] (which WTO

420 Pelkmans and Carzaniga 'The Trade Policy Review of the European Union' (n 417) 98.

421 Kessing, *Improving Trade Policy Reviews in the World Trade Organization* (n 391) 40.

422 George Fane, 'The Trade Policy Review of Indonesia' [1996] The World Economy: Global Trade Policy 110 (hereafter Fane, 'The Trade Policy Review of Indonesia').

423 Fane, 'The Trade Policy Review of Indonesia' (n 420) 110.

424 Kessing, *Improving Trade Policy Reviews in the World Trade Organization* (n 391) 39.

425 Mordechai E Kreinin, 'Israel's Trade Policy Review' [1996] The World Economy: Global Trade Policy 119–32 (hereafter Kreinin, 'Israel's Trade Policy Review').

426 Robert M Stern, 'The Trade Policy Review of Japan' [1996] The World Economy: Global Trade Policy 133–55 (hereafter Stern, 'The Trade Policy Review of Japan').

427 Interview with a former WTO expert, April 2015, 2 (Document on file with the author).

428 Jan Willemn Gunning, 'The Trade Policy Review of Zimbabwe' [1996] The World Economy: Global Trade Policy 157–66 (hereafter Gunning, 'The Trade Policy Review of Zimbabwe'); Kessing, *Improving Trade Policy Reviews in the World Trade Organization* (n 391) 35.

experts explain was due to a lack of available data)[429] and (b) the lack of analysis of key policies raised by the Zimbabwean political and fiscal reforms. In this regard, Professor Gunning took issue with the lack of credibility and sustainability of trade liberalization that ought to be central in the TPR but which was not the case.[430] Nevertheless, WTO experts point to the fact that the TPR was only meant to call the 'promises' of the authorities into question. Furthermore, it is noteworthy that none of the Members present at the TPRB dared to criticize the Zimbabwean authorities.[431]

- In his reading of Costa Rica's TPR of 1995, Kessing bemoaned the fact that nothing was said in the review about the change in US policy in 1993 which required the US Agency for International Development (USAID) to withdraw its support for the main investment and export promotion in Costa Rica.[432]
- In her overview of Sri Lanka's TPR of 1995, Dr Cuthbertson observed that the Secretariat report could have been strengthened with the inclusion of several general and more specific policy points. These include: (a) a mention of the bipartisan nature of economic liberalization; (b) the stated commitment of the new government to lower and harmonize tariffs; and (c) the unilateral nature of Sri Lanka's liberalization.[433]
- In his reading of Côte d'Ivoire's TPR of 1995, Kessing expressed regret at the lack of a description of several problems that pointed to the presence of a muddled, irrational and inconsistent trade policy.[434]
- In his overview of Uganda's TPR of 1995, Professor Collier bemoaned the fact that the TPR did not focus on three core issues. These include: (a) the coffee tax (the report missed the fact that the private sector would disinvest as a result of the tax so that the tax was reducing precisely what the government most wished to encourage; the WTO therefore missed an opportunity to use its authority and expertise to counter the mistaken advice of the IMF to argue for the tax); (b) the general equilibrium irrelevance of switching from export taxes to import taxes[435] (the Secretariat report did not analyse whether there was any rationale for such a switch and missed the point that effective tax rates had risen sharply as a result of the move to a competitive exchange rate); and (c) the need to enhance credibility through WTO lock-in mechanisms (the Secretariat report did not discuss the fact that Uganda had been rated as the riskiest country in Africa three years before the mission).[436]

[429] Interview with a former WTO expert, April 2015, 2 (Document on file with the author).

[430] Gunning, 'The Trade Policy Review of Zimbabwe' (n 426) 161–63; Kessing, *Improving Trade Policy Reviews in the World Trade Organization* (n 391) 27.

[431] Interview with a former WTO expert, April 2015, 3 (Document on file with the author).

[432] Kessing, *Improving Trade Policy Reviews in the World Trade Organization* (n 391) 37.

[433] AG (Sandy) Cuthbertson, 'The Trade Policy Review of Sri Lanka' [1997] The World Economy: Global Trade Policy 635 (hereafter Cuthbertson, 'The Trade Policy Review of Sri Lanka').

[434] Kessing, *Improving Trade Policy Reviews in the World Trade Organization* (n 391) 41.

[435] WTO experts point to the fact that the elasticity of substitution is not necessarily one; Interview with a former WTO expert, April 2015, 3 (Document on file with the author).

[436] Paul Collier, 'The Trade Policy Review of Uganda' [1997] The World Economy: Global Trade Policy 662–63 (hereafter Collier, 'The Trade Policy Review of Uganda').

- In their analysis of the Swiss TPR of 1996, Professor Hauser and Dr Straw cautiously expressed regret for the fact that the report did not explain the reasons for Switzerland's structural crisis or that it failed to emphasize more explicitly the need to strengthen the country's newly enacted liberalization programme.[437]
- In his reading of El Salvador's TPR of 1996, Kessing expressed regret for the fact that nothing was said in the review about the change in US policy in 1993 which required the US Agency for International Development (USAID) to withdraw its support for El Salvador's main investment and export promotion agency.[438]
- In his analysis of Columbia's TPR of 1996, Dr Rajapatirana observed that '*the TPR could have given more weight to analysis by quantifying the nature of the trade regime. It could have provided estimates of the level and variance in effective rates of protection indicated by the movements towards or away from neutrality of incentives between export promoting and import substituting activities and estimated the bias of the regime against exports.*' Moreover, Dr Rajapatirana observed that 'Columbia can do harm to itself by following inappropriate policies that are WTO consistent'. His overview of the TPR seems to point to the lack of adequate alternative policy analysis.[439] In this regard, Dr Rajapatirana emphasized several issues. These include: (a) the remaining agenda for reducing protection (where the reports omits to make a strong note of the use of tariff quotes, selective safeguards, and the recourse to some managed trade); (b) the special case of agriculture (where the report does not cover the issue of implied protection that stems from the price band system for agriculture or does not address the absorption agreements as an attempt at managed trade); (c) the issue of trade preference and integration (where the TPR could have done well to point to the administrative burdens and advantages of simplifying the system by adopting uniform rules of origin); (d) the exchange rate and macro-economic issues (where the TPR did not trace the link between macro-economic factors such as inflation, exchange, and interest rates on the trade policy outcomes); and (e) other institutional and contingent protection issues (where little or no advice was offered on the need for neutral institutions and restraint in the use of contingent protection measures).[440]
- In examining the Dominican Republic's TPR of 1996, Kessing bemoaned the fact that the primary agency responsible for export promotion was not even identified. Such a non-treatment was, moreover, analysed as fairly typical.[441]

[437] Heinz Hauser and Robert Straw, 'Swiss Trade Policy and the 1996 WTO Review' [1997] The World Economy: Global Trade Policy 675–76 and 678–79 (hereafter Hauser and Straw 'Swiss Trade Policy and the 1996 WTO Review').

[438] Kessing, *Improving Trade Policy Reviews in the World Trade Organization* (n 391) 38.

[439] Sarath Rajapatirana, 'Columbian Trade Policies and the 1996 WTO Trade Policy Review' [1998] The World Economy: Global Trade Policy 519 (hereafter Rajapatirana, 'Columbian Trade Policies and the 1996 WTO Trade Policy Review').

[440] Rajapatirana, 'Columbian Trade Policies and the 1996 WTO Trade Policy Review' (n 437) 522–26.

[441] Kessing, *Improving Trade Policy Reviews in the World Trade Organization* (n 391) 37.

- In his overview of the European Union's TPR of 1997, Professor Tharakan stated that a TPR evaluation should go further than the transparency objective and '*use sharper instruments of evaluation*', particularly in its evaluation of the effect of the proliferation of the preferential arrangements and the use of the anti-dumping mechanism.[442]

Academic complaints about TPR assessments which were perceived as too positive or too negative were also often heard.

- Kessing questioned the bias in Morocco's TPRs of 1989 and 1996 as being too positive.[443]According to the author, in spite of the appalling increase in protection, the reports (especially the 1996 report) speak only of the overall policy trend from the early 1980s, which they describe as positive.
- A similar overly positive bias is detected in Chile's TPR of 1991. According to Kessing, this TPR was too generous in complimenting the country's progress towards liberalization, especially since Chile's liberalization of its workforce was far from complete.[444]
- In his reading of India's TPR of 1993, Kessing questioned the Secretariat's bias towards optimism in accepting the country's decades-long use of its precarious balance of payments as an excuse '*for maintaining one of the world's most complicated and oppressive protectionist regimes*'. As such the report was said to fail in taking a sufficiently long-term view.[445]
- In their analysis of the European Union's TPR of 1995, Dr Pelkmans and Mrs Carzaniga complained about double standards in the TPR's coverage. According to the authors, the TPR '*implicitly criticises the Community for rules which allow the authorities to allow anti-absorption duties where exporters have absorbed all or part of an anti-dumping duty but fails to make any reference to the fact the Community is not alone among major trading partners in having introduced the lesser duty rule*'. WTO experts justify this narrow focus simply by pointing to the fact that TPRs should focus on the country under review and not on their peers.[446] Nevertheless, Dr Pelkmans and Mrs Carzaniga also observed that '*the GATT Secretariat has gone through a learning process in understanding the Community and its trade policy*', and they admit that '*the 1995 TPR is authoritative and unbiased*'.[447]
- In his reading of Costa Rica's TPR of 1995, Kessing notices that the TPR of Costa Rica (although on the whole considered to be a good review) was

[442] PKM. Tharakan, 'Beyond Transparency: An Analysis of the Trade Policy Review of the European Union' [1999] The World Economy: Global Trade Policy 835 (hereafter Tharakan, 'Beyond Transparency: An Analysis of the Trade Policy Review of the European Union').

[443] Kessing, *Improving Trade Policy Reviews in the World Trade Organization* (n 391) 31.

[444] Kessing, *Improving Trade Policy Reviews in the World Trade Organization* (n 391) 30.

[445] Kessing, *Improving Trade Policy Reviews in the World Trade Organization* (n 391) 30.

[446] Interview with former WTO expert, April 2015, 1 (Document on file with the author).

[447] Pelkmans and Carzaniga 'The Trade Policy Review of the European Union' (n 417) 98.

insufficiently frank in spelling out the implications of its persistent tendency to pursue inconsistent macro-economic, trade, and social policies.[448]

- In his overview of the Brazilian TPR of 1996, Professor Flores expressed regret at the fact that the report pays too much attention to the macro-economic situation. According to the author, '*alarmist or extremely pessimistic views were out of context in view of Brazil's past experience in coping with heterodox situations*'.[449]
- In his analysis of New Zealand's TPR of 1996, Professor Richardson criticized the TPR's description of the participatory nature of New Zealand's trade policy-making.[450] Furthermore, the author took issue with the TPR's almost central focus on New Zealand's accession to the WTO government procurement agreement. According to Professor Richardson, '*New Zealand's procurement is already very open by international standards and non-discriminatory*'.[451]
- In his overview of India's TPR of 1998, Professor Panagariya argued that the TPR's concerns about the Agreement on Textiles and Clothing (ATC) having a negative impact on India's textiles and clothing were overstated. According to the TPR, the removal of MFA quotas and import liberalization may lead to losses and adjustment problems. According to the author, these fears are overrated. Once the industry is forced to compete and rents disappear, margins for unions to demand high wages will be squeezed and the support for laws mandating a virtual ban on the exit of firms in the organized sector.[452]

Reporting on information and naming and shaming – Between the establishment of the WTO (January 1995) and the end of the period which was covered by the first appraisal (September 1999), 58 TPRs took place and 181 DSB disputes were initiated. Of these, sixteen disputes related to Sanitary and Phytosanitary measures (SPS) whereas twenty-two related to the area of Technical Barriers to Trade (TBT).

Through its focus on the respective DSB and TPR coverage of the same SPS and TBT disputes, this section will analyse individual TPRs' added value in terms of transparency and naming and shaming. It examines the proceeding and succeeding TPR(s) for each of the DSB disputes. For each of these TPRs, the Secretariat report, and the government report, the debates during the TPRB meeting and the written questions and answers are analysed from the angle of transparency (examining whether the respective reports, meeting, or questions explicitly or indirectly managed to refer to elements of the future dispute) and from the perspective of naming

[448] Kessing, *Improving Trade Policy Reviews in the World Trade Organization* (n 391) 41.

[449] Renato G Flores, 'Brazilian Trade Policy and the WTO' [1997] The World Economy: Global Trade Policy 616 (hereafter Flores, 'Brazilian Trade Policy and the WTO').

[450] Martin Richardson, 'New Zealand Trade Policy and the 1996 WTO Review' [1998] The World Economy: Global Trade Policy 533 (hereafter Richardson, 'New Zealand Trade Policy and the 1996 WTO Review').

[451] Richardson, 'New Zealand Trade Policy and the 1996 WTO Review' (n 448) 546

[452] Arvind Panagariya, 'The WTO Trade Policy Review of India, 1998' [1999] The World Economy: Global Trade Policy 799–824 (hereafter Panagariya, 'The WTO Trade Policy Review of India, 1998').

and shaming (examining whether the respective reports, meeting, or questions managed to elicit a defensive stance from the country under review).

- In *US—Standards for Reformulated and Conventional Gasoline*, a case brought in January 1995, Venezuela and Brazil complained about the so-called gasoline rule which amended the US Clean Air Act. This amendment, which had been tabled by the US Environmental Protection Agency in order to reduce toxic motor vehicle pollution, established minimum levels of cleanliness for 'reformulated gasoline' (which could be sold in most polluted parts of the United States) and 'conventional gasoline' (which could be sold elsewhere). Although the rule formally applied to domestic producers and to foreign importers of gasoline, in practice, foreign importers were often faced with a more stringent level of permissible emissions for 'conventional gasoline'. This was so since the permissible emissions for domestic refineries were based on a baseline quality derived from a minimum of a six-months' operation during 1990. Nonetheless, where no 1990 baseline could be established (which—de facto—was more often the case for foreign importers), the Environmental Protection Agency assigned a statutory baseline which reflected the average quality of domestic US gasoline but which was stricter than the baseline of most US refineries. The complainants therefore alleged that the rule was discriminatory and violated Articles I and III of the GATT and Article 2 of the Agreement on Technical Barriers to Trade (TBT).[453]

The initiation of this case was preceded by the TPR of the United States of 1994.[454] This TPR is interesting since its Secretariat report was able to put its finger on the legislative amendment which led to the dispute (the TPRM's transparency objective was therefore met). Nevertheless, the future complainants in the DSB case did not seize the occasion of the review to make their point; as a result, the TPRM's opportunity for naming and shaming was not pursued. The Secretariat's chapter dedicated to trade policies by sector was able to forecast the contours of the dispute to come, even if only indirectly. The Secretariat's analysis dedicated to Chemical and related industries explicitly emphasizes the fact that '*environmental concerns may increasingly impact on the sector*'[455] and even puts some emphasis on the fact that '*the Clean Air Act Amendments of 1990 introduced new standards for gasoline*

[453] WTO, *US—Standards for Reformulated and Conventional Gasoline—Report of the Panel* (29 January 1996), WT/DS2/R; WTO, *US—Standards for Reformulated and Conventional Gasoline—Appellate Body Report* (29 April 1996), WT/DS2/AB/R; Arthur Appleton, 'GATT Article XX's Chapeau: A Disguised 'Necessity' Test?: The WTO Appellate Body's Ruling in United States—Standards for Reformulated and Conventional Gasoline' (1997) 6(2) Review of European Community & International Environmental Law 13–138 (hereafter Appleton, 'GATT Article XX's Chapeau: A Disguised 'Necessity' Test?: The WTO Appellate Body's Ruling in United States—Standards for Reformulated and Conventional Gasoline').

[454] Trade Policy Review of the United States of 16–17 February 1994, Vol II (Documents on file with the author).

[455] Trade Policy Review of the United States of 16–17 February 1994, Vol I, 126–87 (especially at 173) and 192 (Document on file with the author).

quality and sulphur emissions, with refineries needing at times to change their production mix to oxygenate gasoline in conformity with the Act'.[456] The government report, however, remains (completely) silent about the (potential) problem. Furthermore, during the TPRB meeting of 16–17 February 1994,[457] which was dedicated to the examination of US trade policy, the future complainants did not emphasize their concerns (Venezuela was absent from the meeting).[458]

Although the future complainants did not seize the occasion of the 1994 review to name the United States and shame it into better behaviour, they requested further DSB consultations in January 1995. Since these remained unsuccessful, Panels were established and merged. The (joint) Panel consequently found the US regulation to be inconsistent with Article III.4 of the GATT. According to the Panel, imported and domestic gasoline were like products and since, under the baseline establishment methods, imported gasoline was effectively prevented from benefitting from as favourable sales conditions as were afforded to domestic gasoline, imported gasoline was treated less favourably than domestic gasoline. Nonetheless, for reasons of judicial economy, the Panel did not address the claims under the TBT agreement.[459] Following appeal by the United States, the report of the Appellate Body rejected some of the findings of the Panel but still concluded that the US measure was inconsistent with the GATT since it could not be justified under Article XX(g) of the GATT.[460]

The TPR of the United States of 1996 put some weight on the US implementation of the DSB's recommendations.[461] The report of the Secretariat dedicates a sub-section to Standards, technical regulations, and conformity assessment which contains a full description of the trade problem and its unfolding case. According to the sub-section: '*From 1 January 1995, the Gasoline Rule permits only gasoline of a specified cleanliness ('reformulated gasoline') to be sold to consumers in the most polluted areas in the country. In the rest of the country, only gasoline no dirtier than that sold in the base year of 1990 ('conventional gasoline') can be sold. The quality of gasoline sold in 1990 is established on a refinery-specific basis for refineries which operated at least six months during that year. The Environmental Protection Agency (EPA) established a statutory baseline, applied to refiners who were not in operation for at least 6 months in 1990 and imports and blenders. The regulations have been successfully challenged by Brazil and Venezuela in a WTO dispute settlement*'. The sub-section

[456] Trade Policy Review of the United States of 16–17 February 1994, Vol I, 173 (Documents on file with the author).

[457] The official documents contain a factual error with regard to the date of the TPR meeting. Whereas the meeting took place on 16–17 February 1994, the document indicates that the meeting took place one year earlier; Trade Policy Review of the United States of 16–17 February 1994, Vol I, p V (Documents on file with the author).

[458] Trade Policy Review of the United States, Vol II, 16–17 February 1994 (Document on file with the author).

[459] WTO, *US—Standards for Reformulated and Conventional Gasoline—Report of the Panel* (29 January 1996) WT/DS2/R.

[460] WTO, *US—Standards for Reformulated and Conventional Gasoline—Appellate Body Report* (29 April 1996) WT/DS2/AB/R.

[461] Trade Policy Review of the United States of 11–12 November 1996 (Document on file with the author).

moreover highlights the fact that the consultations between the United States and the complainants to implement the recommendations of the DSB continued in October 1996.[462] However, the government report remains silent on the issue. Nonetheless, for the first time, the complainants raised their concerns repeatedly during the meeting of the TPRB. Brazil enquired when the United States intended to implement the final finding of the DSB with regard to the gasoline case[463] whereas Venezuela also underscored its hope that the recommendations of the DSB would be implemented as soon as possible.[464] The United States answered in great detail while emphasizing that it had '*notified the DSB of its intention to implement its recommendations. Moreover, under US law this required a period of notice and comment because the matter arose by reason of administrative regulation. The US Administrative Procedure Act required such a period for notice and comment before the new regulation was formulated. More detail would be provided as the regulatory process developed.*'[465]

Although it is difficult to ascertain whether the TPR's naming and shaming effectively contributed to the intention of the United States to implement the recommendations of the DSB, the United States announced on August 1997 that it would do so.[466]

The issue was therefore raised in a final manner in the US TPR of 1999.[467] The Secretariat's report's sub-section on Standards, sanitary requirements, and environmental regulations (briefly) notes that '*environmental regulation are enforced under . . ., the Energy Policy and Conservation Act, the Clean Air Act, as amended by the Clean Air Act amendments of 1990*'[468] and indicates (in a specific section dedicated to trade disputes) that '*US standards for reformulated and conventional gasoline and the policies adopted by the Environmental Protection Agency, were subject to a complaint in the WTO by Venezuela and Brazil in 1995. The dispute was resolved as the US announced implementation of the recommendations of the DSB as of 19 August 1997.*'[469] On the other hand, the issue was again conspicuously

[462] Trade Policy Review of the United States of 11–12 November 1996, Secretariat report, WT/TPR/S/16, 21 October 1996, 91–98 (especially at 93).

[463] Trade Policy Review of the United States of 11–12 November 1996, Minutes of the Meeting, WT/TPR/M/16, 30 January 1997, 28.

[464] Trade Policy Review of the United States of 11–12 November 1996, Minutes of the Meeting, WT/TPR/M/16, 30 January 1997, 22.

[465] Trade Policy Review of the United States of 11–12 November 1996, Minutes of the Meeting, WT/TPR/M/16, 30 January 1997, 39.

[466] Trade Policy Review of the United States of 12–14 July 1999, Secretariat Report, WT/TPR/S/56, 1 June 1999, 130.

[467] Trade Policy Review of the United States of 12–14 July 1999, Minutes of the Meeting, WT/TPR/M/56, 11 August 1999.

[468] Trade Policy Review of the United States of 12–14 July 1999, Secretariat Report, WT/TPR/S/56, 1 June 1999, 128.

[469] Trade Policy Review of the United States of 12–14 July 1999, Secretariat Report, WT/TPR/S/56, 1 June 1999, 130.

absent from the government report,[470] the TPRB meeting (which took place in absence of Venezuela),[471] or the written questions thereof.[472]

- In *EU—Trade description of scallops*, Canada, Chile, and Peru complained that a French Government order of March 1993 and its amendments laying down the official name and trade description of scallops would hinder and reduce the competitiveness on the French market of their own exported scallops.[473] According to the French Government order, certain imported scallops after 1 January 1996 could no longer be sold as '*Coquille Saint-Jacques*' or as '*Noix de Saint-Jacques*' but only as '*pétoncle*' although the respective products were allegedly like-products. According to the complainants, the French Government order therefore violated Articles I and III of the GATT and Article 2 of the TBT agreement.

The TPR of the European Union of May 1993 was unable to predict the upcoming trade concern.[474] Neither did the future complainants seize the opportunity to name France (or Europe) and shame them into better behaviour. Although the Secretariat's report undertook some analysis on European measures directly affecting imports[475] and developments in agriculture, fisheries, and food production,[476] it did not manage to identify the trade-related shortcomings of the French Government Order. Likewise, the government report contains information on Standards and certification,[477] on Agriculture,[478] and on Rules of origin.[479] Nevertheless, none of these point to the future problem. Moreover, during the TPRB meeting, amongst the three complainants only Chile (generally) alluded to EU-wide restrictions in the fisheries sector.[480]

470 Trade Policy Review of the United States of 12–14 July 1999, Government Report, WT/TPR/G/56, 1 June 1999.

471 Trade Policy Review of the United States of 12–14 July 1999, Minutes of the Meeting, WT/TPR/M/56, 11 August 1999.

472 Trade Policy Review of the United States of 12–14 July 1999, Written questions and answers, WT/TPR/M/56/Add.1, 9 March 2000.

473 WTO, *EC—Trade Description of Scallops—Request for Consultations by Peru* (25 July 1995) WT/DS12/1; WTO, *EC—Trade Description of Scallops—Request for consultations by Canada* (24 May 1995) WT/DS7/R and WT/DS7/1.

474 Trade Policy Review of the European Communities of 17–18 May 1993, Vol II (Document on file with the author).

475 Trade Policy Review of the European Communities of 17–18 May 1993, Vol I, 65–101 (Document on file with the author).

476 Trade Policy Review of the European Communities of 17–18 May 1993, Vol I, 127–65 (particularly as of 158 with regard to fisheries) (Document on file with the author).

477 Trade Policy Review of the European Communities of 17–18 May 1993, Vol II, 45–47 (Document on file with the author).

478 Trade Policy Review of the European Communities of 17–18 May 1993, Vol II, 55–58 (Document on file with the author).

479 Trade Policy Review of the European Communities of 17–18 May 1993, Vol II, 70 (Document on file with the author).

480 Trade Policy Review of the European Communities of 17–18 May 1993, Vol II, 115, 135, and 153 (Document on file with the author).

Since further consultations failed to resolve the issue, two Panels were established to respectively deal with the Canadian complaint (in July 1995) and with the Chilean and Peruvian complaints (in October 1995).[481]

The TPR of the European Union of July 1995 identifies the issue for the first time.[482] Although the Secretariat's report analyses measures directly affecting imports[483] and developments in agriculture, fisheries, and food production,[484] the ongoing consultations of the dispute are only (briefly) mentioned and tabled in a specific section with regard to Dispute settlement under the General Agreement.[485] Although the government's reporting on agriculture (and other overall government's reporting) remains silent on the issue,[486] the topic was raised during the meeting of the TPRB. Of the three complainants, only Canada '*questioned the integrity of the Single Market and the Commission's ability to persuade Member states to amend restrictive practices such as regulations on scallop labelling in France*'.[487]

Although the Panels had concluded their substantive work, proceedings were suspended in (May) 1996 in view of the successful consultations which had resulted in a mutually agreed solution (which was notified to the DSB in July 1996). Brief Panel reports were therefore circulated in August 1996.[488]

The TPR of the European Union of November 1997 succinctly documents the issue in a final manner: its Secretariat report managed to highlight the issue but the complainants in the case did not seize the opportunity of the review to further name and shame France or the European Union into better behaviour. In line with previous practice, the topic is not identified in the Secretariat's reporting contained in the sub-sections on recent developments in other import-related areas[489] or on developments in agriculture.[490] Nonetheless, the issue and its ensuing trade dispute is again mentioned in (tabular form) in a specific section with regard to the Dispute Settlement Body.[491] This reference did not lead to any further follow-up in the

[481] WTO, *EC—Trade Description of Scallops—Constitution of the Panel Established at the Request of Canada* (14 September 1995) WT/DS7/8; WTO, *EC—Trade Description of Scallops—Constitution of the Panel Established at the Requests of Peru and Chile* (26 October 1995) WT/DS12/8 and WT/DS14/7.

[482] Trade Policy Review of the European Union of 24–25 July 1995, Vol II (Document on file with the author).

[483] Trade Policy Review of the European Union of 24–25 July 1995, Secretariat Report, WT/TPR/S/3, 30 June 1995, 51–70.

[484] Trade Policy Review of the European Union of 24–25 July 1995, Secretariat Report, WT/TPR/S/3, 30 June 1995, 79–93 (particularly at 91–93).

[485] Trade Policy Review of the European Union of 24–25 July 1995, Secretariat Report, WT/TPR/S/3, 30 June 1995, 168–72.

[486] Trade Policy Review of the European Union of 24–25 July 1995, Government Report, WT/TPR/G/3, 30 June 1995.

[487] Trade Policy Review of the European Union of 24–25 July 1995, Minutes of the Meeting, WT/TPR/M/3, 4 October 1995, 13.

[488] WTO, *European Communities—Trade Description of Scallops—Report of the Panel* (5 August 1996) WT/DS7/R.

[489] Trade Policy Review of the European Union of 25–26 November 1997, Secretariat Report, WT/TPR/S/30, 20 October 1997, 62–68.

[490] Trade Policy Review of the European Union of 25–26 November 1997, Secretariat Report, WT/TPR/S/30, 20 October 1997, 82–92.

[491] Trade Policy Review of the European Union of 25–26 November 1997, Secretariat Report, WT/TPR/S/30, 20 October 1997, 36–39 (particularly at 38).

government report[492] or by the complainants in the TPRB meeting, which was not attended by Peru.[493]

- In *Australia—Measures Affecting Importation of Salmon*, Canada took issue with the Australian quarantine regime which had resulted in an import ban on its exports of fresh, chilled, and frozen salmon.[494] Although Australia had argued that the ban was created to protect diverse recreational fisheries from exotic disease, Canada disagreed and was of the opinion that salmon products for human consumption were not associated with the spread of salmon disease and that the micro-organisms that were of concern were unlikely to be found in concentration sufficient to transmit exotic diseases in the export products which were subject to the ban.[495] According to Canada, the prohibition was therefore constitutive of a violation of Articles XI and XIII of the GATT 1994 and of the SPS Agreement.

Australia's TPR of February 1994—its last review before the DSB consultations were formally launched in October 1995—dedicates a substantial amount of analysis to the topic.[496] The TPR is noteworthy, not only for the Secretariat's referencing of the concerns which resulted in the DSB case but also for the government report's unusual explicit acknowledgment of the issue. The Secretariat analyses the trade concerns in the report's sections dedicated to measures directly affecting imports[497] and to agriculture, forestry, and fisheries.[498] In the former, the Secretariat only notes, in rather general terms, that '*Australia has maintained import restrictions since 1964 on various animal, mainly marine, products under Article 20 of the GATT*' and that '*the Secretariat has not been informed of any significant policy changes since the initial trade policy review*'. The Secretariat

[492] Trade Policy Review of the European Union of 25–26 November 1997, Government Report, WT/TPR/G/30, 20 October 1997.

[493] Trade Policy Review of the European Union of 25–26 November 1997, Minutes of the Meeting, WT/TPR/M/30, 26 January 1998.

[494] WTO, *Australia—Measures Affecting Importation of Salmon—Report of the Panel* (12 June 1998) WT/DS18/R; WTO, *Australia—Measures Affecting Importation of Salmon—Appellate Body Report* (20 October 1998) WT/DS18/AB/R; Joost Pauwelyn, 'The WTO Agreement on Sanitary and Phytosanitary (SPS) Measures as Applied in the First Three SPS Disputes: EC—Hormones, Australia—Salmon and Japan—Varietals' (1999) 2(4) Journal of International Economic Law 641–64 (hereafter Pauwelyn, 'The WTO Agreement on Sanitary and Phytosanitary (SPS) Measures as Applied in the First Three SPS Disputes: EC—Hormones, Australia—Salmon and Japan—Varietals'); Donna Roberts, 'Preliminary Assessment of the Effects of the WTO Agreement on Sanitary and Phytosanitary Trade Regulations' (1998) 1(3) Journal of International Economic Law 387–96 (hereafter Roberts, 'Preliminary Assessment of the Effects of the WTO Agreement on Sanitary and Phytosanitary Trade Regulations').

[495] Matthew D Taylor, 'The WTO panel decision on Australia's salmon import guidelines: evidence that the SPS agreement can effectively protect human health interests' (2000) 9(2) Pacific Rim Law & Policy Journal Association 473–74 (hereafter Taylor, 'The WTO panel decision on Australia's salmon import guidelines: evidence that the SPS agreement can effectively protect human health interests').

[496] Trade Policy Review of Australia of 3–4 February 1994, Vol II (Document on file with the author).

[497] Trade Policy Review of Australia of 3–4 February 1994, Vol I, 42–69 (particularly at 50 and 52) (Document on file with the author).

[498] Trade Policy Review of Australia of 3–4 February 1994, Vol I, 108–31 (particularly 129) (Document on file with the author).

furthermore details some of the basic features of the Australian quarantine requirements but does not pay any specific attention to the import ban on salmon. However, in the section on agriculture, forestry, and fisheries more detail is provided with the Secretariat underlining that '*Australian fish imports and exports are, in turn, subject to prohibitions and restrictions under the Wildlife Protection Act and Customs Regulations*' and that '*all imports must be inspected at the point of entry to ensure compliance with the Food Standards Code*'. Interestingly, the Secretariat emphasizes explicitly in a footnote, which seems to be limited to the Australian Food Standards Code, that '*Australia has lifted an import ban on uncooked salmonid meat, imports of which may now enter subject to adequate assurances against the introduction of exotic fish diseases*'. The government report highlights and very clearly defends its measures affecting salmon imports.[499] According to the Australian government, absolute import prohibitions occur seldom whereas conditional import prohibitions are often based on health or safety obligations. The Australian government report moreover emphasizes that its quarantine requirements are based on scientific evidence and provide for consultations with all concerned stakeholders. Interestingly, the government report nevertheless admits that '*whilst Australia is either adhering to international standards, or moving in that direction, there will be a few instances where, on scientific grounds, and having regard to local factors, it will be appropriate for Australia to adopt standards that are tighter than international standards.*'[500]

During the meeting of the TPRB, the reports by the Secretariat and the Australian government lead to some critical naming and shaming by Canada but were closely followed by Australian counterarguments. Canada complained about a number of remaining critical standards issues. These included the '*application of restrictive agri-food requirements ... excessive levels of sanitary and phytosanitary protection, for example, heating requirements for ... smoked salmon with an adverse impact on marketability and an uneven application among similar products of disease-related import bans*'.[501] Nevertheless, Australia responded that '*it was inappropriate to judge Australia's animal and plant health regulations without taking into account the specific situation of an island continent. Given the geographic scale of the country, diseases could long remain undiscovered and would be extremely difficult to combat. As a major exporter of many farm products, Australia was compelled to take effective measures, based on scientific evidence and generally recognized standards, to protect its animal and plant health status*'.[502]

[499] Trade Policy Review of Australia of 3–4 February 1994, Vol II, 38–46 (particularly 42 and 43) (Document on file with the author).

[500] Trade Policy Review of Australia of 3–4 February 1994, Vol II, 43 (Document on file with the author).

[501] Trade Policy Review of Australia of 3–4 February 1994, Vol II, 135 (Document on file with the author).

[502] Trade Policy Review of Australia of 3–4 February 1994, Vol II, 141 (Document on file with the author).

Since consultations failed to resolve the issue, a Panel was established in (April) 1997. The Panel report which was rendered in June 1998 considered that the Australian measures were inconsistent with Articles 2 and 5 of the SPS Agreement.[503]

The Australian TPR of 30 June to 2 July 1998 took therefore place after the circulation of the Panel report (ie on 12 June 1998) but before Australia's appeal resulted in a final verdict by the Appellate Body.[504] Its Secretariat report contains various references to the issue and the ensuing DSB case. These encompass the latest update on the DSB case (in a specific section on Dispute settlement)[505] and the sub-section on Standards and quarantine[506] which underlines that '*Because of its stringent testing requirements and effective ban on a number of products due to quarantine considerations, Australia's trading partners have criticised its quarantine laws as being too severe. Australia's import restrictions have also been the subject of WTO consultations requested in 1995 and a Panel was established under the WTO Dispute Settlement Mechanism in 1997 on Australia's restrictions of salmon imports from Canada*'. In a similar vein, Secretariat's reporting on agriculture, fisheries, and forestry[507] indicates that '*Although Australia's tariff restrictions in the sector are low, strict application of quarantine laws restrict a number of imports. .... A recently completed review of aquatic animal health and quarantine recommended a review of the structure of quarantine policies and improved infrastructure arrangements for aquatic animal health. The government has largely adopted the recommendations, including a revised quarantine risk assessment procedure, a review of existing quarantine policies and further development of fish health infrastructure*'. Unsurprisingly, Australia's government report again (vigorously) highlights and defends its quarantine regime.[508] Nevertheless, Canada and Australia both seized the TPRB meeting to air concerns and table justifications. In this regard, Canada's representative to the TPRB complained that '*Australia's quarantine regulations were a persistent and serious impediment to Canadian exports to Australia. In particular, market access for ... salmon was of serious concern. The recent WTO panel finding that Australia's ban on frozen salmon imports was inconsistent with its WTO obligations should encourage Australia to re-examine its approach to quarantine issues*'. Moreover, the Canadian representative '*looked forward to Australia's response to the*

[503] WTO, *Australia—Measures Affecting Importation of Salmon-Report of the Panel* (12 June 1998) WT/DS18/R.

[504] Trade Policy Review of Australia of 30 June–2 July 1998, Minutes of the Meeting, WT/TPR/M/41, 26 October 1998.

[505] Trade Policy Review of Australia of 30 June–2 July 1998, Secretariat Report, WT/TPR/S/41, 10 June 1998, 33–36 (particularly at 33).

[506] Trade Policy Review of Australia of 30 June–2 July 1998, Secretariat Report, WT/TPR/S/ 41, 10 June 1998, 68–75 (particularly at 75).

[507] Trade Policy Review of Australia of 30 June–2 July 1998, Secretariat Report, WT/TPR/S/ 41, 10 June 1998, 96–108 (particularly at 107).

[508] Trade Policy Review of Australia of 30 June–2 July 1998, Government Report, WT/TPR/G/41, 11 June 1998, 13–14.

panel's findings'.[509] Australia reiterated its defensive views with regard to its quarantine regime.[510]

The report of the Appellate Body which was issued in October 1998 reversed some of the Panel's reasoning but confirmed that the Australian measures were inconsistent with Articles 2 and 5 of the SPS Agreement. Following the adoption of the Appellate Body and modified Panel reports, Canada requested arbitration proceedings to determine Australia's reasonable period for implementation of the DSB's recommendations, requested the DSB's approval to suspend concessions to Australia for its protracted non-compliance with the recommendations of the DSB, and entered into compliance proceedings to determine the WTO consistency of the Australian implementing measures, while arbitration on the level of suspension of concessions was temporarily suspended.[511] The report of the compliance Panel was rendered in March 2000. It identified several shortcomings in the Australian implementation measures. These included delays in the entry into force of several implementing measures and the existence of some specific Australian and Tasmanian measures which were not based on risk assessment or on sufficient scientific evidence.[512] However, in May 2000, Canada and Australia announced that they had concluded an agreement to resolve the dispute. Canada stated nevertheless, that it would monitor Australia's commitment to implement the agreement by 1 June 2000 and that it hoped to notify the DSB of a mutually agreed solution soon thereafter.[513]

The Australian TPR of 2002 thus took place after both countries had agreed to solve the dispute.[514] Nevertheless, the review continues to dwell on the case. The Secretariat's reporting refers to the case in the context of its specific section on trade disputes and consultations.[515] In a similar vein, Secretariat's sub-section on standards and other technical requirements[516] indicates that '*following a long running dispute with Canada on the importation of salmon, agreement was reached in May 2002 on a set of least trade restrictive quarantine requirements that ensure Australia's fish health status is protected*'. Nevertheless, in line with its earlier practice, Australia's government report unapologetically continues to defend its strict quarantine regime by

[509] Trade Policy Review of Australia of 30 June–2 July 1998, Minutes of the Meeting, WT/TPR/M/41, 26 October 1998, 14.

[510] Trade Policy Review of Australia of 30 June–2 July 1998, Minutes of the Meeting, WT/TPR/M/41, 26 October 1998, 25, 29, and 37.

[511] WTO, *Australia—Measures Affecting Importation of Salmon—Arbitration under Article 21.3(c) of the Understanding on Rules and Procedures Governing the Settlement of Disputes* (23 February 1999) WT/DS18/9.

[512] WTO, *Australia—Measures Affecting Importation of Salmon—Recourse to Article 21.5 by Canada* (18 February 2000) WT/DS18/RW.

[513] WTO, DSB, Minutes of the Meeting, WT/DSB/M/80, 26 June 2000, 13.

[514] Trade Policy Review of Australia of 23–25 September 2002, Minutes of the Meeting, WT/TPR/M/104, 3 December 2002.

[515] Trade Policy Review of Australia of 23–25 September 2002, Secretariat Report, WT/TPR/S/104, 26 August 2002, 23.

[516] Trade Policy Review of Australia of 23–25 September 2002, Secretariat Report, WT/TPR/S/104, 26 August 2002, 46–53 (particularly at 52).

means of a specific section dedicated to the topic.[517] Moreover, Australia followed the same defensive line during the TPRB meeting.[518]

- In *EC—Measures Concerning Meat and Meat Products*, the United States and Canada took issue with the measures taken by the European Communities under its Council Directive Prohibiting the Use in Livestock Farming of Certain Substances Having a Hormonal Action.[519] This Council Directive banned the sale and marketing of beef treated with any of six growth hormones (ie stradiol, testosterone, progesterone, zeranol, trenbolone acetate, and melengestrol acetate), arguably to address the health concerns of European citizens. Nonetheless, the sixth growth hormones had been approved by the US and Canadian agencies for food and health protection as safe and had consequently been widely used in national meat production.[520] The complainants therefore alleged that the European measures unduly restricted or prohibited their export of meat and meat products. The United States and Canada consequently claimed that the measures were inconsistent with Articles III or XI of the GATT (1994), Articles 2, 3, and 5 of the SPS Agreement, Article 2 of the TBT Agreement, and Article 4 of the Agreement on Agriculture.

The TPR of the European Union of 1995 touches on the trade concerns which led to the initiation of the DSB case.[521] Secretariat's main analysis of the topic is contained in a sub-section detailing quantitative restrictions, trade controls, and surveillance measures which laconically states that '*according to the Commission, apart from measures specifically justified on health, security or environmental grounds, there are at present no EC restrictions, other than those referred below (ie in the section).*'[522] Moreover, the Secretariat's analysis of Standards and other technical requirements, which is contained in the sub-section Recent developments in other imported-related areas,[523] emphasizes that '*EU policies on the use of hormones have remained unchanged. Retaliatory measures taken by the US in the context of the Communities' hormone directive have remained in force, although reduced in scope to take account of*

[517] Trade Policy Review of Australia of 23–25 September 2002, Government Report, WT/TPR/G/104, 26 August 2002, 9–10.

[518] Trade Policy Review of Australia of 23–25 September 2002, Minutes of the Meeting, WT/TPR/M/104, 3 December 2002, 15–19.

[519] WTO, *EC—Measures Concerning Meat and Meat Products—Report of the Panel* (18 August 1997) WT/DS26/R/USA; WTO, *EC—Measures Concerning Meat and Meat Products—Report of the Panel* (18 August 1997) WT/DS48/R/CAN; WTO, *EC—Measures Concerning Meat and Meat Products—Appellate Body Report* (16 January 1998) WT/DS26 and 48/AB/R; Pauwelyn, 'The WTO Agreement on Sanitary and Phytosanitary (SPS) Measures as Applied in the First Three SPS Disputes: EC—Hormones, Australia—Salmon and Japan—Varietals' (n 521) 641–64.

[520] Renée Johnson, 'The U.S.–EU Beef Hormones Dispute' (Report 40449, US Congressional Research Service, 14 January 2015).

[521] Trade Policy Review of the European Union of 24–25 July 1995, Vol II (Document on file with the author).

[522] Trade Policy Review of the European Union of 24–25 July 1995, WT/TPR/S/3, 30 June 1995, 57–60 and 69.

[523] The part on Standards and other technical requirements is not contained in the analytical overview table at the start of Secretariat's report.

US exports of hormone-free beef'.[524] Other sections of the Secretariat report, such as Developments in agriculture, fisheries and food production[525] or Other initiatives to address trade frictions,[526] do not explicitly address the topic. Likewise, the government report remains completely silent on the issue. The topic is therefore neither tackled in the report's section on standards and certification[527] nor in its analysis of European agriculture.[528] Moreover, during the TPRB meeting, Canada and the United States only tackled the problem in very general terms. Canada expressed concern about the EU's implementation of market access commitments in agriculture whereas the United States only mentioned persistent problems in the context of agriculture.[529] In its answers with regard to problems of implementation, standards and certification, and agriculture, the European Union avoided providing any further specific comments on the issue.[530]

In August 1997, two separate Panel reports were issued. Both considered that the EC import ban was inconsistent with Articles 3 and 5 of the SPS Agreement.[531]

The TPR of the European Union of November 1997 focuses on the issue again.[532] In view of the recent publication date of the two Panel reports, the European Union had still not managed to change its course. In line with its earlier practice, the Secretariat's main identification of the trade concern is contained in its report's section on measures directly affecting imports.[533] In this context, the Secretariat's analysis of standards and other technical requirements[534] in the report's sub-section on recent developments in other import-related areas unsurprisingly indicates that '*the EU approach concerning the use of hormones in meat and milk production has remained unchanged since the previous TPR*'. The analysis then confirms that the European Union has appealed against the decision.[535] The Secretariat's sectional

[524] Trade Policy Review of the European Union of 24–25 July 1995, WT/TPR/S/3, 30 June 1995, 71.

[525] Trade Policy Review of the European Union of 24–25 July 1995, WT/TPR/S/3, 30 June 1995, 79–91.

[526] Trade Policy Review of the European Union of 24–25 July 1995, WT/TPR/S/3, 30 June 1995, 176–79.

[527] Trade Policy Review of the European Union of 24–25 July 1995, WT/TPR/G/3, 30 June 1995, 22–23.

[528] Trade Policy Review of the European Union of 24–25 July 1995, WT/TPR/G/3, 30 June 1995, 24–26.

[529] Trade Policy Review of the European Union of 24–25 July 1995, WT/TPR/M/3, 4 October 1995, 13–14.

[530] Trade Policy Review of the European Union of 24–25 July 1995, WT/TPR/M/3, 4 October 1995, 31.

[531] WTO, *EC—Measures Concerning Meat and Meat Products—Report of the Panel* (18 August 1997) WT/DS26/R/USA; WTO, *EC—Measures Concerning Meat and Meat Products—Report of the Panel* (18 August 1997) WT/DS48/R/CAN.

[532] Trade Policy Review of the European Union of 25–26 November 1997, Minutes of the Meeting, WT/TPR/M/30, 26 January 1998.

[533] Trade Policy Review of the European Union of 25–26 November 1997, Secretariat Report, WT/TPR/S/30, 20 October 1997, 44–68.

[534] This analysis is again not mentioned in the analytic overview at the beginning of Secretariat's report.

[535] Trade Policy Review of the European Union of 25–26 November 1997, Secretariat Report, WT/TPR/S/30, 20 October 1997, 67.

analysis of developments in agriculture however remains silent on the issue.[536] The same is once again true of the government's report.[537] Nevertheless, this did not bar Canada's TPRB representative from some general naming and shaming of the European Union. In this regard, the representative emphasized the '*market access issues of bilateral concern regarding agriculture and stressed growing trade effects, in that sector, of EU regulations related to the protection of health, safety and environment*'.[538]

Further to appeal by the European Communities in both cases, the Appellate Body issued a joint report. This report, which was rendered on 16 January 1998, reversed some of the Panel's findings but confirmed the Panel's conclusion that the EC import prohibition was inconsistent with Articles 3.3 and 5.1 of the SPS Agreement.[539] Upon further EC- requested arbitration, the arbitrator determined that the European Communities had to implement the recommendations of the Appellate Body by 13 May 1999.[540] On 3 June 1999, the United States and Canada requested the DSB's authorization for the suspension of concessions to the European Communities. In both cases, the European Communities asked for arbitration on the level of suspension of the concessions. The respective retaliatory suspensions of concessions to the European Communities by the United States and Canada were consequently granted through the DSB's meeting of 26 July 1999.[541]

The TPR of the European Union of 2000 therefore analyses the trade concerns to a substantial degree[542] not only through a specific identification in the Secretariat and government reports (ie in pursuit of the TPRM's transparency objective) but also by means of naming and shaming in the TPRB meeting and in the written questions and answers thereof.

In line with its earlier practice, the Secretariat's main analysis of the issue is contained in the report's section with regard to measures directly affecting imports.[543] In its sub-section on product regulations and standards, the Secretariat first (rather descriptively) sketches the unfolding contours of the issue while indicating that '*Another significant development since the last TPR of the EU in 1997 is the greater visibility of food safety in policy discussions. The Commission is concerned with assuring that the EU has the highest standards of food safety . . . to*

536 Trade Policy Review of the European Union of 25–26 November 1997, Secretariat Report, WT/TPR/S/30, 20 October 1997, 82–89.

537 Trade Policy Review of the European Union of 25–26 November 1997, Government Report, WT/TPR/G/30, 20 October 1997.

538 Trade Policy Review of the European Union of 25–26 November 1997, Minutes of the Meeting, WT/TPR/M/30, 26 January 1998, 8.

539 WTO, *EC—Measures Concerning Meat and Meat Products—Appellate Body Report* (16 January 1998) WT/DS26 and 48/AB/R.

540 WTO, *EC—Measures Concerning Meat and Meat Products—Arbitration under Article 21.3(c) of the Understanding on Rules and Procedures Governing the Settlement of Disputes* (29 May 1998) WT/DS26/15 and WT/DS48/13.

541 WTO, DSB, Minutes of the Meeting, WT/DSB/M/65, 15 September 1999, 17–19

542 Trade Policy Review of the European Communities of 12–14 July 2000, Minutes of the Meeting, WT/TPR/M/72, 26 October 2000.

543 Trade Policy Review of the European Communities of 12–14 July 2000, Secretariat Report, WT/TPR/S/72, 14 June 2000, 40–69.

which end a radical new approach is proposed for consultations and discussions, inviting comments by April 2000. This development is linked to a number of food scares at the Community level, but will also have implications for the imported or exported food given the leading role of the Community in world food trade. The Commission proposes the establishment of an independent European Food Authority to carry out the role of risk assessment and risk communication, building on the reform of the current system for scientific advice introduced in 1997 in the wake of the BSE crisis. The Commission also proposes a Food Action Plan to establish food safety as the primary objective of EU food law and change the regulatory framework accordingly, including the control of foodstuffs through the entire food chain, "from farm to table". Scientific evidence is to underpin the food safety policy, with the precautionary principle to be used where appropriate'. Adopting a neutral position, the Secretariat then sets out to explain how these experiences and new institutional developments relate to the dispute at hand. In this respect, it notes that '*With respect to food regulations and standards, each Member state is represented on the* Codex Alimentarius *Commission, which is a joint FAO/WHO programme to develop an international food code. According to the SPS agreement, as interpreted in the high-profile WTO dispute settlement proceeding on hormone-treated beef, WTO Members that apply Codex Standards or recommendations are considered to meet the obligations of the SPS Agreement. According to the Commission, a WTO Member may only impose more restrictive measures if there is scientific evidence (a risk assessment) justifying measures leading to a higher level of protection than by applying Codex Standards. As a result, the Community, whose exports underwent retaliation by the US and Canada in 1999, was engaged in early 2000 in such a risk assessment for its measures with respect to hormone-treated beef*'.[544] The issue is not tackled in Secretariat's report's analysis with regard to agriculture.[545]

In its chapter which is dedicated to the European Union and the WTO, the government report rather unusually highlights and defends its ongoing DSB case. According to the European Union, '*among the most important among the few cases in which the EU was the defendant, touched upon the increasingly important issues of the protection of human health. In both the "hormones" ... cases, the WTO is called to strike a balance between the sovereign rights of Member states to seek protection of the health of their population on the one hand, and the protection of the negotiated rights of third countries on the other hand. Despite the real difficulties that the EU is encountering in relation to the implementation of the "hormones" ... cases, the EU rests fully committed to implementing the Panels as soon as possible*'.[546] Furthermore, the meeting of the TPRB was used extensively by the complainants in an attempt to name and shame the European Union into more SPS-conforming behaviour. Some of this criticism was directly related to the ongoing dispute, although

[544] Trade Policy Review of the European Communities of 12–14 July 2000, Secretariat Report, WT/TPR/S/72, 14 June 2000, 56–63.

[545] Trade Policy Review of the European Communities of 12–14 July 2000, Secretariat Report, WT/TPR/S/72, 14 June 2000, 89–99.

[546] Trade Policy Review of the European Communities of 12–14 July 2000, Government Report, WT/TPR/G/72, 14 June 2000, 8.

some concerns were worded in general terms. According to the United States, '*Differences between the US and the EU remained. The US was one of the largest exporters of agricultural products in the world, and therefore had a keen interest in the operation of the Common Agricultural Policy (CAP) . . . The US was also concerned with ensuring third-country participation in EU regulatory decision-making, as foreseen by the transparency obligations of the TBT and SPS agreements. The EU should allow WTO Members and affected exporters a meaningful opportunity to comment on regulatory proposals and consider the comments before a final technical regulation was promulgated and enforced*'.[547] Canada was more direct and '*called upon the European Union, as a strong supporter of a vital multilateral trading system, to implement DSB rulings and recommendations*'.[548] It also expressed wider concern on the EU's Common Agricultural Policy[549] while stating that it had '*taken a great interest in the EU's recent food safety difficulties and the erosion of consumer confidence in their food. The Canadian Government commended the EU on its plan to create an independent European Food Safety Authority but had concerns that certain EU regulations involving health, safety, and the environment, had or threatened to have a negative effect on Canadian interests. The Canadian government was not alone in asserting that such measures should be based only on sound science and must be the least trade-distorting possible in their application: the SPS and TBT agreements called for nothing less. This increasingly important area in trade required further international co-operation to address the different approaches of WTO Members in order to avoid further high-profile disputes that could damage the integrity of the multilateral trading system. Co-operation could also address concerns that some countries were taking unilateral actions in the name of food safety or environmental protection as a pretence for measures whose real object was economic protection or advantage. The appropriate manner to address concerns of this nature, whether . . . hormone-treated meat . . . was to develop a rigorous, science-based regulatory response, to potential health and environmental threats. Good governance demanded a rational science-based approach to risk assessment and management, and courage would at times be required by lawmakers and officials in the face of misinformed public opinion*'.[550]

Nevertheless, the European Union counterargued while stating that it '*noted the attention devoted to the issue by authorities of the EU since the creation of the common market, to harmonize standards and foster the free movement of goods, while maintaining a high level of protection of health. Existing EU regulations were being developed by the EU and the Member states and the measures were applied to all products placed on the market without distinction of origin. The evaluation of risk was carried out by the Scientific Committee of the Commission, based on the principles of sound science,*

[547] Trade Policy Review of the European Communities of 12–14 July 2000, Minutes of the Meeting, WT/TPR/M/72, 26 October 2000, 31.

[548] Trade Policy Review of the European Communities of 12–14 July 2000, Minutes of the Meeting, WT/TPR/M/72, 26 October 2000, 32.

[549] Trade Policy Review of the European Communities of 12–14 July 2000, Minutes of the Meeting, WT/TPR/M/72, 26 October 2000, 32–33.

[550] Trade Policy Review of the European Communities of 12–14 July 2000, Minutes of the Meeting, WT/TPR/M/72, 26 October 2000, 33.

which formed the basis of Commission proposals for legislation to the Member states and to the European Parliament, if applicable, and in consultation with representatives of civil society'.[551] The European Union then seized the opportunity of the TPRB meeting to frame its interpretation of the precautionary principle in law while emphasizing that '*it was applied by the EU to cases where relevant scientific evidence was insufficient, in accordance with Article 5.7 of the SPS agreement, as part of a strategy of risk management. The Commission had issued a communication on the subject (COM (2000)1) which placed the precautionary principle in a structured approach to risk assessment and risk management. The Commission was of the view that a regulatory decision was fundamentally a political one when the scientific evidence was insufficient to definitively assess risk. The Commission's communication however established objective criteria to guide the application of the precautionary principle. The EU had actively participated in the discussions on the principle in international fora, notably the* OECD *and the* Codex Alimentarius'.[552]

The United States was not convinced by these arguments and therefore tabled further written questions not only with regard to the EU's interpretation of the precautionary principle[553] but also with regard to the hormones case.[554] Nevertheless, the European Union replied very defensively while emphasizing that '*it should be noted in this respect that under the SPS agreement the US have the same obligation to provide the scientific information requested by the European Commission on these hormones. As the Appellate Body has held in the hormones cases, the US have unjustifiably refused to provide to the EC the requested data on which they have decided to authorise these hormones for animal growth promotion. Despite the fact that such a specific request was made again to the US in 1998–1000, until today they have failed to respect this obligation*'.[555]

No major new legal developments had occurred by the time of the next TPR of the European Union of July 2002.[556] Nevertheless, the review identified the dispute and its wider underlying concerns throughout the reports of the Secretariat and the government as well as through the TPRB meeting.

The Secretariat report's main analysis of the topic is contained in a sub-section specifically dedicated to product regulations and standards (part of the section on measures directly affecting imports).[557] In this context, the Secretariat notes

[551] Trade Policy Review of the European Communities of 12–14 July 2000, Minutes of the Meeting, WT/TPR/M/72, 26 October 2000, 59.

[552] Trade Policy Review of the European Communities of 12–14 July 2000, Minutes of the Meeting, WT/TPR/M/72, 26 October 2000, 59.

[553] Trade Policy Review of the European Communities of 12–14 July 2000, Written questions and answers, WT/TPR/M/72/Add. 1, 26 October 2000, 70 and 183 (with regard to the precautionary principle).

[554] Trade Policy Review of the European Communities of 12–14 July 2000, Written questions and answers, WT/TPR/M/72/Add. 1, 26 October 2000, 71 and 185 (with regard to the hormones case).

[555] Trade Policy Review of the European Communities of 12–14 July 2000, Written questions and answers, WT/TPR/M/72/Add. 1, 26 October 2000, 185.

[556] Trade Policy Review of the European Communities of 24–26 July 2002, Minutes of the Meeting, WT/TPR/M/102, 23 September 2002.

[557] Trade Policy Review of the European Communities of 24–26 July 2002, Secretariat Report, WT/TPR/S/102, 26 June 2002, 26–69 (particularly at 37–46).

that '*the Community is also considering amendments to its legislation banning the use of hormones of growth promoters with the objective of bringing the legislation into compliance with WTO rulings on the matter*'. It also indicates that '*as was noted at the time of its last Review, the EU has been involved in a long-standing WTO dispute settlement proceeding on hormone-treated beef, as a result of which Community export underwent retaliation by the US and Canada in 1999, this continues to be in place. According to the Commission, a WTO Member state may impose more trade restrictive measures if there is scientific evidence (a risk assessment) justifying measures leading to a higher level of protection than by applying Codex Standards. During the period under review, the Community has engaged in risk assessment for its measures with respect to hormone-treated beef, and is considering revisions of legislation banning the use of hormones as growth promoters*'.[558] Furthermore, the Secretariat's chapter on developments in selected sectors[559] and more particularly, its sub-section on agriculture, emphasizes that '*Although not directly related to BSE, the legislation banning hormones as growth promoters was revised of 1 July 2001, on the basis of scientific evidence collected by the Commission. The original legislation was the subject of a WTO dispute settlement proceeding in the context of which certain, mainly agricultural, EU exports have undergone sanctions in Canada and the US. Modifications of the Directive to bring EU legislation into compliance with the WTO ruling are currently under discussion in the Council and the European Parliament*'.

Although the government report does not explicitly raise the issue, it rather cryptically states that '*the EU remains fully committed to the successful resolution of (DSB) cases where the EU is a defendant*'.[560]

During the TPRB meeting, both complainants in the ongoing case tried to name and shame the European Union into better behaviour. In this regard, Canada stated that '*As a major exporter and developer of innovative agricultural products, Canada was concerned that its exports to the EU had declined over the last few years. One reason was the EU's recent trend towards regulations that were an impediment to Canada's exports. Canada was particularly concerned because these regulations were often introduced under the guise of food safety and SPS concerns, but were taken without a sound scientific basis and a due regard for international standards.*'[561]

In a similar vein the United States emphasized that '*Given the steady decline in traditional trade measures as impediments to international commerce, certainly among developed countries, the role of regulatory issues in the shaping of economic relations between countries loomed larger. This was particularly the case of the EU, which through*

[558] Trade Policy Review of the European Communities of 24–26 July 2002, Secretariat Report, WT/TPR/S/102, 26 June 2002, 41 and 44–45.

[559] Trade Policy Review of the European Communities of 24–26 July 2002, Secretariat Report, WT/TPR/S/102, 26 June 2002, 69–103 (particularly at 69–77).

[560] Trade Policy Review of the European Communities 24–26 July 2002, Government Report, WT/TPR/G/102, 26 June 2002, 10.

[561] Trade Policy Review of the European Communities of 24–26 July 2002, Minutes of the Meeting, WT/TPR/M/102, 23 September 2002, 14–15.

its sheer size could have a profound regulatory influence on world trade. US concerns with the EU's policies in this sphere, which had been expressed in previous discussions in the TPRB, remained. Specifically, she (i.e. the US representative to the TPRB) echoed the Secretariat's identification in its report that EU rule-making processes were often perceived by third countries as exclusionary, allowing no meaningful opportunity for non-EU parties to influence the outcome of its regulatory decisions' and thus stated that it '*welcome[s] the current internal debate within the EU on governance, and the need for transparency in rule-making. However, she (i.e. the US representative to the TPRB) called again on the EU to ensure that Members and affected exporters had a meaningful opportunity to comment on regulatory proposals, and that those comments were considered before a final international position on technical regulations was reached*'.[562]

Unsurprisingly, the Commission disagreed with the critical interpretations according to which the European Union had abused the precautionary principle for protectionist purposes. It therefore rebutted these claims with legal arguments. According to the Commission, '*What was being protected was the health of consumers and of the public. Article 2 of the SPS agreement allowed some flexibility for governments to fix their own standards provided the criteria set out therein were met (measures only to the extent necessary and non-discrimination). Members had to base their measures on international standards, but Article 3.3 specifically provided that they might opt for higher standards of protection provided they were scientifically justified. Given the very high level of consumer concerns in the EU following the BSE outbreak, and more recently foot-and-mouth disease in several MS, the EU was politically obliged for the moment to set high standards, but they should also be scientifically justified.*'[563] Further to the comments of Canada and the United States, which had called for greater transparency and participation in regulatory norm setting, the European Union stated that '*there was a trend to increase the scope for third countries' participation as a principle of better governance. For example, the European Food Safety Agency provided for third-country participation in its scientific work*'.[564] Moreover, according to the Commission, '*the EU's approach to precaution involved comprehensive pre-market scientific risk assessment, which was taken into account when the Council took decisions. The same applied to hormones, where the Commission was carrying out further scientific assessments in line with the findings of the dispute settlement Panel, and has invited submissions from any source, including industry. In trying to take the correct approach to precaution, the EU was in the vanguard of those MS who were having to find the appropriate balance between trade and the protection of health and safety, often without clear international consensus on where the balance should be struck. Many*

[562] Trade Policy Review of the European Communities of 24–26 July 2002, Minutes of the Meeting, WT/TPR/M/102, 23 September 2002, 23–24.

[563] Trade Policy Review of the European Communities of 24–26 July 2002, Minutes of the Meeting, WT/TPR/M/102, 23 September 2002, 46.

[564] Trade Policy Review of the European Communities of 24–26 July 2002, Minutes of the Meeting, WT/TPR/M/102, 23 September 2002, 48.

of the issues confronting the European regulator at present would sooner or later confront regulators of other Members'.[565] *The EU furthermore recalled that it 'had offered, before Doha to further codify the WTO approach to precaution set out in the SPS agreement, as clarified by the Appellate Body. As the world's largest agricultural exporter, the EU was perhaps more concerned than anybody else that the application of precaution not be abused or turned into a protectionist weapon that could reduce EU access to third-country markets. The EU needed as much predictability for its traders as possible. Its offers, however, had not been taken up'*. The European Union therefore wondered '*whether Members would now wish to reconsider their positions*'.[566]

At the DSB meeting of 7 November 2003, the European Communities stated that, following the entry into force of its new Directive No 2003/74 regarding the prohibition on the use in stock farming of certain hormones, there was no legal basis for the continued imposition of retaliatory measures by the United States and Canada.[567] One of the reasons cited by the Appellate Body in its ruling against the European Communities was its failure to carry out a risk assessment within the meaning of Articles 5.1 and 5.2 of the SPS Agreement. Nonetheless, according to the European Communities, the new Directive established such assessments to be undertaken by an independent scientific committee on its behalf. Moreover, the scientific findings of this committee had indicated that the hormones in question posed a risk for consumers. The European Communities deemed that it was therefore entitled to demand the immediate lifting of the sanctions.[568] Unsurprisingly, neither the United States nor Canada were in a position to accede to this request. Both countries continued to doubt the scientific basis of the new measure and studies.[569] As a result, the European Communities requested recourse to Article 21.5 of the DSU.[570]

The EU's TPR of October 2004 therefore again) put its finger on the issue.[571] In line with its earlier practice, the Secretariat's main analysis of the problem is contained in its report's chapter on trade policies and practices by measure.[572] One of its sub-sections, specifically dedicated to SPS measures indicates, that '*in response to the WTO ruling on the EC's ban on the use of hormones as growth promoters, the Community adopted a directive seeking to bring its legislation into compliance. The new directive confirms the prohibition of substances having hormonal action for growth*

565 Trade Policy Review of the European Communities of 24–26 July 2002, Minutes of the Meeting, WT/TPR/M/102, 23 September 2002, 49.

566 Trade Policy Review of the European Communities of 24–26 July 2002, Minutes of the Meeting, WT/TPR/M/102, 23 September 2002, 49.

567 It should be noted that the new Directive maintained the prohibition on five of the six hormones and allowed only limited use of the sixth hormone.

568 WTO, DSB, Minutes of the Meeting, WT/DSB/M/157, 18 December 2003, 7.

569 WTO, DSB, Minutes of the Meeting, WT/DSB/M/157, 18 December 2003, 7–8.

570 WTO, DSB, Minutes of the Meeting, WT/DSB/M/159, 15 January 2004, 5.

571 Trade Policy Review of the European Communities of 25–27 October 2004, Minutes of the Meeting, WT/TPR/M/136, 18 January 2005.

572 Trade Policy Review of the European Communities of 25–27 October 2004, Secretariat Report, WT/TPR/S/136, 23 June 2004, 37–83.

promotion and reduces the circumstances under which one of the hormones (oestradiol 17-beta) may be administered to food-producing animals for purposes other than growth promotion. As regard the remaining five hormones, the Commission considers the scientific evidence gathered so far to be insufficient to propose a permanent prohibition. Therefore, the prohibition in the amended directive is provisional. The Commission is to review regularly scientific information that may become available, and seeks to obtain additional information'.[573] The Secretariat's sectional analysis of agriculture in the report's chapter analysing trade policies by sector does not delve further into the issue.[574]

Although the government report remains silent on the issue,[575] both complainants raised the topic in the framework of the TPRB meeting and attempted to name and shame the European Union into more SPS conforming behaviour. Canada emphasized only in general terms that '*the role of regulatory issues had grown in importance, including in the EC: its prominence and commitment to safety, environment, and health could have a profound impact outside its borders*'.[576] The comments of the United States were sharper, even critical of Secretariat's Report. According to the United States, '*the role of non-tariff barriers and regulatory issues in EC trade policy was important to the US. The principal challenges for the US-EC trade relationship would lie in confronting the trade implications of regulatory measures adopted by the EC. The US believed that the report by the Secretariat did not comment extensively enough on whether non-EC parties had a meaningful opportunity to influence the outcome of regulatory decisions. The EC needed to increase transparency and access to increasingly complex regulatory and trade policy process*'.[577] The United States also requested more details on the EU's implementation of the DSB's recommendations in the hormones case, as ascertained by the Secretariat.[578] Nevertheless, the European Union observed rather meaninglessly that '*the Commission carried out a complementary risk assessment, in accordance with the requirements of the Agreement on the application of sanitary and phytosanitary measures as interpreted by the Appellate Body in the Hormones case, of the six hormonal substances (oestradiol, 17B, testosterone, progesterone, trenbolone acetate, zeranol and melengestrol acetate) whose administration for animal growth promotion purposes is prohibited by Directive 96/22/EC. Following completion of*

[573] Trade Policy Review of the European Communities of 25–27 October 2004, Secretariat Report, WT/TPR/S/136, 23 June 2004, 63–65.

[574] Trade Policy Review of the European Communities of 25–27 October 2004, Secretariat Report, WT/TPR/S/136, 23 June 2004, 85–100.

[575] Trade Policy Review of the European Communities of 25–27 October 2004, Government Report, WT/TPR/G/136, 1 October 2004.

[576] Trade Policy Review of the European Communities of 25–27 October 2004, Minutes of the Meeting, WT/TPR/M/136, 18 January 2005, 10.

[577] Trade Policy Review of the European Communities of 25–27 October 2004, Minutes of the Meeting, WT/TPR/M/136, 18 January 2005, 12.

[578] Trade Policy Review of the European Communities of 25–27 October 2004, Secretariat Report, WT/TPR/S/136, 23 June 2004, 65.

the said risk assessment the EU adopted Directive 2003/74/EC of 22 September 2003 amending Council Directive 96/22/EC concerning the prohibition on the use in stock farming of certain substances having a hormonal or thyrostatic action and of beta-agonists'.[579]

In November 2004, the European Communities filed two (separate) requests for consultations with the United States and Canada, asserting that both countries should have removed their retaliatory measures insofar as the European Communities had removed the measures found to be inconsistent with the DSB's recommendations.[580]

The TPR of the European Union of February 2007 focuses for the fifth time on the trade concerns.[581] The Secretariat report clearly identifies the issue and both complainants in the case also seized the TPRB meeting in an attempt to name and shame the European Union into conforming to the SPS Agreement.

In line with its earlier practice, the Secretariat's main analysis of the issue is contained in a sub-section which is specifically dedicated to SPS measures.[582] This sub-section indicates that '*the prohibition on certain substances having hormonal action for growth promotion has remained into force*'. However, the specific trade concern is not analysed in Secretariat's analysis of agriculture and related activities.[583] The same is true for the government report.[584]

Nevertheless, the United States—though not Canada—seized the opportunity of the TPRB meeting in an attempt to name and shame the European Union into behaviour that was more consistent with the SPS Agreement. In this context, the United States stated that '*Excessive sanitary and phytosanitary restrictions ... created enormous burdens for US exporters. Real new trade flows in agriculture would remain difficult to achieve without a transparent regulatory regime based on risk assessments and consistent across Member states. The US urged the EC to comply with the recommendations and ruling of the DSB ... and to work to resolve their long-running beef hormone dispute.*'[585] Nonetheless, the European Communities

[579] Trade Policy Review of the European Communities of 25–27 October 2004, Written questions and answers, WT/TPR/M/136/Add.1, 18 January 2005, 155.

[580] WTO, *European Communities—Measures Concerning Meat and Meat Products (Hormones)—Continued Suspension of Obligations in the EC—Hormones Dispute—Request for Consultations by the European Communities* (9 November 2004) WT/DS321/1; WTO, *European Communities—Measures Concerning Meat and Meat Products (Hormones)—Continued Suspension of Obligations in the EC—Hormones Dispute—Request for Consultations by the European Communities* (10 November 2004) WT/DS320/1.

[581] Trade Policy Review of the European Union of 26–28 February 2007, Minutes of the Meeting, WT/TPR/M/177, 30 April 2007.

[582] Trade Policy Review of the European Union of 26–28 February 2007, Secretariat Report, WT/TPR/S/177, 22 January 2007, 59–61 (particularly at 61).

[583] Trade Policy Review of the European Union of 26–28 February 2007, Secretariat Report, WT/TPR/S/177, 22 January 2007, 79–95.

[584] Trade Policy Review of the European Union, Government Report, WT/TPR/G/177, 22 January 2007.

[585] Trade Policy Review of the European Union of 26–28 February 2007, Minutes of the Meeting, WT/TPR/M/177, 30 April 2007, 13.

answered that '*it was convinced that the EC's SPS measures were based on science, although scientific views in the US could be different in some of the cases. The EC did not foresee any reason for changing the EC's present policies. Regarding the reference made to the regulatory process . . . on which the implementation of the Panel decision was under active discussion between the EC and other parties to the Panel, the EC intended to find ways to comply with the decisions of the Panel*'.[586] None of the complainants attempted to investigate the issue any further by means of written questions.[587]

Since US and Canadian sanctions remained in place in spite of the new EU measures, the European Communities requested consultations with the United States and Canada under Article 21.5 of the DSU.[588] Moreover, Australia and New Zealand successfully asked to join these consultations.

The TPR of the European Union of April 2009 touches on the issue again.[589] Although the Secretariat's report covers the topic in a rather minimalistic way and the government report lacks any reference to the issue, the complainants in the DSB case used the TPRB meeting extensively in an attempt to name and shame the European Union.

The Secretariat's sub-section, which is specifically dedicated to SPS measures[590] and which is again not identified in its analytical overview table at the beginning of the report, succinctly states that '*Imports of meat derived from animals treated with hormonal growth promoters, mechanically recovered meat, and the use of specified risk materials (to reduce the risk of transmissible spongiform encephalopathy) are prohibited. The use of antimicrobial treatment on food of animal origin is also prohibited.*' In line with its earlier practice, the Secretariat's analysis of agriculture and related activities does not refer to the issue.[591] Moreover, the government report omits the issue completely.[592]

This silence did not disbar Canada and the United States from bringing the topic extensively under the attention of the TPRB Membership. In this context, Canada reiterated the fact that '*We have other concerns with significant regulatory impediments. These include the EC ban on the importation of meat derived from animals treated with certain hormone treatments . . . Regarding hormones, we see no*

[586] Trade Policy Review of the European Union of 26–28 February 2007, Minutes of the Meeting, WT/TPR/M/177, 30 April 2007, 27.

[587] Trade Policy Review of the European Union of 26–28 February 2007, Written questions and answers, WT/TPR/M/177/Add. 1, 30 April 2007.

[588] WTO, DSB, Minutes of the Meeting, WT/DSB/M/261, 6 March 2009, 11–17

[589] Trade Policy Review of the European Union of 6–8 April 2009, Minutes of the Meeting, WT/TPR/M/214, 8 June 2009.

[590] Trade Policy Review of the European Union of 6–8 April 2009, Secretariat Report, WT/TPR/S/214, 2 March 2009, 60–65 (particularly at 61–62).

[591] Trade Policy Review of the European Union of 6–8 April 2009, Secretariat Report, WT/TPR/S/214, 2 March 2009, 97–117.

[592] Trade Policy Review of the European Union of 6–8 April 2009, Government Report, WT/TPR/G/214, 2 March 2009.

scientific justification for the EC's hormones ban.'[593] In a similar vein, the United States emphasized that '*Agricultural and food products that the US safely consumes at home and exports to dozens of other Member states have been excluded from the EC market by SPS measures that appear to lack sufficient scientific justification. In some cases, the EC has imposed SPS barriers on products that the EC's own scientists have concluded pose no risk to human, animal, and plant life or health. Because of SPS and other barriers, US agricultural exporters have been unable to access fully the EC's post-Uruguay Round market.*' The United States also stated that '*EC standards, testing, and certification rules and EC regulatory practices have become increasingly important determinants of market access for firms around the world. Unfortunately, we have found that by the time the EC issues public notices on regulatory proposals—some with enormous trade implications—deliberations among EC Member states have progressed too far to allow for meaningful consideration of the views of trading partners. As we have asked for several years, we continue to urge the EC to offer WTO Members and their private sector stakeholders meaningful opportunities to comment on regulatory proposals and assurances that those comments will be taken into consideration before a final regulation is promulgated and enforced*'. Furthermore, '*both in the area of SPS regulations … we continue to be concerned that some measures maintained by the EC on the grounds of food safety or environmental protection may not be appropriately supported by science-based risk assessments*'.[594] Nevertheless, the EC answered (rather evasively) that '*As is well-known, EC legislation bans the use of growth-promoting hormones in beef, whether produced in the EU or imported. After the earlier decision of the DSB, the hormones directive has been modified to reflect the additional scientific proof underpinning its provision. As this has not led to the solution of the debate with the WTO Members concerned, the Appellate Body last year requested us to start compliance proceedings to demonstrate the WTO-consistency of our hormones directive. We have requested consultations with the US and Canada and look forward to settling this long-lasting dispute shortly.*'[595] No further written questions were tabled with regard to the issue.[596]

On 25 September 2009, the European Communities and the United States notified the DSB of a Memorandum of Understanding.[597] The European Union and Canada followed and notified the DSB of their Memorandum of Understanding on 17 March 2011.[598]

[593] Trade Policy Review of the European Union of 6–8 April 2009, Minutes of the Meeting, WT/TPR/M/214, 8 June 2009, 33.

[594] Trade Policy Review of the European Union of 6–8 April 2009, Minutes of the Meeting, WT/TPR/M/214, 8 June 2009, 43–44.

[595] Trade Policy Review of the European Union of 6–8 April 2009, Minutes of the Meeting, WT/TPR/M/214, 8 June 2009, 73.

[596] Trade Policy Review of the European Union of 6–8 April 2009, Written questions and answers, WT/TPR/M/214/Add. 1, 2 July 2009.

[597] WTO, *European Communities—Measures Concerning Meat and Meat Products (Hormones)—Joint Communication from the European Communities and the US* (30 September 2009) WT/DS26/28.

[598] WTO, *European Communities—Measures Concerning Meat and Meat Products (Hormones)—Joint Communication from the European Union and Canada* (22 March 2011) WT/DS48/26.

The TPR of the European Union of July 2011 no longer explicitly highlights the issue.[599] Neither the Secretariat's[600] nor the government's report[601] draws any further attention to the topic.

The complainants in the hormones case therefore used the TPRB meeting not to reiterate complaints about outstanding implementation in the dispute but instead to lament in more general terms about other persisting regulatory SPS barriers. In this regard, Canada stated that '*we nonetheless remain concerned with the growing number of regulatory barriers which hinder or threaten to hinder access to the European market for Canadian business*' and that '*Canada and the EU share the legitimate objectives of protecting human, animal, plant health and the environment. While recognizing that there are different approaches to reaching these objectives, we have the highest expectations that the EU will ensure that any measures it takes are science-based, no more trade-restrictive than necessary and reflect the realities of global trade today. Unfortunately, in too many cases the EU has not lived up to these expectations.*'[602] Similarly, the United States reiterated its regret about the fact that '*food and animal feed products that have been safely consumed in the US for decades, and that the US exports to dozens of other Members, continue to be excluded from the EU market by SPS measures that appear to lack sufficient scientific justification … Because of SPS and other barriers, US agricultural exporters have been unable to take full advantage of the market access the EU offered in the Uruguay Round.*' The United States repeated its institutional concerns while indicating that '*with respect to the EU's overarching policies and procedures, we have found that by the time the EU issues public notices on regulatory proposals—some with enormous trade implications—internal deliberations among EU Member states have progressed too far to allow for meaningful consideration of the views of trading partners. As we have for several years, we continue to urge the EU to offer WTO Members and their private sector stakeholders meaningful opportunities to comment on regulatory proposals, and assurances that those comments will be taken into consideration before final regulations are promulgated and enforced*'.

Furthermore, it added that '*inconsistent implementation of internal market rules continue to constrain trade for EU and foreign producers alike. We applaud the European Commission's efforts to eliminate lingering internal barriers to the free flow of goods, and look forward to hearing how the EU intends to address remaining barriers—including those that are not scientifically justified—to the free flow of goods at the EU and Member state levels*'.[603]

[599] Trade Policy Review of the European Union of 6–8 July 2011, Minutes of the Meeting, WT/TPR/M/248, 14 September 2011.

[600] Trade Policy Review of the European Union of 6–8 July 2011, Secretariat Report, WT/TPR/S/248, 1 June 2011.

[601] Trade Policy Review of the European Union of 6–8 July 2011, Government Report, WT/TPR/G/248, 1 June 2011.

[602] Trade Policy Review of the European Union of 6–8 July 2011, Minutes of the Meeting, WT/TPR/M/248, 14 September 2011, 24.

[603] Trade Policy Review of the European Union of 6–8 July 2011, Minutes of the Meeting, WT/TPR/M/248, 14 September 2011, 29–30 and 69.

The European Union answered in a similar general way and explained that '*the vast majority of EU regulations are based on international standards that by their nature tend to represent middle-way solutions or standards. Such reliance on international standards is, by the way, not the case for several other major WTO Members, complaining about our regime at this forum.*' The European Union stated that '*the EU's legislation seeks to ensure the functioning of the internal market and a high level of consumer and environment protection—frequently higher than in other WTO Members. This is a fundamental point for us, as Article 168 (1) of the Treaty on the Functioning of the European Union provides that "A high level of human health protection shall be ensured in the definition and implementation of all Union policies and activities". Several Members have also recognised ... that public policy concerns relating to food safety, consumer and environmental protection are legitimate*'. With regard to the alleged abuse of SPS standards as obstacles to trade, the European Union referred to '*the huge technical assistance and capacity building efforts, the numerous co-operation programs with developing countries in this area ... If SPS measures were to be such an insurmountable obstacle as claimed by some, all this trade could not have been realized.*'[604] None of the written questions specifically touched on the hormones issue.[605]

The TPR of the European Union of July 2013—the last European TPR which explicitly referred to the dispute—took place without any further legal developments in the hormones case.[606] The Secretariat's reporting, as contained in its subsection on SPS measures,[607] and government's reporting[608] remain once again silent on the dispute.

Furthermore, Canada and the United States followed their earlier practices and only complained in general terms about other persisting SPS regulatory barriers. In this context, Canada emphasized, in similar terms to its earlier intervention on the occasion of the EU's TPR of 2011, that '*under the banner of the legitimate objectives of protecting human, animal, and plant health as well as the environment, which Canada and the EU share, we are concerned that too often, measures proposed or adopted are not science-based. Nor do they meet the test of "not more trade-restrictive than necessary"*'.[609] Similarly, the United States repeated that '*the EU's barriers to our agricultural exports remain a significant concern, both with respect to high tariff*

[604] Trade Policy Review of the European Union of 6–8 July 2011, Minutes of the Meeting, WT/TPR/M/248, 14 September 2011, 62.

[605] Trade Policy Review of the European Union of 6–8 July 2011, Written questions, WT/TPR/M/248/Add. 1, 31 August 2011.

[606] Trade Policy Review of the European Union of 16–18 July 2013, Minutes of the Meeting, WT/TPR/M/284, 23 October 2013.

[607] Trade Policy Review of the European Union of 16–18 July 2013, Secretariat Report, WT/TPR/S/284, 28 May 2013, 64–69; Secretariat's analysis of Agriculture again does not mention the topic; Trade Policy Review of the European Union of 16–18 July 2013, Secretariat Report, WT/TPR/S/284, 28 May 2013, 111–31.

[608] Trade Policy Review of the European Union of 16–18 July, Government Report, WT/TPR/G/284, 28 May 2013.

[609] Trade Policy Review of the European Union of 16–18 July 2013, Minutes of the Meeting, WT/TPR/M/284, 23 October 2013, 33.

protection and non-tariff barriers, including sanitary and phytosanitary measures that are based on science or risk assessment... Because of these and other barriers, US agricultural exporters have been unable to take full advantage of the market access obligations agreed to by the EU during the Uruguay Round'. The United States reiterated its long-held institutional concerns in stating that '*the EU's regulatory and legislative process also do not typically provide essential and meaningful opportunity for WTO Members and their stakeholders to comment on regulatory proposals. Further, we have concerns regarding the apparent lack of mechanisms to ensure that stakeholder comments will be taken into account in final regulations. Our experience has been that internal deliberations with the Commission and among EU Member states on draft regulatory proposals progress much too far before trading partners and their stakeholders can provide views on the proposed text. As a result, by the time the EU considers these views, it is often too late to influence the character of the regulatory proposal, even on matters that have enormous trade implications*'. It repeated that it '*continued to applaud the European Commission's efforts to eliminate lingering internal barriers to the free flow of goods and look forward to hearing how the EU intends to address remaining barriers—including those that are not scientifically justified—to the free flow of goods at the EU and Member State levels*'.[610]

The European Union brushed these general concerns away while noting that '*EU regulations apply irrespective of the origin of the products*', that it '*pays maximum attention that TBT and SPS measures should not create unnecessary obstacles to trade or a disproportionate burden for producers*', and that '*the EU legislative process is highly transparent*'. In addition, it stated that European SPS measures '*are extensively harmonized within the EU*', that '*they are taken on the basis of a thorough risk analysis*' and that they '*avoid the trade disruptive "zero tolerance" approach often used by other countries*'.[611] No further written questions were tabled with regard to the hormone issue.[612]

On 14 April 2014, the European Union and the United States informed the DSB of a revised Memorandum of Understanding.[613]

- In *Argentina—Measures Affecting Imports of Footwear, Textiles, Apparel and Other Items*, the United States took issue with Argentina's imposition of specific duties on these items in excess of the bound rate and with other measures.[614] As a result of Argentina's internal liberalization within the framework of Mercosur, its imports of footwear had increased rapidly. Since Mercosur

[610] Trade Policy Review of the European Union of 16–18 July 2013, Minutes of the Meeting, WT/TPR/M/284, 23 October 2013, 12–13.

[611] Trade Policy Review of the European Union of 16–18 July 2013, Minutes of the Meeting, WT/TPR/M/284, 23 October 2013, 55–56.

[612] Trade Policy Review of the European Union of 16–18 July 2013, Written questions and answers, WT/TPR/M/284/Add. 1 and Add. 1/Rev. 1, 24 October 2013 and 28 November 2013.

[613] WTO, *European Communities—Measures Concerning Meat and Meat Products (Hormones)—Joint Communication from the European Union and the United States* (17 April 2014) WT/DS26/29.

[614] WTO, *Argentina—Measures Affecting Imports of Footwear, Textiles, Apparel and Other Items—Report of the Panel* (25 November 1997) WT/DS56/R; WTO, *Argentina—Measures Affecting Imports of Footwear, Textiles, Apparel and Other Items—Appellate Body Report* (27 March 1998) WT/DS56/AB/R.

lacked an intra-regional safeguard mechanism, Argentina was compensating downward price pressure by applying import relief and safeguard measures on several third countries.[615] The United States interpreted these measures as a series of WTO inconsistencies, including violations of Articles II, VII, VIII, and X of GATT (1994), Article II of the TBT Agreement,[616] Articles 1 to 8 of the Agreement on Customs Valuation, and Article 7 of the Agreement on Textiles and Clothing.[617]

Although Argentina's trade policy had been reviewed by the TPRB before the start of the DSB case, its most recent review was of limited value in this case. Its TPR dated back to 1992 whereas Argentina's measures that led to the dispute stemmed from the period between March 1995 and February 1997.[618]

Since DSB consultations in the case had remained unsuccessful, the Panel rendered its report on 25 November 1997. According to the Panel, the minimum specific duties imposed on textiles and apparel were inconsistent with the requirements of Article 2 of the GATT whereas the imposed statistical tax of 3 per cent *ad valorem* was considered to be incompatible with the requirements of Article VIII of GATT.[619] Moreover, further to appeal by Argentina, the Appellate Body upheld most of the Panel's findings and conclusions.[620] As a consequence, Argentina announced on 22 June 1998 that it had reached an agreement with the United States on the implementation of the DSB's recommendations. In accordance with the agreement, Argentina would cap specific duties on textiles and apparel at 35 per cent by 19 October 1998. It would also reduce its statistical tax to 0.5 per cent by 1 January 1999.[621]

The Secretariat's report for Argentina's TPR of January 1999 and the written questions and answers which resulted from the TPRB meeting discuss the dispute in detail.[622] This contrasts with the government report and the TPRB meeting

[615] Elias Baracat and Julio J Nogués, 'WTO Safeguards and Trade Liberalization—Lessons from the Argentina Footwear Case' (World Bank Policy Research Working Paper, No 3614, 2005) pp ii, 2–3, 15 <http://elibrary.worldbank.org/doi/abs/10.1596/1813-9450-3614> accessed 6 May 2017 (hereafter Baracat and Nogués, 'WTO Safeguards and Trade Liberalization—Lessons from the Argentina Footwear Case').

[616] Nonetheless, the final request for the establishment of a Panel does no longer refer to an alleged violation of the TBT agreement; WTO, *Argentina—Measures Affecting Imports of Footwear, Textiles, Apparel and Other Items—Request for the Establishment of a Panel by the United States* (10 January 1997) WT/DS56/5.

[617] WTO, *Argentina—Measures Affecting Imports of Footwear, Textiles, Apparel and Other Items—Report of the Panel* (25 November 1997) WT/DS56/R; WTO, *Argentina—Measures Affecting Imports of Footwear, Textiles, Apparel and Other Items—Appellate Body Report* (27 March 1998) WT/DS56/AB/R.

[618] Trade Policy Review of Argentina, Vol II, 4–5 March 1991 (Document on file with the author); WTO, Report of the Panel, WT/DS56/R, 25 November 1997, 3.

[619] WTO, *Argentina—Measures Affecting Imports of Footwear, Textiles, Apparel and Other Items—Report of the Panel* (25 November 1997) WT/DS56/R.

[620] WTO, *Argentina—Measures Affecting Imports of Footwear, Textiles, Apparel and Other Items—Appellate Body Report* (27 March 1998) WT/DS56/AB/R.

[621] WTO, *Argentina—Measures Affecting Imports of Footwear, Textiles, Apparel and Other Items—Communication from Argentina* (7 July 1998) WT/DS56/14.

[622] Trade Policy Review of Argentina of 20–22 January 1999, Minutes of the Meeting, WT/TPR/M/47, 1 March 1999.

which both lack any reference to the case. Several sections of the Secretariat's report shed light on the issue.[623] From a legal perspective and a TBT angle, the main gist of the analysis is contained in the report's section specifically dedicated to trade disputes and consultations[624] and in the Secretariat's analysis with regard to marking, labelling, and packaging, contained in the report's sub-section on standards and other technical requirements.[625] The former provides a substantial amount of legal detail while indicating that '*the authorities made a proposal to implement the Appellate Body's conclusions: customs procedures were to be introduced to ensure that the ad valorem equivalent of minimum specific duties would not exceed the bound rate of 35%, and ceilings by range of import value were to be set from January 1999 to ensure that the statistical tax would not exceed USD 500 per shipment. A regulation was issued in July 1998 to ensure that the ad valorem equivalent to the minimum specific duties applied on textiles imports from Members of the WTO do not exceed the bound level of 35%. Customs were instructed to adopt enforcement procedures in this respect. In September 1998, the duration of minimum specific duties affecting textiles and clothing was set until 31 March 2000; the ad valorem equivalent of such duties, depending on the product, must not exceed 35% or 30% until 31 July 1999, and 30% or 26% until their expiry*'. Although the request for the establishment of a Panel no longer referred to an alleged violation of the TBT agreement,[626] the Secretariat's sub-section on standards and other technical requirements correctly emphasizes that '*during the customs clearance process, imported goods are inspected for country-of-origins markings. Special rulings affect products such as ... textile and textile manufacturers ... and shoes.*' It states moreover that '*since July 1996 new labelling requirements on chemical composition, origin, producer, importer and exporter have applied to ... clothing and footwear with a view to improving information available to consumers*'. Nevertheless, the Secretariat's extensive referencing of the topic can be contrasted with the lack of any reference with regard to the subject in the government report.[627]

The United States did not seize the opportunity of the TPRB meeting to name and shame Argentina into better behaviour.[628] Nevertheless, it tabled written questions with regard to the tariff case.[629]

[623] Trade Policy Review of Argentina of 20–22 January 1999, Secretariat Report, WT/TPR/S/47, 2 October 1998, 34–37, 44–53, and 122–24.

[624] Trade Policy Review of Argentina of 20–22 January 1999, Secretariat Report, WT/TPR/S/47, 2 October 1998, 34–37 (especially at 34–35).

[625] Trade Policy Review of Argentina of 20–22 January 1999, Secretariat Report, WT/TPR/S/47, 2 October 1998, 69–72 (especially at 72).

[626] Nonetheless, the final request for the establishment of a panel does no longer refer to an alleged violation of the TBT agreement; WTO, *Argentina—Measures Affecting Imports of Footwear, Textiles, Apparel and Other Items—Request for the Establishment of a Panel by the United States* (10 January 1997), WT/DS56/5, 2.

[627] Trade Policy Review of Argentina of 20–22 January 1999, Government Report, WT/TPR/G/47, 2 October 1998.

[628] Trade Policy Review of Argentina of 20–22 January 1999, Minutes of the Meeting, WT/TPR/M/47, 1 March 1999, 7, 13, 15, 221, and 227.

[629] Trade Policy Review of Argentina of 20–22 January 1999, Minutes of the Meeting, WT/TPR/M/47, 1 March 1999, 47.

At the DSB meeting of 26 May 1999, Argentina announced that Decree 108/99, pursuant to which no import transactions covered by the statistical tax should be taxed in excess of the mutually agreed amounts, would enter into force on 30 May 1999.[630]

Argentina's Trade Policy Review of February 2007 covers the issue but does so in a less prominent way.[631] The Secretariat's earlier sectional reporting on trade disputes has disappeared from the standard structure of its report. The information relating to the dispute is scattered across the report. In this context, the Secretariat notes amongst others that '*in 1998, a WTO panel found that the imposition of the statistical tax was inconsistent with WTO rules since an ad valorem duty with no fixed maximum fee, by its very nature, is not limited in amount to the approximate cost of services rendered. As a result, in 1999, Argentina authorities set caps for the statistical tax depending on the value of imports. In 2005, revenue from the statistical tax amounted to Arg Dollar 96 million*'.[632]

Nevertheless, the issue did not resurface in Argentina's government report,[633] in the complainant's interventions during the TPRB meeting,[634] or in his written questions.[635]

- In *EC—Measures Affecting Butter Products*, New Zealand took issue with the EC's and the UK's decision that New Zealand's butter manufactured by the so-called AMMIX and spreadable butter-making process did not qualify for entry under the country-specific tariff quota (CSTQ) for butter established for New Zealand in the European Communities' WTO Schedule LXXX because butter manufactured by these two processes was not 'manufactured directly from milk or cream' (as required by the terms of the tariff quota).[636] The decision resulted in a situation whereby the two products would be subject to EC levies at a much higher out-of-quota tariff rate. According to New Zealand, these decisions therefore amounted to violations of Articles II, X, and XI of the GATT, Article 2 of the TBT Agreement, and Article 3 of the Agreement on Import Licensing Procedures.

The European Communities underwent a trade policy review prior to the initiation of the case.[637] Nevertheless, this review is of little relevance since the European

[630] WTO, DSB, Minutes of the Meeting, WT/DSB/M/62, 2 July 1999, 4

[631] Trade Policy Review of Argentina of 12–14 February 2007, Minutes of the Meeting, WT/TPR/M/176, 28 March 2007.

[632] Trade Policy Review of Argentina of 12–14 February 2007, Secretariat Report, WT/TPR/S/176, 8 January 2007, 37–48 (particularly at 45).

[633] Trade Policy Review of Argentina of 12–14 February 2007, Government Report, WT/TPR/G/176, 8 January 2007.

[634] Trade Policy Review of Argentina of 12–14 February 2007, Minutes of the Meeting, WT/TPR/M/176, 28 March 2007.

[635] Trade Policy Review of Argentina of 12–14 February 2007, Written questions, WT/TPR/M/176/Add. 1, 16 May 2007.

[636] WTO, *EC—Measures Affecting Butter Products—Report of the Panel* (24 November 1999) WT/DS72/R.

[637] Trade Policy Review of the European Union of 24–25 July 1995, Vol II (Document on file with the author).

decisions which led to the initiation of the DSB case stemmed from the period between July 1996 and January 1997.[638]

On 18 November 1997, a Panel was established.

The TPR of the European Union of November 1997 identifies the issue only briefly in a very succinct way.[639] The Secretariat's report's sub-section on the Dispute Settlement Body simply cites the case without further analysis.[640] Moreover, the report's section on developments in agriculture remains completely silent on the issue.[641] The same is true with regard to the government report.[642] During the TPRB meeting, New Zealand only expressed its general concern on the EU's policies in the agricultural sector; it did not explicitly refer to the case.[643]

Further to several requests of the complainants, tabled from 24 February 1999, the Panel repeatedly suspended its work. During the period of the last suspension, the parties notified the DSB of a mutually agreed solution.[644] As part of this understanding, the EC passed a regulation which clarified that New Zealand exports of spreadable and AMMIX butter did qualify for entry under New Zealand's Country-Specific Tariff Quota for butter.

The TPR of the European Union of July 2000 remains completely silent on the issue.[645] Neither the Secretariat's[646] nor the government's report,[647] the TPRB meeting[648] nor the written question tabled by New Zealand[649]—which acted as the complainant in the DSB case—contain any specific reference to the subject.

- In *Japan—Measures Affecting Agricultural Products*, the United States took issue with respect to Japanese quarantine measures as contained in its Plant Protection Law Enforcement Regulations which had resulted in the ban on

[638] WTO, *EC—Measures Affecting Butter Products—Report of the Panel* (24 November 1999) WT/DS72/R.

[639] Trade Policy Review of the European Union of 25–26 November 1997, Minutes of the Meeting, WT/TPR/M/30, 26 January 1998.

[640] Trade Policy Review of the European Union of 25–26 November 1997, Secretariat Report, WT/TPR/S/30, 20 October 1997, 39.

[641] Trade Policy Review of the European Union of 25–26 November 1997, Secretariat Report, WT/TPR/S/30, 20 October 1997, 82–92.

[642] Trade Policy Review of the European Union of 25–26 November 1997, Government Report, WT/TPR/G/30, 20 October 1997.

[643] Trade Policy Review of the European Union of 25–26 November 1997, Minutes of the Meeting, WT/TPR/M/30, 26 January 1998, 8.

[644] WTO, *EC—Measures Affecting Butter Products—Notification of Mutually Agreed Solution* (18 November 1999) WT/DS72/2.

[645] Trade Policy Review of the European Communities of 12–14 July 2000, Minutes of the Meeting, WT/TPR/M/72, 26 October 2000.

[646] Trade Policy Review of the European Communities of 12–14 July 2000, Secretariat Report, WT/TPR/S/72, 14 June 2000.

[647] Trade Policy Review of the European Communities of 12–14 July 2000, Government Report, WT/TPR/G/72, 14 June 2000.

[648] Trade Policy Review of the European Communities of 12–14 July 2000, Minutes of the Meeting, WT/TPR/M/72, 26 October 2000.

[649] Trade Policy Review of the European Communities of 12–14 July 2000, Written questions and answers, WT/TPR/M/72/Add. 1, 26 October 2000.

> certain agricultural products. Under the quarantine measures, Japan required that the efficacy of a particular quarantine treatment be established for each variety of specific agricultural products before the import of the product was allowed. The United States considered this requirement tantamount to a violation of Articles 2, 5, 7, and 8 of the SPS Agreement, of Article XI of the GATT (1994) and of Article 4 of the Agreement on Agriculture.[650]

The Japanese TPR of April 1995 seemed incapable of fully predicting the issue.[651] Nevertheless, the reports by the Secretariat and the government as well as the TPRB meeting all sketch some of the situational contours which later led to the dispute. The Secretariat's report's section on fruit and vegetables provides some background and indicates that '*In general, plant quarantine is conducted according to the Plant Protection Law and, according to the authorities, is consistent with the International Plant Protection Convention (IPPC). Import bans on a total of 11 items have been lifted since 1992, at the same time, 19 fresh fruit items suspected of oriental fruit fly infestation, including pears, grapes and apples from designated countries, were added to the prohibited list in June 1993.*'[652] Similarly, the government report defensively states that '*Japan has become the largest net importer of agricultural products in the world, and its food self-sufficiency rate of 46 per cent is the lowest among the developed countries. Given these circumstances, the concerns of Japanese citizens about food security are quite high*'.[653] The United States did not seize the opportunity of the TPRB meeting to name and shame Japan into behaviour that conforms to the SPS Agreement.[654] Nevertheless, with regard to standards, Japan itself felt compelled to state that '*concerning animal or plan quarantine, however, these were not fully developed. Japan would contribute to the development of international standards and risk-assessment techniques. In addition, Japan intended to harmonize national SPS measures with international standards, according to the development of international standards. There were some cases were technical consultations had already taken place*'.[655]

A Panel was established on 18 November 1997. According to its report of October 1998, Japan had acted inconsistently with Articles 2 and 5 of the SPS Agreement and Annex B and, consequently, with Article 7 of the SPS Agreement.[656]

[650] WTO, *Japan—Measures Affecting Agricultural Products—Report of the Panel* (27 October 1998) WT/DS76/R; WTO, *Japan—Measures Affecting Agricultural Products—Appellate Body Report* (22 February 1999) WT/DS76/AB/R.

[651] Trade Policy Review of Japan of 4–5 April 1995, Vol II (Document on file with the author).

[652] Trade Policy Review of Japan of 4–5 April 1995, Vol I, 97–157 (particularly at 116–18) (Document on file with the author).

[653] Trade Policy Review of Japan of 4–5 April 1995, Vol II, 13–44 (particularly at 13 and 22) (Document on file with the author).

[654] Trade Policy Review of Japan of 4–5 April 1995, Vol II, 69–70, 76, 78, 79, 83–84, and 86–87 (Document on file with the author).

[655] Trade Policy Review of Japan of 4–5 April 1995, Vol II, 80 (Document on file with the author).

[656] WTO, *Japan—Measures Affecting Agricultural Products—Report of the Panel* (27 October 1998) WT/DS76/R.

The Japanese TPR of January 1998 identifies the trade concerns but its TPRB meeting was barely used in an attempt to name and shame Japan.[657] The Secretariat's report documents the dispute in its *Annex II, Trade disputes and consultations: cases under GAT and WTO provisions, January 1995–July 199.*[658] In addition, it contains a sub-section on standards and regulations, sanitary and phytosanitary procedures which states that '*on (mandatory) regulations and (voluntary) standards, comprising both technical and sanitary-related measures, Japan seeks to coordinate domestic measures with international norms*' and which emphasizes, in the framework of its discussion with regard to SPS procedures, that the '*US requested bilateral consultations pursuant to GATT Article XXIII on nullification or impairment*'.[659] The Secretariat's sectional analysis of agriculture, forestry, and fisheries, however, remains silent on the subject.[660] Similarly and unsurprisingly, the government report abstains from referring to the topic.[661] During the TPRB meeting, the United States did not explicitly raise the dispute but noted nevertheless that '*while some progress had been made in the area of customs clearance times and sanitary inspection procedures, these remained quite high by developed-country standards*'.[662] Nonetheless, Japan itself felt again obliged to emphasize that '*testing by variety of fruit and vegetable was a delicate question. Japan believed that this testing was in conformity with the SPS agreement as was the case for the more general questions on phytosanitary procedures regarding fruit and vegetables. The procedure related to imports of plants was made public: normally, imports of fresh fruit or vegetables did not require inspection at the time of exportation by exporting countries*'.[663]

Further to an appeal by Japan, the Appellate Body deemed Japan's varietal testing of apples, cherries, nectarines, and walnuts to be inconsistent with the requirements of the SPS Agreement.[664] The parties subsequently agreed on a reasonable period of time for the implementation of the recommendations of the DSB. As a result of this agreement, Japan would abolish the varietal testing requirement as well as its 'Experimental Guide' from 31 December 1999.[665] Furthermore, in early 2000,

[657] Trade Policy Review of Japan of 28–29 January 1998, Minutes of the Meeting, WT/TPR/M/32, 8 June 1998.

[658] Trade Policy Review of Japan of 28–28 January 1998, Secretariat Report, WT/TPR/S/32, 5 January 1998, 33–37 (particularly at 34).

[659] Trade Policy Review of Japan of 28–29 January 1998, Secretariat Report, WT/TPR/S/32, 5 January 1998, 37 and 53–58.

[660] Trade Policy Review of Japan of 28–29 January 1998, Secretariat Report, WT/TPR/S/32, 5 January 1998, 88–103.

[661] Trade Policy Review of Japan of 28–29 January 1998, Government Report, WT/TPR/G/32, 5 January 1998.

[662] Trade Policy Review of Japan of 28–29 January 1998, Minutes of the Meeting, WT/TPR/M/32, 8 June 1998, 22–24, 28–29, 33, 35, and 37 (particularly at 23).

[663] Trade Policy Review of Japan of 28–29 January 1998, Minutes of the meeting, WT/TPR/M/32, 8 June 1998, 31.

[664] WTO, *Japan—Measures Affecting Agricultural Products—Appellate Body Report* (22 February 1999) WT/DS76/AB/R.

[665] WTO, *Japan—Measures Affecting Agricultural Products—Agreement under Article 21.3.b of the DSU* (18 June 1999) WT/DS76/9, 1.

Japan initiated consultations with the United States regarding a new Japanese quarantine methodology for products that were subject to import prohibitions because they were considered to be hosts of codling moth.[666]

The Japanese TPR of November 2000 thus devotes a substantial amount of analysis and naming and shaming with regard to the problem, both in the Secretariat's report and in the framework of the TPRB meeting.[667] The Secretariat's reporting on the issue is, as usual, contained in its sub-sectional reporting on standards and SPS measures[668] which dryly details recent developments in Japanese plant and animal quarantine arrangements and explicitly refers to the DSB case. In this context, the sub-section '*on 31 December 1999, Japan announced the immediate abolition of the varietal testing requirement that was in force for eight products, in accordance with the rulings and recommendations adopted by the DSB; Japan has been conducting consultations with the US regarding a new quarantine methodology for the eight products, which are currently subject to import prohibition on the grounds that they are hosts of codling moth*'. In line with its earlier practice, the Secretariat's section analysing agriculture[669] remains silent on the topic, as does the Japanese government's report.[670] Nevertheless, in the framework of the TPRB meeting, the United States conveyed some positive signals when it '*welcomed the measures undertaken to increase the transparency of Japan's regulatory regime*' but was critical in stating that '*the use of administrative guidance made the operation of significant parts of Japan's trade policy non-transparent*'.[671] The United States did not table any further written questions on the topic.[672] Nonetheless, Japan rebutted all arguments and answered that its '*SPS measures were applied only to the extent necessary for the protection of human, animal or plant life or health, in full consistency with the SPS agreement based on scientific principles. Under the Japanese plant protection system, quarantine pests were defined as those liable to cause damage to economic plants if they were to spread, and which met either of the following conditions: those which were not confirmed existing in Japan, or those which were already present in some part of Japan, but for which official controls were undertaken. This definition was based on the standards provided by the International Plant Protection Convention. Under the Plant Protection Law, the importation of plants that served as hosts for pests, such as the Mediterranean fruit fly and Tobacco blue mould were prohibited. Such a quarantine measure was based on scientific evidence*

[666] WTO, *Japan—Measures Affecting Agricultural Products—Communication from Japan* (13 January 2000) WT/DS76/10.

[667] Trade Policy Review of Japan, Minutes of the Meeting of 14–16 November 2000, WT/TPR/M/76, 1 February 2001.

[668] Trade Policy Review of Japan of 14–16 November 2000, Secretariat Report, WT/TPR/S/76, 17 October 2000, 54–57.

[669] Trade Policy Review of Japan of 14–16 November 2000, Secretariat Report, WT/TPR/S/76, 17 October 2000, 81–87.

[670] Trade Policy Review of Japan of 14–16 November 2000, Government Report, WT/TPR/G/76, 17 October 2000.

[671] Trade Policy Review of Japan of 14–16 November 2000, Minutes of the Meeting, WT/TPR/M/76, 1 February 2001, 18 and 31.

[672] Trade Policy Review of Japan of 14–16 November 2000, Written questions and answers, WT/TPR/M/76/Add.1, 13 February 2001.

and was consistent with the WTO/SPS agreement. At the same time, Japan approved the importation of these prohibited plants on the condition that the exporting country had developed an effective method to prevent the invasion of such pests. If a country had a specific request for lifting an import ban, Japan was ready to discuss it from a technical viewpoint.'

Japan stated that '*for the sake of transparency, Japan translated into English the requirements and procedures for lifting the import ban and this was distributed to the various countries' embassies in Tokyo. Japan also provided information on import-prohibited pests and diseases. Furthermore, Japan was prepared to explain at length the details of such requirements, upon request*'. It indicated in addition that '*with regard to plant quarantine, the number of requests for lifting the import ban was increasing. The Standard Examination Procedures regarding Requests for the Lifting of the Import Ban on Plant Quarantine were determined by the Agricultural Minister in September 1999 and were published in the Tsusho Koho, as well as on the MAFF website. The current status of the examination of such requests had also been published in the Tsuho Koho*'.[673]

On 23 August 2001, the parties to the dispute notified the DSB that they had reached a mutually satisfactory solution with respect to the conditions for lifting import prohibitions on the fruits at issue.[674]

The Japanese TPR of (November) 2002 touches on the issue conclusively. The Secretariat's report's sub-section on standards, and sanitary and phytosanitary measures[675] refers to the dispute briefly while noting that '*in a previous dispute between Japan and the US on import quarantine measures on eight products, including apples, the two countries reached agreement on the new quarantine methodologies in August 2001*'.[676] In line with its earlier practice, however, the Secretariat's report's section on agriculture remains silent about the problem.[677] The same is true with regard to the Japanese government's report.[678] Moreover, during the meeting of the TPRB, the United States no longer explicitly referred to the dispute. Nevertheless, it stated in more general terms that it '*was concerned with Japan's use of non-science-based import restrictive measures, affecting the importation of a broad range of agricultural products, and expected Japan to fulfil its obligations under the WTO SPS agreement and employ only the least trade-restrictive sanitary and phytosanitary measures.*'[679] Moreover, the United States tabled further detailed

[673] Trade Policy Review of Japan of 14–16 November 2000, Minutes of the Meeting, WT/TPR/M/76, 1 February 2001, 33.

[674] WTO, *Japan—Measures Affecting Agricultural Products—Communication from Japan and the United States* (30 August 2001) WT/DS76/12, 1.

[675] Trade Policy Review of Japan of 6–8 November 2002, Secretariat Report, WT/TPR/S/107, 9 October 2002, 38–42.

[676] Trade Policy Review of Japan of 6–8 November 2002, Secretariat Report, WT/TPR/S/107, 9 October 2002, 38–42.

[677] Trade Policy Review of Japan of 6–8 November 2002, Secretariat Report, WT/TPR/S/107, 9 October 2002, 54–59.

[678] Trade Policy Review of Japan of 6–8 November 2002, Government Report, WT/TPR/G/107, 9 October 2002.

[679] Trade Policy Review of Japan of 6–8 November 2002, Minutes of the Meeting, WT/TPR/M/107, 4 February 2003, 15 and 22.

written questions and answers with regard to Japan's pest treatment and implementation.[680] Japan rebuffed these comments and answered that '*There had been increasing requests from Japanese consumers to ensure food safety, and to prevent the introduction of pests and infectious diseases from overseas. It was the Government's responsibility to respond to these concerns. Japan's sanitary and phytosanitary measures had been pursued on a scientific basis. Japan constantly ensured that these measures remained at an appropriate level for the protection of human, animal or plant life or health, in conformity with the SPS Agreement. Considering these factors, it was not appropriate to criticize Japan's SPS measures as unjustifiable or excessively restrictive.*'[681] Japan emphasized that it '*was in full agreement with the discussant's statement about balance. There should be balance between protecting consumers as well as human, animal and plant health, and finding a reasonable and appropriate level of protection.*' It noted furthermore that '*Japan was on many fronts a disease/pest-free country, and the introduction of infectious disease or pest, through insufficient quarantine measures, would severely damage the Japanese industry. Once this damage was done it was difficult to recover, and recovery to the previous level of safety was slow. Furthermore, the government was faced with growing public awareness about the safety of the food and the recovery of consumer confidence was even more difficult than the recovery of the material damage to the industry. SPS issues were highly technical in nature and differed from one product to another, or one pest to another. A full, satisfactory response to some of the concerns expressed on SPS-related issues could only be provided through consultations at expert level, including the question of the scientific basis upon which Japan's experts were acting. Japan was prepared to enter into any bilateral consultations at expert level.*'[682]

- In *EC—Measures Affecting Asbestos and Asbestos-Containing Products*, Canada took issue with a French Decree of 24 December 1996, with respect to the prohibition of asbestos and products containing asbestos, including a ban on the import of such goods. Although the Decree foresaw a general interdiction, its Article 2 set out a temporary exception for asbestos chrysotile fibres subject to the fulfilment of certain conditions (including the requirement that no less health-hazardous substitutes were available and that the technical safety guarantees required for the product's ultimate purpose were fulfilled). Canada—which was one of the few remaining asbestos producers and exporters—maintained that chrysotile asbestos was safe in circumstances of properly controlled use (as France itself permitted the use of domestically produced asbestos for certain purposes) and should therefore not be banned outright.[683] According to

[680] Trade Policy Review of Japan, Written questions and answers, WT/TPR/M/107/Add. 1, 6–8 November 2002, 136–52 (Document on file with the author).

[681] Trade Policy Review of Japan of 6–8 November 2002, Minutes of the Meeting, WT/TPR/M/107, 4 February 2003, 21.

[682] Trade Policy Review of Japan of 6–8 November 2002, Minutes of the Meeting, WT/TPR/M/107, 4 February 2003, 23.

[683] Mary Footer and Saman Zia-Zarifi, 'Case Notes—European Communities—Measures Affecting Asbestos and Asbestos-Containing Products, The World Trade Organization on Trial for its Handling of Occupational Health and Safety Issues' (2002) 3(1) Melbourne Journal of International Law

Canada, the French measures therefore amounted to a violation of Articles 2, 3, and 5 of the SPS Agreement, of Article 2 of the TBT Agreement and of Articles III, XI, and XIII of the GATT (1994).[684]

The TPR of the European Union of November 1997 did not explicitly raise the topic.[685] Neither the Secretariat's[686] nor the extremely short government's report identify the issue.[687] Moreover, Canada did not raise the issue during the TPRB meeting.[688] Nevertheless, the European Union itself seemed indirectly to hint at the future problem when it stated that '*In certain cases, Member states could set supplementary requirements for products produced on their own territories but these were not applied to products from other countries. In the framework of regulations for protection of the environment and workplace safety, Member states often set supplementary requirements to those set out in the EU legislation, thus risking the creation of problems for free circulation within the Community market. In such cases, the Community's task was to ensure the removal of such divergences through, for example, the introduction of supplementary regulations.*'[689]

The European Communities' TPR of July 2000 took place after the formal establishment of the DSB's Panel in the asbestos case but before the Panel's circulation of its report.[690] The trade dispute was therefore clearly on the TPR's radar. Secretariat's gist of reporting on the issue is contained in the sub-sectional on prohibitions, restrictions, and licensing requirements which emphasizes that '*in 1999, the EU banned, as from 2005, remaining uses of chrysotile asbestos, invoking the fact that all forms of asbestos are proven carcinogens, and following the bans introduced to some degree by nine of the 15 Member states; five of the six types of asbestos had already been banned in the EU in 1991*'.[691] Moreover, the government report surprisingly touches on the issue, albeit in general terms, while noting that '*the most*

120–42 (hereafter Footer and Zia-Zarifi, 'Case Notes —European Communities—Measures Affecting Asbestos and Asbestos-Containing Products, The World Trade Organization on Trial for its Handling of Occupational Health and Safety Issues').

684 WTO, *EC—Measures Affecting Asbestos and Asbestos-Containing Products—Report of the Panel* (18 September 2000) WT/DS135/R; WTO, *EC—Measures Affecting Asbestos and Asbestos-Containing Products—Appellate Body Report* (12 March 2001) WT/DS135/AB/R; Jochem Wiers, 'Responsible Decision-makers, Do It Yourself: The Panel Report in the Asbestos Case' (2001) 28(1) 117–26.

685 Trade Policy Review of the European Union of 25–26 November 1997, Minutes of the Meeting, WT/TPR/M/30, 26 January 1998.

686 Trade Policy Review of the European Union of 25–26 November 1997, Secretariat Report, WT/TPR/S/30, 20 October 1997, 48–51 and 62–68; Neither is it identified in Secretariat's (sub-sectional) analysis of Manufacturing; Trade Policy Review of the European Union of 25–26 November 1997, Secretariat Report, WT/TPR/S/30, 20 October 1997, 92–106.

687 Trade Policy Review of the European Union of 25–26 November 1997, Government Report, WT/TPR/G/30.

688 Trade Policy Review of the European Union of 25–26 November 1997, Minutes of the Meeting, WT/TPR/M/30, 26 January 1998.

689 Trade Policy Review of the European Union of 25–26 November 1997, Minutes of the Meeting, WT/TPR/M/30, 26 January 1998.

690 Trade Policy Review of the European Communities of 12–14 July 2000, Minutes of the Meeting, WT/TPR/M/72, 26 October 2000.

691 Trade Policy Review of the European Communities of 12–14 July 2000, Secretariat Report, WT/TPR/S/72, 14 June 2000, 51; The sub-section on Developments in selected manufacturing industries

important among the few cases in which the EU was the defendant touched upon the increasingly important issues of the protection of human health. In both ... the asbestos cases, the WTO is called to strike a balance between the sovereign right of Members to seek protection of the health of their population on the one hand, and the protection of the negotiated rights of third countries on the other hand. Despite the real difficulties that the EU is encountering in relation to the implementation of the ... asbestos cases, the EU rests fully committed to implementing the Panels as soon as possible'.[692] During the TPRB meeting, Canada only raised some general issues. In this regard, it noted that the area of the SPS and TBT agreements '*required for further international co-operation to address the different approaches of WTO Members in order to avoid further high-profile disputes that could potentially damage the integrity of the multilateral trading system*' and stated that '*the appropriate manner to address concerns of this nature ... was to develop a rigorous, science-based regulatory response to potential health and environmental threats. Good governance demanded a rational science-based approach to risk assessment and management, and courage would at times be required by lawmakers and officials in the face of misinformed public opinion.*'[693] Nevertheless, it did not table any specific written questions with regard to the ongoing asbestos case.[694]

The Panel report, circulated on 18 September 2000, considered that the French Decree violated Article III:4 of the GATT 1994 but was justified under Article XX(b) of the GATT (1994).[695] Moreover, further to appeal by Canada, the Appellate Body confirmed that the French Decree had not been shown to be WTO-inconsistent.[696]

The TPR of the European Union of July 2002 again put its finger on the issue.[697] The Secretariat's sub-sectional analysis on prohibitions, restrictions, surveillance, and licensing requirements indicates that '*the ban on remaining chrysotyle asbestos, which had been noted in the last review of the EU and which is to be made effective by 2005, was unsuccessfully challenged by Canada under the WTO dispute settlement procedures*'.[698] The government report of the European Union therefore proudly declares that '*the EU would like to underscore the results of the asbestos case (DS 135) which*

does not touch on the subject since it did not look into the sector mainly affected by the use of asbestos; Trade Policy Review of the European Communities of 12–14 July 2000, Secretariat Report, WT/TPR/S/72, 14 June 2000, 99–114.

[692] Trade Policy Review of the European Communities of 12–14 July 2000, Government Report, WT/TPR/G/72, 14 June 2000, 8.

[693] Trade Policy Review of the European Communities of 12–14 July 2000, Minutes of the Meeting, WT/TPR/M/72, 26 October 2000, 9.

[694] Trade Policy Review of the European Communities of 12–14 July 2000, Written questions and answers, WT/TPR/M/72/Add. 1, 26 October 2000, 81–88.

[695] WTO, *EC—Measures Affecting Asbestos and Asbestos-Containing Products—Report of the Panel* (18 September 2000) WT/DS135/R.

[696] WTO, *EC—Measures Affecting Asbestos and Asbestos-Containing Products—Appellate Body Report* (12 March 2000) WT/DS135/AB/R.

[697] Trade Policy Review of the European Communities of 24–26 July 2002, Minutes of the Meeting, WT/TPR/M/102, 23 September 2002.

[698] Trade Policy Review of the European Communities of 24–26 July 2002, Secretariat Report, WT/TPR/S/102, 26 June 2002, 31–36 (particularly at 32).

reaffirmed that health protection can be set as an overriding goal of public policy'.[699] Unsurprisingly, Canada didn't raise the issue any further in the TPRB meeting.[700] Nevertheless, it tabled some further written questions with regard to the topic.[701]

- In *EC—Protection of Trademarks and Geographical Indications for Agricultural Products and Foodstuffs*, the United States and Australia took issue with the amended EC Regulation 2081/92 which allegedly did not provide national treatment with respect to geographical indications and which, according to the complainants, did not provide sufficient protection to pre-existing trademarks which were similar or identical to geographical indications.[702] The United States considered this situation therefore to be in violation of Articles 3, 16, 14, 63, and 65 of the TRIPS Agreement. Likewise, Australia claimed that the EC's position appeared to be inconsistent with the EC's obligations pursuant to Articles I and III of the GATT (1994), Articles 1, 2, 3, 4, 16, 20, 22, 24, 41, 42, 63, and 65 of the TRIPS Agreement, Article 2 of the TBT Agreement and Article XVI:4 of the WTO Agreement.[703]

The TPR of the European Union of November 1997 remains almost silent on the problem.[704] The Secretariat's report's sub-section on intellectual property protection merely lists EC Regulation 2081/92 which resulted in the dispute.[705] Furthermore, in line with its earlier practice, Secretariat's sectional analysis of developments in agriculture remains entirely silent on the issue.[706] In a similar vein, the extremely short government report does not refer to the issue.[707] During the TPRB meeting, Australia did not raise the problem[708] whereas the United States only stated

[699] Trade Policy Review of the European Communities of 24–26 July 2002, Government Report, WT/TPR/G/102, 26 June 2002, 129–45 (particularly at 135).

[700] Trade Policy Review of the European Communities of 24–26 July 2002, Minutes of the Meeting, WT/TPR/M/102, 23 September 2002, 64–66.

[701] Trade Policy Review of the European Communities of 24–26 July 2002, Written questions and answers, WT/TPR/M/102/Add.1, 31 March 2003, 45.

[702] WTO, *EC—Protection of Trademarks and Geographical Indications for Agricultural Products and Foodstuffs—Report of the Panel* (15 March 2005) WT/DS174/R; WTO, *EC—Protection of Trademarks and Geographical Indications for Agricultural Products and Foodstuffs—Report of the Panel* (15 March 2005) WT/DS290/R; Dev Gangjee, 'Quibbling siblings: Conflicts between Trademarks and Geographical Indications' (2007) 82(3) Chicago-Kent Law Review 1276 (hereafter Gangjee, 'Quibbling siblings: Conflicts between Trademarks and Geographical Indications').

[703] WTO, *EC—Protection of Trademarks and Geographical Indications for Agricultural Products and Foodstuffs—Report of the Panel* (15 March 2005) WT/DS174/R; WTO, *EC—Protection of Trademarks and Geographical Indications for Agricultural Products and Foodstuffs—Report of the Panel* (15 March 2005) WT/DS290/R.

[704] Trade Policy Review of the European Union of 25–26 November 1997, Minutes of the Meeting, WT/TPR/M/30, 26 January 1998.

[705] Trade Policy Review of the European Union of 25–26 November 1997, Secretariat Report, WT/TPR/S/30, 20 October 1997, 78–82 (particularly at 81).

[706] Trade Policy Review of the European Union of 25–26 November 1997, Secretariat Report, WT/TPR/S/30, 20 October 1997, 82–92.

[707] Trade Policy Review of the European Union of 25–26 November 1997, Government Report, WT/TPR/G/30, 20 October 1997.

[708] Trade Policy Review of the European Union of 25–26 November 1997, Minutes of the Meeting, WT/TPR/M/30, 26 January 1998.

in very general terms that '*further clarification was sought from the EU on issues such as ... intellectual property right*'.[709]

The Secretariat and government reports for the TPR of the European Communities of July 2000 barely tackle the topic.[710] Although the Secretariat's sub-section on intellectual property rights protection[711] succinctly states that '*Member states register and enforce the protection of geographical indications for products of Community manufacture, subject to the requirements of Community instruments on the matter*', neither this sub-section nor the section on agriculture further explain the problem at hand.[712] In a similar vein, the government report remains completely silent on the subject.[713] Nonetheless, during the meeting of the TPRB, Australia stated that it '*recognized the legitimate public policy concerns surrounding the food safety issue in the EU, but would be concerned if addressing these issues led to the introduction of new complexities in the world agricultural trading environment or the replacement of one set of restrictive measures with another. Australia also placed a high priority on the issues of bio- and food safety, but was equally concerned that a dilution of the scientific input to decision-making on the acceptability of products or the insertion of non-trade concerns could run counter to the overall objective of liberalization*'.[714] Furthermore, the United States requested and obtained extensive written information with regard to the protection of geographical indications and issues of food safety.[715]

The Secretariat and government reports of the TPR of the European Communities of July 2002 do not directly refer to the trade concerns which led to the dispute.[716] However, they both point to the lack of broader WTO negotiations which could have solved the issue. The gist of the Secretariat's reporting on the issue is contained in the report's sub-section on the protection of intellectual property rights which indicates that '*In the TRIPS council, the EU has sought establishment of a multilateral system for the notification and registration of geographical indications for wines and spirits, in accordance with Article 23.4 of the TIRPS agreement, with a possible extension to other products (eg cheese). The Doha Ministerial Declaration provides for the negotiation of*

[709] Trade Policy Review of the European Union of 25–26 November 1997, Minutes of the Meeting, WT/TPR/M/30, 26 January 1998, 11.

[710] Trade Policy Review of the European Communities of 12–14 July 2000, Minutes of the Meeting, WT/TPR/M/72, 26 October 2000.

[711] Trade Policy Review of the European Communities of 12–14 July 2000, Secretariat Report, WT/TPR/S/72, 14 June 2000, 83–88.

[712] Trade Policy Review of the European Communities of 12–14 July 2000, Secretariat Report, WT/TPR/S/72, 14 June 2000, 89–99.

[713] Trade Policy Review of the European Communities of 12–14 July 2000, Government Report, WT/TPR/G/72, 14 June 2000.

[714] Trade Policy Review of the European Communities of 12–14 July 2000, Minutes of the Meeting, WT/TPR/M/72, 26 October 2000, 18.

[715] Trade Policy Review of the European Communities of 12–14 July 2000, Written questions and answers, WT/TPR/M/72/Add. 1, 26 October 2000, 10–11.

[716] Trade Policy Review of the European Communities of 24–26 July 2002, Minutes of the Meeting, WT/TPR/M/102, 23 September 2002.

a system of wines and spirits, while the TRIPS council could take up the issue of other products.'[717]

Nevertheless, the Secretariat's section on agriculture remains silent on the topic,[718] as does the government report. The report repeats nonetheless that 'the Doha declaration contains a clear provision that negotiations on multilateral register will have to be completed by the Fifth WTO Ministerial Conference and refers also to the TRIPS mandate for negotiations on extension of the coverage of geographical indications for the benefit of business and consumers around the world'.[719] Contrary to the Secretariat's and the government's reports, both of which lack any specific reference to the dispute, the complainants in the case (ie Australia and the United States) seized the opportunity of the TPRB meeting to hint at the issue at hand. In this respect, Australia emphasized that '*[t]he EU was also advancing the notion that market access would be based on intellectual property rights, which they would unilaterally determine as owned by EC producers*' and pointed out that '*Australia was concerned with a growing trend in the EU to impose its own rules and regulations on other Members, often in a way that raised real questions of WTO consistency. It viewed European intentions cautiously in areas such as geographical indications, especially when Members were forced to contend at short notice with overly burdensome technical standards, such as wine regulations recently notified by the EU. Australia had serious concerns about the systemic WTO implications of the adoption of regulations seeking to protect domestic producers from competition through labeling requirements and unilateral declarations about intellectual property.*'[720] In a similar vein, the United States lamented that '*In the area of intellectual property protection, the US and the EU had many of the same objectives in the WTO as well as in individual third-country markets. However, the US was again submitting several questions on the operation of the regime for regulating geographic indications on the EU market. It was concerned that foreign persons wishing to obtain protection for their geographical indications faced a non-transparent process that appeared to conflict with the EU's TRIPS obligations.*'[721]

The European Union simply rebuffed the comments by stating that '*since protection of GIs [geographical indications] was recognized in the TRIPS agreement as legitimate, it was not a disguised trade barrier*'.[722] Nevertheless, Australia seized the

[717] Trade Policy Review of the European Communities of 24–26 July 2002, Secretariat Report, WT/TPR/S/102, 26 June 2002, 26–69 (particularly at 63–69).

[718] Trade Policy Review of the European Communities of 24–26 July 2002, Secretariat Report, WT/TPR/S/102, 26 June 2002, 69–77.

[719] Trade Policy Review of the European Communities of 24–26 July 2002, Government Report, WT/TPR/G/102, 26 June 2002, 13.

[720] Trade Policy Review of the European Communities of 24–26 July 2002, Minutes of the Meeting, WT/TPR/M/102, 23 September 2002, 21–22.

[721] Trade Policy Review of the European Communities of 24–26 July 2002, Minutes of the Meeting, WT/TPR/M/102, 23 September 2002, 25.

[722] Trade Policy Review of the European Communities of 24–26 July 2002, Minutes of the Meeting, WT/TPR/M/102, 23 September 2002, 49.

opportunity to table written questions to obtain further information on the topic at hand.[723]

On 4 April 2003, the United States sent an additional request for consultations concerning EC Regulation 2081/92 and its implementing and enforcement measures. This second request for consultations supplemented the 1999 request. The United States was of the opinion that the EC Regulation limited the GIs which the EC would protect and that it also limited the access of nationals of other Members to the EC's GI procedures and protections provided under the Regulation. The United States therefore considered the amended EC Regulation and its implementing and enforcement measures to be in violation of Articles 2, 3, 4, 16, 22, 24, 63, and 65 of the TRIPS Agreement and of Articles I and III:4 of the GATT (1994).[724] On 2 October 2003, a single Panel was established for the two cases. Nonetheless, due to the complexity of the (joint) cases, the Chairman of the Panel informed the DSB on 17 August 2004 that it would not be able to complete its work within six months.[725]

The topic was extensively covered in the Secretariat's and government's reporting for the TPR of the European Communities of October 2004. The Secretariat's subsectional analysis of the European Intellectual Property rights protection tackles the issue in great detail.[726] Somewhat pedagogically, it explains the institutional mechanism behind its GI protection while stating that '*Community-wide rules exist for the protection of geographical designation of origin and indication (GI) for agricultural products and foodstuffs, wines, and spirits. For agricultural products and foodstuffs, there is a Community-wide system of examination and registration. Associations of producers and/or processors working with the same agricultural product or foodstuff, or other natural or legal persons, under certain conditions, are entitled to apply for registration for an EU-wide GI. The application for registration is to be sent either to the relevant Member state, for GIs of products of EC origin, or to the authorities in the country in which the geographical area is located, for GIs of products of non-EC origin. If the EC Member state or the relevant authority in the third country considers that the application meets the requirements for registration, they transmit it to the European Commission, which verifies whether the conditions are met. The application requires a specification containing the name and description of the product; the definition of the geographical area; the methods of preparation; factors relating to the geographic area; the inspection bodies; details of labelling, and any other legislative requirement. If the Commission is satisfied with the application, it publishes its positive conclusions in the Official Journal of the EC and, if no objections are raised (by interested parties from the EU or third countries) within three*

[723] Trade Policy Review of the European Communities of 24–26 July 2002, Written questions, WT/TPR/M/102/Add.2, 31 March 2003, 158–60.

[724] WTO, *EC—Protection of Trademarks and Geographical Indications for Agricultural Products and Foodstuffs—Request for Consultations by the United States—Addendum* (10 April 2003) WT/DS174/1/Add.1, 1.

[725] WTO, *EC—Protection of Trademarks and Geographical Indications for Agricultural Products and Foodstuffs—Communication from the Chairman of the Panel* (19 August 2004) WT/DS174/22, 1.

[726] Trade Policy Review of the European Communities of 25–27 October 2004, Secretariat Report, WT/TPR/S/136, 23 June 2004, 78–83.

months of publication, the product is entered in the Community's register. The Commission examines any objections before taking a decision whether to grant the GI. For wines and spirits, the role of the Commission is less important. Community legislation establishes the general level of protection, leaving responsibility for control and protection of the relevant GIs with Member states. Once communicated to the Commission and published, GIs enjoy EC-wide protection.'

The European Communities then explained some recent modifications to its institutional regime while indicating that '*During the period under review, amendments were made to the regulation establishing common rules on the protection of geographical indications and designations of origin for agricultural products and foodstuffs. The amendments include: changes to the scope of the regulation (inclusion of wine vinegar and removal of mineral water); extension of the list of products covered by Annex I (foodstuffs) and Annex II (agricultural products); empowering the Commission to impose conditions requiring that packaging takes place in the limited geographical area when justified on grounds of safeguarding quality, traceability, and control; and granting WTO Members the right of objection to the registration of EC GIs. Other amendments include provisions for regulating cases where geographical names are entirely or partially homonymous; and rights that have been acquired through use. During the period under review, EC Member states also cleared a short-list of 41 EC regional quality products whose name the EC seeks to recuperate under the on-going multilateral trade negotiations on agriculture. The list is expected to be updated with GIs from the new Member states.*' Nevertheless, in line with its earlier practice, the Secretariat report's section on agriculture does not cover the issue.[727] The same is true with regard to the government report.[728] In its section on the EC and the WTO, the report nevertheless indicates that '*The EC's approach to the multilateral trade negotiations has been to complement further market opening with stronger rules and disciplines. One important subject that combines market-access and rule-making is that of geographical indications. The EC has been at the forefront of efforts to complete negotiations on a multilateral register and the extension of the coverage of geographical indications for the benefit of business and consumers around the world. These efforts have been met by an increasing number of friends of geographical indications. Regrettably some trading partners have refused to engage seriously in this negotiation. The EC has also participated actively in the examination of the relationship between the TRIPS-agreement, the Convention on Biological Diversity and protection of traditional knowledge, reflecting a commitment to developing countries' interests in this area.*'[729]

Australia and the United States therefore extensively seized the TPRB meeting and its written questions in an attempt to name the European Union and

[727] Trade Policy Review of the European Communities of 25–27 October 2004, Secretariat Report, WT/TPR/S/136, 23 January 2004, 85–100.

[728] Trade Policy Review of the European Communities of 25–27 October 2004, Government Report, WT/TPR/G/136, 1 October 2004.

[729] Trade Policy Review of the European Communities of 25–27 October 2004, Government Report, WT/TPR/G/136, 1 October 2004, 12–15.

shame it into behaving more consistently with WTO rules. They both referred to the general setting of GIs but also to the specificity of the ongoing DSB case. In this regard, Australia stated that '*the EC supported GIs, and offered subsidies to their owners to promote them, but it appeared money had been spent. The representative wondered when was the last time that anyone had heard of a government offering money that was not taken up*.'[730] The EC rebuffed this initial remark and stated that '*export credit was provided by the Member states and was not under EC competence*'.[731] Unabated, Australia continued to put pressure on the European Union by emphasizing that it '*had no fundamental difficulty in the EC's approach in terms of protecting intellectual property rights, but it was concerned about how their regulations were applied to third countries. When the TRIPs agreement was adopted, all Members agreed to the principle of territoriality. But, the EC was seeking to export its particular highly regulatory, very burdensome, and bureaucratic approach to the protection of geographical indications (GIs). GIs had become a contentious topic in WTO. More work was needed on whether there was any benefit to be gained from GIs*'. Australia emphasized moreover that '*Within the WTO, the EC sought to increase the protection for all products to the level of protection now accorded to wines and spirits under the TRIPS. The EC also wanted to create this very bureaucratic multilateral register for all GIs to be put on, and to claw back on a number of terms. What it amounted to was a fundamental rewrite of the TRIPS agreement; there was no mandate in the Doha negotiations to do this, though there was a mandate to negotiate on a multilateral register of GIs in the area of wines and spirits. Rewriting the TRIPS agreement was not wise, particularly after having made a decision on the Singapore issues. The representative asked why new issues should be brought in*.' Furthermore, Australia explicitly pointed to the fact that '*A couple of countries had challenged the EC in a dispute examined by a Panel that, even in its own policy, it had discriminated against third countries, and that it was in breach of observing the TRIPS provisions relating to GI's and trademarks. Australia was worried about this GI's agenda because of very strong discussions within the EC Member states concerning particular names and terms. If this process was replicated internationally, the smaller opponent would not win the argument*.'[732] The United States referred to its advance questions with regard to the protection of geographical indications in the EC for non-EC nationals in agricultural products as well as wine and spirits. In this regard, it noted therefore that '*a European Council regulation appeared to require, as a condition for protecting the geographical indications of another WTO Member, that this Member offered equivalent protection to EC products. The US wished to learn how the EC squared that requirement with the*

[730] Trade Policy Review of the European Communities of 25–27 October 2004, Minutes of the Meeting, WT/TPR/M/136, 18 January 2005, 16–18, 32–33, and 35.

[731] Trade Policy Review of the European Communities of 25–27 October 2004, Minutes of the Meeting, WT/TPR/M/136, 18 January 2005, 33.

[732] Trade Policy Review of the European Communities of 25–27 October 2004, Minutes of the Meeting, WT/TPR/M/136, 18 January 2005, 35 and 37.

national treatment obligation under TRIPS.'[733] Nevertheless, the EC dodged the question by answering that '*For other agricultural products and foodstuffs, a 1992 EC regulation had created a framework for its Members to register their geographical indications, and protect them within the single market. Labelling of specific origins and processing methods facilitated exporting and marketing of food products, and generated profits. This was a marketing strategy that could give great market access opportunities, in particular for developing countries. Therefore, to provide sufficient protection for such products, the EC had promoted, in the DDA, an extension of the (already) higher protection level for wines and spirits to other products, and the creation of a system of world-wide registration, first for wines and spirits, later for other products.*'[734] Both Australia and the United States tabled additional highly legal written questions with regard to the EC's protection of geographical indications.[735]

The Panel's report, which was adopted on 20 April 2005, concurred with United States' and Australian views in its consideration that the EC's GI Regulation did not provide national treatment to other WTO Members' rights holders and products.[736] The European Communities therefore stated its intention to implement the DSB's recommendations within a reasonable period of time which would expire on 3 April 2006.[737] On 17 February 2006, the European Communities announced that its new regulation on geographical indications under discussion in the Council of the European Union and the European Parliament would implement the DSB's recommendations and rulings in full.[738] Although this new regulation entered into force on 31 March 2006 (ie before the deadline of the agreed reasonable period of time), Australia and the United States voiced their disagreement about the European Communities' alleged full implementation of the DSB's recommendations and rulings. Both complainants in the case therefore invited the European Communities to revise its new regulation.[739]

As a result, the TPR of the European Union of February 2007 again put its finger on the issue.[740] The Secretariat's sub-section on intellectual property rights clearly identifies the latest developments within the context of GI protection as

[733] Trade Policy Review of the European Communities of 25–27 October 2004, Minutes of the Meeting, WT/TPR/M/136, 18 January 2005, 13.

[734] Trade Policy Review of the European Communities of 25–27 October 2004, Minutes of the Meeting, WT/TPR/M/136, 18 January 2005, 34.

[735] Trade Policy Review of the European Communities of 25–27 October 2004, Questions and answers, WT/TPR/M/136/Add. 1, 18 January 2005, 116–131 (particularly at 125–26) and 131–78 (particularly at 164–69).

[736] WTO, *EC—Protection of Trademarks and Geographical Indications for Agricultural Products and Foodstuffs—Report of the Panel* (15 March 2005) WT/DS174/R; WTO, *EC—Protection of Trademarks and Geographical Indications for Agricultural Products and Foodstuffs—Report of the Panel* (15 March 2005) WT/DS290/R.

[737] WTO, DSB, Minutes of Meeting, WT/DSB/M/189, 17 June 2005, 9.

[738] WTO, DSB, Minutes of Meeting, WT/DSB/M/205, 31 March 2006, 11.

[739] WTO, DSB, Minutes of Meeting, WT/DSB/M/205, 31 March 2006, 11–12; WTO, DSB, Minutes of Meeting, WT/DSB/M/210, 30 May 2006, 6.

[740] Trade Policy Review of the European Union of 26–28 February 2007, Minutes of the Meeting, WT/TPR/M/177, 30 April 2007.

a result of the ongoing proceedings before the DSB.[741] In this regard, the subsection comments that '*Council Regulation No. 510/2006 of 20 March 2006 repealed Council Regulation No. 2081/92 on the protection of geographical indications and designations of origin for agricultural products and foodstuffs, as a consequence of a Panel Report by the Dispute Settlement Body (DSB) on the protection of trademarks and geographical indicators by the EC. The new legislation, i.e. Council Regulation No. 510/2006, addressed the following issues: (i) clarification and simplification of the registration procedure; (ii) a better definition of responsibilities between Member states and the Commission; (iii) the need to clarify that the provisions under Council Regulation No. 2081/92 on equivalence and reciprocity did not apply to GIs corresponding to geographical areas located in other WTO Members; (iv) opening registration directly to producer groups in third countries and not through their national administration; and (v) clarifying the procedures concerning amendments to specifications, objections, or cancellation in the event of failure to respect specifications.*' Nonetheless, in line with its earlier practice, the Secretariat's analysis on agriculture and related activities remains silent on the issue.[742] The same is true with regard to the government report which unsurprisingly lacks any specific references to the DSB litigation.[743] The report nevertheless reiterates that '*geographical indications are part of the single undertaking*' and that '*the EC also supports the extension of the protection given by the register to products other than wines and spirits, and, for a limited number of well-known GIs, a prohibition of their use by others than the right holders, regardless of the exceptions provided for in Article 24 of the TRIPS Agreement.*'[744] During the meeting of the TPRB, neither Australia nor the United States referred to the issue.[745] On the other hand, the European Union itself felt obliged to state that '*geographical indications (GIs) were a means of promoting quality products and rural development, protecting producers against unfair competition, and consumers against misleading information. This was an opportunity for farmers around the world, not a restriction.*'[746] Although Australia did not table any written questions on the topic, the United States requested further information on to the subject.[747]

This analysis yields several conclusions: First, reports of the Secretariat offer excellent added value in terms of transparency. The examples cited earlier demonstrate that

[741] Trade Policy Review of the European Union of 26–28 February 2007, Secretariat Report, WT/TPR/S/177, 22 January 2007, 73–78.

[742] Trade Policy Review of the European Union of 26–28 February 2007, Secretariat Report, WT/TPR/S/177, 22 January 2007, 79–95.

[743] Trade Policy Review of the European Union of 26–28 February 2007, Government Report, WT/TPR/G/177, 22 January 2007.

[744] Trade Policy Review of the European Union of 26–28 February 2007, Government Report, WT/TPR/G/177, 22 January 2007, 12–15 (particularly at 14).

[745] Trade Policy Review of the European Union of 26–28 February 2007, Minutes of the Meeting, WT/TPR/M/177, 30 April 2007, 12 and 13–14, 26 and 29.

[746] Trade Policy Review of the European Union of 26–28 February 2007, Minutes of the Meeting, WT/TPR/M/177, 30 April 2007, 28.

[747] Trade Policy Review of the European Union of 26–28 February 2007, Written questions and answers, WT/TPR/M/177/Add. 1, 30 April 2007, 38–42 and 230, 54–65 (particularly at 61–62) and 129–31 (particularly at 130) and 275.

in most TPRs, these reports were able to point to the contours of the dispute to come. Second, reports of the government under review have minimal added value in terms of transparency. With the exception of a few cases, they were never used to refer to actual or future trade concerns. Third, in terms of naming and shaming, both TPRB meetings and written questions and answers offer clear added value, the former as a forum for some general naming and shaming, the latter as a means which sometimes enables the exchange of highly legalistic requests.

Structure of meetings

During the first years of the TPRs, the internal structure of TPRB meetings gradually improved.[748] Modifications sought to put more emphasis on dialogue and discussion and mainly concerned the preparatory stage of the TPR (improved adherence to the timetables related to the review coupled with the availability of some flexibility for smaller Members), the timing of the review meetings (confirming the existing practice of holding TPR meetings on two successive mornings), the statements in the special Council meetings (providing some guidance with regard to their length, structure, and content), the replies by the country under review, the nature of the Chairman's concluding remarks (which remained the Chairman's own responsibility and were not a negotiated text) and media relations and publication.[749]

With regard to the discussants, parties explicitly recognized that '*the role of discussants was crucial, especially in triggering the debate on the second day of a review meeting*'[750] and reiterated that '*the selection of good discussants is crucial to the success of a review*'.[751] The practice of having two independent discussants for each review and providing them with the opportunity to be rather intrusive vis-à-vis the country under review by allowing them to circulate their full statements to the country under review only just before the meeting was therefore prolonged. Nevertheless, the suggestion of broadening the range of discussants to officials from capitals, well-known academics, or other non-governmental experts was not retained.[752]

After a rather lengthy debate, the first appraisal resulted in some modifications to the structure of the TPR meetings. In this regard, it concluded that two half days were considered to be appropriate for a TPRB review with a day in between desirable. Moreover, it emphasized that '*more interactive discussion was encouraged, as was*

[748] Answers from Mr Frank Wolter (first director of the Trade Policy Review Division, 1989–1991) to a questionnaire of the author (2 April 2014).

[749] Procedures for Review Meetings, Communication from the Chairman (30 April 1993) BISD L/7208, 1–2 (hereafter Procedures for Review Meetings, Communication from the Chairman (30 April 1993)); WTO, TPRB, Procedural Improvements to the Trade Policy Review Mechanism, Note from the Chair, WT/TPR/13, 13 December 1995; WTO, TPRB, Procedural Improvements to the Trade Policy Review Mechanism, Note from the Chair, WT/TPR/20, 19 July 1996.

[750] Trade Policy Review Mechanism—Arrangements for the continued operation of the Mechanism, Decision of 10 May 1994 (11 May 1994) BISD L/7458 (hereafter Trade Policy Review Mechanism—Arrangements for the continued operation of the Mechanism, Decision of 10 May 1994).

[751] WTO, TPRB, Procedural Improvements to the Trade Policy Review Mechanism, Note from the Chair, WT/TPR/13, 13 December 1995.

[752] WTO, TPRB, Procedural Improvements to the Trade Policy Review Mechanism, Note from the Chair, WT/TPR/13, 13 December 1995; WTO, TPRB, Procedural Improvements to the Trade Policy Review Mechanism, Note from the Chair, WT/TPR/20, 19 July 1996, 2

greater participation in reviews of smaller Members'.[753] Furthermore, the appraisal process had found that '*a single discussant, rather than two, might be desirable at certain TPRB reviews, particularly for the larger traders, when a considerable number of interventions could be expected, so as to allow time for a full exchange of views between Members*'.[754] Interestingly, this view was nonetheless not retained in later stages of the review process (which favoured flexibility on the role and number of discussants)[755] or in the final document of the first appraisal.[756]

ii) Overview of developments in the International Trading Environment

The Council's Decision of April 1989 provided for the GATT Council to undertake an overview of developments in the international trading environment, assisted by an annual report of the Director-General setting out major GATT activities and highlighting significant policy issues affecting the multilateral system.[757] Although the objectives of the Council's Decision and those contained in Annex 3 to the Marrakesh Agreement are identical, the Council's Decision explained in addition that '*the enhanced surveillance thus provided would also strengthen the existing "early warning" aspect of the special meetings of the Council*' while indicating that '*it is understood that this overview by the Council, together with the trade policy review mechanism, would replace the existing reviews in special Council meetings established under paragraph 24 of the 1979 Understanding regarding Notification, Consultation, Dispute Settlement and Surveillance.*'

Overviews undertaken in the period between the formal establishment of the WTO (1995) and the end of the first appraisal of the TPRM (1999) tend to be rather positive. Nonetheless, the Overview of 1998 indicates that this positive outlook changed in 1997 and was followed by the 1998 financial crisis and its negative impact on trade.[758] Furthermore, this trend was reconfirmed by the Overview of 1999 which nonetheless also emphasized that the slowdown was halted in 1999.[759]

[753] WTO, Ministerial Conference, Third Session, Seattle 30 November–3 December 1999, Appraisal of the operation of the Trade Policy Review Mechanism, WT/MIN(99)/2, 8 October 1999, 3.

[754] Appraisal of the operation of the TPRM, Draft Report to Ministers, No 3714, 25 June 1999, 4 (Document on file with the author).

[755] Appraisal of the operation of the TPRM, Draft Report to Ministers, No 4428, 16 July 1999, 3–4 (Document on file with the author); Appraisal of the operation of the TPRM, Draft Report to Ministers, No 4921, 30 July 1999, 4 (Document on file with the author); Appraisal of the operation of the TPRM, Draft Report to Ministers, No 5282, 14 September 1999, 4 (Document on file with the author); Appraisal of the operation of the TPRM, Draft Report to Ministers, No 5439, 21 September 1999, 4 (Document on file with the author); Appraisal of the operation of the TPRM, Draft Report to Ministers, No 5545, 23 September 1999, 4 (Document on file with the author).

[756] WTO, Ministerial Conference, Third Session, Seattle 30 November–3 December 1999, Appraisal of the operation of the Trade Policy Review Mechanism, WT/MIN(99)/2, 8 October 1999, 3.

[757] General Agreement on Tariffs and Trade, 12 April 1989 Council, Matters Arising from the December 1988 and April 1989 Meetings of the Trade Negotiations Committee, Communication from the Council Chairman, C/W/585, 31 March 1989.

[758] WTO, TPRB, Overview of developments in international trade and the trading system, Annual Report by the Director-General, WT/TPR/OV/4, 30 November 1998, 1–2.

[759] WTO, TPRB, Overview of developments in international trade and the trading system, Annual Report by the Director-General, WT/TPR/OV/5, 15 October 1999, 1–2.

In spite of these critical assessments, which would result in more transparency and naming and shaming in times of crisis (especially in 1998 and 1999), the structure and coverage of the Overviews evolved in a rather different way. First, only the 1995 Overview contained a specific section dedicated to the analysis of activities undertaken within the framework of individual trade policy reviews. A similar specific section was lacking in the overviews of 1996 to 1999.[760] Second, if some countries' (harmful or positive) trade policies and practices are explicitly highlighted, it is often unclear why these practices and not those of others are cited. For instance, the 1998 Overview's focus on South Asia refers only to India's reduction of its import and investment restrictions whereas Malaysia's cut in import tariffs (1997), Australia tariff reform (1998), and Indonesia's deregulation of trade in agricultural commodities (1998) are not highlighted.[761] The criteria behind increased coverage in Overviews should be consistent for all. Finally, the structural coverage of identified SPS and TBT measures and their potential consecutive follow-up in the respective frameworks of the TPRM and the DSB kept evolving in a rather erratic way. For instance, specific sections were foreseen to cover SPS and TBT measures in the Overview of 1995. Nonetheless, these measures were not covered within the Overview's specific section with regard to the TPRM's activities.[762] The Overview of 1998 no longer provided specific sections to cover SPS and TBT measures. One of its paragraphs which details the TPRM's activities underlines nevertheless that '*liberalization in Latin America has become more complex ... In some cases ... concerns have been expressed over recent increases in ... the introduction of administrative and technical measures against imports*' thus specifically, but indirectly, highlighting TBT issues.[763] As a result, the Overviews of this period fell short of providing coherent and comprehensive coverage of harmful trade practices. These should ideally be covered from their initial identification by the concerned WTO committee(s), to their potential later review by the TPRM, ending with coverage of the DSB's potential litigation over the measure at issue.

[760] The overviews of 1995 does contain a specific section with regard to the TPRM; see WTO, TPRB, Overview of developments in international trade and the trading system, Annual Report by the Director-General, WT/TPR/OV/1, 1 December 1995; On the other hand, although the overview refers to the TPRM's activities, a specific section with regard to the TPRM's activities is lacking in the overviews of 1996, 1997, 1998, and 1999; WTO, TPRB, Overview of developments in international trade and the trading system, Annual Report by the Director-General, WT/TPR/OV/2, 28 November 1996; WTO, TPRB, Overview of developments in international trade and the trading system, Annual Report by the Director-General, WT/TPR/OV/3, 5 December 1997; WTO, TPRB, Overview of developments in international trade and the trading system, Annual Report by the Director-General, WT/TPR/OV/4, 30 November 1998; WTO, TPRB, Overview of developments in international trade and the trading system, Annual Report by the Director-General, WT/TPR/OV/5, 15 October 1999.

[761] WTO, TPRB, Overview of developments in international trade and the trading system, Annual Report by the Director-General, WT/TPR/OV/4, 30 November 1998, 4.

[762] WTO, TPRB, Overview of developments in international trade and the trading system, Annual Report by the Director-General, WT/TPR/OV/1, 1 December 1995, 14–15.

[763] WTO, TPRB, Overview of developments in international trade and the trading system, Annual Report by the Director-General, WT/TPR/OV/4, 30 November 1998, 4.

c) Participation

i) Governments (Government under review and its peers)

In the period between the temporary establishment of the TPRM (by the mid-term review Ministerial of 1988 and the Council Decision of 1989) and its definitive formalization via Annex 3 of the Marrakesh Agreement of 1995), fifty-one Contracting Parties underwent a trade policy review.[764] In the period between the mechanism's formal establishment (1995) and the end of the first appraisal of the TPRM (1999), fifty-eight additional Members were subject to a review.[765] This period witnessed some institutional shifts and political pressures with regards to the governments under review. The first was the enlargement of the European Union which regrettably resulted in the disappearance of new EU Member states from the formal list of WTO Members which were to be reviewed. As a result, the Secretariat could no longer analyse these Member states' individual behind the border measures.[766] Another recurrent pressure was the promotion of reviews of developing and least-developed countries through the planning of development-friendly review schedules and the increased provision of technical assistance.[767] In this regard, the first appraisal formally encouraged a higher participation of smaller Members.[768]

Tables II.1 and II.2 demonstrate that trade policy reviews which took place in the period between 1989 and the end of 1994 were generally well attended. This seems to attest to the TPRD's first director's description of the young TPRM as 'the only show in town'.[769]

TPRs of the Quad countries (ie the major trading entities which are on the two-year review cycle) were the best attended during this period. Of twenty-seven Contracting Parties to the 1993 TPR of the European Communities,[770] the presence of twenty-six Contracting Parties at the 1989 review of the United States,[771] the

[764] That is, the period between the TPR of Australia of 1989 and the review of Israel of 1994; Data of the author; The CD ROM '*20 years of Trade Policy Reviews 1989–2009, Marking the 20th anniversary of the Trade Policy Review Mechanism*'.

[765] That is, the period between the TPR of Cameroon of 1995 and the review of the Philippines of 1999; Although the 1998 review of Burkina Faso and Mali took place as a joint review, these reviews are counted as two separate reviews since they received a different formal numbering; Data of the author; CD ROM '*20 years of Trade Policy Reviews 1989–2009, Marking the 20th anniversary of the Trade Policy Review Mechanism*'.

[766] Answers from Mr Frank Wolter (first director of the Trade Policy Review Division, 1989–1991) to a questionnaire of the author (2 April 2014).

[767] Laird and Valdés, 'The Trade Policy Review Mechanism' (n 149) 479; Appraisal of the operation of the TPRM, Informal Meeting of 21 May 1999, Checklist of Main Points, No 3274, 3 June 1999, 3 (Document on file with the author).

[768] Appraisal of the Operation of the Trade Policy Review Mechanism, Report to Ministers, Ministerial Conference, Third Session, Seattle, 30 November–3 December 1999, WT/MIN(99)/2, 8 October 1999, 3.

[769] Answers from Mr Frank Wolter (first director of the Trade Policy Review Division, 1989–91) to a questionnaire of the author (2 April 2014).

[770] Trade Policy Review of the European Communities of 17–18 May 1993, Vol II (Document on file with the author).

[771] Trade Policy Review of the United States of 14 December 1989 (Document on file with the author).

attendance of twenty-four Contracting Parties to the 1994 TPRs of the European Communities and of the United States,[772] the presence of twenty-one Contracting Parties at the 1992 review of Japan,[773] and the attendance of nineteen Contracting Parties to the 1992 TPR of the United States[774] should be noted. Nevertheless, some high attendance rates of non-Quad reviews also stand out. Mexico's TPR of 1993 (attended by twenty-six Contracting Parties),[775] the 1993 review of Peru, the 1992 TPRs of Egypt and Brazil,[776] and the 1993 review of the Philippines[777] (the latter four all being reviewed in the presence of twenty-one Contracting Parties) are to be noted.

Nine Contracting Parties attended the TPRs of Macau (1994),[778] Iceland (1994),[779] and Nigeria (1991);[780] ten Contracting Parties showed up for the review of New Zealand (1990),[781] and eleven Contracting Parties attended the TPRs of Israel (1994),[782] Ghana (1992),[783] Indonesia (1991),[784] Hong Kong (1990),[785] Columbia (1990),[786] and Sweden (1990).[787] Countries' respective affiliation to a certain review cycle or region cannot therefore fully account for these low attendance rates.

[772] Trade Policy Review of the European Union of 24–25 July 1995, Minutes of the Meeting, WT/TPR/M/3, 4 October 1995; Trade Policy Review of the United States of 16–17 February 1993, Vol II (Documents on file with the author).

[773] Trade Policy Review of Japan of 12–13 October 1992, Vol II (Document on file with the author).

[774] Trade Policy Review of the United States of 11–12 March 1992, Vol II (Document on file with the author).

[775] Trade Policy Review of Mexico of 19–20 April 1993, Vol II (Document on file with the author).

[776] Trade Policy Review of Peru of 7–8 February 1993, Vol II (Document on file with the author); Trade Policy Review of Egypt of 5–6 October 1992, Vol II (Document on file with the author); Trade Policy Review of Brazil of 14–15 October 1992, Vol II (Document on file with the author).

[777] Trade Policy Review of the Philippines of 16–17 February 1993, Vol II (Document on file with the author).

[778] Trade Policy Review of Macao of 27–28 September 1994, Vol II (Document on file with the author).

[779] Trade Policy Review of Iceland of 9–10 February 1994, Vol II (Document on file with the author).

[780] Trade Policy Review of Nigeria of 1–2 October 1991, Vol II (Document on file with the author).

[781] Trade Policy Review of New Zealand of 2–3 August 1990 (Document on file with the author).

[782] Trade Policy Review of Israel of 19–20 December 1994, Vol II (Document on file with the author).

[783] Trade Policy Review of Ghana of 9–10 March 1992, Vol II (Document on file with the author).

[784] Trade Policy Review of Indonesia of 25–26 April 1991, Vol II (Document on file with the author).

[785] Trade Policy Review of Hong Kong of 31 July–1 August 1990 (Document on file with the author).

[786] Trade Policy Review of Colombia of 6–7 June 1990 (Document on file with the author).

[787] Trade Policy Review of Sweden of 5–6 June 1990 (Document on file with the author).

Table II.1

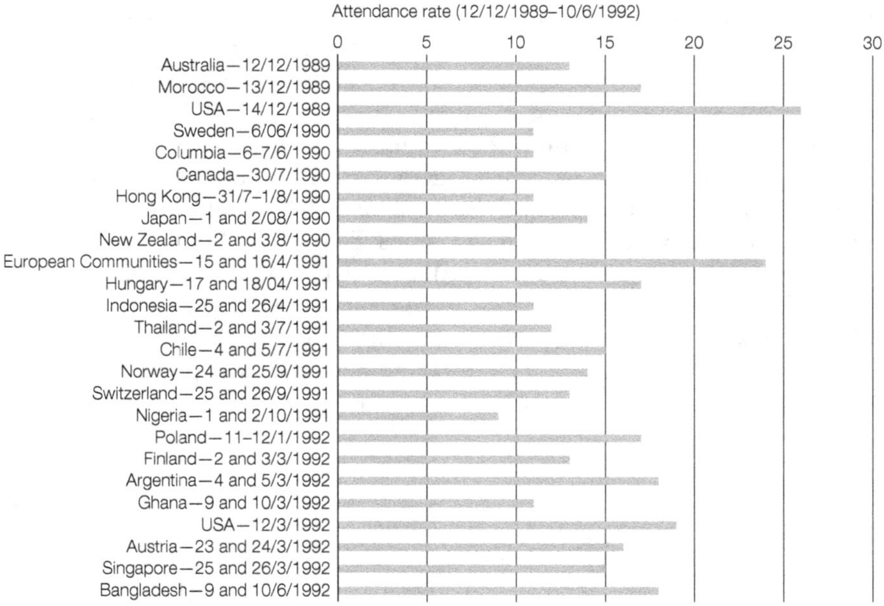

Table II.2

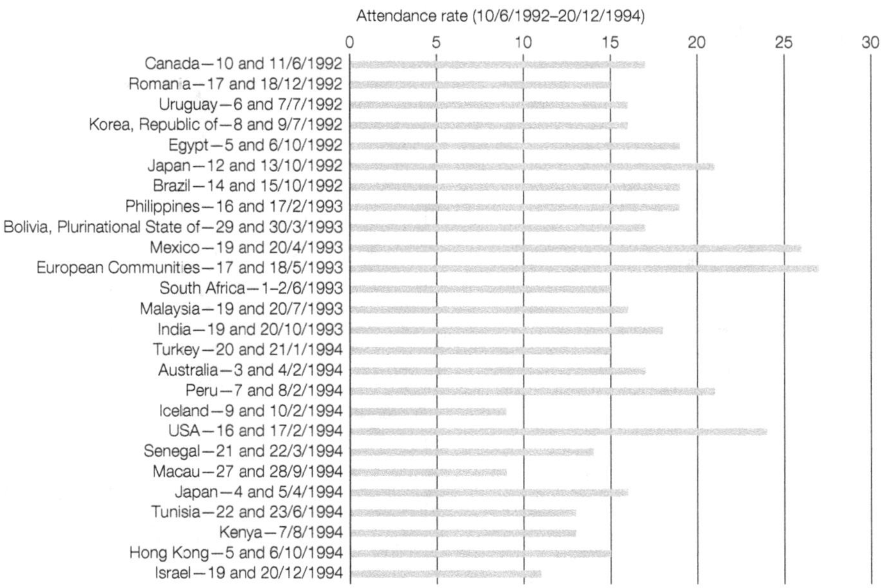

Tables II.3 and II.4 demonstrate that the participation rates of the reviewing peers have varied equally during this period.

Amongst the top five participants were (in a descending order): the European Communities, Canada, and Australia, which participated each in forty-nine out of the fifty-one TPRs of this period; the United States, involved in forty-eight reviews; Japan, which participated in forty-seven TPRs; Switzerland which was involved in forty-three reviews, and India which participated in thirty-seven out of the fifty-one TPRs.[788] The Quad countries and the countries on the second periodicity cycle therefore also ranked amongst the most active TPRM participants. On the other hand, the bottom three countries in terms of their participation rates (in ascending order) were Bangladesh, Cameroon, Guatemala, Nicaragua, Paraguay, and Zambia, each participating in only one out of the fifty-one TPRs of this period. They were followed by Cyprus, El Salvador, Indonesia, the Slovak Republic, and Sri Lanka which were each involved in two reviews, whereas Costa Rica, Côte d'Ivoire, Cuba, Iceland, Israel, Jamaica, Malaysia, the Philippines, Singapore, and Tunisia each participated in three out of the fifty-one TPRs of this period.[789] Although LDCs clearly stand out by their poor participation in trade policy reviews, some of their more developed counterparts also have a poor participation rate.

Table II.3

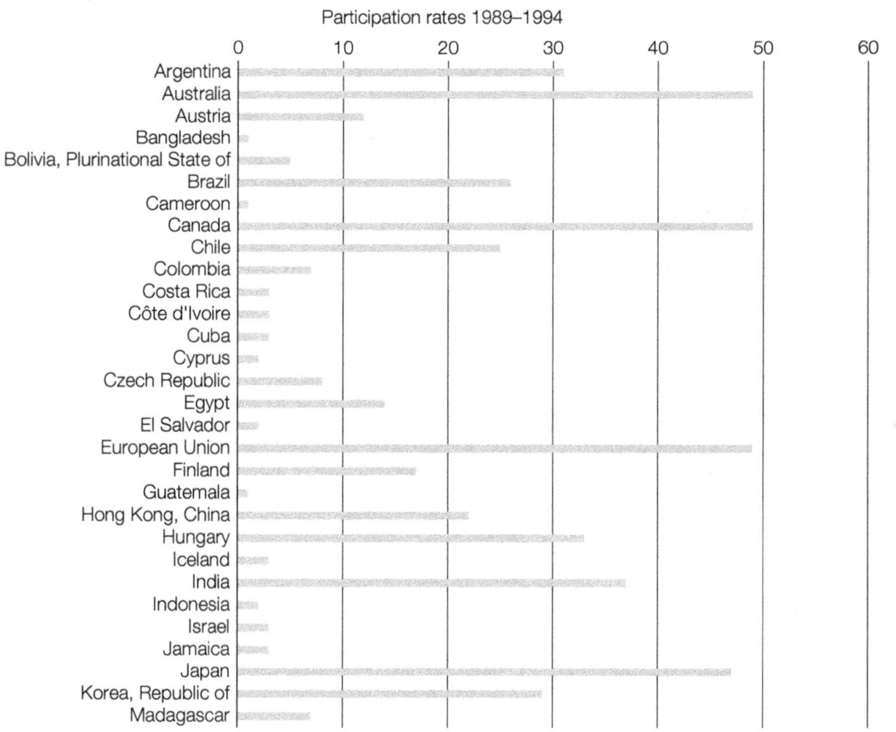

[788] Data on file with the author.

[789] Data on file with the author.

Table II.4

Tables II.5 and II.6 demonstrate how the attendance rates in the period between the definitive establishment of the TPRM (1995) and the end of its first appraisal (1999) continued to vary.

The list of top five well-attended TPRs in this period is constituted (in descending order) by the 1999 TPR of the United States (with twenty-seven Members attending),[790] the 1996 review of the United States (in the presence of twenty-four Members),[791] the TPRs of India (1998) and Bolivia (1999) (each being attended by twenty-three Members),[792] by the 1997 review of the European Union (in presence of twenty-two Members),[793] and by the 1996 TPR of Norway (attended by twenty-one Members).[794] Again, participation levels for reviews of Quad countries were relatively high.

[790] Trade Policy Review of the United States of 12–14 July 1999, Minutes of the Meeting, WT/TPR/M/56, 11 August 1999.

[791] Trade Policy Review of the United States of 11–12 November 1996, Minutes of the Meeting, WT/TPR/M/16, 30 January 1997.

[792] Trade Policy Review of India of 16–17 April 1998, Minutes of the Meeting, WT/TPR/M/33, 22 September 1998; Trade Policy Review of Bolivia of 19–21 July 1999, Minutes of the Meeting, WT/TPR/M/57, 15 September 1999.

[793] Trade Policy Review of the European Union of 25–26 November 1997, Minutes of the Meeting, WT/TPR/M/30, 26 January 1998.

[794] Trade Policy Review of Norway of 11–12 June 1996, Minutes of the Meeting, WT/TPR/M/15, 5 August 1996.

Table II.5

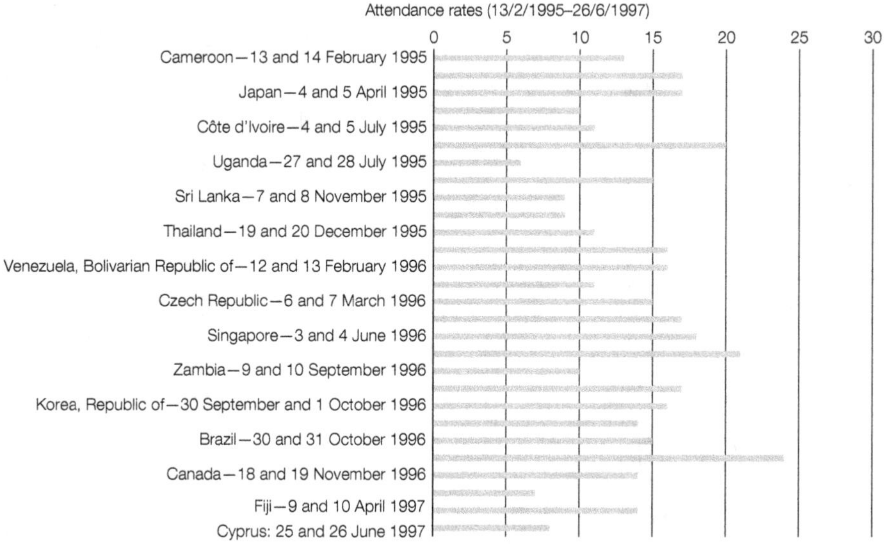

Table II.6

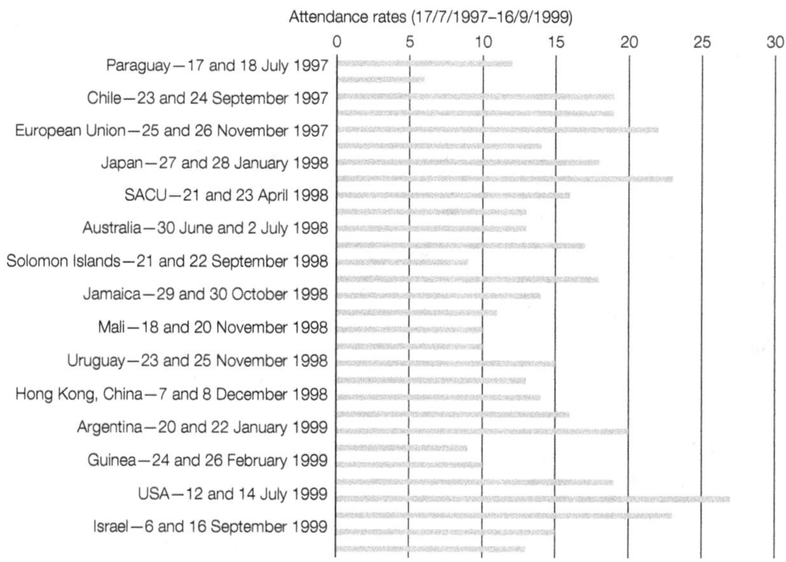

On the other hand, the list of the least well-attended (in ascending order) was constituted by the TPRs of Benin (1997) and Uganda (1995) (each being attended by six Members),[795] by the reviews of El Salvador (1996) and Cyprus (1997) (each

[795] Trade Policy Review of Benin of 15–16 September 1997, Minutes of the Meeting, WT/TPR/M/27, 14 October 1997; Trade Policy Review of Uganda of 27–28 July 1995, Minutes of the Meeting, WT/TPR/M/4, 5 October 1995.

in presence of seven Members),[796] and by the TPRs of Togo (1999), the Solomon Islands (1998), the Slovak Republic (1995), and Sri Lanka (1995) (each being attended by nine Members).[797]

Table II.7

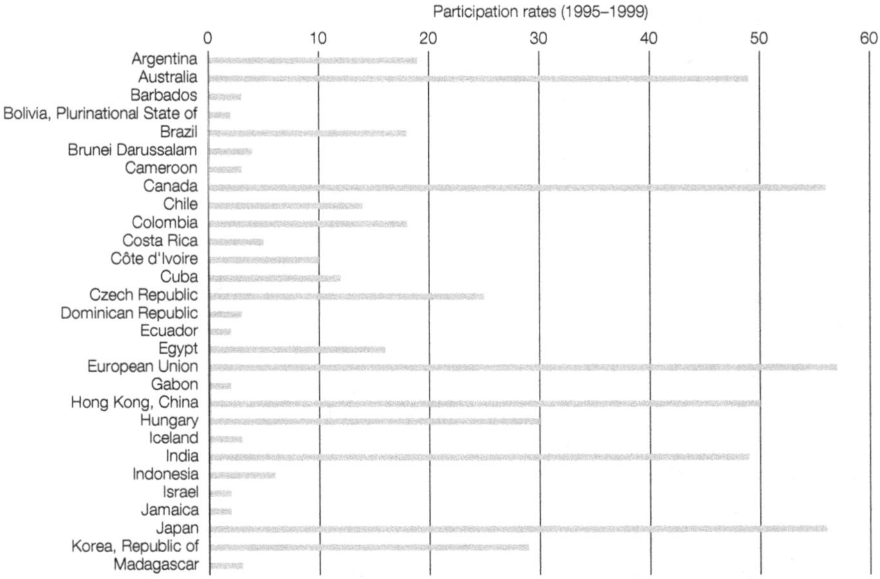

Tables II.7 and II.8 show the national participation rates in the period between the TPRM's formal establishment (1995) and the end of its first appraisal (1999).

The list of the top five TPR participants in this period was (again) almost entirely constituted by members of the Quad. The European Union took part in fifty-seven out of the fifty-eight TPRs of this period. Several other Quad countries (the United States, Japan, and Canada) followed, each with an involvement in fifty-six reviews. Hong Kong China participated in fifty TPRs, whereas India and Australia each took part in forty-nine reviews. New Zealand finished the list with a participation in thirty-=eight out of the fifty-eight TPRs of this period.[798]

[796] Trade Policy Review of El Salvador of 25–26 November 1996, Minutes of the Meeting, WT/TPR/M/23, 27 January 1997; Trade Policy Review of Cyprus of 25–26 June 1997, Minutes of the Meeting, WT/TPR/M/25, 22 July 1997.

[797] Trade Policy Review of Togo of 27–28 January 1999, Minutes of the Meeting, WT/TPR/M/48, 9 April 1999; Trade Policy Review of the Solomon Islands of 21–22 September 1998, Minutes of the Meeting, WT/TPR/M/45, 27 November 1998; Trade Policy Review of the Slovak Republic of 5–6 December 1995, Minutes of the Meeting, WT/TPR/M/7, 22 March 1996; Trade Policy Review of Sri Lanka of 7–8 November 1995, Minutes of the Meeting, WT/TPR/M/6, 7 December 1995.

[798] Data on file with the author.

Table II.8

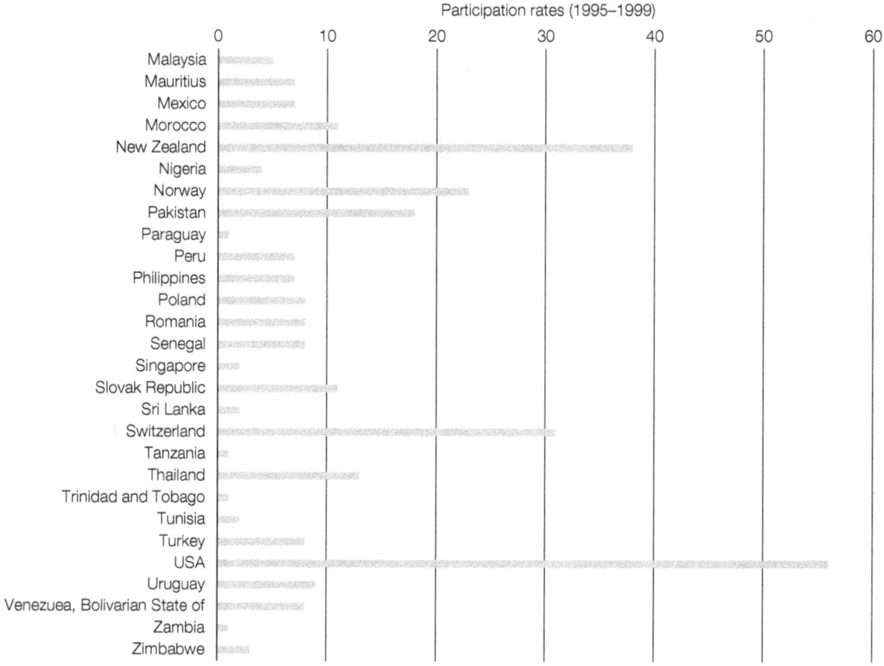

Countries which participated in the least numbers of TPRs were (in ascending order): Honduras, Paraguay, Tanzania, Trinidad and Tobago plus Zambia took each part in only one TPR, with Bolivia, Ecuador, Gabon, Israel, Jamaica, Sri Lanka, Singapore, and Tunisia following. Each of these participated in two reviews. The list ends with Barbados, Cameroon, the Dominican Republic, Iceland, Madagascar, and Zimbabwe. Each of these countries was involved in three TPRs.[799]

	1990	1991	1992	1993	1994	1995	1996	1997	1998	1999
Average attendance rate	12.0	14.3	16.6	19.7	14.7	12.5	15.4	14.2	14.4	14.5
Percentage	12%	14.3%	16%	17.5%	11.6%	9%	11%	10%	10%	10%

Yearly attendance rates in the period covered by the first appraisal (ie starting with the Mechanism's first full year of operation (1990) until the end of 1999) were volatile. Nevertheless, while yearly attendance rates expressed in relative terms had increased at the end of this period, yearly attendance rates expressed in absolute terms had dropped. Moreover, 1993 was a peak year in relative and absolute terms while 1995 saw a substantial dip in both regards.[800]

[799] Data on file with the author.

[800] Data on file with the author.

ii) Secretariat

Table II.9

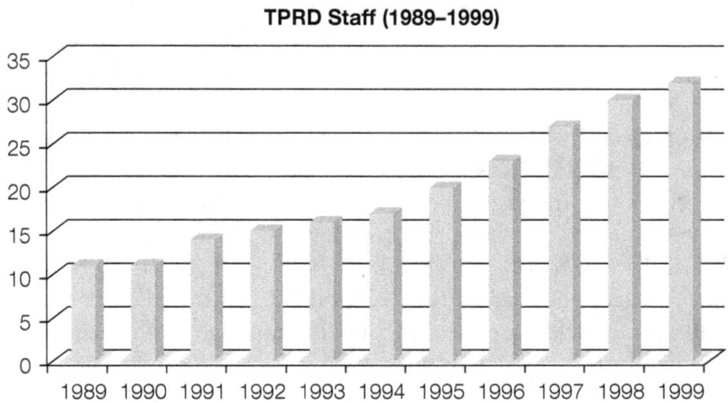

During the period between the temporary establishment of the TPRM (by the mid-term review Ministerial of 1988 and the Council Decision of 1989) and the end of the first appraisal of the TPRM (1999), the staff of the TPRD increased from eleven to thirty-two individuals. This included only a handful of experts with a legal background.[801] Furthermore, in this period, the percentage of staff allocated to the TPRD never amounted to more than 6 per cent of overall WTO staff. In 1990, which was the TPRB's first full year of operation, TPRD staff amounted only to 4 per cent of all WTO staff (an all-time record).[802]

The GATT budget estimates for the financial year 1989 amounted to CHF 65.163.000, including a provision of CHF 750.000 for the potential establishment of a Trade Policy Review Mechanism, subject to a positive decision at the Montreal Ministerial meeting.[803] According to the Secretariat, the amount budgeted '*was meant to be a contingency provision because it was difficult to estimate the precise cost*'.[804] Nevertheless, one Contracting Party reserved his delegation's position on the proposal with the argument that the 'best information available at this time did not suggest that expenditure for this purpose could reasonable be anticipated during 1989' and that '*if an amount were to be included in the budget, it should not specifically be for a TPRM but a contingency amount for implementation of any decision made by the Trade Negotiations Committee at the Montreal Ministerial meeting, which required implementation in 1989*'.[805] A revised allocation of CHF 500.000

[801] Answers from the Human Resources Department of the WTO to questions of the author (4 December 2015).

[802] Answers from the Human Resources Department of the WTO to questions of the author (4 December 2015).

[803] Budget Estimates for the Financial Year 1989 (13 September 1988) BISD L/6390, 3; Report of the Committee on Budget, Finance and Administration (7 October 1988) BISD L/6408, 4 (hereafter Report of the Committee on Budget, Finance and Administration (7 October 1988)).

[804] Report of the Committee on Budget, Finance and Administration (7 October 1988) (n 801) 12.

[805] Report of the Committee on Budget, Finance and Administration (7 October 1988) (n 801) 12.

was therefore presented with the assumption that, in the event of a favourable decision by the Montreal mid-term review, '*the TPRM work could be started later than originally foreseen and that some of the preparatory work could be done using existing staff resources*'.[806] Of the CHF 500.000 only CHF 474.000 were subsequently approved by the Council upon recommendation of the Budget Committee.[807] Nevertheless, 1989 resulted in a final TPRM-related expenditure amounting to CHF 538.529.[808] This compared to an overall appropriated GATT budget for 1989 of CHF 65.186.802.[809] The GATT's initial budgetary estimates for 990) amounted to CHF 75.063.000. This included an estimated CHF 2.394.000 for the TPRM's first full year of operation.[810] Nevertheless, final TPRM expenditure in 1990 amounted to CHF 2.411.434.[811] This compared to an overall appropriated GATT budget for 1990 of CHF 74.832.327.[812] In 1991, the GATT's budgetary estimates increased further to CHF 78.724.000. Of this amount, CHF 2.955.000 was set aside for the TPRM's functioning.[813] Nonetheless, the final TPRM expenditure in 1991 only amounted to CHF 2.663.303 since savings had resulted from delays in recruitment in 1991. In addition, provision was made in the 1991 budget for the production of eleven reports, whereas only eight reports were finally reproduced of which three corresponded to reviews conducted in 1990.[814] This compared to an overall appropriated GATT budget for 1991 of CHF 78.724.802.[815] The GATT's budget estimates for financial year 1992 amounted to CHF 88.017.327, including CHF 4.234.000 for the TPRM.[816] Nevertheless, the final TPRM expenditure in 1992 amounted only to CHF 3.596.554 since savings had been realized under salaries from temporary assistance and the United Nations Joint Staff (UNJS) Pension Fund contributions due to a lower exchange rate and posts being vacant, as well as other Common staff costs related to these posts.[817] This is compared to an overall appropriated GATT budget for 1992 of

806 Report of the Committee on Budget, Finance and Administration (7 October 1988) (n 801) 13.

807 Administrative and Financial Questions, Final Position of the 1989 Budget of the GATT (26 April 1990) BISD L/6668, 1.

808 Budget Estimates for the Financial Year 1992 (30 September 1991) BISD L/6900, 45 (hereafter Budget Estimates for the Financial Year 1992 (30 September 1991)).

809 Answers from the Budgetary Department of the WTO to questions of the author (29 January 2016).

810 Budget Estimates for the Financial Year 1990 (22 August 1989) BISD L/6550, 3 and 9.

811 Budget Estimates for the Financial Year 1992 (30 September 1991) (n 806) 45.

812 Answers from the Budgetary Department of the WTO to questions of the author (29 January 2016).

813 Budget Estimates for the Financial Year 1991 (4 June 1991) BISD L/6850, 7.

814 Administrative and Financial Questions, Final Position of the 1991 Budget (15 September 1992) BISD L/7077, 2; Budget Estimates for the Financial Year 1993 (18 September 1992) BISD L/7070, 43 (hereafter Administrative and Financial Questions, Final Position of the 1991 Budget (15 September 1992)); Data of the author.

815 Answers from the Budgetary Department of the WTO to questions of the author (29 January 2016).

816 Budget Estimates for the Financial Year 1992 (30 September 1991) (n 806) 45.

817 Administrative and Financial Questions, Final Position of the 1992 Budget (14 July 1993) BISD L/7258, 2; Budget Estimates for the Financial Year 1994 (24 September 1993) BISD L/7300, 42 (hereafter Budget Estimates for the Financial Year 1994 (24 September 1993)).

CHF 85.973.327.[818] In 1993, the GATT budgetary estimates amounted to CHF 90.794.000. Of this amount, CHF 3.746.000 was set aside for the TPRM's functioning.[819] Nonetheless, the final TPRM expenditure in 1993 amounted to CHF 268,051 less than the amount initially approved since savings had resulted from salaries to temporary assistance (vacant posts) and the Common staff costs related to these posts such as missions, by reducing the number of staff members needed for each mission, and travel on home leave.[820] This can be compared to an overall appropriated GATT budget for 1993 of CHF 89.850.075.[821] The GATT budget estimates for the financial year 1994 amounted to CHF 98.769.000, including CHF 3.927.000 for the TPRM.[822] Nevertheless, the final TPRM expenditure in 1994 amounted to CHF 4.074.028 because of rental outside the Centre William Rappard and payments for statutory Common staff costs mainly due to unforeseen departures.[823] This can be compared to an overall appropriated GATT budget for 1994 of CHF 94.140.000.[824]

In 1995, WTO budgetary estimates amounted to CHF 131.466.500 (encompassing provisions for the core budget as well as those for extraordinary provisions).[825] Nevertheless, for the first time in the budgetary history of the GATT/WTO, these estimates did not encompass any specific indications with regard to the budgetary needs of the TPRD. Neither are there any data available with regard to the TPRD's actual expenditure for 1995.[826] The WTO budget which was finally appropriated in 1995—the first budget after the formal establishment of the WTO—amounted to CHF 105.389.500.[827] The WTO's budgetary estimates for 1996 amounted to CHF 121.552.703[828] including CHF 4.619.500 for the TPRD.[829] This stands in comparison to an appropriated WTO budget of CHF 115.693.503 for 1996.[830] Again, no data are available with regard to the

[818] Answers from the Budgetary Department of the WTO to questions of the author (29 January 2016).

[819] Administrative and Financial Questions, Final Position of the 1991 Budget (15 September 1992) (n 812) 8.

[820] Administrative and Financial Questions, Final Position of the 1993 Budget (18 May 1994) BISD L/7456, 2.

[821] Answers from the Budgetary Department of the WTO to questions of the author (29 January 2016).

[822] Budget Estimates for the Financial Year 1994 (24 September 1993) (n 815) 7.

[823] Administrative and Financial Questions, Final Position on the 1994 Budget (13 April 1995) BISD L/7627, 3.

[824] Answers from the Budgetary Department of the WTO to questions of the author (29 January 2016).

[825] Budget Estimates 1995 (17 October 1994) BISD L/7550, 3.

[826] This lack of data has been explicitly acknowledged by the Budgetary Department of the WTO; Answers from the Budgetary Department of the WTO to questions of the author (23 July 2015 and 24 January 2016).

[827] WTO, Committee on Budget, Finance and Administration, Mid-term review biennium 2014–15, WT/BFA/W/339, 29 October 2014, 27.

[828] WTO, Budget Estimates 1996, WT/BFA/10 and L/7640, 14 September 1995, 5.

[829] WTO, Budget Estimates 1996, WT/BFA/10 and L/7640, 14 September 1995, 79.

[830] WTO, Committee on Budget, Finance and Administration, Mid-term review biennium 2014–15, WT/BFA/W/339, 29 October 2014, 27.

TPRD's actual expenditure in 1996.[831] In 1997, the WTO budget was initially estimated at CHF 118.944.750.[832] Of this amount, CHF 3.318.100 was set aside for the TPRM's functioning.[833] The WTO budget which was finally appropriated in 1997 amounted to CHF 115.692.750.[834] The WTO's initial budget estimates for 1998—the last year of the period which was covered by the first appraisal—amounted to CHF 117.729.500 including CHF 3.365.500 for the TPRD.[835] This stands in comparison with an appropriated WTO budget of CHF 115.978.850 for 1998.[836] Here again, there are no available data with regard to the specific actual expenditure of the TPRD in 1997 and 1998.[837]

During their informal meeting of 12 May 1999, Members saw some positive budgetary implications resulting from a better relation with the IMF and the World Bank, although independent analysis by the WTO was required.[838] The Secretariat had repeatedly expressed concern with regard to its expanding workload as a result of the increasing WTO Membership. The implication of this was that as many as thirty reviews per year might be required whereas the then resources of the TPRD only allowed for the conduct of about thirteen to fifteen yearly reviews.[839] Although the first appraisal had estimated that only about 5 per cent of the WTO's annual budget was spent on the TPRM, cost efficiencies through (1) grouped reviews; (2) an increased use of consultants; and (3) shorter reports and meetings were encouraged.[840] Moreover, occasionally some Members provided extra-budgetary means on a project- or trust-fund basis. For instance, in 1997 Denmark and Australia paid for the fees of external consultants involved in TPR work under the close supervision of the Secretariat.

[831] This lack of data has been explicitly acknowledged by the Budgetary Department of the WTO; Answers from the Budgetary Department of the WTO to questions of the author (23 July 2015 and 24 January 2016).

[832] WTO, Budget Estimates 1997, Proposals by the Director-General, WT/BFA/27, 9 September 1996, 5.

[833] WTO, Budget Estimates 1997, Proposals by the Director-General, WT/BFA/27, 9 September 1996, 85.

[834] WTO, Committee on Budget, Finance and Administration, Mid-term review biennium 2014–2015, WT/BFA/W/339, 29 October 2014, 27.

[835] WTO, Budget Estimates 1998, Proposals by the Director-General, WT/BFA/W/20, 5 September 1997, 5 and 78.

[836] WTO, Committee on Budget, Finance and Administration, Mid-term review biennium 2014–2015, WT/BFA/W/339, 29 October 2014, 27.

[837] This lack of data has been explicitly acknowledged by the Budgetary Department of the WTO; Answers from the Budgetary Department of the WTO to questions of the author (23 July 2015 and 24 January 2016).

[838] Appraisal of the operation of the TPRM, Informal Meeting of 12 May 1999, Checklist of Main Points, No 2933, 20 May 1999, 3 (Document on file with the author).

[839] Trade Policy Review Mechanism, Report of the Trade Policy Review Body for 1997, Trade Policy Review Body, WT/TPR/41, 28 November 1997, 4; Trade Policy Review Mechanism, Report of the Trade Policy Review Body for 1998, Trade Policy Review Body, WT/TPR/59, 27 November 1998, 2; Trade Policy Review Mechanism, Report of the Trade Policy Review Body for 1999, WT/TPR/69, 7 October 1999, 2; Appraisal of the operation of the TPRM, Informal Meeting of 21 May 1999, Checklist of Main Points, No 3274, 3 June 1999, 3 (Document on file with the author).

[840] WTO, Ministerial Conference, Third Session, Seattle 30 November–3 December 1999, Appraisal of the operation of the Trade Policy Review Mechanism, WT/MIN(99)/2, 8 October 1999, 3.

Within the administrative settings of the WTO, the TPRD has always maintained close links with other departments, in particular with the Development Division, the Technical Co-operation Division, and the Secretariat Working Group (SWG) on Integrated Framework and LDC Issues.[841] Moreover, the TPRD also exchanged information and input with two other Divisions, namely, the Translation and Documentation Division and the division dealing with the media.[842] Nonetheless, as TPRs became more complex, the number of WTO Divisions involved with the elaboration of TPRs gradually increased. The internal flow of information also became politically sensitive, especially between the TPRD and the Integrated Database, containing information on WTO Members' imports and tariffs.[843] The first appraisal therefore explicitly suggested improving the two-way flow of information between the TPRD and other parts of the WTO Secretariat while also cautioning against both the spread of restricted information and trespassing on Member's rights and obligations.[844]

Initially, the Secretariat was fairly independent in its reporting. Unlike the reports prepared by some other intergovernmental organizations, its reports were not negotiated documents. Despite the fact that this was agreed to in principle during the negotiations of the FOGS group, it took some time for governments to become comfortable with the notion of being investigated and criticized by the Secretariat.[845]

iii) Discussants

In the period before the formal establishment of the WTO (ie the period between the first Australian TPR of 1989[846] and the Israeli review of 1994[847]), all TPRs were based on the participation of two discussants. The first was to provide a developed country's perspective on the trade policies and practices under review, while the second was to complement and contrast these views with a developing country's perspective. Moreover, in the first years after the TPRM's provisional establishment, discussants intervened repeatedly over the course of the review's meeting, not simply once during the first day of the review and once again during the review's final day.

[841] Axel Borrmann, Georg Koopmann, *Adapting the WTO Trade Policy Reviews to the Needs of Developing Countries: Starting Points and Options* (Hamburg Institute of International Economics 2002), 30 (hereafter Borrmann and Koopmann, *Adapting the WTO Trade Policy Reviews to the Needs of Developing Countries*).

[842] Answers from Mr Frank Wolter (first director of the Trade Policy Review Division, 1989–1991) to a questionnaire of the author (2 April 2014).

[843] Borrmann and Koopmann, *Adapting the WTO Trade Policy Reviews to the Needs of Developing Countries* (n 839) 30.

[844] WTO, Ministerial Conference, Third Session, Seattle 30 November–3 December 1999, Appraisal of the operation of the Trade Policy Review Mechanism, WT/MIN(99)/2, 8 October 1999, 2.

[845] Answers from Mr Frank Wolter (first director of the Trade Policy Review Division, 1989–91) to a questionnaire of the author (2 April 2014).

[846] Trade Policy Review of Australia, 12 December 1989 (Document on file with the author).

[847] Trade Policy Review of Israel, Vol II, 19–20 December 1994 (Document on file with the author).

The 1993 rules of procedure for review meetings establish some specific guidance with regard to the discussants. This includes the requirement that '*discussants continue to be nominated keeping in view their competence for the task. They act in their personal capacity and not as representatives of their governments*' as well as the hope that a discussant would be able to serve for more than one review.[848] This procedural guidance was initially followed well. In the period under analysis, the governmental affiliation of the respective discussants was never mentioned, with the exception of the TPR of Turkey of 1994[849] and the five consecutive reviews (including the TPR of Macao of 1994).[850]

Moreover, discussants tended to be fairly independent: the number of discussants who based their assessments explicitly on the Secretariat's or the government's reporting and those who did not was almost equally divided. Slightly more than half the discussants who covered TPRs in this period referred, directly or indirectly, to the Secretariat's reporting (52 out of the 102 discussants who covered the 51 TPRs of this period or 50 per cent) rather than to governmental reporting (49 out of the 102 discussants or 48 per cent).[851] Furthermore, discussants dared to take critical positions. Although none initially dared to venture criticism of the Secretariat's reporting, governmental reporting in the period was not spared, albeit on a rather exceptional basis. For instance, in the TPR of the United States of 1989, the first discussant stated that '*the recent OECD report gives a favourable assessment of US trade performance and presents a relatively optimistic view on the continued reduction of the huge deficits in merchandise trade and current account, but only if the US does not fail to reduce its budget deficit*'. He then went on to contrast the findings of the OECD with the government report where he found '*only a rather brief description which seems to suggest that the principal factors for the trade deficit are to be found outside the US and that the persistence of the deficit alone can explain the increased pressure for protectionist trade measures*'.[852] In a similar vein, the first discussant of the TPR of the European Communities of 1992 stated that '*the Communities report emphasizes that it regards regional trade arrangements as a complement to the multilateral system. It seems to me that there are questions about what appears to be a less than central role for the MFN principle and about the cumulative impact on the global system. Put another way, is the multilateral track of trade liberalization getting enough attention relative to competing trade policy initiatives of the Communities?*'[853] Another example can be found in the second discussant of Austria's TPR of 1992 who openly criticized national governmental reporting (though not Austria's) while noting that

[848] *Procedures for Review Meetings, Communication from the Chairman* (30 April 1993) (n 776) 1.

[849] Trade Policy Review of Turkey of 20–21 January 1994, Vol II (Document on file with the author).

[850] Trade Policy Review of Macao of 27–28 September 1994, Vol II (Document on file with the author).

[851] Data on file with the author.

[852] Trade Policy Review of the United States of 14 December 1989 (Document on file with the author).

[853] Trade Policy Review of the European Communities of 15–16 April 1991, Minutes of the Meeting, C/RM/M/10, 2 July 1991, 10.

'*doubt has been expressed regarding the usefulness of national TPRM reports, as they sometimes added little in terms of information or opinion*'.[854] Furthermore, in twelve out of the fifty-one TPRs of this period (ie 23 per cent), the discussants referred to external studies which shed some additional light on the trade policies and practices of the country under review.[855]

Interestingly, in this initial period, issues of dispute settlement were mentioned only in the review of the European Communities of 1991.[856] In this context, the discussant noted that he '*was interested to note that two-fifths of all GATT Article XXIII cases of dispute settlement since 1960 have involved the Communities, either as a complainant or a defendant. While this may suggest the importance of having an effective GATT dispute settlement in managing trade relations with a trading unit as big and as complex as the Communities. I have questions about the reference in the Communities' report to the possibility of a protracted internal decision-making process in handling dispute cases as well as the possibility of blocking power by the minority. I wonder whether the fact that the European Court of Justice has determined that the GATT is binding on the EC has any practical implication on the handling of disputes. The fact that agriculture has been the source of half of all GATT disputes involving the Communities is also interesting to note*'.

In the period after the formal establishment of the TPRM and the end of the first appraisal (ie the period between the TPR of Cameroon of 1995[857] and the review of the Philippines of 1999[858]), the intensity of the WTO's process for peer review started to change.

The number of discussants diminished since the participation of two discussants in any TPR was no longer guaranteed.[859] Moreover, the remaining discussant(s) became more independent. Fewer than half of the discussants who covered the TPRs of this period referred, directly or indirectly, to Secretariat's reporting (50 out of the 116 discussants who covered the 58 TPRs of this period or 43 per cent). This number decreased even further with regard to governmental reporting (only 28 out of the 116 discussants or 24 per cent).[860] In line with previous practice, none of the discussants dared to criticize the consecutive reports of the Secretariat. Nonetheless, government reporting was repeatedly subject to criticism, albeit again still on a relatively exceptional basis. For instance, in the TPR of Hong Kong of 1998, the discussant stated that '*the notion of "one country, two systems"*

854 Trade Policy Review of Austria, Vol II, 23–24 March 1992 (Document on file with the author).

855 Data on file with the author.

856 Trade Policy Review of the European Communities of 15–16 April 1991, Minutes of the Meeting, C/RM/M/10, 2 July 1991, 11.

857 Trade Policy Review of Cameroon of 13–14 February 1995, Vol II (Document on file with the author).

858 Trade Policy Review of the Philippines of 27–29 September 1999, Minutes of the Meeting, WT/TPR/M/59, 15 November 1999.

859 Nevertheless, the (joint) TPR of Burkina Faso and Mali was even covered by three discussants; Trade Policy Review of Burkina Faso and Mali, Minutes of the Meeting of 18–20 November 1998, WT/TPR/M/43, and WT/TPR/M/46, 25 February 1999; The TPR of the SACU was also covered by three discussants; Trade Policy Review of the SACU of 21–23 April 1998, Minutes of the Meeting, WT/TPR/M/34, WT/TPR/M/35, WT/TPR/M/36, WT/TPR/M/37, WT/TPR/M/38, 15 December 1998.

860 Data on file with the author.

would presumably require a fair amount of flexibility, and correspondingly, a lack of orthodox ideology for it to be successful. Quoting the government report para. 1, "in all then, we have the full backing of the Central People's Government of the PRC which in accordance with the Basic Law, has left the Government of the HSKAR to manage our economic and trade affairs entirely as we think fit", and para. 10, "in accordance with the relevant provisions of the Basic Law, the government of the HSKAR has been authorized by the CPG to conclude . . . ", he asked about consistency between the expressions "entirely as we think fit" and "has been authorized by the CPG to conclude"'.[861] In a similar vein, the second discussant in the TPR of Mexico of 1997 asked the Mexican delegation '*for reconciliation of the amount of foreign direct investment reported by the delegation (US 3.1 billion between 1994 and 1996) and the figures in the Secretariat report (US 18.7 billion USD)*'.[862] In twelve out of the fifty-eight TPRs of this period (ie 20 per cent), the discussants also referred to external studies which shed additional light on the trade policies and practices of the country under review.[863]

Discussants increasingly raised questions with regard to compliance and/or dispute settlement. For instance, in the TPR of the United States of 1996, the second discussant noted the extra-territorial nature of some environmental regulations and then observed that '*these regulations might be in violation of GATT/WTO Agreements*'.[864] Moreover, in the TPR of Australia of 1998, the second discussant stated that '*while it was difficult to compare the international equivalence of quarantine standards, Australia's stringent SPS measures and a commitment to increase funds to strengthen quarantine raised a number of concerns, including the consistency of restrictions with international agreements: and the question of transparency during the consultation process which could be detrimental to Australian imports. While recognizing Australia's geographical need to prevent pest and disease encroachment, questions remained as to how Australia decided on the suitability of established quarantine restrictions, especially those beyond internationally acceptable norms, and how domestic industries without scientific knowledge, contributed to the process. He asked for comments on a recent panel report, in circulation but not yet adopted, which had found that some Australian SPS measures may be inconsistent with WTO agreements*'.[865] Furthermore, the first discussant in the TPR of the United States of 1999 '*paid tribute to the US for faithfully complying with rulings even when they had gone against US claims*'.[866] However, several discussants clearly demonstrated their willingness to avoid any discussions about dispute

[861] Trade Policy Review of Hong Kong, Minutes of the Meeting of 7–8 December 1998, WT/TPR/M/52, 12 April 1999.

[862] Trade Policy Review of Mexico of 7–8 October 1997, Minutes of the Meeting, WT/TPR/M/29, 16 December 1997, 10.

[863] Data on file with the author.

[864] Trade Policy Review of the United States of 11–12 November 1996, Minutes of the Meeting, WT/TPR/M/16, 30 January 1997, 11–12.

[865] Trade Policy Review of Australia of 30 June–2 July 1998, Minutes of the Meeting, WT/TPR/M/41, 26 October 1998, 12.

[866] Trade Policy Review of the United States of 12–14 July 1999, Minutes of the Meeting, WT/TPR/M/56, 11 August 1999,10.

settlement. For instance, in the TPR of Singapore of 1996, the second discussant clearly stated that '*the TPRM was a learning experience, not a forum for judging implementation or raising dispute settlement questions, but rather one in which experiences could be shared and to try to learn from the practices of others*'.[867] In a similar vein, the first discussant in the TPR of the United States of 1996 mentioned the Helms–Burton Act but then indicated that '*as the matter has already been raised in the Dispute Settlement Body, the formal and legal discussion of this matter was left to that body*'.[868]

The first appraisal itself favoured continued flexibility with regard to the number and the role of discussants. Furthermore, it urged that 'steps should be taken to make review meetings more interactive, with greater participation by Members'.[869]

2. Second appraisal of the operation of the Trade Policy Review Mechanism (May–July 2005): review of the TPRM's functioning between September 1999 and September 2005

On 31 May 2005, the TPRB agreed on a procedure to carry out its second appraisal of the operation of the TPRM.[870] Like the first review, the second appraisal started with the elaboration of a questionnaire (a non-paper) by the Secretariat.[871] Four informal meetings followed in the period from May to July 2005.[872]

a) Objectives

The earlier academic debate between the proponents of the TPRM as an exclusive transparency mechanism and those who saw a prime or partial/indirect objective of naming and shaming in the TPRM gave rise to further academic analysis in the period between September 1999 and September 2005.

In his revised paper on the TPRM, Francois took a relatively incremental approach in acknowledging the usage of the TPRM as a vehicle for peer pressure. In this regard, he states that '*the TPRM is at its heart a vehicle for providing information. In its present form, it is not meant to be used for policy recommendations. The WTO Members said as much when stating, in Annex 3 of the Uruguay Round Agreements*

[867] Trade Policy Review of Singapore of 3–4 June 1996, Minutes of the Meeting, WT/TPR/M/14, 6 August 1996, 6.

[868] Trade Policy Review of the United States of 11–12 November 1996, Minutes of the Meeting, WT/TPR/M/16, 30 January 1997, 10.

[869] WTO, Ministerial Conference, Third Session, Seattle 30 November–3 December 1999, Appraisal of the operation of the Trade Policy Review Mechanism, WT/MIN(99)/2, 8 October 1999, 3.

[870] *Second appraisal of the operation of the Trade Policy Review Mechanism—Report to Ministers* (21 September 2005) WT/MIN(05)/1, 1 (hereafter *Second appraisal of the operation of the Trade Policy Review Mechanism 2005*).

[871] Possible points for the appraisal of the operation of the trade policy review mechanism (TPRM), Non-paper, 10 May 2005 (Document on file with the author).

[872] *Second appraisal of the operation of the Trade Policy Review Mechanism 2005* (n 868).

defining the TPRM, that the TPRM is 'not intended to serve as a basis for the enforcement of specific obligations under the Agreements or for dispute settlement procedures, or to impose new policy commitments on Members', but then also adds that '*even so, it does serve as a basis for WTO-centred peer pressure and periodic airing of the extent to which Members are adhering to obligations*'.[873] Ratnesh took a more radical stance in describing the TPRM as a '*weapon of enforcing discipline*' or even as an '*extended wing of the Dispute Settlement Mechanism*'[874] whereas the TPRM's review procedures were almost melodramatically described as '*kowtowing genuflexion, self-inflicted rape of our vast polity*' and '*surrender*'.[875] Nonetheless, it seems difficult to support these claims by the author's own analysis of some twenty-two TPRs which did not result in any links with the Dispute Settlement Body, either specific or general.[876] Moreover, the above assessment of the TPRM also contrasts with the author's depiction of the TPRM as a toothless entity, describing her as '*the overlooking Old Dame in the Big House*'.[877]

Other academics ventured forth in a more empiric way and started to analyse under what organizational conditions and through which mechanisms the TPRM's state reporting procedures could contribute to *compliance* with international rules. This literature concluded that the TPRM *already* pursued some form of *compliance*. In Conzelmann's view, the TPRM is a mechanism for *soft compliance*. According to the author, '*the basic idea was to supplement the dispute settlement system by an instrument that would regularly assess the broad picture of Member states practices in the light of GATT rules, but to keep the authority of interpretation of compliant or non-compliant behaviour in single cases firmly within the community of states. Hence, the TPRM is intended to do "more" than the Dispute Settlement Body (DSB) in the sense of covering not only single cases, but also "less" than the DSB in the sense of not delegating the judgement on compliance or non-compliance to a third party. The* additional *[emphasis added] function of the TPRM, then, is to generate information*

[873] Francois, 'Maximizing the Benefits of the Trade Policy Review Mechanism for Developing Countries' (n 37) 9, versus Francois, 'Trade Policy Transparency and Investor Confidence: Some Implications for an Effective Trade Policy Review Mechanism' (n 37) 312; Interestingly, this position (generally held by economists) is closer to the (earlier expressed) views of Mavroidis (a lawyer) who had already identified several functions within existing surveillance schemes: a review function (comparing a national policy instrument with an international standard and making a judgement as to whether the policy instrument conforms to the international standard), a corrective function (recommending a change in national policy when a national policy instrument is found to be contrary to the international legal obligations of the country under review), and a creative function (providing interpretation). In particular, the corrective function is closely related to the compliance objective; Mavroidis, 'Surveillance Schemes: The GATT's New Trade Policy Review Mechanism' (n 6) 408.

[874] Kumar Ratnesh, *WTO (World Trade Organization): Structure, Functions, Tasks and Challenges* (New Delhi 2002) 42 (hereafter Ratnesh, *WTO (World Trade Organization): Structure, Functions, Tasks and Challenges*).

[875] Ratnesh, *WTO (World Trade Organization): Structure, Functions, Tasks and Challenges* (n 872) 43–44.

[876] Ratnesh, *WTO (World Trade Organization): Structure, Functions, Tasks and Challenges* (n 872) 46–71.

[877] Ratnesh, *WTO (World Trade Organization): Structure, Functions, Tasks and Challenges* (n 872) 43–44.

on the overall conduct of WTO Members with regard to their duties under the WTO rules'.[878] Although Conzelmann repeatedly admits that more empirical work is needed, the author already points to some elements which blur the traditional/formal distinction between the TPRM's goal of transparency and its objective of naming and shaming. These include: the existence of specific policy recommendations by the Chairperson of the TPRB (since the right to interpret the GATT, GATS, and TRIPS rests exclusively with the Contracting Parties and, in some cases, with the DSB), the more-than-factual reporting of the Secretariat (since Secretariat's reporting is not supposed to be prescriptive), or the TPRM's (apparent) inability to respect its formal delinkage from dispute settlement procedures (since Annex 3 of the Marrakesh agreement is not a covered agreement).[879]

Nonetheless, the numerous trade policy reviews which had been produced in the meantime could still be contrasted with the lack of any final conclusions—based on conclusive scientific and empirical analysis—with regard to the implementation of the TPRM's stated objectives and its respective degree of focus on transparency and/or naming and shaming objective. In addition, other WTO entities such as the WTO Working Group on the Interaction between Trade and Competition Policy maintained adherence to the traditional view that '*peer review and dispute settlement are separate and autonomous mechanisms that may, but need not, stand by side*'.[880]

The second appraisal therefore resulted in an almost identical assessment of the TPRM's mission and objectives as its predecessor. The formal description of the value added by the TPRM's mission and objectives was identical (in this regard, the second appraisal focused on the TPRM's public-good aspect, its value as a vehicle for reflection, as input provider to policy formulation, and as a means to follow up on technical assistance needs) although the number of critical points relating to the TPRM's mission and objectives decreased (the only remaining point still urged the review of all Members, at least once and as soon as possible).[881]

It should be remembered that the TPRM and the DSB were conceived as two separately functioning entities. Paragraph A of Annex 3 to the Marrakesh Agreement is very clear in stating that the TPRM '*is not, however, intended to serve as a basis for the enforcement of specific obligations under the Agreements or for dispute settlement procedures, or to impose new policy commitments on Members*'.[882] In addition, Annex 3 to the Marrakesh Agreement is not a covered agreement under Appendix

[878] Conzelmann, 'Beyond the Carrot and the Stick—(How) Do State Reporting Procedures Matter?' (n 219) 1 and 12.

[879] Conzelmann, 'Beyond the Carrot and the Stick—(How) Do State Reporting Procedures Matter?' (n 219) 15–19; Some elements were subsequently revised in Thomas Conzelmann, 'Beyond the carrot and the stick: The authority of peer reviews in the WTO and the OECD' (Paper for presentation at the ECPR Standing Group for International Relations, 2010), 11–17 (hereafter Conzelmann, 'Beyond the carrot and the stick: The authority of peer reviews in the WTO and the OECD').

[880] WTO, Communication from the Working Group on the Interaction between Trade and Competition Policy (WT/WGTCP/W/244) (n 22).

[881] *Second appraisal of the operation of the Trade Policy Review Mechanism 2005* (n 868) 2.

[882] The Trade Policy Review Mechanism (n 151).

I to Annex II to the Marrakesh Agreement which embodies the Understanding on Rules and Procedures Governing the Settlement of Disputes.[883] As a result, the TPRM and its findings should in principle not be invoked within the proceedings of the Dispute Settlement Body. Nevertheless, in spite of all this, in the period covered by the second appraisal the number of references to findings of the TPRM increased to seven panel proceedings (covering 4.6 per cent of all disputes which originated in this period).[884] Further to the views of Argentina, according to which a TPR review '*undeniably provides for a thorough examination of the trade policies of Members and the extent to which they have adapted or failed to adapt to GATT/WTO rules*', the Panel in *Chile—Price Band System and Safeguard Measures Relating to Certain Agricultural Products* felt compelled to make it clear that the '*report should not be taken into account in the context of dispute settlement proceedings*'.[885] Moreover, in *US—Continued Suspension of Obligations in the EC—Hormones Dispute*, the Appellate Body implicitly warned that Trade Policy Review meetings should not be turned into '*a fertile source of comments that . . . could constitute determinations actionable under Article 23.2(a) (of the DSU)*'.[886]

b) Structure

i) Individual trade policy reviews

Periodicity

The second appraisal of the TPRM (ie September 1999– to September 2005) covered six years during which the TPRM functioned. Although the Secretariat's annual forecast of the number of TPRs which would be implemented in the coming year was correct in three years (ie in 2000, 2001, and 2003),[887] in the remaining three years (ie in 2002, 2004, and 2005) the number of implemented TPRs fell below the

[883] The Marrakesh Agreement (n 353).

[884] WTO, *Chile—Price Band System and Safeguard Measures Relating to Certain Agricultural Products—Report of the Panel* (3 May 2002) WT/DS207/R, 175; WTO, *Chile —Price Band System and Safeguard Measures Relating to Certain Agricultural Products— Appellate Body Report* (23 September 2002) WT/DS207/AB/R, 7; WTO, *EC—Conditions for Granting Tariff Preferences to Developing Countries—Report of the Panel* (1 December 2003) WT/DS246/R, B-94 and B-95; WTO, *Korea—Measures Affecting Trade in Commercial Vessels—Report of the Panel* (7 March 2005) WT/DS273/R, 151; WTO, *US—Measures Affecting the Cross-Border Supply of Gambling and Betting Services—Report of the Panel* (10 November 2004) WT/DS285/R, 109 and 238; WTO, *EC —Selected Customs Matters—Report of the Panel* (16 June 2006) WT/DS315/R, F-5; WTO, *EC—Hormones Dispute—US—Continued Suspension of Obligations—Report of the Panel* (31 March 2008) WT/DS320/R, 71; WTO, *EC—Hormones Dispute—US—Continued Suspension of Obligations—Appellate Body Report* (16 October 2008) WT/DS320/AB/R, 167; WTO, *EC—Hormones Dispute—Canada—Continued Suspension of Obligations—Report of the Panel* (31 March 2008) WT/DS321/R, 69; WTO, *EC—Hormones Dispute—Canada—Continued Suspension of Obligations—Appellate Body Report* (16 October 2008) WT/DS321/AB/R, 167.

[885] WTO, *Chile—Price Band System and Safeguard Measures Relating to Certain Agricultural Products—Report of the Panel* (3 May 2002) WT/DS207/R, 46 and 147.

[886] WTO, *EC—Hormones Dispute—US—Continued Suspension of Obligations—Appellate Body Report* (16 October 2008) WT/DS320/AB/R, 167.

[887] For 2000 see: WTO, TPRB, Draft Report of the Trade Policy Review Body for 1999, Trade Policy Review Mechanism, WT/TPR/W/23, 30 September 1999, 5; WTO, TPRB, Trade Policy Review Mechanism, Draft Programme of Reviews for 2000, Trade Policy Review Body, WT/TPR/W/

Secretariat's initial estimates.[888] The Secretariat's annual reporting on the TPRM between September 1999 and September 2005 included a categorization of the countries under review by their cyclical periodicity. Although the TPRM's periodicity is based on the annual review of two Quad countries and four countries of the group of sixteen which are on the four-year cycle,[889] the number of countries reviewed under the two-year cycle varied between one (in 2001, 2003, and 2005) and three in 2000. Likewise, the number of countries reviewed under the four-year cycle varied between zero (in 2005) to six (in 2000 and 2004).

Furthermore, in the period covered by the second appraisal, it became even more difficult to predict when and/or which country would be subject to review under the different cycles of periodicity. First, the 2005 rules of procedure stated that the periodicity contained in paragraph C(ii) of the TPRM would be applied '*with a general flexibility of up to six months, if and as may be necessary*'.[890] Second, in the aftermath of China's WTO accession, it replaced Canada in 2003 as the fourth Member of the Quad.[891] Third, as a result of the volatility of the commodity prices and due to the enlargement process of the European Union, the composition of the list of countries which were on the four- or six-year cycles was also modified.[892] In addition, it should be noted that the Secretariat still based its determination of a country's review cycle on that country's representative share of world trade of finalized goods and services over a fixed period of three years. Nevertheless, this determination is methodologically blind to the gradual proliferation of global value chains as well as to intellectual property's growing importance in international trade.[893]

25, 9 November 1999, 1; Data of the author. For 2001 see: WTO, TPRB, Draft Report of the Trade Policy Review Body for 2000, Trade Policy Review Body, WT/TPR/W/27/Rev. 1, 6 October 2000, 2; Data of the author; WTO, TPRB, Draft Report of the Trade Policy Review Body for 2001, Trade Policy Review Mechanism, WT/TPR/W/28, 11 September 2001, 1. For 2003 see: WTO, TPRB, Report of the Trade Policy Review Body for 2002, Trade Policy Review Body, WT/TPR/W/29, 7 October 2002, 2; Data of the author; WTO, TPRB, Draft Report of the Trade Policy Review Body for 2003, Trade Policy Review Mechanism, WT/TPR/W/31, 28 October 2003, 1 and 6.

888 For 2002 see: WTO, TPRB, Draft Report of the Trade Policy Review Body for 2001, Trade Policy Review Mechanism, WT/TPR/W/28, 11 September 2001, 2; Data of the author; WTO, TPRB, Report of the Trade Policy Review Body for 2002, Trade Policy Review Body, WT/TPR/W/29, 7 October 2002, 1. For 2004 see: WTO, TPRB, Draft Report of the Trade Policy Review Body for 2003, Trade Policy Review Mechanism, WT/TPR/W/31, 28 October 2003, 2; Data of the author; WTO, TPRB, Draft Report of the Trade Policy Review Body for 2004, Trade Policy Review Mechanism, WT/TPR/W/32, 18 October 2004, 2 and 6. For 2005 see: WTO, TPRB, Draft Report of the Trade Policy Review Body for 2004, Trade Policy Review Mechanism, WT/TPR/W/32, 18 October 2004, 2 and 6; Data of the author; WTO, TPRB, Draft Trade Policy Review Mechanism, Report of the Trade Policy Review Body for 2005, WT/TPR/W/35, 12 October 2005, 1 and 6.

889 Laird, 'The WTO's Trade Policy Review Mechanism—From Through the Looking Glass' (n 370) 746.

890 WTO, TPRB, Draft Rules of Procedure for Meetings of the Trade Policy Review Body, WT/TPR/W/34, 6 September 2005, 1.

891 Laird and Valdés, 'The Trade Policy Review Mechanism' (n 149).

892 Laird and Valdés, 'The Trade Policy Review Mechanism' (n 149) 463–84.

893 As attested by the World Intellectual Property Organization's (WIPO) increasing activities and the formalization of the WTO's TRIPS Agreement as contained in Annex 1C of the Marrakesh Agreement Establishing the World Trade Organization; <www.wipo.int/> accessed 17 May 2017 and

Although the second appraisal process raised the question of whether '*the role of the TPRM was the same in respect of the major traders, middle-level economies, developing countries, transition economies and least-developed countries*',[894] its final report did not specifically touch on the question of a potentially revised periodicity.[895]

Reporting

While competition issues were not formally part of the TPRM mandate, the Secretariat and the countries under review increasingly sought to report on them as they related to trade in goods and services and regulatory reforms.[896] During the informal meetings which led to the second review, Members again discussed whether TPRs should examine new issues such as the links between trade and social policy issues (eg trade and gender or trade and health).[897]

As a result of the review process, the second appraisal indicated that governmental reporting should retain the same almost absolute freedom as before. The review emphasized that it was satisfied with the current structure, contents, and quality of Secretariat's reporting. It indicated nevertheless that it saw scope for these reports to have a more uniform coverage, to be more reader friendly, to contain links to the Internet and a summary of the outcomes of previous reviews.[898] Interestingly, the TPR of Tanzania (2000) was the first LDC review in which the Secretariat report contained a specific section with regard to trade-related assistance.[899]

TPR's informational value – The period covered by the second appraisal (ie September 1999 to September 2005) resulted in extensive academic output which analysed the information contained in the Secretariat's (and sometimes governmental) reporting within the context of individual TPRs.

The remainder of this section will examine those views. In order to do so, it divides the academic views on the TPRs' added informational value into three categories: (a) TPRs with missing information; (b) TPRs which according to academia contain a too positive or a too negative assessment of the situation; and (c) TPRs with incorrect information. Moreover, for each of these three categories, this section contrasts the views of external academics where possible with the anonymous perspectives of WTO staff with regard to the same point.

WTO, 'Trade-Related Aspects of Intellectual Property Rights' <https://www.wto.org/english/docs_e/legal_e/27-trips_01_e.htm> accessed 8 July 2017

[894] Possible points for the appraisal of the operation of the trade policy review mechanism (TPRM), Non-paper, 10 May 2005, 2 (Document on file with the author).

[895] *Second appraisal of the operation of the Trade Policy Review Mechanism 2005* (n 868).

[896] WTO, Communication from the Working Group on the Interaction between Trade and Competition Policy (WT/WGTCP/W/244) (n 22) 9.

[897] Possible points for the appraisal of the operation of the trade policy review mechanism (TPRM), Non-paper, 10 May 2005, 2 (Document on file with the author).

[898] Second Appraisal of the Operation of the Trade Policy Review Mechanism, Ministerial Conference, Sixth Session, Hong Kong, 13–18 December 2005, WT/MIN(05)/1, 21 September 2005, 2; *Second appraisal of the operation of the Trade Policy Review Mechanism 2005* (n 868) 2.

[899] Borrmann and Koopmann, *Adapting the WTO Trade Policy Reviews to the Needs of Developing Countries: Starting Points and Options* (n 868) 34; Trade Policy Review of Tanzania of 2–3 March 2000, Minutes of the Meeting, WT/TPR/M/66, 2 May 2000.

In line with earlier findings, all observers of this period were positive or even enthusiastic about the successive TPRs' overall added value in terms of fostering increased transparency. Nevertheless, a clear majority of the academics also complained about missing information. Experts' complaints about TPR assessments which were perceived as too positive or too negative were also often heard. Furthermore, for the first time, academia drew attention to a TPR which contained incorrect information.

Most academic literature complained about TPRs' lack of certain specific information:

- In his analysis of Argentina's TPR of 1999, Professor Berlinski expressed regret that the purely descriptive TPR analysis of Argentina's special legal regimes did not shed any light on the '*extent to which authorities have been able to audit whether the objectives of the regimes were accomplished*'.[900] The cost of protection of these special regimes and restrictions to the mobility of goods and services in Mercosur was therefore often unclear.[901] Nevertheless, WTO experts pointed to the fact that there was a lack of available data in this regard.[902]
- In his overview of Poland's TPR of 2000, Professor Hare stated that the Secretariat report did not analyse the likelihood that dispersed tariff rates facilitated corruption by customs officials through the improper classification of products for tariff purposes (although such an analysis was made by the EC).[903]
- In his analysis of Malaysia's TPR of 2001, Professor Athukorala raised several critical points. These included: (a) the rather sketchy discussion of Malaysia's capital control-based recovery package; (b) the (purely) descriptive nature and listing of non-tariff barriers and commodities covered; (c) a lack of substantial analysis of the reasons that lay behind Malaysia's decision not to apply anti-dumping or other contingency measures; (d) the lack of thorough analysis with regard to Malaysian export subsidies; and (e) the lack of detailed analysis with regard to the implications of Malaysia's trade policy for the global trading system.[904] According to the author, the TPR's coverage was too much focused on tariffs.
- In his overview of Burundi's TPR of 2004, Professor Milner argued that '*neither political stability nor further trade policy reform are likely to be sufficient to induce significant export growth and diversifications*'. The author therefore argued that '*a greater emphasis be given by TPRs in particular to identifying the other necessary ingredients of a reform programme (including measures to increase human capital*

[900] Julio Berlinski, 'The WTO Trade Policy Review of Argentina' [2000] The World Economy: Global Trade Policy 1207 (hereafter Berlinski, 'The WTO Trade Policy Review of Argentina').
[901] Berlinski, 'The WTO Trade Policy Review of Argentina' (n 898) 1211.
[902] Interview with a former WTO expert, April 2015, 4 (Document on file with the author).
[903] Paul G Hare, 'Trade Policy Review of Poland, 2000' [2001] The World Economy: Global Trade Policy 1191.
[904] Prema-chandra Athukorala, 'Malaysian Trade Policy and the 2001 WTO Trade Policy Review' [2002] The World Economy: Global Trade Policy 1314–16.

development, to improve business Organizations, to upgrade infrastructure and to improve institutional support for trade development)'.[905]

- In his analysis of the Maldives' TPR of 2003, Professor Athukorala pointed to several omissions in the Secretariat's report. These included: (a) the lack of analysis with regard to the political patronage that State Owned Enterprises (SOEs) often provide;[906] (b) the lack of analysis with regard to the impact of bilateral trading agreements, free trade areas, and GSP (Generalised Scheme of Preferences) on the Maldives trade performance; (c) the lack of any discussion on the implementing issues relating to the WTO agreement on Sanitary and Phytosanitary measures (this should be important in view of the fact that the Maldives relies heavily on its exports of fish products); (d) a lack of analysis of the environmental dimension of its trade and investment policy; and (e) the absence of any mention of the impact of the Maldives' graduation from LDC status for export performance.[907]
- In his overview of the Gambia's TPR of 2004, Professor McKay pointed to some issues which were not discussed in the Secretariat's report. These included (a) the accuracy of trade data (especially in view of the porous borders and the importance of re-exports) and (b) the need for a better delineation of the Gambia's technical assistance needs (a point stressed by the discussant but not resolved in the meeting).[908]
- In his analysis of Turkey's TPR of 2003, Professor Togan bemoaned the fact that the issue of the Turkish current account was largely neglected in the TPR.[909]
- In his overview of the TPR of the United States of 2004, Professor Prusa raised several critical points. These included the limited coverage in the government report of the US Farm Bill (which starkly contrasts with the dozens of pages of questions and comments by other Members on the Bill).[910]
- In his analysis of Europe's TPR of 2004, Professor Tharakan raised the question of whether the TPR clearly managed to identify the EU's major problem areas. The author concludes that although the Secretariat reporting seemed to contain more economic analysis, the comments made by Members still seemed to leave out the broader implication of those issues. As such Professor Tharakan argued for a greater role for the discussant

[905] Chris Milner, 'Trade Policy in Burundi: Reform Without Political Stability' [2004] The World Economy: Global Trade Policy 1376.

[906] Nonetheless, WTO experts point to the fact that Secretariat's coverage of political patronage and/or corruption increased over time; Interview with a former WTO expert, April 2015, 5 (Document on file with the author).

[907] Prema-chandra Athukorala, 'Trade Policy Making in a Small Island Economy: The WTO Review of the Maldives' [2004] The World Economy: Global Trade Policy 1413, 1416, and 1418.

[908] Andrew McKay, 'Trade Policy Issues in a Small African Economy: The Trade Policy Review of the Gambia 2004' [2005] The World Economy: Global Trade Policy 1198 and 1200.

[909] Sübidey Togan, 'Turkey: Trade Policy Review' [2005] The World Economy: Global Trade Policy 1229.

[910] Thomas J Prusa, '2004 Trade Policy Review—The United States' [2005] The World Economy: Global Trade Policy 1263–75.

whereby relevant issues are analysed in depth and with sufficient economic basis.[911]

Academic complaints about TPR assessments which were perceived as too positive or too negative were also often heard:

- In his overview of Thailand's TPR of 1999, Professor Warr noted '*the heavy reliance on government sources for the TPR's information*'.[912]
- In their analysis of Slovenia's TPR of 2002, Professors Damijan and Majcen pointed to the fact that within Slovenia several views exist with regard to the reasons for its persistently high inflation. The professors' analysis questioned the TPRs' focus on only one of these perspectives.[913] WTO experts justified this stance by reference to the WTO's traditional reliance on IMF data.[914] Moreover, in its discussion of tariff policy for the import of raw materials, intermediate, and capital goods for export-oriented production, the report argued that it was WTO inconsistent. Nevertheless, Professors Damijna and Majcen stressed the fact that discrimination was probably the only way to expand exports during the time when Slovenia suffered from both the loss of Yugoslav markets and the depression that accompanied its transition to statehood.[915] However, WTO experts stressed the fact that the WTO Secretariat simply cannot advocate for WTO-inconsistent policy-making.[916]

One TPR of this period was identified as containing incorrect information:

- In his overview of Norway's TPR of 2004, Melchior pointed out that incorrect tariff averages had been used in analysing the agricultural sector. Trade policy reviews have made a useful contribution by presenting tariff averages based on *ad valorem* equivalent (AVE) estimates. In the review, these AVE estimates were based on import price data supplied by Norway although for some items no imports existed. The WTO Secretariat therefore had to rely on world market prices, which independent academics found to be resulting in lower averages than those which really existed.[917]

Reporting on information and naming and shaming – Between the start (September 1999) and the end (September 2005) of the period which was covered by the second appraisal, 93 TPRs took place and 152 DSB disputes were litigated. Of these, fourteen

[911] PKM. Tharakan, 'Storm Signals: An Analysis of the Trade Policy Review of the European Communities' [2006] The World Economy: Global Trade Policy 1301, 1309.

[912] Peter G Warr, 'Thailand's Post-Crisis Trade Policies, The 1999 WTO Review' [2000] The World Economy: Global Trade Policy 1216.

[913] Joze P Damijan and Boris Majcen, 'Trade Policy in a Small Advanced Transition Economy: Trade Policy Review of Slovenia, 2002' [2002] The World Economy: Global Trade Policy 1377 (hereafter Damijan and Majcen, 'Trade Policy in a Small Advanced Transition Economy: Trade Policy Review of Slovenia, 2002').

[914] Interview with a former WTO expert, April 2015, 4 (Document on file with the author).

[915] Damijan and Majcen, 'Trade Policy in a Small Advanced Transition Economy: Trade Policy Review of Slovenia, 2002' (n 911) 1380.

[916] Interview with a former WTO expert, April 2015, 4 (Document on file with the author).

[917] Arne Melchior, 'The Most and Least Favoured Nations: Norway's Trade Policy in Perspective' [2006] The World Economy: Global Trade Policy 1342.

disputes related to Sanitary and Phytosanitary measures (SPS) whereas eleven disputes related to Technical Barriers to Trade (TBT).

Through its focus on the respective DSB and TPR coverage of the same SPS and TBT disputes, this section will analyse individual TPRs' added value in terms of transparency and naming and shaming. In order to do so, for each of the DSB disputes, this section examines the proceeding and succeeding TPR(s). For each of these, the Secretariat report and the government report, the debates during the TPRB meeting, and the written questions and answers are analysed from a transparency angle (examining whether the respective reports, meeting, or questions explicitly or indirectly managed to refer to elements of the dispute to come) and from the perspective of naming and shaming (questioning whether the respective reports, meeting, or questions managed to elicit some defensive stance from the country under review).

- In *EC—Trade Description of Sardines*, Peru took issue with EC Regulation No 2136/89 which allegedly prevented Peruvian exporters to continue to use the trade description 'sardines' for their products.[918] According to the European Union, only the species '*Sardina pilchardus*' could be marketed under the name 'sardines'. It should be noted that this species can be found in European waters and is largely fished by EC vessels.[919] Nevertheless, according to Peru, according to the relevant *Codex Alimentarius* standards (STAN 94-181 rev. 1995), the species '*sardinops sagax sagax*' was listed among those species which can (also) be traded as '*sardines*'. Peru was therefore of the view that EC Regulation 2136/89 was an unjustifiable trade barrier in clear violation of Articles 2 and 12 of the TBT Agreement and of Article XI:1 of the GATT (1994). Peru also argued that the Regulation was inconsistent with the principle of non-discrimination, and therefore in breach of Articles I and III of the GATT (1994).

The case was preceded by the TPR of the European Communities of (July) 2000.[920] Nevertheless, neither its Secretariat's[921] or government's report[922] nor its TRPB meeting[923] or written questions thereof[924] were able to shed any light or put any pressure on the nascent trade problem.

[918] WTO, *EC—Trade Description of Sardines—Report of the Panel* (29 May 2002) WT/DS231/R; WTO, *EC—Trade Description of Sardines—Appellate Body Report* (26 September 2002) WT/DS231/AB/R; Robert Howse, 'The Sardines Panel and AB Rulings – Some Preliminary Reactions' (2002) 29(3) Legal Issues of Economic Integration 247–54.

[919] Gregory Shaffer, Victor Mosoti, and Asif Qureshi, 'Towards A Development-Supportive Dispute Settlement System in the WTO' (2003) 5 ICTSD Resource Paper 35.

[920] Trade Policy Review of the European Communities of 12–14 July 2000, Minutes of the Meeting, WT/TPR/M/72, 26 October 2000.

[921] Trade Policy Review of the European Communities of 12–14 July 2000, Secretariat Report, WT/TPR/S/72, 14 June 2000, 56–63; Likewise, the Secretariat's sectional reporting on Agriculture remains silent on the subject; Trade Policy Review of the European Communities of 12–14 July 2000, Secretariat Report, WT/TPR/S/72, 14 June 2000, 89–99.

[922] Trade Policy Review of the European Communities of 12–14 July 2000, Government Report, WT/TPR/G/72, 14 June 2000.

[923] Trade Policy Review of the European Communities of 12–14 July 2000, Minutes of the Meeting, WT/TPR/M/72, 26 October 2000 (Document on file with the author).

[924] Trade Policy Review of the European Communities of 12–14 July 2000, Written questions and answers, WT/TPR/M/72/Add. 1, 26 October 2000.

In May 2002, a Panel report concluded that the EC Regulation was inconsistent with Article 2.4 of the TBT Agreement.[925]

Nevertheless, the TPR of the European Communities of July 2002 remained again silent on the issue.[926] Neither its Secretariat's[927] nor government's reports[928] nor the TPRB meeting, at which Peru was absent,[929] nor the written questions thereof[930] contained any highlighting or referencing of the topic.

The report of the Appellate Body (which was adopted on 23 October 2002) reversed some of the findings of the Panel but upheld the latter's conclusion that the EC's disputed Regulation was inconsistent with Article 2.4 of the TBT Agreement.[931] Nevertheless, on 25 July 2003, the European Communities and Peru informed the DSB that they had reached a mutually agreed solution.[932]

The TPR of the European Communities of October 2004—the last which touched on the issue—remains largely though not entirely silent on the dispute.[933] The Secretariat's analysis with regard to technical barriers to trade, sanitary and phytosanitary measures, or with regard to fisheries remains silent on the issue.[934] The same is true with regard to the government report.[935] Nonetheless, during the TPRB meeting, Peru tabled some general complaints while stating that '*the EC was Peru's second market for exports. Peru's exports had been facing obstacles due to the implementation of stringent TBT and SPS measures; a number of conditions were not clearly laid out in EC directives.*'[936] Moreover, Peru's written questions pointed more explicitly to the underlying issue behind its DSB dispute.[937] In this regard, Peru asked '*why is the EU resisting the development of a CODEX food standard for sardines that would expand the scope of species covered, and thus provide*

[925] WTO, *EC—Trade Description of Sardines—Report of the Panel* (29 May 2002) WT/DS231/R.

[926] Trade Policy Review of the European Communities of 24–26 July 2002, Minutes of the Meeting, WT/TPR/M/102, 23 September 2002.

[927] Trade Policy Review of the European Communities of 24–26 July 2002, Secretariat Report, WT/TPR/S/102, 26 June 2002, 37–46; Neither is the topic raised in Secretariat's (sectional) analysis of Fisheries; Trade Policy Review of the European Communities of 24–26 July 2002, Secretariat Report, WT/TPR/S/102, 26 June 2002, 77–83.

[928] Trade Policy Review of the European Communities of 24–26 July 2002, Government Report, WT/TPR/G/102, 26 June 2002.

[929] Trade Policy Review of the European Communities of 24–26 July 2002, Minutes of the Meeting, WT/TPR/M/102, 23 September 2002.

[930] Trade Policy Review of the European Communities of 24–26 July 2002, Written questions, WT/TPR/M/102/Add.1, 31 March 2003.

[931] WTO, *EC—Trade Description of Sardines—Appellate Body Report* (26 September 2002) WT/DS231/AB/R.

[932] WTO, *EC—Trade Description of Sardines—Notification of Mutually Agreed Solution* (29 July 2003) WT/DS231/18.

[933] Trade Policy Review of the European Communities of 25–27 October 2004, Minutes of the Meeting, WT/TPR/M/136, 18 January 2005.

[934] Trade Policy Review of the European Communities of 25–27 October 2004, Secretariat's Report, WT/TPR/S/136, 23 June 2004, 59–62, 63–66, and 100–07.

[935] Trade Policy Review of the European Communities of 25–27 October 2004, Government's Report, WT/TPR/G/ 136, 1 October 2004.

[936] Trade Policy Review of the European Communities of 25–27 October 2004, Minutes of the Meeting, WT/TPR/M/136, 18 January 2005, 14.

[937] Trade Policy Review of the European Communities of 25–27 October 2004, Written questions and answers, WT/TPR/M/136/Add. 1, 18 January 2005, 111–16.

significant commercial benefits to developing countries in South America and Africa?' Peru furthermore asked the European Union to '*comment on the requirement in EC Regulation 1181/2003 (amending Regulation 2136/89 establishing common marketing standards for preserved sardines) that requires that sardine producers re-label their product before marketing in the EU market. In particular, does the EC believe that adding the scientific names of non-European sardine species to sardine labels really provide useful information to the consumer. Is this requirement aimed at making non-European species less commercially viable? Is the typical European consumer familiar with the scientific genus and species nomenclature for fish?*' The European Union answered the question, while indicating that it considered that '*the methodology detailed in the CODEX standard for Canned Sardines and Sardine-Type Products is inappropriate as it has allowed fishes such as Sprats, Anchovies and Herrings to be sold as sardines when they are canned whereas they are sold under their own names when salted. The EU thinks that this approach is totally misleading for consumers. The EU would therefore favour the revision of the criteria to include fish species in the list of species allowed to be sold as sardines and a revision of the existing list prior to the possible inclusion of Clupea Bentincki*'.[938] With regard to Peru's second question, the European Union answered that '*The new rules were the subject of a joint notification of Peru and the European Union in the WTO, within the framework of the dispute on the trade description of sardines and of sardine-type products. The two parties considered that the new European Regulation fulfilled the requirements of the Dispute Settlement Body rulings. The new EC Regulation is based on the relevant standard of the* Codex Alimentarius. *Among the possibilities offered by the standard of the* Codex, *the European Union did choose one that guarantees the most complete information and that avoids the risks of confusion between the various species of fish. The European consumer is increasingly demanding when commercial information is involved and with regard to the quality of the products. Even so, the Regulation does not establish one obligation to use the scientific name in all cases, provided the used commercial name is sufficiently distinctive. It was certainly not the intention of the European Union to make non-European species less commercially viable. The European Union sought to ensure a maximum of transparency in the drafting of its new Regulation allowing WTO Members to express their views on the subjects.*'[939]

- In *Japan—Measures Affecting the Importation of Apples*, the United States took issue with certain Japanese quarantine measures on American apples which had been allegedly installed to protect Japan from the introduction of fire blight. The United States complained that the nine disputed measures imposed an overly restrictive quarantine regime and were maintained without sufficient scientific evidence. These measures included: (1) the prohibition to import apples from orchards in which any fire blight was detected, (2) the requirement

[938] Trade Policy Review of the European Communities of 25–27 October 2004, Written questions and answers, WT/TPR/M/136/Add. 1, 18 January 2005, 154.

[939] Trade Policy Review of the European Communities of 25–27 October 2004, Written questions and answers, WT/TPR/M/136/Add. 1, 18 January 2005, 172–73.

that export orchards be inspected three times yearly for the presence of fire blight, and (3) the disqualification of any orchard from exporting to Japan should fire blight be detected within a 500-metre buffer zone surrounding such orchard.[940] According to the United States these measures violated Article XI of the GATT (1994), Articles 2.2 and 3, 5.1 to 5.3 and 5.6, 6.1 and 6.2, and Article 7 and Annex B of the SPS Agreement and Article 14 of the Agreement on Agriculture.

The initiation of the DSB case was preceded by the TPR of Japan of November 2000.[941] Nonetheless, neither its Secretariat's report[942] nor its government's report[943] were able to identify the nascent contours of the dispute. However, during the TPRB meeting, Japan itself felt obliged to underline that '*Japan's SPS measures were applied only to the extent necessary for the protection of human, animal or plant life or health, in full consistency with the SPS agreement based on scientific principles. Under the Japanese plant protection system, quarantine pests were defined as those liable to cause damage to economic plants if they were to spread, and which met either of following conditions: those which were not confirmed as existing in Japan, or those which were already present in some part of Japan, but for which official controls were undertaken. This definition was based on the standards provided by the International Plant Protection Convention*.'[944] Nevertheless, the United States did not seize the opportunity of this Japanese statement to table any further written question with regard to the topic.[945]

The TPR of Japan of November 2002 became more explicit with regard to the case.[946] The Secretariat's sub-sectional reporting on Standards and SPS measures simply indicates that '*on 1 March, the US requested consultations with Japan with respect to restrictions on Japan's import of apples*'.[947] However, the Japanese

[940] WTO, *Japan—Measures Affecting the Importation of Apples—Report of the Panel* (15 July 2003), WT/DS245/R; WTO, *Japan—Measures Affecting the Importation of Apples—Appellate Body Report* (26 November 2003) WT/DS245/AB/R; Gavin Goh, 'Tipping the Apple Cart: The Limits of Science and Law in the SPS Agreement after Japan – Apples' (2006) 40(4) Journal of World Trade 655–686 (hereafter Goh, 'Tipping the Apple Cart: The Limits of Science and Law in the SPS Agreement after Japan – Apples').

[941] Trade Policy Review of Japan of 14–16 November 2000, Minutes of the Meeting, WT/TPR/M/76, 1 February 2001.

[942] Trade Policy Review of Japan of 14–16 November 2000, Secretariat Report, WT/TPR/S/76, 17 October 2000, 54–57, 45–49, and 44; Similarly, the topic is not mentioned in Secretariat's analysis of Agriculture; Trade Policy Review of Japan of 14–16 November 2000, Secretariat Report, WT/TPR/S/76, 17 October 2000, 81–87.

[943] Trade Policy Review of Japan of 14–16 November 2000, Government Report, WT/TPR/G/76, 17 October 2000.

[944] Trade Policy Review of Japan of 14–16 November 2000, Minutes of the Meeting, WT/TPR/M/76, 1 February 2001, 33

[945] Trade Policy Review of Japan of 14–16 November 2000, Written questions and answers, WT/TPR/M/76/Add. 1, 13 February 2001.

[946] Trade Policy Review of Japan of 6–8 November 2002, Minutes of the Meeting, WT/TPR/M/107, 4 February 2003.

[947] Trade Policy Review of Japan of 6–8 November 2002, Secretariat Report, WT/TPR/S/107, 9 October 2002, 38–42 (particularly at 41); Nonetheless, Secretariat's (sectional) reporting on Agriculture remains (again) silent on the problem; Trade Policy Review of Japan of 6–8 November 2002, Secretariat Report, WT/TPR/S/107, 9 October 2002, 54–59.

government's report does not dwell on the issue at all.[948] This silence did not stop the United States from raising the issue during the TPRB meeting. In this regard, the United States repeatedly stated in general terms that it '*was concerned with Japan's use of non-science-based import restrictive measures, affecting the importation of a broad range of agricultural products, and expected Japan to fulfil its obligations under the WTO SPS agreement and employ only the least trade-restrictive sanitary and phytosanitary measures*'.[949] Japan answered that it was '*on many fronts a disease/pest-free country, and the introduction of infectious disease or pest, through insufficient quarantine measures, would severely damage the Japanese industry. Once this damage was done it was difficult to recover, and recovery to the previous level of safety was slow. Furthermore, the government was faced with growing public awareness about the safety of the food and the recovery of consumer confidence was even more difficult than the recovery of the material damage to the industry. SPS measures were highly technical in nature and differed from one product to another, or one pest to another. A full satisfactory response to some of the concerns expressed on SPS-related issues could only be provided through consultations at expert level, including the question of the scientific basis upon which experts were acting. Japan was prepared to enter into any bilateral consultations at expert level*'.[950]

On 15 July 2003, the Panel report was circulated to Members.[951] According to the Panel, Japan's imposition of its phytosanitary quarantine measures on imports of apples from the United States was contrary to Articles 2.2, 5.1, and 5.7 of the SPS Agreement. Moreover, this finding was confirmed by the Appellate Body.[952] The parties therefore agreed to a reasonable period of time to implement the recommendations which would expire on 30 June 2004.[953] Nevertheless, on 19 July 2004, the United States considered that Japan had failed to implement the DSB's recommendations. It therefore requested a compliance Panel to look into Japan's alleged continued violation of Articles 2.2 and 3, 5.1 to 5.3, 5.5, and 6.1 and 6.2 of the SPS Agreement, Article XI of the GATT (1994) and Article 4.2 of the Agreement on Agriculture.[954] Simultaneously with its request to establish a compliance Panel, the United States requested the DSB to authorize its suspension of concessions or other obligations with respect to Japan. Since Japan objected, the DSB meeting of 30 July 2004 agreed that the matter would be referred to arbitration.[955] Nevertheless, on 4

[948] Trade Policy Review of Japan of 6–8 November 2002, Government Report, WT/TPR/G/107, 9 October 2002, 95–106.

[949] Trade Policy Review of Japan of 6–8 November 2002, Minutes of the Meeting, WT/TPR/M/107, 4 February 2003, 15.

[950] Trade Policy Review of Japan of 6–8 November 2002, Minutes of the Meeting, WT/TPR/M/107, 4 February 2003, 23.

[951] WTO, *Japan—Measures Affecting the Importation of Apples—Report of the Panel* (15 July 2003) WT/DS245/R.

[952] WTO, *Japan—Measures Affecting the Importation of Apples—Appellate Body Report* (26 November 2003) WT/DS245/AB/R.

[953] WTO, *Japan—Measures Affecting the Importation of Apples—Agreement under Article 21.3(b) of the DSU* (12 February 2004) WT/DS245/9, 1.

[954] WTO, *Japan—Measures Affecting the Importation of Apples—Recourse to Article 21.5 of the DSU by the United States* (23 June 2005) WT/DS245/RW.

[955] WTO, Minutes of Meeting, WT/DSB/M/174, 1 September 2004.

August 2004, Japan and the United States tabled a request to suspend the arbitration proceeding until the DSB's adoption of the recommendations and the rulings of the compliance Panel.[956]

The TPR of Japan of January 2005 took therefore place before the compliance Panel had issued its conclusions.[957] Unlike the Secretariat's succinct previous reporting on the case (ie in 2002), its report for the 2005 TPR remains surprisingly silent on the DSB case.[958] Neither is the topic contained in the Japanese government's report.[959] Nevertheless, this silence did not stop the United States from raising the topic in general terms during the TPRB meeting. In this regard, the United States emphasized that it was '*concerned about Japan's use of non-science based sanitary and phytosanitary measures, which restricted the importation of a broad range of agricultural products, such as beef, poultry, and apples; as a global leader in trade, Japan was expected to fulfil its obligations under the WTO SPS agreement and employ only the least trade-restrictive SPS measures. The US considered that the defensive posture on agriculture continued to hold Japan from being a more active player in the DDA negotiations. It encouraged Japan to take a forward-looking stance, by expanding market access on agricultural imports, cutting trade-distorting subsidies to farmers, and implementing SPS measures in an appropriate and science-based manner*'.[960] Moreover, the subject was also raised throughout the written questions, though not by the United States.[961]

On 23 June 2005, the compliance report was circulated. According to the compliance Panel, Japan's imposition of phytosanitary measure on imports of apples from the United States was contrary to Articles 2.2 and 5.1 of the SPS Agreement. Moreover, the Panel considered that if the United States only exported mature, symptomless apples, the alternative measures which had been proposed by the United States met the requirement of Article 5.6 of the SPS Agreement.[962] As a result, on 30 August 2005, Japan and the United States informed the DSB that they had reached a mutually agreed solution.[963]

[956] WTO, *Japan—Measures Affecting the Importation of Apples—Request by Japan for Arbitration under Article 22.6 of the DSU* (10 August 2004) WT/DS245/16.

[957] Trade Policy Review of Japan of 25–27 January 2005, Minutes of the Meeting, WT/TPR/M/142, 1 April 2005.

[958] Trade Policy Review of Japan of 25–27 January 2005, Secretariat Report, WT/TPR/S/142, 17 December 2004, 37–40; Likewise, the Secretariat's analysis of Agriculture does not deal with the subject; Trade Policy Review of Japan of 25–27 January 2005, Secretariat Report, WT/TPR/S/142, 17 December 2004, 59–64.

[959] Trade Policy Review of Japan of 25–27 January 2005, Government Report, WT/TPR/G/142, 17 December 2004.

[960] Trade Policy Review of Japan of 25–27 January 2005, Minutes of the Meeting, WT/TPR/M/142, 1 April 2005, 13.

[961] Trade Policy Review of Japan of 25–27 January 2005, Written questions and answers, WT/TPR/M/142/Add. 1, 12 April 2005, 102 and 238.

[962] WTO, *Japan—Measures Affecting the Importation of Apples—Recourse to Article 21.5 of the DSU by the United States* (23 June 2005) WT/DS245/RW.

[963] WTO, *Japan—Measures Affecting the Importation of Apples—Notification of Mutually Agreed solution* (2 September 2005) WT/DS245/21.

Japan's TPR of February 2007 no longer revisits the issue,[964] neither via the Secretariat's report[965] nor by means of the Japanese government's report.[966] In a similar vein, the United States used the meeting of the TPRB to table general complaints only about restrictive SPS measures; it no longer specifically referred to the apples dispute,[967] nor did the it table any further written questions with regard to the subject.[968]

- In *EC—Measures Affecting the Approval and Marketing of Biotech Products*, the United States, Canada, and Argentina took issue with certain measures by the European Community and its Member states which impeded their national export of Genetically Modified Organisms (GMO) and GMO-related products.[969] Regarding EC-level measures, a moratorium applied by the EC since October 1998 on the approval of biotech products had restricted imports of agricultural and food products. With regard to Member state-level measures, a number of EC Member states maintained national marketing and import bans on biotech products even though these products had already been approved by the EC for import and marketing in the EC.[970] The United States, Canada, and Argentina therefore alleged that the measures at issue were inconsistent with the EC's obligations under Articles 2, 5, 7, and 8, and Annexes B and C of the SPS Agreement, with Articles I, III, X, and XI of the GATT (1994), with Article 4 of the Agreement on Agriculture, and with Articles 2 and 5 of the TBT Agreement. According to Argentina, the measures were, in addition, inconsistent with Article 10 of the SPS Agreement and with Article 7 of the TBT Agreement.

Although the TPR of the European Communities of July 2002[971] preceded the launch of formal consultations in this dispute,[972] its Secretariat report already

[964] Trade Policy Review of Japan of 31 January–2 February 2007, Minutes of the Meeting, WT/TPR/M/175, 28 March 2007.

[965] Trade Policy Review of Japan of 31 January–2 February 2007, Secretariat Report, WT/TPR/S/175, 19 December 2006, 31–47 (particularly at 42–46); Likewise, Secretariat's analysis of Agriculture did not raise the issue of the dispute; Trade Policy Review of Japan of 31 January–2 February 2007, Secretariat Report, WT/TPR/S/175, 19 December 2006, 62–69.

[966] Trade Policy Review of Japan of 31 January–2 February 2007, Government Report, WT/TPR/G/175, 19 December 2006.

[967] Trade Policy Review of Japan of 31 February–2 February 2007, Minutes of the Meeting, WT/TPR/M/175, 28 March 2007, 13–14 and 23.

[968] Trade Policy Review of Japan of 31 February–2 February 2007, Written questions and answers, WT/TPR/M/175/Add. 1, 5 April 2007, 273.

[969] WTO, *EC—Measures Affecting the Approval and Marketing of Biotech Products—Report of the Panel* (29 September 2006) WT/DS291-DS292-DS293/R; Denise Prévost, 'Opening Pandora's Box: The Panel's Findings in the EC–Biotech Products Dispute' (2007) 34, Legal Issues of Economic Integration 67–101.

[970] David Wirth, 'The World Trade Organization Dispute Over Genetically Modified Organisms: The Precautionary Principle Meets International Trade Law' (2013) 4 Vermont Law Review 1177.

[971] Trade Policy Review of the European Communities of 24–26 July 2002, Minutes of the Meeting, WT/TPR/M/102, 23 September 2002.

[972] WTO, *EC—Measures Affecting the Approval and Marketing of Biotech Products—Request for Consultations* (20 May 2003) WT/DS291.

sheds considerable light on the topic. The Secretariat's sub-section on Product regulations and standards indicates that '*As was noted at the time of the previous review, a number of food scares at the Community level, as well as controversies over the placement of novel foods on the market, had led to a debate on the issue of food safety. Changes were also made to the legislative framework for the placement on the market of genetically modified organisms (GMOs) and products that may contain GMO or GMO derivatives, which was noted as an area of controversy at the time of the last review, both within the EU and between the EU and the United States. Although 18 authorizations for placement on the Community market had been issued in the course of the 1990s, the process of marketing new products throughout the Member states was effectively frozen since 1998. The new legislation tightens authorization procedures, which are to be time-bound and provides for mandatory labelling. However, certain Member states have continued to oppose the licensing of GMOs, pending the introduction of traceability on labels.*'[973] The sub-section moreover underlines that 'the Commission has also proposed comprehensive traceability labelling requirements for products containing, or produced from GMOs'. However, the government report did not raise the topic.[974]

Nevertheless, all three future complainants in the case (the United States, Canada, and Australia) used the TPRB meeting in an attempt to name and shame the European Union into a better behaviour. The United States stated that '*Concerns with EU regulatory approaches had come up in several other areas. Unfortunately, there had been little progress since the EU's last TPR on agricultural biotechnology, where the EU continued to ignore its international obligations, refusing to make final decisions on approvals of agricultural biotechnology products, even where no health risks had been identified through scientific review. The situation was becoming even more discouraging as the EU appeared bent on instituting a mandatory labelling and traceability scheme for biotechnology products that the United States believed would be prone to fraud and basically inoperable, posing a new barrier to the development of this promising technology.*'[975] In a similar vein, Canada noted that '*As a major exporter and developer of innovative agricultural products, Canada was concerned that its exports to the EU had declined over the last few years. One reason was the EU's recent trends towards regulations that were an impediment to Canada's exports. Canada was particularly concerned because these regulations were often introduced under the guise of food safety and SPS concerns, but were taken without a sound scientific basis and a due regard for international standards. One example was the EU's management of agricultural biotechnology: the approval process had been stalled for*

[973] Trade Policy Review of the European Communities of 24–26 July 2002, Secretariat Report, WT/TPR/S/102, 26 June 2002, 37–46 (particularly at 39 and 41–42); As usual, the section on Agriculture does not address the future dispute; Trade Policy Review of the European Communities of 24–26 July 2002, Secretariat Report, WT/TPR/S/102, 26 June 2002, 69–77.

[974] Trade Policy Review of the European Communities of 24–26 July 2002, Government Report, WT/TPR/G/102.

[975] Trade Policy Review of the European Communities of 24–26 July 2002, Minutes of the Meeting, WT/TPR/M/102, 23 September 2002, 24.

four years, although there was no evidence to such that foods obtained through biotechnology, which had been approved under an internationally recognized approach, such as those developed by the OECD and the FAO/WHO, were any less safe than their conventional counterparts.'[976] Argentina intervened in a similar critical vein while noting that it was '*also concerned by the proposed EU Regulation on labelling and traceability of food and feed products produced from genetically modified organisms (GMOs), whose implementation would have adverse implications for exporters of products that contained or were produced from GMOs. Argentina had submitted its comments on this regulatory proposal to the SPS Committee and the TBT committee*'.[977] Nonetheless, the European Union brushed these criticisms aside, while emphasizing that '*A number of concerns were expressed about the European approach to risk assessment and precaution, for example as regards genetically modified organisms (GMOs). The EU's approach to precaution involved comprehensive pre-market scientific risk assessment, which was taken into account when the Council took decisions ... In trying to take the correct approach to precaution, the EU was in the vanguard of those Members who were having to find the appropriate balance between trade and the protection of health and safety, often without clear international consensus on where the balance should be struck. Many of the issues confronting the European regulator at present would sooner or later confront regulators of other Members.*'[978]

This response prompted counterarguments by Argentina and the United States. Argentina noted that '*although it was true that the SPS agreement permitted standards of a higher level than international ones to be applied, its Article 3.3 stipulated that they had to be based on a scientific risk assessment*'.[979] The United States shared '*other delegations concerns on the EU's handling of the debate on GMOs and risk assessment and noted the importance of risk management*'.[980] The European Union therefore felt obliged to clarify that '*traceability and labelling were not one and the same matter. Labelling was generally not linked to food safety, but was related to the need to provide consumers with information, while traceability was linked to food safety. The Commission understood the need for consideration of the full implications of the proposed measures on GMOs, but noted that the EU parliament wished to restrict the presence of GMOs in the food chain even further. There was clearly a link between approval of the traceability and labelling regulations and political support for restarting the approval of new GMOs*'.[981]

[976] Trade Policy Review of the European Communities of 24–26 July 2002, Minutes of the Meeting, WT/TPR/M/102, 23 September 2002, 14–15.

[977] Trade Policy Review of the European Communities of 24–26 July 2002, Minutes of the Meeting, WT/TPR/M/102, 23 September 2002, 29.

[978] Trade Policy Review of the European Communities of 24–26 July 2002, Minutes of the Meeting, WT/TPR/M/102, 23 September 2002, 49.

[979] Trade Policy Review of the European Communities of 24–26 July 2002, Minutes of the Meeting, WT/TPR/M/102, 23 September 2002, 52.

[980] Trade Policy Review of the European Communities of 24–26 July 2002, Minutes of the Meeting, WT/TPR/M/102, 23 September 2002, 53.

[981] Trade Policy Review of the European Communities of 24–26 July 2002, Minutes of the Meeting, WT/TPR/M/102, 23 September 2002, 55.

Further to the requests of the United States, Canada, and Argentina, on 4 March 2004 the Director-General composed a joint Panel.[982]

The TPR of the European Communities of October 2004 took place before the Panel had issued its report.[983] Nevertheless, the Secretariat report's sub-section on SPS measures[984] pedagogically analyses new legal developments in the context while noting that '*Since its last TPR, the EC has adopted two Regulations related to food and feed products produced from genetically modified organisms (GMOs).*[985] *Under a Regulation adopted on 22 September 2003, applications for authorization to place genetically modified food and feed products on the EC market are to be lodged with the European Food Safety Authority (EFSA) through a competent national authority. The EFSA is expected to give its opinion to the Commission within six months. On the basis of the EFSA's opinion and 'other factors' (not specified), the Commission is empowered to take a decision in consultation with the Committee on Food Chain and Animal Health within three months. The implementation of the 2003 Regulation should pave the way for lifting the moratorium on new authorizations. The second Regulation concerns the traceability and labelling of GMOs, and the traceability of food and feed products produced from GMOs.*[986] *According to this Regulation, when placing a genetically modified product on the Community market, operators must transmit to those receiving the product certain details indicating that it contains GMOs. Operators are also required to have in place systems and procedures that support the holding of this information for a five-year period. Operators are also required to ensure that products containing GMOs be labelled as such.*' Unsurprisingly, the government report remains silent on the subject.[987]

This did not stop the majority of the complainants from referring to the allegedly problematic GMO-labelling schemes and/or to the DSB case during the TPRB meeting. The United States stated in this regard that it '*remained discouraged that the EC appeared determined to implement a mandatory labelling and traceability scheme for biotechnology products*'.[988] Similarly, Canada emphasized that it '*was a major*

[982] WTO, *EC—Measures Affecting the Approval and Marketing of Biotech Products—Constitution of the Panel Established at the Requests of the United States, Canada and Argentina* (5 March 2004) WT/DS291/24-WT/DS292/18 and WT/DS293/18, 5 March 2004, 1.

[983] Trade Policy Review of the European Communities of 25–27 October 2004, Minutes of the Meeting, WT/TPR/M/136, 18 January 2005.

[984] Trade Policy Review of the European Communities of 25–27 October 2004, Secretariat Report, WT/TPR/S/136, 23 June 2004, 63–66 and 65; On the other hand, Secretariat's sectional reporting on Agriculture (again) remains silent on the subject; Trade Policy Review of the European Communities of 25–27 October 2004, Secretariat Report, WT/TPR/S/136, 23 June 2004, 85–100.

[985] Council Regulation (EC) 1829/2003 on genetically modified food and feed [2003] OJ L/268/1 (hereafter EC Regulation on genetically modified food 2003).

[986] Council Regulation (EC) 1830/2003 concerning the traceability and labelling of genetically modified organisms and the traceability of food and feed products produced from genetically modified organisms and amending Directive 2001/18/EC [2003] OJ L268/24 (hereafter EC Regulation concerning the traceability and labelling of genetically modified organisms 2003).

[987] Trade Policy Review of the European Communities of 25–27 October 2004, Government Report, WT/TPR/G/136, 1 October 2004.

[988] Trade Policy Review of the European Communities of 25–27 October 2004, Minutes of the Meeting, WT/TPR/M/136, 18 January 2005, 12–13, 31, and 35 (particularly at 13 and 31).

exporter of agricultural products derived through modern bio-technologies. It remained concerned about regulations that impeded trade for these products (for example, the EC's moratorium on the approval process for agricultural biotech products); since 2002, little progress in this area had been observed. On GMOs, the EC labelling and traceability measures were creating uncertainty for Canadian exporters. Canada was concerned about how the traceability and detection requirements would be implemented given the lack of internationally-accepted testing and sampling methodologies to validate the presence of GMOs'.[989] Furthermore, Argentina and the United States tabled detailed additional written questions with regard to the issue.[990]

In the meantime, the deadline for the circulation of the Panel report was repeatedly delayed throughout 2004, 2005, and 2006. Finally, on 29 September 2006, the Panel report was circulated.[991] The Panel deemed that the European Communities had applied a general de facto moratorium on the approval of biotech products between June 1999 and August 2003. The Panel moreover considered that, by applying this moratorium, the European Communities had acted inconsistently with its obligations under Annex C(1)(a), first clause, and with Article 8 of the SPS Agreement because the de facto moratorium led to undue delays in the completion of EC approval procedures. With regard to the product-specific EC measures, the Panel found that the European Community had acted inconsistently with its obligations under Annex C(1)(a), first clause, and with Article 8 of the SPS Agreement in respect of the approval procedures concerning twenty-four out of the twenty-seven biotech products as identified by the complaining parties because there were undue delays in the completion of the approval procedures for each of these products. With regard to the EC Member state safeguard measures, the Panel found that the European Community had acted inconsistently with its obligations under Articles 2.2 and 5.1 of the SPS Agreement with regard to all of the safeguard measures at issue, because these measures were not based on risk assessments in conformity with the SPS Agreement. At its meeting on 21 November 2006, the DSB adopted the Panel report.[992] In December 2006, the parties started to discuss a reasonable period of time for implementation of the Panel's recommendations.

The TPR of the European Union of February 2007 points again to the issue.[993] The Secretariat's and the government's report both highlight the topic. Surprisingly, the Secretariat's reporting on the subject is not contained within its sub-sectional analysis of SPS measures[994] (which had been Secretariat's standard

[989] Trade Policy Review of the European Communities of 25–27 October 2004, Minutes of the Meeting, WT/TPR/M/136, 18 January 2005, 9–10 (particularly at 9).

[990] Trade Policy Review of the European Communities of 25–27 October 2004, Written questions and answers, WT/TPR/M/136/Add. 1, 18 January 2005, 178–81 and 154–55.

[991] WTO, *EC—Measures Affecting the Approval and Marketing of Biotech Products—Report of the Panel* (29 September 2006) WT/DS291-DS292-DS293/R.

[992] WTO, DSB, Minutes of Meeting, WT/DSB/M/222, 12 January 2007, 17.

[993] Trade Policy Review of the European Union of 26–28 February 2007, Minutes of the Meeting, WT/TPR/M/177, 30 April 2007.

[994] Trade Policy Review of the European Union of 26–28 February 2007, Secretariat Report, WT/TPR/S/177, 22 January 2007, 59–61.

practice) but in the report's section on documentation of European Agriculture and related activities.[995] The latter indicates that '*In April 2004, Regulation (EC) No. 1829/2003 on genetically modified (GM) food and feed came into force, introducing a labelling requirement for GM feed, as well as an exemption from labelling GM food and feed containing adventitious or technically unavoidable traces of GMOs up to 0.9%. Regulation (EC) No. 1830/2003 on the traceability and labelling of GMOs and the traceability of food and feed goods produced from GMOs entered into force in 2004. It introduced specific requirements on the traceability and labelling of GM food and feed.*' Moreover, the TPR's government report also underlines in general terms that '*the EC attached the greatest importance to the timely implementation and compliance with all WTO agreements ... For this, the EC has focussed on strict coherence between the rules governing its Internal Market and the relevant WTO agreements, including, for example, the TBT, SPS and TRIPS agreements. In the past, third countries have been concerned with some of the EC's legislative initiatives, for example on ... genetically modified organisms ... These measures have, however, the legitimate aim of ensuring a high level of protection of health and the environment and are by no means intended to impede circulation of goods in the Internal Market or external trade*'.[996]

During the TPRB meeting, the majority of complainants in the DSB case directly or indirectly referred to the case. The United States '*urged the EC to comply with the recommendations and rulings of the DSB in the Biotech Products dispute*'. It also asked '*what the EC was doing to address situations such as biotech approval or approval of the use of entire macrobiotic treatments for use on poultry*'.[997] Argentina stated only that '*the EC was an important importer of agricultural and fisheries products, however this should not be measured in absolute terms but in terms of specific restrictions that remained and that hampered the formation of prices based on supply and demand.*'[998] Nevertheless, the EC answered rather meaninglessly that '*regarding the reference made to the regulatory process, which could also apply to the GMO issue, on which the implementation of the Panel decision was under active discussion between the EC and other parties to the panel, the EC intended to find ways to comply with the decisions of the Panel.*'[999] None of the three complainants in the DSB case tabled any further written questions on the subject.[1000]

[995] Trade Policy Review of the European Union of 26–28 February 2007, Secretariat Report, WT/TPR/S/177, 22 January 2007, 79–95 (particularly at 85–86).

[996] Trade Policy Review of the European Union of 26–28 February 2007, Government Report, WT/TPR/G/177, 22 January 2007, 15.

[997] Trade Policy Review of the European Union of 26–28 February 2007, Minutes of the Meeting, WT/TPR/M/177, 30 April 2007, 14 and 26.

[998] Trade Policy Review of the European Union of 26–28 February 2007, Minutes of the Meeting, WT/TPR/M/177, 30 April 2007, 11.

[999] Trade Policy Review of the European Union of 26–28 February 2007, Minutes of the Meeting, WT/TPR/M/177, 30 April 2007, 27.

[1000] Trade Policy Review of the European Union of 26–28 February 2007, Written questions and answers, WT/TPR/M/177/Add. 1, 30 April 2007.

The parties to the dispute had initially all agreed that the reasonable period of time (RPT) to implement the DSB's recommendations would expire on 21 November 2007.[1001] Nonetheless, this RPT was later modified to expire on 11 January 2008.[1002] The RPT which had been agreed between Canada and the European Community was then repeatedly prolonged.[1003] Likewise, the RPT between Argentina and the European Community was subject to prolongation.[1004] On 14 January 2008, the European Community and the United States informed the DSB that they had reached an agreement on procedures under Articles 21 and 22 of the DSU.[1005] Nevertheless, on 6 February 2008, the European Community objected to the United States' request for authorization to suspend concessions and other obligations and referred the matter to arbitration under Article 22.6 of the DSU.[1006] In conformity with their agreed procedures, the European Community and the United States consequently asked the Arbitrator to suspend its work.[1007]

The TPR of the European Union of April 2009 took place before the European RPTs with Canada and Argentina had expired and pending suspended arbitration procedures with the United States. The TPR clearly touched on the dispute.[1008] The Secretariat report's sub-section on Technical regulations and other technical requirements provides an extensive overview of the legal and institutional framework with regard to Genetically Modified Organisms (GMOs).[1009] According to the Secretariat, it covered 'inter alia, laboratory research with GMOs (Directive 1990/219); the experimental release of GMOs into the environment (e.g. field testing) (Directive 2001/18); marketing of genetically modified seeds; marketing of food or feed containing, consisting or produced from GMOs (Regulation 1829/2003); and traceability and labelling (Regulation 1830/2003).[1010] Genetically modified seed varieties (and other plant-propagating material) must be authorized for cultivation under Directive 2001/18 on the deliberate

[1001] WTO, *EC—Measures Affecting the Approval and Marketing of Biotech Products—Agreement under Article 21.3(b) of the WTO* (26 June 2007) WT/DS291/35; WTO, *EC—Measures Affecting the Approval and Marketing of Biotech Products—Agreement under Article 21.3(b) of the DSU* (26 June 2007) WT/DS292/29.

[1002] WTO, *EC—Measures Affecting the Approval and Marketing of Biotech Products—Modification of the Agreement under Article 21.3(b) of the DSU* (23 November 2007) WT/DS291/36; WTO, *EC—Measures Affecting the Approval and Marketing of Biotech Products—Modification of the Agreement under Article 21.3(b) of the DSU* (23 November 2007) WT/DS292/30; WTO, *EC—Measures Affecting the Approval and Marketing of Biotech Products—Modification of the Agreement under Article 21.3(b) of the DSU* (23 November 2007) WT/DS293/30.

[1003] WTO, *EC—Measures Affecting the Approval and Marketing of Biotech Products—Modification of the Agreement under Article 21.3(b) of the DSU* (19 December 2008) WT/DS292/36.

[1004] WTO, *EC—Measures Affecting the Approval and Marketing of Biotech Products—Modification of the Agreement under Article 21.3(b) of the DSU* (1 March 2010) WT/DS293/40.

[1005] WTO, *EC—Measures Affecting the Approval and Marketing of Biotech Products—Understanding between the European Communities and the United States Regarding Procedures under Articles 21 and 22 of the DSU* (17 January 2008) WT/DS291/38.

[1006] WTO, *EC—Measures Affecting the Approval and Marketing of Biotech Products—Request by the European Communities for Arbitration under Article 22.6 of the DSU* (7 February 2008) WT/DS291/40.

[1007] WTO, *EC—Measures Affecting the Approval and Marketing of Biotech Products—Recourse by the European Communities to Article 22.6 of the DSU* (19 February 2008) WT/DS291/42.

[1008] Trade Policy Review of the European Union of 6–8 April 2009, Minutes of the Meeting, WT/TPR/M/214, 8 June 2009.

[1009] Trade Policy Review of the European Union of 6–8 April 2009, Secretariat Report, WT/TPR/S/214, 2 March 2009, 56–65 (particularly at 64–65); On the other hand, Secretariat's (sectional) analysis of Agriculture remains silent on the issue; Trade Policy Review of the European Union of 6–8 April 2009, Secretariat Report, WT/TPR/S/214, 2 March 2009, 97–114.

[1010] EC Regulation on genetically modified food 2003 (n 983).

release of GMOs into the environment or under Regulation 1829/2003 on genetically modified food and feed. Authorization is only granted after a positive assessment by the EFSA, including the environmental risk assessment carried out by a competent national authority that no unacceptable risks to the environment or human health is likely to appear. So far only one "GM event" (MON 810 maize) is authorized in the EC for cultivation, import, and processing. MON 810 (and various varieties of this 'event') are currently inscribed in the common catalogue for seed. Under EC Regulation 1829/2003, applications for authorization to market GM food and feed products in the EC are to be lodged with the EFSA through a competent national authority. The EFSA is expected to give its opinion to the Commission within six months, provided the application is complete and no further information is necessary. On the basis of the EFSA's opinion and any other "legitimate factors", the Commission should submit a proposal granting or rejecting the authorization to the Standing Committee on Food Chain and Animal Health within three months. Products derived from various genetically modified "events", including cotton, maize, oilseed, rape, soybean, sugar beet, and yeast and bacterial biomass have been authorized to be used in foodstuff or feed. Approval of other GMOs and their use for food or feed processing is pending; there appear to be considerable delays in reaching final decisions on GMO approvals. However, according to the Commission, the EC is looking for technical solutions that would limit trade disruption due to such time-lag without compromising its high level of protection. The EC has established traceability requirements for GM food and feed to facilitate the withdrawal of products in case of unforeseen adverse effects on human and animal health, or the environment, and to facilitate labelling of GMOs. Traceability applies to all stages of production and distribution of the product concerned.[1011] Operators are required to inform those receiving the product that it contains GMOs, and must keep information on the supplier and buyer of the product for five years. Operators are also required to ensure that products containing, consisting of or produced from GMOs are labelled accordingly. An exemption to the labelling and traceability requirements is foreseen for the adventitious presence and technically unavoidable presence (up to 0.9%) of products containing, consisting of or produced from authorized GMOs. The placing on the EC market of food, feed, and seeds that contain non-authorized GMOs is prohibited. It is intended that conventional seeds must be labelled if they contain genetically modified seeds; establishment of threshold levels is pending'. The government report does not touch on the issue.[1012]

During the TPRB meeting, the majority of complainants in the case attempted to name and shame the European Union into a better behaviour. They therefore indirectly or directly referred to the ongoing case. The United States complained that 'both in the area of SPS regulations and with respect to the standards applied to manufactured products, we continue to be concerned that some measures maintained by the EC on the grounds of food safety or environmental protection may not be appropriately supported by science-based risk assessments'.[1013] Canada was

[1011] EC Regulation concerning the traceability and labelling of genetically modified organisms 2003 (n 984).

[1012] Trade Policy Review of the European Union of 6–8 April 2009, Government Report, WT/TPR/G/214, 2 March 2009.

[1013] Trade Policy Review of the European Union of 6–8 April 2009, Minutes of the Meeting, WT/TPR/M/214, 8 June 2009, 43–44 and 81–82 (particularly at 43–44).

even more direct and emphasized that '*On the biotech dispute, while noting that some progress has been made, Canada expects the EC to fully comply with the Panel's recommendations. We expect the EC to ensure that the approval process for GMOs functions in a manner that is timely, predictable, and based on science. The recent approval of a GM canola of interest to Canada was a welcome development, but it took over 4 years, and some EC Member states continue to slow down the process and maintain unjustified and illegal bans on the marketing of certain GMOs.*'[1014] Furthermore, all complainants in the case tabled additional detailed legalistic written questions with regard to the topic.[1015] Nonetheless, the European Union rebutted all comments and noted that it '*would like to reiterate that EC's regulatory system for authorizing GMOs is in line with the WTO rules, as confirmed by the DSU case. Some Members commented that the authorization procedures for individual GMOs are slow. I will have to recall that authorisation of GMOs proceeds according to timetables established in the EC legislation, and delays are often due to the lack of complete information from the applicant. In any event, the European Food Safety Agency is working with applicants to improve applications so as to avoid any delays in the processing of applications. 21 authorisations have been granted since 2004*'.[1016]

On 15 July 2009, Canada and the European Communities notified the DSB of a mutually agreed solution.[1017] The parties thereby agreed to establish a bilateral dialogue on agricultural biotech market access issues of mutual interest. On 19 March 2010, Argentina and the European Union notified the DSB of a similar mutually agreed solution.[1018]

The issue is again highlighted in conclusion in the Secretariat's, though not government's,[1019] reporting for the TPR of the European Union of July 2011.[1020] Secretariat report's sub-section on SPS measures[1021] provides extensive institutional and legal background to the issue while neutrally stating that '*The use of genetically modified organisms (GMOs) is regulated at EU level on the basis of Regulation No. 1829/2003 on genetically modified food and feed, Directive 2001/18/EC on the deliberate release of GMOs into the environment, and Regulation 1830/2003 on the*

[1014] Trade Policy Review of the European Union, Minutes of the Meeting of 6–8 April 2009, WT/TPR/M/214, 8 June 2009, 32–34 and 82 (particularly at 33).

[1015] Trade Policy Review of the European Union of 6–8 April 2009, Written questions and answers, WT/TPR/M/214/Add. 1, 2 July 2009, respectively at 287–88, 217–20, and 348

[1016] Trade Policy Review of the European Union, Minutes of the Meeting of 6–8 April 2009, WT/TPR/M/214, 8 June 2009, 73.

[1017] WTO, *EC—Measures Affecting the Approval and Marketing of Biotech Products—Notification of a Mutually Agreed Solution* (17 July 2009) WT/DS292/40.

[1018] WTO, *EC—Measures Affecting the Approval and Marketing of Biotech Products—Notification of a Mutually Agreed Solution* (23 March 2010) WT/DS293/41.

[1019] Trade Policy Review of the European Union, Government Report of 6–8 July 2011, WT/TPR/G/248, 1 June 2011.

[1020] Trade Policy Review of the European Union of 6–8 July 2011, Minutes of the Meeting, WT/TPR/M/248, 14 September 2011.

[1021] Trade Policy Review of the European Union of 6–8 July 2011, Secretariat Report, WT/TPR/S/248, 1 June 2011, 55–60, especially at 60; On the other hand, the Secretariat Report's analysis on Agriculture is (again) silent on the topic; Trade Policy Review of the European Union of 6–8 July 2011, Secretariat Report, WT/TPR/S/248, 1 June 2011, 101–16.

traceability and labelling of GMOs, and food and feed produced from GMOs.[1022] *Member states may not legislate with respect to the cultivation of GMOs, only to their use. In July 2010, the European Commission adopted a proposed Regulation to amend Directive 2001/18/EC to allow Member states to restrict or prohibit the cultivation in all or part of their territories of GMOs authorized at the EU level. Under the proposed Regulation, Member states may adopt measures with respect to the cultivation of GMOs in their territories, but not with respect to the import into the EU of authorized GM seeds and plant propagating material, and the products of their harvest. Prohibitions or restrictions would be based on grounds other than those covered by the environmental and health risk assessment under the existing EU authorization system for GMOs. According to this system, the level of protection of human and animal health and of the environment chosen in the EU may not be revised by a Member State. Under the proposed Regulation, Member states must notify measures they intend to adopt, and the reasons for adopting them, to the Commission and to the other Member states one month prior to their adoption. The proposed legislation does not change the authorization procedure for GMOs. The Commission's legislative proposal is subject to the procedure on co-decision with the European Parliament and the Council. According to the Commission, the new approach is necessary "to achieve the right balance between maintaining the EU system of authorisations based on scientific assessment of health and environmental risks and the need to grant freedom to Member states to address specific national, regional or local issues raised by the cultivation of GMOs". Several Member states have prohibited or restricted cultivation of GMOs authorized at the EU level. For example, Austria, France, Germany, Hungary, and Lithuania have prohibited maize MON 810; Austria has prohibited maize T 25; and Austria, Hungary, and Luxembourg have prohibited Amflora potato.'* The Secretariat's report goes so far as indirectly to assess the illegality of these measures by some institutional referencing. In this regard, the report emphasizes that, '*according to the scientific opinion of the European Food Safety Agency, "these measures were not based on new or additional scientific information since the authorizations were granted and therefore such measures were not justified from a legal point of view." A judgement issued by the Court of Justice of the European Union in July 2009 considered that legislation adopted by Poland to prohibit the marketing of GM seeds was contrary to EU law.*'[1023] Although none of the complainants explicitly referred to the dispute, the majority of them seized the TPRB meeting in an attempt to name and shame the European Union into better behaviour. In this regard, the United States lamented the fact that '*food and animal feed products that have been safely consumed in the United States for decades, and that the United States exports to dozens of other Members, continue to be excluded from the EU market by SPS measures that appear to lack sufficient scientific justification.*

[1022] EC Regulation on genetically modified food 2003 (n 1012); Directive 2001/18/EC of the European Parliament and of the Council of 12 March 2001 on the deliberate release into the environment of genetically modified organisms and repealing Council Directive 90/220/EEC [2001] OJ L106; EC Regulation concerning the traceability and labelling of genetically modified organisms 2003 (n 984).

[1023] Case C-165/08 *Commission of the European Communities v Republic of Poland* [2009] ECR I-06843.

For example, the EU has restricted the import and marketing of certain products of agricultural biotechnology, and forbidden the use on food of certain pathogen reduction treatments, that the EU's own scientists have concluded pose no risk to human, animal, and plant life or health. Because of SPS and other barriers, U.S. agricultural exporters have been unable to take full advantage of the market access the EU offered in the Uruguay Round'. The United States indicated moreover that '*In the area of sanitary and phytosanitary measures, an area in which many Members have expressed concern in this review, we continue to urge the EU to implement a regulatory regime that complies with the EU's own statutory deadlines and in which regulatory decisions are consistent with the outcomes of risk assessments based on science and are consistently applied across Member states.*'[1024] Along similar lines, Canada stated that '*Canada and the EU share the legitimate objectives of protecting human, animal, plant health and the environment. While recognizing that there are different approaches to reaching these objectives, we have the highest expectations that the EU will ensure that any measures it takes are science-based, no more trade-restrictive than necessary and reflect the realities of global trade today. Unfortunately, in too many cases the EU has not lived up to these expectations.*' Moreover, Canada regretted that '*other measures that lack a scientific basis and that are of concern to Canada include the EU's policies and decisions regarding genetically modified organisms, as well as its ban on ractopamine, and the associated efforts to introduce regional issues that are not considered legitimate into the context of Codex decision-making.*'[1025] Each of the three complainants in the case tabled further detailed written questions on the subject.[1026] The EU rebutted these comments and answered briefly that '*Concerning GMOs specifically, our legislative framework is currently subject to two evaluations: 1) evaluation of the EU legislative framework on GM food and feed; and 2) evaluation of the EU legislative Framework in the Field of Cultivation of GMOs under Directive 2001/18/EC and Regulation (EC) No. 1829/2003 and marketing of their other uses under Directive 2001/18/EC. The final reports of these two evaluations are due to be published soon. It is on the basis of these reports that it will be considered whether there is a need to review the current EU policy on GMOs.*'[1027]

This analysis leads to several conclusions. First, reports of the Secretariat offer excellent added value in terms of transparency. These examples demonstrated that for most TPRs (especially those which took place after the formal request for DSB consultations had been tabled), the Secretariat's reporting was able to refer to the contours of the future dispute. Second, reports of the government under review again have a minimalistic added value in terms of transparency. With the exception of one case, they were never used to refer to actual or future trade concerns. Third, in terms of naming and shaming,

[1024] Trade Policy Review of the European Union of 6–8 July 2011, Minutes of the Meeting, WT/TPR/M/248, 14 September 2011, 28–30 and 68–70 (particularly at 29 and 69).

[1025] Trade Policy Review of the European Union of 6–8 July 2011, Minutes of the Meeting, WT/TPR/M/248, 14 September 2011, 24–25, and 71 (particularly at 24–25).

[1026] Trade Policy Review of the European Union of 6–8 July 2011, Written questions and answers, WT/TPR/M/248/Add.1, 31 August 2011, respectively at 250 and 253–54, 212–14, and 312–13.

[1027] Trade Policy Review of the European Union of 6–8 July 2011, Minutes of the Meeting, WT/TPR/M/248, 14 September 2011, 32–33 and 64.

both TPRB meetings and written questions and answers offer added value, the former as a forum for some general naming and shaming, the latter as a means which is sometimes used to put pressure on ongoing DSB litigation.

Structure of meeting

In the years which were covered by the second appraisal (ie 1999 to 2005), the structure of the TPR meetings barely changed. Most annual reports of this period therefore systematically repeat that '*procedures for the reviews have generally run smoothly*'.[1028] Moreover, the questions which inspired the structural discussions of the second appraisal were more or less equal to those which had driven its predecessor.[1029] As a result, the second appraisal resulted in some procedural changes concerning the run-up to the TPR meeting (the lead times before the review changed and the time lines for the written question and answer process were modified) but no modifications were made with regard to the structure of the meeting itself (where the second appraisal maintained the time frame for TPRs, as determined by the first review, and again urged a more interactive discussion during the second part of the TPR session).[1030] The 2005 rules of procedure therefore resulted in a simple update of the rules of procedure for meetings of the TPRB.[1031]

ii) Overview of developments in the International Trading Environment

Overviews undertaken towards the beginning of this period tend to echo the recovery of the world economy and global trade while at the same time warning about the continued significant risks.[1032] The Overviews for 2003 and 2004 stress the continued positive economic expectations for the future.[1033]

The structure and coverage of the yearly Overviews continued to evolve in a rather arbitrary way. First, in line with the Overviews taking place at the end of the period which was covered by the first appraisal, none of the five Overviews drafted

[1028] WTO, TPRB, Draft Report of the Trade Policy Review Body for 2000, Trade Policy Review Body, WT/TPR/W/27, 28 September 2000, 2; WTO, TPRB, Draft Report of the Trade Policy Review Body for 2000, Trade Policy Review Body, WT/TPR/W/27/Rev. 1, 6 October 2000, 2; WTO, TPRB, Draft Report of the Trade Policy Review Body for 2001, Trade Policy Review Mechanism, WT/TPR/W/28, 11 September 2001, 2; WTO, TPRB, Report of the Trade Policy Review Body for 2002, Trade Policy Review Body, WT/TPR/W/29, 7 October 2002, 2; WTO, TPRB, Draft Report of the Trade Policy Review Body for 2003, Trade Policy Review Mechanism, WT/TPR/W/31, 28 October 2003, 2; WTO, TPRB, Draft Report of the Trade Policy Review Body for 2004, Trade Policy Review Mechanism, WT/TPR/W/32, 18 October 2004, 2.

[1029] Possible points for the appraisal of the operation of the trade policy review mechanism (TPRM), Non-paper, 10 May 2005, 3–4 (Document on file with the author).

[1030] Second Appraisal of the Operation of the Trade Policy Review Mechanism—Draft Report to Ministers, WT/TPR/W/33, 12 August 2005, 1 and 3; *Second appraisal of the operation of the Trade Policy Review Mechanism 2005* (n 868) 1 and 3.

[1031] WTO, Draft Rules of Procedure for Meetings of the Trade Policy Review Body, Trade Policy Review Body, WT/TPR/W/34, 6 September 2005.

[1032] WTO, TPRB, Overview of developments in international trade and the trading system, Annual Report by the Director-General, WT/TPR/OV/6, 22 November 2000, 5; WTO, TPRB, Overview of developments in international trade and the trading system, Annual Report by the Director-General, WT/TPR/OV/7, 10 December 2001, 1.

[1033] WTO, TPRB, Overview of developments in international trade and the trading system, Annual Report by the Director-General, WT/TPR/OV/9, 20 February 2004, 1; WTO, TPRB, Overview of developments in international trade and the trading system, Annual Report by the Director-General, WT/TPR/OV/10, 15 November 2004, 1.

throughout the period covered by the second appraisal contained a specific section dedicated to the general analysis of activities undertaken within the framework of individual trade policy reviews.[1034] Nevertheless, all the Overviews explicitly singled out several individual countries' trade policies and practices. As a result, the information obtained throughout the TPRs which took place in the period covered by the second appraisal is extremely scattered over the reporting of the consecutive Overviews.[1035] Second, if some specific national trade policies and practices were highlighted, the (specific/general) criteria for doing so often remained unclear. For instance, the 2004 overview chooses to highlight south–south co-operation through the angle of investment in Mauritius—information which was (also) contained in Mauritius' TPR of 2001.[1036] However, the Overview could equally have chosen to highlight Cameroon's south–south co-operation—information which was included in Cameroon's review of the same year. Finally, the coverage of identified SPS and TBT measures and their potential follow-up in the respective framework of the TPRM and/or the DSB kept evolving in a rather erratic way. For instance, the Overview of 2000 dedicated a specific section to SPS and TBT measures.[1037] Nevertheless, this section did not contain any reference to SPS and/or TBT concerns as raised within the framework of the TPRM. The same is true for the overviews of 2001 and 2002.[1038] Nonetheless, in these two reviews the growing importance of SPS and TBT concerns, and the need for complete and comprehensive coverage by the Overviews, was twice underscored by a specific reference to their further follow-up within the framework of the DSB. The comprehensive nature of the Overviews' coverage increased with the Overview of 2004.[1039] This review is noteworthy, not

[1034] WTO, TPRB, Overview of developments in international trade and the trading system, Annual Report by the Director-General, WT/TPR/OV/6, 22 November 2000; WTO, TPRB, Overview of developments in international trade and the trading system, Annual Report by the Director-General, WT/TPR/OV/7, 10 December 2001; WTO, TPRB, Overview of developments in international trade and the trading system, Annual Report by the Director-General, WT/TPR/OV/8, 15 November 2002; WTO, TPRB, Overview of developments in international trade and the trading system, Annual Report by the Director-General, WT/TPR/OV/9, 20 February 2004; WTO, TPRB, Overview of developments in international trade and the trading system, Annual Report by the Director-General, WT/TPR/OV/10, 15 November 2004.

[1035] WTO, TPRB, Overview of developments in international trade and the trading system, Annual Report by the Director-General, WT/TPR/OV/6, 22 November 2000, 18–19 and 26–29; WTO, TPRB, Overview of developments in international trade and the trading system, Annual Report by the Director-General, WT/TPR/OV/7, 10 December 2001, 30–31, 38–40, 55, 74; WTO, TPRB, Overview of developments in international trade and the trading system, Annual Report by the Director-General, WT/TPR/OV/8, 15 November 2002, 9, 14, 19–21, 24, 26 and 32–34; WTO, TPRB, Overview of developments in international trade and the trading system, Annual Report by the Director-General, WT/TPR/OV/9, 20 February 2004, 2, 7, 13–14, 17–18, 20, 23, 25, 28, 29 and 35; WTO, TPRB, Overview of developments in international trade and the trading system, Annual Report by the Director-General, WT/TPR/OV/10, 15 November 2004, 4, 14, 16, 27, 29 and 32.

[1036] WTO, TPRB, Overview of developments in international trade and the trading system, Annual Report by the Director-General, WT/TPR/OV/10, 15 November 2004, 27.

[1037] WTO, TPRB, Overview of developments in international trade and the trading system, Annual Report by the Director-General, WT/TPR/OV/6, 22 November 2000, 24.

[1038] WTO, TPRB, Overview of developments in international trade and the trading system, Annual Report by the Director-General, WT/TPR/OV/7, 10 December 2001, 36–37; WTO, TPRB, Overview of developments in international trade and the trading system, Annual Report by the Director-General, WT/TPR/OV/8, 15 November 2002, 23.

[1039] WTO, TPRB, Overview of developments in international trade and the trading system, Annual Report by the Director-General, WT/TPR/OV/9, 20 February 2004, 28–30.

only because it contained yet another specific section on technical regulations and SPS measures but also in view of the its explicit reference to these concerns as they were treated in the respective frameworks of the TPRM and the DSB.[1040]

c) *Participation*

i) Governments (Government under review and its peers)

In the period covered by the second appraisal (ie the period between September 1999 and September 2005), ninety-three Members underwent a trade policy review.[1041]

Tables II.10 to II.13 demonstrate the volatility of the attendance rates to TPRs which took place in this period.

The top five well-attended TPRs comprised (in descending order) the 2004 TPR of the United States (with forty Members attending),[1042] the 2004 review of the European Communities (in the presence of thirty-eight Members),[1043] the 2002 TPR of the European Communities (with thirty-five Members attending),[1044] the respective 2000 and 2003 reviews of the European Community and Canada (both in presence of thirty-three Members),[1045] and the 2002 TPR of India (which was attended by thirty-one Members).[1046] In line with earlier findings, TPRs of the Quad countries received the highest attendance.

On the other hand, the least well-attended TPRs in this period were (in ascending order) the 1999 TPR of Nicaragua (with five Members attending),[1047] the 2001 review of Macao (in the presence of seven Members),[1048] and by the TPRs of Sierra Leona (2005), the Gambia (2004), and Papua New Guinea (1999) (each of which were attended by eight Members).[1049] In line with earlier findings, it seems rather difficult to attribute these low attendance rates solely to the specific geographical affiliations of the countries under review.

[1040] WTO, TPRB, Overview of developments in international trade and the trading system, Annual Report by the Director-General, WT/TPR/OV/9, 20 February 2004, 28–29.

[1041] That is, the period between the TPR of Romania of 1999 and the review of Trinidad and Tobago of 2005; Data of the author; See CD ROM '*20 years of Trade Policy Reviews 1989–2009, Marking the 20th anniversary of the Trade Policy Review Mechanism*'.

[1042] Trade Policy Review of the United States of 14–16 January 2004, Minutes of the Meeting, WT/TPR/M/126, 15 March 2004.

[1043] Trade Policy Review of the European Communities of 25–27 October 2004, Minutes of the Meeting, WT/TPR/M/136, 18 January 2005.

[1044] Trade Policy Review of the European Communities of 24–26 July 2002, Minutes of the Meeting, WT/TPR/M/102, 23 September 2002.

[1045] Trade Policy Review of the European Communities of 12–14 July 2000, Minutes of the Meeting, WT/TPR/M/72, 26 October 2000; Trade Policy Review of Canada of 12–14 March 2003, Minutes of the Meeting, WT/TPR/M/112, 12 May 2003.

[1046] Trade Policy review of India of 19–21 June 2002, Minutes of the Meeting, WT/TPR/M/100, 1 August 2002.

[1047] Trade Policy Review of Nicaragua of 25–27 October 1999, Minutes of the Meeting, WT/TPR/M/61, 24 November 1999.

[1048] Trade Policy Review of Macao of 19–21 March 2001, Minutes of the Meeting, WT/TPR/M/82, 24 April 2001.

[1049] Trade Policy Review of Sierra Leona of 9–11 February 2005, Minutes of the Meeting, WT/TPR/M/143, 29 March 2005; Trade Policy Review of the Gambia of 4–6 February 2004, Minutes of the Meeting, WT/TPR/M/127, 29 March 2004; Trade Policy Review of Papua New Guinea of 15–17 November 1999, Minutes of the Meeting, WT/TPR/M/62, 4 January 2000.

Table II.10

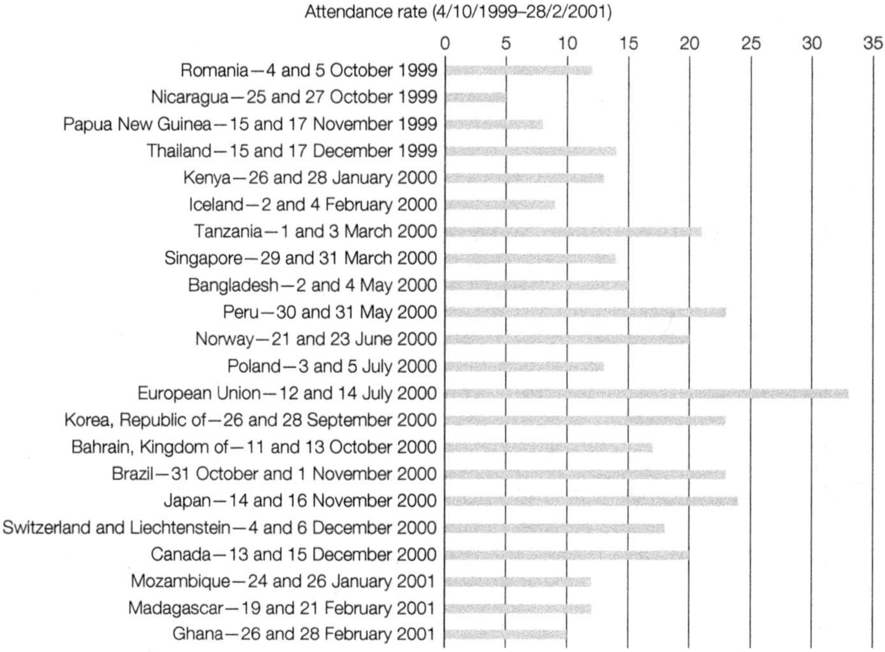

Table II.11

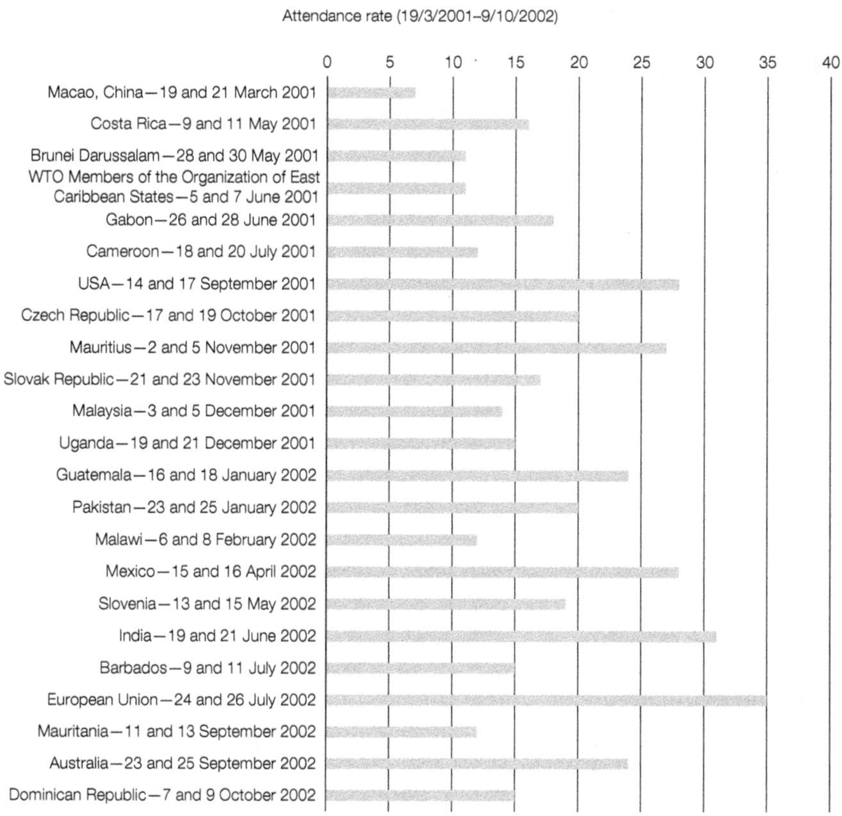

Table II.12

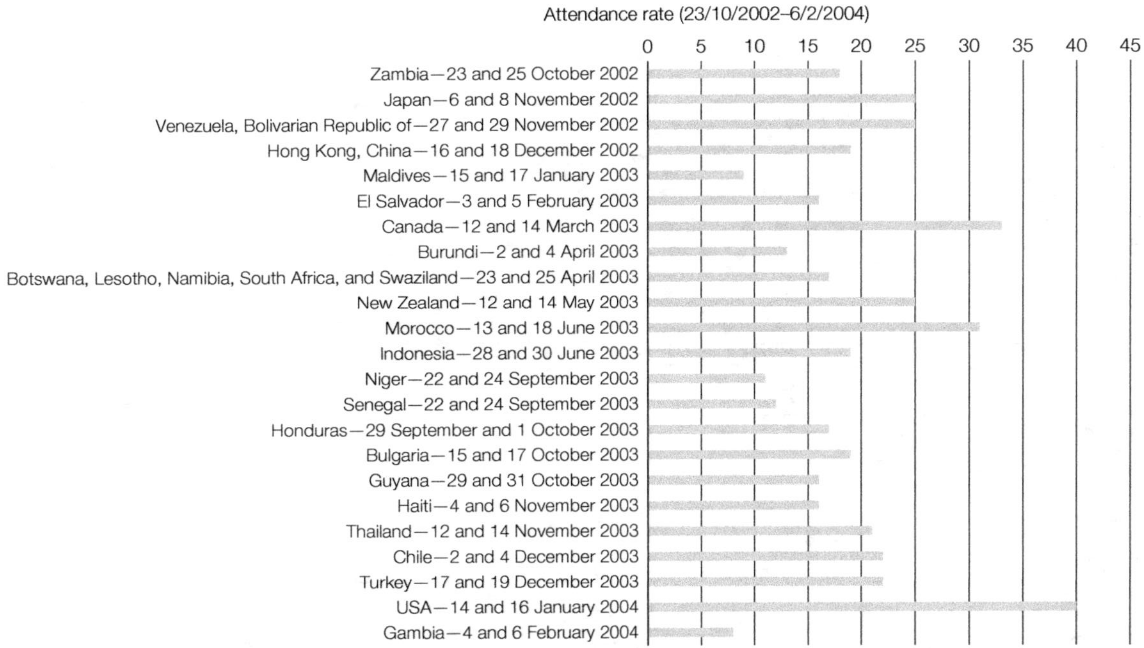

Attendance rate (23/10/2002–6/2/2004)
0
5
10
15
20
25
30
35
40
45
Zambia—23 and 25 October 2002
Japan—6 and 8 November 2002
Venezuela, Bolivarian Republic of—27 and 29 November 2002
Hong Kong, China—16 and 18 December 2002
Maldives—15 and 17 January 2003
El Salvador—3 and 5 February 2003
Canada—12 and 14 March 2003
Burundi—2 and 4 April 2003
Botswana, Lesotho, Namibia, South Africa, and Swaziland—23 and 25 April 2003
New Zealand—12 and 14 May 2003
Morocco—13 and 18 June 2003
Indonesia—28 and 30 June 2003
Niger—22 and 24 September 2003
Senegal—22 and 24 September 2003
Honduras—29 September and 1 October 2003
Bulgaria—15 and 17 October 2003
Guyana—29 and 31 October 2003
Haiti—4 and 6 November 2003
Thailand—12 and 14 November 2003
Chile—2 and 4 December 2003
Turkey—17 and 19 December 2003
USA—14 and 16 January 2004
Gambia—4 and 6 February 2004

Table II.13

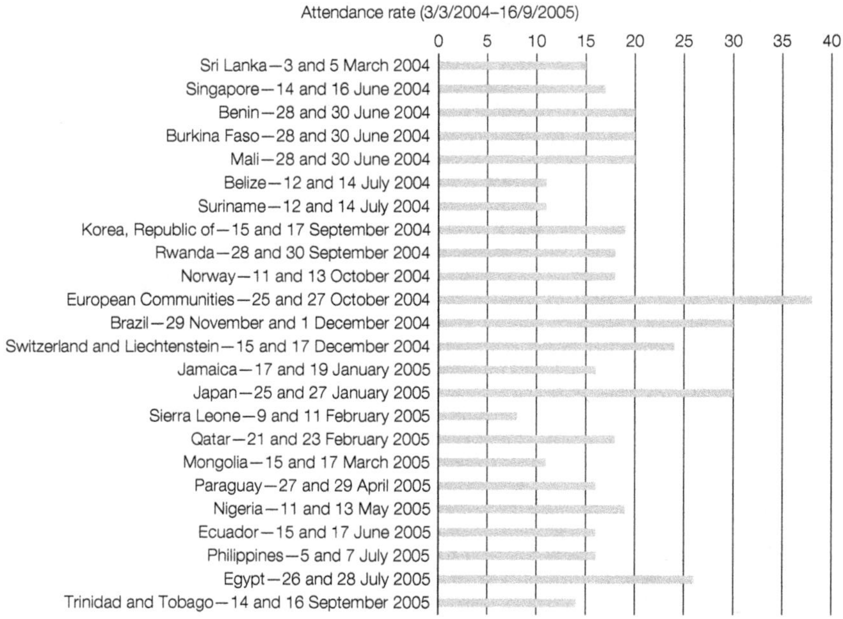

Table II.14

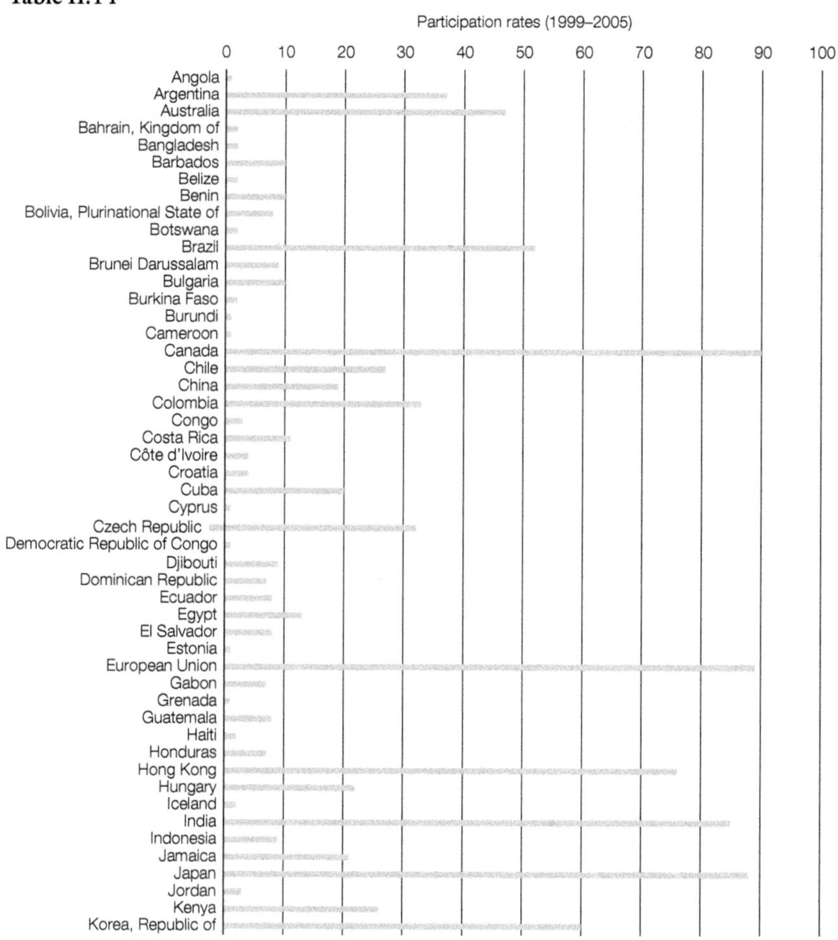

Tables II.14 and II.15 demonstrate the participation rates of individual countries in the period covered by the second appraisal (ie the period between September 1999 and September 2005).

The top five participants of this period are again almost entirely Quad countries. Amongst these countries (in descending order), Canada participated in ninety out of the ninety-three TPRs of this period; the United States and the European Union were each involved in eighty-nine reviews; Japan took part in eighty-eight TPRs; India was involved in eighty-five reviews, and Hong Kong which closed the rankings participating in seventy-six out of the ninety-three TPRs of this period.[1050]

Table II.15

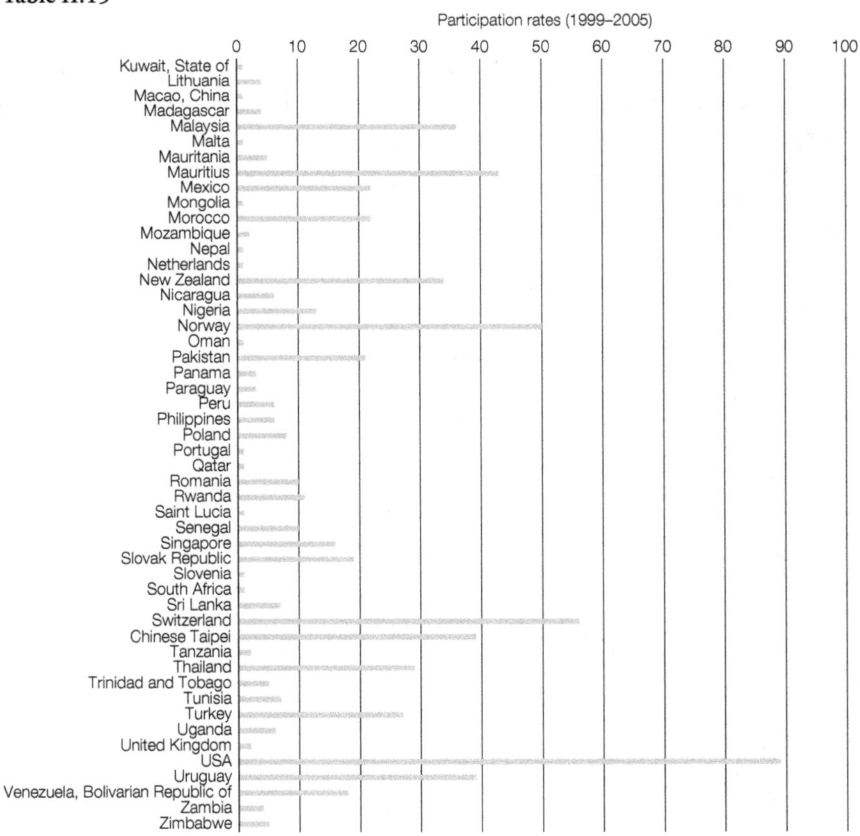

[1050] Data on file with the author.

Angola, Burundi, Cameroon, Cyprus, the Democratic Republic of Congo, Estonia, Grenada, the State of Kuwait, Macao, Malta, Mongolia, Nepal, The Netherlands, Oman, Portugal, Qatar, Saint Lucia, Slovenia, and South Africa participated in only one TPR each. The Kingdom of Bahrain, Bangladesh, Belize, Botswana, Burkina Faso, Haiti, Iceland, Mozambique, Tanzania, and the United Kingdom were involved in two reviews each. Congo, Jordan, Panama, and Paraguay closed the list, participating in three TPRs each.[1051]

	2000	2001	2002	2003	2004	2005
Average Attendance	19.0	15.3	21.0	19.1	21.5	16.9
Percentage	13.5%	10%	14%	13%	14%	11.3%

Yearly attendance rates in the period covered by the second appraisal (ie September 1999 to September 2005) were volatile, though less so than in the period covered by the first appraisal and with relative stagnation occurring as of 2002. Nevertheless, yearly attendance rates at the end of this period had dropped, both in relative and absolute terms.[1052]

ii) Secretariat

Table II.16

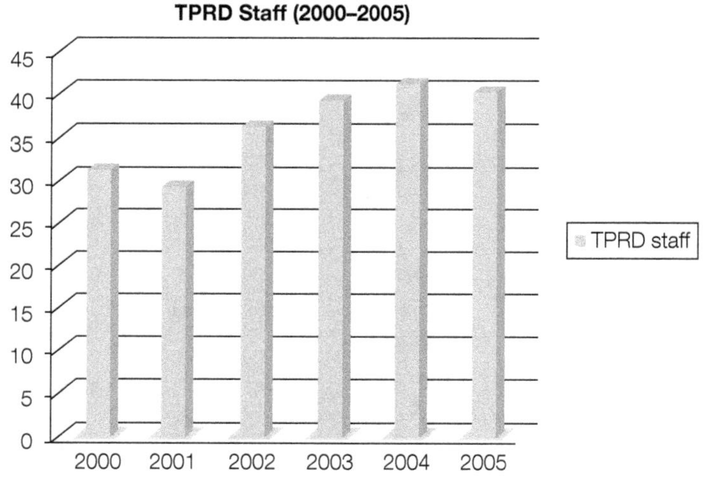

By the end of the period covered by the second appraisal (ie the period between September 1999 and September 2005), TPRD staff had increased to forty experts. With the exception of 2001 (when the department's staff decreased to twenty-nine individuals) and 2005 (when its staffing was reduced from forty-one to forty

[1051] Data on file with the author.

[1052] Data on file with the author.

individuals), the trend in staffing levels was positive. Furthermore, in this period, the overall percentage of staff allocated to the TPRD never amounted to more than 6 per cent of overall WTO staff.[1053]

During the period covered by the second appraisal, estimates were systematically provided for the general WTO budget and for the TPRD budget. Nevertheless, there continued to be a lack of formal data with regard to actual TPRD-related expenditure.[1054] The availability of formal data for the TPRD's actual expenditure for 2001 constitutes an exception.

In 1999, WTO budgetary estimates amounted initially to CHF 127.546.100. Of this total, CHF 3.380.250 was set aside for the TPRD's functioning.[1055] In addition to this estimated core funding, Denmark and Australia contributed respectively CHF 230.663,05 and CHF 82.622,09 of extra-budgetary funding for the TPRs of Burkina Faso, Guinea, Mali, Togo, Tanzania, and Papua New Guinea.[1056] This compared to an overall appropriated WTO budget of CHF 122.195.450 for 1999.[1057] The initial WTO budget estimates for 2000 amounted to CHF 131.068.660 including 3.210.850 for the TPRD.[1058] In addition to its estimated core funding, Germany, The Netherlands, and the United Kingdom also respectively contributed CHF 123.608,67, CHF 6.396,85, and CHF 15.685,90 of extra-budgetary funding for the respective TPRs of Madagascar, Mozambique, Bahrain, and the OECS.[1059] This is in comparison to an overall appropriated WTO budget for 2000 of CHF 127.697.010.[1060] In 2001, the WTO budgetary estimates amounted initially to CHF 158.115.600. Of this amount, CHF 3.247.950 was set aside for the TPRD's functioning.[1061] Nevertheless, the TPRD's approved budget for 2001 (ie CHF 3.511.700) fell

[1053] Answers from the Human Resource Department of the WTO to questions of the author (4 December 2015).

[1054] This lack of formal data has been repeatedly acknowledged by the Budgetary Department of the WTO; Answers from the Budgetary Department of the WTO to questions of the author (23 July 2015 and 24 January 2016); Interestingly, Ghosh provides some informal figures for 1999 and 2000 which would respectively amount to CHF 4.27 million and to CHF 4.42 million. For 2002 and 2003, these data would amount to CHF 5.27 million and to CHF 5.54 million. In 2004 and 2005, these informal figures would respectively amount to CHF 5.93 million and to CHF 6.72 million; Ghosh, 'Developing Countries in the WTO Trade Policy Review Mechanism' (n 166) 446.

[1055] WTO, Budget Estimate 1999, Proposals by the Director-General, WT/BFA/W/27, 4 September 1998, 6 and 103.

[1056] WTO, Report on Extra-Budgetary Funds for 1999, WT/BFA/W/44, 5 October 2000, 23 and 83.

[1057] WTO, Committee on Budget, Finance and Administration, Mid-term review biennium 2014–2015, WT/BFA/W/339, 29 October 2014, 27.

[1058] WTO, Budget Estimate 2000, Proposals by the Director-General, WT/BFA/SPEC/37, 6 September 1999, 7 and 108.

[1059] WTO, Report on Extra-Budgetary Funds for 2000, WT/BFA/W/59, 11 July 2001, 11, 22 and 55; WTO, TPRB, Report of the Trade Policy Review Body for 2001, Trade Policy Review Body, WT/TPR/101, 18 October 2001, 2.

[1060] WTO, Committee on Budget, Finance and Administration, Mid-term review biennium 2014–2015, WT/BFA/W/339, 29 October 2014, 27.

[1061] WTO, Budget Estimates 2001, Proposals by the Director-General, WT/BFA/SPEC/49, 11 September 2000, 6 and 149; Nevertheless, this budgetary estimate did not include any budgetary allocations for missions (ie one of the biggest components of the budget), which were to be allocated at a later date.

below its final expenditure of CHF 3.527.365.[1062] In addition, to its estimated core funding, Germany and Switzerland also contributed respectively CHF 123.142,03 and CHF 386.710,57 of extra-budgetary funding for the respective TPRs of Uganda and Haiti.[1063] This compared to an overall appropriated WTO budget for 2001 of CHF 134.083.610.[1064] The initial WTO budgetary estimates for 2002 amounted to CHF 139.650.850 including 3.412.100 for the TPRD.[1065] The total overall appropriated expenditure of the WTO in 2002 amounted to CHF 160.826.740 (ie CHF 144.197.758 under the annual regular budget and 16.628.982 under various trust funds; the latter included contributions from Germany, Finland, and Sweden which amounted to respectively CHF 54.691,29, CHF 17.000,35, and CHF 18.808,06 of extra-budgetary funding for the preparation of several TPR reports, including those of Honduras[1066]).[1067] The appropriated TPRD's budget for 2002 (ie CHF 4.358.300) was in excess of its final expenditure of CHF 4.014.228.[1068]

In 2003, the WTO budget was initially estimated to amount to CHF 165.7 million.[1069] Of this amount, CHF 4.265.000 was set aside for the TPRD's functioning. Nevertheless, the overall estimate for the WTO budget was later downwards revised to CHF 156.154.650.[1070] This is in comparison with an appropriated WTO budget for 2003 which amounted to CHF 174.486.843 (ie CHF 154.078.369 under the annual budget and CHF 20.408.474 under the various trust funds, including a contribution from Germany over a four-year period to undertake reviews of developing countries and to improve the TPRM with the objective to improve its adaptation to the requirements of developing countries[1071]).[1072] Here, again, there is a lack of data with regard to the TPRD's appropriated and actual expenditure.[1073]

[1062] WTO, Divisional Reporting on Objectives and Expenditure, WT/BFA/W/73, 15 October 2002, 71; Ghosh provides informal figures of CHF 5.24 million for 2001; Ghosh, 'Developing Countries in the WTO Trade Policy Review Mechanism' (n 166) 443.

[1063] WTO, Report on Extra-Budgetary Funds for 2001, WT/BFA/W/74, 11 July 2002, 47 and 90; WTO, TPRB, Report of the Trade Policy Review Body for 2001, Trade Policy Review Body, WT/TPR/101, 18 October 2001, 2.

[1064] WTO, Committee on Budget, Finance and Administration, Mid-term review biennium 2014–2015, WT/BFA/W/339, 29 October 2014, 27.

[1065] WTO, Budget Estimates 2002, Proposals by the Director-General, WT/BFA/SPEC/63, 5 October 2001, 5 and 130.

[1066] WTO, Director General's Report on Extra-Budgetary Funds for 2002, WT/BFA/W/99, 8 July 2003, 92, 97, and 116.

[1067] WTO, Director General's Budgetary and Financial Report for 2002 and Report of the External Auditor Thereon, WT/BFA/W/97, 10 July 2003, 3; Interestingly, other formal data state explicitly that the appropriated regular WTO budget for 2002 would correspond to CHF 143.129.850; WTO, Committee on Budget, Finance and Administration, Mid-term review biennium 2014–2015, WT/BFA/W/339, 29 October 2014, 27.

[1068] WTO, Divisional Reporting on Objectives and Expenditure, WT/BFA/W/98, 8 July 2003, 81.

[1069] WTO, Budget Estimates 2003, Proposals by the Director-General, WT/BFA/SPEC/82, 16 October 2002, 7.

[1070] WTO, Director-General's Revised Proposal for 2003 Budget, WT/BFA/W/85, 27 November 2002, 2.

[1071] WTO, TPRB, Report of the Trade Policy Review Body for 2000, Trade Policy Review Body, WT/TPR/86, 13 October 2000, 2.

[1072] WTO, Director General's Budgetary and Financial Report for 2003 and Report of the External Auditor Thereon, WT/BFA/W/114, 16 Augustus 2004, 3; Interestingly, other formal data state explicitly that the appropriated regular WTO budget for 2003 would correspond to CHF 154.954.350; WTO, Committee on Budget, Finance and Administration, Mid-term review biennium 2014–2015, WT/BFA/W/339, 29 October 2014, 27.

[1073] This lack of data has been explicitly acknowledged by the Budgetary Department of the WTO; Answers from the Budgetary Department of the WTO to questions of the author (23 July 2015 and 24 January 2016).

The initially foreseen WTO budgetary estimates for 2004–5 amounted to CHF 165.65 million including CHF 4.196.400 for the TPRD.[1074] The budget estimates of these years provide a rather worrying picture in underlining that '*With 146 Members, under the frequency requirements of Annex 3 of the Uruguay Round, the TPRB should be doing Reviews of some 23 Members a year (counting the EU as one). The Division is not close to being able to meet this target; moreover, resources were cut in the 2003 budget . . . Further, the Director-General's Annual Overview has taken on added importance. In this overall context, the Division is badly understaffed. Thus, for 2004 only 13 Review dates—covering at most 17 Members—have been scheduled (down from an average of 16 dates in previous years, due to 2003 budget cuts). Lost ground will need to be recovered—and there is growing demand for this—in 2004–2006. Reviews take 8–10 months to prepare, which means that recovery will need to start in 2004 and continue in 2005; in addition, work will need to begin in 2004 on the first Review of China, which will be difficult and resource-intensive, and in 2005 work will start on the first Review of Chinese Taipei. The "normal" pattern—given the frequency demands under Annex 3 for Members reviewed at least once—for 2005 requires the review of 18 Members (with Cyprus, Hungary and Poland "dropping-out" because of their accession to the EU) without counting Members not previously reviewed; there is a similar demand in 2006. In 2005 this will require at least 16 Review dates; in 2006 at least 17 Review dates will be needed*'.[1075] The budgetary estimates compare to an overall appropriated WTO budget which was CHF 161.776.500 in 2004 and to CHF 168.703.400 in 2005.[1076] In addition to the regular budget, contributions from the German Trust Fund facilitated the preparation of the TPRs from Benin, Burkina Faso, and Mali in 2004.[1077] In 2005, Dutch and German extra-budgetary financing enabled the preparation of the reviews of Guinea, Mongolia, and Sierra Leone.[1078] Here, again, in line with earlier practice, there is a lack of formal data with regard to the TPRD's appropriated and actual expenditure.[1079]

The second appraisal dedicated some analysis to the budgetary needs of the TPRM. In this regard, the non-paper which initiated the process clearly asked '*how do the resources put into the TPRM by the Secretariat and by Governments measure up to the benefits of the Mechanism?*' In addition, the paper asked '*what need is seen for assistance to developing counties and LDC/small countries following the meetings? Could funding for this purpose be identified, given the many competing demands for development assistance*' or '*are the resources devoted to this purpose by the*

[1074] WTO, 2004–2005 Budget Estimates, Proposals by the Director-General, WT/BFA/SPEC/100, 3 November 2003, 6 and 150.

[1075] WTO, 2004–2005 Budget Estimates, Proposals by the Director-General, WT/BFA/SPEC/100, 3 November 2003, 150.

[1076] WTO, Committee on Budget, Finance and Administration, Mid-term review biennium 2014–2015, WT/BFA/W/339, 29 October 2014, 27.

[1077] WTO, TPRB, Report of the Trade Policy Review Body for 2004, Trade Policy Review Body, WT/TPR/154, 28 October 2004, 2.

[1078] WTO, TPRB, Report of the Trade Policy Review Body for 2005, Trade Policy Review Body, WT/TPR/173, 8 November 2005, 1.

[1079] This lack of data has been explicitly acknowledged by the Budgetary Department of the WTO; Answers from the Budgetary Department of the WTO to questions of the author (23 July 2015 and 24 January 2016); According to the calculations of the Budgetary Department of the WTO, the TPRD department received a budgetary allocation of CHF 220.000 in 2005. Nevertheless, this amount does not include allocations for missions.

Secretariat and Member Governments sufficient? Would any of the proposed improvements to the operation of the Mechanism require an increase in resources?'[1080] The appraisal process itself concluded that '*the resource-intensive nature of the TPRM means that all efforts should be made for maximum efficiency in the use of resources.*' These included, '*the resource-saving aspects of using, under the authority of Annex 3, trade-relevant information from other intergovernmental organizations*' and the use of grouped reviews.[1081]

During the period which was covered by the second appraisal, the number of WTO Divisions involved with the elaboration of TPRs grew further as reviews became more complex and voluminous. Notable additions of divisions which exchanged information and input with the TPRD were those covering Research and Statistics, Rules, Agriculture, and Services.[1082] Nonetheless, in order to ensure maximum efficiency in the use of resources and to avoid duplication, the second appraisal urges that '*the two way flow of information between the TPRD and other parts of the WTO Secretariat should continue while preserving restricted information and Members' rights and obligations*'.[1083] Moreover, from an internal point of view, the third TPRD director introduced regional sections within the TPRD in order to start generating institutional memory.[1084] Furthermore, from an external point of view, the Secretariat was urged to keep its own capacity for analysis though it was simultaneously encouraged to make use—for reasons of cost-efficiency—of relevant information generated by other intergovernmental organizations.[1085]

The value of the Secretariat's reporting was to a large extent dependent on its relative independency and intrusiveness. It is therefore not surprising that the yearly TPRB reports which were drafted in the period covered by the second appraisal repeatedly urge Members to cooperate with the Secretariat.[1086] Likewise, the TPRB reports for 2003 and 2004 started to warn the Members and the Secretariat that '*close contact with the Member under review is necessary to help ensure the factual*

1080 Possible points for the appraisal of the operation of the trade policy review mechanism (TPRM), Non-paper, 10 May 2005, 3–4 (Document on file with the author).

1081 *Second appraisal of the operation of the Trade Policy Review Mechanism 2005* (n 868) 2–3.

1082 Interview with Dr Clemens Boonekamp, third director of the Trade Policy Review Department, WTO (Geneva, July 2015).

1083 *Second appraisal of the operation of the Trade Policy Review Mechanism 2005* (n 868) 2.

1084 Interview with Dr Clemens Boonekamp, third director of the Trade Policy Review Department, WTO (Geneva, July 2015).

1085 *Second appraisal of the operation of the Trade Policy Review Mechanism 2005* (n 868) 2.

1086 WTO, TPRB, Draft Report of the Trade Policy Review Body for 2000, Trade Policy Review Body, WT/TPR/W/27, 28 September 2000, 4; WTO, TPRB, Draft Report of the Trade Policy Review Body for 2000, Trade Policy Review Body, WT/TPR/W/27/Rev. 1, 6 October 2000, 4; WTO, TPRB, Draft Report of the Trade Policy Review Body for 2001, Trade Policy Review Mechanism, WT/TPR/W/28, 11 September 2001, 4; WTO, TPRB, Report of the Trade Policy Review Body for 2002, Trade Policy Review Body, WT/TPR/W/29, 7 October 2002, 4; WTO, TPRB, Report of the Trade Policy Review Body for January–July 2003, Trade Policy Review Body, WT/TPR/W/30, 27 June 2003, 4; WTO, TPRB, Draft Report of the Trade Policy Review Body for 2003, Trade Policy Review Mechanism, WT/TPR/W/31, 28 October 2003, 4; WTO, TPRB, Draft Report of the Trade Policy Review Body for 2004, Trade Policy Review Mechanism, WT/TPR/W/32, 18 October 2004, 4.

accuracy and clarity of the documentation prepared for the review'.[1087] The second appraisal therefore also resulted in a couple of recommendations to the Secretariat including the request that it '*prepare general guidelines on the process of preparing a review*' and that it '*should continue to prepare . . . objective reports*'.[1088]

iii) Discussants

In the period covered by the second appraisal (ie the period between the TPR of Romania of 1999[1089] and the review of Trinidad and Tobago of 2005[1090]), most though not all TPRs were based on the participation of only one discussant. The TPRs of Romania of 1998 and of the European Communities of 2000 were exceptions: the first was still covered by two discussants, the second by none.[1091] Moreover, out of the eighty-eight discussants of this period, fifty-two had an industrialized background whereas only thirty-five originated in developing countries.[1092] As a result of these two evolutions, perspectives of developing countries risked becoming relatively side-lined or even fully absent from TPRB debates.

Nevertheless, in order to increase the reviews' internal interaction, the 2005 rules of procedure stipulated that discussants must circulate—at least one week before the meeting—an outline of the main points they intend to raise. Paradoxically, the same rules of procedure also seem to mitigate against a too-spontaneous or intrusive interaction during the meeting. In this regard, they emphasize that the discussants' full statements, which should be designed to provide specific themes for discussion, should be given to the Member under review shortly before the meeting (thus limiting the preparation times for an adequate response)[1093] and stress that discussants' statements should not exceed that by the Member under review in length.[1094]

Moreover, compared to the period covered by the first appraisal, discussants increasingly relied on the Secretariat's reporting. More than half of the discussants who covered TPRs in this period referred, directly or indirectly, to the Secretariat's

1087 WTO, TPRB, Draft Report of the Trade Policy Review Body for 2003, Trade Policy Review Mechanism, WT/TPR/W/31, 28 October 2003, 2; WTO, TPRB, Draft Report of the Trade Policy Review Body for 2004, Trade Policy Review Mechanism, WT/TPR/W/32, 18 October 2004, 2.

1088 *Second appraisal of the operation of the Trade Policy Review Mechanism 2005* (n 868) 2.

1089 Trade Policy Review of Romania of 4–5 October 1999, Minutes of the Meeting, WT/TPR/M/60, 4 January 2000.

1090 Trade Policy Review of Trinidad and Tobago of 14–16 September 2000, Minutes of the Meeting, WT/TPR/M/151, 2 November 2005.

1091 Trade Policy Review of the European Communities or 12–14 July 2000, Minutes of the Meeting, WT/TPR/M/72, 26 October 2000.

1092 There are (still) no WTO definitions of 'developed' and 'developing' countries. The distinction which is (currently) applied is therefore based on the methodology applied in the World Trade Report for 2014. This report applies a judgment call and qualifies all Member states of the EU, other non-EU western European countries and territories (principally Iceland, Norway, and Switzerland), Australia, Canada, Japan, New Zealand, and the United States as developed. All other countries and territories are collectively referred to as 'developing economies'; WTO, *Trade and development: recent trends and the role of the WTO* (WTO 2014), 54.

1093 WTO, TPRB, Draft Rules of Procedure for Meetings of the Trade Policy Review Body, WT/TPR/W/34, 6 September 2005, 2.

1094 WTO, TPRB, Draft Rules of Procedure for Meetings of the Trade Policy Review Body, WT/TPR/W/34, 6 September 2005, 2.

reporting (forty-nine out of the eighty-eight discussants who covered the eighty-eight TPRs of this period or 55 per cent). Nevertheless, compared to the period covered by the first half of the first appraisal (ie before the formal establishment of the WTO), discussants who intervened in TPRs which took place during the period covered by the second appraisal were less keen on referencing governmental reporting (thus further attesting to this reporting's limited added value). Only twenty-eight out of the eighty-eight discussants (ie 31 per cent) who covered the eighty-eight88 TPRs of this period referred to governmental reporting.[1095] Moreover, for the first time, discussants began to criticize the reporting by the Secretariat (albeit only in a few exceptional instances). For instance, in the TPR of Hong Kong of 2002 the Chilean discussant referred to the Secretariat report '*which implied that the absence of a competition law may have some negative effects in Hong Kong, China's economy*' and stated that '*he did not see any evidence of that happening*'.[1096] Similarly, the Indian discussant in the TPR of the Maldives of 2003 criticized the Secretariat's report and stated that conventional analysis of the Maldives trade and economic policies needed to be tempered, while indicating that '*suggestions that tariffs risked distorting resource allocations by protecting inefficient industries failed to appreciate the country's import dependency and that the relatively high import duties were applied primarily for revenue reasons to meet developmental needs and to forestall increased fiscal deficits.*'[1097] In a similar vein, the discussant in the TPR of Brazil of 2004 noted that '*the secretariat report noted that the (alcohol-fuel) industry, connected to agricultural production, had been largely liberalized.*' He then suggested that '*the Brazilian delegation might wish to confirm this*'.[1098] Furthermore, in line with earlier discussants' practice, governmental reporting unsurprisingly came up for continued criticism. For instance, in the TPR of Kenya of 2000, the discussant was '*struck by paragraph 60 of the Kenyan government report, which lamented the very high level of tariffs on the agricultural products of developing countries like Kenya resulting from post-Uruguay Round tariffication. This seemed at odds with the Secretariat report, which suggested that Kenya's main agricultural and horticultural exports received preferential treatment under the GSP or the Lomé Convention in all the major developed country markets.*'[1099] Moreover, the discussant in the TPR of New Zealand of 2003 noted that '*New Zealand stated that it did not maintain local-content requirements, however, local manufacturers could claim concessions upon demonstrating that the domestic content of a locally produced product*

[1095] Data on file with the author.

[1096] Trade Policy Review of Hong Kong of 16–18 December 2002, Minutes of the Meeting, WT/TPR/M/109, 17 February 2003, 8.

[1097] Trade Policy Review of the Maldives of 15–17 January 2003, Minutes of the Meeting, WT/TPR/M/110, 5 March 2003, 5.

[1098] Trade Policy Review of Brazil of 29 November–1 December 2004, Minutes of the Meeting, WT/TPR/M/140, 24 January 2005, 10.

[1099] Trade Policy Review of Kenya of 26–28 January 2000, Minutes of the Meeting, WT/TPR/M/64, 29 February 2000, 8.

was not less than 25% of the ex-factory cost of production'.[1100] Similarly, in the TPR of the European Union of 2002, the Republic of South Africa (RSA) discussant emphasized that '*the EU claimed that the sustained vitality of its rural communities was an important societal goal: the discussant asked whether the EU had undertaken any studies to educate its Member states on the impact of the CAP on the live hoods of rural communities in developing countries*'.[1101] In twenty-three out of the eighty-eight TPRs of this period (ie 31%), the discussants even referred to other external studies which shed some additional light on the trade policies and practices of the country under review.[1102] This is a marked increased compared to the period covered by the first appraisal.

The discussants of this period were often keener to touch on issues of dispute settlement rather than to delve into other subjects whose sensitive character was explicitly acknowledged. For instance, the UK discussant of the TPR of Kenya of 2000 explicitly stated that '*the Secretariat report suggested a number of causes for this disappointing investment picture on which it would be inappropriate to dwell in a Trade Policy Review, eg: concerns about security and governance, labour unrest, inadequacies in the business infrastructure, flaws in the legal system and judicial procedures, investment licensing requirements which had proved to be a restraint, a financial structure which was in need of strengthening, and setbacks and lack of progress in implementing the privatization programme*'.[1103] Similarly, the discussant of the TPR of the Southern African Customs Union (SACU) of 2003 explicitly emphasized that certain issues were not yet ripe for negotiation in the WTO in noting that '*SACU Members had been in the forefront of WTO discussions on existing commitments, special and differential treatment, and implementation issues and concerns*'. The discussant would therefore '*leave for others the question of how to address possible new commitments, given the already overflowing dish of negotiations*'.[1104] These examples of marked reserve contrast with some discussants' eagerness to discuss issues relating to dispute settlement. For instance, in the TPR of Korea of 2000, the discussant noted that '*protection afforded to the agricultural sector was high and has led Korea to two dispute settlement cases at the WTO. This situation explained the number of advance questions on several agricultural issues submitted to Korea by participants in its Trade Policy Review.*'[1105] In a similar vein, the discussant in the TPR of the OECS of 2001 even stated that '*it would be interesting to know how the DSB would have ruled if the initiative of the OECD, and most of its Member states, had been brought before the WTO. It was true*

[1100] Trade Policy Review of New Zealand of 12–14 May 2003, Minutes of the Meeting, WT/TPR/M/115, 17 June 2003, 8.

[1101] Trade Policy Review of the European Communities of 24–26 July 2002, Minutes of the Meeting, WT/TPR/M/102, 23 September 2002, 10.

[1102] Data on file with the author.

[1103] Trade Policy Review of Kenya of 26–28 January 2000, Minutes of the Meeting, WT/TPR/M/64, 29 February 2000, 7.

[1104] Trade Policy Review of the SACU of 23–25 April 2003, Minutes of the Meeting, WT/TPR/M/114, 11 June 2003, 7.

[1105] Trade Policy Review of Korea of 26–28 September 2000, Minutes of the Meeting, WT/TPR/M/73, 31 October 2000, 6.

that the WTO had only existed since 1995, but nevertheless, one wondered why the States whose tax administrations felt that they had been injured had not brought their complaint before the WTO. Did they fear the independence of a panel ruling?'[1106] Moreover, the discussant in the TPR of the United States of 2001 explicitly praised '*the US for effective and timely implementation of its WTO commitments, and of the Dispute Settlement Body (DSB) rulings and recommendations*'.[1107] Likewise, the Icelandic discussant in the TPR of Canada of 2003 was interested in the implementation of the WTO Panel's ruling with respect to stockpiling by generic manufacturers of patented medicines, resulting the passing of new Regulations.[1108] Such a request for information on the implementation of a DSB ruling was even more accentuated in the TPR of the United States of 2004 with the discussant commenting that '*Another issue of systemic interest for the WTO was the proper implementation of Panel and Appellate Body rulings. Unfortunately, concern about the US' failure to implement several of these rulings involving legislative change had been a constant feature of the regular Dispute Settlement Body (DSB) meetings for quite a long time. Of particular concern was the lack of compliance with regard to the cases involving the FSC and the Continued Dumping and Subsidy Offset Act (CDSOA) of 2000. As the issue of implementation of DSB rulings and recommendations directly affected the credibility of the multilateral trading system itself, he requested the view of the US as to what institutional challenges might be possible so as to ensure timely implementation.*'[1109] Nevertheless, in spite of their clearly underused potential, the second appraisal barely dwells on the institutional role of the discussants. Instead, the appraisal succinctly states that '*a more interactive discussion*' could result from '*a more pro-active participation by discussants*'.[1110]

3. Third appraisal of the operation of the Trade Policy Review Mechanism (January–October 2008): review of TPRM's functioning between September 2005 and October 2008

On 10 December 2007, the TPRB agreed to undertake its third appraisal of the operation of the TPRM.[1111] In line with its practice acquired under the first and second appraisal, the third review started with the elaboration of a questionnaire—the so-called non-paper by the Secretariat. This non-paper gradually morphed into the final report of the third appraisal but also resulted in another modification to the

[1106] Trade Policy Review of the OECS of 5–7 June 2001, Minutes of the Meeting, WT/TPR/M/85, 15 August 2001, 23.

[1107] Trade Policy Review of the United States of 14–17 September 2001, Minutes of the Meeting, WT/TPR/M/88, 4 January 2002, 13

[1108] Trade Policy Review of Canada of 12–14 March 2003, Minutes of the Meeting, WT/TPR/M/112, 12 May 2003, 9.

[1109] Trade Policy Review of the United States of 14–16 January 2004, Minutes of the Meeting, WT/TPR/M/126, 15 March 2004, 14.

[1110] *Second appraisal of the operation of the Trade Policy Review Mechanism 2005* (n 868) 3.

[1111] *Draft – Third Appraisal of the Operation of the Trade Policy Review Mechanism* (15 October 2008) WT/TPR/W/38, 1 (hereafter *Draft—Third Appraisal of the Operation of the Trade Policy Review Mechanism 2008*).

TPRB's rules of procedure.[1112] Four informal meetings were therefore held in the period from January to October 2008.[1113]

a) Objectives

The earlier academic debate between the proponents of the TPRM as an exclusive mechanism for transparency and those who considered the TPRM as a prime or partial/indirect mechanism for naming and shaming resulted in further analysis in the period between September 2005 and October 2008.

The 2007 World Trade Report's discussion of transparency in the WTO is emblematic.[1114] It lists the TPRM as one of the WTO's five categorical transparency provisions but also emphasizes its surveillance function. Although the latter is not further elaborated—contrary to its analysis of surveillance under the IMF's Article IV consultations—the report (succinctly) recognizes that '*there is an important link between the observance of transparency by Members, their ability to provide timely and accurate notifications to various WTO organs and the quality of the surveillance function of the WTO*'.[1115]

Moreover, academic claims which specifically looked into the TPRM's value as a mechanism for naming and shaming were analysed and supported by a still limited but gradually increasing amount of empirical data. In this regard, Chaisse and Chakraborty were the first—in 2007—to analyse the relationship between TPR findings and the outcome of cases lodged at the DSB. Based on their sample analysis of eighteen TPRs involving Brazil (1996, 2000, and 2004), India (1998 and 2002), the EC (1997, 2000, 2002, and 2004), Japan (1998, 2000, 2002, and 2004) and the United States (1996, 1999, 2001, 2003, and 2006), the authors managed to demonstrate '*that many issues raised by the TPRs of selected Members have been successfully challenged at the WTO, as a result of which areas of concern had been rectified in the subsequent period*'.[1116] The authors concluded that the TPRM may be considered an enforcement mechanism and wondered whether the TPRM and the DSB did not enjoy a closer relationship than was frequently assumed.[1117] In

[1112] Possible points for the third appraisal of the operation of the trade policy review mechanism, Non-paper, 7 December 2007 (Document on file with the author); *Third Appraisal of the Operation of the Trade Policy Review Mechanism* (11 November 2008) WT/TPR/229 (hereafter *Third Appraisal of the Operation of the Trade Policy Review Mechanism 2008)*; WTO, TPRB, Draft Rules of Procedure for Meetings of the Trade Policy Review Body, WT/TPR/W/39, 15 October 2008.

[1113] *Draft—Third Appraisal of the Operation of the Trade Policy Review Mechanism 2008* (n 1109) 1.

[1114] WTO, *Sixty Years of the Multilateral Trading System: Achievements and Challenges* (WTO 2007), 163–67.

[1115] The others being (a) tariff and services schedules which codify Member's commitments; (b) publication and notification; (c) the transparency of the WTO to its Members (internal transparency); and (d) transparency vis-à-vis civil society (external transparency); Robert Wolfe, 'Regulatory Transparency, Developing Countries and the WTO' (2003) 2(2) World Trade Review 157–82.

[1116] Julien Chaisse and Debashis Chakraborty, 'Implementing WTO Rules Through Negotiations and Sanctions: The Role of Trade Policy Review Mechanism and Dispute Settlement System' (2007) 28(1) Pennsylvania Journal of International Economic Law 155, 170, and 172–75.

[1117] Marc D Froese, 'Trade policy review and dispute settlement at the WTO', in David A Deese (eds), *Handbook of the International Political Economy of Trade* (Edward Elgar Publishing 2012), 354 (hereafter Froese, 'Trade policy review and dispute settlement at the WTO').

2008, Ghosh undertook a similar exercise comparing issues raised in some 190 TPRs between 1995 and 2007 and the subsequent filling of disputes (resulting in a total of 172 dispute dyads).[1118] Based on this empirical methodology, the author was able to estimate that a slight majority (ie 53 per cent) of the cases brought to the DSB contained some law or policy which had somehow been referenced in earlier TPR reporting by the Secretariat. Nevertheless, the relationship between the TPRM and the DSB remained rather distant. According to Ghosh's analysis, future DSB complainants sent advance questions to the party under review in only a quarter of the analysed cases. Moreover, TPR reports which were issued after DSB litigation contained increased coverage of the disputed policies but remained low on critical analysis.[1119] Ghosh therefore concluded that '*although TPR reports seek to present a comprehensive picture of a Member's policies, in many cases the most contentious policies barely get a mention and are not subject to detailed analysis*'.[1120]

Nevertheless, in spite of academia's growing attention to the value of the TPRM as a prime or partial/indirect mechanism for naming and shaming, the third appraisal merely reworded the mechanism's objectives as contained in paragraphs A and B of Annex 3 to the Marrakesh Agreement. Moreover, contrary to the second appraisal, the third appraisal no longer retained any critical elements in its assessment of the TPRB's achievement of its objectives.[1121]

The TPRM and the DSB were conceived as two separately functioning entities. Paragraph A of Annex 3 to the Marrakesh Agreement is very clear in stating that the TPRM '*is not, however, intended to serve as a basis for the enforcement of specific obligations under the Agreements or for dispute settlement procedures, or to impose new policy commitments on Members*'.[1122] In addition, Annex 3 to the Marrakesh Agreement is not a covered agreement under Appendix I to Annex II to the Marrakesh Agreement which embodies the Understanding on Rules and Procedures Governing the Settlement of Disputes.[1123] As a result, the TPRM and its findings should in principle not be invoked within the proceedings of the Dispute Settlement Body. Nevertheless, in the period which was covered by the third appraisal, findings of the TPRM had been invoked in five panel proceedings (covering 10.4 per cent of all disputes covered in this period).[1124] In these cases, findings which had

[1118] The author bars nine apparently random cases where some documents were missing; Ghosh, 'Developing Countries in the WTO Trade Policy Review Mechanism' (n 166) 443.

[1119] VanGrasstek, *The History and Future of the World Trade Organization* (n 56) 288; Ghosh's 2008 analysis is also contained in Ghosh, 'Developing Countries in the WTO Trade Policy Review Mechanism' (n 166) 439–45 and in Arunabha Ghosh, 'Strengthening WTO surveillance: making transparency work for developing countries', in Carolyn Deere Birbeck (eds), *Making global trade governance work for development: perspectives and priorities from developing countries* (Cambridge University Press 2011), 400 (hereafter Ghosh, 'Strengthening WTO surveillance: making transparency work for developing countries').

[1120] Ghosh, 'Strengthening WTO surveillance: making transparency work for developing countries' (n 1117) 400.

[1121] *Third Appraisal of the Operation of the Trade Policy Review Mechanism 2008* (n 1110) 1.

[1122] The Trade Policy Review Mechanism (n 151).

[1123] The Marrakesh Agreement (n 353).

[1124] WTO, *Turkey—Measures Affecting the Importation of Rice—Report of the Panel* (21 September 2007) WT/DS334/R; WTO, *US—Continued Existence and Application of Zeroing Methodology—Report*

originated within the framework of the TPRM were invoked as factual—though not as legal—claims.

b) Structure

i) Individual trade policy reviews

Periodicity

The third appraisal of the TPRM (ie September 2005– to October 2008) covered three years wherein the TPRM functioned. In each of these years, the Secretariat's forecasting of the amount of TPRs which would be implemented in the coming year was correct.[1125] Moreover, between September 2005 and October 2008, Secretariat's annual reporting on the TPRM did include a categorization of the countries under review by their cyclical periodicity. Throughout the period, the Secretariat managed to fulfil normal expectations and undertake yearly reviews of two Quad countries. Nevertheless, the number of countries subject to the four-year cycle varied between four in 2006 and seven in 2007 which was not in line with the normal practice of yearly reviews of four countries on the four-year cycle.[1126] Furthermore, the third appraisal notes that '*in certain cases significant trade-related changes took place between the finalization of the reports and the corresponding TPRB meeting*'. The normal sequence of periodic reporting alone could therefore not guarantee to provide a full picture of the trade policies and practices under review. In case of (sudden) significant trade-related changes, Members were consequently urged to inform the Secretariat for the Secretariat to produce an addendum to its report referencing the changes.[1127]

of the Panel (1 October 2008) WT/DS350/R, A-108; WTO, *India—Additional and Extra-Additional Duties on Imports from the United States—Report of the Panel* (9 June 2008) WT/DS360/R, 22 and 56–57; WTO, *China—Measures Affecting the Protection and Enforcement of Intellectual Property Rights—Report of the Panel* (26 January 2009) WT/DS362/R, 87; WTO, *China—Measures Affecting Trading Rights and Distribution Services for Certain Publications and Audio-visual Entertainment Products—Report of the Panel* (12 August 2009) WT/DS363/R, 424.

[1125] For 2006: WTO, TPRB, Draft Trade Policy Review Mechanism, Report of the Trade Policy Review Body for 2005, WT/TPR/W/35, 12 October 2005, 2 and 6.; Data of the author; WTO, TPRB, Report of the Trade Policy Review Body for 2005, Trade Policy Review Body, WT/TPR/173, 8 November 2005, 2; WTO, TPRB, Draft Report of the Trade Policy Review Body for 2006, Trade Policy Review Mechanism, WT/TPR/W/36, 23 October 2006, 1. For 2007: WTO, TPRB, Draft Report of the Trade Policy Review Body for 2006, Trade Policy Review Mechanism, WT/TPR/W/36, 23 October 2006, 2 and 6; WTO, TPRB, Report of the Trade Policy Review Body for 2006, Trade Policy Review Body, WT/TPR/192, 31 October 2006, 2 and 6; Data of the author; WTO, TPRB, Draft Report of the Trade Policy Review Body for 2007, Trade Policy Review Mechanism, WT/TPR/W/37, 26 October 2007, 1. For 2008: WTO, TPRB, Draft Report of the Trade Policy Review Body for 2007, Trade Policy Review Mechanism, WT/TPR/W/37, 26 October 2007, 2 and 6; WTO, TPRB, Report of the Trade Policy Review Body for 2007, Trade Policy Review Body, WT/TPR/213, 12 November 2007, 2 and 6; Data of the author; WTO, TPRB, Draft Report of the Trade Policy Review Body for 2008, Trade Policy Review Mechanism, WT/TPR/W/40, 15 October 2008, 1 and 6; WTO, TPRB, Report of the Trade Policy Review Body for 2008, Trade Policy Review Body, WT/TPR/232, 14 November 2008, 1 and 6.

[1126] Data of the author.

[1127] *Third Appraisal of the Operation of the Trade Policy Review Mechanism 2008* (n 1110) 2.

Reporting

During the informal meetings which resulted in the third review, Members were not so much focused on the question as to whether TPRs should examine new issues.[1128] On the other hand, some reflection was undertaken with regard to the Secretariat's reporting on Aid for Trade. Prior to the 2005 Hong Kong Ministerial Declaration, the TPRM considered the economic and development needs of Members but analysed the response to those needs primarily through the lens of the support offered to developing countries to adhere to WTO rules and through the work of the Integrated Framework on LDCs. Moreover, the TPR of Tanzania (2000) was the first LDC review in which the Secretariat report had contained a specific section with regard to trade-related assistance. This changed, first with the recommendations of the Task Force on Aid for Trade, which indicated, amongst others things, that '*an assessment of Aid for Trade—either as a donor or as a recipient—should be included in the WTO Trade Policy Reviews*',[1129] then with the December 2006 General Council, where Members agreed that a general assessment of Aid for Trade would be included in future Trade Policy Reviews. As a result, the first review whose Secretariat's report contained a specific section on Aid for Trade was the TPR of Malawi of 2010.[1130]

As a result of the third appraisal, governments remained free to decide on the structure and coverage of their reporting. However, the appraisal made a renewed call on the Secretariat to highlight more explicitly the significant changes made by the Members under review since the last review.[1131]

TPRs informational value – Compared to the period which was covered by the second appraisal, the period covered by the third appraisal (ie September 2005 to October 2008) resulted in a substantially reduced amount of academic output which analysed the information contained in the Secretariat's (and sometimes governmental) reporting within the context of individual TPRs.

The remainder of this section analyses those rare views. In order to do so, it ranks the academic views on the TPRs' added informational value into three categories: (a) TPRs with missing information; (b) TPRs which according to academia contain a too positive or a too negative assessment; and (c) TPRs with incorrect information. Moreover, for each of these three categories, this section contrasts the views of the external academics where possible with the anonymous perspectives of WTO staff with regard to the same point.

In line with earlier academic views, it should be emphasized that the only academic writing of this period (analysing the US TPR of 2006) was positive about the review's added value in terms of transparency. Nevertheless, it also complained about the TPR's lack of certain specific information. In this regard, Professor Leoma's analysis of the US TPR points to several missing references. These include (a) an analysis

[1128] Possible points for the third appraisal of the operation of the trade policy review mechanism, Non-paper, 7 December 2007 (Document on file with the author).

[1129] WTO, Recommendations of the Task Force on Aid for Trade, WT/AFT/1, 27 July 2006, 8.

[1130] Trade Policy Review of Malawi of 9–11 June 2010, Secretariat Report, WT/TPR/S/231, 5 May 2010, 54–61.

[1131] *Third Appraisal of the Operation of the Trade Policy Review Mechanism 2008* (n 1110) 3.

of several economic macro-economic trends which had contributed to increased US protectionism; (b) a missing reference to the rising income inequality and loss of manufacturing jobs; (c) an inadequate analysis describing how increased bilateralism might lead to the erosion of political support for further multilateral liberalization; and (d) a missing reference to security-related customs procedures and food regulations.[1132]

Reporting on information and naming and shaming – Between the start (September 2005) and the end (October 2008) of the period which was covered by the third appraisal, fifty-three TPRs took place and forty-eight DSB disputes were litigated. Of these, only one dispute related to Sanitary and Phytosanitary measures (SPS) whereas two disputes related to the area of Technical Barriers to Trade (TBT).

Through its focus on the respective DSB and TPR coverage of the same SPS and TBT disputes, this section again analyses individual TPRs' added value in terms of transparency and naming and shaming. In order to do so, for each of the DSB disputes, this section examines the proceeding and succeeding TPR(s). For each of these TPRs, the Secretariat report and the government report, the debates during the TPRB meeting, and the written questions and answers are analysed from a transparency angle (questioning whether the respective reports, meetings, or questions explicitly or indirectly managed to refer to elements of the future dispute) and from the perspective of naming and shaming (analysing whether the respective reports, meetings, or questions managed to elicit a defensive stance from the country under review).

- In *Australia—Measures Affecting the Importation of Apples from New Zealand*, New Zealand took issue with Australia's Quarantine Act (1908) and the application of its phytosanitary measures as specified in its Final Import Risk Analysis (IRA) report of November 2006 for apples from New Zealand.[1133] New Zealand claimed that these sixteen measures—which resembled the quarantine measures of the largely similar US–Japan dispute—were unduly trade restrictive and that they were not based on proper scientific risk assessment.[1134] According to New Zealand, these measures were therefore inconsistent with Australia's obligations under Articles 2.1, 2.2, 2.3, 5.1, 5.2, 5.3, 5.5, 5.6, 8, and Annex C of the SPS agreement.

Australia's TPR of March 2007 preceded the initiation of formal DSB consultations.[1135] Its Secretariat report's sub-section on Standards and other technical

[1132] Rodney D Ludema, 'Allies and Friends: The Trade Policy Review of the United States, 2006' [2007] The World Economy: Global Trade Policy 1211, 1214, and 1220.

[1133] WTO, *Australia—Measures Affecting the Importation of Apples from New Zealand—Report of the Panel* (9 August 2010) WT/DS367/R; WTO, *Australia—Measures Affecting the Importation of Apples from New Zealand—Appellate Body Report* (29 November 2010) WT/DS367/AB/R, 163; Goh, 'Tipping the Apple Cart: The Limits of Science and Law in the SPS Agreement after Japan—Apples' (n 938) 681–85.

[1134] Meredith Kolsky Lewis, 'Australians Get Their First Taste of New Zealand Apples in Ninety Years,' (2011) 25(25) American Society of International Law, Insights.

[1135] Trade Policy Review of Australia of 5–7 March 2007, Minutes of the Meeting, WT/TPR/M/178, 18 April 2007; WTO, *Australia—Measures Affecting the Importation of Apples from New Zealand—Request for Consultations by New Zealand* (4 September 2007) WT/DS367/1.

requirements[1136] clearly emphasizes the origin of the dispute in noting that '*Australia has a strict sanitary and phytosanitary regime. The authorities justify this by maintaining that Australia has unique and diverse flora and fauna, is a major exporter of agricultural products, and is relatively free from serious pests and diseases. Under quarantine policy, commodities may not be imported unless the quarantine risks are reduced to a level consistent with Australia's appropriate level of protection (ALOP), which is described as "providing a high level of sanitary and phytosanitary protection aimed at reducing risk to a very low level, but not zero". However, if the SPS regime is unduly strict, it may constitute an import restriction or prohibition. Some WTO Members have raised concerns about the strictness of the Australian regime in the Committee on Sanitary and Phytosanitary Measures, covering, inter alia … fresh fruits and vegetables.*' The TPR's succinct government report, however, does not refer to the issue. Moreover, New Zealand seized the TPRB meeting to alert Australia of its possible intentions in terms of litigation. In this regard, it commented that '*In general the two countries had a close and collaborative relationship on bio-security issues. New Zealand believed that recent changes to Australia's import risk analysis process would lead to increased transparency and predictability for processing bio-security market access requests. However, Australia had almost completed its process for the market access request for New Zealand's apples, and the proposed market access conditions were disappointing. The Australian measures were not justified, and New Zealand was still considering all its options.*'[1137] Nevertheless, New Zealand did not raise any additional written questions with regard to the topic.[1138] Nonetheless, in spite of these comments, Australia unabatedly defended its position and responded that it '*was not apologetic about its conservative approach to quarantine: its approach to quarantine was due to its relatively favourable pest- and disease-free status, and its diverse range of unique flora and fauna, which required responsible quarantine stewardship. Nonetheless, Australia was also a strong supporter of trade in agricultural products, and was committed to its obligations under the WTO SPS Agreement, including not adopting measures that were more trade restrictive than required to meets its appropriate level of protection (ALOP).*' Moreover, with regard to the issue of New Zealand's apples Australia emphasized that '*Bio-security Australia had released the final Impact Risk Analysis (IRA) report on 30 November 2006. Stakeholders had until 12 January 2007 to submit appeals; three had been submitted. On 26 February 2007, it was announced that the Import Risk Analysis Appeal Panel which was independent of Bio-security Australia, had disallowed all claims and found one claim outside the grounds of appeal. The Panel's findings helped to prove that the recommendations in*

[1136] Trade Policy Review of Australia of 5–7 March 2007, Secretariat Report, WT/TPR/S/178, 29 January 2007, 43–50 (particularly at 46); On the other hand, the section on Agriculture, livestock, forestry, and fisheries remains silent on the subject; Trade Policy Review of Australia of 5–7 March 2007, Secretariat Report, WT/TPR/S/178, 29 January 2007, 74–81.

[1137] Trade Policy Review of Australia of 5–7 March 2007, Minutes of the Meeting, WT/TPR/M/178, 18 April 2007, 14–15.

[1138] Trade Policy Review of Australia of 5–7 March 2007, Written questions and answers, WT/TPR/M/178/Add. 1, 2 May 2007.

the final report were the result of a sound process based on science. The next step was for Australia's Director of Quarantine to make a policy determination regarding the importation of New Zealand apples.'[1139]

On 21 January 2008, a Panel was established.[1140] Nevertheless, due to the complex nature, the scope of the dispute, and some further organizational difficulties, the Panel took more time than expected and prolonged its deliberation until 9 August 2010. However, the final Panel report addressed all sixteen phytosanitary measures adopted by Australia and found that these were inconsistent with Articles 2.2, 5.1, and 5.2 of the SPS Agreement. Additionally, the Panel found that thirteen of the sixteen measures (namely the pest-specific ones) were more trade-restrictive than required to achieve Australia's appropriate level of phytosanitary protection (ALOP), and were therefore also inconsistent with Article 5.6 of the SPS Agreement.[1141] Moreover, the Appellate Body's report (which was circulated on 29 November 2010) upheld the Panel's findings under which the sixteen Australian measures were not based on a proper risk assessment and were therefore inconsistent with Articles 2.2, 5.1, and 5.2 of the SPS Agreement.[1142] The parties therefore agreed on a reasonable period of time which would expire on 17 August 2011 and which would allow Australia to be in a position to issue import permits for New Zealand's apples from that date based on any conditions which would arise out of the current review.[1143]

The TPR of Australia of April 2011 touches on the subject at length.[1144] The Secretariat's and the government's report both identify the issue. Secretariat's subsection on Standards and other technical regulations first provides some institutional background in explaining that '*during the review period, Australia conducted science-based risk assessments, including import risk analyses (IRAs) under a regulated process, and developed recommendations on import conditions that would meet Australia's appropriate level of protection (ALOP). IRAs completed during the review period included apples from New Zealand ... Australia is a major exporter of agricultural commodities and agri-food products and, has maintained its strict sanitary and phytosanitary (SPS) regime, which the authorities consider proportionate and matching their appropriate level of protection (ALOP).*'[1145] The Secretariat then provides some (indirect) criticism in noting that 'the authorities maintain that

[1139] Trade Policy Review of Australia of 5–7 March 2007, Minutes of the Meeting, WT/TPR/M/178, 18 April 2007, 17

[1140] WTO, *Australia—Measures Affecting the Importation of Apples from New Zealand—Report of the Panel* (9 August 2010) WT/DS367/R.

[1141] WTO, *Australia—Measures Affecting the Importation of Apples from New Zealand—Report of the Panel* (9 August 2010) WT/DS367/R.

[1142] WTO, *Australia—Measures Affecting the Importation of Apples from New Zealand—Appellate Body Report* (29 November 2010) WT/DS367/AB/R, 163.

[1143] WTO, *Australia—Measures Affecting the Importation of Apples from New Zealand—Agreement under Article 21.3(b) of the DSU* (1 February 2011) WT/DS367/19

[1144] Trade Policy Review of Australia of 5–7 April 2011, Minutes of the Meeting, WT/TPR/M/244, 6 May 2011.

[1145] Trade Policy Review of Australia of 5–7 April 2011, Secretariat Report, WT/TPR/S/244, 1 March 2011, 47–54 (particularly at 51 and 53); On the other hand, Secretariat's (sectional) reporting on

SPS measures are based on science and aim to reduce the risk of exotic pests and diseases to a very low level acceptable to Australia (but not zero). Nevertheless, Australia has been criticized by certain trading partners on the grounds that they are unduly stringent and therefore protectionist; during the review period, complaints were related to quarantine procedures and apple imports.'[1146] The Secretariat moreover notes in this context that '*since 2004, an Eminent Scientists Group (ESG), a high level review group independent of Bio-security Australia, has been tasked with providing external scientific and economic scrutiny of significant import risk analyses. Its role was strengthened in September 2007, and again in July 2009, to take account of relevant new information brought to its attention, including assessing conflicting scientific views provided to it.*' The Secretariat then rather surprisingly notes that '*however, it appears that so far no unified analytical framework has been used to assess the costs and benefits of SPS measures for stakeholders along the supply chain, such as domestic consumers, producers and governments, or foreign suppliers, or, where relevant, foreign consumers and governments. Trade effects are part of the assessment, as measures have an impact on trade as conduit of the externality, but trade effects are not the sole focus.*' The Secretariat moreover engages in some quasi-legalistic assessment while indicating in this regard that '*the authorities consider that the WTO SPS Agreement provisions do not require such analysis, and that the only direction as to relevant economic consequences to be taken into account in a risk assessment is found in Article 5.3 of the Agreement. Australia's risk import assessments address the issue of economic consequences to relevant stakeholders.*'[1147] In line with its earlier practice, the Australian government made use of its report to defend its position at some length. In this regard, the report states that '*In 2008, the Australian Government commissioned an independent review of Australia's quarantine and bio-security arrangements. The review received 220 submissions and held 170 meetings, including with trading partners. It reported in September 2008, finding that Australia operates a good bio-security system but that improvements could be made. The review*

Agriculture, livestock, forestry, and fisheries remains (again) silent on the subject; Trade Policy Review of Australia of 5–7 April 2011, Secretariat Report, WT/TPR/S/244, 1 March 2011, 86–94.

[1146] In this regard, the Secretariat report mentions the following:

> At end-December 2009, 4 out of 15 WTO panels established to examine SPS-related dispute cases were on complaints against Australia. The cases involved complaints by: Canada and the United States against Australia's restrictions on imports of fresh, chilled or frozen salmon (mutually agreed solution, 2000); the Philippines against Australia's restrictions on fresh fruits and vegetables, including bananas (panel established in 2003); the EU against Australia's quarantine procedures (mutually agreed solution, 2007); and New Zealand against Australia's restrictions on apples (Chapter II) (WTO document G/SPS/53, 3 May 2010).

[1147] In this regard, the Secretariat reports provides the following legalistic points:

> Article 5.3 of the SPS Agreement allows for cost-effectiveness analysis to be applied to evaluating alternative measures to reducing pest and disease risk to the appropriate level of protection (ALOP) in line with the objective of minimizing negative trade effects. Cost-effectiveness analysis involves an evaluation of the costs of different measures in addressing a particular benefit. A measure is chosen on the basis that it involves the least aggregated cost. Although falling short of cost-benefit analysis, the application by regulators of cost - effectiveness' analysis can at least facilitate the selection of measures that are consistent with achieving a desired risk target at low cost.

highlighted the need for improvements to better deal with increasing risks, arising from climate change, globalisation and increased passenger and cargo movements. Its recommendations were designed to improve the good aspects of the current system and to rectify any shortcomings. In December 2008, the Government agreed in principle to all the recommendations. The Australian Government is progressing a range of bio-security reforms to improve the system's efficiency and effectiveness and its ability to adjust to ever-changing bio-security risks. Work is under way in a number of areas to build a better bio-security system that fosters partnerships, improves governance structures and targets risks. However, reforms will take some time and changes will be incremental. Reform activities will be staged in a sensible manner so that Australia's bio-security is not compromised during the process. Trading partners will be kept informed of changes.' Furthermore, the Australian government's report explicitly counters the Secretariat's legal analysis while extensively emphasizing that '*On the suggestion of applying a cost benefit analysis to Australia's bio-security regime, it is important to recognise that the SPS Agreement limits the factors that can be taken into account in imposing measures on imports. This point was noted in the Independent Review of Australia's Quarantine and Bio-security Arrangements (2008), which concluded that: "Perhaps paradoxically, but quite intentionally, the SPS Agreement excludes consideration of economic losses or gains arising from the import itself as distinct from the potential harm from pests or diseases." This, together with the requirement that any measures should not be more trade restrictive than required, ensures that trade issues are not brought to bear in a way that increases the risk of SPS measures being used as non-tariff barriers.*'[1148]

Nevertheless, during the TPRB meeting, New Zealand referred to the dispute while reiterating that it '*enjoys a close and collaborative relationship with Australia on bio-security issues. We welcome the close co-operation and constructive bilateral dialogue following the release of the WTO Appellate Body's report on the Australia-apples case and we look forward to implementation of the findings within the agreed timeframe*'.[1149] Contrary to the European Union, New Zealand refrained from tabling any further specific questions with regard to the case.[1150]

On 2 September 2011, Australia reported that it had adopted the measures necessary to comply with the DSB's recommendations and rulings and that Australian imports of New Zealand's apples had therefore resumed as of 19 August 2011. Nevertheless, New Zealand explicitly questioned whether Australia had fully complied with the DSB's recommendations and rulings.[1151] New Zealand and Australia therefore informed the DSB of Agreed Procedures under Articles 21 and 22 of the DSU.[1152]

[1148] Trade Policy Review of Australia of 5–7 April 2011, Government Report, WT/TPR/G/244, 1 March 2011, 9–10.

[1149] Trade Policy Review of Australia of 5–7 April 2011, Minutes of the Meeting, WT/TPR/M/244, 6 May 2011, 32.

[1150] Trade Policy Review of Australia of 5–7 April 2011, Questions and answers, WT/TPR/M/244/Add. 1, 16 May 2011, 152–53.

[1151] WTO, DSB, Minutes of Meeting, WT/DSB/M/302, 28 October 2011, 9.

[1152] WTO, *Australia—Measures Affecting the Importation of Apples from New Zealand—Understanding between New Zealand and Australia Regarding Procedures under Article 21 and 22 of the DSU* (19 September 2011) WT/DS367/21.

- Australia's TPR of 21–23 April 2015 again highlights the issue.[1153] Secretariat's analysis with regard to Sanitary and Phytosanitary Regulations notes in this regard that' *Australia, a major exporter of agricultural commodities and agri-food products, has maintained its generally strict sanitary and phytosanitary (SPS) regime, which the authorities consider proportionate and matching their relevant appropriate level of protection. The authorities maintain that SPS measures are based on science and aim to reduce the risk of exotic pests and diseases to a very low level acceptable to Australia (but not zero). During the review period, there have been no complaints related to Australia's SPS regime at the WTO; in the past Australia had been criticized by certain trading partners on the grounds that it was unduly stringent and therefore protectionist. Although the role of the Eminent Scientists Group (ESG) (a high-level review group tasked with providing external scientific and economic scrutiny of significant import risk analyses) was strengthened in the past, so far, no unified analytical framework has been used to assess the costs and benefits of SPS measures for stakeholders along the supply chain, such as domestic consumers, producers and governments, or foreign suppliers or, where relevant, foreign consumers and governments. Trade effects are part of the assessment but are not its sole focus. The authorities consider that the WTO SPS Agreement provisions do not require such analysis, and that the only direction as to relevant economic consequences to be taken into account in a risk assessment is found in Article 5.3 of the Agreement.*'[1154,1155]

  The Secretariat's import risk analysis, which is also contained in the report's subsection on Standards and other technical requirements, comments succinctly that '*assessing risk may also take the form of a non-regulated analysis of existing import policy. Between 2011 and August 2014, a number of non-regulated risk analyses were undertaken, including... apples from New Zealand.*'[1156] In line with its earlier practice, Australian governmental reporting proudly defends its quarantine arrangements. In this regard, it commented that' *Australia manages its bio-security risks offshore, at the border, and within Australia—the bio-security continuum. This framework manages bio-security risks at the point where intervention is most effective. Several historical reviews have identified improvements to Australia's bio-security system. Australia's bio-security system is continuously reformed to ensure it keeps pace with the dynamic bio-security environment. Central to these reform activities has been the focus on managing risks at all points on the bio-security continuum. There is an emphasis on prevention, preparedness and early intervention. This includes activities offshore to reduce risks before they reach the border, actions*

[1153] Trade Policy Review of Australia of 21–23 April 2015, Minutes of the Meeting, WT/TPR/M/321, 24 June 2015.

[1154] In addition to Article 5.3, Article 5.6 of the SPS Agreement states that in establishing SPS measures to achieve the ALOP, Members shall ensure that the measures are not more trade-restrictive than required.

[1155] Trade Policy Review of Australia of 21–23 April 2015, Secretariat Report, WT/TPR/S/312, 3 March 2015, 56.

[1156] Trade Policy Review of Australia of 21–23 April 2015, Secretariat Report, WT/TPR/S/312, 3 March 2015, 53–61 (particularly at 58).

at the border to deal with risks, and managing activities within Australia to minimise the impact of incursions and to facilitate trade. There is also a focus on aligning resources and regulatory effort based on the level of risk. This approach includes ensuring sustainable funding, improving legislative frameworks, modernising information and communications technology systems and enhancing the management of established pests and diseases. The Australian Government introduced the Bio-security Bill in 2014 to replace the Quarantine Act 1908. The Bio-security Bill simplifies Australia's bio-security laws while maintaining the standard of protection for human, animal, plant life and the environment ... The Australian Government examined import risk analysis (IRA) processes in 2014 to ensure arrangements are sufficiently robust to minimise the risk of exotic pests and disease incursions in Australia. The Department of Agriculture sought input from stakeholders and trading partners on specific elements of the IRA process. Recommendations for administrative and regulatory improvements are being considered in the context of developing regulations and policies for import risk analyses under the Bio-security Bill 2014.'[1157] During the TPRB meeting, New Zealand explicitly commended Australia 'on its development of a modern regulatory framework to simplify and streamline bio-security processes while maintaining strong bio-security standards'.[1158] Nevertheless, it tabled several additional written questions with regard to the evolving Australian bio-security framework.[1159]

- In *US—Measures Concerning the Importation, Marketing and Sale of Tuna and Tuna Products*, Mexico took issue with several US measures.[1160] These included: (i) the Dolphin Protection Consumer Information, (ii) the Dolphin safe labelling standards and Dolphin safe requirements for tuna harvested in the Eastern Tropical Pacific Ocean by large purse-seine vessels, and (iii) US Court of Appeal's ruling in *Earth Island Institute v Hogarth*. Mexican fishing practices generally did not adhere to these measures even though they complied with dolphin-safe standards provided in an international conservation treaty to protect dolphins which had been negotiated among the United States, Mexico, and twelve other countries that border or fish for tuna in the Eastern Tropical Pacific Ocean.[1161] According to Mexico, these US measures were therefore

[1157] Trade Policy Review of Australia of 21–23 April 2015, Government Report, WT/TPR/G/312, 3 March 2015, 12.

[1158] Trade Policy Review of Australia of 21–23 April 2015, Minutes of the Meeting, WT/TPR/M/312, 24 June 2015, 15.

[1159] Trade Policy Review of Australia of 21–23 April 2015, Written questions and answers, WT/TPR/M/312/Add.1, 25 June 2015, 145.

[1160] WTO, *US—Measures Concerning the Importation, Marketing and Sale of Tuna and Tuna Products—Report of the Panel* (15 September 2011) WT/DS381/R; WTO, *US—Measures Concerning the Importation, Marketing and Sale of Tuna and Tuna Products—Appellate Body Report* (16 May 2012) WT/DS381/AB/R; Laurens J Ankersmit and Jesicca C Lawrence, 'The Future of Environmental Labelling: US—Tuna II and the Scope of the TBT' (2012) 39 Legal Issues of Economic Integration 127–47.

[1161] Gregory Shaffer, 'The WTO Tuna-Dolphin II Case: United States—Measures Concerning the Importation, Marketing and Sale of Tuna and Tuna Products' (2013), Issue 1, American Journal of International Law.

inconsistent, amongst others, with Articles I:1 and III:4 of the GATT (1994), and with Article 2.1, 2.2, and 2.4 of the TBT Agreement.

The TPR of the United States of June 2008 took place before the initiation of formal consultations in the future case.[1162] Nevertheless, several parts of its Secretariat's report already touch directly and indirectly on the contours of the future dispute. The Secretariat's analysis of trade policies and practices by measure briefly mentions that '*non-tariff import restrictions are maintained largely for non-commercial purposes. This includes a ban on imports of marine mammal products, shrimp, and tuna from countries found not to be in compliance with U.S. environmental provisions.*'[1163] Moreover, the report's sub-section on quantitative restrictions and licensing[1164] states that '*The Marine Mammal Protection Act (MMPA) prohibits the importation of marine mammals and their parts or products into the United States. However, the Secretary of Commerce may issue permits allowing imports of living marine mammals for scientific research, enhancement, or public display. Parts and products may be imported for scientific research. Under the MMPA, yellow fin tuna from the eastern tropical Pacific can only be imported if it comes from a country with an "affirmative finding". Four countries have such a finding: Ecuador, El Salvador, Mexico, and Spain. Tuna from these countries can only be labelled as "dolphin safe" if caught without the chase and encirclement of dolphins in the entire trip and without killing or seriously injuring any dolphins in the set in which the tuna was caught. A 2002 finding by the Secretary of Commerce, which would have changed the definition of dolphin-safe to cover tuna caught by the chase and encirclement of dolphins, as long as there were no observed dolphin mortalities or serious injury, was found by a federal appeals court, in April 2007, to be "arbitrary and capricious".*'

Although the Secretariat's sub-sectional analysis of food labelling—as contained in the report's section on agriculture—contains some details on fish labelling and its economic costs, it remains silent on the issue of tuna.[1165] Neither the government's report[1166] nor Mexico's interventions at the TPRB meeting[1167] nor its written questions[1168] raise the topic any further.

[1162] Trade Policy Review of the United States of 9–11 June 2008, Minutes of the Meeting, WT/TPR/M/200, 4 August 2008; WTO, *US—Measures Concerning the Importation, Marketing and Sale of Tuna and Tuna Products—Request for Consultations by Mexico* (28 October 2008) WT/DS381/R/1.

[1163] Trade Policy Review of the United States of 9–11 June 2008, Secretariat Report, WT/TPR/S/200, 5 May 2008, 23.

[1164] Trade Policy Review of the United States of 9–11 June 2008, Secretariat Report, WT/TPR/S/200, 5 May 2008, 44–46 (particularly at 45).

[1165] Trade Policy Review of the United States of 9–11 June 2008, Secretariat Report, WT/TPR/S/200, 5 May 2008, 81–89 (particularly at 88–89).

[1166] Trade Policy Review of the United States of 9–11 June 2008, Government Report, WT/TPR/G/200, 5 May 2008.

[1167] Trade Policy Review of the United States of 9–11 June 2008, Minutes of the Meeting, WT/TPR/M/200, 4 August 2008 12–14.

[1168] Trade Policy Review of the United States of 9–11 June 2008, Questions and answers, WT/TPR/M/200/Add. 1, 9 September 2008 and WT/TPR/M/Add. 2, 9 September 2008.

The TPR of the United States of October 2010 took place before the Panel had reached its conclusions.[1169] Nevertheless, the TPR again put its finger on the issue. The Secretariat's only reference to the case is contained in the report's sub-section on technical regulations and standards which succinctly indicates that '*Yellow fin tuna sold in the U.S. market can only be labelled as "dolphin safe" if caught without the chase and encirclement of dolphins and without killing or seriously injuring any dolphins in the net in which the tuna was caught. Following a request by Mexico, a WTO panel was established in April 2009 to review the consistency with WTO rules of U.S. dolphin safe labelling provisions.*'[1170] The government report contains no reference to the topic.[1171] Nevertheless, this silence did not disbar Mexico from raising the dispute during the TPRB meeting[1172] (though not throughout its additional written questions).[1173] In the meeting, Mexico enumerated several disputes. With regard to the Tuna dispute, it stated clearly that '*the dispute with the US goes back more than 20 years and during that time the tuna caught by the Mexican fishing fleet has faced various restrictions which are currently being maintained by a label erroneously called "dolphin-safe" that is currently restricting access to the US market through the use of clearly discriminatory measures. Mexico considers these measures to be inconsistent with the GATT and the TBT. The US should amend the regulations on "dolphin-safe" labels and allow effective access that complies with international guidelines agreed by the US for the protection of dolphins*'.

Due to the complexity of the case, the Panel report was only circulated on 15 September 2011. The report concluded that Mexico had effectively demonstrated that the US dolphin-safe labelling provisions were more trade-restrictive than necessary in order to fulfil their legitimate objectives.[1174] Moreover, on 31 October 2011, the parties requested the DSB to adopt a draft decision extending the normal sixty-day time period for appeals to 20 January 2012.[1175] Further to appeal by the United States and a counter-appeal by Mexico, the Appellate Body deemed that the US measure was inconsistent with Article 2.1 of the TBT Agreement. Nevertheless, the Appellate Body also rejected the two Mexican grounds for counter-appeal, namely, Mexico's claim that the Panel had erred in finding that the US' dolphin protection objective was a legitimate objective, and that the Panel had erred in proceeding to examine whether there was a less trade-restrictive alternative measure after it had found that the measure at issue could at best only partially fulfil

[1169] Trade Policy Review of the United States of 29 September–1 October 2010, Minutes of the Meeting, WT/TPR/M/235, 1 November 2010.

[1170] Trade Policy Review of the United States of 29 September–1 October 2010, Secretariat Report, WT/TPR/S/235, 25 August 2010, 35–40.

[1171] Trade Policy Review of the United States of 29 September–1 October 2010, Government Report, WT/TPR/G/235, 25 August 2010.

[1172] Trade Policy Review of the United States of 29 September–1 October 2010, Minutes of the Meeting, WT/TPR/M/235, 1 November 2010, 16–18.

[1173] Trade Policy Review of the United States of 29 September–1 October 2010, Questions and answers, WT/TPR/M/235/Add. 1, 1 November 2010.

[1174] WTO, *US—Measures Concerning the Importation, Marketing and Sale of Tuna and Tuna Products—Report of the Panel* (15 September 2011) WT/DS381/R.

[1175] WTO, *US—Measures Concerning the Importation, Marketing and Sale of Tuna and Tuna Products—Joint Request by Mexico and the United States for a Decision by the DSB* (1 November 2011) WT/DS381/9.

US' objectives.[1176] The parties to the dispute informed the DSB on 17 September 2012 therefore that they had agreed that the reasonable period of time for the United States to implement the DSB's recommendations and rulings would expire on 13 July 2013.[1177]

The TPR of the United States of December 2012 reiterates the issue succinctly.[1178] The Secretariat's sole reference to the dispute is contained in its sub-sectional reporting on technical regulations and standards[1179] which states that '*WTO Members have used the TBT Committee to raise a number of concerns about TBT measures taken by the United States, and three dispute settlement proceedings in the WTO were taken against the United States under the TBT Agreement during the period under review*'.[1180] Moreover, the government report—unsurprisingly—does not touch on the dispute.[1181] The same is true for Mexico's intervention at the TPRB meeting[1182] and its written questions.[1183]

On 23 July 2013, the United States stated that it had implemented the DSB's recommendations.[1184] Nonetheless, on 14 November 2013, Mexico requested the establishment of a compliance Panel.[1185] Although this Panel was composed on 27 January 2014, the Chair of the compliance Panel subsequently informed the DSB that the Panel expected to issue its final report to the parties by December 2014, in accordance with the timetable adopted after consultation with the parties.[1186]

The TPR of the United States of December 2014 was the last US TPR in which the issue was raised.[1187] The Secretariat's only reference to the issue is contained in the report's sub-section on technical regulations and standards[1188] which succinctly

[1176] WTO, *US—Measures Concerning the Importation, Marketing and Sale of Tuna and Tuna Products—Appellate Body Report* (16 May 2012) WT/DS381/AB/R.

[1177] WTO, *US—Measures Concerning the Importation Marketing and Sale of Tuna and Tuna Products—Agreement under Article 21.3(b) of the DSU* (19 September 2012) WT/DS381/17.

[1178] Trade Policy Review of the United States of 18–20 December 2012, Minutes of the Meeting, WT/TPR/M/275, 30 April 2013.

[1179] Trade Policy Review of the United States of 18–20 December 2012, Secretariat Report, WT/TPR/S/275, 13 November 2012, 58–61 (particularly at 58), on the other hand, Secretariat's sectional analysis of Fisheries is again silent on the subject; Trade Policy Review of the United States of 18–20 December 2012, Secretariat Report, WT/TPR/S/275, 18–20 December 2012; 111–17.

[1180] In this regard, the Secretariat report refers to several cases: '*US—Clove Cigarettes (DS406), US—Country of Origin Labelling (COOL) (DS386 and DS384), and US-Tuna II (DS381)*'.

[1181] Trade Policy Review of the United States of 18–20 December 2012, Government Report, WT/TPR/G/275, 13 November 2012.

[1182] Trade Policy Review of the United States of 18–20 December 2012, Minutes of the Meeting, WT/TPR/M/275, 30 April 2013, 33–35.

[1183] Trade Policy Review of the United States of 18–20 December 2012, Questions and answers, WT/TPR/M/275/Add.1, 15 May 2013.

[1184] WTO, DSB, Minutes of Meeting, WT/DSB/M/334, 2 October 2013, 9.

[1185] WTO, *US—Measures Concerning the Importation, Marketing and Sale of Tuna and Tuna Products—Recourse to Article 21.5 of the DSU by Mexico* (14 April 2015) WT/DS381/RW.

[1186] WTO, *US—Measures Concerning the Importation, Marketing and Sale of Tuna and Tuna Products—Recourse to Article 21.5 of the DSU by Mexico, Communication from the Panel* (17 April 2014) WT/DS381/22.

[1187] Trade Policy Review of the United States of 16–18 December 2014, Minutes of the Meeting, WT/TPR/M/307, 9 February 2015.

[1188] Trade Policy Review of the United States of 16–18 December 2014, Secretariat Report, WT/TPR/S/307, 11 November 2014, 66–69 (particularly at 68).

states that '*since the last Review of the United States, five specific trade concerns have been raised in the TBT Committee against measures taken by the United States. Furthermore, three WTO dispute settlement proceedings taken against the United States under the TBT Agreement are pending.*'[1189] In line with its earlier practice, however, the government report does not pay any attention to the subject.[1190] Moreover, Mexico did not refer to the dispute during the meeting of the TPRB.[1191] Contrary to Brazil and China, Mexico was also not interested in further written information on the subject.[1192]

This analysis yields several conclusions: First, reports of the Secretariat offer excellent added value in terms of transparency. These examples have demonstrated that for all TPRs, these reports were again able either to identify or to predict the contours of the (future) dispute. Second, reports of the government under review have minimal added value in terms of transparency. With the exception of one case, they were never used to refer to actual or future trade concerns. Third, in terms of naming and shaming, both TPRB meetings and written questions and answers offer clear added value in terms of naming and shaming, especially in TPRs which took place after the dispute had been initiated.

Structure of meetings

In the years which were covered by the third appraisal (ie 2005 to 2008), the structure of the TPR meetings remained almost unaltered. Most annual reports of this period systematically keep reiterating that '*procedures for the reviews have generally run smoothly*'.[1193] Moreover, the questions which inspired the structural discussions of the third appraisal were more general than those which had animated the discussions of the second appraisal (questioning for instance, how the interaction between Members could be improved or whether any changes were required to the structure of meetings).[1194] Nevertheless, these questions also sought to examine the effectiveness of the new requirements for the written question and answer process which had been introduced as a result of the second appraisal.

[1189] In this regard, the Secretariat report referred to several cases: *US—Measures Concerning the Importation, Marketing and Sale of Tuna and Tuna Products (Tuna II) (DS381); US—Certain Country of Origin Labelling (COOL) Requirements (DS386 and DS384)*; and *US—Measures Affecting the Production and Sale of Clove Cigarettes (DS406).*

[1190] Trade Policy Review of the United States of 16–18 December 2014, Government Report, WT/TPR/G/307, 11 November 2014.

[1191] Trade Policy Review of the United States of 16–18 December 2014, Minutes of the Meeting, WT/TPR/M/307, 9 February 2015, 35–36.

[1192] Trade Policy Review of the United States of 16–18 December 2014, Questions and answers, WT/TPR/M/307/Add. 1, 16 February 2015, 79 and 144.

[1193] WTO, TPRB, Draft Trade Policy Review Mechanism, Report of the Trade Policy Review Body for 2005, WT/TPR/W/35, 12 October 2005, 2; WTO, TPRB, Draft Report of the Trade Policy Review Body for 2006, Trade Policy Review Mechanism, WT/TPR/W/36, 23 October 2006, 2; WTO, TPRB, Draft Report of the Trade Policy Review Body for 2007, Trade Policy Review Mechanism, WT/TPR/W/37, 26 October 2007, 2.

[1194] Possible points for the third appraisal of the operation of the trade policy review mechanism, Non-paper, 7 December 2007, 2–3 (Document on file with the author).

As a result, the third appraisal pays a substantial amount of attention to the process of preparing reviews (judging that earlier modifications operated satisfactorily) whereas it only succinctly covers the structure of the TPRB meetings.[1195] Moreover, with regard to the latter, the appraisal process underlines on one hand that it needed to promote more interactive discussions among Members and that discussants should continue to articulate '*thought-provoking ideas*'. However, the same appraisal process recognizes explicitly that it could not reach consensus on how more interaction might be achieved. In addition, it decided to do away with the communication from the discussant.[1196] In line with earlier practice, the third appraisal resulted in (another) update of the TPRB's rules of procedure.[1197]

ii) Overview of developments in the International Trading Environment

The Overview of 2005 describes a world economy with a regionally varied recovery rate but still marred by some serious downside risks.[1198] Nevertheless, due to their duplication with other WTO publications such as the World Trade Report and the Annual Activities Report, the publication of Overviews was temporarily suspended after 2005. The 2005 Overview was therefore the only one which was drafted in the period which was covered by the third appraisal.

The structure and coverage of the 2005 Overview remained in line with earlier practice and therefore did not encompass a specific section dedicated to the general analysis of activities undertaken within the framework of individual trade policy reviews.[1199] Nevertheless, the Overview explicitly points to several individual countries' trade policies and practices.[1200] However, the (specific/general) criteria for doing so often remain unclear. For instance, making use of information contained in Nigeria's review of 2005, the Overview chooses to highlight the country as an example which demonstrates the strategic importance of increasing the efficiency of a country's maritime port system.[1201] Nonetheless, with the availability of information contained in Sierra Leone's review of 2005, the Overview could have chosen Sierra Leone's efforts as an equally valid example. Interestingly, the 2005 Overview encompasses a full coverage of identified SPS and TBT measures and their further follow-up in the respective frameworks of the TPRM and the DSB. In this regard, the 2005 Overview's specific section on SPS and TBT

1195 *Draft—Third Appraisal of the Operation of the Trade Policy Review Mechanism 2008* (n 1138) 1–2 vs p 3.

1196 *Draft—Third Appraisal of the Operation of the Trade Policy Review Mechanism 2008* (n 1109) 2–3.

1197 WTO, TPRB, Draft Rules of Procedure for Meetings of the Trade Policy Review Body, WT/TPR/W/39, 15 October 2008.

1198 WTO, TPRB, Overview of developments in the International trading environment, Annual Report by the Director-General, WT/TPR/OV/11, 6 February 2006, 1–2.

1199 WTO, TPRB, Overview of developments in the International trading environment, Annual Report by the Director-General, WT/TPR/OV/11, 6 February 2006, 51.

1200 WTO, TPRB, Overview of developments in the International trading environment, Annual Report by the Director-General, WT/TPR/OV/11, 6 February 2006, 4, 40, 42, and 45.

1201 WTO, TPRB, Overview of developments in the International trading environment, Annual Report by the Director-General, WT/TPR/OV/11, 6 February 2006, 4, 40, 42, and 45.

measures[1202] refers at length not only to the coverage of these measures in the framework of the TPRM[1203] but also to their follow-up, where applicable, in the context of the DSB.[1204] Nevertheless, Overviews were temporarily suspended after 2005. It is therefore impossible to assess whether the holistic coverage of SPS and TBT issues (ie including their potential coverage by the TPRM and the DSB) which was adopted by the 2005 Overview had an ad hoc nature or a structural character.

c) Participation

i) Governments (Government under review and its peers)

In the period covered by the third appraisal (ie the period between September 2005 and October 2008), fifty-three Members underwent a trade policy review.[1205]

Tables II.17 and II.18 demonstrate the attendance rates to TPRs which took place in this period.

The attendance rates in this period once again centred on the reviews of Quad countries. In this period, it involved the (descending) attendance by forty-three Members to the TPR of the United States of 2006,[1206] the presence of thirty-eight Members at the review of the United States of 2008,[1207] the attendance by thirty-four Members to the respective TPRs of the European Union (2007) and China (2008),[1208] the presence of thirty-five Members at the review of Columbia (2006),[1209] and the attendance of thirty-two Members to the respective TPRs of India (2007) and Mexico (2008).[1210]

The least-well-attended TPRs during the same period were: eleven Members to the TPRs of Macau (2007), the Kirgiz Republic (2006), and Togo (2006),[1211] the presence of only thirteen Members at the respective reviews of the OECS (2007), Congo

[1202] WTO, TPRB, Overview of developments in the International trading environment, Annual Report by the Director-General, WT/TPR/OV/11, 6 February 2006, 39–43.

[1203] WTO, TPRB, Overview of developments in the International trading environment, Annual Report by the Director-General, WT/TPR/OV/11, 6 February 2006, 40–41.

[1204] WTO, TPRB, Overview of developments in the International trading environment, Annual Report by the Director-General, WT/TPR/OV/11, 6 February 2006, 41.

[1205] ie the period between the TPR of Tunisia of 2005 and the review of Norway of 2008; Data of the author; The CD ROM '*20 years of Trade Policy Reviews 1989–2009, Marking the 20th anniversary of the Trade Policy Review Mechanism*'.

[1206] Trade Policy Review of the United States of 22–24 March 2006, Minutes of the Meeting, WT/TPR/M/160, 9 June 2006.

[1207] Trade Policy Review of the United States of 9–11 June 2008, Minutes of the Meeting, WT/TPR/M/200, 4 August 2008.

[1208] Trade Policy Review of the European Union of 26–28 February 2007, Minutes of the Meeting, WT/TPR/M/177, 30 April 2007; Trade Policy Review of China of 21–23 March 2008, Minutes of the Meeting, WT/TPR/M/199, 24 July 2008.

[1209] Trade Policy Review of Colombia of 22–24 November 2006, Minutes of the Meeting, WT/TPR/M/172, 28 March 2007.

[1210] Trade Policy Review of India of 23–25 May 2007, Minutes of the Meeting, WT/TPR/M/182, 9 July 2007; Trade Policy Review of Mexico of 11–13 February 2008, Minutes of the Meeting, WT/TPR/M/195, 14 April 2008.

[1211] Trade Policy Review of Macao of 30 April–2 May 2007, Minutes of the Meeting, WT/TPR/M/181, 12 June 2007; Trade Policy Review of the Kirgiz Republic of 9–11 October 2006, Minutes of

Table II.17

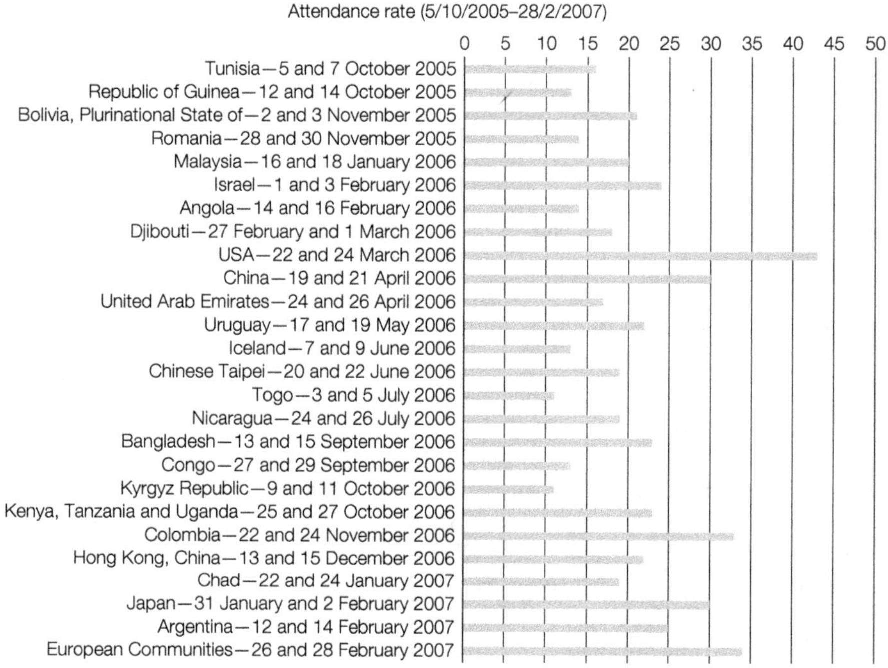

Table II.18

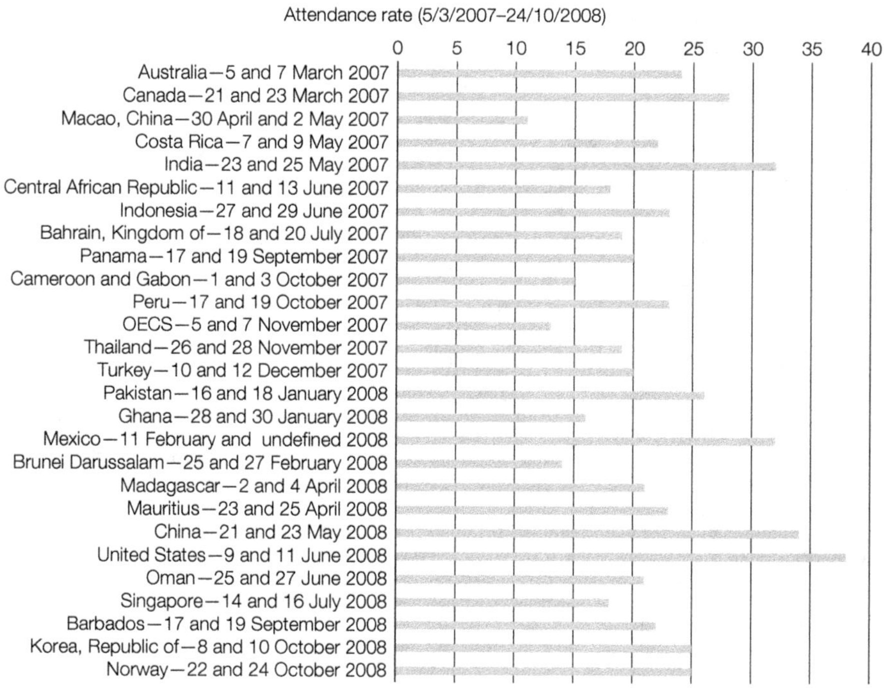

(2006), Iceland (2006), and Guinea (2005),[1212] and only fourteen Members attending the TPRs of Brunei Darussalam (2008), Angola (2006), and Romania (2005).[1213] Again, these low attendance rates cannot be explained solely by the respective Members' affiliation to certain review cycles nor by their regional affiliation.

Tables II.19 and II.20 demonstrate that national participation rates have varied greatly throughout this period.

Table II.19

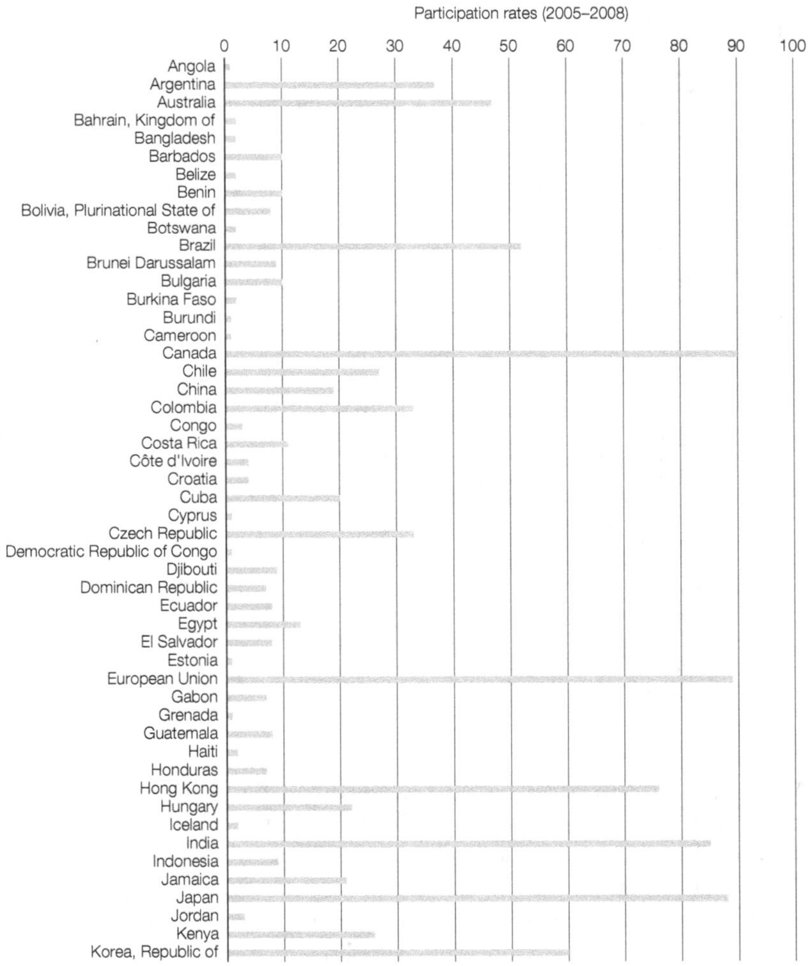

the Meeting, WT/TPR/M/170, 13 December 2006; Trade Policy Review of Togo of 3–5 July 2006, Minutes of the Meeting, WT/TPR/M/166, 29 August 2006.

1212 Trade Policy Review of the OECS of 5–7 November 2007, Minutes of the Meeting, WT/TPR/M/190, 14 December 2007; Trade Policy Review of the Congo of 27–29 September 2006, Minutes of the Meeting, WT/TPR/M/169, 12 December 2006; Trade Policy Review of Iceland of 7–9 June 2006, Minutes of the Meeting, WT/TPR/M/164, 4 August 2006; Trade Policy Review of Guinea of 12–14 October 2005, Minutes of the Meeting, WT/TPR/M/153, 1 December 2005.

1213 Trade Policy Review of Brunei Darussalam of 25–27 February 2008, Minutes of the Meeting, WT/TPR/M/196, 10 April 2008; Trade Policy Review of Angola of 14–16 February 2006, Minutes of

Table II.20

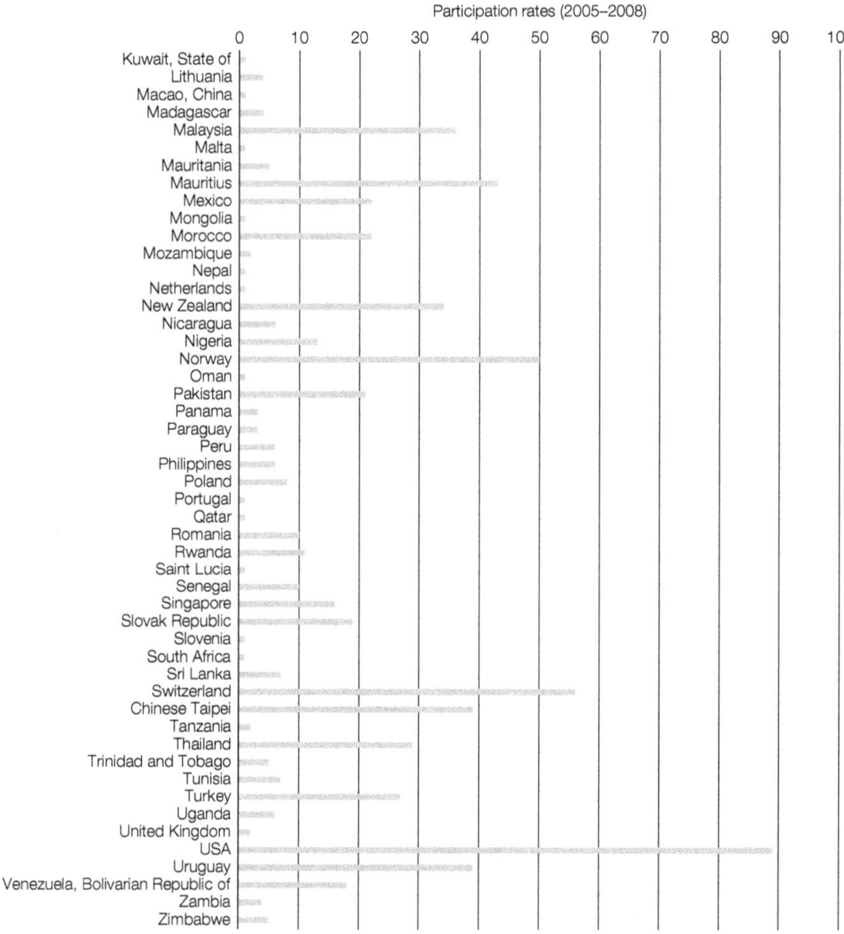

Amongst the top five participants (in descending order) were the following countries. Brazil came first and took part in all the fifty-three TPRs which took place in this period. The European Union and Japan followed. Each was involved in fifty-two reviews. Canada and the United States came third, each with a participation in fifty-one out of the fifty-three TPRs of this period. Chinese Taipei was involved in forty-seven reviews, and Columbia closed the list which a participation in forty-five TPRs out of the fifty-three TPRs of this period.[1214]

On the other hand, the lowest participation rates comprised the following (in ascending order). Togo, Saudi Arabia, Romania, Qatar, the Philippines,

the Meeting, WT/TPR/M/158, 6 April 2006; Trade Policy Review of Romania of 28–30 November 2005, Minutes of the Meeting, WT/TPR/M/155, 18 January 2006.

1214 Data on file with the author.

Namibia, Macau, Lesotho, Kuwait, Hungary, Tunisia, Chad, Bangladesh, and Bahrain took each part in only one TPR throughout the whole period. Venezuela, Trinidad and Tobago, Tanzania, Oman, Madagascar, Israel, Indonesia, Gabon, Egypt, Djibouti, Congo, Bulgaria, and Angola followed. Each of these countries was involved in two reviews. Rwanda, Panama, Haiti, and Cameroon closed the list. These countries participated each in three out of the fifty-three TPRs of the period.[1215] Interestingly, some LDCs stand to be characterized (again) by their poor participation level. Nevertheless, these data demonstrate that some of their more developed counterparts also had a rather poor participation record in this period.

	2006	2007	2008
Average Attendance	20.8	21.9	24.1
Percentage	13.9%	14.5%	15.7%

Yearly attendance rates in the period covered by the third appraisal (ie September 2005 to October 2008) continued to be marked by a small degree of volatility. Nevertheless, yearly attendance rates at the end of this period had increased, both in relative and absolute terms.[1216]

ii) Secretariat

Table II.21

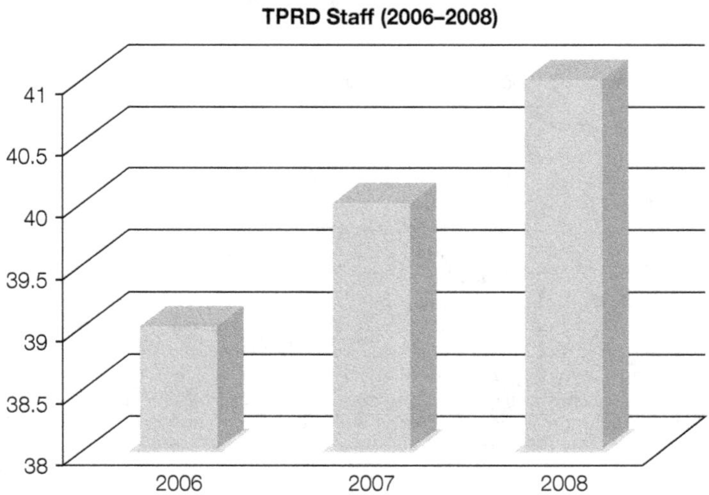

[1215] Data on file with the author.

[1216] Data on file with the author.

During the period covered by the third appraisal of the TPRM (ie between September 2005 and October 2008), the staffing level of the TPRD increased from thirty-nine to forty-one individuals. This increase was linear. Moreover, a clear majority of TPRD personnel still had no legal background. Furthermore, in this period, the overall percentage of staff allocated to the TPRD never amounted to more than 6 per cent of overall WTO staff.[1217]

Since the 2004–5 budget of the WTO was partly linked to the period which was covered by the second appraisal (ie the period between September 1999 and September 2005), it was analysed earlier. In 2006–07, the WTO budget which was initially estimated amounted to CHF 361.97 million.[1218] Members approved CHF 175.000.150 and CHF 181.976.450 for 2006 and 2007 respectively.[1219] Moreover, extra-budgetary contributions from several bilateral donors such as Germany and The Netherlands to the DDA Global Trust Fund facilitated the preparations of the (2006) reviews of Angola, Congo, Djibouti, the East African Community, the Kyrgyz Republic, Nicaragua, and Togo, the (2007) reviews of Cameroon, the Central African Republic, Chad, Gabon, and the OECS and the (2008) reviews of Ghana, Madagascar, Mauritius, and Pakistan.[1220] Nonetheless, in line with previous budgetary practice, the budget for 2006–07 did not include any formal data with regard to the appropriated or actual expenditure of the TPRD.[1221]

The third appraisal looked again into budgetary issues. Although the non-paper which facilitated the review process had only asked whether '*for less developed countries there are now, normally, two visits to capitals—is this suitable and, if so, how should the visits be funded*',[1222] the outcome document urged again '*that all efforts should continue to be made for maximum efficiency in the use of resources, and to minimize the burden on Members under review*'. In this context, the TPRB welcomed the time-saving use by the Secretariat of information sources such as the Internet.[1223]

1217 Answers from the Human Resources Department of the WTO to questions of the author (4 December 2015).

1218 WTO, 2006–2007 Budget Estimates, Proposals by the Director-General, WT/BFA/SPEC/134, 13 October 2005, 5.

1219 WTO, Director-General's Budgetary and Financial Report for 2006 and Report of the External Auditor Thereon, WT/BFA/W/157, 19 September 2007, 3.

1220 WTO, TPRB, Report of the Trade Policy Review Body for 2006, Trade Policy Review Body, WT/TPR.192, 31 October 2006, 1–2; WTO, TPRB, Report of the Trade Policy Review Body for 2007, Trade Policy Review Body, WT/TPR/213, 12 November 2007, 1; WTO, TPRB, Report of the Trade Policy Review Body for 2008, Trade Policy Review Body, WT/TPR/232, 14 November 2008, 1–2; WTO, Director-General's Report on Extra-Budgetary Funds for 2006 and Report of the External Auditor Thereon, WT/BFA/W/158, 19 September 2008, 3; WTO, Director-General's Report on Extra-Budgetary Funds for 2007 and Report of the External Auditor Thereon, WT/BFA/W/169, 16 September 2008, 8.

1221 This lack of data has been repeatedly acknowledged by the Budgetary Department of the WTO, Answers from the Budgetary Department of the WTO to questions of the author (23 July 2015 and 24 January 2016); According to the calculations of the Budgetary Department of the WTO, the TPRD department received a budgetary allocation of CHF 260.000 in 2006 and of CHF 280.000 in 2007. Nevertheless, this amount does not include allocations for missions; Interestingly, Ghosh provides another informal figure of CHF 7.01 million for 2006; Ghosh, 'Developing Countries in the WTO Trade Policy Review Mechanism' (n 166) 446.

1222 Possible points for the third appraisal of the operation of the trade policy review mechanism, Non-paper, 7 December 2007, 2 (Document on file with the author).

1223 *Third Appraisal of the Operation of the Trade Policy Review Mechanism* 2008 (n 1110) 2–3.

During the period which was covered by the third appraisal, the number of WTO Divisions involved in the elaboration of TPRs slowly stagnated. In this regard, it is interesting to note that the third appraisal, contrary to earlier ones, makes no specific recommendations with regard to the need for further internal Divisional streamlining or synergies for the production of Secretariat's reports.[1224] Nevertheless, the 2005, 2006, 2007, and 2008 reports all deserve a specific mention for the TPRD's collaboration with the WTO's Development Division, with the Institute for Training, and with the Technical Co-operation Division.[1225]

In the meantime, the added value provided by the Secretariat's reporting continued to be largely dependent on the Secretariat's independency and intrusiveness. It is therefore not surprising that the yearly TPRB reports which were drafted in the period covered by the third appraisal continued urged Members to cooperate with the Secretariat.[1226] Nevertheless, the TPRB reports for 2005, 2006, 2007, and 2008 almost automatically continued to warn the Members and the Secretariat that 'close contact with the Member under review is necessary to help ensure the factual accuracy and clarity of the documentation prepared for the review'.[1227] Moreover, the appraisal process considered whether the Secretariat's reports should be more critical. Tellingly, no agreement was reached on this point.[1228]

iii) Discussants

In the period covered by the third appraisal (ie the period between the TPR of Tunisia of 2005[1229] and the review of Norway of 2008),[1230] all TPRs were based on the participation of only one discussant. Contrary to the period covered by the second appraisal, the number of discussants with an industrialized background (twenty-two out of the fifty-three) did not exceed those from a developing country (the remaining

[1224] *Third Appraisal of the Operation of the Trade Policy Review Mechanism* 2008 (n 1110).

[1225] WTO, TPRB, Draft Trade Policy Review Mechanism, Report of the Trade Policy Review Body for 2005, WT/TPR/W/35, 12 October 2005, 4; WTO, TPRB, Draft Report of the Trade Policy Review Body for 2006, Trade Policy Review Mechanism, WT/TPR/W/36, 23 October 2006, 4; WTO, TPRB, Draft Report of the Trade Policy Review Body for 2007, Trade Policy Review Mechanism, WT/TPR/W/37, 26 October 2007, 4; WTO, TPRB, Draft Report of the Trade Policy Review Body for 2008, Trade Policy Review Mechanism, WT/TPR/W/40, 15 October 2008, 4.

[1226] WTO, TPRB, Draft Trade Policy Review Mechanism, Report of the Trade Policy Review Body for 2005, WT/TPR/W/35, 12 October 2005, 4; WTO, TPRB, Draft Report of the Trade Policy Review Body for 2006, Trade Policy Review Mechanism, WT/TPR/W/36, 23 October 2006, 4; WTO, TPRB, Draft Report of the Trade Policy Review Body for 2007, Trade Policy Review Mechanism, WT/TPR/W/37, 26 October 2007, 4; WTO, TPRB, Draft Report of the Trade Policy Review Body for 2008, Trade Policy Review Mechanism, WT/TPR/W/40, 15 October 2008, 4.

[1227] WTO, TPRB, Draft Trade Policy Review Mechanism, Report of the Trade Policy Review Body for 2005, WT/TPR/W/35, 12 October 2005, 2; WTO, TPRB, Draft Report of the Trade Policy Review Body for 2006, Trade Policy Review Mechanism, WT/TPR/W/36, 23 October 2006, 2; WTO, TPRB, Draft Report of the Trade Policy Review Body for 2007, Trade Policy Review Mechanism, WT/TPR/W/37, 26 October 2007, 2; WTO, TPRB, Draft Report of the Trade Policy Review Body for 2008, Trade Policy Review Mechanism, WT/TPR/W/40, 15 October 2008, 2.

[1228] *Third Appraisal of the Operation of the Trade Policy Review Mechanism 2008* (n 1110) 3.

[1229] Trade Policy Review of Tunisia of 5–7 October 2005, Minutes of the Meeting, WT/TPR/M/152, 7 November 2005.

[1230] Trade Policy Review of Norway of 22–24 November 2008, Minutes of the Meeting, WT/TPR/M/205, 10 December 2008.

thirty-one). As a result, developing countries' perspectives were relatively better articulated and heard.

Discussants grew substantially more independent. On the one hand, the 2008 rules of procedure had explicitly emphasized that '*discussants' statements should not exceed in length that by the Member under review*'.[1231] As a result, the scope for a deep interactive debate sparked by the discussant was formally weakened. On the other hand, discussants of this period relied substantially less on the Secretariat's reporting. Fewer than half the discussants referred, directly or indirectly, to the Secretariat's reporting (twenty-one out of the fifty-three discussants who covered the fifty-three TPRs of this period or 39 per cent). Moreover, in line with earlier practice, discussants referring to governmental reporting was even lower (twelve out of the fifty-three discussants or 22 per cent).[1232] The Secretariat's reporting, however, continued to be the subject of some criticism, albeit on a somewhat exceptional basis. For instance, the discussant in the TPR of Macau of 2007 commented that the '*Secretariat report stated [on page 43] that, according to the authorities, Macao did not provide any export subsidies, but [on page 28] that "various tax incentives are made available for projects that encourage exports"*'.[1233] Nevertheless, in line with acquired practice, governmental reporting came even more often under fire by discussants. For instance, the discussant of the TPR of the Kyrgyz Republic of 2006 noted that '*according to the government report, foreign investors could own 100% of property in all sectors. However, according to the Economist Intelligence Unit, legal entities and foreign corporations could not purchase land.*'[1234] In seventeen out of the fifty-three TPRs of this period (ie 32 per cent), the discussants referred to other external studies which shed some additional light on the trade policies and practices of the country under review.[1235] The period covered by the third appraisal thus attested to the presence of increasingly critical discussants.

Issues with regard to dispute settlement also resurfaced on a more regular basis. In this regard, the focus was often on failing US compliance in the context of dispute settlement. For instance, the discussant in the TPR of the United States of 2006 stated that '*it was important to stress that during the period under review, the US had issued legislation to abide by DSB rulings in two prominent anti-dumping cases: the anti-dumping Act of 1916 had been repealed, as had the Byrd amendment. Members had noted with some concern, however, that in the case of the Byrd Amendment anti-dumping duties would continue to be distributed to the domestic industry until 1 October 2007, creating further trade distortions; she enquired about*

[1231] WTO, TPRB, Draft Rules of Procedure for Meetings of the Trade Policy Review Body, WT/TPR/W/39, 15 October 2008, 2.

[1232] Data on file with the author.

[1233] Trade Policy Review of Macau of 30 April–2 May 2007, Minutes of the Meeting, WT/TPR/M/181, 12 June 2007, 6.

[1234] Trade Policy Review of the Kyrgyz Republic of 9–11 October 2006, Minutes of the Meeting, WT/TPR/M/170, 13 December 2006, 7.

[1235] Data on file with the author.

the choice of a date that seemed so relatively far in the future'.[1236] The discussant also noted that '*US implementation of Panel and Appellate Body rulings was of systemic importance to the WTO. Concerns about the failure by the US to implement several rulings had been voiced in previous US reviews. During the period under review, a compliance Panel had found that legislation repealing the US tax code's extra-territorial income provisions had failed to implement fully previous WTO rulings. At the same time, as noted in the Report by the US, the US had announced in 2005 that it was undertaking a number of measures to comply with the WTO ruling in upland cotton, including the adoption of a risk-based fee structure for certain export credit guarantee programmes. More recently, the President had signed legislation to eliminate Step 2 export subsidies for upland cotton and the Byrd amendment.*' In a similar vein, the discussant in the TPR of the United States of 2008 stated that '*while compliance with DSB resolutions and decisions has been good, implementation of some DSB recommendations were still pending, such as the cases dealing with Article 211 of the Omnibus Act of 1998, some aspects of anti-dumping investigations on certain steel hot rolled products originating from Japan, and section 110 (5) of the Copyright Law*'.[1237] The discussant highlighted the fact that '*the use of "zeroing" when calculating the margin of dumping had been the subject of several disputes under the DSB, and on each occasion, the DSB had found the practice to be contrary to the ADA. Although the Byrd amendment had been revoked in 2005, AD and CVD assessed before October 2007 were still being distributed to US producers who had supported the request*'. The discussant also noted that the 'implementation of the DSB recommendations on gambling and betting were still outstanding'. Similarly, the discussant in the TPR of Colombia of 2006 wrote that*Colombia implemented the Andean price band system, a variable levy system applied on a broad range of agricultural products. Although this system had not been challenged in the WTO, a WTO Panel had ruled against an apparently similar system operated by another Member.*'[1238] The discussant then '*enquired about the difficulties that this ruling raised for the continuation the Andean price band system, and whether Colombia planned to modify its system in light of the panel ruling*'.

In spite of the discussants' underused institutional potential, the third appraisal hardly dwelt on this issue. Although it still '*deemed it appropriate for discussants to continue to articulate though-provoking ideas*', the appraisal saw no further justification to keep the '*communication from the discussant*' and decided to abolish this requirement.[1239]

[1236] Trade Policy Review of the United States of 22–24 March 2006, Minutes of the Meeting, WT/TPR/M/160, 9 June 2006.

[1237] Trade Policy Review of the United States of 9–11 June 2008, Minutes of the Meeting, WT/TPR/M/200, 4 August 2008, 8–11.

[1238] Trade Policy Review of Columbia of 22–24 November 2006, Minutes of the Meeting, WT/TPR/M/172, 28 March 2007, 7.

[1239] *Third Appraisal of the Operation of the Trade Policy Review Mechanism 2008* (n 1110) 2–4.

4. Fourth appraisal of the operation of the Trade Policy Review Mechanism (July–November 2011): review of TPRM's functioning between October 2008 and November 2011

On 3 April 2011, the Chairperson of the TPRB announced his intention to begin the fourth appraisal of the operation of the TPRM.[1240] In line with the TPRB's practice acquired during earlier appraisals, a non-paper with questions and suggestions guided the process.[1241] As a result, informal TPRB meetings were held between July and November 2011.[1242]

The fourth appraisal is noteworthy for the rather unusual depth of its debate which resulted in several new proposals by the Members. These included China's proposals to further operationalize the principle of special and differential treatment for developing country Members[1243] and Argentina's proposal to provide the WTO with a more solid institutional basis strengthening its role in the monitoring and surveillance of international trade.[1244] Further to these discussions, the rules of procedure for meetings of the Trade Policy Review Body were also revised.[1245]

a) Objectives

The earlier academic debate between the proponents of the TPRM as an exclusive mechanism for transparency and the advocates of the TPRM as a prime or partial/indirect mechanism for naming and shaming resulted in some further academic analysis between October 2008 and November 2011.

This renewed academic interest in the TPRM was partly sparked by the financial and economic crisis of 2008. As a result, some of the academic literature was largely inspired by the wish to increase the practical added value and political clout of the TPRM in shaping domestic politics to counter protectionism.[1246]

[1240] Fourth Appraisal of the Trade Policy Review Mechanism, Report on the Meeting, WT/TPR/R/5, 9 December 2011, 1.

[1241] Fourth Appraisal of the Operation of the TPRM, informal WTO document (Document on file with the author).

[1242] *Fourth Appraisal of the Operation of the Trade Policy Review Mechanism* (17 November 2011) WT/TPR/W/44, 1 (hereafter *Fourth Appraisal of the Operation of the Trade Policy Review Mechanism 2011*); Fourth Appraisal of the Trade Policy Review Mechanism, Report on the Meeting, WT/TPR/R/5, 9 December 2011, 1.

[1243] Fourth Appraisal of The Trade Policy Review Mechanism, Comments and Suggestions of China, Non–paper, JOB/TPR/1, 30 August 2011; Fourth Appraisal of The Trade Policy Review Mechanism, Comments and Suggestions of China, Non-paper, JOB/TPR/2, 13 September 2011; The Chinese proposal was an (unsuccessful) part of the ongoing attempts to replace current and ineffective models of S&D; Thomas Cottier, 'Preparing for structural reform in the WTO' (2007) 10(3) Journal of International Economic Law 502.

[1244] Ideas for Strengthening of The WTO: Monitoring and Surveillance, Communication from Argentina, WT/GC/W/639, 3 October 2011; Informal meeting of the TPRB (18 October 2011): Non-paper by the EU, 17 October 2011.

[1245] WTO, TPRB, Rules of Procedure for Meetings of the Trade Policy Review Body, WT/TPR/6/Rev.3, 31 January 2012.

[1246] Valentin Zahrnt, 'The WTO's Trade Policy Review Mechanism: How to Create Political Will for Liberalization' (2009) 11, ECIPE Working Paper <http://www.ecipe.org/app/uploads/2014/12/

According to Zahrnt, '*no official document defines and prioritizes the objectives of the TPRM in detail or identifies the channels through which the mechanism shall obtain its results*'.[1247] Zahrnt therefore argued for an explicit commitment of the TPRM to convince readers of the benefits of liberal reform and to serve as a reference in domestic policy debates. Interestingly, Zahrnt's conclusion that the TPRM could serve as a reference in domestic policy debates contradicts with Carmichael's earlier findings according to which '*experience has shown that the TPRM has done nothing to ease the negative pressures governments face at home, from protected domestic producers seeking to avoid the adjustment liberalisation involves for them*'.[1248] In any case, Zahrnt's ensuing suggestions were largely political in nature and made no difference to the degree to which the respective transparency and/or the naming and shaming objectives were pursued in practice.

Nevertheless, other academic literature in this period refocused on the traditional cleavage between the transparency and surveillance objectives. In this regard, Conzelmann emphasized the TPRM's relative dichotomy stating on the one hand that 'Members of the WTO division dealing with the TPRM highlight that the procedure would largely lose in value if it would be used as a pre-stage to enforcement, and that the Dispute Settlement Body declines to use information generated through the TPRM within its work' while affirming on the other that '*academic observes point out that it is highly unlikely for a DSB hearing to disregard a discussion of the respective topic in previous reviews*', with the latter view being confirmed by most Geneva delegations.[1249] The author therefore concluded that '*the two processes operate largely in insulation from one another, thus taking a potential sword out of the hands of the TPRM*'.

Ghosh managed to surpass the traditional cleavage between the TPRM's two objectives.[1250] In evaluating the TPRM's performance against its given mandate of increasing transparency to promote improved adherence with trade rules, the author demonstrated empirically that the TPRM does not generate information specific to the needs of developing countries and that much of the WTO Membership does not participate in review meetings.[1251] Ghosh imputes this double failure to several factors including a weak mandate, a repeated lack of analysis with regard to salient trade features, and a poor capacity and lack of willingness of the Members to

the-wto2019s-trade-policy-review-mechanism-how-to-create-political-will-for-liberalization-1.pdf> accessed 6 May 2017 (hereafter Zahrnt, *The WTO's Trade Policy Review Mechanism*).

[1247] Zahrnt, *The WTO's Trade Policy Review Mechanism* (n 1244) 6.

[1248] Bill Carmichael, 'Trade Policy at the Cross-Roads' (2005) Australian National University, Pacific Economic Papers, No 351 <https://crawford.anu.edu.au/pdf/pep/pep-351.pdf> accessed 17 June 2017.

[1249] Conzelmann, 'Beyond the carrot and the stick: The authority of peer reviews in the WTO and the OECD' (n 877) 13; Data of the author.

[1250] Ghosh, 'Developing Countries in the WTO Trade Policy Review Mechanism' (n 166) 419–455; Ghosh, 'Strengthening WTO surveillance: making transparency work for developing countries' (n 1117) 394–441.

[1251] Ghosh, 'Developing Countries in the WTO Trade Policy Review Mechanism' (n 166) 419 and 450.

participate in TPRM reviews.[1252] The author moreover acknowledges that these elements were not remedied by the mechanism's successive reforms.[1253]

Whether as a result of this academic criticism or not, the fourth appraisal was relatively more elaborate than earlier appraisals in its assessment of the TPRM's objectives. It reiterates all the TPRM's known objectives contained in paragraph A and B of Annex 3 to the Marrakesh Agreement. In addition, it stresses the TPRM's role in providing technical assistance to developing country Members and emphasizes the need for reviews of Members that have not yet been reviewed. For the first time, however, the appraisal also explicitly emphasized that Members sometimes saw a considerable room for improvement of the transparency objective:*In anticipation of the mandated rise in the number of Trade Policy Reviews in accordance with the 2–4–6 year frequency (which Members broadly agreed to maintain, with the existing flexibility) and consequent burden on Members (including their role as discussants), the Chairperson and the Secretariat, it was agreed that the main purpose of this Fourth Appraisal would be to streamline the existing TPRM in order to make it even more effective in achieving its objectives.*'[1254] Moreover, the fourth appraisal paid specific attention to the secondary objective of naming and shaming. In this regard, the appraisal explicitly notes that '*the collective appreciation and evaluation of the impact of the trade policies and practices of the Member under review on the functioning of the multilateral trading system, which is one of the mandated objectives of the TPRM seems often to play a distant, secondary role*'.[1255] Nevertheless, it is careful to delineate the official borders of naming and shaming, indicating that '*enhanced transparency could act as a catalyst for action by Members under Review. At the same time, however, any proposals in this regard should not affect the existing rights and obligations of Members. Nor should they expand the Secretariat's role in the TPRM.*'[1256] The substantial number of 'best-effort' guidelines in the context of naming and shaming therefore include: (a) the recommendation to Members to exercise self-discipline and common sense in the types and number of written questions and (b) the request that Members should refrain from posing questions on matters undergoing dispute settlement, including those matters under consultation. A similar explicit warning to steer clear of legal comments is addressed to the Chairperson.[1257] Furthermore, the appraisal states that information tabled and/or requested in the framework of the TPRM should not be misused for other purposes, including those of a more compliance-related nature.

1252 Ghosh, 'Strengthening WTO surveillance: making transparency work for developing countries' (n 1117) 398–403.

1253 Ghosh, 'Strengthening WTO surveillance: making transparency work for developing countries' (n 1117) 405–12.

1254 *Fourth Appraisal of the Operation of the Trade Policy Review Mechanism 2011* (n 1240) 5

1255 *Fourth Appraisal of the Operation of the Trade Policy Review Mechanism 2011* (n 1240) 4.

1256 *Fourth Appraisal of the Operation of the Trade Policy Review Mechanism 2011* (n 1240) 5.

1257 Fourth Appraisal of the Trade Policy Review Mechanism, Ministerial Conference, Eighth Session, Geneva, 15–17 December 2011, WT/MIN(11)/6, 29 November 2011, 7.

Again, it should be remembered that the TPRM and the DSB were conceived as two separately functioning entities. Paragraph A of Annex 3 to the Marrakesh Agreement is very clear in stating that the TPRM '*is not, however, intended to serve as a basis for the enforcement of specific obligations under the Agreements or for dispute settlement procedures, or to impose new policy commitments on Members*'.[1258] In addition, Annex 3 to the Marrakesh Agreement is not a covered agreement under Appendix I to Annex II to the Marrakesh Agreement which embodies the Understanding on Rules and Procedures Governing the Settlement of Disputes.[1259] As a result, the TPRM and its findings should in principle not be invoked within the proceedings of the Dispute Settlement Body. Nevertheless, in the period which was covered by the fourth appraisal, findings of the TPRM had been invoked in seven panel proceedings (reaching a maximum of 15.2 per cent of all disputes covered in this period).[1260] In these cases, findings which had been originated within the framework of the TPRM were invoked as factual though not as legal claims.

b) Structure

i) Individual trade policy reviews

Periodicity

The fourth appraisal of the TPRM (ie October 2008 to November 2011) covered three years during which the TPRM functioned (2009, 2010, and 2011). In these years, the Secretariat correctly estimated the number of TPRs it would implement in 2010.[1261] However, it overestimated the number of TPRs it was able to implement in 2011[1262] and underestimated the number of reviews it undertook in 2009.[1263]

[1258] Trade Policy Review Mechanism (n 151).

[1259] The Marrakesh Agreement (n 353).

[1260] WTO, *US—Anti-Dumping Administrative Reviews and Other Measures Related to Imports of Certain Orange Juice from Brazil—Report of the Panel* (25 March 2011) WT/DS382/R; WTO, *European Communities—Measures Prohibiting the Importation and Marketing of Seal Products—Report of the Panel* (25 November 2013) WT/DS400 and DS401/R; WTO, *Dominican Republic—Safeguard Measures on Imports of Polypropylene Bags and Tubular Fabric—Report of the Panel* (31 January 2012) WT/DS415-DS416-DS417-DS418, 117.

[1261] For 2010 see: WTO, TPRB, Report of the Trade Policy Review Body for 2009, Trade Policy Review Body, WT/TPR/249, 29 October 2009, 1 and 7; Data of the author; WTO, TPRB, Draft Report of the Trade Policy Review Body for 2010, Trade Policy Review Mechanism, WT/TPR/W/42, 28 October 2010, 1 and 4; WTO, TPRB, Report of the Trade Policy Review Body for 2010, Trade Policy Review Body, WT/TPR/269, 29 November 2010, 1 and 4.

[1262] For 2011 see: WTO, TPRB, Report of the Trade Policy Review Body for 2010, Trade Policy Review Body, WT/TPR/269, 29 November 2010, 2 and 4; Data of the author; WTO, TPRB, Draft Report of the Trade Policy Review Body for 2011, Trade Policy Review Mechanism, WT/TPR/W/43, 4 November 2011, 1 and 4; WTO, TPRB, Report of the Trade Policy Review Body for 2011, Trade Policy Review Body, WT/TPR/284, 15 November 2011, 1 and 4.

[1263] For 2009 see: WTO, TPRB, Report of the Trade Policy Review Body for 2008, Trade Policy Review Body, WT/TPR/232, 14 November 2008, 2 and 6; Data of the author; WTO, TPRB, Draft Report of the Trade Policy Review Body for 2009, Trade Policy Review Mechanism, WT/TPR/W/41, 8 October 2009, 1 and 7; WTO, TPRB, Report of the Trade Policy Review Body for 2009, Trade Policy Review Body, WT/TPR/249, 29 October 2009, 1 and 7.

Between October 2008 and November 2011, Secretariat's annual reporting on the TPRM included a categorization of the countries under review by their cyclical periodicity. Nevertheless, although the Secretariat again successfully managed to fulfil normal expectations and review two Quad countries in each year throughout the whole period, it was not able to muster yearly reviews of four countries of the four-year cycle. Instead, the number of yearly reviewed countries on the four-year cycle varied between one in 2009 and three in 2011.[1264]

The Secretariat also modified how it counted joint reviews. In the past, it had counted joint reviews (for instance those of 1998, 2000, 2001, 2003, 2004, 2006, 2007, and 2008) as one review. However, in 2009, it counted joint reviews separately (eg in 2009 the Secretariat stated that it had undertaken twenty-one reviews, whereas it had only undertaken sixteen reviews including the two joint reviews of the SACU and of Niger and Senegal).[1265] This practice continued in 2011, where the Secretariat stated that it had undertaken fourteen reviews but which included the joint review of Guinea–Conakry and Mauritania.[1266] In 2012, the Secretariat's counting of reviews reverted arbitrarily back to its traditional way of counting joint reviews as one review.[1267]

Members still agreed with the existing periodicity of reviews. Moreover, the summary of main issues discussed in the first informal meeting of the fourth appraisal clearly emphasized the value of flexibility. It stated that '*the TPRM does allow for some flexibility. For example, a period longer than six years can be (and has been) allowed for LDCs. Moreover, an additional 6 months has, in practice, been allowed sometimes for 2- and 4-year Members.*'[1268] Furthermore, in order to operationalize the principle of special and differential treatment within the context of the appraisal, China attempted to tinker further with the existing periodicity. It proposed that '*The frequency of a developing country Member of the first 4 trading entities and the following 16 may be adjusted to 3 years and 6 years respectively, with other developing country Members reviewed every 8 years and least-developed country Members even longer. Meanwhile, whenever a developing country Member, particularly a least developed country Member expresses its willingness to have its review at a shorter interval, the review should be arranged as early as possible.*'[1269] Although the Chinese proposal was largely rejected, the concept of periodicity continued to be applied in a very flexible way.[1270]

1264 Data of the author.

1265 WTO, TPRB, Draft Report of the Trade Policy Review Body for 2009, Trade Policy Review Mechanism, WT/TPR/W/41, 8 October 2009, 1.

1266 WTO, TPRB, Draft Report of the Trade Policy Review Body for 2011, Trade Policy Review Mechanism, WT/TPR/W/43, 4 November 2011, 1; WTO, TPRB, Report of the Trade Policy Review Body for 2011, Trade Policy Review Body, WT/TPR/284, 15 November 2011, 1.

1267 WTO, TPRB, Report of the Trade Policy Review Body for 2012, Trade Policy Review Body, WT/TPR/306, 23 November 2012, 1 and 5.

1268 Fourth Appraisal of the Trade Policy Review Mechanism, Summary of Main Issues discussed in First Informal Meeting, Rough Draft, 18 July 2011, 2 (Document on file with the author).

1269 Fourth Appraisal of the Trade Policy Review Mechanism, Comments and Suggestions of China, Non–paper, JOB/TPR/1, 30 August 2011, 1–2.

1270 Fourth Appraisal of the TPRM, Informal open-ended meeting, 23 September 2011, 9 (Document on file with the author).

Reporting
Although the fourth appraisal did not raise the question of whether the TPRM should undertake analysis of new topics, it saw some room for improvement in the Secretariat's reporting by providing a greater coverage of matters such as trade policy's role in sustainable development, Aid for Trade, and the implementation of trade policies at the sub-federal level.[1271]

Moreover, governments remained free to decide on the structure and coverage of their reporting. On the other hand, the Secretariat's reporting came under fire by China and by the rest of the TPRB's Membership. In order to operationalize the principle of special and differential treatment within the context of the TPRB, China made a failed attempt to limit the structural invasiveness and coverage of the Secretariat's reporting by proposing that the Secretariat agree in advance with the reviewed Member on a list of official annual publications where much information requested would already be available or by attempting to curtail the existing question-and-answer approach.[1272] Nevertheless, the fourth appraisal also resulted in several other TPRB recommendations which were successfully adopted in order to enhance the Secretariat's reporting. These include the recommendations (a) for a higher consistency in Secretariat's reporting across all Members (especially those in the same cycle) in terms of comprehensiveness, accuracy, and detailed analysis—especially in the context of the Secretariat's summary observations; (b) for an increased focus on changes or new developments since previous reviews; and (c) for more detail in the Secretariat's report of the extent to which requested information or data were not available from Members under review.[1273]

TPR's informational value – Compared to the period covered by the third appraisal, the period covered by the fourth appraisal (ie October 2008 to November 2011) yielded no further academic literature analysing the information contained in the Secretariat's (and sometimes governmental) reporting within the context of individual TPRs.

Reporting on information and naming and shaming – Between the start (October 2008) and the end (November 2011) of the period which was covered by the fourth appraisal, fifty TPRs took place and forty-six DSB disputes were initiated. Of these, six disputes related to sanitary and phytosanitary measures (SPS) whereas six related to the area of technical barriers to trade (TBT).

Through its focus on the respective DSB and TPR coverage of the same SPS and TBT disputes, this section again analyses individual TPRs' added value in terms of transparency and naming and shaming. In order to do so, for each of the DSB

[1271] Fourth Appraisal of the Trade Policy Review Mechanism, Summary of Main Issues discussed in First Informal Meeting, Rough Draft, 18 July 2011, 1 (Document on file with the author).

[1272] Fourth Appraisal of the Trade Policy Review Mechanism, Comments and Suggestions of China, Non–paper, JOB/TPR/2, 13 September 2011, 1–3.

[1273] Fourth Appraisal of the Trade Policy Review Mechanism, Summary of Main Issues discussed in First Informal Meeting, Rough Draft, 18 July 2011, 1 (Document on file with the author); *Fourth Appraisal of the Operation of the Trade Policy Review Mechanism 2011* (n 1240) 5; Fourth Appraisal of the Trade Policy Review Mechanism, Ministerial Conference, Eighth Session, Geneva, 15–17 December 2011, WT/MIN(11)/6, 29 November 2011, 5.

disputes, this section examines the proceeding and succeeding TPR(s). For each of these TPRs, the Secretariat report and the government report, the debates during the TPRB meeting, and the written questions and answers will be analysed from a transparency angle (questioning whether the respective reports, meetings, or questions explicitly or indirectly managed to refer to elements of the future dispute) and from the perspective of naming and shaming (analysing whether the respective reports, meetings, or questions managed to elicit a defensive stance from the country under review).

- In *US—Certain Country of Origin Labelling (COOL) requirements*, Canada and Mexico took issue with several American country-of-origin-labelling (COOL) provisions which had a mandatory nature.[1274] These measures included the obligation to inform consumers at the retail level of the country of origin in respect of the covered commodities, including beef and pork. Moreover, according to the provisions, the eligibility for a designation of a covered commodity as exclusively having a US origin could only be derived from an animal that was exclusively born, raised, and slaughtered in the United States. As a result, this requirement would exclude such a designation in respect of beef or pork derived from livestock that was exported to the United States for feed or immediate slaughter.[1275] Furthermore, in the case of certain products, the determination of nationality deviated considerably from international country-of-origin labelling standards. According to Canada and Mexico, the COOL provisions were therefore inconsistent with Articles III, IX, and X of the GATT (1994) and with Article 2 of the TBT Agreement, or, alternatively, with Articles 2, 5, and 7 of the SPS Agreement and with Article 2 of the Agreement on Rules of Origin. After both parties' initial request for consultations had been tabled, Canada and Mexico also requested additional consultations concerning related US amendments and measures.

The TPR of the United States of (June) 2008, which took place before the formal DSB consultations had been initiated, clearly identifies the issues which led to the dispute.[1276] The Secretariat's coverage of the issue is mainly contained in its report's sub-section on technical regulations, conformity assessments, and standards.[1277] This sub-section states that '*between July 2005 and July 2007, WTO Members raised concerns in the Committee on Technical Barriers to Trade regarding... country of origin*

[1274] WTO, *US—Certain Country of Origin Labelling (COOL) requirements—Report of the Panel* (18 November 2011) WT/DS384 and DS 386/R; WTO, *US—Certain Country of Origin Labelling (COOL) requirements—Appellate Body Report* (29 June 2012) WT/DS384 and DS 386/AB/R.

[1275] Joel L Greene, 'Country-of-Origin Labelling for Food and the WTO Trade Dispute on Meat Labelling' (Report 7-5700, US Congressional Research Service, 5 November 2014).

[1276] WTO, *US—Certain Country of Origin Labelling (COOL) requirements—Request for Consultations by Canada* (4 December 2008) WT/DS384/1; WTO, *US—Certain Country of Origin Labelling (COOL) requirements—Request for Consultations by Canada* (22 December 2008) WT/DS386/1; Trade Policy Review of the United States of 9–11 June 2008, Minutes of the Meeting, WT/TPR/M/200, 4 August 2008.

[1277] Trade Policy Review of the United States of 9–11 June 2008, Secretariat Report, WT/TPR/S/200, 5 May 2008, 46–50 (particularly at 47).

labelling regulations.[1278] *Only the concern relating to country of origin labelling has been raised in a subsequent Committee meeting; none of the concerns has been followed by formal dispute settlement.*' Country-of-origin labelling for beef is also briefly mentioned in the Secretariat report's section on agriculture.[1279] The government report, unsurprisingly, remains silent on the topic.[1280] This silence did not stop Canada from voicing its concerns on the subject during the TPRB meeting. It used the meeting to state that it '*was very concerned and disappointed with the 2008 Farm Bill, which lacked any meaningful reform and represented a missed opportunity for the US to show real leadership in agricultural reform. Amongst Canada's concerns were mandatory country-of-origin labellings… The amendments to mandatory country-of-origin labelling represented only an incremental improvement to the provisions in the previous bill, and the legislation still contained fisheries, agriculture, and agri-food product labelling requirements that were arbitrary and flawed, and which ignored the reality of an integrated North American market*'.[1281] Canada tabled additional written questions on the topic.[1282]

At its meeting on 19 November 2009, the DSB established a single Panel to examine both disputes.[1283] On 10 May 2010, the Panel was composed by the Director-General.[1284]

The TPR of the United States of October 2010 took place after the Panel had been established.[1285] As a result, the Secretariat paid a considerable amount of attention to the dispute. While the Secretariat report's sub-section on technical regulations and standards[1286] succinctly indicates that '*there are also country-of-origin labelling requirements for certain agricultural products and fish*', the report's section on agriculture[1287] added further detail in stating that '*The 2008 Farm Act added chicken, goat meat, ginseng, pecans and macadamia nuts to the list of commodities covered by*

[1278] In this regard, the Secretariat reports refer to the following: '*WTO documents G/TBT/M/41, 12 June 2007; G/TBT/M/39, 31 July 2006; G/TBT/M/38, 23 May 2006; G/TBT/M/37, 22 December 2005 and G/TBT/M/36, 4 August 2005*'.

[1279] Trade Policy Review of the United States of 9–11 June 2008, Secretariat Report, WT/TPR/S/200, 5 May 2008, 81–89 particularly at 89.

[1280] Trade Policy Review of the United States of 9–11 June 2008, Government Report, WT/TPR/S/200, 5 May 2008.

[1281] Trade Policy Review of the United States of 9–11 June 2008, Minutes of the Meeting, WT/TPR/M/200, 4 August 2008, 20–22 (particularly at 21); During the TPRB meeting, Mexico remained silent on the subject; Trade Policy Review of the United States of 9–11 June 2008, Minutes of the Meeting, WT/TPR/M/200, 4 August 2008, 12–14.

[1282] Trade Policy Review of the United States of 9–11 June 2008, Questions and answers, WT/TPR/M/200/Add. 1, 9 September 2008, 51 and 155.

[1283] WTO, DSB, Minutes of Meeting, WT/DSB/M/276, 29 January 2010, 12–14.

[1284] WTO, *US—Certain Country of Origin Labelling (COOL) Requirements—Constitution of the Panel Established at the Requests of Canada and Mexico, Note by the Secretariat* (11 May 2010) WT/DS384/9 and WT/DS386/8.

[1285] Trade Policy Review of the United States of 29 September–1 October 2010, Minutes of the Meeting, WT/TPR/M/235, 1 November 2010.

[1286] Trade Policy Review of the United States of 29 September–1 October 2010, Secretariat Report, WT/TPR/S/235, 25 August 2010, 39.

[1287] Trade Policy Review of the United States of 29 September–1 October 2010, Secretariat Report, WT/TPR/S/235, 25 August 2010, 80–94 (particularly at paragraph 9.89).

the country-of-origin labelling provisions. It also introduced different categories of labels depending on whether the animal was born, raised and/or slaughtered in the United States. On 19 November 2009, the DSB established a panel to hear complaints from Canada and Mexico on the country-of-origin labelling provisions.'[1288]

Conforming with its earlier practice, the government's report remains silent on the issue.[1289] Nevertheless, during the TPRB meeting, both complainants in the case reiterated their concerns about the ongoing country-of-origin dispute. Canada stated that its '*relationship on agriculture is very positive, but there are issues of concern. Canada is challenging the Country-of-origin Labelling (COOL) requirement that has negatively affected exports of Canadian livestock to the US.*'[1290] Mexico commented in similar terms that '*another dispute with the US resolves around the establishment of country of origin labelling requirements (COOL), protectionist and unjustified requirements that violate several provisions of the GATT 1994 and the Agreement on Technical Barriers to Trade.*' The Mexican representative did not '*propose to give details of the serious harm that this practice is doing to Mexican exports*' but stated that*it has damaged the integrated production chain that existed between the two countries. The government of Mexico would like to encourage the US to review the regulations and adhere to the provisions of the GATT and the Agreement on Technical Barriers to Trade, since the COOL requirements do not promote any legitimate interests and are eminently protectionist in nature in favour of the livestock producers of the US.*[1291] *Mexico also tabled some additional written questions on the topic*'.[1292]

On 18 November 2011, the Panel report was circulated to Members.[1293] It found that the COOL measures, by according less favourable treatment to imported cattle and hog products than to like domestic products, amounted to a violation of Article 2.1 of the TBT Agreement. The Panel also considered that the COOL measures did not fulfil their legitimate objectives of providing consumers with information on origin and therefore violated Article 2.2 of the TBT Agreement. Nevertheless, throughout March 2012, the parties to the dispute notified the DSB of their respective decisions to appeal the report.[1294] On 29 June 2012, the Appellate Body report

[1288] In this regard, the Secretariat reports refer to '*WTO document series WT/DS/384 and WT/DS/386; and WT/DSB/M/276, 29 January 2010*'.

[1289] Trade Policy Review of the United States of 29 September–1 October 2010, Government Report, WT/TPR/G/235, 25 August 2010.

[1290] Trade Policy Review of the United States of 29 September–1 October 2010, Minutes of the Meeting, WT/TPR/M/235, 1 November 2010, 47–48 (particularly at 48).

[1291] Trade Policy Review of the United States of 29 September–1 October 2010, Minutes of the Meeting, WT/TPR/M/235, 1 November 2010, 16–18 (particularly at 17).

[1292] Trade Policy Review of the United States of 29 September–1 October 2010, Written questions and answers, WT/TPR/M/235/Add. 1, 1 November 2010, 313.

[1293] WTO, *US—Certain Country of Origin Labelling (COOL) requirements—Report of the Panel* (18 November 2011) WT/DS384 and DS386/R.

[1294] WTO, *US—Certain Country of Origin Labelling (COOL) Requirements—Notification of an Appeal by the US under Article 16.4 and Article 17 of the Understanding on Rules and Procedures Governing the Settlement of Disputes (DSU), and under Rule 20(1) of the Working Procedures for Appellate Review* (28 March 2011) WT/DS384/12 and WT/DS386/11; WTO, *US—Certain Country of Origin Labelling (COOL) Requirements— Notification of an Appeal by Canada under Article 16.4 and Article 17 of the Understanding on Rules and Procedures Governing the Settlement of Disputes (DSU), and under Rule 23(1) of the Working Procedures for Appellate Review* (2 April 2012) WT/DS384/13.

was circulated.[1295] The report confirmed the Panel's finding that the COOL measures violated Article 2.1 of the TBT Agreement by according less favourable treatment to imported cattle and hogs than to similar domestic cattle and hogs. The United States therefore informed the DSB on 21 August 2012 that it intended to implement the DSB's recommendations and rulings but that it would need a reasonable period of time to do so.[1296] On 13 September 2012, Canada and Mexico requested that the reasonable period of time be determined through arbitration. On 4 December 2012, the arbitration determined that the RPT was ten months from the date of adoption of the Panel and Appellate Body reports. It would therefore expire on 23 May 2013.[1297]

The TPR of the United States of December 2012 revisits the issue.[1298] The Secretariat's only reference to the dispute is contained in a sub-section on technical regulations and standards[1299] which states that '*WTO Members have used the TBT Committee to raise a number of concerns about TBT measures taken by the United States, and three dispute settlement proceedings in the WTO were taken against the United States under the TBT Agreement during the period under review*'.[1300] The government report remains unsurprisingly silent on the issue.[1301] During the TPRB meeting, only Canada raised the matter of the dispute while noting that it was '*pleased that the US has now indicated its intention to bring this measure into conformity. We look forward to the US making the required changes to the relevant statute, which Canada views as necessary to comply with the decision of the Appellate Body and to restore the integrity of North American livestock sector.*'[1302] In addition, Canada tabled written questions on the topic.[1303]

At the DSB meeting of 24 May 2013, the United States informed the Members of the DSB that it had made changes to the COOL requirements which had been found to be inconsistent with Article 2.1 of the TBT Agreement. The United

[1295] WTO, *US – Certain Country of Origin Labelling (COOL) requirements—Appellate Body Report* (29 June 2012) WT/DS384 and DS386/AB/R.

[1296] WTO, *US—Certain Country of Origin Labelling (COOL) Requirements—Communication from the US* (23 August 2012) WT/DS384/19 and WT/DS386/18.

[1297] WTO, *US—Certain Country of Origin Labelling (COOL) requirements—Arbitration under Article 21.3(c) of the Understanding on Rules and Procedures Governing the Settlement of Disputes* (4 December 2012) WT/DS384/24 and WT/DS386/23.

[1298] Trade Policy Review of the United States of 18–20 December 2012, Minutes of the Meeting, WT/TPR/M/275, 30 April 2013.

[1299] Trade Policy Review of the United States of 18–20 December 2012, Secretariat Report, WT/TPR/S/275, 13 November 2012, 58–61 (particularly at 58); Secretariat's (sectional) analysis of Agriculture is silent on the topic; Trade Policy Review of the United States of 18–20 December 2012, Secretariat Report, WT/TPR/S/275, 13 November 2012, 99–111

[1300] In this regard, the Secretariat report refers to '*US—Clove Cigarettes (DS406), US—Country of Origin Labelling (COOL) (DS386 and DS384), and US—Tuna II (DS381)*'.

[1301] Trade Policy Review of the United States of 18–20 December 2012, Government Report, WT/TPR/G/275, 13 November 2012.

[1302] Trade Policy Review of the United States of 18–20 December 2012, Minutes of the Meeting, WT/TPR/M/275, 30 April 2013, 27–29 (particularly at 28).

[1303] Trade Policy Review of the United States of 18–20 December 2012, Written questions, WT/TPR/M/275/Add.1, 15 May 2013, 70.

States was of the view that it had brought its COOL requirements into compliance with the DSB's recommendations and rulings. Nevertheless, Canada and Mexico disagreed. According to both complainants, the amendments were more restrictive and caused further harm.[1304] Canada and Mexico therefore requested the establishment of a compliance Panel.[1305] On 20 October 2014, the report of this joint compliance Panel report was circulated to Members.[1306] The compliance Panel deemed that the amended COOL measures violated Article 2.1 of the TBT Agreement and Article III.4 of the GATT (1994). Nonetheless, on 28 November 2014, the United States notified the DSB of its decision to appeal certain issues of law covered in the compliance Panel report and certain legal interpretations developed by the Panel.[1307]

The TPR of the United States of December 2014 is the last US TPR which clearly focuses on the dispute.[1308] Secretariat report's sub-sectional on technical regulations and standards mentions that '*since the last Review of the US, five specific trade concerns have been raised in the TBT Committee against measures taken by the US. Furthermore, three WTO dispute settlement proceedings against the US under the TBT agreement are pending (including the COOL case).*'[1309] In line with its earlier practice, the government's reporting remains completely silent on the issue.[1310] Nevertheless, during the TPRB meeting, Canada explicitly raised the dispute.[1311] In this regard, it stated that it '*fully expects the United States to live up to its international trade obligations. Multiple WTO rulings have confirmed Canada's long-standing view that the U.S. COOL measure is protectionist and prevents both of our countries from enjoying the benefits of freer and more open trade in the livestock sector. We are therefore disappointed that the United States has decided to appeal again the latest ruling, which will only further delay the inevitable resolution of this dispute*'.

1304 WTO, DSB, Minutes of Meeting, WT/DSB/M/332, 31 July 2013, 22–23.

1305 WTO, *US—Certain Country of Origin Labelling (COOL) Requirements—Recourse to Article 21.5 of the DSU by Canada* (20 August 2013) WT/DS384/26; WTO, *US—Certain Country of Origin Labelling (COOL) Requirements—Recourse to Article 21.5 of the DSU by Mexico* (20 August 2013) WT/DS386/25.

1306 WTO, *US—Certain Country of Origin Labelling (COOL) requirements—Recourse to Article 21.5 of the DSU by Canada and Mexico* (20 October 2014) WT/DS384 and DS386/RW.

1307 WTO, *US—Certain Country of Origin Labelling (COOL) Requirements—Recourse to Article 21.5 of the DSU by Canada and Mexico, Notification of an Appeal by the United States under Article 16.4 and Article 17 of the Understanding on Rules and Procedures Governing the Settlement of Disputes (DSU), and under Rule 20(1) of the Working Procedures for Appellate Review* (2 December 2014) WT/DS384/29 and WT/DS386/28.

1308 Trade Policy Review of the United States of 16–18 December 2014, Minutes of the Meeting, WT/TPR/M/307, 9 February 2015.

1309 Trade Policy Review of the United States of 16–18 December 2014, Secretariat Report, WT/TPR/S/307, 11 November 2014, 66–69 (particularly at 68); On the other hand, the dispute is not tackled in Secretariat's (sectional) analysis of Agriculture; Trade Policy Review of the United States of 16–18 December 2014, Secretariat Report, WT/TPR/S/307, 11 November 2014, 101–17.

1310 Trade Policy Review of the United States of 16–18 December 2014, Government Report, WT/TPR/G/307, 11 November 2014.

1311 Trade Policy Review of the United States of 16–18 December 2014, Minutes of the Meeting, WT/TPR/M/307, 9 February 2015, 37–39 (particularly at 37).

Contrary to Brazil or China, the complainants in the dispute did not raise any further written questions.[1312]

- In *Korea—Measures Affecting the Importation of Bovine Meat and Meat Products from Canada*, Canada took issue with certain Korean measures affecting the importation of its bovine meat and meat products.[1313] According to Canada, Korea prohibited the importation of Canadian bovine meat and meat products allegedly on the basis to protect itself against risks arising from Bovine Spongiform Encephalopathy (BSE) which had been prevalent amongst North American producers. Nevertheless, in 2003, after tests on cattle herds showed that all tested animals were free from BSE, many countries started to ease restrictions on Canadian beef. Nonetheless, South Korea maintained the original ban, even after the World Organization for Animal Health (OIE) had classified Canada in 2007 as a zone with controlled BSE risk.[1314] In Canada's view, the Korean measures were therefore inconsistent with Articles 2.2, 2.3, 3.1, 3.3, 5.1, 5.5, 5.6, 5.7, 6.1, 8 and Annex C of the SPS Agreement and with Articles I.1, III.4, and XI.1 of the GATT (1994).

The TPR of Korea of October 2008 focused on the issue.[1315] The Secretariat report's sub-section on standards and other technical requirements[1316] indicates that '*since April 2004, three Members have raised specific concerns in the SPS Committee about measures maintained by Korea.1317 Korea bans imports, for example, of live cattle, sheep, and goats, and certain products from countries where BSE and foot and mouth diseases are known to occur.*' The government report does not touch on the issue.[1318] This silence did not stop Canada from seizing the opportunity of the TPRB meeting in an attempt to name and shame Korea into better behaviour. Canada therefore (explicitly) pointed to the dispute and took note '*with concern of Korea's import*

[1312] Trade Policy Review of the United States of 16–18 December 2014, Written questions and answers, WT/TPR/M/307/Add. 1, 16 February 2015, 79 and 144.

[1313] WTO, *Korea—Measures Affecting the Importation of Bovine Meat and Meat Products from Canada—Report of the Panel* (3 July 2012) WT/DS391/R.

[1314] *Canada challenges Korean Beef Ban at the WTO* (2009) 13(14) Bridges; *South Korea Lifts Ban on Canadian Beef Imports* (2012) 16(3) Bridges, 1.

[1315] Trade Policy Review of Korea of 8–10 October 2008, Minutes of the Meeting, WT/TPR/M/204, 1 December 2008.

[1316] Trade Policy Review of Korea of 8–10 October 2008, Secretariat Report, WT/TPR/S/204, 3 September 2008, 59–66 (particularly at 64); On the other hand, Secretariat's sectional analysis on Agriculture again remains silent on the issue; Trade Policy Review of Korea of 8–10 October 2008, Secretariat Report, WT/TPR/S/204, 3 September 2008, 91–101.

[1317] In this regard, the Secretariat report states the following:

The United States raised a concern related to citrus exports from California, which Korea has banned since April 2004 due to concerns related to the presence of certain fungi. This concern was subsequently reported as resolved. In 2007, Canada, supported by the European Communities, raised a concern regarding Korea's BSE-related measures. Canada had formally requested a justification of this measure, which went beyond international standards. Also in 2007, Brazil expressed concerns about Korea's lack of recognition of regionalization (Article 6 of the SPS Agreement) with respect to foot-and-mouth disease. These concerns have apparently not yet been resolved.

[1318] Trade Policy Review of Korea of 8–10 October 2008, Government Report, WT/TPR/G/204, 3 September 2008.

policies on beef, which it considered discriminatory and which led Korean consumers paying significantly higher than world prices for domestic beef at a time of high food prices.' Moreover, '*it appeared that Korea was basing its beef import policy decisions on domestic politics and producers' interests instead of science and global trading principles. He [ie the Canadian representative] noted that it was important that Korea ensured that its beef import regime was consistent with global trading rules.*'[1319] Canada also tabled extensive written questions with regard to the existence of BSE as the alleged justification for Korea's import ban.[1320] Nevertheless, Korea defended its rules as being SPS-consistent.[1321]

At its meeting of 31 August 2009, the DSB established a Panel.[1322] Due to the complexity of the dispute, the Panel indicated that it would need additional time to complete its tasks. Nonetheless, a Canadian request to suspend the proceedings of the Panel pursuant to Article 12.12 of the DSU was later followed by a mutually agreed solution between the parties to the dispute. The Panel report of 3 July 2012 was therefore confined to a brief description of the case and a report that a solution has been reached.[1323]

The TPR of Korea of September 2012 raises the dispute extensively.[1324] Several sections of the Secretariat's reporting touch on the issue. Its report's sub-section on standards and other technical requirements indicates again that 'Korea bans import of animals and their products from countries affected by exotic animal diseases such as foot-and-mouth disease and BSE' and that '*according to the authorities, Korea applies the same animal quarantine and livestock product health requirements to domestic production and imports.*[1325] *Canada's complaint against Korea's measures affecting imports of its bovine meat and meat products led to the establishment of a WTO dispute settlement panel in August 2009*'. Moreover, Secretariat's sectional analysis of agriculture and livestock states that '*at the end of 2011, Korea ended an eight-year ban on imports of Canadian beef by passing import health requirements for Canadian beef under 30 months of age; Korea was the last major beef-importing country to agree to relax its restrictions on Canadian beef*'.[1326] In line with its earlier practice, the government's report does not refer to the dispute.[1327] This silence did

[1319] Trade Policy Review of Korea of 8–10 October 2008, Minutes of the Meeting, WT/TPR/M/204, 1 December 2008, 10.

[1320] Trade Policy Review of Korea of 8–10 October 2008, Minutes of the Meeting, WT/TPR/M/204, 8 December 2008, 32, 34–35, 152–54, and 156.

[1321] Trade Policy Review of Korea of 8–10 October 2008, Minutes of the Meeting, WT/TPR/M/204, 1 December 2008, 16.

[1322] WTO, DSB, Minutes of Meeting, WT/DSB/M/273, 6 November 2009, 3.

[1323] WTO, *Korea—Measures Affecting the Importation of Bovine Meat and Meat Products from Canada—Report of the Panel* (3 July 2012) WT/DS391/R.

[1324] Trade Policy Review of Korea of 19–21 September 2012, Minutes of the Meeting, WT/TPR/M/268, 12 November 2012.

[1325] Trade Policy Review of Korea of 19–21 September 2012, Secretariat Report, WT/TPR/S/268, 15 August 2012, 66–76 (particularly at 74).

[1326] Trade Policy Review of Korea of 19–21 September 2012, Secretariat Report, WT/TPR/S/268, 15 August 2012, 111–21 (particularly at 121).

[1327] Trade Policy Review of Korea of 19–21 September 2012, Government Report, WT/TPR/G/268, 15 August 2012.

not disbar Canada from using the TPRB meeting to remind Korea that it should stick to a more SPS-consistent behaviour. Canada emphasized that '*another positive development in the Canada–Korea bilateral relationship was the restoration of access for Canadian beef earlier this year, following a bilateral settlement that resulted in Canada's decision to terminate the WTO panel regarding Measures Affecting the Importation of Bovine Meat and Meat Products from Canada. We look forward to continuing to work with Korea to further re-establish Canadian beef in the Korean market as a safe and high-quality product, following an import ban on nearly 10 years.*'[1328]
Canada did not table any further written questions with regard to the dispute.[1329]

- In *US—Certain Measures Affecting Imports of Poultry from China*, China took issue with several US measures which primarily included Section 727 of the Omnibus Appropriations Act of 2009. This measure effectively prohibited the establishment or implementation of any measures that would allow Chinese poultry to be imported into the United States since the measure denied the use of any funding of the US Department for Agriculture (USDA) for this purpose.[1330] China was therefore of the view that the measure and any closely related measures constituted a violation, at a minimum, of Articles I.1 and XI.1 of the GATT (1994) and of Article 4.2 of the Agreement on Agriculture. In addition, China specified that although it did not believe that the US measure or any closely related measures at issue constituted sanitary and phytosanitary measures within the meaning of the SPS Agreement, if it were nevertheless demonstrated that any such measure was an SPS measure, China would consider such measure also to be in violation of US obligations under various provisions of the SPS Agreement.[1331]

The TPR of the United States of June 2008 preceded the formal request for consultations in the case.[1332] Nevertheless, the contours of the situation that resulted in the dispute were already identified by Secretariat's reporting on Sanitary and phytosanitary standards.[1333] The sub-section underlines in this regard that' *Before imports of meat, poultry, or egg products are allowed, Food Safety and Inspection Service (FSIS) evaluates whether a country's regulatory system for these products attains the same level of protection as the United States. If the system is deemed equivalent,*

[1328] Trade Policy Review of Korea of 19–21 September 2012, Minutes of the Meeting, WT/TPR/M/268, 12 November 2012, 20.

[1329] Trade Policy Review of Korea of 19–21 September 2012, Written questions and answers, WT/TPR/M/268/Add. 1, 23 November 2012.

[1330] Donald H Regan, 'United States—Certain Measures Affecting Imports of Poultry from China: The Fascinating Case that Wasn't' (2012) 11(2) World Trade Review 274–77.

[1331] WTO, *US—Certain Measures Affecting Imports of Poultry from China—Report of the Panel* (29 September 2010) WT/DS392/R.

[1332] Trade Policy Review of the United States of 9–11 June 2008, Minutes of the Meeting, WT/TPR/M/200, 4 August 2008; WTO, *US—Certain Measures Affecting Imports of Poultry from China—Request for Consultations by China* (21 April 2009) WT/DS392/1.

[1333] Trade Policy Review of the United States of 9–11 June 2008, Secretariat Report, WT/TPR/S/200, 5 May 2008; On the other hand, Secretariat's sectional analysis on Agriculture remains again silent on the subject; Trade Policy Review of the United States of 9–11 June 2008, Secretariat Report, WT/TPR/S/200, 5 May 2008, 81–89.

U.S. regulations are amended to allow for imports. FSIS has published the process whereby it assesses the equivalence of foreign meat and poultry regulatory systems. The United States has recognized 34 foreign systems as equivalent to the U.S. meat, poultry, and/or egg products regulatory systems. Only meat, poultry, and egg products from facilities certified by the FSIS-recognized competent authority of the foreign country can be imported into the United States.' The government report does not touch on the subject.[1334] Nevertheless, this silence did not stop China from tabling the issue in the context of the TPRB meeting. It therefore stated that '*A number of TBT/SPS measures applied without sound rationale were inconsistent with international standards, and were de facto obstacles undermining imports. In particular, Article 733 of the Agricultural Allocation Bill for the fiscal year 2008, passed at the end of 2007, stipulated that the appropriation under this bill should not be used to design or implement policies on the import of cooked poultry from China. While bilaterally, the US had stated several times that there were no "technical problem" in the import of Chinese cooked poultry products and that this issue would be solved as soon as possible, domestically it had kept using administrative measures to regulate trade, which were not consistent with WTO rules. China urged the US to terminate these measures as soon as possible.*' Moreover, '*China asked about the science underlying the provision in the Agriculture Appropriations Bill, which did not allow appropriations to be used to implement rules allowing imports of cooked poultry from China. He [i.e. China's representative] sought information regarding the possible extension of this provision beyond the end of the fiscal year, and asked about measures to ensure that this conformed to WTO rules. On SPS, risk assessment was being abused by the US and constituted a de facto barrier to international trade.*'[1335] In addition, China tabled written questions with regard to the situation which would result in the dispute.[1336]

At its meeting of 31 July 2009, the DSB established a Panel. Nonetheless, due to the complexity of the case, the Panel's report was only circulated on 29 September 2010.[1337] According to the Panel, Section 727 was inconsistent with Articles 2.2, 2.3, 5.1, 5.2, 5.5 and 8 of the SPS Agreement, and with Articles I.1, XI.1, and XX (b) of the GATT (1994). Nevertheless, Section 727 had expired in the meantime. The Panel therefore did not recommend that the DSB request the United States to bring Section 727 into conformity with its obligations.

The TPR of the United States of the beginning of October 2010 reiterates the facts of the dispute.[1338] The Secretariat's report managed to put its finger on

[1334] Trade Policy Review of the United States of 9–11 June 2008, Government Report, WT/TPR/S/200, 5 May 2008.

[1335] Trade Policy Review of the United States of 9–11 June 2008, Minutes of the Meeting, WT/TPR/M/200, 4 August 2008, 24–26 (particularly at 26 and 44–45).

[1336] Trade Policy Review of the United States of 9–11 June 2008, Written questions and answers, WT/TPR/M/200/Add. 1, 9 September 2008, 66 and 185–86.

[1337] WTO, *US—Certain Measures Affecting Imports of Poultry from China—Report of the Panel* (29 September 2010) WT/DS392/R.

[1338] Trade Policy Review of the United States of 29 September–1 October 2010, Minutes of the Meeting, WT/TPR/M/235, 1 November 2010.

the issue in its sub-sectional analysis of SPS measures[1339] which describes the regulation of poultry imports and explicitly stated that '*on 17 April 2009, China requested consultations under the Dispute Settlement system on measures taken by the United States affecting the import of poultry products from China. China went on to request that a panel be established and, on 31 July 2009, at the second request, the DSB established a panel.*'[1340] Unsurprisingly, the US government report did not refer to the issue.[1341] Nevertheless, in line with its earlier practice, China seized the opportunity of the TPRB meeting in an attempt to name and shame the United States into more SPS-consistent behaviour. In this regard, China stated that '*the WTO recently ruled that the US Omnibus Appropriations Act of 2009 violated relevant WTO rules on MFN, elimination of quantitative restrictions, and animal and plant quarantine. However, section 743 of the Consolidated Appropriations Act, 2010 still contained a number of additional restrictive measures against exports of Chinese products to the US, and clearly indicates that the US administration does not take the application for the import of Chinese poultry products into consideration at first place. Such a practice that seriously departs from the WTO rules should be changed as soon as possible*'.

The United States rebutted these arguments and stated that its measures applied to all countries and not particularly to China. China answered and stated that '*the explanation of the US does not well address our concern. This is a discriminatory measure against China and will seriously impede China's poultry products export to the US. The chapeau of Section 743 clearly indicated that "none of the funds made available by this Act may be used to poultry imports from China".*' Nonetheless, the United States again rebuffed these remarks while stating that 'the most important aspect of this dispute is that the measure only applied in the fiscal year 2009. The measure was replaced in fiscal year 2010 with language permitting the use of the funds under certain conditions, and those conditions have been met. As a result, there is no current funding restriction affecting the Department of Agriculture's considerations of poultry from China.'[1342] China tabled some additional written questions on the topic.[1343]

The TPR of the United States of December 2012 took place after the adoption of the Panel's report.[1344] Nevertheless, its Secretariat's reporting and written

[1339] Trade Policy Review of the United States of 29 September–1 October 2010, Secretariat Report, WT/TPR/S/235, 25 August 2010, 40–46 (particularly at 40–41 and 43); On the other hand, Secretariat's sectional analysis of Agriculture remains silent on the topic; Trade Policy Review of the United States of 29 September–1 October 2010, Secretariat Report, WT/TPR/S/235, 25 August 2010, 80–94.

[1340] In this regard, the Secretariat reports refer to '*WTO documents WT/DS392/1, 2 and 3*'.

[1341] Trade Policy Review of the United States of 29 September–1 October 2010, Government Report, WT/TPR/G/235, 25 August 2010.

[1342] Trade Policy Review of the United States of 29 September–1 October 2010, Minutes of the Meeting, WT/TPR/M/235, 1 November 2010, 21–23 (particularly at 23), 70–72 (particularly at 71) and 73.

[1343] Trade Policy Review of the United States of 29 September–1 October 2010, Written questions and answers, WT/TPR/M/235/Add. 1, 1 November 2010, 101–03.

[1344] Trade Policy Review of the United States of 18–20 December 2012, Minutes of the Meeting, WT/TPR/M/275, 30 April 2013; WTO, *US—Certain Measures Affecting Imports of Poultry from China—Report of the Panel* (29 September 2010) WT/DS392/R.

questions still explicitly refer to the dispute in a final way.[1345] Secretariat's sub-sectional analysis of SPS measures[1346] succinctly mentions the dispute again while indicating that 'the SPS Agreement was also cited in a dispute settlement cases taken against the United States on poultry'.[1347,1348] In a similar vein, China used its written questions to request further details with regard to the US follow-up on the case.[1349]

- In *EC—Measures Prohibiting the Importation and Marketing of Seal Products*, Canada and Norway took issue with EC Regulation No 1007/2009 on the trade in seal products and with its implementing legislation as contained in EC Regulation No 737/2010.[1350] According to the complainants, the Regulation prohibited the importation and the placing on the EC market of all seal products while containing certain exceptions that afforded privileged EU market access to seal products originating in the EC and in certain third countries.[1351] Canada and Norway therefore alleged that the measures were inconsistent with Articles 2.1, 2.2, 5.1, 5.2, 5.4, 5.6, 6.1, 6.2, 7.1, 7.2, 7.4, 7.5, 8.1, and 8.2 of the TBT Agreement, with Articles I.1, III.4, and XI.1 of the GATT (1994) and with Article 4.2 of the Agreement on Agriculture.

The TPR of the European Union of April 2009 already managed to identify the upcoming issue and attempted to name and shame the European Union into behaviour more consistent with WTO rules.[1352] In this regard, Secretariat's sub-sectional

[1345] The TPR of the United States of 16–18 December 2014 details that '*There are no major new developments regarding FSIS import requirements since the last review of the United States*'; Trade Policy Review of the United States of 16–18 December 2014, Secretariat Report, WT/TPR/S/307, 11 November 2014, 70.

[1346] Trade Policy Review of the United States of 18–20 December 2012, Secretariat Report, WT/TPR/S/275, 13 November 2012, 61–65 (particularly at 64); On the other hand, Secretariat's sectional analysis of Agriculture remains again silent on the issue; Trade Policy Review of the United States of 18–20 December 2012, Secretariat Report, WT/TPR/S/275, 13 November 2012, 99–111.

[1347] In this regard, the Secretariat report refers to '*DS392 United States—Certain Measures Affecting Imports of Poultry from China*'.

[1348] In this regard, the Secretariat reports states: 'The SPS Agreement was also cited in the request for consultations in another case on clove cigarettes (DS406 United States-Measures Affecting the Production and Sale of Clove Cigarettes), but the Panel noted that 'no analysis or request for findings was made in respect to [the] conditional SPS claims' (WT/DS406/R para. 7.9) and they were not examined.'

[1349] Trade Policy Review of the United States of 18–20 December 2012, Written questions and answers, WT/TPR/M/275/Add.1, 15 May 2013, 134–135.

[1350] WTO, *European Communities—Measures Prohibiting the Importation and Marketing of Seal Products—Report of the Panel* (25 November 2013) WT/DS400 and DS401/R; WTO, *EC—Measures Prohibiting the Importation and Marketing of Seal Products—Appellate Body Report* (22 May 2014) WT/DS400 and DS401/AB/R; Philip I Levy and Donald H Regan, 'EC—Seal Products: Seals and Sensibilities (TBT Aspects of the Panel and Appellate Body Reports)' (2014), European University Institute, Working Papers, RSCAS 2014/108 <http://cadmus.eui.eu/bitstream/handle/1814/33774/RSCAS_2014_108.pdf;sequence=1> accessed 17 June 2017.

[1351] Rob Howse, Joanna Langille, and Katie Sykes, 'Sealing the Deal: The WTO's Appellate Body Report in EC – Seal Products' (2014) 18(12) American Society of International Law, Insights.

[1352] Trade Policy Review of the European Union of 6–8 April 2009, Minutes of the Meeting, WT/TPR/M/214, 8 June 2009.

reporting on technical regulations and other technical requirements[1353] succinctly indicates that '*a number of Members have raised concerns in the TBT Committee regarding technical regulations maintained or proposed by the EC or its Member states, which (could) act as unnecessary barriers to trade in . . . seal products*'.[1354] The EU's government report remains silent on the subject, however.[1355] This silence did not bar Canada and Norway from raising the issue during the TPRB meeting. In this context, Canada commented that '*It is also very important . . . to note that the recent developments pushing for bans on the import and use of all seal products, at the Member State and EC levels, is another area of great concern for Canada. The proposed measures to ban the importation of seal products are inconsistent with the EC's WTO obligations. The Canadian seal hunts are humane, sustainable, well-managed and well-regulated. We are pleased that the European Commission itself has recognized that there is no conservation threat to the seal population. Therefore, we call on the EC and its Member states to recognize that there is no scientific or legal basis to prohibit trade of seal products and to stop their efforts to do so. The only acceptable solution is to develop reasonable international welfare standards, which can only be achieved through dialogue and collaboration.*'[1356] In a similar vein, Norway commented that it '*had taken due note of the EC notification concerning trade in seal products and we have raised our concerns in the TBT committee. We understand that neither the notified proposed Regulation, nor the proposed Regulation adopted by the Internal Market Committee of the European Parliament may be the final version. Both versions, however pose challenges to Norway's exports and raise doubts about the WTO consistency of such trade restrictions. Furthermore, it sets a dangerous precedent in the matter of sustainable harvesting of renewable resources. While hoping that this issue could be solved through dialogue between close partners, the Norwegian government has decided to initiate consultations under the DSU should the EC take a decision along the lines that now seem to be developing*'.[1357] Nevertheless, neither Canada nor Norway tabled additional written questions on the issue.[1358]

At its meeting of 25 March 2011, the DSB established a Panel in dispute DS400.[1359] At its meeting on 21 April 2011, the DSB established a Panel in dispute DS401. The DSB consequently agreed to join both Panels pursuant to Article 9.1 of the DSU.

[1353] Trade Policy Review of the European Union of 6–8 April 2009, Secretariat Report, WT/TPR/S/214, 2 March 2009, 56–65 (particularly at 58); On the other hand, Secretariat's section to agriculture and related activities remains again silent on the issue; Trade Policy Review of the European Union of 6–8 April 2009, Secretariat Report, WT/TPR/S/214, 2 March 2009; 97–117 (particularly at 113–17).

[1354] In this regard, the Secretariat report refers to '*WTO document G/TBT/GEN/74, 25 September 2008*'.

[1355] Trade Policy Review of the European Union of 6–8 April 2009, Government Report, WT/TPR/G/214, 2 March 2009.

[1356] Trade Policy Review of the European Union of 6–8 April 2009, Minutes of the Meeting, WT/TPR/M/214, 8 June 2009, 32–34 (particularly at 34).

[1357] Trade Policy Review of the European Union of 6–8 April 2009, Minutes of the Meeting, WT/TPR/M/214, 8 June 2009, 21–23 (particularly at 22–23).

[1358] Trade Policy Review of the European Union of 6–8 April 2009, Written questions and answers, WT/TPR/M/214/Add. 1, 2 July 2009.

[1359] WTO, DSB, Minutes of Meeting, WT/DSB/M/294, 9 June 2011, 12–13.

The dispute resurfaced in the TPR of the European Union of July 2011.[1360] In line with its earlier practice, Secretariat's sub-sectional reporting on technical regulations and standards mentions the EC's notification of its technical regulations on seal products.[1361] Unsurprisingly, the EU's government report remains silent on the subject.[1362] Nevertheless, Canada emphasized during the TPRB meeting that it '*and the EU share the legitimate objectives of protecting human, animal, plant health and the environment. While recognizing that there are different approaches to reaching these objectives, we have the highest expectations that the EU will ensure that any measures it takes are science-based, no more trade-restrictive than necessary and reflect the realities of global trade today. Unfortunately, in too many cases, the EU has not lived up to these expectations. For instance, Canada reiterates its deep disappointment that the EC has chosen to place severe restrictions on the trade of seal products, despite the facts that the Canadian seal harvest is lawful sustainable, human, strictly regulated and monitored and guided by rigorous animal welfare principles*'.[1363] In addition, Canada tabled written questions with regard to the issue.[1364] Norway was not present at the TPRB meeting and tabled no specific questions which related to the dispute.[1365]

The TPR of the European Union of July 2013 took place after Canada and Norway had formally requested the Director-General to determine the composition of the panel.[1366] Nevertheless, neither the TPR's Secretariat's nor its government's report dwell extensively on the issue. However, the parties in the dispute seized the opportunity of the TPRB meeting again in an attempt to name and shame the European Union into behaving in line with WTO rules. The Secretariat's sub-sectional reporting on technical regulations and standards[1367] and its sectional analysis of fisheries[1368] do not mention the dispute. Nevertheless, the Secretariat still identifies the technical regulations and the dispute, albeit only in tabular

1360 Trade Policy Review of the European Union of 6–8 July 2011, Minutes of the Meeting, WT/TPR/M/248, 14 September 2011.

1361 Trade Policy Review of the European Union of 6–8 July 2011, Secretariat Report, WT/TPR/S/248, 1 June 2011, 45–55 (particularly at 46–48); On the other hand, Secretariat's section dedicated to Agriculture makes no mention at all of the issue; Trade Policy Review of the European Union of 6–8 July 2011, Secretariat Report, WT/TPR/S/248, 1 June 2011, 101–16.

1362 Trade Policy Review of the European Union of 6–8 July 2011, Government Report, WT/TPR/G/248, 1 June 2011.

1363 Trade Policy Review of the European Union of 6–8 July 2011, Minutes of the Meeting, WT/TPR/M/248, 14 September 2011, 24–25; Norway was not present at the meeting.

1364 Trade Policy Review of the European Union of 6–8 July 2011, Written questions, WT/TPR/M/248/Add. 1, 31 August 2011, 210.

1365 Trade Policy Review of the European Union of 6–8 July 2011, Written questions, WT/TPR/M/248/Add. 1, 31 August 2011, 405–6.

1366 Trade Policy Review of the European Union of 16–18 July 2013, Minutes of the Meeting, WT/TPR/M/284, 23 October 2013; WTO, *EC—Measures Prohibiting the Importation and Marketing of Seal Products- Constitution of the Panel Established at the Requests of Canada and Norway* (5 October 2012) WT/DS400/5 and WT/DS401/6.

1367 Trade Policy Review of the European Union of 16–18 July 2013, Secretariat Report, WT/TPR/S/284, 28 May 2013, 57–64.

1368 Trade Policy Review of the European Union of 16–18 July 2013, Secretariat Report, WT/TPR/S/284, 28 May 2013, 123–31.

form.[1369] Nonetheless, in line with its earlier practice, the EU's government report remains completely silent on the dispute.[1370] During the TPRB meeting, Canada voiced its concerns about several SPS issues, though not about the seal dispute.[1371] Norway, however, did not hesitate to name and shame the European Union, stating that '*the ban on trade and sale of seal products imposed by the European Union is an unfortunate example of disturbances in our otherwise excellent trading relations. Norway believes that the measures are inconsistent with WTO rules on several grounds, and is pursuing the case at the DSB.*'[1372] None of the parties tabled any further written questions on the subject.[1373]

On 25 November 2013, the Panel report was circulated.[1374] It concluded that the European ban was justified but also found that the European exception provided to its indigenous communities (IC) and their seal products originating in Greenland (specifically its Inuit population) violated Article I.1 of the GATT (1994) because the exception was not accorded immediately and unconditionally to similar products originating elsewhere. With respect to the European exception for the purpose of maritime resource management (MRM), the Panel found that it violated Article III.4 of the GATT (1994) because it accorded imported seal products treatment less favourable than that accorded to like domestic seal products. Further to the respective appeals, the report of the Appellate Body was circulated on 22 May 2014.[1375] The Appellate Body confirmed the Panel's main conclusion that the European ban was justified but reversed some of the Panel's other findings. The Appellate Body also upheld the Panel's conclusion that the European exceptions were inconsistent with WTO rules. The parties to the dispute therefore agreed to a reasonable period of time for the European Union to implement the DSB's recommendations.[1376] This period would expire on 18 October 2015.

The TPR of the European Union of 6 to 8 July 2015 barely refers to the dispute. Secretariat's only reference to the dispute is in a table.[1377] Unsurprisingly, the EU government report remains silent on the case. Nevertheless, this silence did not disbar Canada from raising the dispute. In this regard, it commented that '*it continues*

[1369] Trade Policy Review of the European Union of 16–18 July 2013, Secretariat Report, WT/TPR/S/284, 28 May 2013, 184 and 190.

[1370] Trade Policy Review of the European Union of 16–18 July 2013, Government Report, WT/TPR/G/284, 28 May 2013.

[1371] Trade Policy Review of the European Union of 16–18 July 2013, Minutes of the Meeting, WT/TPR/M/284, 23 October 2013, 32–33.

[1372] Trade Policy Review of the European Union of 16–18 July 2013, Minutes of the Meeting, WT/TPR/M/284, 23 October 2013, 29–31.

[1373] Trade Policy Review of the European Union of 16–18 July 2013, Written questions and answers, WT/TPR/M/284/Add. 1/Rev. 1, 24 October 2013.

[1374] WTO, *EC—Measures Prohibiting the Importation and Marketing of Seal Products—Report of the Panel* (25 November 2013) WT/DS400 and DS401/R.

[1375] WTO, *EC—Measures Prohibiting the Importation and Marketing of Seal Products—Appellate Body Report* (22 May 2014) WT/DS400 and DS401/AB/R.

[1376] WTO, *EC—Measures Prohibiting the Importation and Marketing of Seal Products—Agreement under Article 21.3(b) of the DSU* (8 September 2014) WT/DS400/15.

[1377] Trade Policy Review of the European Union of 6–8 July 2015, Secretariat Report, WT/TPR/S/317, 18 May 2015, 186–87.

to monitor the EU's efforts to implement the rulings and recommendations of the DSB concerning the EU Seal Regime. At the same time, Canada is also working to operationalize the indigenous exemption under that regime. Any amendments to the EU Seal Regime must be implemented in a manner that does not adversely affect the Inuit and other indigenous communities.'[1378] None of the complainants raised any further written questions.

- In *US—Measures Affecting the Production and Sale of Clove Cigarettes*, Indonesia took issue with the US Family Smoking Prevention Tobacco Control Act of 2009 which banned clove cigarettes.[1379] According to Indonesia, Section 907 prohibited, among other things, the production or sale in the United States of cigarettes containing certain additives, including clove, but would continue—at the same time—to permit the production and sale of other cigarettes, including cigarettes containing menthol (which were often domestically produced). Indonesia alleged therefore that Section 907 was inconsistent, inter alia, with Article III.4 of the GATT (1994), with Article 2 of the TBT Agreement and with various provisions of the SPS Agreement.

The TPR of the United States of June 2008 took place before Section 907 was drafted and thus remained completely silent on the issue.[1380]

Nevertheless, the US' next TPR of October 2010 took place after the parties had agreed on the composition of the Panel.[1381] The Secretariat's report's sub-section on technical regulations and standards was therefore able to shed some light on the issue which resulted in the dispute.[1382] It succinctly stated that '*approximately 40% of notifications were by sub-federal entities, and covered products like . . . cigarettes*'. The TPR's government's report,[1383] the TPRB meeting (at which Indonesia was absent),[1384] and its written questions[1385] do not refer to the subject.

[1378] Trade Policy Review of the European Union of 6–8 July 2015, Minutes of the Meeting, WT/TPR/M/317, 12 October 2015, 18.

[1379] WTO, *US—Measures Affecting the Production and Sale of Clove Cigarettes—Report of the Panel* (2 September 2011) WT/DS406/R; WTO, *US—Measures Affecting the Production and Sale of Clove Cigarettes—Appellate Body Report* (4 April 2012) WT/DS406/AB/R; Lucas Ballet, 'Losing Flavour: Indonesia's WTO Complaint Against the US Ban on Clove Cigarettes' (2011) 26(2) American University International Law Review 515–41.

[1380] Trade Policy Review of the United States of 9–11 June 2008, Minutes of the Meeting, WT/TPR/M/200, 4 August 2008; WTO, *US—Measures Affecting the Production and Sale of Clove Cigarettes—Report of the Panel* (2 September 2011) WT/DS406/R.

[1381] Trade Policy Review of the United States of 29 September – 1 October 2010, Minutes of the Meeting, WT/TPR/M/235, 1 November 2010; WTO, *US—Measures Affecting the Production and Sale of Clove Cigarettes—Report of the Panel* (2 September 2011) WT/DS406/R.

[1382] Trade Policy Review of the United States of 29 September–1 October 2010, Secretariat Report, WT/TPR/S/235, 25 August 2010, 35–40; On the other hand, Secretariat's sectional analysis of Agriculture again remains silent on the subject; Trade Policy Review of the United States of 29 September–1 October 2010, Secretariat Report, WT/TPR/S/235, 25 August 2010, 80–94.

[1383] Trade Policy Review of the United States of 29 September–1 October 2010, Government Report, WT/TPR/G/235, 25 August 2010.

[1384] Trade Policy Review of the United States of 29 September–1 October 2010, Minutes of the Meeting, WT/TPR/M/235, 1 November 2010.

[1385] Trade Policy Review of the United States of 29 September–1 October 2010, Written questions and answers, WT/TPR/M/235/Add. 1, 1 November 2010.

On 2 September 2011, the Panel report was circulated.[1386] According to the report, the US ban was inconsistent with Article 2.1, 2.9.2, and 2.12 of the TBT agreement. Further to a US appeal, the Appellate Body issued its report on 4 April 2012.[1387] The Appellate Body reversed some of the findings of the Panel but still considered that Section 907(a)(1)(A) was inconsistent with Article 2.1 and 2.12 of the TBT agreement. The parties to the dispute therefore agreed on a reasonable period of time for implementation which would expire on 24 July 2013.[1388]

The topic is further highlighted in the TPR of the US of December 2012.[1389] The Secretariat's reporting repeatedly identifies the dispute. The report's sub-section on technical regulations and standards underlines in this regard that '*WTO Members have used the TBT Committee to raise a number of concerns about TBT measures taken by the United States, and three dispute settlement proceedings in the WTO were taken against the United States under the TBT Agreement during the period under review*'[1390] whereas the report's sub-section on sanitary and phytosanitary measures also notes that the SPS agreement was cited in the clove cigarettes case.[1391] The US government's report remains silent on the issue.[1392] During the meeting of the TPRB, Indonesia noted that it and the US had agreed to implement the recommendations and that it was monitoring the follow-up activities closely.[1393] Moreover, it tabled detailed written questions to ask how the United States intended to implement the recommendations of the DSB.[1394]

On 12 August 2013, Indonesia requested the authorization of the DSB to suspend concessions or other obligations to the United States. Since the United States objected, the matter was referred to arbitration.[1395] Nevertheless, arbitration proceedings were suspended on 24 June 2014 further to the joint request of the parties. On 3 October 2014, the parties to the dispute notified the DSB that they had reached a mutually agreed solution. Since arbitration was no longer necessary, the

[1386] WTO, *US—Measures Affecting the Production and Sale of Clove Cigarettes—Report of the Panel* (2 September 2011) WT/DS406/R

[1387] WTO, *US—Measures Affecting the Production and Sale of Clove Cigarettes—Appellate Body Report* (4 April 2012) WT/DS406/AB/R.

[1388] WTO, *US—Measures Affecting the Production and Sale of Clove Cigarettes—Agreement under Article 21.3(b) of the DSU* (19 June 2012) WT/DS406/10.

[1389] Trade Policy Review of the United States of 18–20 December 2012, Minutes of the Meeting, WT/TPR/M/275, 30 April 2013.

[1390] Trade Policy Review of the United States of 18–20 December 2012, Secretariat Report, WT/TPR/S/275, 13 November 2012, 58–61.

[1391] Trade Policy Review of the United States of 18–20 December 2012, Secretariat Report, WT/TPR/S/275, 13 November 2012, 64.

[1392] Trade Policy Review of the United States of 18–20 December 2012, Government Report, WT/TPR/S/275, 13 November 2012.

[1393] Trade Policy Review of the United States of 18–20 December 2012, Minutes of the Meeting, WT/TPR/M/275, 30 April 2012, 42.

[1394] Trade Policy Review of the United States of 18–20 December 2012, Written questions and answers, WT/TPR/M/275/Add.1, 15 May 2013, 257.

[1395] WTO, *US—Measures Affecting the Production and Sale of Clove Cigarettes—Recourse to Article 22.2 of the DSU by Indonesia* (13 August 2013) WT/DS406/12.

Chair of the Arbitration Panel notified the DSB on 8 October 2014 that he considered that the arbitration Panel had completed its work.[1396]

Nevertheless, the TPR of the United States of (December) 2014 tackles the issue again.[1397] In its report, the Secretariat's sub-section on technical regulations and standards directly mentions the issue.[1398] It states that '*three WTO dispute settlement proceedings taken against the United States under the TBT Agreement are pending*'. The TPR's government report, however, does not touch on the issue.[1399] Moreover, Indonesia did not raise the dispute during the TPRB meeting[1400] and, contrary to Brazil, China, and India, who all tabled (direct or indirect) questions with regard to the dispute, it did not raise any written questions with regard to the subject.[1401]

This analysis leads to several conclusions: First, reports Reports of the Secretariat again stand to be characterized by their excellent added value in terms of transparency. These examples have demonstrated that for all analysed TPRs bar one, the Secretariat's reports were able either to predict or to identify the contours of the future dispute. Second, reports of the government under review offer only minimal added value in terms of transparency. None of the analysed reports was used to refer to actual or to future trade concerns. Third, in terms of naming and shaming, both TPRB meetings and written questions and answers offer clear added value in terms of naming and shaming, the former in terms of general naming and shaming, the latter often even in the context of very specific DSB related questioning.

Structure of meetings

In the years covered by the fourth appraisal (ie 2008 to 2011), the structure of TPR meetings barely changed. Most annual reports which were drafted in this period therefore systematically kept to their traditional line in reiterating that '*procedures for the reviews have generally run smoothly*'.[1402] Nevertheless, compared to the questions which animated the discussions of the third appraisal, the Secretariat's suggestions and questions for the discussions of the fourth appraisal contained some

[1396] WTO, *US—Measures Affecting the Production and Sale of Clove Cigarettes—Recourse to Article 22.6 of the DSU by the United States, Communication from the Arbitrator* (9 October 2014) WT/DS406/18.

[1397] Trade Policy Review of the United States of 16–18 December 2014, Minutes of the Meeting, WT/TPR/M/307, 9 February 2015.

[1398] Trade Policy Review of the United States of 16–18 December 2014, Secretariat Report, WT/TPR/S/307, 11 November 2014, 66–69 (particularly at 68); On the other hand, Secretariat's section on agriculture remains again silent on the issue; Trade Policy Review of the United States of 16–18 December 2014, Secretariat Report, WT/TPR/S/307, 11 November 2014, 101–146.

[1399] Trade Policy Review of the United States of 16–18 December 2014, Government Report, WT/TPR/G/307, 11 November 2014.

[1400] Trade Policy Review of the United States of 16–18 December 2014, Minutes of the Meeting, WT/TPR/M/307, 9 February 2015, 43–44.

[1401] Trade Policy Review of the United States of 16–18 December 2014, Written questions and answers, WT/TPR/M/307/Add. 1, 16 February 2015, 78, 144 and 272.

[1402] WTO, TPRB, Draft Report of the Trade Policy Review Body for 2008, Trade Policy Review Mechanism, WT/TPR/W/40, 15 October 2008, 2; WTO, TPRB, Draft Report of the Trade Policy Review Body for 2009, Trade Policy Review Mechanism, WT/TPR/W/41, 8 October 2009, 2; WTO, TPRB, Draft Report of the Trade Policy Review Body for 2010, Trade Policy Review Mechanism, WT/TPR/W/42, 28 October 2010, 2.

very specific ideas with regard to the structure of the meetings. These included the proposal to hold a one day meeting instead of two half-day meetings (with a day in between), the suggestion to supplement the Chairman's introductory remarks with a main issues note (which would distinguish topics which were systemic from those which were specific to the country under review), and the proposal to have a note prepared by the discussant (appointed by the Chair rather than by the Member under review) to be distributed to Members before the meeting (the latter suggestion was based on the understanding that the discussant might be someone other than a delegate).[1403]

Contrary to previous appraisals, the fourth appraisal contains some substantial analysis of the results of the previous 2008 appraisal.[1404] Moreover, the appraisal clearly underlines the value of a well-functioning question and answer process. Nevertheless, this consideration is coupled with the explicit acknowledgement that '*the TPRB had recognized the need to promote more interactive discussions among Members. In practice, however, little seems to have changed over the past years.*'[1405]

As a result, the fourth appraisal made a further attempt to streamline the efficiency of the question and answer process. This modification was based on the appraisal's assessment that the lack of respect for the existing procedural time-lines of the TPRM's question and answer process led to capacity problems for Members on the two- and four-year cycles (who often received a substantial amount of questions) and for those on the six-year cycle (who had only a limited availability of resources to respond).[1406] Members therefore agreed to provide more time for the question and answer process in a pilot.[1407]

The fourth appraisal also tinkered with the organization and structure of TPRB meetings.[1408] Not only did the appraisal detail the respective roles of the participants involved in reviews, including an explicit call for a reinforcement of the discussant's

[1403] Fourth Appraisal of the Operation of the TPRM, informal WTO document (Document on file with the author).

[1404] Fourth Appraisal of the Trade Policy Review Mechanism, Ministerial Conference, Eighth Session, Geneva, 15–17 December 2011, WT/MIN(11)/6, 29 November 2011, 1–2.

[1405] Fourth Appraisal of the Trade Policy Review Mechanism, Ministerial Conference, Eighth Session, Geneva, 15–17 December 2011, WT/MIN(11)/6, 29 November 2011, 3.

[1406] Fourth Appraisal of the Trade Policy Review Mechanism, Summary of Main Issues discussed in First Informal Meeting, Rough Draft, 18 July 2011, 2–3 (Document on file with the author).

[1407] The fourth review provided members in this regard with the possibility—to be implemented on a voluntary pilot basis—to choose between alternative timelines. Under the current timelines, the Secretariat's and government's reports were to be sent for translation nine weeks before the TPRB. This was extended to eleven weeks under the revised timelines. Under the current timelines, the reports were then to be circulated to Members five weeks before the TPRB whereas the revised timelines foresaw two additional weeks. Under the current timelines, written questions had to be tabled two weeks before the TPRB whereas they were to be tabled four weeks under the revised timelines. Under the current timelines, Members States under review had to answer the written questions by the start of the meeting. The revised timelines stipulated that Members provide answers within one week. Under the current timelines, written answers were to be provided during the meeting whereas the revised timelines foresaw them to be provided within four weeks; *Fourth Appraisal of the Operation of the Trade Policy Review Mechanism 2011* (n 1240) 6; Fourth Appraisal of the Trade Policy Review Mechanism, Ministerial Conference, Eighth Session, Geneva, 15–17 December 2011, WT/MIN(11)/6, 29 November 2011, 6.

[1408] Fourth Appraisal of the Trade Policy Review Mechanism, Ministerial Conference, Eighth Session, Geneva, 15–17 December 2011, WT/MIN(11)/6, 29 November 2011, 7–8.

role, it also focused on the length and structure of TPRB meetings. The cost of keeping delegations in Geneva for the two-day TPR meeting was important for some delegations.[1409] The fourth appraisal therefore offered the opportunity—again on a pilot basis—to hold a one-day meeting at the request of the Member under review and after consultations with the TPRB Membership.[1410] In addition, the appraisal resulted in some structural proposals to make TPRB meetings more interactive. These included: (a) an (unsuccessful) suggestion to divide each TPRB meeting into formal (morning) and informal (afternoon) sessions and (b) the (failed) proposal to hold TPRB meetings in the territory of Member(s) under review.[1411] The proposal to dedicate the first session of the TPRB meeting to questions and answers, and, with the assent of the Member(s) under review, to focus on a more in-depth exchange of views during the second session was retained.[1412] In line with earlier practice, the TPRB's rules of procedure were updated to reflect the modifications resulting from the fourth appraisal.[1413]

ii) Overview of developments in the International Trading Environment

The Overviews of the period covered by the fourth appraisal covered a world where '*the financial crisis and consequent collapse of aggregate demand in Europe and North America created a global economic recession that has dragged down the volume of merchandise trade by over 10 per cent in 2009, back to the level at which it stood in 2005*'.[1414] Nevertheless, by July 2010, '*world trade volume had recovered roughly to its level of July 2008 and was close to its pre-crisis peak in April of that year*'.[1415] This positive trend weakened the next year with global activity slowing down, the presence of an uneven economic performance across countries, rising debt levels and financial volatility, the persistence of high unemployment in many countries, and a sharp reduction in economic confidence.[1416] As a result of these developments, a substantial amount of attention was (re)paid to the TPRM as the WTO's transparency vehicle which could possibly prevent or mitigate the risks of rising global protectionism.

The structure and coverage of the Overviews of this period attempted to keep track with these macro-economic developments. First, contrary to the preceding

[1409] Fourth Appraisal of the Trade Policy Review Mechanism, Summary of Main Issues discussed in First Informal Meeting, Rough Draft, 18 July 2011, 2 (Document on file with the author).

[1410] *Fourth Appraisal of the Operation of the Trade Policy Review Mechanism 2011* (n 1240) 8; Fourth Appraisal of the Trade Policy Review Mechanism, Ministerial Conference, Eighth Session, Geneva, 15–17 December 2011, WT/MIN(11)/6, 29 November 2011, 5 and 8.

[1411] Fourth Appraisal of the Trade Policy Review Mechanism, Summary of Main Issues discussed in First Informal Meeting, Rough Draft, 18 July 2011, 4 (Document on file with the author).

[1412] *Fourth Appraisal of the Operation of the Trade Policy Review Mechanism 2011* (n 1240) 8; Fourth Appraisal of the Trade Policy Review Mechanism, Ministerial Conference, Eighth Session, Geneva, 15–17 December 2011, WT/MIN(11)/6, 29 November 2011, 8.

[1413] WTO, TPRB, Rules of Procedure for Meetings of the Trade Policy Review Body, WT/TPR/6/Rev.3, 31 January 2012.

[1414] WTO, TPRB, Overview of developments in the International trading environment, Annual Report by the Director-General, WT/TPR/OV/12, 18 November 2009, A-3.

[1415] WTO, TPRB, Overview of developments in the International trading environment, Annual Report by the Director-General, WT/TPR/OV/13, 24 November 2010, 2.

[1416] WTO, TPRB, Overview of developments in the International trading environment, Annual Report by the Director-General, WT/TPR/OV/14, 21 November 2011, 2.

2005 Overview, all Overviews which took place in this period (ie those of 2009, 2010, and 2011) contained a specific section with extensive analysis of individual trade policy reviews undertaken during the period.[1417] The effects of the global crisis and the twentieth anniversary of the operation of the TPRM undoubtedly mattered.

Nevertheless, contrary to the preceding 2005 Overview, the Overviews' coverage of identified SPS and TBT measures succeeded by their potential follow-up within the respective frameworks of the TPRM and the DSB was not always guaranteed. The complete and comprehensive nature of the 2005 Overview therefore proved to be rather ad hoc. For instance, the 2009 Overview's sections on sanitary and phytosanitary measures and on technical barriers to trade do not explicitly refer to their review in the framework of the TPRM. Nevertheless, both sections contain several comments that were the result of the TPRM's activities in this context.[1418] Moreover, the annual Overview's specific section on the TPRM's activities explicitly refers to the SPS and TBT concerns raised in the context of the EC's review.[1419] Nonetheless, neither the Overview's sections on SPS and TBT measures nor its section with regard to the activities of the TPRM refer to a further follow-up of SPS and/or TBT measures in the context of the DSB. Likewise, the sections of the 2010 and 2011 Overviews with regard to sanitary and phytosanitary measures and with regard to technical barriers to trade do not explicitly refer to the TPRM's activities. However, both sections of these Overviews again contain several findings which were the direct or indirect result of the TPRM's activities in this context.[1420] Furthermore, the 2010 Overview's section on the TPRM's activities specifically underlines the SPS and TBT concerns which had been raised in the context of Croatia's TPR,[1421] whereas the 2011 Overview underlines similar concerns tabled in the contexts of the TPRs of Japan, Australia, India, Cambodia, Jamaica, Canada, the European Union, and Zimbabwe.[1422] Nevertheless, neither the Overview of 2010 nor the Overview of 2011 contain any standardized referencing of further follow-up of SPS and/or TBT measures by the DSB. Although the 2010 Overview's sections on SPS and TBT measures remain silent on their further follow-up within the context of the DSB,

[1417] WTO, TPRB, Overview of developments In the International trading environment, Annual Report by the Director-General, WT/TPR/OV/12, 18 November 2009, A33–A36; WTO, TPRB, Overview of developments in the International trading environment, Annual Report by the Director-General, WT/TPR/OV/13, 24 November 2010, 43–46; WTO, TPRB, Overview of developments in the International trading environment, Annual Report by the Director-General, WT/TPR/OV/14, 21 November 2011, 35–39 and 58–62. In particular, the 2011 overview is noteworthy. This overview pays not only attention to the TPRM as an institutional entity but also extensively covers the TPRM's individual reviews.

[1418] WTO, TPRB, Overview of developments in the International trading environment, Annual Report by the Director-General, WT/TPR/OV/12, 18 November 2009, A31–A32.

[1419] WTO, TPRB, Overview of developments in the International trading environment, Annual Report by the Director-General, WT/TPR/OV/12, 18 November 2009, A35.

[1420] WTO, TPRB, Overview of developments in the International trading environment, Annual Report by the Director-General, WT/TPR/OV/13, 24 November 2010, 33–35; WTO, TPRB, Overview of developments in the International trading environment, Annual Report by the Director-General, WT/TPR/OV/14, 21 November 2011, 27–33.

[1421] WTO, TPRB, Overview of developments in the International trading environment, Annual Report by the Director-General, WT/TPR/OV/13, 24 November 2010, 45.

[1422] WTO, TPRB, Overview of developments in the International trading environment, Annual Report by the Director-General, WT/TPR/OV/14, 21 November 2011, 36, 37, 38 and 39.

the report's section on the activities of the TPRM refers explicitly to the US' failure to implement certain dispute settlement rulings.[1423] In a similar vein, the 2011 Overview's sections on TBT measures and the TPRM both refer to the further DSB follow-up of some of the issues which had been raised in these respective contexts. In this regard, the former section states that '*very few of the Specific Trade Concerns (STCs) discussed to date end up in dispute settlement proceedings which suggests that the TBT committee is effectively contributing to the multilateral review of non-tariff measures maintained by Members' and that Members refer to co-operation between and among Members as "regulatory co-operation"... Effective co-operation should function as a means of reducing the number of trade concerns that arise in the TBT Committee and that could potentially lead to formal dispute settlement proceedings.*'[1424] However, the Overview's section on the TPRM explicitly emphasizes that the review mechanism '*is insulated from the judicial and rule-making functions of the WTO which enables it to focus more easily on policy transparency and analysis*'.[1425] While this statement is undoubtedly correct, a coherent and comprehensive way of covering trade issues (for instance, in the context of SPS, TBT, or others) would dictate that the measures in question be covered in a standardized way. This would encompass the Overviews' reporting on the measures' successive coverage by the respective committee(s), on their coverage by the TPRM, and on their (potential) litigation within the context of the DSB.

c) Participation

i) Governments (Government under review and its peers)

In the period which was covered by the fourth appraisal (ie the period between October 2008 and November 2011), fifty Contracting Parties underwent a trade policy review.[1426]

Tables II.22 and II.23 demonstrate that the attendance rates to individual reviews in this period varied to a great extent.

The top five well-attended TPRs in the period are again mainly constituted by reviews of Quad countries. These involve (in descending order): the attendance of forty-three Members to the TPR of India (2011);[1427] the presence of forty Members at the respective reviews of Brazil (2009), the European Union (2009), and the US (2009);[1428] the attendance of thirty-seven Members to the TPR of the European Union

[1423] WTO, TPRB, Overview of developments in the International trading environment, Annual Report by the Director-General, WT/TPR/OV/13, 24 November 2010, 44.

[1424] WTO, TPRB, Overview of developments in the International trading environment, Annual Report by the Director-General, WT/TPR/OV/14, 21 November 2011, 32–33.

[1425] WTO, TPRB, Overview of developments in the International trading environment, Annual Report by the Director-General, WT/TPR/OV/14, 21 November 2011, 58.

[1426] That is, the period between the TPR of Jordan of 2008 and the review of Thailand of 2011 (the joint 2011 review of Mauritania and Guinea being counted as two reviews); Data of the author; See CD ROM *20 years of Trade Policy Reviews 1989–2009, Marking the 20th anniversary of the Trade Policy Review Mechanism.*

[1427] Trade Policy Review of India of 14–16 September 2011, Minutes of the Meeting, WT/TPR/M/249, 14 October 2011.

[1428] Trade Policy Review of Brazil of 9–11 March 2012, Minutes of the Meeting, WT/TPR/M/212, 3 June 2009; Trade Policy Review of the European Union of 6–8 April 2009, Minutes of the Meeting, WT/TPR/M/214, 8 June 2009; Trade Policy Review of the United States of 29 September–1 October 2010, Minutes of the Meeting, WT/TPR/M/235, 1 November 2010.

Table II.22

Table II.23

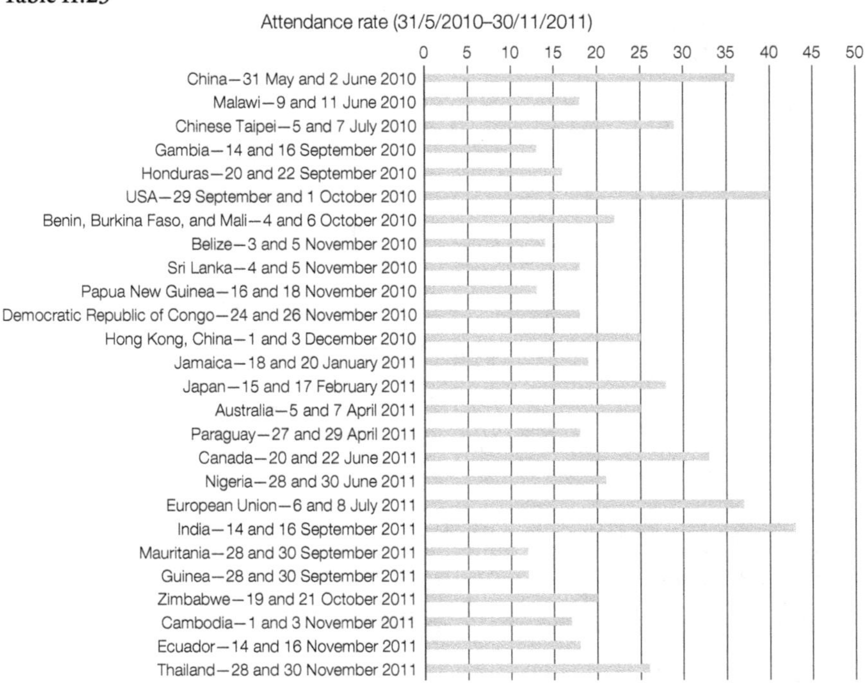

(2011);[1429] the presence of thirty-six Members at the review of China (2010),[1430] and the attendance of thirty-four Members to the TPR of Chile (2009).[1431]

The least well-attended TPRs in this period consists (in ascending order) of the TPR of Georgia (2009)[1432] which was attended by ten countries; the review of Armenia (2010)[1433] which took place in the presence of eleven Members, and of the joint TPR of Guinea and Mauritania (2011) which was attended by twelve countries.[1434]

Tables II.24 and II.25 highlight the national participation rates in the period covered by the fourth appraisal (ie the period between October 2008 and November 2011).

Table II.24

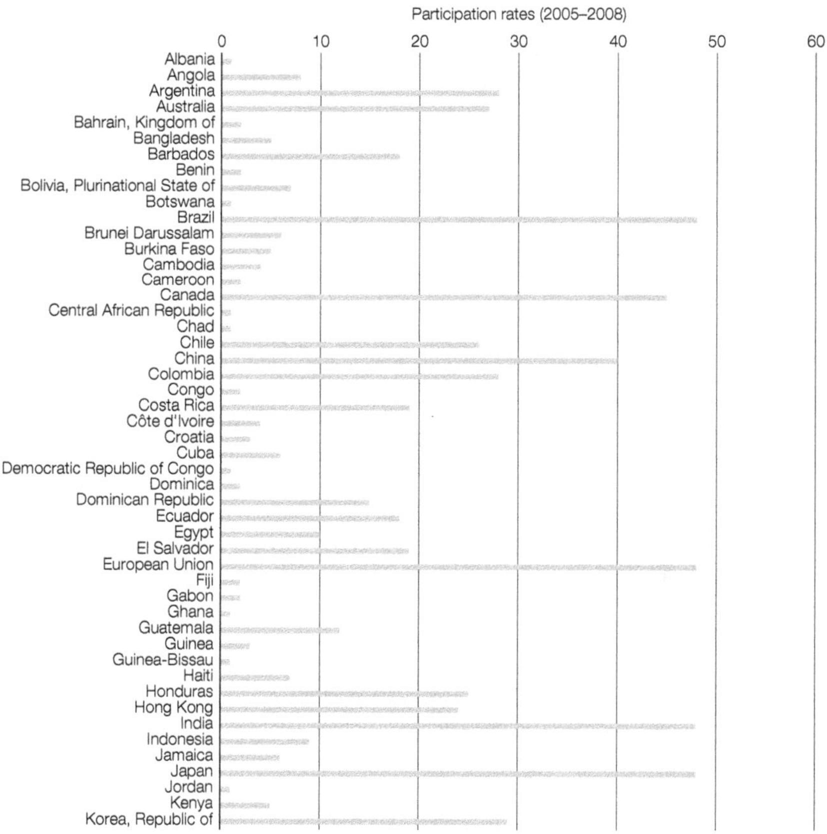

[1429] Trade Policy Review of the European Union of 6–8 July 2011, Minutes of the Meeting, WT/TPR/M/248, 14 September 2011.

[1430] Trade Policy Review of China of 31 May–2 June 2010, Minutes of the Meeting, WT/TPR/M/230, 29 June 2010.

[1431] Trade Policy Review of Chile of 7–9 October 2005, Minutes of the Meeting, WT/TPR/M/220, 17 December 2009.

[1432] Trade Policy Review of Georgia of 8–10 December 2009, Minutes of the Meeting, WT/TPR/M/224, 8 February 2010.

[1433] Trade Policy Review of Armenia of 6–8 April 2010, Minutes of the Meeting, WT/TPR/M/228, 30 April 2010.

[1434] Trade Policy Review of Guinea and Mauritania of 28–30 September 2011, Minutes of the Meeting, WT/TPR/M/250 and WT/TPR/M/251, 18 November 2011.

Table II.25

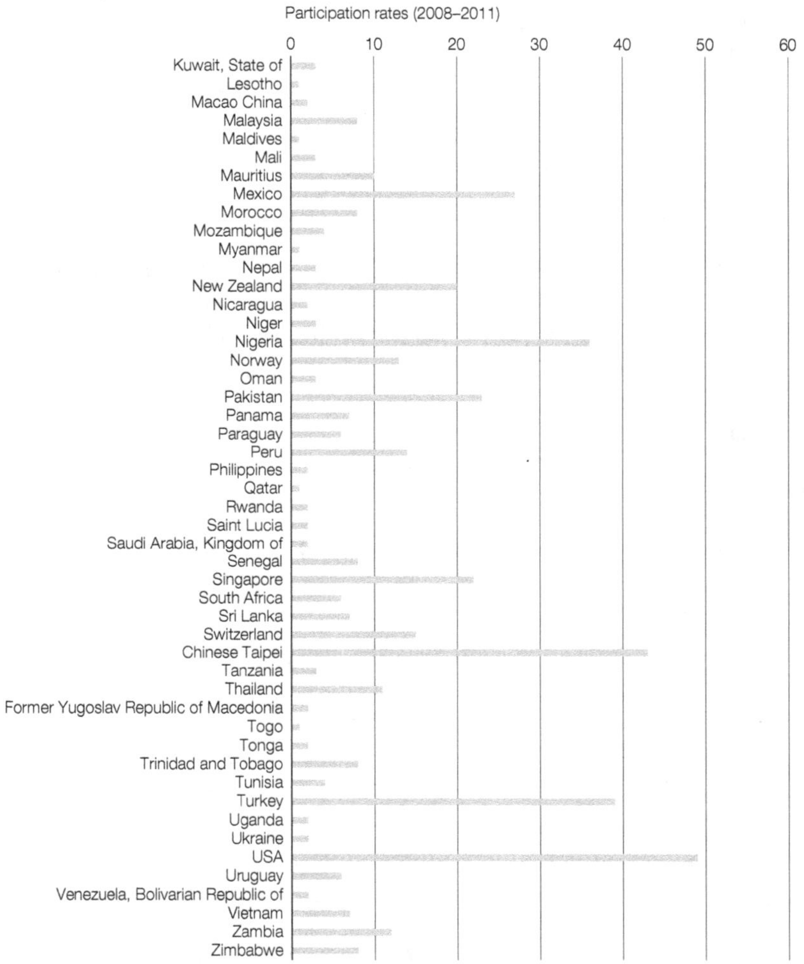

The top five participants in this period were again almost entirely constituted by Quad countries. The United States took part in each of the fifty TPRs which were organized in this period. Brazil, the European Union, India, and Japan followed. Each of these countries was involved in forty-eight reviews. Canada took part in forty-five TPRs of the period. Chinese Taipei ranked fourth and was involved in forty-three reviews. China closed the list and took part in forty out of the fifty TPRs of this period.[1435]

The lowest participation rates during this period were by the following countries. Togo, Qatar, Myanmar, the Maldives, Lesotho, Jordan, Guinea-Bissau, Ghana, the DRC, Chad, the Central African Republic, Botswana, and Albania took each part in only one TPR. Venezuela, Ukraine, Uganda, Togo, FYROM, Saudi Arabia, Saint-Lucia, Rwanda, the Philippines, Nicaragua, Macau, Gabon, Fiji, Dominica, Congo, Cameroon, Benin, and Bahrain followed and were each involved in two reviews.

[1435] Data on file with the author.

Tanzania, Oman, Niger, Nepal, Mali, Kuwait, Guinea, and Croatia closed the list. Each took part in three TPRs.[1436] LDCs and developing countries therefore again stand out by their low participation rates.

	2009	2010	2011
Average Attendance	24.0	20.4	23.5
Percentage	15.6%	13.3%	15.3%

Yearly attendance rates in the period covered by the fourth appraisal (ie October 2008 to November 2011) continued to be marked by their relative lack of volatility. Nevertheless, yearly attendance rates at the end of this period had decreased again, both in relative and in absolute terms.[1437]

ii) Secretariat

Table II.26

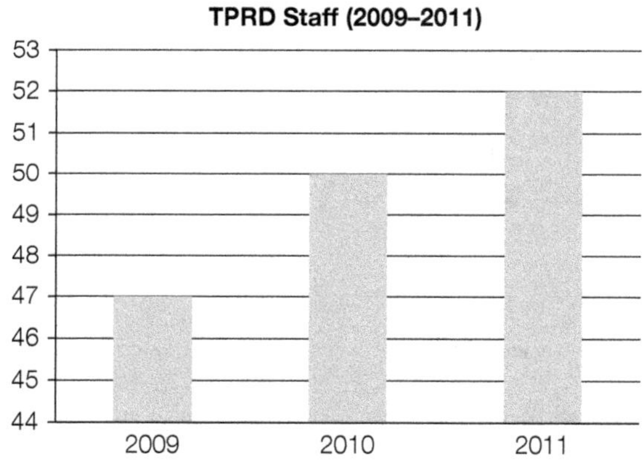

In the period covered by the fourth appraisal (ie the period between October 2008 and November 2011), TPRD staff numbers increased from forty-seven to fifty-two experts. This increase was linear throughout the whole period. Furthermore, the overall percentage of staff allocated to the TPRD never amounted to more than 8 per cent of overall WTO staff.[1438]

The period which was covered by the fourth appraisal again stands to be characterized by a complete lack of formal data with regard to the estimated, appropriated, and actual expenditure of the TPRD.[1439]

1436 Data on file with the author. 1437 Data on file with the author.

1438 Answers from the Human Resources Department of the WTO to questions of the author (4 December 2015).

1439 This lack of data has been explicitly acknowledged by the Budgetary Department of the WTO, Answers from the Budgetary Department of the WTO to questions of the author (23 July

The initial WTO budget estimates for 2008–09 amounted to CHF 376 million.[1440] Members finally appropriated CHF 184.891.500 and CHF 190.780.000 for the respective years of 2008 and 2009.[1441] In addition to the regular budget, Dutch and German financing facilitated the TPRs of Ghana, Madagascar, Mauritius and Pakistan in 2008.[1442] Likewise, Dutch and German extra-budgetary funding enabled the preparation of the 2009 reviews for Georgia, Guatemala, Fiji, the Maldives, Mozambique, Niger, Senegal, SACU, the Solomon Islands, and Zambia.[1443]

In 2010–11, the initial WTO budgetary estimates amounted respectively to CHF 195.642.200 and to CHF 201.824.100.[1444] The consolidated budget for 2010 amounts to CHF 193.989.500[1445] whereas its consolidated successor for 2011 amounts to CHF 196.003.900.[1446] In addition to the regular budget, Dutch and German extra-budgetary funding (again) enabled the preparation of the 2010 TPRs of Benin, Burkina Faso, Malawi, Papua New Guinea, and the Gambia.[1447] The annual report of the TPRB for 2011 no longer refers to the availability of any extra-budgetary funding.[1448]

The fourth appraisal paid renewed attention to budgetary issues. During the appraisal's first informal meeting, Members felt that it should be possible to complete TPRs successfully in a single day since several Members considered the additional cost in keeping their delegation from capital in Geneva quite high for the extra two days. On the other hand, there appeared to be almost no support for holding TPRB meetings in the territory of the country under review in order to reduce financial costs.[1449] Moreover, the appraisal's outcome document stresses that the increase in the number of yearly reviews would place pressure on the Secretariat's resources.[1450]

2015 and 24 January 2016); According to the calculations of the Budgetary Department of the WTO, the TPRD department received a budgetary allocation of CHF 300.000 in 2008, of 330.000 in 2009, and of 300.00 in 2010 and 2011. Nevertheless, this amount does not include allocations for missions.

1440 WTO, 2008–2009, Budget Estimates, Proposals by the Director-General, WT/BFA/SPEC/171, 1 November 2007, 6.

1441 WTO, Director-General's Budgetary and Financial Report, WT/BFA/W/181, 28 September 2009, 3. Interestingly, other formal data state explicitly that the appropriated regular WTO budget for 2009 would correspond to CHF 189.257.600 ; WTO, Committee on Budget, Finance and Administration, Mid-term review biennium 2014–2015, WT/BFA/W/339, 29 October 2014, 27.

1442 WTO, TPRB, Report of the Trade Policy Review Body for 2008, Trade Policy Review Body, WT/TPR/232, 14 November 2008, 1–2.

1443 WTO, TPRB, Draft Report of the Trade Policy Review Body for 2009, Trade Policy Review Mechanism, WT/TPR/W/41, 8 October 2009, 1–2.

1444 WTO, 2010–2011 Budget Proposals, WT/BFA/W/189, 23 October 2009.

1445 WTO, WTO Budgetary and Financial Progress Report, WT/BFA/W/231, 7 March 2011, 1.

1446 WTO, WTO Budgetary and Financial Progress Report, WT/BFA/W/242, 10 June 2011, 1.

1447 WTO, TPRB, Report of the Trade Policy Review Body for 2009, Trade Policy Review Body, WT/TPR/249, 29 October 2009, 1–2; WTO, TPRB, Report of the Trade Policy Review Body for 2010, Trade Policy Review Body, WT/TPR/269, 29 November 2010, 1–2.

1448 WTO, TPRB, Report of the Trade Policy Review Body for 2011, Trade Policy Review Body, WT/TPR/284, 15 November 2011.

1449 Fourth Appraisal of the Trade Policy Review Mechanism, Summary of Main Issues discussed in First Informal Meeting, Rough Draft, 18 July 2011, 2, 5 (Document on file with the author).

1450 Fourth Appraisal of the Trade Policy Review Mechanism, Ministerial Conference, Eighth Session, Geneva, 15–17 December 2011, WT/MIN(11)/6, 29 November 2011, 3.

During the period covered by the fourth appraisal, the number of WTO Divisions involved with the elaboration of TPRs remained unchanged. In this regard, it is interesting to note that the fourth appraisal still saw no need to make specific recommendations with regard to the need for further internal Divisional streamlining or synergies for the production of Secretariat's reports.[1451] Nevertheless, the 2009 report again reserves a specific mention for the TPRD's collaboration with the WTO's Development Division, the Institute for Training, and the Technical Co-operation Division.[1452]

In the meantime, the added value of Secretariat's reporting continued to be largely dependent on the Secretariat's independence and intrusiveness. It is therefore not surprising that the yearly TPRB reports which were drafted in the period covered by the third appraisal kept urging Members to cooperate with the Secretariat.[1453] Nevertheless, the TPRB reports for 2009 also continued to warn the Members and the Secretariat that '*close contact with the Member under review is necessary to help ensure the factual accuracy and clarity of the documentation prepared for the review*'.[1454] Moreover, the fourth appraisal requires the Secretariat to seek to ensure that its reports are factual and objective and that, subject to each Member providing the data and information that a thorough trade policy review requires, the Secretariat treats Members even-handedly, particularly when they are reviewed on the same cycle.[1455] In sum, Members were not interested either in increasing Secretariat's role (as the appraisal explicitly stated)[1456] or in diminishing its capacity (as the unsuccessful Chinese proposal aimed at operationalizing the principle of special and differential treatment in the context of the TPRM had attempted to do).[1457]

iii) Discussants

In the period covered by the fourth appraisal (ie the period between the TPR of Jordan of 2008[1458] and the review of Thailand of 2011[1459]), all TPRs involved the participation of only one discussant. As in the period covered by the third appraisal,

[1451] Fourth Appraisal of the Trade Policy Review Mechanism, Ministerial Conference, Eighth Session, Geneva, 15–17 December 2011, WT/MIN(11)/6, 29 November 2011.

[1452] WTO, TPRB, Draft Report of the Trade Policy Review Body for 2009, Trade Policy Review Mechanism, WT/TPR/W/41, 8 October 2009, 4; WTO, TPRB, Draft Report of the Trade Policy Review Body for 2010, Trade Policy Review Mechanism, WT/TPR/W/42, 28 October 2010, 2.

[1453] WTO, TPRB, Draft Report of the Trade Policy Review Body for 2009, Trade Policy Review Mechanism, WT/TPR/W/41, 8 October 2009, 5.

[1454] WTO, TPRB, Draft Report of the Trade Policy Review Body for 2009, Trade Policy Review Mechanism, WT/TPR/W/41, 8 October 2009, 2; WTO, TPRB, Draft Report of the Trade Policy Review Body for 2010, Trade Policy Review Mechanism, WT/TPR/W/42, 28 October 2010, 2.

[1455] Fourth Appraisal of the Trade Policy Review Mechanism, Ministerial Conference, Eighth Session, Geneva, 15–17 December 2011, WT/MIN(11)/6, 29 November 2011, 2.

[1456] *Fourth Appraisal of the Operation of the Trade Policy Review Mechanism 2011* (n 1240) 5.

[1457] See infra; Fourth Appraisal of the Trade Policy Review Mechanism, Comments and Suggestions of China, Non–paper, JOB/TPR/1, 30 August 2011, 1.

[1458] Trade Policy Review of Jordan of 10–12 November 2008, Minutes of the Meeting, WT/TPR/M/206, 19 December 2008.

[1459] Trade Policy Review of Thailand of 28–30 November 2011, Minutes of the Meeting, WT/TPR/M/255, 30 January 2012.

a majority of discussants originated from developing countries (twenty-nine out of forty-nine).[1460] As a result, developing countries' views were relatively better voiced.

Discussants who participated in reviews in this period relied substantially more on reporting available within the framework of the TPRM than their predecessors had during the previous period. A majority of the discussants who participated in the TPRs referred (directly or indirectly) to the Secretariat's reporting (thirty-five out of the forty-nine discussants, covering the fifty TPRs of this period or 71 per cent). In line with earlier practice, however, fewer than half of the discussants referred to governmental reporting (twenty-two out of the forty-nine discussants or 44 per cent).[1461] Moreover, whereas the Secretariat's reporting continued to be criticized, the discussants' appetite for criticism of governmental reporting sharply reduced. The Secretariat's reporting was repeatedly criticized. For instance, the discussant in the TPR of Paraguay of 2010 commented that '*para 8 in Chapter I of the Secretariat report states that next exports of goods and services contributed negatively to GDP due to "strong import growth"*'. The discussant then stated that '*a distinction must be made between the definition of "next exports" used by the Secretariat, ie the current account balance (total exports less total imports) and "net exports" meaning total exports less imports used to produce the exports*' and explained that '*with a definition such as this, exports contributed very positively to GDP growth*'.[1462] Moreover, the discussant in the TPR of Zimbabwe of 2011 indicated that '*on tariffs the usual presumption that developing countries favour high tariffs vis-à-vis liberalisation has to be recast in its proper context. Most developing countries impose tariffs and other restrictions on international trade as both a source of public revenue, as well as to protect fragile domestic producers from being undercut by the more experienced foreign competitors. Contrary to this logic, neo-classical trade theory dictates that these restrictions create distortions in the economy on the grounds that protecting inefficient producers leads to net welfare losses. This is the logic pursued in the Secretariat's report on the point that I mentioned earlier in regarding high tariffs and FDI inflows. It can be convincingly argued that, liberalisation, important as it is, cannot occur in a void. All attendant considerations have to be taken into account. Negotiations on liberalisation in the Doha round are quite telling on this issue. The concern that the neo-classical trade theory has not been able to accommodate, relates to the need to cushion those that are losing as a result of changes while nurturing those that are gaining, during the transition phase. The need for the management of adjustment costs is another consideration. If transaction is to be made in trade liberalisation, developing countries, such as Zimbabwe, would need some support for the management of the adjustment costs in their various manifestations such as employment, and in the case of agriculture, the rural livelihood in general. Perhaps this consideration should guide efforts to liberalize in current and future WTO Rounds*'.[1463] Furthermore, the

1460 Data on file with the author.

1461 Data on file with the author.

1462 Trade Policy Review of Paraguay of 27–29 April 2011, Minutes of the Meeting, WT/TPR/M/245, 25 May 2011, 7.

1463 Trade Policy Review of Zimbabwe of 19–21 October 2011, Minutes of the Meeting, WT/TPR/M/252, 28 November 2011, 10–11.

discussant in the TPR of Ecuador of 2011 was equally critical, stating that he did '*not intend to be as categorical as the Secretariat report, which on p. 8 and 83 states that more state intervention in the economy (priority sectors, selective substitution and social welfare) does not necessarily contribute to a more efficient allocation of resources and has not lead to major productivity gains, and hence improved international competitiveness, when for Ecuador we are referring to an extremely short period of time in which to assess these effects. Furthermore, the recent global financial crisis has taught us that the invisible hand of the market is not so invisible to some, that it does not always efficiently allocate resources because of the imperfections in the data transmitted, not showing information that is only possessed by private interest groups*'.[1464] On the other hand, contrary to the previous period, no governmental reporting was criticized in the period covered by the fourth appraisal. Nevertheless, discussants' trend towards more reliance on available reporting by the Secretariat and the governments under review was combined with the fact that thirty-two out of the forty-nine discussants of this period (ie 65 per cent) referred to other external studies which shed some additional light on the trade policies and practices of the country under review.[1465]

Issues with regard to dispute settlement also resurfaced during this period. For instance, the discussant in the TPR of Chile of 2009 emphasized that '*there is a system of price bands applied to imports of wheat, wheat flour and sugar, which vary with changes in international market prices. Reflecting high world prices, the system has resulted in applied tariffs below 6% for much of the review period. However, two panels have found this system WTO inconsistent. A draft law was introduced in Congress in 2007, to bring the system into conformity with WTO rules by replacing the price band system for wheat and flour with compound tariffs. Could Chile explain the possible benefits arising from a change in this system*'.[1466] Likewise, in the TPR of the US of 2010, the discussant commented that '*some concerns remain on the US Administration's implementation of the Panel or Appellate Body rulings, therefore it would be meaningful for Members to hear of the difficulties faced by the US and what their plans are to address these difficulties*'.[1467]

Contrary to earlier appraisals, the fourth appraisal elaborated on the role of discussants at some length. In this regard, the non-paper which had initiated the appraisal had already suggested that '*a note prepared by the discussant (appointed by the Chair rather than the Member under review) would also be distributed to Members before the meeting*' and that '*the discussant might possibly be someone other than a delegate*'.[1468] Moreover, throughout the appraisal process, several Members had called for the discussant's role to be reinforced. Among the suggestions floated, were the

[1464] Trade Policy Review of Ecuador of 14–16 November 2011, Minutes of the Meeting, WT/TPR/M/254, 9 January 2012, 12.

[1465] Data on file with the author.

[1466] Trade Policy Review of Chile of 7–9 October 2009, Minutes of the Meeting, WT/TPR/M/220, 17 December 2009, 8–9.

[1467] Trade Policy Review of the United States of 29 September–1 October 2010, Minutes of the Meeting, WT/TPR/M/235, 1 November 2010, 11.

[1468] Fourth Appraisal of the Operation of the TPRM, informal WTO document (Document on file with the author).

recommendations: (1) that the discussant's intervention should focus on the main challenges and actions required to meet them, rather than by merely summarizing the Secretariat and government reports; (2) that the discussant should review the conclusions from previous TPRs and the subsequent response of the reviewed Members; (3) that the discussant assess the quality of the oral and written responses provided by the reviewed Member and would have the opportunity to request, when needed, further clarification of answers; (4) that the discussant should make concluding remarks to complement those by the Chairperson; and (5) to assign the discussant's role to a well-known trade policy academic (if only occasionally).[1469] Although Members did not manage to agree on all proposals, the fourth appraisal explicitly requested the role of the discussant to be reinforced. In this regard, it notes that '*without limiting Discussant's freedom, in line with the TPRM's mandate, Members suggested that the discussant, in coordination with the Chairperson, might usefully identify and build on the key themes, focus on the main challenges, and review policy changes since the previous TPR*'.[1470]

5. Fifth appraisal of the operation of the Trade Policy Review Mechanism (July–October 2013): review of the TPRM's functioning between November 2011 and October 2013

On 2 July 2013, the Chairperson of the TPRB announced his intention to launch the fifth appraisal of the operation of the TPRM.[1471] Informal meetings of the TPRB were consequently organized between July and October 2013.[1472]

In view of the substantive modifications to the TPRM which had been introduced as a result of the fourth appraisal, due to the short time span that separated the fifth appraisal from its predecessor and in view of the preparations for the ninth WTO Ministerial, the fifth appraisal remained rather low-profile. The Members therefore agreed to continue to apply the proposed modifications of the fourth appraisal on a provisional basis and to decide on them finally during the following appraisal, due to take place not later than within five years and preferably not in the lead-up to a WTO Ministerial.[1473]

[1469] Fourth Appraisal of the TPRM, Informal open-ended meeting, 23 September 2011, 7–8 (Document on file with the author); Fourth appraisal of the TPRM, Informal meeting, 4 October 2011, 8 (Document on file with the author).

[1470] *Fourth Appraisal of the Operation of the Trade Policy Review Mechanism 2011* (n 1240) 7; Fourth Appraisal of the Trade Policy Review Mechanism, Ministerial Conference, Eighth Session, Geneva, 15–17 December 2011, WT/MIN(11)/6, 29 November 2011, 8.

[1471] Fifth Appraisal of the Trade Policy Review Mechanism, Ministerial Conference, Ninth Session, Bali, 3–6 December 2013, WT/MIN(13)/5, 28 October 2013, 1 (hereafter *Fifth Appraisal of the Trade Policy Review Mechanism 2013*).

[1472] Unofficial room documents, Trade Policy Review Body, RD/TPR/225*, 27 September 2013 (Document on file with the author); Unofficial room documents, Trade Policy Review Body, RD/TPR/225/Rev.1*, 11 October 2013 (Document on file with the author); *Fifth Appraisal of the Trade Policy Review Mechanism 2013* (n 1469).

[1473] *Fifth Appraisal of the Trade Policy Review Mechanism 2013* (n 1469) 6.

a) Objectives

The earlier academic debate between the proponents of the TPRM as an exclusive mechanism for transparency and those who considered the TPRM as a prime or partial/indirect mechanism for naming and shaming led to further analysis in the period between November 2011 and October 2013. Academic writings of this period seemed to oscillate between the formal speculation that the WTO's Membership would somehow not be interested in properly analysing/solving the problem, a further (limited though laudable) attempt to quantify the TPRM's simultaneous pursuit of its transparency and naming and shaming objectives, the repeated acknowledgement that the relationship between the TPRM and the DSB remained delicate and complex, and a proposal to extend and refine the role of the TPRM in order to keep the mechanism relevant.

Laird and Valdés referred to the old academic debates concerning the practical interpretation of the TPRM's objectives while repeating that some (ie Blackhurst, Curzon Price, and the United States during the FOGS negotiations) had highlighted the transparency and other non-legal objectives of the mechanism whereas others (ie Qureshi and India during the FOGS negotiations) had advocated the mechanism's importance as part of the enforcement of GATT/WTO legal obligations.[1474] Nevertheless, these authors rather ironically acknowledged that '*Members themselves pay attention to legal issues during the review meetings, routinely questioning the Members under review on its compliance with WTO agreements. However, rather than clarifying the objectives set up in Annex 3 and their revealed interest on compliance issues, Members have preferred to simply reaffirm 'the relevance of TPRM's mission as defined in Annex 3 of the Marrakesh Agreement*.'[1475] Luckily, academia has been less complacent than the WTO Membership. Some of the academic literature in the period therefore paid (a renewed) attention to the analysis of empirical data with regard to the relationship between the TPRM and the DSB. Refreshingly, some of the academics of this period started their analysis not with another theoretical debate about the TPRM's transparency objective versus its goal in terms of naming and shaming (and the links with the DSB) but with the simple observation that '*given the fact that much of this interest in the TPRM occurred before the WTO's Dispute Settlement Mechanism (DSM) was created, very little attention has been devoted to the study of policy review as its functions relate to the DSM*'.[1476] Froese examined the relationship between barriers to trade which were flagged by the TPRM and subsequent challenges brought to the Dispute Settlement Body.[1477] In examining sixteen TPRs which involved Canada (1996, 1998, 2000, 2003, 2007, and 2011), the United States (1996, 1999, 2001, 2004, 2006, 2008, 2010), and Mexico (1997, 2002, and 2008), the author managed to demonstrate the relatively limited efficacy of TPRs in predicting future trade litigation between Canada, the

[1474] Laird and Valdés, 'The Trade Policy Review Mechanism' (n 149) 466–68
[1475] Laird and Valdés, 'The Trade Policy Review Mechanism' (n 149) 467.
[1476] Froese, 'Trade policy review and dispute settlement at the WTO' (n 1115) 349.
[1477] Froese, 'Trade policy review and dispute settlement at the WTO' (n 1115) 349–97.

United Sates, and Mexico. The author concluded that '*issues raised by the TPRM are not very good predictors of future trade challenges, at least not in that sense that Members raise individual issues that correlate closely with future complainants at the DSB. However, the TPRM is a good predictor of Member sentiment in the sense that issues that dominate TPRs tend also to be challenged at the DSM.*'[1478] Nevertheless, Froese's analysis also showed that the relationship between the TPRM and the DSB should not be read in the framework of prediction of trade litigation but rather in the context of a more holistic understanding which showed that the TPRM '*ought not to be considered as related only to the liberalization negotiation process, nor ought it to be considered in somewhat simple terms of a disciplinary function*'. The author analyses the TPRM rather as operating '*in the liminal space between transparency and surveillance, in which it simultaneously offers Members greater access to information and opportunity to meet treaty obligations*'. This academic literature therefore suggests that transparency and surveillance should be considered as two sides of the same coin.[1479]

Other authors of this period tend to repeat the (rather) traditional delineation between the TPRM and the DSB. VanGrasstek notes for instance that '*the relationship between the TPRM and the Dispute Settlement Understanding (DSU) is complex and delicate*'.[1480] In this regard, the author emphasizes that, according to Annex 3 of the Marrakesh Agreement, '*nothing cited in a TPR can, by itself, form the basis of a complaint under the Dispute Settlement Understanding*' but also states that '*this is not to say that when a measure is mentioned in a TPR report, it somehow enjoys a safe harbour; a measure that is so listed may give a "heads-up" to other Members, and if they wish to pursue the matter in dispute settlement they need only verify the information through some other source*'.[1481] Although VanGrasstek refers to Ghosh's earlier statistical analysis which covered TPRs taking place in the period between 1995 and 2007,[1482] he acknowledges the still substantial lack of data by stating that '*it is impossible to know how often, if ever, TPR reports, have brought a matter to the attention of a future complainant for the first time*'.

In order to keep the mechanism's relevancy, Chaisse and Matsushita make the proposal to extend and to refine its role.[1483] Their proposal is based on the premise that since the Doha Development Agenda negotiations keep stagnating, the WTO Membership might consider modifying the TPRM's role with regard to the harmonization and coordination of preferential trade agreements and the convergence of environmental policy measures. In this perspective, the TPRM's continued

[1478] Froese, 'Trade policy review and dispute settlement at the WTO' (n 1115) 369.

[1479] Froese, 'Trade policy review and dispute settlement at the WTO' (n 1115) 371–73.

[1480] VanGrasstek, *The History and Future of the World Trade Organization* (n 56) 288.

[1481] VanGrasstek, *The History and Future of the World Trade Organization* (n 56) 288.

[1482] Ghosh, 'Developing Countries in the WTO Trade Policy Review Mechanism' (n 166) 419–55.

[1483] Julien Chaisse and Mitsuo Matsuhita, 'Maintaining the WTO's Supremacy in the International Trade Order: A Proposal to Refine and Revise the Role of the Trade Policy Review Mechanism' (2013) 16(1) Journal of International Economic Law, 9–36; The same idea has also been described in Mitsuo Matsushita, 'A View on Future Roles of the WTO: Should There be More Soft Law in The WTO' (2014) 17 Journal of International Economic Law 701–15.

relevancy is closely related to its ability (or rather that of the WTO Membership's) to adapt the mechanism as a transparency tool that is capable of covering new contemporary economic concerns.

In spite of the renewed academic analysis of the TPRM's objectives and contrary to earlier appraisals, the fifth appraisal no longer dedicates a specific section to the analysis of the TPRM's objectives.[1484] In this regard, the appraisal only acknowledges that '*the TPRM had proven all the more vital in recent years in the aftermath of the economic crisis and in the collective efforts to keep protectionism at bay*' and therefore stresses '*the need to ensure the proper operation of the TPRM, including through the full participation of all Members*'.[1485]

The TPRM and the DSB were conceived as two separately functioning entities. The Dispute Settlement Body has therefore rather successfully attempted to guarantee that the TPRM and its findings would not be invoked within its context. Nevertheless, in the period which was covered by the fifth appraisal, Members again, directly or indirectly, invoked findings of the TPRM in five panel proceedings (reaching a maximum of 12.5 per cent of all disputes covered in this period).[1486] Interestingly, in *China—Measures Related to the Exportation of Rare Earths, Tungsten and Molybdenum,* China, in framing the legal contours of its own Accession Protocol, even explicitly referred to the earlier mentioned legal separation between the TPRM and the DSB. In this context, it noted that '*the list of covered agreements in Appendix 1 of the DSU is exhaustive ... China recalls in this context that the Trade Policy Review Mechanism (TPRM), governed by Annex 3 of the WTO Agreement is equally an integral part of the latter according to the express terms of Article II:2 of the WTO Agreement. However, the TPRM is not a covered agreement since it does not figure in Appendix 1 of the DSU.*'

b) Structure

i) **Individual trade policy reviews**

Periodicity

The fifth appraisal of the TPRM (ie November 2011 to October 2013) covered three years wherein the TPRM functioned (2012, 2013, and 2014). The quality of the Secretariat's forecasting again varied in each of these years. Its forecast for 2012 was correct.[1487] Nevertheless, its forecasting for 2013 and 2014 was again

[1484] Although the importance of the TPRM for the functioning of the Multilateral trading system by achieving greater transparency in, and mutual understanding of, the trade policies and practices of Members is (succinctly) recalled; *Fifth Appraisal of the Trade Policy Review Mechanism 2013* (n 1469) 4.

[1485] *Fifth Appraisal of the Trade Policy Review Mechanism 2013* (n 1469) 6.

[1486] WTO, *China—Measures Related to the Exportation of Rare Earths, Tungsten and Molybdenum—Reports of the Panel, Addendum* (26 March 2014) WT/DS431-DS432-DS433/R/Add.1, B-76; WTO, *China—Measures Relating to the Production and Exportation of Apparel and Textile Products—Request for Consultations by Mexico* (18 October 2012) WT/DS451/1, 12; WTO, *Argentina—Measures Relating to Trade in Goods and Services—Report of the Panel, Addendum* (30 September 2015) WT/DS453/R/Add. 1, B-41.

[1487] For 2012 see: WTO, TPRB, Draft Report of the Trade Policy Review Body for 2011, Trade Policy Review Mechanism, WT/TPR/W/43, 4 November 2011, 1 and 4; Data of the author; WTO, TPRB, Report of the Trade Policy Review Body for 2012, Trade Policy Review Body, WT/TPR/306, 23 November 2012, 1 and 5.

based on overestimates.[1488] Moreover, between November 2011 and October 2013, the Secretariat's annual reporting on the TPRM included a categorization of the countries under review by their cyclical periodicity. Throughout the period, the Secretariat again successfully managed to review two Quad countries in each year. Nevertheless, the number of countries subject to the four-year cycle which were effectively reviewed in this period varied between three in 2014 and five in 2012, respectively less and more than normally required.[1489] Moreover, the fifth appraisal explicitly noted that the TPRs of several Members, including Angola, the Plurinational State of Bolivia, Cuba (which had never been subject to a single TPR), Egypt, Haiti, Moldova, and the Bolivarian Republic of Venezuela was overdue.[1490]

From a methodological point of view, it should be noted that the Secretariat still based its determination of a country's review cycle on that country's representative share of world trade of finalized goods and services over a fixed period of three years. Nevertheless, the substantial presence of global supply chains renders this measurement increasingly outdated from a statistical angle and completely arbitrary from a political perspective.[1491] As the IMF notes that '*the growing importance of global supply chains further increases the international transmission of shocks*', the 'automatic' character of the current periodic cycles may therefore need to be readjusted. In addition, the importance of intellectual property is (still) not reflected in these determinations.[1492]

Reporting

During the fifth appraisal, Members did not raise the question as to whether the Secretariat should delve into new issues in its reporting. Moreover, although the 2011 World Trade Report had still stated that '*the WTO, for its part, is progressively regionalizing its Trade Policy Reviews and is now encouraging the regionalization of Aid for Trade*',[1493] the Secretariat's specific reporting on Aid for Trade was discontinued after Myanmar's TPR of 2014.[1494] However, the appraisal renews the

[1488] For 2013 see: WTO, TPRB, Report of the Trade Policy Review Body for 2012, Trade Policy Review Body, WT/TPR/306, 23 November 2012, 1 and 6; Data of the author; WTO, TPRB, Draft Report of the Trade Policy Review Body for 2013, Trade Policy Review Mechanism, WT/TPR/W/49, 15 August 2013, 4. For 2014 see: WTO, TPRB, Draft Report of the Trade Policy Review Body for 2013, Trade Policy Review Mechanism, WT/TPR/W/49, 15 August 2013, 2 and 5; Data of the author; WTO, TPRB, Draft Report of the Trade Policy Review Body for 2014, Trade Policy Review Mechanism, WT/TPR/W/71/Rev. 1, 4 November 2014, 4.

[1489] Data of the author.

[1490] *Fifth Appraisal of the Trade Policy Review Mechanism 2013* (n 1469) 4.

[1491] International Monetary Fund—Strategy, Policy and Review Department, *Changing Patterns of Global Trade* (IMF 2012), 12–22 and 54 <https://www.imf.org/external/pubs/ft/dp/2012/dp1201.pdf> accessed 17 June 2017

[1492] John M Curtis, 'Intellectual Property Rights and International Trade: An Overview' (2012) The Centre for International Governance Innovation CIGI Papers No 3; United Nations System Task Team on the Post-2015 UN Development Agenda, Science, technology and innovation and intellectual property rights: The vision for development, 2012.

[1493] WTO, *The WTO and Preferential Trade Agreements: From Co-existence to Coherence* (WTO 2011), 153.

[1494] Trade Policy Review of Myanmar, Minutes of the Meeting, WT/TPR/M/293, 11–13 March 2014.

recommendation that the Secretariat improves its coverage of central and (where relevant, feasible, and possible) sub-central behind-the-border measures on trade in goods and services, especially with regard to regulatory measures, subsidies and state aid, state trading, and government procurement.[1495]

The fifth appraisal remains silent on governmental reporting and makes an overwhelmingly positive analysis of the Secretariat's reporting while noting that it had implemented most of the recommendations resulting from the fourth appraisal. The appraisal rather meaninglessly invited the Secretariat '*to continue to explore ways to improve and streamline its reports in order to make them more effective in achieving the objectives of the TPRM and, at the same time, help reduce documentation and translation costs of the TPRB*'.[1496]

TPR's informational value – Similar to the fourth appraisal, the period covered by the fifth appraisal (ie November 2011 to October 2013) did not result in any academic output analysing the information contained in the Secretariat's (and sometimes governmental) reporting within the context of individual TPRs.

Reporting on information and naming and shaming – Between the start (ie November 2011) and the end (ie October 2013) of the period which was covered by the fifth appraisal, thirty-two TPRs took place and forty DSB disputes were initiated. Of these, three disputes related to Sanitary and Phytosanitary measures whereas eight related to the area of Technical Barriers to Trade.

Through its focus on the respective DSB and TPR coverage of the same SPS and TBT disputes, the remainder of this section analyses individual TPRs' added value in terms of transparency and naming and shaming. In order to do so, for each of the DSB disputes, this section examines the proceeding and succeeding TPR(s). For each of these TPRs, the Secretariat report and the government report, the debates during the TPRB meeting, and the written questions and answers are analysed from a transparency angle (questioning whether the respective reports, meetings, or questions explicitly or indirectly managed to refer to elements of the future dispute) and from the perspective of naming and shaming (examining whether the respective reports, meetings, or questions managed to elicit some (defensive) stance from the country under review).

- In *India—Measures Concerning the Importation of Certain Agricultural Products*, the United States took issue with a series of Indian measures (ie a number of orders issued by India's Department of Animal Husbandry, Dairying, and Fisheries pursuant to the Livestock Importation Act (1898), as well as any amendments, related measures, or implementing measures thereof, and the Statutory Order (2011)) with regard to the importation of various agricultural products from the United States, purportedly because of concerns related to Avian Influenza.[1497] India continued to impose these measures despite

[1495] *Fifth Appraisal of the Trade Policy Review Mechanism 2013* (n 1469) 6.
[1496] *Fifth Appraisal of the Trade Policy Review Mechanism 2013* (n 1469) 6.
[1497] WTO, *India—Measures Concerning the Importation of Certain Agricultural Products—Report of the Panel* (14 October 2014) WT/DS430/R.

reassurances from the World Organization for Animal Health (OIE) Code Commission (which is amongst others tasked with setting health standards for trade in animals and animal products) according to which low pathogenic influenza allows for trade. Moreover, the United States had notified the OIE of cases of low-pathogenic avian flu but did not experience any outbreak of high-pathogenic avian flu since 2004. This contrasts which the over ninety outbreaks which India had seen on a domestic level between 2003 and 2013.[1498] The United States therefore concluded that the continued imposition of the Indian measures constituted a violation of Articles 2.2, 2.3, 3.1, 5.1, 5.2, 5.5, 5.6, 5.7, 6.1, 6.2 and 7; of Annex B, paragraphs 2, 5, and 6 of the SPS Agreement and of Articles I and XI of the GATT (1994).

The TPR of India of September 2011 highlights the problem at length.[1499] Several sub-sections of the Secretariat's report managed to identify the issue. The report's sub-section on import prohibitions, restrictions and licensing succinctly indicates that '*for sanitary reasons, India has continued to ban imports of certain avian livestock and livestock products*'.[1500] Moreover, the report's sub-sectional analysis of SPS measures contains a more detailed description of the Livestock Importation Act of 1898.[1501] Furthermore, the report's section on agriculture explains in general terms that '*Imports of animal products into India require sanitary import permits issued by the Department of Animal Husbandry, Dairy and Fisheries; permits must be obtained prior to shipment from the country of origin. The Department approves or rejects the application based on an import risk analysis on a case by case basis. Sanitary import permits are not import licences, they are certificates verifying that India's sanitary requirements are fulfilled. Some imports of animal products also require an import licence issued by the Director General of Foreign Trade. Imports of animal and fish products are only allowed through designated ports where animal quarantine and certification services exist.*'[1502] However, in line with its earlier practice, the government report remains silent on the topic.[1503] Nevertheless, during the TPRB meeting, the United States referred to the problem in general terms only when it listed several challenges including the fact that '*this would include significant, long-term reductions in agricultural tariffs, and removal of unjustifiable SPS and TBT impediments on agricultural imports, both of which can help food price inflation*'.[1504] It tabled written

[1498] *WTO Panel Grants US Victory in India Poultry Ban Dispute* (2014) 18(34), Bridges.

[1499] Trade Policy Review of India of 14–16 September 2011, Minutes of the Meeting, WT/TPR/M/249, 14 October 2011.

[1500] Trade Policy Review of India of 14–16 September 2011, Secretariat Report, WT/TPR/S/249, 10 August 2011, 53–58 (particularly at 53).

[1501] Trade Policy Review of India of 14–16 September 2011, Secretariat Report, WT/TPR/S/249, 10 August 2011, 71–74 (particularly at 72).

[1502] Trade Policy Review of India of 14–16 September 2011, Secretariat Report, WT/TPR/S/249, 10 August 2011, 126–138 (particularly at 131).

[1503] Trade Policy Review of India of 14–16 September 2011, Government Report, WT/TPR/G/249, 10 August 2011.

[1504] Trade Policy Review of India of 14–16 September 2011, Minutes of the Meeting, WT/TPR/M/249, 14 October 2011, 16–19 and 67–68.

questions to request additional specific details on Indian SPS measures which had been allegedly taken to combat avian influenza.[1505]

On 18 February 2013, the Panel was composed. Nonetheless, due to the complexity of the case, the Panel report was only circulated on 14 October 2014.[1506] It considered that India's measures were inconsistent with Articles 2.2, 2.3, 3.1, 3.2, 5.1, 5.2, 5.6, 6.1, 6.2, 7 and Annex B of the SPS Agreement. Further to the request of both parties, a DSB meeting of 18 November 2014 agreed that the normal sixty-day deadline for appeals would be extended to 26 January 2015.[1507] India used the final day of this extension period to launch an appeal.[1508] The Appellate Body therefore issued its report on 4 June 2015, thus coinciding with the Indian TPR.[1509] The Appellate Bodies' report largely upheld the Panel's findings and confirmed that the Indian measures were not based on international standards. As a result, the measures were found to be inconsistent with Articles 2.3, 5.1, 5.2, 5.6, 6.1 and 6.2 of the SPS agreement.[1510]

The dispute resurfaced in the TPR of India of 2 to 4 June 2015.[1511] Although the report's sub-sectional analysis of sanitary and phytosanitary requirements remains silent on the case,[1512] the dispute is referenced in a table in the Secretariat's report sub-sectional analysis of India's involvement in the WTO.[1513] In line with its earlier practice, however, the government report remains silent on the topic.[1514] The United States therefore seized the TPRB meeting in an attempt to name and shame India into behaviour consistent with the SPS Agreement. In this regard, it noted in general terms that it '*invites India to consider how additional steps to open the country's trading regime can help India harness the benefits of trade to drive up investment and create jobs? This would include ... removal of unjustifiable SPS and TBT impediments on agricultural imports, both of which can help address food price inflation*',[1515] and that '*products often face obstacles in the form of SPS and*

[1505] Trade Policy Review of India of 14–16 September 2011, Written questions and answers, WT/TPR/M/249/Add. 1, 14 October 2011, 285 and Trade Policy Review of India of 14–16 September 2011, Written questions and answers, WT/TPR/M/249/Add. 2, 28 October 2011, 42–43.

[1506] WTO, *India—Measures Concerning the Importation of Certain Agricultural Products—Report of the Panel* (14 October 2014) WT/DS430/R.

[1507] WTO, DSB, Minutes of Meeting, WT/DSB/M/352, 30 January 2015, 12–13.

[1508] WTO, *India—Measures Concerning the Importation of Certain Agricultural Products—Notification of an Appeal by India under Article 16.4 and Article 17 of the Understanding on Rules and Procedures Governing the Settlement of Disputes (DSU) and under Rule 20(1) of the Working Procedures for Appellate Review* (2 February 2015) WT/DS430/8.

[1509] WTO, *India—Measures Concerning the Importation of Certain Agricultural Products—Appellate Body Report* (4 June 2015) WT/DS430/AB/R.

[1510] *WTO Affirms US Victory in India Poultry Ban Case* (2015) 19(21) Bridges.

[1511] Trade Policy Review of India of 2–4 June 2015, Minutes of the Meeting, WT/TPR/M/313, 20 July 2015.

[1512] Trade Policy Review of India of 2–4 June 2015, Secretariat Report, WT/TPR/S/313, 28 April 2015, 62–64.

[1513] Trade Policy Review of India of 2–4 June 2015, Secretariat Report, WT/TPR/S/313, 28 April 2015, 29.

[1514] Trade Policy Review of India of 2–4 June 2015, Government Report, WT/TPR/G/313, 28 April 2015.

[1515] Trade Policy Review of India of 2–4 June 2015, Minutes of the Meeting, WT/TPR/M/313, 20 July 2015, 20.

TBT measures that appear to have no scientific or other justifiable basis under the WTO Agreements'.[1516] Nevertheless, the United States tabled no further written questions.[1517]

This analysis yields several conclusions: First, reports of the Secretariat still offer excellent added value in terms of transparency. This example again managed to demonstrate that the TPRs were either able to identify or to refer to the contours of the (future) dispute. Second, reports of the government under review have no added value in terms of transparency. Neither of the two reports of the Indian government referred to the trade concerns. Third, in terms of naming and shaming, both TPRB meetings and written questions and answers again offer added value in terms of naming and shaming.

Structure of meetings

In the years covered by the fifth appraisal (ie 2011–13), the structure of TPR meetings did not change. Annual reports drafted during this period therefore kept repeating that '*procedures for the reviews have generally run smoothly*'.[1518] In line with its practice as acquired under the fourth appraisal, the fifth appraisal lists the results of its predecessor and attempts to analyse ensuing progress and developments.[1519] In this regard, the appraisal concludes that the substantive modifications resulting from the fourth appraisal, including the structural changes to the question and answer process and the TPRB meetings, '*worked satisfactory but that more time was needed to fully appreciate all aspects before agreeing to make them definitive*'.[1520]

On the other hand, the appraisal also acknowledges that the proposed structural modification with regard to the reduced length of TPRB meetings still failed to materialize (since the proposal of the fourth appraisal to hold single-day TPRs on a pilot basis had not been retained by a single Member).[1521] Moreover, the fifth appraisal also kept urging Members to make the TPRB meetings as interactive as possible '*by focussing on the main trade and trade-related policy changes since the last reviews and areas of systemic importance, and keeping to a minimum, to the extent possible, diplomatic courtesy and extensive routine description of bilateral relations*'. Furthermore, Members themselves explicitly expressed the desire to reflect longer on several points, including on how the meetings could be made more interactive.[1522]

1516 Trade Policy Review of India of 2–4 June 2015, Minutes of the Meeting, WT/TPR/M/313, 20 July 2015, 21.

1517 Trade Policy Review of India of 2–4 June 2015, Minutes of the Meeting, WT/TPR/M/313/Add. 1, 31 July 2015.

1518 WTO, TPRB, Draft Report of the Trade Policy Review Body for 2011, Trade Policy Review Mechanism, WT/TPR/W/43, 4 November 2011, 2; WTO, TPRB, Report of the Trade Policy Review Body for 2012, Trade Policy Review Body, WT/TPR/306, 23 November 2012, 1; WTO, TPRB, Draft Report of the Trade Policy Review Body for 2013, Trade Policy Review Mechanism, WT/TPR/W/49, 15 August 2013, 1; WTO, TPRB, Report of the Trade Policy Review Body for 2013, Trade Policy Review Body, WT/TPR/321, 8 October 2013, 1.

1519 *Fifth Appraisal of the Trade Policy Review Mechanism 2013* (n 1469) 1–5.

1520 *Fifth Appraisal of the Trade Policy Review Mechanism 2013* (n 1469) 5.

1521 *Fifth Appraisal of the Trade Policy Review Mechanism 2013* (n 1469) 3.

1522 *Fifth Appraisal of the Trade Policy Review Mechanism 2013* (n 1469) 5–6.

ii) Overview of developments in the International Trading Environment

The Overviews of the period covered by the fifth appraisal still paint a bleak picture but start to hint at a slow recovery of the world economy. In this regard, the 2012 Overview states that '*the outlook is worse than at the time of issuance of the previous trade monitoring report in June 2012 due, among other things, to budget developments and the persistent debt crisis in some major economies. Output and employment trends in many countries have continued to be negative, despite the many measures implemented to contain the slowdown in economic growth.*'[1523] The Overview of 2013 indicates that '*trade growth in 2013 reflected the slow and uneven growth that we saw in the global economy. The volume of merchandise trade expanded by less than 2.5% last year. It is projected to grow by between 4.0% and 4.5% in 2014 but that is still below the historical average since 1990 of 5.5%.*'[1524]

The structure and coverage of the Overviews of this period gradually began to assume a standard format and line, undoubtedly partly influenced by the still uncertain macro-economic developments. First, like their predecessors, the Overviews of 2012 and 2013 (the latter issued at the end of January 2014) continue to dedicate a specific section to the general analysis of the TPRM's activities.[1525] In this regard, the Overview of 2012 clearly refers to the TPRM in emphasizing that '*the trade monitoring exercise and the individual Trade Policy Reviews undertaken in 2012 show that, on the whole, governments have continued to resist domestic pressures to erect trade barriers, although some of them have put in place trade-restrictive measures*'.[1526] In a similar vein, the 2013 Overview remarks that 'individual Trade Policy Reviews undertaken in 2013 have shown that WTO Members are making efforts to resist domestic pressures to erect trade barriers. Some slippage is perhaps inevitable.'[1527] Second, the 2012 and 2013 Overviews' coverage of identified SPS and TBT measures and their further follow-up in the respective frameworks of the TPRM and the DSB became more standardized. Although the 2012 and 2013 Overviews' sections with regard to sanitary and phytosanitary measures and to technical barriers to trade do not explicitly refer to the TPRM's activities, they contain several comments that were the direct or indirect result of the TPRM's activities in their regard.[1528] Furthermore, the 2012 Overview's section with regard to the TPRM's activities specifically underlines SPS

[1523] WTO, TPRB, Overview of developments in the International trading environment, Annual Report by the Director-General, WT/TPR/OV/15, 29 November 2012, 2.

[1524] WTO, TPRB, Overview of developments in the International trading environment, Annual Report by the Director-General, WT/TPR/OV/16, 31 January 2014, 3.

[1525] WTO, TPRB, Overview of developments in the International trading environment, Annual Report by the Director-General, WT/TPR/OV/15, 29 November 2012, 60–66; WTO, TPRB, Overview of developments in the International trading environment, Annual Report by the Director-General, WT/TPR/OV/16, 31 January 2014, 45–53.

[1526] WTO, TPRB, Overview of developments in the International trading environment, Annual Report by the Director-General, WT/TPR/OV/15, 29 November 2012, 2.

[1527] WTO, TPRB, Overview of developments in the International trading environment, Annual Report by the Director-General, WT/TPR/OV/16, 31 January 2014, 3.

[1528] WTO, TPRB, Overview of developments in the International trading environment, Annual Report by the Director-General, WT/TPR/OV/15, 29 November 2012, 27–36.

WTO, TPRB, Overview of developments in the International trading environment, Annual Report by the Director-General, WT/TPR/OV/16, 31 January 2014, 23–36.

and/or TBT concerns raised in the context of the reviews of Uruguay, Colombia, Turkey, Saudi Arabia, Kuwait, the UAE, Bangladesh, Korea, Singapore, China, the Philippines, Nepal, and the EAC.[1529] The 2013 Overview's section on the TPRM's activities includes SPS and TBT concerns as recurring in several of the TPRs which had been undertaken during the year. These concerns are highlighted in the framework of the reviews of Israel, Iceland, Japan, Indonesia, Mexico, Switzerland, Macao China, the European Union, the CEMAC, Vietnam, Peru, the Kirgiz Republic, and FYROM.[1530] However, neither the Overview of 2012 nor that of 2013 contain any standardized referencing to the potential further follow-up of SPS and/or TBT issues by the DSB. Although the 2012 and 2013 Overviews' specific sections on SPS measures and on the TPRM remain silent on such a potential further DSB follow-up of issues which had been raised, both Overviews' sections on TBT measures repeatedly make the link with the DSB. In this regard, the 2012 Overview explicitly notes that '*the fact that very few of the 356 Specific Trade Concerns (STCs) discussed to date end up in formal dispute settlement proceedings suggests that the Committee's multilateral review of measures may be contributing to pre-empting trade conflicts*'.[1531] The 2013 Overview indicates furthermore that '*since the last monitoring report, four new disputes involving measures which have been discussed as STCs in previous TBT committee meetings have been the subject of consultation requests. Two involve Australian measures on plain packaging for tobacco products, while the other two involve Russia's recycling fee on motor vehicles and certain EU measures relating to the import, consumption, and production of biodiesel. For all four of these disputes, consultations are still pending*'.[1532] Again, a coherent and comprehensive way of reporting would dictate that identified SPS and/or TBT issues ought to be referenced in a standardized way. This would involve the Overview's referencing of the concerned measure's successive coverage by the respective committee(s), by the TPRM, and, where possible, also by the DSB.

c) *Participation*

i) Governments (Government under review and its peers)

In the period covered by the fifth appraisal (ie the period between November 2011 and October 2013), thirty-two Members underwent a trade policy review.[1533]

Tables II.27 and II.28 show the attendance rates to TPRs which took place in this period.

1529 WTO, TPRB, Overview of developments in the International trading environment, Annual Report by the Director-General, WT/TPR/OV/15, 29 November 2012, 61–65.

1530 WTO, TPRB, Overview of developments in the International trading environment, Annual Report by the Director-General, WT/TPR/OV/16, 31 January 2014, 45–53.

1531 WTO, TPRB, Overview of developments in the International trading environment, Annual Report by the Director-General, WT/TPR/OV/15, 29 November 2012, 34.

1532 WTO, TPRB, Overview of developments in the International trading environment, Annual Report by the Director-General, WT/TPR/OV/16, 31 January 2014, 31.

1533 That is, the period between the TPR of the Kingdom of Saudi Arabia of 2012 and the review of Costa Rica of 2013; Data of the author; See the CD ROM *20 years of Trade Policy Reviews 1989–2009, Marking the 20th anniversary of the Trade Policy Review Mechanism.*

Table II.27

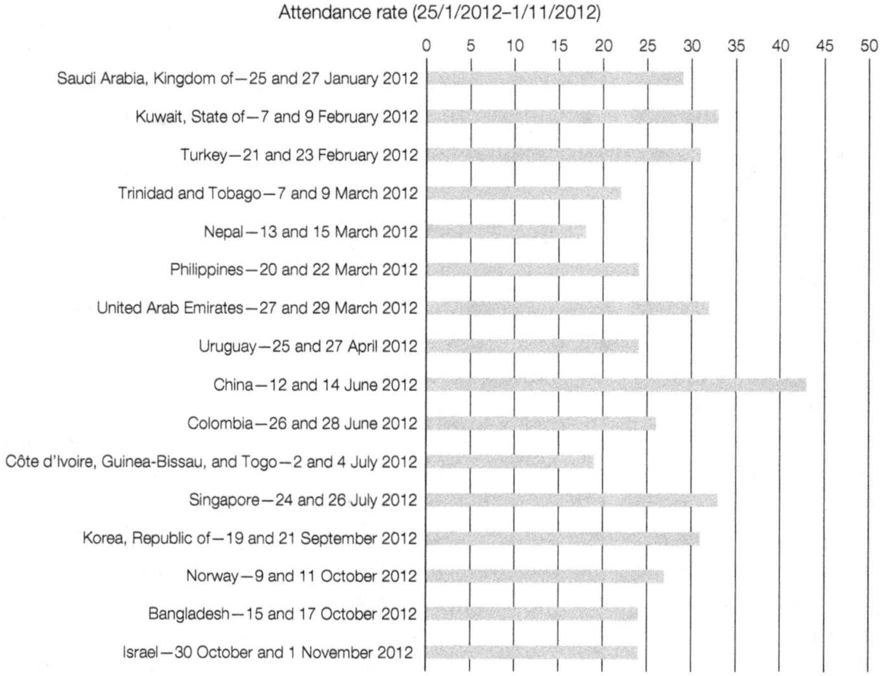

Table II.28

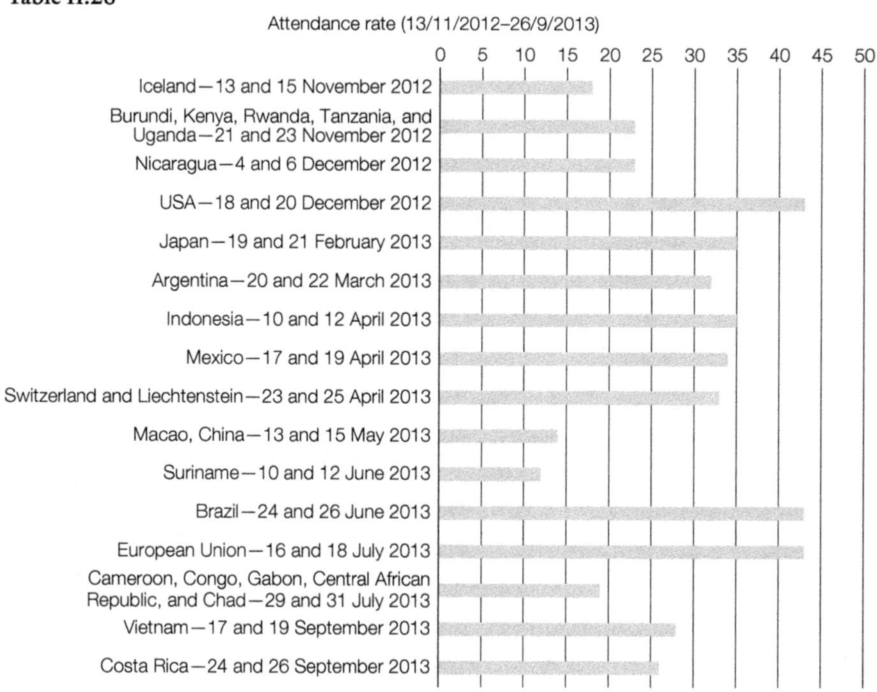

TPRs attracting the most attendees are again centred around reviews of Quad countries. In this period, they involved the (descending) attendance by forty-three Members to the TPRs of China (2012), the United States (2012), Brazil (2013), and the European Union (2013);[1534] the presence of thirty-five countries at the reviews of Japan (2013) and Indonesia (2013);[1535] the attendance by thirty-four Members to the TPR of Mexico (2013);[1536] the presence of thirty-three countries at the respective reviews of Kuwait (2012), Singapore (2012), and Switzerland (2013),[1537] and the attendance by thirty-two Members to the TPRs of the United Arab Emirates (2012) and Argentina (2013).[1538]

On the other hand, the least well-attended TPRs consist (in ascending order) of the review of Suriname (2013)[1539] which was attended by twelve countries; of the TPR of Macao (2013)[1540] in the presence of fourteen Members; and of the respective reviews of Iceland (2012) and Nepal (2012) which were each attended by eighteen countries.[1541]

Tables II.29 and II.30 highlight the national participation rates in the period covered by the fifth appraisal.

The list of top five participants in this period was again almost entirely constituted by Quad countries. India took part in each of the thirty-two TPRs organized throughout the period. Brazil and the United States followed. Each was involved in thirty-one reviews. Canada, the European Union, and Chinese Taipei took each part in thirty TPRs. Japan came fourth and was involved in twenty-nine reviews. Argentina and China closed the list, each taking part in twenty-eight out of the thirty-two TPRs of this period.[1542]

On the other hand, countries attending the fewest TPRs were Rwanda, Mauritius, Guinea-Bissau, Ghana, Gabon, Dominica, Croatia, Burkina Faso, Botswana, and Bahrain, all of whom each took part in only a single TPR. Uganda, Togo, Sri Lanka,

1534 Trade Policy Review of China of 12–14 June 2012, Minutes of the Meeting, WT/TPR/M/264, 17 July 2012; Trade Policy Review of the United States of 18–20 December 2012, Minutes of the Meeting, WT/TPR/M/275, 30 April 2013; Trade Policy Review of Brazil of 24–26 June 2013, Minutes of the Meeting, WT/TPR/M/283, 11 October 2013; Trade Policy Review of the European Union of 16–18 July 2013, Minutes of the Meeting, WT/TPR/M/284, 23 October 2013.

1535 Trade Policy Review of Japan of 19–21 February 2013, Minutes of the Meeting, WT/TPR/M/276, 13 June 2013; Trade Policy Review of Indonesia of 10–12 April 2013, Minutes of the Meeting, WT/TPR/M/278, 1 August 2013.

1536 Trade Policy Review of Mexico of 4 September 2013, Minutes of the Meeting, WT/TPR/M/279, 4 September 2013.

1537 Trade Policy Review of Kuwait of 7–9 February 2012, Minutes of the Meeting, WT/TPR/M/258, 26 March 2012; Trade Policy Review of Singapore of 24–26 July 2012, Minutes of the Meeting, WT/TPR/M/267, 8 October 2012; Trade Policy Review of Switzerland and Liechtenstein of 23–25 April 2013, Minutes of the Meeting, WT/TPR/M/280, 12 September 2013.

1538 Trade Policy Review of the United Arab Emirates of 27–29 March 2012, Minutes of the Meeting, WT/TPR/M/262, 9 May 2012; Trade Policy Review of Argentina of 20–22 March 2013, Minutes of the Meeting, WT/TPR/M/277, 18 July 2013.

1539 Trade Policy Review of Suriname of 10–12 June 2013, Minutes of the Meeting, WT/TPR/M/282, 3 October 2013.

1540 Trade Policy Review of Macao of 13–15 May 2013, Minutes of the Meeting, WT/TPR/M/281, 13 September 2013.

1541 Trade Policy Review of Iceland of 13–15 November 2012, Minutes of the Meeting, WT/TPR/M/273, 25 February 2013; Trade Policy Review of Nepal of 13–15 March 2012, Minutes of the Meeting, WT/TPR/M/257, 16 April 2012.

1542 Data on file with the author.

Table II.29

Senegal, the Russian Federation, Panama, Kuwait, Israel, Iceland, Haiti, Côte d'Ivoire, Cambodia, Angola, and Albania followed. Each of these countries was involved in two reviews. Zambia, Guinea, and Egypt closed the list, each participating in only three TPRs.[1543] As before, LDCs and developing countries were overrepresented on this list.

	2011	2012
Average Attendance	23.5	27.3
Percentage	15.3%	17.3%

[1543] Data on file with the author.

Table II.30

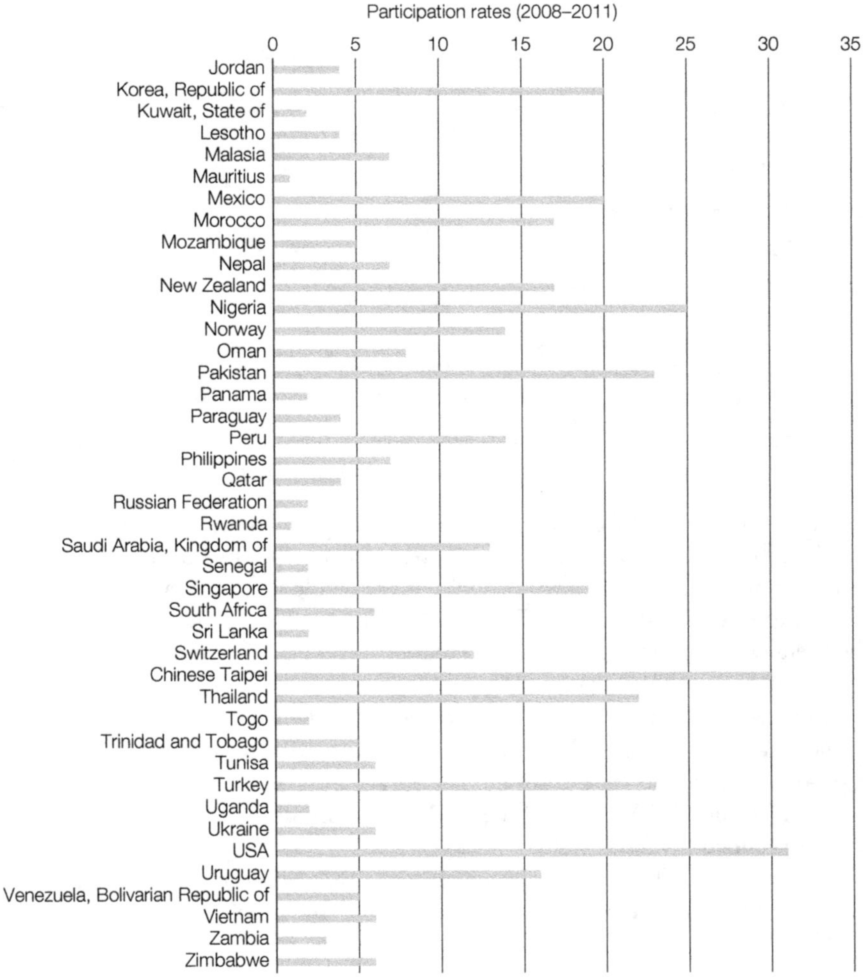

Yearly attendance rates in the period covered by the fifth appraisal (ie November 2011 to October 2013) continued to be marked by a minor degree of volatility. Nevertheless, yearly attendance rates at the end of this period had increased again, both in relative and absolute terms.[1544]

[1544] Data on file with the author.

ii) Secretariat

Table II.31

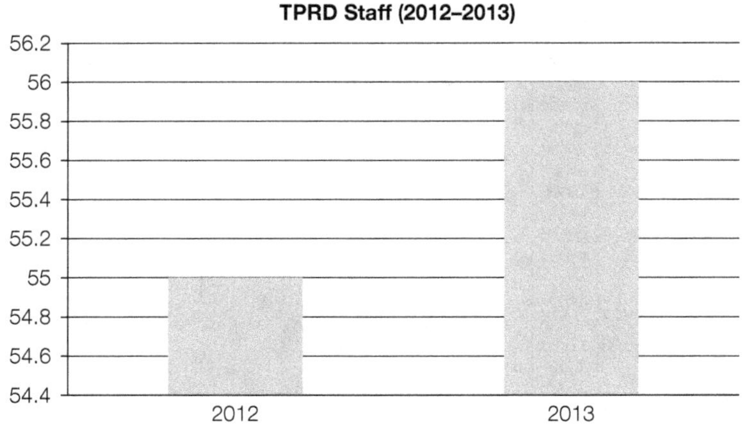

In the period covered by the fifth appraisal (ie the period between November 2011 and October 2013), TPRD staff had increased from fifty-five to fifty-six experts. This staffing increase was linear throughout the whole period. Nevertheless, it was still rather exceptional to find TPRD experts with a legal background.[1545] Moreover, the overall percentage of staff allocated to the TPRD never amounted to more than 8 per cent of overall WTO staff.[1546]

In line with earlier budgetary practice, the period which was covered by the fifth appraisal once again completely lacks formal data with regard to the estimated, appropriated and real expenditure of the TPRD.[1547] Moreover, neither the 2011 nor the 2012 nor 2013 reports of the TPRB mention the existence or availability of any extra-budgetary funding.[1548]

The initial WTO budgetary estimates for 2012–13 amounted respectively to CHF 196.003.900 and to CHF 199.677.700.[1549] The quasi-permanent growth of the WTO Membership continued to result—through the periodicity requirements

[1545] Interview with Mr Willy Alfaro, fifth director of the Trade Policy Review Department, WTO (Geneva, July 2015).

[1546] Answers from the Human Resources Department of the WTO to questions of the author (4 December 2015).

[1547] This lack of data has been explicitly acknowledged by the Budgetary Department of the WTO, Answers from the Budgetary Department of the WTO to questions of the author (23 July 2015 and 24 January 2016); According to the calculations of the Budgetary Department of the WTO, the TPRD department received a budgetary allocation of CHF 300.000 in 2011, CHF 400.000 in 2012, and CHF 500.000 in 2013. Nevertheless, this amount does not include allocations for missions.

[1548] WTO, TPRB, Draft Report of the Trade Policy Review Body for 2011, Trade Policy Review Mechanism, WT/TPR/W/43, 4 November 2011; WTO, TPRB, Report of the Trade Policy Review Body for 2011, Trade Policy Review Body, WT/TPR/284, 15 November 2011; WTO, TPRB, Report of the Trade Policy Review Body for 2012, Trade Policy Review Body, WT/TPR/306, 23 November 2012; WTO, TPRB, Report of the Trade Policy Review Body for 2013, Trade Policy Review Body, WT/TPR/321, 8 October 2013.

[1549] WTO, 2012–2013 Budget Proposals, WT/BFA/W/250, 21 October 2011, 7.

of the TPRM—in a further yearly increase in TPRs. In this regard, it is noteworthy that the budget estimates for 2012–13 indicate that the*Doha Development Agenda (DDA) Global Trust Fund is also currently funding mission travel related to Trade Policy Reviews that fall within the mandate of the regular work of the WTO Secretariat. The proposal is to shift that expenditure, amounting to some CHF 300,000 per year, gradually from the DDA Global Trust Fund to the regular WTO budget. The aim is to have all travel expenditure related to Trade Policy Reviews funded through the regular budget by 2013. The rise in the number of Trade Policy Reviews conducted every year will result into additional travel expenditure that will be funded partly through an increase in the travel budget.*'[1550] Finally, the General Council approved the fifth WTO biennial budget (which covered 2012 and 2013) in allocating respectively CHF 196.003.900 and CHF 197.203.900.[1551] Moreover, budgetary expenditure in 2013 amounted to CHF 187 million.[1552]

In order to achieve the necessary level of austerity required by the 2012–13 budget, the General Council requested cost savings in document production and meetings.[1553] As a consequence, the fifth appraisal acknowledges that the Chair of the TPRB undertook successful consultations which resulted in a reduction of the volume of documentation by switching to an increasingly paperless working environment.[1554] However, Members were unable to reach agreement on some of the proposals for cost-savings such as whether podcasts might allow for the discontinuation of the production of minutes of the TPRB meetings.[1555]

During the period which was covered by the appraisal, the number of WTO Divisions that interacted with the TPRD remained unaltered. In this regard, it is interesting to note that the fifth appraisal saw no need to make any specific recommendations with regard to the need for further internal divisional streamlining or synergies for the production of the Secretariat's reports.[1556] Nevertheless, where the 2011 report again reserves a standardized specific mention for the TPRD's collaboration with the WTO's Development Division, the Institute for Training, and the Technical Co-operation Division,[1557] this comment has been dropped from the 2012 and the 2013 reports.[1558]

[1550] WTO, 2012–2013 Budget Proposals, WT/BFA/W/250, 21 October 2011, 37–38.

[1551] WTO, Mid-Term Review Biennium 2012–2013, WT/BFA/W/290, 6 November 2012, 4.

[1552] WTO, Committee on Budget, Finance and Administration, Report on the Meeting held on 17 September 2014, WT/BFA/144, 15 October 2014, 1.

[1553] Unofficial Room Documents, Trade Policy Review Body, RD/TPR/124, 6 March 2013 (Document on file with the author).

[1554] *Fifth Appraisal of the Trade Policy Review Mechanism 2013* (n 1469) 3; WTO, TPRB, Revised Secretariat Procedures for Distribution of the Record of the Meeting of the TPR Reviews, WT/TPR/INF/2, 8 February 2012.

[1555] The use of podcasts might reduce the translation costs of the minutes of the TPRB meetings which were estimated at about CHF 400.000.

[1556] *Fifth Appraisal of the Trade Policy Review Mechanism 2013* (n 1469).

[1557] WTO, TPRB, Draft Report of the Trade Policy Review Body for 2011, Trade Policy Review Mechanism, WT/TPR/W/43, 4 November 2011, 2.

[1558] WTO, TPRB, Report of the Trade Policy Review Body for 2012, Trade Policy Review Body, WT/TPR/306, 23 November 2012; WTO, TPRB, Report of the Trade Policy Review Body for 2013, Trade Policy Review Body, WT/TPR/321, 8 October 2013.

In the meantime, the added value of the Secretariat's reporting continued to be largely dependent on the Secretariat's independency and intrusiveness. Nevertheless, contrary to the previous period, the yearly reports of 2011, 2012, and 2013 no longer explicitly urge Members to cooperate with the Secretariat. However, the TPRB reports for 2011, 2012, 2013, and the appraisal itself continued to warn the Members and the Secretariat that '*close contact with the Member under review is necessary to help ensure the factual accuracy and clarity of the documentation prepared for the review*'.[1559]

iii) Discussants

In the period covered by the fifth appraisal (ie the period between the TPR of Saudi Arabia of 2012[1560] and the review of Costa Rica of 2013[1561]), all TPRs involved the participation of only a single discussant. In line with the periods covered by the third and fourth appraisals, a majority of discussants again originated in developing countries (twenty out of the thirty-two TPRs of this period).[1562] As a result, developing countries' perspectives were relatively better voiced.

Compared to the previous period, discussants relied even more on Secretariat's reporting but slightly less on available reporting by the governments under review. First, a majority of discussants participating in TPRs which took place in this period referred (directly or indirectly) to Secretariat's reporting (twenty-five out of the thirty-two discussants covering the thirty-two TPRs of this period or 78 per cent). Fewer than half of the discussants was interested in making any reference to governmental reporting (fourteen out of the thirty-two discussants or 43 per cent). This is not altogether unsurprising in view of the limited informational added value of government's reporting. Second, the Secretariat's reporting was rarely criticized in the period covered by the fifth appraisal. For instance, the Danish discussant in China's TPR of 2012 emphasized that he '*was struck by several instances in which the Secretariat concludes that it was not able to gather sufficient information to do its job properly, to describe clearly and fully all of the trade and trade-related measures that it encountered and the ways in which they are applied. It seems that some important policies, laws and regulations remain complex or not sufficiently transparent to the outside observer, that the implementation of laws in some cases is unclear, or that the local administration or imports or investments in some instances is cumbersome*'.[1563] Similarly, governmental reporting in the period was subject to criticism only in exceptional cases. For example, the discussant in Norway's TPR of 2012 highlighted

[1559] WTO, TPRB, Draft Report of the Trade Policy Review Body for 2011, Trade Policy Review Mechanism, WT/TPR/W/43, 4 November 2011, 1; WTO, TPRB, Report of the Trade Policy Review Body for 2012, Trade Policy Review Body, WT/TPR/306, 23 November 2012, 2; WTO, TPRB, Report of the Trade Policy Review Body for 2013, Trade Policy Review Body, WT/TPR/321, 8 October 2013, 2; *Fifth Appraisal of the Trade Policy Review Mechanism 2013* (n 1469) 3.

[1560] Trade Policy Review of Saudi Arabia of 25–27 January 2012, Minutes of the Meeting, WT/TPR/M/256, 6 March 2012.

[1561] Trade Policy Review of Costa Rica of 24–26 September 2013, Minutes of the Meeting, WT/TPR/M/286, 9 December 2012.

[1562] Data on file with the author.

[1563] Trade Policy Review of China of 12–14 June 2012, Minutes of the Meeting, WT/TPR/M/264, 17 July 2012, 10.

that he 'would be very happy to hear why Norway has opted to leaving out agriculture in its report for the TPR'.[1564] Nevertheless, discussants' trend towards more reliance on formal reporting of the TPRM, which had started during the period covered by the fourth appraisal, was bucked again by the their eagerness to quote other reference documents. In twenty-one out of the thirty-two TPRs of this period (ie in 65 per cent), discussants referred to external studies which shed some additional light on the trade policies and practices of the country under review.[1565] This is the highest number of references to external studies across all periods which had been covered by the five consecutive appraisals. In addition, some of the discussants even started to explore news ways of reviewing countries. For instance, the discussant in Japan's TPR of 2012 used some visual aids to support his statement.[1566] In a similar vein, the discussant in the TPR of Costa Rica of 2013 used about fourteen to fifteen slides drawn from external sources.[1567]

Although issues regarding dispute settlement had been emphasized in most of the previous TPRs of the United States, the US review of 2012 was mute in this regard.[1568] In general, during the period covered by the fifth appraisal, compliance and/or issues with regard to dispute settlement were not raised by the discussants.

[1564] Trade Policy Review of Norway of 9–11 October 2012, Minutes of the Meeting, WT/TPR/M/269, 19 November 2012.

[1565] Data on file with the author.

[1566] Trade Policy Review of Japan of 19–21 February 2013, Minutes of the Meeting, WT/TPR/M/276, 13 June 2013, 9–13.

[1567] Trade Policy Review of Costa Rica of 24–26 September 2013, Minutes of the Meeting, WT/TPR/M/286, 9 December 2013, 8.

[1568] Trade Policy Review of the United States of 18–20 December 2012, Minutes of the Meeting, WT/TPR/M/275, 30 April 2013.

III
Conclusions

> The surest way to corrupt a youth is to instruct him to hold in higher esteem those who think alike than those who think differently.
>
> Friedrich Nietzsche

This book has attempted to analyse *whether* and/or *to what degree* the widespread narrative according to which the TPRM has functioned well as the WTO's mechanism for peer review can be substantiated by the facts.

It has done so following a threefold approach. First, throughout its review of a series of generally recognized mechanisms for peer review in the respective frameworks of the IMF, the OECD, the FSB, the APRM, the UPR, and the respective structures for climate change mitigation as contained in the UNFCCC and its Kyoto Protocol, it has demonstrated that these mechanisms have certain elements in common (ie objectives, structure, and participation). The first part of Chapter II then showed that these features gradually appeared throughout the five defining institutional steps which preceded the TPRM's formal establishment as the WTO's mechanism for peer review (ie Article X of the GATT 1947; the Understanding regarding Notification, Consultation, Dispute Settlement and Surveillance (1979); the Leutwiler Report 'Trade policies for a better future: Proposals for Action' (1983–85); the Functioning of the GATT Negotiations (FOGS) (1986–88) and the Mid-Term Review (1989)).

The second part of Chapter II concluded this analysis and demonstrated that the WTO Membership and most external observers generally adhered to an overall positive assessment of the TPRM's performance as the WTO's mechanism for peer review. Throughout the consecutive appraisal processes, they agreed that the TPRM's objectives, structure, and participation have all performed relatively well. In terms of objectives, the WTO Membership and most external observers have agreed that transparency is the TPRM's exclusive or main goal and that this objective has been successfully pursued. With regard to the mechanism's structure, the WTO Membership has expressed appreciation for the TPRM's structure, repeatedly stating that '*the procedures for the TPRB reviews have run smoothly*'. In addition, compared to the important structural modifications to the nascent TPRM prior to its mid-term review, the mechanism's first five appraisals rarely resulted in substantial changes to the structure of TPRB meetings *senso strictu*.[1] Moreover, reporting requirements figure among the most important structural features of the TPRM. Since transparency is rightly considered to be the TPRM's primary objective, reporting requirements regulate transparencies' structure and scope directly, mainly through the form and content of the Secretariat and the government reports. This is generally thought to be very good news, both among the WTO Membership as well as in academic circles. Among the WTO Membership, the first five appraisals have resulted in few substantial changes to the TPRM's formal reporting requirements which, as a result, still date back to 1989 or to 1990 for LDCs). Within academic circles, the transparency value of several specific TPRs has been explicitly acknowledged. Finally, in terms of participation, the consecutive appraisals have resulted in a repeated general positive assessment with regard to the attendance and interactivity of the TPRs.

However, the second part of Chapter II has also demonstrated that this positive assessment should be qualified, both from a national angle as from an international perspective. First, an empirical and general in-depth analysis of the TPRs' impact on countries' respective policies has never been undertaken.[2] This gap is all the more surprising in view of the fact that the national and international impact of several other international mechanisms for peer review has been assiduously studied thereby sometimes leading to significant institutional modifications to the concerned mechanism(s) for peer review.[3] Second, even from an international perspective, the effectiveness of the individual building blocks (ie objectives, structure, and participation) of the TPRM as the WTO's mechanism for peer review has not always been guaranteed, as even some of the appraisals themselves seem to imply. These findings raise the question of how far the TPRM has really been able to perform successfully as the WTO's mechanism for peer review.

[1] Arguably, the most important modification to the TPRM's present structure—*senso lato*—would result from the fourth appraisal's modifications to the TPRM's written question and answer process.

[2] Arguably it would be difficult to prove the (exclusive positive) causal effect between the TPRs' conclusions and domestic policy changes empirically; Sam Laird, 'The WTO's Trade Policy Review Mechanism—From Through the Looking Glass' (1999) 22(6) The World Economy 761 (hereafter Laird, 'The WTO's Trade Policy Review Mechanism—From Through the Looking Glass'); Francois details the 'formalization of some (*hoped for*) effects of the TPRM' [emphasis added], cf Joseph F Francois, 'Trade Policy Transparency and Investor Confidence: Some Implications for an Effective Trade Policy Review Mechanism' (2001) 9(2) Review of International Economics 304–16; Zahrnt even states that 'TPRs are deemed to have *no discernible effect* on trade policies' [emphasis added], cf Valentin Zahrnt, 'The WTO's Trade Policy Review Mechanism: How to Create Political Will for Liberalization' (2009) 11 ECIPE Working Paper 2 <http://www.ecipe.org/app/uploads/2014/12/the-wto2019s-trade-policy-review-mechanism-how-to-create-political-will-for-liberalization-1.pdf> accessed 6 May 2017 (hereafter Zahrnt, 'The WTO's Trade Policy Review Mechanism: How to Create Political Will for Liberalization'); Moreover, some authors *completely doubt* the TPRM's added value for domestic transparency; cf Bill Carmichael, 'Trade Policy at the Cross-Roads' (2005) Australian National University, Pacific Economic Papers No. 351, 7 <https://crawford.anu.edu.au/pdf/pep/pep-351.pdf> accessed 17 June 2017; On the other hand, the yearly Overviews imply (or even state) that the TPRM's activities have an unquestionable positive effect on domestic economies.

[3] Answers from Frank Wolter (first director of the Trade Policy Review Division, 1989–91) to a questionnaire of the author (2 April 2014); For examples of studies of the national impact of other international mechanisms for peer review, see A Chayes and AH Chayes, *The New Sovereignty—Compliance With International Regulatory Agreements* (Harvard University Press 1995) 236–37.

A. Objectives

Although the majority of the first five appraisals of the TPRM spent some time analysing the TPRM's transparency objective and emphasizing that the TPRM was and is not about enforcement, these appraisals paid almost *no* attention to the analysis of the TPRM's other stated purpose.[4] This lacuna seems to arise mainly for three reasons: the undeniable institutional priority (as embodied in Annex 3 of the Marrakesh Agreement) of the TPRM's first objective—transparency—over its second goal of naming and shaming, the (still current) relative lack of lawyers at the Trade Policy Review Division, and the TPRM's mainly diplomatic working environment. Nevertheless, this gap in the institutional analysis of the WTO can be contrasted with available academic literature which has paid an initially isolated but gradually growing attention to the analysis of the TPRM's other stated purpose and even to its potential link to the DSB.[5] Nonetheless, as this book has demonstrated, this kind of academic output still remains relatively limited. Most early academic literature on the TPRM (ie literature dating back to the period covered by the first appraisal) was either concerned with analysing how the mechanism's transparency function as materialized through several specific TPRs had been implemented[6] or

[4] *Appraisal of the Operation of the Trade Policy Review Mechanism—Draft Report to Ministers* (30 September 1999) WT/TPR/W/24; *Appraisal of the Operation of the Trade Policy Review Mechanism, Ministerial Conference, Third Session, Seattle, 30 November—3 December 1999* (8 October 1999) WT/MIN(1999)/2; *Second Appraisal of the Operation of the Trade Policy Review Mechanism—Draft Report to Ministers* (12 August 2005) WT/TPR/W/33; *Second Appraisal of the Operation of the Trade Policy Review Mechanism—Report to Ministers* (21 September 2005) WT/MIN(05)/1; *Draft—Third Appraisal of the Operation of the Trade Policy Review Mechanism* (15 October 2008) WT/TPR/W/38; *Third Appraisal of the Operation of the Trade Policy Review Mechanism* (11 November 2008) WT/TPR/229; *Fourth Appraisal of the Operation of the Trade Policy Review Mechanism* (17 November 2011) WT/TPR/W/44; *Fourth Appraisal of the Trade Policy Review Mechanism, Ministerial Conference, Eighth Session, Geneva, 15–17 December 2011* (29 November 2011) WT/MIN(11)/6; *Fifth Appraisal of the Trade Policy Review Mechanism, Ministerial Conference, Ninth Session, Bali, 3–6 December 2013* (28 October 2013) WT/MIN(13)/5.

[5] Especially, Asif H Qureshi, 'The New GATT Trade Policy Review Mechanism: An Exercise in Transparency or "Enforcement"' (1990) June, Journal of World Trade 149–60 (hereafter Qureshi, 'The New GATT Trade Policy Review Mechanism: An Exercise in Transparency or "Enforcement"'); Asif H Quereshi, 'Some Reflections on the GATT TPRM, in the Light of the Trade Policy Review of the European Communities—A Legal Perspective' (1992) 26(6) Journal of World Trade, 103–20; Asif H Qureshi, 'Some Lessons From "Developing Countries" Trade Policy Reviews in the GATT Framework: An Enforcement Perspective' (1995) 18(3) The World Economy, 489–503; Julien Chaisse and Debashis Chakraborty, 'Implementing WTO Rules Through Negotiations and Sanctions: The Role of Trade Policy Review Mechanism and Dispute Settlement System' (2007) 28(1) Pennsylvania Journal of International Economic Law, 153–86 (hereafter Chaisse and Chakraborty, 'Implementing WTO Rules Through Negotiations and Sanctions: The Role of Trade Policy Review Mechanism and Dispute Settlement System'); Marc D. Froese, 'Trade Policy Review and Dispute Settlement at the WTO', in David A Deese (ed), *Handbook of the International Political Economy of Trade* (Edward Elgar Publishing 2012) 349–97 (hereafter Froese, 'Trade Policy Review and Dispute Settlement at the WTO').

[6] Anne O Krueger, 'US Trade Policy and the GATT Review' [1995] The World Economy: Global Trade Policy 65; VN Balasubramanyam, 'India's Trade Policy Review' [1995] The World Economy: Global Trade Policy 79; Kym Anderson, 'The GATT's Review of Australian Trade Policy' [1995] The World Economy: Global Trade Policy 91; Sübidey Togan, 'Trade Policy Review of the Republic of Turkey' [1995] The World Economy: Global Trade Policy 107; Merle Holden, 'GATT Trade Policy Review—South Africa: 1993' [1995] The World Economy: Global Trade Policy 121; Timothy J Kehoe, 'A Review of Mexico's Trade Policy from 1982 to 1994' [1995] The World Economy: Global Trade Policy 135; Mathias

provided a more general evaluation of the TPRM's transparency objective.[7] This was not all together unsurprising since the TPRM's transparency objective is clearly enunciated in Annex 3 to the Marrakesh Agreement. Subsequent academic analysis (ie output which originated in the period covered by the second appraisal) started

Kende, 'Monetary Affairs in the WTO Trade Policy Review Mechanism' in Thomas Cottier, Rosa M Lastra, Christian Tietje, and Lucia Satragno (eds), *The Rule of Law in Monetary Affairs* (Cambridge University Press 2014) 384; Ronald J Wonnacott, 'Canadian Trade Policy: The GATT's 1995 Review' [1996] The World Economy: Global Trade Policy 67; Jacques Pelkmans and Antonia Giulia Carzaniga, 'The Trade Policy Review of the European Union' [1996] The World Economy: Global Trade Policy 81; George Fane, 'The Trade Policy Review of Indonesia' [1996] The World Economy: Global Trade Policy 101; Mordechai E Kreinin, 'Israel's Trade Policy Review' [1996] The World Economy: Global Trade Policy 119; Robert M Stern, 'The Trade Policy Review of Japan' [1996] The World Economy: Global Trade Policy 133; Jan Willemn Gunning, 'The Trade Policy Review of Zimbabwe' [1996] The World Economy: Global Trade Policy 157; Renato G Flores, 'Brazilian Trade Policy and the WTO' [1997] The World Economy: Global Trade Policy 615; AG (Sandy) Cuthbertson, 'The Trade Policy Review of Sri Lanka' [1997] The World Economy: Global Trade Policy 633; Paul Collier, 'The Trade Policy Review of Uganda' [1997] The World Economy: Global Trade Policy 649; Heinz Hauser and Robert Straw, 'Swiss Trade Policy and the 1996 WTO Review' [1997] The World Economy: Global Trade Policy 665; Robert M Stern, 'The WTO Trade Policy Review of the United States' [1998] The World Economy: Global Trade Policy 483; Sarath Rajapatirana, 'Columbian Trade Policies and the 1996 WTO Trade Policy Review' [1998] The World Economy: Global Trade Policy 515; Martin Richardson, 'New Zealand Trade Policy and the 1996 WTO Review' [1998] The World Economy: Global Trade Policy 529; Arvind Panagariya, 'The WTO Trade Policy Review of India, 1998' [1999] The World Economy: Global Trade Policy 799; PKM Tharakan, 'Beyond Transparency: An Analysis of the Trade Policy Review of the European Union' [1999] The World Economy: Global Trade Policy 825; Julio Berlinski, 'The WTO Trade Policy Review of Argentina' [2000] The World Economy: Global Trade Policy 1195; Peter G Warr, 'Thailand's Post-crisis Trade Policies, The 1999 WTO Review' [2000] The World Economy: Global Trade Policy 1215; Paul G Hare, 'Trade Policy Review of Poland, 2000' [2001] The World Economy: Global Trade Policy 1179; Kumar Ratnesh, *WTO (World Trade Organization): Structure, Functions, Tasks and Challenges* (New Delhi 2002); Prema-chandra Athukorala, 'Malaysian Trade Policy and the 2001 WTO Trade Policy Review' [2002] The World Economy: Global Trade Policy 1297; Francis Teal, 'Export Growth and Trade Policy in Ghana in the Twentieth Century' [2002] The World Economy: Global Trade Policy 1319; VN Balasubramanyam, 'India: Trade Policy Review' [2002], The World Economy: Global Trade Policy 1357; Joze P Damijan and Boris Majcen, 'Trade Policy in a Small Advanced Transition Economy: Trade Policy Review of Slovenia, 2002' [2002] The World Economy: Global Trade Policy 1369; Chris Milner, 'Trade Policy in Burundi: Reform Without Political Stability' [2004] The World Economy: Global Trade Policy 1363; Keith Head and John Ries, 'Regionalism Within Multilateralism: The WTO Trade Policy Review of Canada' [2004] The World Economy: Global Trade Policy 1377; Prema-chandra Athukorala, 'Trade Policy Making in a Small Island Economy: The WTO Review of the Maldives' [2004] The World Economy: Global Trade Policy 1401; Andrew McKay, 'Trade Policy Issues in a Small African Economy: The Trade Policy Review of The Gambia 2004' [2005] The World Economy: Global Trade Policy 1197; SM Thangavelu and Mun-Heng Toh, 'Bilateral WTO-Plus Free Trade Agreements: The WTO Trade Policy Review of Singapore 2004' [2005] The World Economy: Global Trade Policy 1211; Sübidey Togan, 'Turkey: Trade Policy Review' [2005] The World Economy: Global Trade Policy 1229; Thomas J Prusa, '2004 Trade Policy Review—The United States' [2005] The World Economy: Global Trade Policy 1263; PKM Tharakan, 'Storm Signals: An Analysis of the Trade Policy Review of the European Communities' [2006] The World Economy: Global Trade Policy 1301; Jong-Eun Lee, 'Identifying Trade Structure and Macroeconomic Caveats: The Post-crisis of Korea' [2006] The World Economy: Global Trade Policy 1311; Arne Melchior, 'The Most and Least Favoured Nations: Norway's Trade Policy in Perspective' [2006] The World Economy: Global Trade Policy 1329; Bala Ramasamy and Matthew Yeung, 'Malaysia—Trade Policy Review 2006' [2007] The World Economy: Global Trade Policy 1193; Rodney D Ludema, 'Allies and Friends: The Trade Policy Review of the United States, 2006' [2007] The World Economy: Global Trade Policy 1209; Michael Henry, 'Formulating Trade Policy in a Small Hydrocarbon-dependent Economy: The Case of Trinidad and Tobago' [2007] The World Economy: Global Trade Policy 1222.

[7] As the criticism of Abbot on the writings of Quereshi have demonstrated; Roderick Abbot, 'GATT and the Trade Policy Review Mechanism: Further Reflections on Earlier Reflections' (1993) 27(3) Journal of World Trade 117–19.

to undertake prudent attempts to map the TPRM's implementation of its secondary goal of naming and shaming. Although the TPRM's transparency function still kept its (rightly) primary importance in academic circles, a few academics of this period (predominantly with a background in political science) did not shy away from analysing the TPRM as a '*compliance mechanism*' or even as an '*extended wing of the DSB*'.[8] During the period covered by the third appraisal, academia went a step further and started to analyse the relationship between the TPRM and the DSB empirically. Nonetheless, most articles of this period were confronted with a prevailing lack of formal data and analysis to support their claims.[9] In the period covered by the fourth appraisal, academic findings became more straightforward. For the first time, these included rather critical views according to which (a) the TPRM's objectives did not fully work as they were supposed to (a view which was at loggerheads with the formal views of the WTO Membership as expressed during the appraisal process);[10] (b) the TPRM should be reformed in light of the increased risk of protectionism which resulted from the global financial and economic crisis (ie an acknowledgement that the wider review system did not fully work as it was supposed to);[11] and (c) that the TPRM had an untapped surveillance potential (ie a view that implicitly seemed to acknowledge the TPRM's added value in terms of naming and shaming).[12] Academic writing in the period covered by the fifth appraisal appeared to oscillate between two positions. Some academics seemed to be satisfied with the status quo. These authors either acknowledged that the relationship between the TPRM and the DSB remained 'delicate and complex'[13] or even speculated that the WTO's Membership would somehow not be interested in properly analysing/solving the problem.[14] Others proposed expanding the

[8] Thomas Conzelmann, 'Beyond the Carrot and the Stick—(How) Do State Reporting Procedures Matter?' (ECPR Uppsala Joint Sessions, 2004) 15–19 <https://ecpr.eu/Filestore/PaperProposal/8e9b4d5a-1ba2-4933-af69-c2c59f40f368.pdf> accessed 6 May 2017 (hereafter Conzelmann, 'Beyond the Carrot and the Stick—(How) Do State Reporting Procedures Matter?'); Some elements were subsequently revised in Thomas Conzelmann, 'Beyond the Carrot and the Stick: The Authority of Peer Reviews in the WTO and the OECD' (Paper presented at the ECPR Standing Group for International Relations, 2010) 11–17 (hereafter Conzelmann, 'Beyond the Carrot and the Stick: The Authority of Peer Reviews in the WTO and the OECD'); Kumar Ratnesh, *WTO (World Trade Organization): Structure, Functions, Tasks and Challenges* (New Delhi 2002) 42–72.

[9] Chaisse and Chakraborty, 'Implementing WTO Rules Through Negotiations and Sanctions: The Role of Trade Policy Review Mechanism and Dispute Settlement System' (n 5) 155, 170 and 172–75; Arunabha Ghosh, 'Developing Countries in the WTO Trade Policy Review Mechanism' (2010) 9(3) World Trade Review 419–55 (hereafter Ghosh, 'Developing Countries in the WTO Trade Policy Review Mechanism'), Ghosh based his findings on empirical evidence from all TPRs conducted between 1995 and 2007.

[10] Arunabha Ghosh, 'Strengthening WTO Surveillance: Making Transparency Work for Developing Countries', in Carolyn Deere Birbeck (ed), *Making Global Trade Governance Work for Development: Perspectives and Priorities from Developing Countries* (Cambridge University Press 2011) 400–3 (hereafter Ghosh, 'Strengthening WTO Surveillance: Making Transparency Work for Developing Countries').

[11] Zahrnt, 'The WTO's Trade Policy Review Mechanism: How to Create Political Will for Liberalization' (n 2).

[12] Conzelmann, 'Beyond the Carrot and the Stick: The Authority of Peer Reviews in the WTO and the OECD' (n 8) 13.

[13] Craig VanGrasstek, *The History and Future of the World Trade Organization* (WTO 2013) 288 (hereafter VanGrasstek, *The History and Future of the World Trade Organization*)

[14] Sam Laird and Raymundo Valdés, 'The Trade Policy Review Mechanism', in A Narlikar, M Daunton, and RM Stern (eds), *The Oxford Handbook on The World Trade Organization* (Oxford University Press 2012) 467.

institutional status and role of the TPRM in order to keep the mechanism relevant, either by further attempts to quantify the TPRM's simultaneous pursuit of its transparency and naming and shaming objectives[15] or by proposing new objectives for the TPRM.[16] Throughout these periods, the scope of the TPRM's objectives has always been questioned.

Moreover, academia was not alone. In spite of the Members' repeated emphasis on the TPRM's primary objective (ie increased transparency) within the framework of consecutive appraisals, the Membership itself seemed to entertain other thoughts when it came to litigation. Whatever the theoretical value attached to the mechanisms' primary goal of transparency, the legally conceived dichotomy between peer review and litigation—in principle guaranteed by Annex 3 to the Marrakesh Agreement and Appendix I to Annex II[17]—was never strictly adhered to by the Member states. Throughout the entire process of the five consecutive appraisals, Members have repeatedly attempted to invoke the findings of the TPRM within the context of the DSB. In a similar vein, they have not shied away from bringing DSB-related arguments to the framework of the TPRM. Arthur Dunkel's words, according to which the TPRM is a '*long-term enterprise*' in which '*transparency and legal assessment will become more indistinguishable with the latter eventually replacing the former*', seems thus to be vindicated, at least in part.[18]

The exclusive theoretical acknowledgement or practical pursuit of the TPRM's transparency objective *alone* runs the risk of rendering the mechanism increasingly irrelevant or even obsolete. As a start, the TPRM's secondary goal of naming and shaming should therefore be more widely acknowledged, studied, and applied. In analysing all TPRs conducted between 1995 and 2007, Ghosh came to the conclusion that the TPRM has 'a weak mandate'.[19] This book has demonstrated that this finding is equally valid for the interpretation and application of the mechanism's goals after 2007, and certainly for the whole period between 1989 and 2013. Moreover, any institutional tinkering with the mechanism's dual objectives should take into account that transparency is and will remain a *conditio sine qua non* to naming and shaming.[20] If there is an intentional or unintentional lack of transparency, it

[15] Froese, 'Trade Policy Review and Dispute Settlement at the WTO' (n 5) 349.

[16] Julien Chaisse and Mitsuo Matsuhita, 'Maintaining the WTO's Supremacy in the International Trade Order: A Proposal to Refine and Revise the Role of the Trade Policy Review Mechanism' (2013) 16(1) Journal of International Economic Law 9–36 (hereafter Chaisse and Matsushita, 'Maintaining the WTO's Supremacy in the International Trade Order: A Proposal to Refine and Revise the Role of the Trade Policy Review Mechanism'); The same idea has also been described in Mitsuo Matsushita, 'A View on Future Roles of the WTO: Should There be More Soft Law in The WTO' (2014) 17 Journal of International Economic Law 701–15 (hereafter Matsushita, 'A View on Future Roles of the WTO: Should There be More Soft Law in The WTO').

[17] Marrakesh Agreement Establishing the World Trade Organization (15 April 1994) <https://www.wto.org/english/docs_e/legal_e/legal_e.htm> accessed 20 May 2017 (hereafter Marrakesh Agreement Establishing the World Trade Organization).

[18] Petros Mavroidis, 'Surveillance Schemes: The GATT's New Trade Policy Review Mechanism' (1992) 13(2) Michigan Journal of International Law 413.

[19] Ghosh, 'Strengthening WTO Surveillance: Making Transparency Work for Developing Countries' (n 10) 398–403.

[20] Qureshi, 'The New GATT Trade Policy Review Mechanism: An Exercise in Transparency or "Enforcement"' (n 5) 149–60.

will be difficult to pursue naming and shaming effectively. On the other hand, if too much emphasis is put on the goal of naming and shaming, participants may be less inclined to volunteer for full transparency.

This situation has not changed in the lead-up to the last (sixth) appraisal of the TPRM whose results precede the Eleventh WTO Ministerial (December 2017). The yearly reports of the TPRB for 2015 and 2016 still do not delve into an analysis of the TPRM's implementation of its second objective of naming and shaming, nor do they provide any comments thereof,[21] neither did the Members themselves seize the opportunity of the last appraisal process in order to table any proposal which focused on the TPRM's secondary objective. On the contrary, the background and objectives of several Japanese proposals were aimed at achieving a higher degree of transparency throughout the TPRM's functioning[22] or its appraisal.[23] In a similar vein, the objectives of a Swiss communication, a submission of the United States, and a communication from Australia tabled during the sixth appraisal process were all aimed mainly at the transparency aspect of the TPRM.[24] It is therefore not surprising that the results of the sixth appraisal still do not focus on the mechanism's pursuit of its *double* objectives.[25] In the author's views, this persistent lack of analysis of the TPRM's secondary goal of naming and shaming is regrettable. From a historical point of view, such a limited analysis not only runs counter some of the more recent academic perspectives but also offers limited added value from the perspective of several Members who seemed to have crossed the line between naming and shaming and formal litigation. Moreover, in view of the fact that the results of the sixth appraisal process of the TPRM will (probably) be one of the main or even the only substantial 'housekeeping' issue of the Eleventh Ministerial, it would be rather disappointing not to analyse the mechanism's pursuit of its secondary objective a little further. With regard to the future, this conclusion may even be more valid in view of the increasingly critical view of some of the founding GATT/WTO Members vis-à-vis the legitimacy of the WTO's dispute settlement system. The TPRM currently has untapped potential in terms of naming and shaming. It would be regrettable not to start using it or at least formally recognizing it, especially if the WTO's dispute settlement function comes under fire.

[21] Report of the Trade Policy Review Body for 2015, WT/TPR/361, 23 October 2015; Report of the Trade Policy Review Body for 2016, WT/TPR/387, 7 November 2016.

[22] Sixth Appraisal of the WTO Trade Policy Review Mechanism, Communication from Japan, RD/TPR/694, 7 October 2016; Sixth Appraisal of the WTO Trade Policy Review Mechanism, Communication from Japan, Revision, RD/TPR/694/Rev.1, 28 October 2016; Interview with EU experts, July 2017.

[23] Sixth Appraisal of the WTO Trade Policy Review Mechanism, Communication from Japan, RD/TPR/728, 24 November 2016; Interview with EU experts, July 2017.

[24] Sixth Appraisal of the WTO Trade Policy Review Mechanism, Communication from Switzerland, RD/TPR/695, 10 October 2016; Sixth Appraisal of the WTO Trade Policy Review Mechanism, Submission from the United States, RD/TPR/704, 20 October 2016; Sixth Appraisal of the WTO Trade Policy Review Mechanism, Communication from Australia, RD/TPR/705, 20 October 2016.

[25] *Sixth Appraisal of the Trade Policy Review Mechanism* (22 December 2016) WT/TPR/389 (hereafter *Sixth Appraisal of the Trade Policy Review Mechanism 2016*).

B. Structure

This book has demonstrated that some of the mechanism's structural elements, such as the periodicity requirements for individual TPRs, did not seem to function as initially conceived or that they could be improved, such the structural reporting requirements for individual TPRs or yearly Overviews and the structure of the review meetings. These elements should therefore be modified not only to increase transparency but also to pay an increased level of attention to the mechanism's currently underrated potential in terms of naming and shaming. In addition, the overview of structural elements which are typical for mechanisms of peer review lead to the conclusion that some of these elements, such as the investigative procedure(s) or the follow-up structure, had been relatively neglected during the institutional development of the TPRM into the WTO's mechanism for peer review. As a result, more political attention might be provided to the further development of these two structural features.

1. The first structural element: periodicity

The periodicity regulating structure of the TPRM is contained in Paragraph C (ii) and (iv) of Annex 3 to the Marrakesh Agreement. Although Members had consistently expressed satisfaction with the underlying principles and practical modalities of the TPRM's periodicity, this book has raised several questions.

First, the justification for an automatic periodicity is based on the assumption that this institutional characteristic would enhance the predictability of reviews and would simultaneously lower the organizational and political cost of negotiations which would otherwise be required on a yearly basis in order to identify the WTO Members which are to be reviewed. Nevertheless, as this book has demonstrated, the Secretariat often unintentionally overestimates and sometimes underestimates the number of reviews to be undertaken in the next year. Moreover, in almost each year of the TPRM's functioning, there have been subsequent modifications to the initial list of countries which had been selected for review. The reasons behind these modifications not only relate to normal changes in world trade (such as China's replacement of Canada as a Member of the Quad in the aftermath of China's WTO accession) but also to internal (technical, political, or socio-economic) problems[26] or to a procedurally enhanced flexibility (as a result of the 2005 rules of procedure). The system is therefore not ideal in terms of predictability or cost-effectiveness.

Second, the current periodicity cycles are based on the principle that the biggest traders (ie the Quad countries) are more prone to provoke or to be engaged in protectionism than their smaller counterparts and, hence, need to be subjected to surveillance on a more frequent basis. Nonetheless, this principle does not necessarily

[26] For instance, the cancellation of Sierra Leona's TPR of 2014 due to the Ebola outbreak; cf WTO, TPRB, Report of the Trade Policy Review Body for 2014, Trade Policy Review Mechanism, WT/TPR/340, 21 November 2014, 2.

correspond to economic reality. First, most big traders are anyhow under more public scrutiny and may therefore behave better, irrespective of the effectiveness of the TPRM. Second, the inversion of this principle, according to which smaller countries would be less prone to protectionism and should therefore be subject to a less intensive form of surveillance, may not live up to its premise. Instead, some countries which stand to be characterized by their (extremely) small share of world trade might be categorized as such precisely because of their pursuit of very protectionist trade instincts. In this regard, Cuba serves as an example.[27]

Third, the determination of the respective periodic cycle of a country hinges upon that country's representative share of world trade in finalized goods and services over a fixed reference period of three years. This determination is outdated and arbitrary. First, world trade is increasingly made up by intermediated products and by non-tangible commodities such as intellectual property. As the 2013 World Trade Report indicates, '*international supply chains play a major role in today's world economy: trade goods and services contain inputs that may come from many different countries, and traditional trade statistics misleadingly attribute the full transaction value of trade products to the last economy in the production process*'.[28] Moreover, intellectual property plays an increasingly important role in world trade and should be taken into account in the context of the determination of a country's representative share of world trade. Second, there is no economic basis for arguing that the three-year reference period which originated in the FOGS negotiations is fundamentally correct.[29]

Fourth, cycles of two and four years are difficult to service and to maintain in practical terms. These periodicity cycles are based (a) upon the yearly review of two Quad countries and (b) upon the yearly review of four countries of the group of sixteen countries which are on the four-year cycle.[30] As of 1998, Secretariat's annual reporting on the TPRM started to contain a categorization of the countries under review as ranked by their cyclical periodicity. Nevertheless, the availability of such a standardized overview has not altered the fact—as attested by this book's findings relating to the period covered by the fifth appraisal—that some of the ideal periodicity requirements (ie especially those for countries subject to the four-year cycle) are still hard to meet.

Fifth, the analysis of the first five appraisals led to the conclusion that the WTO Membership itself might be ready for an altered periodicity. All Quad countries have already complained about the two-year periodicity of their reviews (considered to be too intensive) and have also complained about the cycle's replacement by interim reviews (which then became as comprehensive in scope as the original

[27] Cuba's share of world trade is rather small as a result of several factors, including the (former) US trade embargo and its persistent economic structure as a non-market economy. In spite of its WTO accession in 1995, Cuba did so far not undergo a single TPR (although the country is a candidate for review in 2017); WTO, TPRB, Report of the Trade Policy Review Body for 2015, Trade Policy Review Mechanism, WT/TPR/W/89/Rev.1, 14 October 2015, 7.

[28] WTO, *Factors Shaping the Future of World Trade* (WTO 2013), 6.

[29] See '*The Functioning of the GATT System (FOGS) Negotiations (1986)*'.

[30] Laird, 'The WTO's Trade Policy Review Mechanism—From Through the Looking Glass' (n 2) 746.

two-yearly reviews).[31] Moreover, at the other end of the spectrum, LDC countries have similarly lamented that they did not have the technical means to prepare for TPRs properly. At the same time, the Secretariat's specific TPR reporting on Aid for Trade—which had been contained in LDC reviews and which was perceived to be useful precisely in order to remedy this situation—was interrupted in 2014.[32] Furthermore, some diplomats have complained that a periodicity which spans more than six years cannot be read as a guarantee for continuity of the reviews.[33]

One could therefore suggest that the TPRB either adopt a completely flexible periodicity (ie a cycle determined completely by ad hoc political decision-making) or at least adopt a mixed, flexible periodicity (ie a cycle combining automatic review with some political decision-making). In this context, the analysis of the periodicity structures of the APRM and the FSB could provide some inspiration.[34] A new periodicity model might be developed, based on: (1) an obligatory base review to be carried out within a predetermined period after the country's accession to the WTO (ie in line with the existing requirements of Annex 3 of the Marrakesh Agreement to guarantee that there are no (new) freeriders of the global trading system); (2) reviews that may be provoked by early signs of impending economic distress (ie to overcome the current hurdles of automatic periodicity which may result in a country which is in need of review being 'overlooked' by the current periodicity cycles);[35] and (3) a flexible selection, based on formal criteria, for the remaining countries which should be reviewed.[36] This kind of cyclical model would balance respect for equal treatment of all Members' sovereign equality with the need to focus on particular Members with protectionist trade instincts which may prompt an economic crisis for that particular country.[37]

The sixth TPRM appraisal's main suggestion to alter the existing periodicity cycles (of two, four, and six years) into review cycles of three, five, and seven years (starting in 2019) conforms to formal expectations but it is rather disappointing from a substantive perspective. Current periodicity cycles are supposed to result into twenty-four TPRs per year, taxing for both Members and the Secretariat, and this will supposedly increase to thirty TPRs a year as a result of new WTO accessions, themselves unsustainable in the long run if budgetary allowances are not increased.[38] Although the threshold argument for thirty TPRs a year is consistent and has been raised from the first appraisal, in the author's view the proposed modification is disappointing[39] as it will inevitably lead to less transparency since the periodicity of

[31] Interview with a diplomat of the Delegation of the European Union (Geneva, 27 January 2014); Interviews with diplomats of the respective Delegations of China, Japan and the United States (Geneva, July 2014).

[32] Trade Policy Review of Myanmar, Minutes of the Meeting, WT/TPR/M/293, 11–13 March 2014.

[33] Data of the author.

[34] See 'Mechanisms for peer review—theoretical core elements'.

[35] Arguably this second category would weaken the usefulness of the mechanism as a—continuous—vector for domestic policy reform. Nevertheless, it has been difficult to empirically prove the (exclusive) positive causal effect between TPRs' outcomes and domestic policy changes; see (n 2).

[36] In this regard, the periodicity cycles could be linked with the respective growth rates of the Members.

[37] Based on an analogy with the periodicity requirements of a hypothetical competition policy review mechanism, cfr Communication from the Working Group on the Interaction between Trade and Competition Policy, WT/WGTCP/W/243, 28 July 2003, 6 (hereafter WTO, Communication from the Working Group on the Interaction between Trade and Competition Policy (WT/WGTCP/W/243)).

[38] *Sixth Appraisal of the Trade Policy Review Mechanism 2016* (n 25) 2.

[39] Appraisal of the operation of the TPRM, Informal Meeting of 21 May 1999, Checklist of Main points, No. 3274, 3 June 1999, 3.

each of the three specific review cycles is extended. In addition, the altered periodicity does not provide adequate answers to the first three concerns mentioned earlier. As Table III.1 demonstrates, throughout the functioning of the Trade Policy Review, the number of TPRs effectively undertaken has often been lower than the number of those planned. The proposed changes in periodicity as a result of the sixth appraisal are a priori neutral in this regard. As a result, the predictability of the TPRM will probably not be affected.[40] Moreover, in terms of cost efficiency, the proposed changes might be inevitable in view of the limited available budgets, at least in the near future, but they offer no incentive to Members to change future funding for the TPRM. Furthermore, the sixth appraisal's changed periodicity is not based on a radically altered approach which would treat bigger and smaller traders on a more equal basis or which would more adequately reflect the ongoing changes to the structure of international trade.

Table III.1

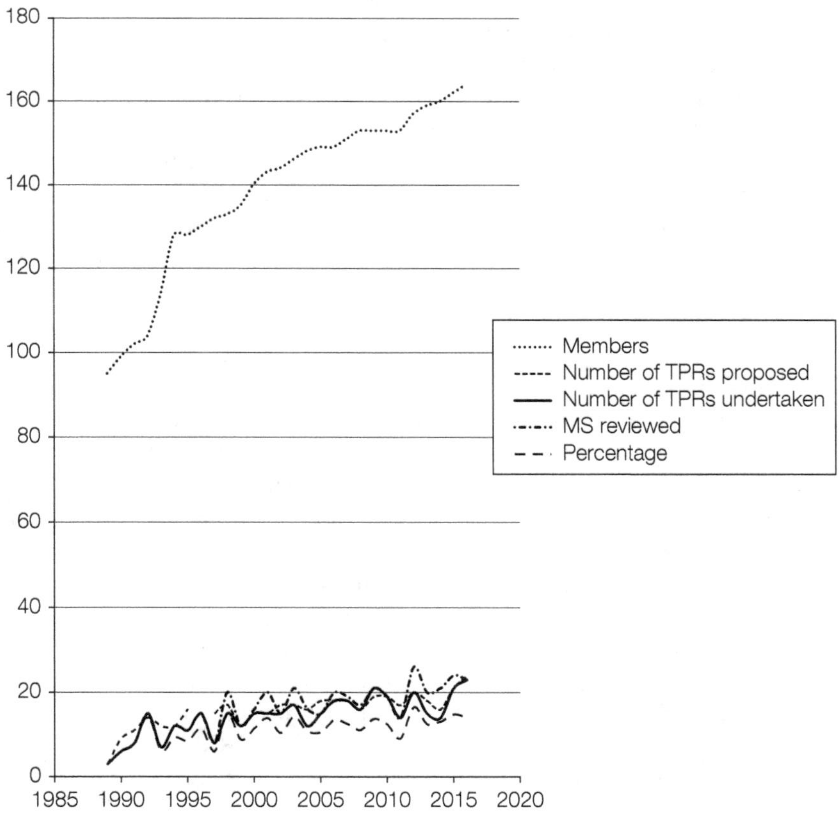

[40] The Sixth Appraisal itself notes that there had been eight cases of deviation from the review cycles (amongst which six deviations of one or two years whereas the remaining two cases had been outstanding for more than eight years because the Members concerned had not agreed to be reviewed); Sixth Appraisal of the Trade Policy Review Mechanism, Issues Discussed, RD/TPR/702, 14 October 2016.

2. Second structural element: investigative procedure(s)

The second structural element (ie the existence of an investigative procedure(s) in order to obtain the information needed for the peer review) has been relatively neglected throughout the institutional development and functioning of the TPRM as the WTO's mechanism for peer review. The TPRM's investigative procedures result mainly from guidance developed during the FOGS negotiations and in the course of some of the appraisals. Although the effectiveness, in terms of transparency and peer pressure, and the legitimacy of a mechanism for peer review directly depends on the quality of its investigative procedure(s), the complexity, specificity, and formality of the TPRM's investigative procedures pale in comparison with those that are applied in the respective frameworks of Article IV consultations of the IMF, peer reviews of the OECD's DAC, the APRM, and the FSB.

In this context, the latest TPRB reports for 2015 and 2016 only mention, repeatedly, that the review process, from the preparatory stage to the meeting, has run relatively smoothly. The Secretariat's reports continue to be prepared in close consultation with the authorities of the Member under review. Responses to requests for data, documentation, and information have generally been provided with the suggested deadlines. In preparing its reports, the Secretariat has continued its efforts to reduce the burden on Members under review by using, to the extent possible, other sources of documentation, including Members' official websites or other credible websites.[41] However, the TPRB report of 2015 stated that '*this has not always been possible for all Members under review, and requests for documentation continue to be followed up with a questionnaire when sufficient information is not available from alternative sources*'. The report also warned that '*the comments by the authorities on the draft reports and visits to capitals by teams from the Secretariat remain essential to the TPR process*'.[42] In a similar vein, the Report of the Trade Policy Review Body for 2016 emphasizes that responsiveness from Members remains essential.[43] The Secretariat's warning with regard to the trade monitoring exercise (as part of the sixth appraisal process) is even sterner: '*in preparing these reports, the Secretariat has to rely on Members to provide accurate information and verify all the measures recorded for their economies. The response rate, however, is often unsatisfactory.*'[44]

In short, the Members under review and the Secretariat have a shared responsibility for the provision of information in the context of the review processes under Annex 3 of the Marrakesh Agreement, with the country under review having a preponderant weight in this process. More political attention to the further elaboration and implementation of the TPRM's investigative procedures is therefore merited, not least in the aftermath of the sixth appraisal of the TPRM which remains neutral on the topic. In this regard, it might be interesting to sharpen the investigative

[41] Report of the Trade Policy Review Body for 2015, WT/TPR/361, 23 October 2015, 1; Report of the Trade Policy Review Body for 2016, WT/TPR/387, 1.

[42] Report of the Trade Policy Review Body for 2015, WT/TPR/361, 23 October 2015, 1.

[43] Report of the Trade Policy Review Body for 2016, WT/TPR/387, 1.

[44] Sixth Appraisal of the Trade Policy Review Mechanism, Issues Discussed, RD/TPR/702, 14 October 2016; *Sixth Appraisal of the Trade Policy Review Mechanism 2016* (n 25) 6.

procedures with further input from the relevant market participants, following the institutional example set by the FSB, and civil society, following the institutional example of the APRM.

3. Third structural element: reporting requirements, the structure of the review meeting, and a follow-up structure

a) *Reporting requirements*

The reporting requirements for individual TPRs and for yearly Overviews of developments in the International Trading Environment are contained in paragraph C(v) and (vi), paragraph D, and paragraph G of Annex 3 to the Marrakesh Agreement.

Members did not object to the continued application of the old formal reporting requirements for individual TPRs which, as a result, essentially still date back to 1989. Neither did the Membership formally amend these requirements in any substantial way. Likewise, the yearly Overviews have evolved in a rather arbitrary way, relatively free from any stringent requirements with regard to their structure and content of reporting. These features are therefore at loggerheads with some of the early academic policy suggestions for the creation of an effective GATT surveillance mechanism which had explicitly pleaded that the surveillance '*focuses on a more or less narrow and well defined policy area, and (that) those carrying out the surveillance have a relatively concrete mandate*'.[45] In general, these characteristics also seem to square uneasy with the principle of equality which would dictate that Members subject themselves to reviews on the understanding that their reviewing peers will later undergo a similar degree of enquiry and peer pressure. After all, peer review can only be effective if it is based on value sharing, an adequate level of commitment, mutual trust, and credibility.[46] However, in the words of the fourth appraisal, Members '*saw room for improvement in (Secretariat's reporting) in several respects, including in consistency across all Members (especially those in the same cycle) in terms of comprehensiveness, accuracy and detailed analysis*'.[47] Reporting requirements which are not very stringent for individual TPRs and which are completely absent from the framework of the yearly Overviews should therefore be adopted, strengthened, or standardized with a view to increase transparency (and comparability of reporting) and potential naming and shaming.

i) Current reporting requirements for individual TPRs

Several questions could be raised with regard to the current reporting requirements for individual TPRs: (a) governments have remained completely free to report as

[45] Richard Blackhurst, 'Strengthening GATT Surveillance of Trade-Related Policies' in Meinhard Hilf and Ernst-Ulrich Petersman (eds), *The New GATT Round of Multilateral Trade Negotiations: Legal and Economic Aspects* (Kluwer Law and Taxation Publishers 1988) 143 (hereafter Blackhurst, 'Strengthening GATT Surveillance of Trade-Related Policies').

[46] Fabrizio Pagani, 'Peer Review: A Tool for Co-operation and Change—An Analysis of an OECD Working Method' (OECD, 2002) 4–5.

[47] Fourth Appraisal of the Trade Policy Review Mechanism, Ministerial Conference, Eighth Session, Geneva, 15–17 December 2011, WT/MIN(11)/6, 29 November 2011, 5

they saw fit (leading to the fact that these reports have been informally described by certain diplomats as '*pure state propaganda*');[48] (b) the Secretariat continues to report subject to the initial reporting requirements of 1989 and 1990 in combination with a rather minimalistic degree of guidance as contained in the successive appraisals (Members thus did not seem interested either in increasing the Secretariat's role, as the fourth appraisal explicitly stated, nor in diminishing its capacity, as the rejection of the Chinese proposal with regard to the TPRM's potential in terms of special and differential treatment had demonstrated); whereas (c) the written questions and answers are subject to an even smaller degree of guidance (as contained in certain appraisals). Nevertheless, in spite of these relative shortcomings, individual TPRs' added value has been positively acclaimed, as attested to by the numerous academic writings to this effect.

This assessment is overrated insofar as it has been exclusively based on existing academic literature. Countries are subject to periodic review since their trade practices and policies continuously evolve. Nevertheless, most academic writings have assessed the overall value of the TPRM by analysing individual TPR reports which would at maximum lead to a snapshot assessment of a country's situation. Moreover, the TPRM's output is based upon four different building blocks (ie Secretariat's report, the government report, the minutes of the meeting, and the TPRM's written questions and answers) whereas academic output has almost always been limited to an analysis of the Secretariat's and sometimes governmental TPR reporting. As a result, it is relatively rare to find an analysis of the TPRs' minutes of the meeting and even exceptional to stumble upon an academic examination of the TPRs' question and answers. Furthermore, a couple of (rare) academic articles were relatively critical with regard to the specific informational added value of particular TPRs. Nevertheless, this kind of criticism was often loaded with '*personal, subjective or even idealized comments*' which did not always live up to scientific and factual counterarguments by the WTO Secretariat.[49]

Yet, the academics' positive assessment is underrated if the whole picture is duly taken into account—not only the TPRM's implementation of its primary objective of increased transparency but also its pursuit of its secondary goal of naming and shaming. This book has therefore attempted to apply a broader analysis of the TPRM's dual objectives to its structural functioning. In this regard, it has looked into the TPRM's reporting from a transparency angle and from the perspective of naming and shaming. Moreover, contrary to existing academic writing, this book paid specific attention to all the TPRM's four building blocks (ie the Secretariat report, the government report, the minutes of the meeting, and the written questions and answers). In doing so it has found that the TPRM's added value in terms of naming and shaming is positive but underrated. In addition, this book's analysis has, rather unsurprisingly, been able to confirm the TPRM's positive added value in providing an increased level of transparency.

[48] Data of the author.

[49] Laird, 'The WTO's Trade Policy Review Mechanism—From Through the Looking Glass' (n 2) 753.

For a majority of the analysed cases, the Secretariat was able, directly or indirectly, to sketch the contours of the situation which would lead to the future DSB dispute. Moreover, in almost all cases, the Secretariat continued to report on the issue which had led to the dispute after the parties to the dispute had initiated formal DSB consultations. On the other hand, the informational added value of governmental reporting remains extremely limited. For almost all analysed cases, governmental TPR reporting, both preceding and succeeding DSB consultations, offered no or limited new insights. The few governments which used their reporting to highlight a (potential) trade dispute seem to have done so either because the likelihood of formal initiation of a trade dispute seemed very high,[50] because the trade dispute was highly likely to be or had already been settled in their favour,[51] or because of the perceived political importance to underscore certain general values, which anyhow would result in a very limited informational added value.[52] Moreover, for a majority of analysed DSB cases, the future complainants effectively seized the opportunity of the TPR which preceded the request for formal DSB consultations to name and shame the future defendant within the context of the TPRB meeting into behaviour more consistent with WTO rules. It was exceptional, however, that future complainants in a DSB case seized the opportunity of a TPRB meeting to table a nascent trade concern in the absence of any reference to the future problem in the report of the Secretariat. In addition, there are several examples of discussants who did not shy away from tabling questions which border naming and shaming and the provision of a purely legal assessment.[53] The discussants' respective interventions in the TPR of the OECs (2001), in the review of Canada (2003), and in the TPR of Chile (2009) are emblematic in this regard. In the first review, the discussant stated

[50] For the Australian Government's defence of its quarantine regime on salmon from Canada, see Trade Policy Review of Australia of 3–4 February 1994, Vol II, 38–46 (particularly 42 and 43) (Document on file with the author); Trade Policy Review of Australia of 30 June–2 July 1998, Government Report, WT/TPR/G/41, 11 June 1998, 13–14 and Trade Policy Review of Australia of 23–25 September 2002, Government Report, WT/TPR/G/104, 26 August 2002, 9–10; For the Australian Government's defence of its quarantine regime on Apples from New Zealand, see Trade Policy Review of Australia of 5–7 April 2011, Government Report, WT/TPR/G/244, 1 March 2011, 9–10 and Trade Policy Review of Australia of 21–23 April 2015, Government Report, WT/TPR/G/312, 3 March 2015, 12.

[51] Asbestos Trade Policy Review of the European Communities of 12–14 July 2000, Government Report, WT/TPR/G/72, 14 June 2000, 8 and Trade Policy Review of the European Communities of 24–26 July 2002, Government Report, WT/TPR/G/102, 26 June 2002, 129–45 (particularly at 135).

[52] For the EU's position on Hormones, see Trade Policy Review of the European Communities of 12–14 July 2000, Government Report, WT/TPR/G/72, 14 June 2000, 8; For the EU's position on GIs see Trade Policy Review of the European Communities of 24–26 July 2002, Government Report, WT/TPR/G/102, 26 June 2002, 13; Trade Policy Review of the European Communities of 25–27 October 2004, Government Report, WT/TPR/G/136, 1 October 2004, 12–15; Trade Policy Review of the European Union of 26–28 February 2007, Government Report, WT/TPR/G/177, 22 January 2007, 12–15 and particularly at 14; For the EU's position on biotech see, Trade Policy Review of the European Union of 26–28 February 2007, Government Report, WT/TPR/G/177, 22 January 2007, 15.

[53] Trade Policy Review of the European Communities of 15–16 April 1991, Minutes of the Meeting, C/RM/M/10, 2 July 1991, 11; Trade Policy Review of the United States of 11–12 November 1996, Minutes of the Meeting, WT/TPR/M/16, 30 January 1997, 11–12; Trade Policy Review of Australia of 30 June–2 July 1998, Minutes of the Meeting, WT/TPR/M/41, 26 October 1998, 12; Trade Policy Review of the United States of 12–14 July 1999, Minutes of the Meeting, WT/TPR/M/56, 11 August 1999, 10.

rather bluntly that*it would be interesting to know how the DSB would have ruled if the initiative of the OECD, and most of its Member states, had been brought before the WTO. It was true that the WTO had only existed since 1995, but nevertheless, one wondered why the States whose tax administrations felt that they had been injured had not brought their complaint before the WTO. Did they fear the independence of a panel ruling?*'[54] In the second TPR, the discussant was interested in the implementation of the WTO Panel's ruling with respect to stockpiling by generic manufacturers of patented medicines, resulting the passing of new regulations.[55] In the third review, the discussant was interested in DSB follow-up while commenting that*there is a system of price bands applied to imports of wheat, wheat flour and sugar, which vary with changes in international market prices. Reflecting high world prices, the system has resulted in applied tariffs below 6% for much of the review period. However, two Panels have found this system WTO inconsistent. A draft law was introduced in Congress in 2007, to bring the system into conformity with WTO rules by replacing the price band system for wheat and flour with compound tariffs. Could Chile explain the possible benefits arising from a change in this system*'.[56] These three discussants were therefore clearly inspired by, but also more intrepid than, the Communication from the Nordics who—as early as the FOGS negotiations—had declared that '*the surveillance mechanism should from a legal point of view be distinct from all existing legal GATT mechanisms, e.g. existing surveillance, dispute settlement procedures, notification requirements*' but which had simultaneously noted that '*if the review reveals anything which other Contracting Parties want to complain about, the normal consultation and Panel procedures could be followed*'.[57] Furthermore, this book's analysis has been able to demonstrate that written questions and answers that were tabled in TPRs which took place after the initiation of a DSB case were often characterized by their highly legalistic nature.[58]

With regard to individual TPRs, it is regrettable that the Secretariat's reporting no longer contains a section specifically dedicated to the analysis of trade disputes. The Secretariat's tabular referencing of trade disputes is only partially able to remedy this situation since it does not contain any analysis. Moreover, in view of the increase in trade-related developments in fields which are outside the TPRM's current thematic mandate or which are even (partly) foreign to the WTO's multilateral character, it might be useful to revert to the practice of the

[54] Trade Policy Review of the OECS of 5–7 June 2001, Minutes of the Meeting, WT/TPR/M/85, 15 August 2001, 23.

[55] Trade Policy Review of Canada of 12–14 March 2003, Minutes of the Meeting, WT/TPR/M/112, 12 May 2003, 9.

[56] Trade Policy Review of Chile of 7–9 October 2009, Minutes of the Meeting, WT/TPR/M/220, 17 December 2009, 8–9.

[57] Multilateral Trade Negotiations, The Uruguay Round, Negotiating Group on Functioning of the GATT System, Communication from the Nordic Countries, MTN.GNG/NG14/W/17, 28 January 1988, 2.

[58] Trade Policy Review of the European Communities of 25–27 October 2004, Questions and answers, WT/TPR/M/136/Add. 1, 18 January 2005, 116–31 (particularly at 125–26) and 131–78 (particularly at 164–69); Trade Policy Review of the European Union of 6–8 April 2009, Written questions and answers, WT/TPR/M/214/Add. 1, 2 July 2009, respectively at 287–88, 217–20, and 348.

first and second appraisal whereby some discussion on the question of the added value of reporting on traditional versus new topics took place. Furthermore, written questions and answers frequently suffer from a lack of standardization. Their added value—informational or in terms of naming and shaming—would be higher if formal guidance was greater than that currently contained in the consecutive appraisals, especially since these questions and answers often constitute a rich source of information for potential DSB litigation. This situation was acknowledged by the discussant in the Korea's TPR of 2000 who drew attention to the fact that '*protection afforded to the agricultural sector was high and has led Korea to two dispute settlement cases at the WTO. This situation explained the number of advance questions on several agricultural issues submitted to Korea by participants in its Trade Policy Review.*'[59]

The results of the sixth appraisal do not contain substantial surprises with regard to the reporting requirements for individual TPRs. The Secretariat keeps its nominal independence in terms of determining the breadth and depth of its reports whereas governmental sovereignty in terms of reporting remains equally unchallenged, although the appraisal explicitly mentions that some Members had explicitly identified government reports as a '*burden*' or had characterized them as providing '*limited added value*'.[60]

It is unfortunate that the European, Canadian, or Japanese proposals to render the Secretariat reports' coverage more interesting were unsuccessful.[61] It is also disappointing that none of the proposals specifically focuses on the development of precise reporting requirements with regard to the follow-up to be accorded to TPR reports. In this regard, the FSB and the APRM constitute useful examples. FSB reporting requirements foresee the elaboration of analytical sections which describe recent accomplishments and evaluate areas where progress is lagging as well as a concluding section with recommendations. Moreover, in the FSB context, these analytical sections are to distinguish, where appropriate, weak compliance or performance caused by capacity or legislative constraints from that caused by unwillingness or other factors.[62] In a similar vein, APRM reporting requirements provide that where problems are identified the APRM reports need to assess the political willingness for reform and financial requirements for its implementation.[63]

As a result of the activism of some of the Members,[64] the sixth appraisal uses some hortatory though non-binding language with regard to the coverage of LDC and

[59] Trade Policy Review of Korea of 26–28 September 2000, Minutes of the Meeting, WT/TPR/M/73, 31 October 2000, 6.

[60] *Sixth Appraisal of the Trade Policy Review Mechanism 2016* (n 25) 2.

[61] Sixth Appraisal of the Trade Policy Review Mechanism, RD/TPR/693, 7 October 2016; Sixth Appraisal of the Trade Policy Review Mechanism, RD/TPR/691/Rev.1, 5 October 2016; Sixth Appraisal of the WTO Trade Policy Review Mechanism, Communication from Japan, RD/TPR/694, 7 October 2016; Interview with EU experts, July 2017.

[62] See section 2 of Chapter II, 'Mechanisms for peer review—theoretical core elements'.

[63] See section 2 of Chapter II 'Mechanisms for peer review—theoretical core elements'.

[64] Sixth Appraisal of the Trade Policy Review Mechanism, Communication from Australia, RD/TPR/705, 20 October 2016.

Aid for Trade elements in Secretariat and governmental reports, which is undoubtedly a welcome step into the right direction.

ii) Current structure and reporting requirements of the consecutive yearly overviews

Several questions could be raised with regard to the current structure and reporting requirements of the consecutive yearly Overviews. An examination of the Overviews led to the conclusion that some of their features tend to function in a suboptimal way. First, not all yearly Overviews have contained specific sections dedicated to the TPRM's annual activities. This is at loggerheads with the need for the development of a standardized way of reporting. Second, some national trade practices and policies were singled out as examples. This raises the question as to which specific criteria should be observed to decide upon a higher (anecdotal or exemplary) level of transparency and naming and shaming. Finally, most overviews lacked a coherent and comprehensive coverage of trade measures which had been identified as harmful. In this regard, most yearly Overviews lacked reporting on the identified measures' consecutive coverage, first by the committee(s) concerned, potentially followed by the measure's coverage in the respective frameworks of the TPRM and where applicable also of the DSB.

In a similar vein, the informational value of Overviews of developments of the international trading environment would probably be greater if all Overviews systematically contained a separate section specifically dedicated to cover activities which had been undertaken in the framework of the TPRM's work. The fact that the yearly Overviews have started to pay renewed and increased attention to the TPRM's functioning in the aftermath of the global crisis can only underscore this recommendation.[65] Moreover, the Overviews additional added value in terms of naming and shaming might be increased if their sections also systematically cross-referred to respective coverage of measures—by the committee(s), by the TPRM, and, where possible, also by the DSB. The overviews of 2004, 2005, 2011, and 2013 are emblematic in this regard.[66] The overview of 2011 correctly reports that the '*TPRM is insulated from the judicial and rule-making functions of*

[65] WTO, TPRB, Overview of Developments in the International Trading Environment, Annual Report by the Director-General, WT/TPR/OV/12, 18 November 2009, pp A33–A36; WTO, TPRB, Overview of Developments in the International Trading Environment, Annual Report by the Director-General, WT/TPR/OV/13, 24 November 2010, 43–46; WTO, TPRB, Overview of Developments in the International Trading Environment, Annual Report by the Director-General, WT/TPR/OV/14, 21 November 2011, 35–39 and 58–62; WTO, TPRB, Overview of Developments in the International Trading Environment, Annual Report by the Director-General, WT/TPR/OV/15, 29 November 2012, 60–66; WTO, TPRB, Overview of Developments in the International Trading Environment, Annual Report by the Director-General, WT/TPR/OV/16, 31 January 2014, 45–53.

[66] WTO, TPRB, Overview of Developments in the International Trading Environment, Annual Report by the Director-General, WT/TPR/OV/9, 20 February 2004, 28–30; WTO, TPRB, Overview of Developments in the International Trading Environment, Annual Report by the Director-General, WT/TPR/OV/11, 6 February 2006, 39–41; WTO, TPRB, Overview of Developments in the International Trading Environment, Annual Report by the Director-General, WT/TPR/OV/14, 21 November 2011, 32–33 and 58; WTO, TPRB, Overview of Developments in the International Trading Environment, Annual Report by the Director-General, WT/TPR/OV/16, 31 January 2014, 31.

the WTO which enables it to focus more easily on policy transparency and analysis'. Nevertheless, the analysis of a trade concern—from its first analysis by an SPS, TBT, or other committee(s) through its consecutive assessment by the TPRM and its potential further follow-up by the DSB—would lead to more transparency and to greater naming and shaming. This understanding was implicitly contained in the Overview of 2013 which noted that '*since the last monitoring report, four new disputes involving measures which have been discussed as Specific Trade Concerns (STCs) in previous TBT committee meetings have been the subject of consultation requests*'. Likewise, the report of the Trade Policy Review Body for 2014 reflects the fact that the trade monitoring report of 2014 pays an increased attention to the objective of naming and shaming. In this regard, it states that '*the report also underscored the need for greater transparency regarding those measures, and highlighted some areas where the record of Members' compliance [emphasis added] with their WTO notification obligations could be improved*'.[67]

The results of the sixth appraisal of the TPRM seek to ensure consistency in the format and length of information provided by the Members in the framework of the Overviews by means of the potential development by the Secretariat of a standardized questionnaire. In view of the earlier remarks this proposal is very welcome. Further measures should equally be taken to ensure that such a standardized set of data by the Members flows into an equally standardized reporting format for the Overviews. Contrary to their predecessors, the yearly overviews for 2014, 2015, and 2016 all contain specific sections encompassing an overview of Trade Policy Reviews.[68] Nevertheless, although these sections have increased coverage with regard to the reviews undertaken in the respective periods, most of them still did not cover all TPRs undertaken, thus still providing a higher anecdotal or exemplary level of transparency and naming and shaming with regard to some of the reviews.[69] Likewise, the Overviews of 2014, 2015, and 2016 still lack standardized reporting on the identified measures' consecutive coverage, first by the committee(s) concerned, potentially followed by the measure's coverage in the respective frameworks of the TPRM and, where applicable, also of the DSB.

b) The structure for the review meetings of individual reviews

The structure for the meetings of individual reviews has been elaborated throughout the TPRM's successive rules of procedure, enacted in conformity with paragraph C

[67] Report of the Trade Policy Review Body for 2014, WT/TPR/340, 21 November 2014, 2.

[68] WTO, TPRB, Overview of Developments in the International Trading Environment, Annual Report by the Director-General, WT/TPR/OV/17, 24 November 2014, 2 and 70–79; WTO, TPRB, Overview of Developments in the International Trading Environment, Annual Report by the Director-General, WT/TPR/OV/18, 17 November 2015, 1 and 54–65; WTO, TPRB, Overview of Developments in the International Trading Environment, Annual Report by the Director-General, WT/TPR/OV/19, 21 November 2016, 1 and 64–78.

[69] The Overview of Developments in the International Trading Environment of 2015 covers eighteen out of the eighteen reviews undertaken. On the other hand, the Overviews of 2014 and 2016 still have a less comprehensive coverage.

(iii) of Annex 3 to the Marrakesh Agreement and often modified as a result of the ongoing appraisal process.

If reporting requirements are crucial for the pursuit of the TPRM's transparency objective, the structure of TPRB meetings is essential for the TPRM's implementation of its secondary goal of naming and shaming.

In this regard, the structure of TPRB meetings, *senso strictu*, has barely changed throughout the history of the consecutive appraisals. Contrary to the TPRM's first years of functioning in which several of the mechanism's institutional features were enacted and improved, the fourth and fifth appraisals of the TPRM have mainly lead to modifications to the mechanism's written question and answer process (ie preceding the meeting)[70] rather than to the structure of its review meetings itself, *senso strictu*. Moreover, even with regard to the TPRM's written question and answer process, some points may be raised. On the one hand, longer procedural time-frames would theoretically enable a better attendance of and participation in TPRB meetings. On the other, the modifications to the TPRM's written question and answer process have not yet resulted in a substantially increased level of attendance and participation by smaller Members, these being two of the main concerns expressed during the first, second, and third appraisals.

Second, even the full effects of the limited number of proposed structural modifications are not yet clear. After the first five appraisals of the TPRM, the proposal to hold one-day TPRB meetings had not been retained by a single Member whereas those proposals which could have effectively resulted in a substantially increased degree of attendance at and/or participation in TPRs (ie the proposals to hold TPRB meetings in the territory of Members under review or the suggestion to divide each TPRB meeting into formal and informal sessions) were rejected outright.[71]

Third, the consecutive appraisals' thinking vis-à-vis the structural position of the discussant(s)—a potential key element with regard to the level of interactivity of TPRB meetings—has been ambiguous. Members have specifically and repeatedly pleaded for a reinforced role of the discussants and, more generally, for more interactive meetings. However, the first appraisal witnessed a proposal to reduce the number of the discussants whereas the third appraisal abolished the communication of the discussant(s). Moreover, several of the proposals which had been tabled during the fourth appraisal specifically in order to reinforce the discussants' institutional standing failed to reach consensus while the proposal to enlarge the circle of discussants to include outsiders, potentially leading to more interactivity, has been repeatedly rejected.

The structure of review meetings should therefore be improved. Effectively structured TPR meetings result in an increased level of transparency and in an adequate

[70] Nevertheless, another structural element which is required for the preparation of review meetings—that is, a formal investigative procedure (ie the second structural element inherent in mechanisms for peer review)—continues to be (relatively) neglected in the absence of any formal and regularly updated TPRD guidelines to this regard; See section 2 of Chapter II, 'Mechanisms for peer review—theoretical core elements' and '*The Functioning of the GATT System (FOGS) Negotiations (1986)*'.

[71] Fourth Appraisal of the Trade Policy Review Mechanism, Summary of Main Issues discussed in First Informal Meeting, Rough Draft, 18 July 2011 (Document on file with the author).

degree of naming and shaming. In this regard, it is not sufficient to maintain the practice (introduced by the fourth appraisal and maintained under the fifth appraisal) simply to analyse progress and developments which resulted from structural modifications as introduced by the previous appraisal. Lessons learned and best practices noted are always important steps to increase the efficiency of meetings. It is therefore important, as this book has demonstrated, to keep tinkering, especially with those structural elements which had been gradually watered down, such as the discussants' overall institutional standing in the meetings or the discussants' ability to intervene,[72] or which had even been rejected, such as the proposal to divide the review meeting in formal and informal parts.

In this regard, the results of the sixth appraisal constitute another step in the right direction. Several proposals clearly aimed at increasing the level of transparency and naming and shaming of the review meeting. These include the extension of timelines for submitting questions and answers and the maintenance of the current and alternative timelines for questioning, further technical improvements to the question-and-answer process, and the possibility of including innovative elements to the programme for the reviews, albeit on a voluntary, informal basis. It is unfortunate that the institutional position and role of the discussant is still not upgraded as a result of the appraisal. In this regard, it is nevertheless a hopeful sign that the sixth appraisal at least specifically acknowledges that '*Members considered that, in some cases, having two discussants for a TPR could enrich the discussion*' or '*that they saw value in encouraging the discussants to share their views and questions with all Members in advance of TPR meetings*'.[73]

c) *Follow-up structure*

During the institutional development of the TPRM, the elaboration of a structure for a guaranteed follow-up was not sought.[74] The Contracting Parties to the GATT were simply not interested in developing another forum for legal enforcement. Moreover, contrary to the peer review mechanisms of the OECD's DAC, the FSB, and the UPR, the concluding remarks of the TPRM's Chairperson are not based on a requirement for formal unanimity or consensus. As a result, the political value of a TPR's recommendations is often diminished. In addition, the reviewed country's position with regard to its TPR's concluding remarks, recommendations and suggestions is a priori less clear. Furthermore, the only guarantee for further follow-up to the TPRM's recommendations is indirectly contained in the mechanism's periodicity structure. Nevertheless, this book has already concluded that this structure could do better. As a result, the TPRM's institutional capacity and guarantee for

[72] In the first years of the TPRM's functioning, discussants intervened repeatedly over the course of the review's meeting. Over time, this practice was watered down with the discussant now only intervening once during the first day of the review and once more during the review's final day.

[73] *Sixth Appraisal of the Trade Policy Review Mechanism 2016* (n 25) 4.

[74] See section 2 of Chapter II, 'Mechanisms for peer review—theoretical core elements'.

further follow-up to its recommendations pales in comparison to those of the FSB and the UPR.

Political attention to the establishment of a structure for reinforced and specific follow-up to the TPR's recommendations is therefore warranted, particularly in the aftermath of the adoption of the results of the sixth appraisal of the TPRM which remain almost non-committal on this topic (with the exception of the proposal to change the TPRs periodicity as well as with regard to the organization of follow-up seminars to TPRs on an ad hoc basis).

4. Fourth structural element: formal review of peer review

Although the first five appraisals have provided a positive picture of the TPRM, a substantial caveat applies. TPR appraisals are indeed based on a relatively unsophisticated and (so far) unaltered appraisal process. Although the TPRM's current appraisal structure is in line with the relatively simple appraisal processes of the FSB or the UPR,[75] it pales in comparison with the highly sophisticated review structures embodied by the IMF's Triennial Surveillance Reviews (TSRs).[76] These review structures are elaborate, not only with regard to the timing of the next review(s) but also with regard to the multitude of entities and experts which are to undertake or which will be implicated in the review process. In order to keep the TPRM as relevant for the WTO Membership as the Article IV consultations are for the Members of the IMF, the elaboration of a more ambitious appraisal structure is therefore highly welcome. Contrary to the TSRs, the TPRM's current appraisals are conducted primarily in retrospect, are based on a collection of the Membership's and the Secretariat's inside views, not the views of external experts who might provide a fresh point of view, as is the case for TSRs, and rarely adjust the review structure on the basis of previous experience. Moreover, the proposals of the Members which feed into the appraisal process remain restricted for some time before they are made public. As a result, it is not surprising that the traditional output of the TPRM's appraisal structure tends to be overly positive and is shielded from public criticism in the period when it is most relevant. This can be underscored by academic writing which cynically emphasized, as early as 2009, that '*the self-assessments of the Trade Policy Review Body offer much praise and no evidence, while the academic literature is largely descriptive and out-dated*'.[77]

This situation has not changed in the aftermath of the sixth appraisal of the TPRM. In this regard, the last appraisal applies the same standard language in terms of agenda setting and scope for the seventh appraisal. The only new element simply verbally reinforces the next appraisal's usual focus on the TPRM's transparency aspect.[78]

[75] See section 2 of Chapter II, 'Mechanisms for peer review—theoretical core elements'.

[76] See section 2 of Chapter II, 'Mechanisms for peer review—theoretical core elements'.

[77] Zahrnt, 'The WTO's Trade Policy Review Mechanism: How to Create Political Will for Liberalization' (n 2) 2.

[78] Sixth Appraisal of the Trade Policy Review Mechanism, Communication from Japan, RD/TPR/728, 24 November 2016; Sixth Appraisal of the Trade Policy Review Mechanism, Issues Discussed,

C. Participation

The effectiveness of a mechanism for peer review stands or falls with its attendance and participation rates. Peer reviews which are well-attended and interactive automatically yield a greater transparency and a higher level of peer pressure on the country under review. In order to increase these and to keep the mechanism politically relevant, the review process could be made more trenchant. In this regard, more leeway might be provided for some of the actual participants in the review. In addition, the additional participation of business, social partners, and civil society (in the widest sense of the word) might be considered.

1. Governmental representation

In the early days of the WTO, the TPRB had noted in its report to the Singapore Ministerial (1996) that the level of governmental representation had not always been matched by its participation, either in terms of numbers or level.[79] This is still very much the case. TPRs of Quad countries initially obtained the best attendance rates. This seemed to alter gradually in the periods covered by the fourth and fifth appraisal (ie the period between October 2008 and November 2011 and the period between November 2011 and October 2013), with the best attendance rates now going to the BRICs including India (2011), Brazil (2009 and 2013), and China (2010 and 2012). Reviews with the worst attendance rates were common amongst LDCs and developing countries but also included the reviews of some developed Members (including the review of Iceland (1994)). Moreover, Quad countries have permanently figured among the most active participants in the TPRM. Unsurprisingly, the most active non-Quad participants can be found amongst countries on the four-year cycle (Australia and Canada) and the BRICs (especially Brazil and India). Nevertheless, this book has also demonstrated that some countries such as Colombia, Hong Kong, and New Zealand punch well above their weight in terms of participation. Most of these are economies with a vested interest in open trade. Low participation rates were well-represented amongst LDCs and developing countries but are also characteristic for some of their developed counterparts (such as Iceland and Israel). This book has shown furthermore that Members' attendance levels have neither decreased nor substantially increased. While Ghosh's findings according to which '*much of the WTO Membership does not participate in review meetings*' are undoubtedly still true, this book's assessment is more optimistic.[80] The TPRM's initial years

Marked-up version, Revision, RD/TPR/703/Rev.3, 2 December 2016 (hereafter Sixth Appraisal of the Trade Policy Review Mechanism, Issues Discussed, Marked-up version, Revision 3); *Sixth Appraisal of the Trade Policy Review Mechanism 2016* (n 25) 7.

[79] WTO, TPRB, Trade Policy Review Mechanism, Report to the Singapore Ministerial Conference, WT/TPR/27, 28 October 1996.

[80] Ghosh, 'Developing Countries in the WTO Trade Policy Review Mechanism' (n 9) 442–45 and 450.

of functioning (ie 1990 to 1993) saw a marked increase in relative and absolute attendance levels to TPRs. After a substantial dip in 1995, yearly attendance levels tended to stagnate, initially between 10 per cent and 13.5 per cent (1996 to 2001), then between 11.3 per cent and 15.7 per cent (2002 to 2009). Between 2010 and 2012, yearly attendance rates increased again to 17.3 per cent which is not far below the historic maximum attendance level of 17.7 per cent (1993). In spite of an increasing choice and variety of often more important parallel meetings at the WTO and elsewhere, Members thus seemed to have voted 'with their feet' for '*the continuation of a relative participatory success of the TPRM. Nevertheless, in the period covered by the first five appraisals, attendance and participation levels between developed and developing countries have continued to differ widely.*'

Governmental naming and shaming of reviewed peers might be improved by analysing the review process as an exercise in group psychology with the intention of maximizing peer pressure on the government under review. Whether this succeeds will depend upon influence and persuasion entailing quantitative aspects, including the size of the group, and certain qualitative features, including the level of expertise present in the group and the potential prevalence of the negative glasshouse effect whereby peers' restraint from naming and shaming originates in their fear for retribution at a later stage.[81]

This leads to the question of whether the mixed pursuit of the TPRM's dual objectives would not be more successfully pursued by smaller country groupings which would, in addition, be limited to a more homogenous group of peers. Such a setting would be similar to the IMF's Executive Boards' discussions within the framework of its Article IV consultations. In this context, full transparency is temporarily sacrificed on the altar of efficiency and potentially more direct naming and shaming. The distribution of Article IV reports at a later stage remedies this temporary lack of full transparency. In a similar way, the example of the peer review process of the OECD's DAC demonstrates that a greater homogeneity amongst peers is conducive to a higher level of transparency and to more intrusive naming and shaming.[82] Some countries and regions (such as South America) already have a tendency for higher attendance and participation rates in reviews of countries that are more or less homogeneous or with whom trading partners have closer (regional) ties.[83] As a result, the argument for reviews based on smaller country groupings limited to a more homogenous group of peers may possibly be easier to accept in practice.

Nevertheless, whether governments will attend and participate in TPRs ultimately depends on two factors: their financial and technical capacity to do so and their willingness to invest money and time. Whereas the former mainly depends upon their own available budget and/or available support, the latter may be increased by further tinkering with the TPRM's institutional parameters in order to provide more added value in terms of transparency and naming and shaming. In this regard, it is to be

[81] WTO, Communication from the Working Group on the Interaction between Trade and Competition Policy (WT/WGTCP/W/243) (n 37) 13.

[82] Conzelmann, 'Beyond the Carrot and the Stick: The Authority of Peer Reviews in the WTO and the OECD' (n 8) 22.

[83] WTO, TPRB, Trade Policy Review Mechanism, Report to the Singapore Ministerial Conference, WT/TPR/27, 28 October 1996.

welcomed that Members continued to use the sixth appraisal in order to discuss how the problem of unsatisfactory attendance and participation should be addressed, at least with regard to day two of the TPRM.[84] However, this discussion was inconclusive.

2. The Secretariat

The Secretariat's overall participation in the TPRM is based on several factors: its staffing and budget but also upon its internal interaction with other WTO divisions and its exchange(s) with the Member(s) under review, mainly through the elaboration of the Secretariat's report.

In terms of staffing, although the TPRD's personnel has increased over the years, its total staffing levels have remained relatively stable in absolute terms while never amounting to more than 8 per cent of overall WTO Staff. This is a positive result, especially in comparison to the human resources in other comparably important WTO entities (such as the DSB). However, the situation is bleaker with regard to the TPRD's budget, which has remained under constant pressure. In addition, the TPRD's budgetary transparency is somewhat questionable.

First, in spite of the continued growth of the WTO Membership (from 97 Members in 1997 to 149 in 2005), there was no corresponding increase in the initially foreseen expenditure for the TPRD (amounting to 2.394.000 CHF in 1997 and 4.196.400 CHF in 2004–5). Moreover, the generous amount of extra-budgetary funding which had been available for the TPRD's activities (particularly present in most years between 1999 and 2005 and in 2008–9) has dwindled in the aftermath of the global financial crisis. In the meantime, the WTO Membership continued to grow while TPR reporting has become more complex and voluminous.

Second, the TPRD's budgetary transparency can be called into question. It is impossible to trace the TPRD's exact level of real expenditure in a linear way between 1989 and 2013. These formal data were indeed only available for a handful of years (1989 to 1992, 1994, and 2001 to 2002). The situation is even worse with regard to the TPRD's appropriated level of expenditure. In this context, data are only available for a couple of years (1989 and 2001 to 2002). Several factors have aggravated this lack of budgetary transparency with regard to the TPRD. These elements include the existence of extra-budgetary funding for the TPRM's activities—often available on a multi-year basis (between 1999 and 2001, in 2004–5, and between 2008 and 2010),[85] a changing budgetary structure for the regular budget (as of 2004–5), and a change in the software which is used for WTO budgetary purposes.[86]

[84] Sixth Appraisal of the Trade Policy Review Mechanism, Issues Discussed, Marked-up version, Revision 3 (n 78); *Sixth Appraisal of the Trade Policy Review Mechanism 2016* (n 25) 4.

[85] Extra budgetary funding contained in Trust Funds is subject to specific budgetary rules. The regular budget functions upon an annual basis. Therefore, unspent allocations go to the budgetary surplus. On the other hand, Trust Funds often function on a multi-year budget with the possibility of budgetary transfers. The proposal, contained in the WTO budget estimates for 2012–13, to shift the DDA Global Trust Fund's current funding of mission travel related to TPRs that fall within the mandate of the regular work of the WTO Secretariat to the regular WTO budget was therefore a (first) step in the right direction.

[86] These difficulties have repeatedly been acknowledged by the Budgetary Department of the WTO, Answers from the Budgetary Department of the WTO to questions of the author (23 July 2015 and 24 January 2016).

With regard to the internal and external interactions of the Secretariat, this book has demonstrated that the Secretariat's initial liberty and intrusiveness has gradually diminished. Not only through a growing number of internal checks and balances on the Secretariat's increasing interactions with other WTO divisions and departments but also through the Secretariat's pursuit of a more deferential style of TPR reporting vis-à-vis the WTO Membership.

In the aftermath of the global financial crisis and in the context of the ongoing relative normative stalemate of the WTO,[87] Members' available WTO budget will probably not increase for the foreseeable future. Moreover, the TPRD's specific budgetary transparency is still not great. As a consequence, prime political emphasis might not immediately be put on an increased budget or staffing level for the TPRD but rather on further clarification of the budgetary rules and transparency with regard to the TPRD's functioning.

In this regard, it should be emphasized that throughout the period 2015–16, the Trade Policy Review Division still remained one of the largest WTO Divisions (with 51.9 experts in 2015 and 2016).[88] Moreover, the TPRD's budgetary transparency and specificity improved substantially as a result of the 2016–17 budget proposals (which specifically highlighted that the Monitoring of Trade Policies would cost 26.000 CHF in the budgets of 2016 and 2017). Nevertheless, the level of the TPRD's budgetary transparency and specificity still remains far below that of the DSB.[89]

3. Discussants

Discussants' actual contribution to interactive TPR debates has gradually withered. From a quantitative point of view, the number of discussants that are due to take part in each review has halved over time. From a qualitative point, the discussant was asked to provide some advance warning of the main points he intended to raise. In addition, it was requested that the discussant's statement not exceed in length that by the Member under review. Moreover, most remaining discussants originated in a developing country which carried the risk of steadily undermining the originally conceived balance between the provision of developed and developing country views. Furthermore, and with the exception of the period just after the formal establishment of the WTO and the period which was covered by the third appraisal, discussants have increasingly referred to the Secretariat's reporting to ask questions and

[87] Chaisse and Matsushita, 'Maintaining the WTO's Supremacy in the International Trade Order: A Proposal to Refine and Revise the Role of the Trade Policy Review Mechanism' (n 16) 10; Simon J Evenett and Alejandro Jara, 'Building on Bali—A Work Programme for the WTO' (Centre for Economic Policy Research, A VoxEU.org eBook, 2013) vii and 37; <http://voxeu.org/content/building-bali-work-programme-wto> accessed 25 May 2017; Matsushita, 'A View on Future Roles of the WTO: Should there be More Soft Law in the WTO' (n 16) 701.

[88] 2014–2015 Budget Proposals, WT/BFA/W/309, 2 October 2013, 36; 2016–2017 Budget Proposals by the Director-General, WT/BFA/W/374, 5 October 2015, 42; Mid-Term Review, Biennium 2016–2017, WT/BFA/W/402, 21 October 2016, 26.

[89] 2016–2017 Budget Proposals by the Director-General, WT/BFA/W/374, 5 October 2015, 36 and 37.

provide comments. Nevertheless, this increased reliance on available analysis by the Secretariat seems to be somewhat counterbalanced by a steadily increasing trend of references to external studies and by a permanent distrust of governmental reporting (discussants' referencing of governmental reporting has always remained below 50 per cent in all periods which were covered by the first five appraisals). In addition, proposals to offer discussant(s) stronger clout, including the possibility of assigning the discussant's role to a well-known trade policy academic (if only occasionally), have repeatedly been rejected.[90]

Although the WTO Membership has persistently claimed that it wanted to make reviews as interactive as possible, it paid lip-service only to the possibility of actually achieving this goal by simply reinforcing the discussants' institutional status. The practice of IMF Executive Board discussions within the context of Article IV consultations has demonstrated that the appointment of reviewers is no *conditio sine qua non* for a frank process as long as the participation to the discussion is limited.[91] Moreover, in more open settings, the examples of the peer review mechanisms of the OECD's DAC (where two examiners act), the FSB (where a team leader intervenes, assisted as needs be by other Members), and the UPR (where Troikas facilitate the discussion) seem to suggest that a minimum of two discussants or examiners is the minimum to guarantee an interactive and balanced discussion. However, at present, TPRs are not organized in a limited setting (enabling a franker discussion; all WTO delegations can participate), nor are they characterized by a multitude of discussants (possibly resulting in a more interactive and balanced discussion). The participation of a single discussant is therefore no guarantee for the quality, interactivity, and balance of the discussion.

Nevertheless, amongst the WTO Membership itself, there seems to be some informal consensus on what it takes to be a 'good discussant'.[92] According to this perspective, a good discussant is a discussant (a) who knows the trade policies and practices of the country under review; (b) who manages to create some discussion during the debate; and (c) who is at the same time well-aware of the typical procedural and diplomatic characteristics of the TPRM. Since most discussants have at least read the reports of the Secretariat and the government under review, the first condition is generally met. The second condition is relatively easy to fulfil, either by contrasting the respective reports, by highlighting (perceived or real) errors, or by elaborating upon external studies which had not been included in the respective reports. In this regard, this book has demonstrated that very few discussants have actually applied all three techniques simultaneously. Respect for the second condition could therefore be ascertained by the elaboration of some binding code of conduct. In a similar vein, respect for the third condition (ie awareness of the institutional and diplomatic

[90] Academia has an enormous and still relatively untapped added value in the diplomatic trade community; Thomas Cottier, 'Preparing for Structural Reform in the WTO' (2007) 10(3) Journal of International Economic Law 504.

[91] See section 2 of Chapter II, 'Mechanisms for peer review—theoretical core elements'.

[92] Interview with a diplomat of the Delegation of the European Union (Geneva, 27 January 2014); Interviews with diplomats of the respective Delegations of China, Japan, and the United States (Geneva, July 2014).

TPRM environment) could easily be guaranteed by the formal establishment of a formal roster of discussants, similar to that of DSB panellists, with proven knowledge of the procedural and diplomatic intricacies of the TPRM. Moreover, such a proposal would find (historic) inspiration in the FOGS Communication of the Nordics which had elaborated the concept of the examiners.[93]

Nevertheless, in this context, the results of the sixth appraisal are rather disappointing. Although the appraisal states that Members considered that, in some cases (such as group reviews), having two discussants for a TPR could enrich the discussion, the appraisal does not recommend any changes to the status quo.[94] More ambitious proposals, such as that of the European Union, had unfortunately been discarded.[95]

4. Towards the inclusion of business, social partners, and civil society?

Certain intergovernmental organizations (including the IMF, the OECD, and UNCTAD) are already entitled to participate in TPRB meetings as observers.[96] However, in order to foster an increased level of transparency and a more intrusive degree of naming and shaming, the TPRB should consider opening itself up to business, social partners, and civil society.

This could be done at the preparation stage (finding inspiration in the UPRs practice whereby the Office of the High Commissioner for Human Rights compiles a summary of other stakeholder information), during the TPR itself (in this context, the non-exhaustive and periodically reviewed participation list for FSB reviews could serve as an example), or in the aftermath of the review (by means of increased outreach during the follow-up seminars).[97]

Such an inclusion may assuage some country's civil society's current fears and criticisms with regard to free trade and increase the legitimacy of global trade policy. At the same time, it may allay business concerns according to which the TPRM is still too focused on the multilateral rulebook (thereby omitting to pay enough attention to an ever-increasing series of new FTAs and FTA-related developments). Moreover, this proposal would not only be in line with some earlier academic recommendations (some even TPRB-specific)[98] and a similar trend in the context of

[93] Multilateral Trade Negotiations, The Uruguay Round, Negotiating Group on Functioning of the GATT System, Communication from the Nordic Countries, MTN.GNG/NG14/W/17, 28 January 1988, 2.

[94] Sixth Appraisal of the Trade Policy Review Mechanism, Issues Discussed, Marked-up version, Revision 3 (n 78); *Sixth Appraisal of the Trade Policy Review Mechanism 2016* (n 25) 4.

[95] Sixth Appraisal of the Trade Policy Review Mechanism, Issues Discussed, RD/TPR/702, 14 October 2016.

[96] Laird, 'The WTO's Trade Policy Review Mechanism—From Through the Looking Glass' (n 2) 750.

[97] See section 2 of Chapter II, 'Mechanisms for peer review—theoretical core elements'; Sixth Appraisal of the Trade Policy Review Mechanism, RD/TPR/693, 7 October 2016.

[98] Schafer Armin, 'A New Form of Governance? Comparing the Open Method of Coordination to Multilateral Surveillance by the IMF and the OECD' (2006) 13(1) Journal of European Public Policy 70–88; Zahrnt, 'The WTO's Trade Policy Review Mechanism: How to Create Political Will for Liberalization' (n 2) 3.

the Dispute Settlement Body[99] but also with the more general policy recommendations of the Oxford Martin Commission for Future Generations (which included former WTO Director-General Lamy) to open up politics and '*optimize new forms of political participation, transparency and accountability, whilst amplifying the voices of global citizens*'.[100]

[99] For an analogy with the hypothetical competition peer review mechanism, see WTO, Communication from the Working Group on the Interaction between Trade and Competition Policy (WT/WGTCP/W/243) (n 37) 9; Thomas Cottier, 'The Common Law of International Trade and the Future of the World Trade Organization' (2015) 18 Journal of International Economic Law 4.

[100] University of Oxford, *The Report of the Oxford Martin Commission for Future Generations* (Oxford Martin School, October 2013), 59.

Postscript

This analysis led to the conclusion that the TPRM *should* and *could* do better. This is not to underestimate or to diminish the TPRM's current value but rather to ensure that the mechanism will remain politically relevant in the future.

If the course of current trade developments is not radically altered, the TPRM should keep doing better with less. In organizational terms, its relatively constant staffing levels and possibly diminishing budget will necessarily need to match the requirements and needs of a growing WTO Membership. In terms of substance, the TPRM will need to prove that it still has the analytical and political firepower to remain the WTO's transparency forum par excellence. It will therefore increasingly need to show (a) that it will not gradually be overshadowed by more recent WTO fora for transparency (such as the transparency mechanism for special and differential treatment or the transparency mechanism for regional trade agreements)[1] and (b) that the mechanism will maintain its relevance as the WTO's foremost trade transparency forum in a world which is increasingly dominated by trade-related developments in fields beyond the TPRM's traditional thematic mandate (such as labour, environment, regulatory compatibility, or e-commerce),[2] or in areas which are increasingly foreign to the WTO's multilateral character, such as the rapidly growing body of regional Free Trade Agreements.[3]

[1] WTO, Transparency Mechanism for Regional Trade Agreements, Decision of 14 December 2006, WT/L/671; 18 December 2016; WTO, Monitoring Mechanism on Special and Differential Treatment, Ministerial Decision of 7 December 2013, Ministerial Conference, Ninth Session, Bali, 3–6 December 2013, WT/MIN(13)/45, WT/L/920, 11 December 2013.

[2] Nonetheless, the OECD has made the proposal that TPRs should examine compliance with fundamental labour standards in certain exporting industries or free trade zones, also involving the International Labour Organisation (ILO) in drawing up the relevant passages in the Secretariat Report, cf Organisation for Economic Co-operation and Development, *Trade, Employment and Labour Standards, A Study of Core Workers' Rights and International Trade* (OECD, 9 September 1996); In a similar vein, the European Commission has supported the (voluntary) inclusion of labour rights in the TPRM and itself includes labour rights in its own report, see Thomas Greven, 'Social Standards in Bilateral and Regional Trade and Investment Agreements—Instruments, Enforcement and Policy Options for Trade Unions' (Friedrich Ebert Stiftung, No 16, March 2005) 42; Adriano Opromolla, 'Enhancing Labour Rights in a Globalised World: A Comparative Transatlantic Perspective' (CRIDHO Working Paper, No 4, 2007) 3 and 25; For a similar suggestion that the TPRM would henceforth analyse the environmental impact of trade agreements within individual countries, see Tilman Santarius, Holger Dalkmann, Makrus Steigenberger, and Karin Vogelpohl, 'Balancing Trade and Environment—An Ecological Reform of the WTO as a Challenge in Sustainable Global Governance' (Wuppertal Institute for Climate, Environment and Energy, 2004), 1 and 50; Chaisse and Matsushita, 'Maintaining the WTO's Supremacy in the International Trade Order: A Proposal to Refine and Revise the Role of the Trade Policy Review Mechanism' (n 16) 31–33; World Economic Forum, *Mega-Regional Trade Agreements—Game Changers or Costly Distractions for the World Trading System* <http://www3.weforum.org/docs/GAC/2014/WEF_GAC_TradeFDI_MegaRegionalTradeAgreements_Report_2014.pdf> accessed 25 May 2017 (hereafter World Economic Forum, *Mega-Regional Trade Agreements—Game Changers or Costly Distractions for the World Trading System*).

[3] World Economic Forum, *Mega-Regional Trade Agreements—Game Changers or Costly Distractions for the World Trading System* (n 102).

Without more intrusive institutional modifications to the TPRM (and, according to the author, the results of the sixth appraisal can only offer temporary relief), its future looks less than assured. This book has therefore offered some avenues for further potential improvement. Nevertheless, as a first step to potential change, the WTO Membership itself needs to be fully aware and appraised of the mechanism's current challenges. This book, written by a professional diplomat who participated in two formal appraisals rich in diplomatic courtesy and in four years of WTO/TPRB meetings often littered with platitudes, has attempted to do just this. It ends with a passionate plea for more study of the TPRM.

Bibliography

A. WTO-RELATED SOURCES

1. Primary sources

a) Legal texts

Marrakesh Agreement Establishing the World Trade Organization (15 April 1994) <https://www.wto.org/english/docs_e/legal_e/legal_e.htm> accessed 20 May 2017

b) TPRM-related documents

i) Foundational and budgetary documentation

Trends in International Trade: Contracting Parties to the General Agreement on Tariffs and Trade, a report by a panel of experts (Geneva, 1958) 138 pp

Statement by the representative of Canada on 28 June 1977—Notification, Consultation, Surveillance and Dispute Settlement, Multilateral Trade Negotiations, Group 'Safeguards', MTN/SG/W/36, 6 June 1977, 4 pp

Outline Regarding Institutions, Consultations, Dispute Settlement and Surveillance in Code for Preventing Technical Barriers to Trade, Multilateral Trade Negotiations, Group 'Non-Tariff Measures', Sub-Group 'Technical Barriers to Trade', MTN/NTN/W/144, 13 March 1978, 2 pp

The Tokyo Round, Statement by GATT Director-General and Publication of Agreements, Press Release, GATT/1234, 12 April 1979, 28 pp

GATT Annual Sessions Acts on Tokyo Round Results and Sets Future Work Programme, Press Release of 30 November 1979, GATT/1253, 30 November 1979, 9 pp

Understanding Regarding Notification, Consultation, Dispute Settlement and Surveillance (28 November 1979) BISD L/4907, 10 pp

Summary Record of Fourth Meeting, Held in the Palais des Nations, Geneva on Wednesday, 28 November 1979, Contracting Parties, Thirty-Fifth Session, SR. 35/4, 18 December 1979, 62 pp

Notification and Surveillance, Proposal by the Director-General (26 March 1980) BISD C/111, 20 pp

Ministerial Declaration (1982) BISD L/5424, 16 pp

Trade Policies for a Better Future, Proposals for Action, Geneva (Geneva: GATT, 1985) 60 pp

Draft Ministerial Declaration on the Uruguay Round (20 September 1986) BISD Min (86)/W/19, 20 pp

GATT Information, The Uruguay Round—Decisions of 28 January 1987, GATT/1405, 5 February 1987, 26 pp

Multilateral Trade Negotiations, The Uruguay Round, Negotiating Group on Functioning of the GATT System, Communication from Australia, MTN.GNG/NG14/W/1, 3 April 1987, 6 pp

Multilateral Trade Negotiations, The Uruguay Round, Negotiating Group on Functioning of the GATT System, Meeting of 7 April 1987, Note by the Secretariat, MTN.GNG/NG14/1, 10 April 1987, 4 pp

Multilateral Trade Negotiations, The Uruguay Round, Negotiating Group on Functioning of the GATT System, Existing Surveillance Functions in the GATT, Note by the Secretariat, MTN/GNG/NG14/W/3, 9 June 1987, 5 pp

Multilateral Trade Negotiations, The Uruguay Round, Negotiating Group on Functioning of the GATT System, Communication from Switzerland, MTN.GNG/NG14/W/7, 18 June 1987, 2 pp

Multilateral Trade Negotiations, the Uruguay Round, Negotiating Group on Functioning of the GATT System, Communication from Japan, MTN.GNG/NG14/W/8, 23 June 1987, 3 pp

Multilateral Trade Negotiations, The Uruguay Round, Negotiating Group on Functioning of the GATT System, Communication from the United States, MTN.GNG/NG14/W/9, 23 June 1987, 5 pp

Multilateral Trade Negotiations, The Uruguay Round, Negotiating Group on Functioning of the GATT System, Note by the Secretariat, MTN.GNG/NG14/2, 26 June 1987, 4 pp

Multilateral Trade Negotiations, The Uruguay Round, Negotiating Group on Functioning of the GATT System, Communication from Canada, MTN.GNG/NG14/W/10, 2 July 1987, 4 pp

Multilateral Trade Negotiations, The Uruguay Round, Negotiating Group on Functioning of the GATT System, Communication from Jamaica, MTN.GNG/NG14/W/11, 8 July 1987, 3 pp

Multilateral Trade Negotiations, The Uruguay Round, Negotiating Group on Functioning of the GATT System, The 1954/55 Review Session, Note by the Secretariat, MTN.GNG/NG14/W/12, 14 August 1987, 4 pp

Multilateral Trade Negotiations, The Uruguay Round, Negotiating Group on Functioning of the GATT System, Communication by New Zealand, MTN.GNG/NG14/W/13, 25 September 1987, 4 pp

Multilateral Trade Negotiations, the Uruguay Round, Negotiating Group on Functioning of the GATT System, Meeting of 28 September 1987, Note by the Secretariat, MTN.GNG/NG14/3, 8 October 1987, 3 pp

Multilateral Trade Negotiations, the Uruguay Round, Negotiating Group on Functioning of the GATT System, Summary of points made in the Group concerning 'Surveillance', Note by the Secretariat, MTN.GNG/NG14/W/14, 21 October 1987, 6 pp

Multilateral Trade Negotiations, The Uruguay Round, Negotiating Group on Functioning of the GATT System, Meeting of 3 and 4 November 1987, Note by the Secretariat, MTN.GNG/NG14/4, 30 November 1987, 8 pp

Multilateral Trade Negotiations, The Uruguay Round, Negotiating Group on Functioning of the GATT System, Communication from the Nordic Countries, MTN.GNG/NG14/W/17, 28 January 1988, 6 pp

Multilateral Trade Negotiations, The Uruguay Round, Negotiating Group on Functioning of the GATT System, Meeting of 25–28 January 1988, Note by the Secretariat, MTN.GNG/NG14/5, 16 February 1988, 6 pp

Multilateral Trade Negotiations, The Uruguay Round, Negotiating Group on Functioning of the GATT System, Multilateral Surveillance Activities in Other International Organizations, Note by the Secretariat, MTN.GNG/NG14/W/19, 18 March 1988, 9 pp

Multilateral Trade Negotiations, The Uruguay Round, Negotiating Group on Functioning of the GATT System, Communication from the European Community, MTN.GNG/NG14/W/20, 22 March 1988, 9 pp

Multilateral Trade Negotiations, The Uruguay Round, Negotiating Group on Functioning of the GATT System, Meeting of 21–23 March 1988, Note by the Secretariat, MTN. GNG/NG14/6, 15 April 1988, 8 pp

Multilateral Trade Negotiations, The Uruguay Round, Negotiating Group on Functioning of the GATT System, Communication from Jamaica, MTN.GNG/NG14/W/22, 16 May 1988, 5 pp

Multilateral Trade Negotiations, The Uruguay Round, Negotiating Group on Functioning of the GATT System, Meeting of 2–3 May 1988, Note by the Secretariat, MTN.GNG/NG14/7, 26 May 1988, 16 pp

Multilateral Trade Negotiations, The Uruguay Round, Negotiating Group on Functioning of the GATT System, Communication from the Delegation of India, MTN.GNG/NG14/W/23, 22 June 1988, 4 pp

Multilateral Trade Negotiations, The Uruguay Round, Negotiating Group on Functioning of the GATT System, Meeting of 20 and 22 June 1988, Note by the Secretariat, MTN. GNG/NG14/8, 13 July 1988, 16 pp

Multilateral Trade Negotiations, The Uruguay Round, Negotiating Group on Functioning of the GATT System, Proposal by the Nordic Countries, MTN.GNG/NG14/W/25, 11 August 1988, 2 pp

Budget Estimates for The Financial Year 1989 (13 September 1988) BISD L/6390, 58 pp

Report of the Committee on Budget, Finance and Administration (7 October 1988) BISD L/6408, 30 pp

Multilateral Trade Negotiations, The Uruguay Round, Negotiating Group on Functioning of the GATT System, Meeting of 26–30 September 1988, Note by the Secretariat, MTN. GNG/NG14/9, 18 October 1988, 12 pp

Multilateral Trade Negotiations, The Uruguay Round, Negotiating Group on Functioning of the GATT System, Communication from a number of Contracting Parties, MTN. GNG/NG14/W/30, 24 October 1988, 11 pp

Multilateral Trade Negotiations, The Uruguay Round, Negotiating Group on Functioning of the GATT System, Meeting of 24–28 October 1988, Note by the Secretariat, MTN. GNG/NG14/10, 14 November 1988, 7 pp

Multilateral Trade Negotiations, The Uruguay Round, Report to the Trade Negotiations Committee meeting at Ministerial level, Montreal, December 1988, Group of Negotiations on Goods, MTN.GNG/13, 22 November 1988, 77 pp

Reports finalized for Montreal TNC Meeting, News of the Uruguay Round of Multilateral Trade Negotiations, News of the Uruguay Round of Multilateral Trade Negotiations, NUR 022, 30 November 1988, 2 pp

Multilateral Trade Negotiations, The Uruguay Round, Trade Negotiations Committee Meeting at Ministerial level, Montreal, December 1988, MTN.TNC/7(Min) 9 December 1988, 43 pp

Montreal Meeting of the Trade Negotiations Committee, News of the Uruguay Round of Multilateral Trade Negotiations, NUR 023, 14 December 1988, 43 pp

Consultations continue in Geneva in effort to free Montreal Package, News of the Uruguay Round of Multilateral Trade Negotiations, NUR 024, 23 February 1989, 3 pp

GATT/AIR/2746, 31 March 1989, 1 p

General Agreement on Tariffs and Trade, 12 April 1989 Council, Matters Arising from the December 1988 and April 1989 Meetings of the Trade Negotiations Committee, Communication from the Council Chairman, C/W/585, 31 March 1989, 13 pp

Multilateral Trade Negotiations, The Uruguay Round, Trade Negotiations Committee Meeting at level of High Officials, Geneva, 5–8 April 1989, MTN.TNC/9, 11 April 1989, 10 pp

Decisions of 12 April 1989 (13 April 1989) BISD L/6490, 5 pp

GATT, Budget Estimate for the Trade Policy Review Mechanism, Note by the Secretariat, Spec(89)20, 21 April 1989, 8 pp

Multilateral Trade Negotiations, The Uruguay Round, Mid-Term Meeting, MTN.TNC/11, 21 April 1989, 41 pp

Mid-term Review Agreements, News of the Uruguay Round of Multilateral Trade Negotiations, NUR 027, 24 April 1989, 42 pp

Multilateral Trade Negotiations, The Uruguay Round, Negotiating Group on Functioning of the GATT System, Communication from Canada, MTN.GNG/NG14/W/33, 24 April 1989, 4 pp

General Agreement on Tariffs and Trade, Council, Minutes of Meeting, Held in Centre William Rappard on 12 April 1989, C/M/231, 2 May 1989, 19 pp

Multilateral Trade Negotiations, The Uruguay Round, Negotiating Group on Functioning of the GATT System, Meeting of 1 and 3 May 1989, Note by the Secretariat, MTN. GNG/NG14/11, 23 May 1989, 4 pp

Multilateral Trade Negotiations, The Uruguay Round, Negotiating Group on Functioning of the GATT System, Meeting of 19–20 June 1989, Note by the Secretariat, MTN.GNG/NG14/12, 30 June 1989, 9 pp

Budget Estimates for The Financial Year 1990 (22 August 1989) BISD L/6550, 73 pp

Multilateral Trade Negotiations, The Uruguay Round, Negotiating Group on Functioning of the GATT System, Meeting of 6 and 9 November 1989, Note by the Secretariat, MTN. GNG/NG14/13, 12 December 1989, 33 pp

Multilateral Trade Negotiations, The Uruguay Round, Negotiating Group on the Functioning of the GATT System, Meeting of 15 December 1989, Note by the Secretariat, MTN. GNG/NG14/14, 12 February 1990, 12 pp

Multilateral Trade Negotiations, The Uruguay Round, Negotiating Group Functioning of the GATT System, Communication from the European Community, MTN.GNG/NG14/W/40, 13 March 1990, 8 pp

Administrative and Financial Questions, Final Position of the 1989 Budget of the GATT (26 April 1990) BISD L/6668, 12 pp

Multilateral Trade Negotiations, The Uruguay Round, Negotiating Group on the Functioning of the GATT System, Meeting of 2 April 1990, Note by the Secretariat, MTN.GNG/NG14/16, 9 May 1990, 16 pp

Multilateral Trade Negotiations, The Uruguay Round, Negotiating Group Functioning of the GATT System, Communication from Switzerland, MTN.GNG/NG14/W/41, 17 May 1990, 9 pp

Multilateral Trade Negotiations, The Uruguay Round, Negotiating Group Functioning of the GATT System, Meeting of 22–23 May 1990, Note by the Secretariat, MTN.GNG/NG14/17, 19 June 1990, 11 pp

Multilateral Trade Negotiations, The Uruguay Round, Negotiating Group Functioning of the GATT System, Meeting of 25–26 June 1990, Note by the Secretariat, MTN.GNG/NG14/18, 9 July 1990, 16 pp

Draft Final Act Embodying the Results of the Uruguay Round of Multilateral Trade Negotiations, Revision, MTN.TNC/W/35/Rev.1, 3 December 1990, 392 pp

Budget Estimates for the Financial Year 1991 (4 June 1991) BISD L/6850, 74 pp

Budget Estimates for the Financial Year 1992 (30 September 1991) BISD L/6900, 71 pp

Draft Final Act Embodying the Results of the Uruguay Round of Multilateral Trade Negotiations, MTN.TNC/W/FA, 20 December 1991, 442 pp
Administrative and Financial Questions, Final Position of the 1991 Budget (15 September 1992) BISD L/7077, 11 pp
Budget Estimates for the Financial Year 1993 (18 September 1992) BISD L/7070, 70 pp
Administrative and Financial Questions, Final Position of the 1992 Budget (14 July 1993) BISD L/7258, 12 pp
Budget Estimates for the Financial Year 1994 (24 September 1993) BISD L/7300, 70 pp
Trade Policy Review Mechanism—Arrangements for the continued operation of the Mechanism, Decision of 10 May 1994 (11 May 1994) BISD L/7458, 2 pp
Administrative and Financial Questions, Final Position of the 1993 Budget (18 May 1994) BISD L/7456, 13 pp
Administrative and Financial Questions, Final Position on the 1994 Budget (13 April 1995) BISD L/7627, 12 pp
WTO, Budget Estimates 1996, WT/BFA/10 and L/7640, 14 September 1995, 85 pp
WTO, Budget Estimates 1997, Proposals by the Director-General, WT/BFA/27, 9 September 1996, 92 pp
WTO, Budget Estimates 1998, Proposals by the Director-General, WT/BFA/W/20, 5 September 1997, 100 pp
WTO, Budget Estimates 1999, Proposals by the Director-General, WT/BFA/W/27, 4 September 1998, 108 pp
WTO, Budget Estimates 2000, Proposals by the Director-General, WT/BFA/SPEC/37, 6 September 1999, 115 pp
WTO, Budget Estimates 2001, Proposals by the Director-General, WT/BFA/SPEC/49, 11 September 2000, 157 pp
WTO, Report on Extra-Budgetary Funds for 1999, WT/BFA/W/44, 5 October 2000, 109 pp
WTO, Report on Extra-Budgetary Funds for 2000, WT/BFA/W/59, 11 July 2001, 126 pp
WTO, Budget Estimates 2002, Proposals by the Director-General, WT/BFA/SPEC/63, 5 October 2001, 137 pp
WTO, Report on Extra-Budgetary Funds for 2001, WT/BFA/W/74, 11 July 2002, 110 pp
WTO, Divisional Reporting on Objectives and Expenditure, WT/BFA/W/73, 15 October 2002, 81 pp
WTO, Budget Estimates 2003, Proposals by the Director-General, WT/BFA/SPEC/82, 16 October 2002, 131 pp
WTO, Director-General's Revised Proposal for 2003 Budget, WT/BFA/W/85, 27 November 2002, 5 pp
WTO, Divisional Reporting on Objectives and Expenditure, WT/BFA/W/98, 8 July 2003, 92 pp
WTO, Director General's Report on Extra-Budgetary Funds for 2002, WT/BFA/W/99, 8 July 2003, 143 pp
WTO, Director General's Budgetary and Financial Report for 2002 and Report of the External Auditor Thereon, WT/BFA/W/97, 10 July 2003, 40 pp
WTO, 2004–2005 Budget Estimates, Proposals by the Director-General, WT/BFA/SPEC/100, 3 November 2003, 152 pp
WTO, Director General's Budgetary and Financial Report for 2003 and Report of the External Auditor Thereon, WT/BFA/W/114, 16 August 2004, 6 pp
WTO, 2006–2007 Budget Estimates, Proposals by the Director-General, WT/BFA/SPEC/134, 13 October 2005, 67 pp

WTO, Director-General's Budgetary and Financial Report for 2005 and Report of the External Auditor Thereon, WT/BFA/W/142, 29 November 2006, 52 pp

WTO, Director-General's Budgetary and Financial Report for 2006 and Report of the External Auditor Thereon, WT/BFA/W/157, 19 September 2007, 52 pp

WTO, 2008–2009, Budget Estimates, Proposals by the Director-General, WT/BFA/SPEC/171, 1 November 2007, 75 pp

WTO, Director-General's Report on Extra-Budgetary Funds for 2007 and Report of the External Auditor Thereon, WT/BFA/W/169, 16 September 2008, 28 pp

WTO, Director-General's Report on Extra-Budgetary Funds for 2006 and Report of the External Auditor Thereon, WT/BFA/W/158, 19 September 2008, 25 pp

WTO, Director-General's Budgetary and Financial Report, WT/BFA/W/181, 28 September 2009, 40 pp

WTO, 2010–2011 Budget Proposals, WT/BFA/W/189, 23 October 2009, 57 pp

WTO, WTO Budgetary and Financial Progress Report, WT/BFA/W/231, 7 March 2011, 5 pp

WTO, WTO Budgetary and Financial Progress Report, WT/BFA/W/242, 10 June 2011, 3 pp

WTO, 2012–2013 Budget Proposals, WT/BFA/W/250, 21 October 2011, 58 pp

WTO, WTO Budget and Finance Report, WT/BFA/W/277, 17 July 2012, 3 pp

WTO, Mid-Term Review Biennium 2012–2013, WT/BFA/W/290, 6 November 2012, 31 pp

Unofficial Room Documents, Trade Policy Review Body, RD/TPR/124, 6 March 2013, 4 pp (Document on file with the author)

WTO, Committee on Budget, Finance and Administration, Report on the Meeting held on 17 September 2014, WT/BFA/144, 15 October 2014, 6 pp

WTO, Committee on Budget, Finance and Administration, Mid-term review biennium 2014–2015, WT/BFA/W/339, 29 October 2014, 30 pp

WTO, 2014–2015 Budget Proposals, WT/BFA/W/309, 2 October 2013, 42 pp

WTO, Committee on Budget, Finance and Administration, Draft Recommendation on the WTO 2014–2015 Budget Proposals, WT/BFA/W/311, 23 October 2013, 9 pp

WTO, 2016–2017 Budget Proposals by the Director-General, WT/BFA/W/374, 5 October 2015, 47 pp

WTO, Committee on Budget, Finance and Administration, Revised Budget Proposals by the Director-General, WT/BFA/W/374/Rev.1, 9 November 2015, 9 pp

ii) Rules of procedure

General Agreement on Tariffs and Trade, Council, Trade Policy Review Mechanism, Procedures for Review Meetings, Communication from the Chairman, L/7208, 30 April 1993, 2 pp

WTO, TPRB, Procedural Improvements to the Trade Policy Review Mechanism, Note from the Chair, WT/TPR/13, 13 December 1995, 3 pp

WTO, TPRB, Procedural Improvements to the Trade Policy Review Mechanism, Note from the Chair, WT/TPR/20, 19 July 1996, 2 pp

WTO, TPRB, Draft Rules of Procedure for Meetings of the Trade Policy Review Body, WT/TPR/W/34, 6 September 2005, 3 pp

WTO, TPRB, Draft Rules of Procedure for Meetings of the Trade Policy Review Body, Trade Policy Review Body, WT/TPR/W/39, 15 October 2008, 3 pp

WTO, TPRB, Rules of Procedure for Meetings of the Trade Policy Review Body, WT/TPR/6/Rev.3, 31 January 2012, 6 pp

WTO, TPRB, Revised Secretariat Procedures for Distribution of the Record of the Meeting of the TPR Reviews, WT/TPR/INF/2, 8 February 2012, 1 p

WTO, TPRB, Draft Revision to the Rules of Procedure for Meetings of the Trade Policy Review Body, RD/TPR/745, 12 January 2017, 7 pp

iii) Trade policy reviews

Most TPRM-related information is available on the following WTO website: <https://www.wto.org/english/tratop_e/tpr_e/tpr_e.htm> accessed 1 June 2017

The CD ROM '*20 years of Trade Policy Reviews 1989–2009, Marking the 20th anniversary of the Trade Policy Review Mechanism*' contains a compilation of all 305 Trade Policy Reviews undertaken between 1989 and 2009. Nevertheless, the CD ROM is not text-sensitive and it is incomplete (CD ROM on file with the author)

Trade Policy Review of Australia of 12 December 1989, 420 pp

Trade Policy Review of the United States of 14 December 1989, 364 pp

Trade Policy Review of Sweden of 5–6 June 1990, 314 pp

Trade Policy Review of Colombia of 6–7 June 1990, 271 pp

Trade Policy Review of Hong Kong of 31 July–1 August 1990, 344 pp

Trade Policy Review of New Zealand of 2–3 August 1990, 329 pp

Trade Policy Review of Argentina of 4–5 March 1991, Vol II, 142 pp

Trade Policy Review of the European Communities of 15–16 April 1991, Minutes of the Meeting, C/RM/M/10, 2 July 1991, 51 pp

Trade Policy Review of Indonesia of 25–26 April 1991, Vol II, 109 pp

Trade Policy Review of Nigeria of 1–2 October 1991, Vol II, 152 pp

Trade Policy Review of Ghana of 9–10 March 1992, Vol II, 96 pp

Trade Policy Review of the United States of 11–12 March 1992, Vol II, 92 pp

Trade Policy Review of Austria of 23–24 March 1992, Vol II, 89 pp

Trade Policy Review of Egypt of 5–6 October 1992, Vol II, 72 pp

Trade Policy Review of Japan of 12–13 October 1992, Vol II, 162 pp

Trade Policy Review of Brazil of 14–15 October 1992, Vol II, 124 pp

Trade Policy Review of Peru of 7–8 February 1993, Vol II, 94 pp

Trade Policy Review of the Philippines of 16–17 February 1993, Vol II, 87 pp

Trade Policy Review of Mexico of 19–20 April 1993, Vol II, 122 pp

Trade Policy Review of the European Communities of 17–18 May 1993, Vol II, 153 pp

Trade Policy Review of Turkey of 20–21 January 1994, Vol II, 85 pp

Trade Policy Review of Australia of 3–4 February 1994, Vol II, 144 pp

Trade Policy Review of Iceland of 9–10 February 1994, Vol II, 103 pp

Trade Policy Review of the United States of 16–17 February 1994, Vol II, 179 pp

Trade Policy Review of Macao of 27–28 September 1994, Vol II, 134 pp

Trade Policy Review of Israel of 19–20 December 1994, Vol II, 290 pp

Trade Policy Review of Cameroon of 13–14 February 1995, Vol II, 180 pp

Trade Policy Review of Japan of 4–5 April 1995, Vol II, 87 pp

Trade Policy Review of the European Union of 24–25 July 1995, Minutes of the Meeting, WT/TPR/M/3, 4 October 1995, 43 pp

Trade Policy Review of Uganda of 27–28 July 1995, Minutes of the Meeting, WT/TPR/M/4, 5 October 1995, 14 pp

Trade Policy Review of Sri Lanka of 7–8 November 1995, Minutes of the Meeting, WT/TPR/M/6, 7 December 1995, 17 pp

Trade Policy Review of the Slovak Republic of 5–6 December 1995, Minutes of the Meeting, WT/TPR/M/7, 22 March 1996, 21 pp

Trade Policy Review of Singapore 3–4 June 1996, Minutes of the Meeting, WT/TPR/M/14, 6 August 1996, 19 pp
Trade Policy Review of Norway of 11–12 June 1996, Minutes of the Meeting, WT/TPR/M/15, 5 August 1996, 35 pp
Trade Policy Review of the United States of 11–12 November 1996, Minutes of the Meeting, WT/TPR/M/16, 30 January 1997, 58 pp
Trade Policy Review of El Salvador of 25–26 November 1996, Minutes of the Meeting, WT/TPR/M/23, 27 January 1997, 28 pp
Trade Policy Review of Cyprus of 25–26 June 1997, Minutes of the Meeting, WT/TPR/M/25, 22 July 1997, 20 pp
Trade Policy Review of Benin of 15–16 September 1997, Minutes of the Meeting, WT/TPR/M/27, 14 October 1997, 21 pp
Trade Policy Review of Mexico of 7–8 October 1997, Minutes of the Meeting, WT/TPR/M/29, 16 December 1997, 231 pp
Trade Policy Review of the European Union of 25–26 November 1997, Minutes of the Meeting, WT/TPR/M/30, 26 January 1998, 30 pp
Trade Policy Review of Japan of 28–29 January 1998, Minutes of the Meeting, WT/TPR/M/32, 8 June 1998, 43 pp
Trade Policy Review of India of 16–17 April 1998, Minutes of the Meeting, WT/TPR/M/33, 22 September 1998, 32 pp
Trade Policy Review of the SACU of 21–23 April 1998, Minutes of the Meeting, WT/TPR/M/34, WT/TPR/M/35, WT/TPR/M/36, WT/TPR/M/37, WT/TPR/M/38, 15 December 1998, 40 pp
Trade Policy Review of Australia of 30 June–2 July 1998, Minutes of the Meeting, WT/TPR/M/41, 26 October 1998, 39 pp
Trade Policy Review of Burkina Faso and Mali of 18–20 November 1998, Minutes of the Meeting, WT/TPR/M/43 and WT/TPR/M/46, 25 February 1999, 31 pp
Trade Policy Review of the Solomon Islands of 21–22 September 1998, Minutes of the Meeting, WT/TPR/M/45, 27 November 1998, 12 pp
Trade Policy Review of Argentina of 20–22 January 1999, Minutes of the Meeting, WT/TPR/M/47, 1 March 1999, 98 pp
Trade Policy Review of Togo of 27–28 January 1999, Minutes of the Meeting, WT/TPR/M/48, 9 April 1999, 30 pp
Trade Policy Review of Hong Kong of 7–8 December 1998, Minutes of the Meeting, WT/TPR/M/52, 12 April 1999, 83 pp
Trade Policy Review of the United States of 12–14 July 1999, Minutes of the Meeting, WT/TPR/M/56, 11 August 1999, 103 pp
Trade Policy Review of Bolivia of 19–21 July 1999, Minutes of the Meeting, WT/TPR/M/57, 15 September 1999, 52 pp
Trade Policy Review of the Philippines of 27–29 September 1999, Minutes of the Meeting, WT/TPR/M/59, 15 November 1999, 72 pp
Trade Policy Review of Romania of 4–5 October 1999, Minutes of the Meeting, WT/TPR/M/60, 4 January 2000, 39 pp
Trade Policy Review of Nicaragua of 25–27 October 1999, Minutes of the Meeting, WT/TPR/M/61, 24 November 1999, 35 pp
Trade Policy Review of Papua New Guinea of 15–17 November 1999, Minutes of the Meeting, WT/TPR/M/62, 4 January 2000, 26 pp
Trade Policy Review of Kenya of 26–28 January 2000, Minutes of the Meeting, WT/TPR/M/64, 29 February 2000, 68 pp

Trade Policy Review of Tanzania of 2–3 March 2000, Minutes of the Meeting, WT/TPR/M/66, 2 May 2000, 27 pp
Trade Policy Review of the European Communities of 12–14 July 2000, Minutes of the Meeting, WT/TPR/M/72, 26 October 2000, 40 pp
Trade Policy Review of Korea of 26–28 September 2000, Minutes of the Meeting, WT/TPR/M/73, 31 October 2000, 109 pp
Trade Policy Review of Japan of 14–16 November 2000, Minutes of the Meeting, WT/TPR/M/76, 1 February 2001, 44 pp
Trade Policy Review of Mozambique of 24–26 January 2001, Minutes of the Meeting, WT/TPR/M/79, 3 April 2001, 48 pp
Trade Policy Review of Madagascar of 19–21 February 2001, Minutes of the Meeting, WT/TPR/M/80, 11 June 2001, 40 pp
Trade Policy Review of Macao of 19–21 March 2001, Minutes of the Meeting, WT/TPR/M/82, 24 April 2001, 56 pp
Trade Policy Review of the OECS of 5–7 June 2001, Minutes of the Meeting, WT/TPR/M/85, 15 August 2001, 68 pp
Trade Policy Review of the United States of 14–17 September 2001, Minutes of the Meeting, WT/TPR/M/88, 4 January 2002, 39 pp
Trade Policy review of India of 19–21 June 2002, Minutes of the Meeting, WT/TPR/M/100, 1 August 2002, 36 pp
Trade Policy Review of the European Communities of 24–26 July 2002, Minutes of the Meeting, WT/TPR/M/102, 23 September 2002, 58 pp
Trade Policy Review of Australia of 23–25 September 2002, Minutes of the Meeting, WT/TPR/M/104, 3 December 2002, 21 pp
Trade Policy Review of Japan of 6–8 November 2002, Minutes of the Meeting, WT/TPR/M/107, 4 February 2003, 28 pp
Trade Policy Review of Hong Kong of 16–18 December 2002, Minutes of the Meeting, WT/TPR/M/109, 17 February 2003, 25 pp
Trade Policy Review of the Maldives of 15–17 January 2003, Minutes of the Meeting, WT/TPR/M/110, 5 March 2003, 12 pp
Trade Policy Review of Canada of 12–14 March 2003, Minutes of the Meeting, WT/TPR/M/112, 12 May 2003, 33 pp
Trade Policy Review of the SACU of 23–25 April 2003, Minutes of the Meeting, WT/TPR/M/114, 11 June 2003, 18 pp
Trade Policy Review of New Zealand of 12–14 May 2003, Minutes of the Meeting, WT/TPR/M/115, 17 June 2003, 25 pp
Trade Policy Review of Turkey of 17–19 December 2003, Minutes of the Meeting, WT/TPR/M/125, 9 February 2004, 19 pp
Trade Policy Review of the United States of 14–16 January 2004, Minutes of the Meeting, WT/TPR/M/126, 15 March 2004, 65 pp
Trade Policy Review of Gambia of 4–6 February 2004, Minutes of the Meeting, WT/TPR/M/127, 29 March 2004, 15 pp
Trade Policy Review of the European Communities of 25–27 October 2004, Minutes of the Meeting, WT/TPR/M/136, 18 January 2005, 38 pp
Trade Policy Review of Brazil of 29 November–1 December 2004, Minutes of the Meeting, WT/TPR/M/140, 24 January 2005, 41 pp
Trade Policy Review of Japan of 25–27 January 2005, Minutes of the Meeting, WT/TPR/M/142, 1 April 2005, 27 pp

Trade Policy Review of Sierra Leone of 9–11 February 2005, Minutes of the Meeting, WT/TPR/M/143, 29 March 2005, 17 pp
Trade Policy Review of Trinidad and Tobago of 14–16 September 2005, Minutes of the Meeting, WT/TPR/M/151, 2 November 2005, 24 pp
Trade Policy Review of Tunisia of 5–7 October 2005, Minutes of the Meeting, WT/TPR/M/152, 7 November 2005, 17 pp
Trade Policy Review of Guinea of 12–14 October 2005, Minutes of the Meeting, WT/TPR/M/153, 1 December 2005, 15 pp
Trade Policy Review of Romania of 28–30 November 2005, Minutes of the Meeting, WT/TPR/M/155, 18 January 2006, 15 pp
Trade Policy Review of Angola of 14–16 February 2006, Minutes of the Meeting, WT/TPR/M/158, 6 April 2006, 16 pp
Trade Policy Review of the United States of 22–24 March 2006, Minutes of the Meeting, WT/TPR/M/160, 9 June 2006, 50 pp
Trade Policy Review of Iceland of 7–9 June 2006, Minutes of the Meeting, WT/TPR/M/164, 4 August 2006, 23 pp
Trade Policy Review of Togo of 3–5 July 2006, Minutes of the Meeting, WT/TPR/M/166, 29 August 2006, 12 pp
Trade Policy Review of the Congo of 27–29 September 2006, Minutes of the Meeting, WT/TPR/M/169, 12 December 2006, 14 pp
Trade Policy Review of the Kirgiz Republic of 9–11 October 2006, Minutes of the Meeting, WT/TPR/M/170, 13 December 2006, 20 pp
Trade Policy Review of Colombia of 22–24 November 2006, Minutes of the Meeting, WT/TPR/M/172, 28 March 2007, 25 pp
Trade Policy Review of Japan of 31 January–2 February 2007, Minutes of the Meeting, WT/TPR/M/175, 28 March 2007, 25 pp
Trade Policy Review of Argentina of 12–14 February 2007, Minutes of the Meeting, WT/TPR/M/176, 28 March 2007, 35 pp
Trade Policy Review of the European Union of 26–28 February 2007, Minutes of the Meeting, WT/TPR/M/177, 30 April 2007, 32 pp
Trade Policy Review of Australia of 5–7 March 2007, Minutes of the Meeting, WT/TPR/M/178, 18 April 2007, 24 pp
Trade Policy Review of Macao of 30 April–2 May 2007, Minutes of the Meeting, WT/TPR/M/181, 12 June 2007, 17 pp
Trade Policy Review of India of 23–25 May 2007, Minutes of the Meeting, WT/TPR/M/182, 9 July 2007, 31 pp
Trade Policy Review of the OECS of 5–7 November 2007, Minutes of the Meeting, WT/TPR/M/190, 14 December 2007, 36 pp
Trade Policy Review of Mexico of 11–13 February 2008, Minutes of the Meeting, WT/TPR/M/195, 14 April 2008, 25 pp
Trade Policy Review of Brunei Darussalam of 25–27 February 2008, Minutes of the Meeting, WT/TPR/M/196, 10 April 2008, 18 pp
Trade Policy Review of China of 21–23 March 2008, Minutes of the Meeting, WT/TPR/M/199, 24 July 2008, 33 pp
Trade Policy Review of the United States of 9–11 June 2008, Minutes of the Meeting, WT/TPR/M/200, 4 August 2008, 50 pp
Trade Policy Review of Korea of 8–10 October 2008, Minutes of the Meeting, WT/TPR/M/204, 1 December 2008, 20 pp

Trade Policy Review of Norway of 22–24 November 2008, Minutes of the Meeting, WT/TPR/M/205, 10 December 2008, 30 pp
Trade Policy Review of Jordan of 10–12 November 2008, Minutes of the Meeting, WT/TPR/M/206, 19 December 2008, 25 pp
Trade Policy Review of Brazil of 9–11 March 2012, Minutes of the Meeting, WT/TPR/M/212, 3 June 2009, 70 pp
Trade Policy Review of the European Union of 6–8 April 2009, Minutes of the Meeting, WT/TPR/M/214, 8 June 2009, 86 pp
Trade Policy Review of Chile of 7–9 October 2005, Minutes of the Meeting, WT/TPR/M/220, 17 December 2009, 53 pp
Trade Policy Review of Georgia of 8–10 December 2009, Minutes of the Meeting, WT/TPR/M/224, 8 February 2010, 29 pp
Trade Policy Review of Armenia of 6–8 April 2010, Minutes of the Meeting, WT/TPR/M/228, 30 April 2010, 22 pp
Trade Policy Review of China of 31 May – 2 June 2010, Minutes of the Meeting, WT/TPR/M/230, 29 June 2010, 66 pp
Trade Policy Review of Malawi of 9–11 June 2010, Secretariat Report, WT/TPR/S/231 and WT/TPR/S/231/Rev.1, 5 May 2010 and 14 July 2010, 83 pp. and 81 pp
Trade Policy Review of the United States of 29 September–1 October 2010, Minutes of the Meeting, WT/TPR/M/235, 1 November 2010, 76 pp
Trade Policy Review of Australia of 5–7 April 2011, Minutes of the Meeting, WT/TPR/M/244, 6 May 2011, 40 pp
Trade Policy Review of Paraguay of 27–29 April 2011, Minutes of the Meeting, WT/TPR/M/245, 25 May 2011, 33 pp
Trade Policy Review of the European Union of 6–8 July 2011, Minutes of the Meeting, WT/TPR/M/248, 14 September 2011, 76 pp
Trade Policy Review of India of 14–16 September 2011, Minutes of the Meeting, WT/TPR/M/249, 14 October 2011, 71 pp
Trade Policy Review of Guinea and Mauritania of 28–30 September 2011, Minutes of the Meeting, WT/TPR/M/250 and WT/TPR/M/251, 18 November 2011, 34 pp
Trade Policy Review of Zimbabwe of 19–21 October 2011, Minutes of the Meeting, WT/TPR/M/252, 28 November 2011, 43 pp
Trade Policy Review of Ecuador of 14–16 November 2011, Minutes of the Meeting, WT/TPR/M/254, 9 January 2012, 46 pp
Trade Policy Review of Thailand of 28–30 November 2011, Minutes of the Meeting, WT/TPR/M/255, 30 January 2012, 42 pp
Trade Policy Review of Saudi Arabia of 25–27 January 2012, Minutes of the Meeting, WT/TPR/M/256, 6 March 2012, 42 pp
Trade Policy Review of Nepal of 13–15 March 2012, Minutes of the Meeting, WT/TPR/M/257, 16 April 2012, 33 pp
Trade Policy Review of Kuwait of 7–9 February 2012, Minutes of the Meeting, WT/TPR/M/258, 26 March 2012, 39 pp
Trade Policy Review of the United Arab Emirates of 27–29 March 2012, Minutes of the Meeting, WT/TPR/M/262, 9 May 2012, 41 pp
Trade Policy Review of China of 12–14 June 2012, Minutes of the Meeting, WT/TPR/M/264, 17 July 2012, 70 pp
Trade Policy Review of Singapore of 24–26 July 2012, Minutes of the Meeting, WT/TPR/M/267, 8 October 2012, 45 pp

Trade Policy Review of Korea of 19–21 September 2012, Minutes of the Meeting, WT/TPR/M/268, 12 November 2012, 48 pp
Trade Policy Review of Norway of 9–11 October 2012, Minutes of the Meeting, WT/TPR/M/269, 19 November 2012, 46 pp
Trade Policy Review of Iceland of 13–15 November 2012, Minutes of the Meeting, WT/TPR/M/273, 25 February 2013, 32 pp
Trade Policy Review of the United States of 18–20 December 2012, Minutes of the Meeting, WT/TPR/M/275, 30 April 2013, 75 pp
Trade Policy Review of Japan of 19–21 February 2013, Minutes of the Meeting, WT/TPR/M/276, 13 June 2013, 61 pp
Trade Policy Review of Argentina of 20–22 March 2013, Minutes of the Meeting, WT/TPR/M/277, 18 July 2013, 52 pp
Trade Policy Review of Indonesia of 10–12 April 2013, Minutes of the Meeting, WT/TPR/M/278, 1 August 2013, 50 pp
Trade Policy Review of Mexico of 4 September 2013, Minutes of the Meeting, WT/TPR/M/279, 4 September 2013, 51 pp
Trade Policy Review of Switzerland and Liechtenstein of 23–25 April 2013, Minutes of the Meeting, WT/TPR/M/280, 12 September 2013, 51 pp
Trade Policy Review of Macao of 13–15 May 2013, Minutes of the Meeting, WT/TPR/M/281, 13 September 2013, 24 pp
Trade Policy Review of Suriname of 10–12 June 2013, Minutes of the Meeting, WT/TPR/M/282, 3 October 2013, 19 pp
Trade Policy Review of Brazil of 24–26 June 2013, Minutes of the Meeting, WT/TPR/M/283, 11 October 2013, 59 pp
Trade Policy Review of the European Union of 16–18 July 2013, Minutes of the Meeting, WT/TPR/M/284, 23 October 2013, 69 pp
Trade Policy Review of Costa Rica of 24–26 September 2013, Minutes of the Meeting, WT/TPR/M/286, 9 December 2013, 41 pp
Trade Policy Review of Myanmar of 11–13 March 2014, Minutes of the Meeting, WT/TPR/M/293, 23 April 2014, 40 pp
Trade Policy Review of the United States of 16–18 December 2014, Minutes of the Meeting, WT/TPR/M/307, 9 February 2015, 76 pp
Trade Policy Review of Australia of 21–23 April 2015, Minutes of the Meeting, WT/TPR/M/312, 24 June 2015, 48 pp
Trade Policy Review of India of 2–4 June 2015, Minutes of the Meeting, WT/TPR/M/313, 20 July 2015, 58 pp
Trade Policy Review of the European Union of 6–8 July 2015, Minutes of the Meeting, WT/TPR/M/317, 12 October 2015, 83 pp

iv) Review programmes and Annual reports of the TPRB

GATT, Council, Trade Policy Review Mechanism, Program of Reviews, Communication from the Chairman, Council, C/W/603, 7 July 1989, 2 pp
GATT, Trade Policy Review Mechanism, Programme of Reviews—1989 and 1990, Decision of 19 July 1989, Addendum, L/6554/Add. 1, 28 July 1989, 1 p
GATT, Council, Trade Policy Review Mechanism, Programme of Reviews, Communication from the Chairman, C/W/642, 4 July 1990, 2 pp
GATT, Trade Policy Review Mechanism, Programme of Reviews for 1991, Decision of 11 July 1990, L/6701, 13 July 1990, 1 p

GATT, Trade Policy Review Mechanism, Programme of Reviews for 1991, Decision of 11 July 1990, L/6701/Add. 1, 19 September 1990, 1 p

GATT, Council, Trade Policy Review Mechanism, Programme of Reviews for 1991, Review of Bangladesh, Communication from the Chairman, C/W/664, 25 January 1991, 1 p

GATT, Council, Trade Policy Review Mechanism, Programme of Reviews for 1992, L/6887, 17 July 1991, 1 p

GATT, Trade Policy Review Mechanism, Programme of Reviews for 1991, Addendum, L/6701/Add. 2, 11 December 1991, 1 p

GATT, Council, Trade Policy Review Mechanism, Programme of reviews for 1993, L/7040, 24 June 1992, 1 p

GATT, Council, Trade Policy Review Mechanism, Programme of Reviews for 1994, L/7285, 22 July 1993, 1 p

GATT, Trade Policy Review Mechanism, Programme of Reviews for 1995, L/7494, 22 July 1994, 1 p

WTO, TPRB, Trade Policy Review Mechanism, Report to the Singapore Ministerial Conference, WT/TPR/27, 28 October 1996, 5 pp

WTO, TPRB, Report on the meeting held on 10 March 1997, Trade Policy Review Body, WT/TPR/R/1, 20 March 1997, 4 pp

WTO, TPRB, Trade Policy Review Mechanism, Report of the Trade Policy Review Body for 1997, Trade Policy Review Body, WT/TPR/41, 28 November 1997, 6 pp

WTO, TPRB, Draft Report of the Trade Policy Review Body for 1998, Trade Policy Review Mechanism, WT/TPR/W/21, 11 November 1998, 6 pp

WTO, TPRB, Trade Policy Review Mechanism, Report of the Trade Policy Review Body for 1998, Trade Policy Review Body, WT/TPR/59, 27 November 1998, 7 pp

WTO, TPRB, Draft Report of the Trade Policy Review Body for 1999, Trade Policy Review Mechanism, WT/TPR/W/23, 30 September 1999, 5 pp

WTO, TPRB, Report of the Trade Policy Review Body for 1999, Trade Policy Review Body, WT/TPR/69, 7 October 1999, 5 pp

WTO, TPRB, Trade Policy Review Mechanism, Draft Programme of Reviews for 2000, Trade Policy Review Body, WT/TPR/W/25, 9 November 1999, 1 p

WTO, TPRB, Report on the meeting held on 15 and 17 November 1999, WT/TPR/R/4, 23 November 1999, 1 p

WTO, TPRB, Draft Report of the Trade Policy Review Body for 2000, Trade Policy Review Body, WT/TPR/W/27, 28 September 2000, 6 pp

WTO, TPRB, Draft Report of the Trade Policy Review Body for 2000, Trade Policy Review Body, WT/TPR/W/27/Rev.1, 6 October 2000, 6 pp

WTO, TPRB, Report of the Trade Policy Review Body for 2000, Trade Policy Review Body, WT/TPR/86, 13 October 2000, 6 pp

WTO, TPRB, Draft Report of the Trade Policy Review Body for 2001, Trade Policy Review Mechanism, WT/TPR/W/28, 11 September 2001, 6 pp

WTO, TPRB, Report of the Trade Policy Review Body for 2001, Trade Policy Review Body, WT/TPR/101, 18 October 2001, 6 pp

WTO, TPRB, Report of the Trade Policy Review Body for 2002, Trade Policy Review Body, WT/TPR/W/29, 7 October 2002, 6 pp

WTO, TPRB, Report of the Trade Policy Review Body for 2002, Trade Policy Review Body, WT/TPR/122, 11 October 2002, 6 pp

WTO, TPRB, Report of the Trade Policy Review Body for January–July 2003, Trade Policy Review Body, WT/TPR/W/30, 27 June 2003, 6 pp

WTO, TPRB, Draft Report of the Trade Policy Review Body for 2003, Trade Policy Review Mechanism, WT/TPR/W/31, 28 October 2003, 6 pp
WTO, TPRB, Report of the Trade Policy Review Body for 2003, Trade Policy Review Body, WT/TPR/140, 31 October 2003, 6 pp
WTO, TPRB, Draft Report of the Trade Policy Review Body for 2004, Trade Policy Review Mechanism, WT/TPR/W/32, 18 October 2004, 6 pp
WTO, TPRB, Report of the Trade Policy Review Body for 2004, Trade Policy Review Body, WT/TPR/154, 28 October 2004, 6 pp
WTO, TPRB, Draft Trade Policy Review Mechanism, Report of the Trade Policy Review Body for 2005, WT/TPR/W/35, 12 October 2005, 6 pp
WTO, TPRB, Report of the Trade Policy Review Body for 2005, Trade Policy Review Body, WT/TPR/173, 8 November 2005, 6 pp
WTO, TPRB, Draft Report of the Trade Policy Review Body for 2006, Trade Policy Review Mechanism, WT/TPR/W/36, 23 October 2006, 6 pp
WTO, TPRB, Report of the Trade Policy Review Body for 2006, Trade Policy Review Body, WT/TPR/192, 31 October 2006, 6 pp
WTO, TPRB, Draft Report of the Trade Policy Review Body for 2007, Trade Policy Review Mechanism, WT/TPR/W/37, 26 October 2007, 6 pp
WTO, TPRB, Report of the Trade Policy Review Body for 2007, Trade Policy Review Body, WT/TPR/213, 12 November 2007, 6 pp
WTO, TPRB, Draft Report of the Trade Policy Review Body for 2008, Trade Policy Review Mechanism, WT/TPR/W/40, 15 October 2008, 6 pp
WTO, TPRB, Report of the Trade Policy Review Body for 2008, Trade Policy Review Body, WT/TPR/232, 14 November 2008, 6 pp
WTO, TPRB, Draft Report of the Trade Policy Review Body for 2009, Trade Policy Review Mechanism, WT/TPR/W/41, 8 October 2009, 7 pp
WTO, TPRB, Report of the Trade Policy Review Body for 2009, Trade Policy Review Body, WT/TPR/249, 29 October 2009, 7 pp
WTO, TPRB, Draft Report of the Trade Policy Review Body for 2010, Trade Policy Review Mechanism, WT/TPR/W/42, 28 October 2010, 4 pp
WTO, TPRB, Report of the Trade Policy Review Body for 2010, Trade Policy Review Body, WT/TPR/269, 29 November 2010, 4 pp
WTO, TPRB, Draft Report of the Trade Policy Review Body for 2011, Trade Policy Review Mechanism, WT/TPR/W/43, 4 November 2011, 4 pp
WTO, TPRB, Report of the Trade Policy Review Body for 2011, Trade Policy Review Body, WT/TPR/284, 15 November 2011, 4 pp
WTO, TPRB, Report of the Trade Policy Review Body for 2012, Trade Policy Review Body, WT/TPR/306, 23 November 2012, 7 pp
WTO, TPRB, Draft Report of the Trade Policy Review Body for 2013, Trade Policy Review Mechanism, WT/TPR/W/49, 15 August 2013, 6 pp
WTO, TPRB, Report of the Trade Policy Review Body for 2013, Trade Policy Review Body, WT/TPR/321, 8 October 2013, 6 pp
WTO, TPRB, Draft Report of the Trade Policy Review Body for 2014, Trade Policy Review Mechanism, WT/TPR/W/71/Rev.1, 4 November 2014, 6 pp
WTO, TPRB, Report of the Trade Policy Review Body for 2014, Trade Policy Review Mechanism, WT/TPR/340, 21 November 2014, 6 pp
WTO, TPRB, Draft Report of the Trade Policy Review Body for 2015, Trade Policy Review Mechanism, WT/TPR/W/89/Rev.1, 14 October 2015, 7 pp

WTO, TPRB, Report of the Trade Policy Review Body for 2015, Trade Policy Review Mechanism, WT/TPR/361, 23 October 2015, 6 pp
WTO, TPRB, Draft Report of the Trade Policy Review Body for 2016, Trade Policy Review Mechanism, WT/TPR/W/114, 7 October 2016, 6 pp
WTO, TPRB, Report of the Trade Policy Review Body for 2016, Trade Policy Review Mechanism, WT/TPR/387, 7 November 2016, 6 pp

v) Appraisal of the TPRM

Appraisal of the operation of the TPRM, Informal Meeting of 12 May 1999, Checklist of Main Points, No 2933, 20 May 1999, 4 pp
Appraisal of the operation of the TPRM, Informal Meeting of 21 May 1999, Checklist of Main Points, No 3274, 3 June 1999, 4 pp
Appraisal of the operation of the TPRM, Draft Report to Ministers, No 3714, 25 June 1999, 5 pp
Appraisal of the operation of the TPRM, Draft Report to Ministers, No 4428, 16 July 1999, 5 pp
Appraisal of the operation of the TPRM, Draft Report to Ministers, No 4921, 30 July 1999, 5 pp
Appraisal of the operation of the TPRM, Draft Report to Ministers, No 5282, 14 September 1999, 5 pp
Appraisal of the operation of the TPRM, Draft Report to Ministers, No 5439, 21 September 1999, 5 pp
Appraisal of the operation of the TPRM, Draft Report to Ministers, No 5545, 23 September 1999, 5 pp
WTO, TPRB, Trade Policy Review Mechanism, Draft Report of the Trade Policy Review Body for 1999, WT/TPR/W/23, 30 September 1999, 5 pp
WTO, TPRB, Appraisal of the operation of the Trade Policy Review Mechanism, Draft Report to Ministers, WT/TPR/W/24, 30 September 1999, 4 pp
WTO, Ministerial Conference, Third Session, Seattle 30 November–3 December 1999, Appraisal of the operation of the Trade Policy Review Mechanism, WT/MIN(99)/2, 8 October 1999, 4 pp
Possible points for the appraisal of the operation of the Trade Policy Review Mechanism (TPRM) Non-paper, 10 May 2005, 4 pp
Second appraisal of the operation of the Trade Policy Review Mechanism—Draft Report to Ministers, WT/TPR/W/33, 12 August 2005, 4 pp
Second appraisal of the operation of the Trade Policy Review Mechanism, Report to Ministers, WT/MIN(05)/1, 21 September 2005, 4 pp
Possible points for the third appraisal of the operation of the Trade Policy Review Mechanism, Non-paper, 7 December 2007, 3 pp
Draft—Third appraisal of the operation of the Trade Policy Review Mechanism, WT/TPR/W/38, 15 October 2008, 4 pp
Third appraisal of the operation of the Trade Policy Review Mechanism, WT/TPR/229, 11 November 2008, 4 pp
Fourth appraisal of the operation of the TPRM, informal WTO document, 1 p
Fourth appraisal of the Trade Policy Review Mechanism, Summary of Main Issues discussed in First Informal Meeting, Rough Draft, 18 July 2011, 7 pp
Fourth appraisal of the Trade Policy Review Mechanism, Comments and Suggestions of China, Non–paper, JOB/TPR/1, 30 August 2011, 4 pp

Fourth appraisal of the Trade Policy Review Mechanism, Comments and Suggestions of China, Non-paper, JOB/TPR/2, 13 September 2011, 1 p

Fourth appraisal of the TPRM, Informal open-ended meeting, 23 September 2011, 18 pp

Ideas for Strengthening of the WTO: Monitoring and Surveillance, Communication from Argentina, WT/GC/W/639, 3 October 2011, 3 pp

Fourth appraisal of the TPRM, Informal meeting, 4 October 2011, 16 pp

Informal meeting of the TPRB (18 October 2011): Non-paper by the EU, 17 October 2011, 1 p

Fourth appraisal of the operation of the Trade Policy Review Mechanism, WT/TPR/W/44, 17 November 2011, 11 pp

Fourth appraisal of the Trade Policy Review Mechanism, Ministerial Conference, Eighth Session, Geneva, 15–17 December 2011, WT/MIN(11)/6, 29 November 2011, 11 pp

Fourth appraisal of the Trade Policy Review Mechanism, Report on the Meeting, WT/TPR/R/5, 9 December 2011, 2 pp

Unofficial room documents, Trade Policy Review Body, RD/TPR/225*, 27 September 2013, 7 pp

Unofficial room documents, Trade Policy Review Body, RD/TPR/225/Rev.1*, 11 October 2013, 7 pp

Unofficial room documents, Trade Policy Review Body, 15 October 2013, 7 pp

Fifth appraisal of the Trade Policy Review Mechanism, Ministerial Conference, Ninth Session, Bali, 3–6 December 2013, WT/MIN(13)/5, 28 October 2013, 6 pp

Sixth appraisal of the Trade Policy Review Mechanism, Communication from the European Union, RD/TPR/693, 7 October 2016, 4 pp

Sixth appraisal of the Trade Policy Review Mechanism, Communication from Japan, RD/TPR/694, 7 October 2016, 2 pp

Sixth appraisal of the Trade Policy Review Mechanism, Communication from Switzerland, RD/TPR/695, 10 October 2016, 2 pp

Sixth appraisal of the Trade Policy Review Mechanism, Presentation—Timeframes, RD/TPR/697, 11 October 2016, 2 pp

Sixth appraisal of the Trade Policy Review Mechanism, Issues Discussed, RD/TPR/702, 14 October 2016, 10 pp

Sixth appraisal of the Trade Policy Review Mechanism, Issues Discussed, Marked-up version, RD/TPR/703, 14 October 2016, 10 pp

Sixth appraisal of the Trade Policy Review Mechanism, Communication from Australia, RD/TPR/705, 20 October 2016, 3 pp

Sixth appraisal of the Trade Policy Review Mechanism, Submission from the United States, Trade Monitoring (Part G of Annex 3) RD/TPR/704, 20 October 2016, 2 pp

Sixth appraisal of the Trade Policy Review Mechanism, Communication from Australia, RD/TPR/705, 20 October 2016, 3 pp

Sixth appraisal of the WTO Trade Policy Review Mechanism, Communication from Japan, Revision, RD/TPR/694/Rev.1, 28 October 2016, 2 pp

Sixth appraisal of the Trade Policy Review Mechanism, Issues Discussed, Revision, RD/TPR/702/Rev.1, 4 November 2016, 10 pp

Sixth appraisal of the Trade Policy Review Mechanism, Issues Discussed, Marked-up version, Revision, RD/TPR/703/Rev.1, 4 November 2016, 12 pp

Sixth appraisal of the Trade Policy Review Mechanism, Issues Discussed, Revision, RD/TPR/702/Rev.2, 18 November 2016, 10 pp

Sixth appraisal of the Trade Policy Review Mechanism, Issues Discussed, Marked-up version, Revision, RD/TPR/703/Rev.2, 18 November 2016, 11 pp

Sixth appraisal of the Trade Policy Review Mechanism, Final Stage Timetable, RD/TPR/724, 18 November 2016, 2 pp
Sixth appraisal of the Trade Policy Review Mechanism, Communication from Japan, RD/TPR/728, 24 November 2016, 2 pp
Sixth appraisal of the Trade Policy Review Mechanism, Issues Discussed, Marked-up version, Revision, RD/TPR/703/Rev.3, 2 December 2016, 10 pp
Sixth appraisal of the Trade Policy Review Mechanism, Draft Report, Corrigendum, WT/TPR/W/118/Corr.1, 7 December 2016, 1 p
Sixth appraisal of the Trade Policy Review Mechanism, WT/TPR/389, 22 December 2016, 8 pp
Amendment of the Trade Policy Review Mechanism, Note from the Chairperson, RD/TPR/744, 12 January 2017, 3 pp

vi) Overview of developments in the International Trading Environment

General Agreement on Tariffs and Trade, Council, 11 December 1989, Council Overview of Developments in the International Trading Environment, Annual Report by the Director-General, C/171, 5 December 1989, 19 pp
WTO, TPRB, Overview of developments in international trade and the trading system, Annual Report by the Director-General, WT/TPR/OV/1, 1 December 1995, 32 pp
WTO, TPRB, Overview of developments in international trade and the trading system, Annual Report by the Director-General, WT/TPR/OV/2, 28 November 1996, 8 pp
WTO, TPRB, Overview of developments in international trade and the trading system, Annual Report by the Director-General, WT/TPR/OV/3, 5 December 1997, 7 pp
WTO, TPRB, Overview of developments in international trade and the trading system, Annual Report by the Director-General, WT/TPR/OV/4, 30 November 1998, 9 pp
WTO, TPRB, Overview of developments in international trade and the trading system, Annual Report by the Director-General, WT/TPR/OV/5, 15 October 1999, 15 pp
WTO, TPRB, Overview of developments in international trade and the trading system, Annual Report by the Director-General, WT/TPR/OV/6, 22 November 2000, 42 pp
WTO, TPRB, Overview of developments in international trade and the trading system, Annual Report by the Director-General, WT/TPR/OV/7, 10 December 2001, 102 pp
WTO, TPRB, Overview of developments in international trade and the trading system, Annual Report by the Director-General, WT/TPR/OV/8, 15 November 2002, 46 pp
WTO, TPRB, Overview of developments in international trade and the trading system, Annual Report by the Director-General, WT/TPR/OV/9, 20 February 2004, 52 pp
WTO, TPRB, Overview of developments in international trade and the trading system, Annual Report by the Director-General, WT/TPR/OV/10, 15 November 2004, 47 pp
WTO, TPRB, Overview of developments in the International trading environment, Annual Report by the Director-General, WT/TPR/OV/11, 6 February 2006, 51 pp
WTO, TPRB, Overview of developments in the International trading environment, Annual Report by the Director-General, WT/TPR/OV/12, 18 November 2009, 154 pp
WTO, TPRB, Overview of developments in the International trading environment, Annual Report by the Director-General, WT/TPR/OV/13, 24 November 2010, 114 pp
WTO, TPRB, Overview of developments in the International trading environment, Annual Report by the Director-General, WT/TPR/OV/14, 21 November 2011, 118 pp
WTO, TPRB, Overview of developments in the International trading environment, Annual Report by the Director-General, WT/TPR/OV/15, 29 November 2012, 138 pp
WTO, TPRB, Overview of developments in the International trading environment, Annual Report by the Director-General, WT/TPR/OV/16, 31 January 2014, 140 pp

WTO, TPRB, Overview of developments in the International trading environment, Annual Report by the Director-General, WT/TPR/OV/17, 24 November 2014, 178 pp

WTO, TPRB, Overview of developments in the International trading environment, Annual Report by the Director-General, WT/TPR/OV/18, 17 November 2015, 191 pp

WTO, TPRB, Overview of developments in the International trading environment, Annual Report by the Director-General, WT/TPR/OV/19, 21 November 2016, 209 pp

c) World Trade Reports

WTO, *Exploring the Links between Subsidies, Trade and the WTO* (WTO 2006) 266 pp

WTO, *Sixty Years of the Multilateral Trading System: Achievements and Challenges* (WTO 2007) 436 pp

WTO, *The WTO and Preferential Trade Agreements: From Co-existence to Coherence* (WTO 2011) 256 pp

WTO, *Trade and Public Policies: A Closer Look at Non-tariff Measures in the 21st Century* (WTO 2012) 248 pp

WTO, *Factors Shaping the Future of World Trade* (WTO 2013) 340 pp

WTO, *Trade and Development: Recent Trends and the Role of the WTO* (WTO 2014) 242 pp

d) Jurisprudence

WTO, *US—Standards for Reformulated and Conventional Gasoline—Note by the Secretariat* (4 July 1995) WT/DS2/4, 1 p

WTO, *US—Standards for Reformulated and Conventional Gasoline—Report of the Panel* (29 January 1996) WT/DS2/R, 47 pp

WTO, *US—Standards for Reformulated and Conventional Gasoline—Appellate Body Report* (29 April 1996) WT/DS2/AB/R 30 pp

WTO, *EC—Trade Description of Scallops—Request for consultations by Canada* (24 May 1995) WT/DS7/1, 2 pp

WTO, *EC—Trade Description of Scallops—Constitution of the Panel Established at the Request of Canada* (14 September 1995) WT/DS7/8, 1 p

WTO, *EC—Trade Description of Scallops-Request for Consultations by Peru* (25 July 1995) WT/DS12/1, 1 p

WTO, *EC—Trade Description of Scallops—Constitution of the Panel Established at the Requests of Peru and Chile* (26 October 1995) WT/DS12/8 and WT/DS14/7, 1 p

WTO, *Australia—Measures Affecting Importation of Salmon—Report of the Panel* (12 June 1998) WT/DS18/R, 263 pp

WTO, *Australia—Measures Affecting Importation of Salmon—Appellate Body Report* (20 October 1998) WT/DS18/AB/R, 84 pp

WTO, *Australia—Measures Affecting Importation of Salmon—Arbitration under Article 21.3(c) of the Understanding on Rules and Procedures Governing the Settlement of Disputes* (23 February 1999) WT/DS18/9, 12 pp

WTO, *Australia—Measures Affecting Importation of Salmon—Recourse to Article 21.5 by Canada* (18 February 2000) WT/DS18/RW, 167 pp

WTO, *United States—Restrictions on Imports of Cotton and Man-made Fibre Underwear—Appellate Body Report* (10 February 1997) WT/DS24/AB/R, 23 pp

WTO, *EC—Measures Concerning Meat and Meat Products—Report of the Panel* (18 August 1997) WT/DS26/R/USA, 365 pp

WTO, *EC—Measures Concerning Meat and Meat Products—Report of the Panel* (18 August 1997) WT/DS48/R/CAN, 395 pp

WTO, *EC—Measures Concerning Meat and Meat Products—Appellate Body Report* (16 January 1998) WT/DS26 and 48/AB/R, 105 pp

WTO, *EC—Measures Concerning Meat and Meat Products—Arbitration under Article 21.3(c) of the Understanding on Rules and Procedures Governing the Settlement of Disputes* (29 May 1998) WT/DS26/15 and WT/DS48/13, 20 pp

WTO, *EC—Measures Concerning Meat and Meat Products—Recourse to Arbitration by the European Communities under Article 22.6 of the DSU* (12 July 1999) WT/DS26/ARB, 22 pp

WTO, *European Communities—Measures Concerning Meat and Meat Products (Hormones)—Joint Communication from the European Communities and the US* (30 September 2009) WT/DS26/28, 7 pp

WTO, *European Communities—Measures Concerning Meat and Meat Products (Hormones)—Joint Communication from the European Union and the United States* (17 April 2014) WT/DS26/29, 5 pp

WTO, *EC—Measures Concerning Meat and Meat Products—Recourse to Arbitration by the European Communities under Article 22.6 of the DSU* (12 July 1999) WT/DS48/ARB, 17 pp

WTO, *European Communities—Measures Concerning Meat and Meat Products (Hormones)—Joint Communication from the European Union and Canada* (22 March 2011) WT/DS48/26, 6 pp

WTO, *Turkey—Restrictions on Imports of Textile and Clothing Products—Report of the Panel* (31 May 1999) WT/DS34/R, 155 pp

WTO, *Argentina—Measures Affecting Imports of Footwear, Textiles, Apparel and Other Items—Request for the Establishment of a Panel by the United States* (10 January 1997) WT/DS56/5, 2 pp

WTO, *Argentina—Measures Affecting Imports of Footwear, Textiles, Apparel and Other Items—Report of the Panel* (25 November 1997) WT/DS56/R, 105 pp

WTO, *Argentina—Measures Affecting Imports of Footwear, Textiles, Apparel and Other Items—Appellate Body Report* (27 March 1998) WT/DS56/AB/R, 33 pp

WTO, *Argentina—Measures Affecting Imports of Footwear, Textiles, Apparel and Other Items—Communication from Argentina* (7 July 1998) WT/DS56/14, 4 pp

WTO, *Canada—Measures Affecting the Export of Civilian Aircraft—Report of the Panel* (14 April 1999) WT/DS70/R, 235 pp

WTO, *EC—Measures Affecting Butter Products—Notification of Mutually Agreed Solution* (18 November 1999) WT/DS72/2, 4 pp

WTO, *EC—Measures Affecting Butter Products—Report of the Panel* (24 November 1999) WT/DS72/R, 3 pp

WTO, *Japan—Measures Affecting Agricultural Products—Report of the Panel* (27 October 1998) WT/DS76/R, 170 pp

WTO, *Japan—Measures Affecting Agricultural Products—Appellate Body Report* (22 February 1999) WT/DS76/AB/R, 42 pp

WTO, *Japan—Measures Affecting Agricultural Products—Agreement under Article 21.3.b of the DSU* (18 June 1999) WT/DS76/9, 1 p

WTO, *Japan—Measures Affecting Agricultural Products—Communication from Japan* (13 January 2000) WT/DS76/10, 1 p

WTO, *Japan—Measures Affecting Agricultural Products—Communication from Japan and the United States* (30 August 2001) WT/DS76/12, 1 p

WTO, *India—Quantitative Restrictions on Imports of Agricultural, Textile and Industrial Products—Report of the Panel* (6 April 1999) WT/DS90/R, 189 pp

WTO, *EC—Measures Affecting Asbestos and Asbestos-Containing Products—Report of the Panel* (18 September 2000) WT/DS135/R, 465 pp

WTO, *EC—Measures Affecting Asbestos and Asbestos-Containing Products—Appellate Body Report* (12 March 2000) WT/DS135/AB/R, 71 pp

WTO, *India—Measures Affecting the Automotive Sector—Report of the Panel* (21 December 2001) WT/DS146 and DS175/R, 183 pp

WTO, *European Communities—Protection of Trademarks and Geographical Indications for Agricultural Products and Foodstuffs—Request for Consultations by the United States—Addendum* (10 April 2003) WT/DS174/1/Add.1, 1 p

WTO, *European Communities—Protection of Trademarks and Geographical Indications for Agricultural Products and Foodstuffs—Communication from the Chairman of the Panel* (19 August 2004) WT/DS174/22, 1 p

WTO, *EC—Protection of Trademarks and Geographical Indications for Agricultural Products and Foodstuffs—Report of the Panel* (15 March 2005) WT/DS174/R, 168 pp

WTO, *Chile—Price Band System and Safeguard Measures Relating to Certain Agricultural Products—Report of the Panel* (3 May 2002) WT/DS207/R, 175 pp

WTO, *Chile—Price Band System and Safeguard Measures Relating to Certain Agricultural Products—Appellate Body Report* (23 September 2002) WT/DS207/AB/R, 93 pp

WTO, *EC—Trade Description of Sardines—Report of the Panel* (29 May 2002) WT/DS231/R, 101 pp

WTO, *EC—Trade Description of Sardines—Appellate Body Report* (26 September 2002) WT/DS231/AB/R, 98 pp

WTO, *EC—Trade Description of Sardines—Notification of Mutually Agreed Solution* (29 July 2003) WT/DS231/18, 6 pp

WTO, *Japan—Measures Affecting the Importation of Apples—Report of the Panel* (15 July 2003) WT/DS245/R, 280 pp

WTO, *Japan—Measures Affecting the Importation of Apples—Appellate Body Report* (26 November 2003) WT/DS245/AB/R, 93 pp

WTO, *Japan—Measures Affecting the Importation of Apples—Agreement under Article 21.3(b) of the DSU* (12 February 2004) WT/DS245/9, 1 p

WTO, *Japan—Measures Affecting the Importation of Apples—Request by Japan for Arbitration under Article 22.6 of the DSU* (10 August 2004) WT/DS245/16, 1 p

WTO, *Japan—Measures Affecting the Importation of Apples—Recourse to Article 21.5 of the DSU by the United States* (23 June 2005) WT/DS245/RW, 170 pp

WTO, *Japan—Measures Affecting the Importation of Apples—Notification of Mutually Agreed solution* (2 September 2005) WT/DS245/21, 2 pp

WTO, *EC—Conditions for Granting Tariff Preferences to Developing Countries- Report of the Panel* (1 December 2003) WT/DS246/R, 402 pp

WTO, *Korea—Measures Affecting Trade in Commercial Vessels—Report of the Panel* (7 March 2005) WT/DS273/R, 619 pp

WTO, *US—Measures Affecting the Cross-Border Supply of Gambling and Betting Services—Report of the Panel* (10 November 2004) WT/DS285/R, 451 pp

WTO, *EC—Protection of Trademarks and Geographical Indications for Agricultural Products and Foodstuffs—Report of the Panel* (15 March 2005) WT/DS290/R, 167 pp

WTO, *EC—Measures Affecting the Approval and Marketing of Biotech Products—Request for Consultations* (20 May 2003) WT/DS291, 10 pp

WTO, *European Communities—Measures Affecting the Approval and Marketing of Biotech Products—Constitution of the Panel Established at the Requests of the United States, Canada and Argentina* (5 March 2004) WT/DS291/24-WT/DS292/18 and WT/DS293/18, 5 March 2004, 2 pp

WTO, *EC—Measures Affecting the Approval and Marketing of Biotech Products—Report of the Panel* (29 September 2006) WT/DS291-DS292-DS293/R, 1200 pp

WTO, *European Communities—Measures Affecting the Approval and Marketing of Biotech Products—Agreement under Article 21.3(b) of the WTO* (26 June 2007) WT/DS291/35, 1 p

WTO, *European Communities—Measures Affecting the Approval and Marketing of Biotech Products—Modification of the Agreement under Article 21.3(b) of the DSU* (23 November 2007) WT/DS291/36, 1 p

WTO, *European Communities—Measures Affecting the Approval and Marketing of Biotech Products—Understanding between the European Communities and the United States Regarding Procedures under Articles 21 and 22 of the DSU* (17 January 2008) WT/DS291/38, 3 pp

WTO, *European Communities—Measures Affecting the Approval and Marketing of Biotech Products—Request by the European Communities for Arbitration under Article 22.6 of the DSU* (7 February 2008) WT/DS291/40, 1 p

WTO, *European Communities—Measures Affecting the Approval and Marketing of Biotech Products—Recourse by the European Communities to Article 22.6 of the DSU* (19 February 2008) WT/DS291/42, 1 p

WTO, *European Communities—Measures Affecting the Approval and Marketing of Biotech Products—Agreement under Article 21.3(b) of the DSU* (26 June 2007) WT/DS292/29, 1 p

WTO, *European Communities—Measures Affecting the Approval and Marketing of Biotech Products—Modification of the Agreement under Article 21.3(b) of the DSU* (23 November 2007) WT/DS292/30, 1 p

WTO, *European Communities—Measures Affecting the Approval and Marketing of Biotech Products—Modification of the Agreement under Article 21.3(b) of the DSU* (19 December 2008) WT/DS292/36, 1 p

WTO, *European Communities—Measures Affecting the Approval and Marketing of Biotech Products—Notification of a Mutually Agreed Solution* (17 July 2009) WT/DS292/40, 3 pp

WTO, *European Communities—Measures Affecting the Approval and Marketing of Biotech Products—Agreement under Article 21.3(b) of the DSU* (26 June 2007) WT/DS293/29, 1 p

WTO, *European Communities—Measures Affecting the Approval and Marketing of Biotech Products—Modification of the Agreement under Article 21.3(b) of the DSU* (23 November 2007) WT/DS293/30, 1 p

WTO, *European Communities—Measures Affecting the Approval and Marketing of Biotech Products—Modification of the Agreement under Article 21.3(b) of the DSU* (1 March 2010) WT/DS293/40, 1 p

WTO, *European Communities—Measures Affecting the Approval and Marketing of Biotech Products—Notification of a Mutually Agreed Solution* (23 March 2010) WT/DS293/41, 4 pp

WTO, *EC—Selected Customs Matters—Report of the Panel* (16 June 2006) WT/DS315/R, 639 pp

WTO, *European Communities—Measures Concerning Meat and Meat Products (Hormones)—Continued Suspension of Obligations in the EC—Hormones Dispute—Request for Consultations by the European Communities* (10 November 2004) WT/DS320/1, 3 pp

WTO, *EC—Hormones Dispute—US—Continued Suspension of Obligations—Report of the Panel* (31 March 2008) WT/DS320/R, 332 pp

WTO, *EC—Hormones Dispute—US—Continued Suspension of Obligations—Appellate Body Report* (16 October 2008) WT/DS320/AB/R, 333 pp

WTO, *European Communities—Measures Concerning Meat and Meat Products (Hormones)-Continued Suspension of Obligations in the EC—Hormones Dispute—Request for Consultations by the European Communities* (9 November 2004) WT/DS321/1, 3 pp

WTO, *EC—Hormones Dispute—Canada—Continued Suspension of Obligations- Report of the Panel* (31 March 2008) WT/DS321/R, 325 pp

WTO, *Turkey—Measures Affecting the Importation of Rice—Report of the Panel* (21 September 2007) WT/DS334/R, 435 pp

WTO, *US—Continued Existence and Application of Zeroing Methodology—Report of the Panel* (1 October 2008) WT/DS350/R, 445 pp

WTO, *India—Additional and Extra-Additional Duties on Imports from the United States—Report of the Panel* (9 June 2008) WT/DS360/R, 182 pp

WTO, *China—Measures Affecting the Protection and Enforcement of Intellectual Property Rights—Report of the Panel* (26 January 2009) WT/DS362/R, 315 pp

WTO, *China—Measures Affecting Trading Rights and Distribution Services for Certain Publications and Audio-visual Entertainment Products—Report of the Panel* (12 August 2009) WT/DS363/R, 499 pp

WTO, *Australia—Measures Affecting the Importation of Apples from New Zealand—Report of the Panel* (9 August 2010) WT/DS367/R, 598 pp

WTO, *Australia—Measures Affecting the Importation of Apples from New Zealand—Appellate Body Report* (29 November 2010) WT/DS367/AB/R, 163 pp

WTO, *Australia—Measures Affecting the Importation of Apples from New Zealand—Request for Consultations by New Zealand* (4 September 2007) WT/DS367/1, 1 p

WTO, *Australia—Measures Affecting the Importation of Apples from New Zealand—Agreement under Article 21.3(b) of the DSU* (1 February 2011) WT/DS367/19, 1 p

WTO, *Australia—Measures Affecting the Importation of Apples from New Zealand—Understanding between New Zealand and Australia Regarding Procedures under Article 21 and 22 of the DSU* (19 September 2011) WT/DS367/21, 3 pp

WTO, *US—Measures Concerning the Importation, Marketing and Sale of Tuna and Tuna Products—Request for Consultations by Mexico* (28 October 2008) WT/DS381/R/1, 2 pp

WTO, *US—Measures Concerning the Importation, Marketing and Sale of Tuna and Tuna Products—Report of the Panel* (15 September 2011) WT/DS381/R, 292 pp

WTO, *US—Measures Concerning the Importation, Marketing and Sale of Tuna and Tuna Products—Joint Request by Mexico and the United States for a Decision by the DSB* (1 November 2011) WT/DS381/9, 1 p

WTO, *US—Measures Concerning the Importation, Marketing and Sale of Tuna and Tuna Products—Appellate Body Report* (16 May 2012) WT/DS381/AB/R, 161 pp

WTO, *US—Measures Concerning the Importation Marketing and Sale of Tuna and Tuna Products—Agreement under Article 21.3(b) of the DSU* (19 September 2012) WT/DS381/17, 1 p

WTO, *US—Anti-Dumping Administrative Reviews and Other Measures Related to Imports of Certain Orange Juice from Brazil—Report of the Panel* (25 March 2011) WT/DS382/R, 202 pp

WTO, *US—Certain Country of Origin Labelling (COOL) Requirements—Request for Consultations by Canada* (4 December 2008) WT/DS384/1, 2 pp

WTO, *US—Certain Country of Origin Labelling (COOL) Requirements—Request for Consultations by Canada* (22 December 2008) WT/DS386/1, 2 pp

WTO, *US—Certain Country of Origin Labelling (COOL) Requirements—Constitution of the Panel Established at the Requests of Canada and Mexico, Note by the Secretariat* (11 May 2010) WT/DS384/9 and WT/DS386/8, 1 p

WTO, *US—Certain Country of Origin Labelling (COOL) Requirements—Notification of an Appeal by the US under Article 16.4 and Article 17 of the Understanding on Rules and Procedures Governing the Settlement of Disputes (DSU) and under Rule 20(1) of the Working Procedures for Appellate Review* (28 March 2011) WT/DS384/12 and WT/DS386/11, 1 p

WTO, *US—Certain Country of Origin Labelling (COOL) requirements—Report of the Panel* (18 November 2011) WT/DS384 and DS386/R, 432 pp

WTO, *US—Certain Country of Origin Labelling (COOL) Requirements—Notification of an Appeal by Canada under Article 16.4 and Article 17 of the Understanding on Rules and Procedures Governing the Settlement of Disputes (DSU) and under Rule 23(1) of the Working Procedures for Appellate Review* (2 April 2012) WT/DS384/13, 2 pp

WTO, *US—Certain Country of Origin Labelling (COOL) requirements—Appellate Body Report* (29 June 2012) WT/DS384 and DS386/AB/R, 232 pp

WTO, *US—Certain Country of Origin Labelling (COOL) Requirements—Communication from the US* (23 August 2012) WT/DS384/19 and WT/DS386/18, 1 p

WTO, *US—Certain Country of Origin Labelling (COOL) requirements—Arbitration under Article 21.3(c) of the Understanding on Rules and Procedures Governing the Settlement of Disputes* (4 December 2012) WT/DS384/24 and WT/DS386/23, 58 pp

WTO, *US—Certain Country of Origin Labelling (COOL) Requirements—Recourse to Article 21.5 of the DSU by Canada* (20 August 2013) WT/DS384/26, 3 pp

WTO, *US—Certain Country of Origin Labelling (COOL) Requirements—Recourse to Article 21.5 of the DSU by Mexico* (20 August 2013) WT/DS386/25, 3 pp

WTO, *US—Certain Country of Origin Labelling (COOL) Requirements—Recourse to Article 21.5 of the DSU by Canada and Mexico* (20 October 2014) WT/DS384 and DS386/RW, 206 pp

WTO, *US—Certain Country of Origin Labelling (COOL) Requirements—Recourse to Article 21.5 of the DSU by Canada and Mexico, Notification of an Appeal by the United States under Article 16.4 and Article 17 of the Understanding on Rules and Procedures Governing the Settlement of Disputes (DSU) and under Rule 20(1) of the Working Procedures for Appellate Review* (2 December 2014) WT/DS384/29 and WT/DS386/28, 2 pp

WTO, *Korea—Measures Affecting the Importation of Bovine Meat and Meat Products from Canada—Report of the Panel* (3 July 2012) WT/DS391/R, 4 pp

WTO, *US—Certain Measures Affecting Imports of Poultry from China—Request for Consultations by China* (21 April 2009) WT/DS392/1, 2 pp

WTO, *US—Certain Measures Affecting Imports of Poultry from China—Report of the Panel* (29 September 2010) WT/DS392/R, 184 pp

WTO, *European Communities—Measures Prohibiting the Importation and Marketing of Seal Products—Constitution of the Panel Established at the Requests of Canada and Norway* (5 October 2012) WT/DS400/5 and WT/DS401/6, 2 pp

WTO, *European Communities—Measures Prohibiting the Importation and Marketing of Seal Products—Report of the Panel* (25 November 2013) WT/DS400 and DS401/R, 186 pp

WTO, *EC—Measures Prohibiting the Importation and Marketing of Seal Products—Appellate Body Report* (22 May 2014) WT/DS400 and DS401/AB/R, 208 pp

WTO, *European Communities—Measures Prohibiting the Importation and Marketing of Seal Products—Agreement under Article 21.3(b) of the DSU* (8 September 2014) WT/DS400/15, 1 p

WTO, *US—Measures Affecting the Production and Sale of Clove Cigarettes—Report of the Panel* (2 September 2011) WT/DS406/R, 285 pp

WTO, *US—Measures Affecting the Production and Sale of Clove Cigarettes—Appellate Body Report* (4 April 2012) WT/DS406/AB/R, 106 pp

WTO, *US—Measures Affecting the Production and Sale of Clove Cigarettes—Agreement under Article 21.3(b) of the DSU* (19 June 2012) WT/DS406/10, 1 p

WTO, *US—Measures Affecting the Production and Sale of Clove Cigarettes—Recourse to Article 22.2 of the DSU by Indonesia* (13 August 2013) WT/DS406/12, 2 pp

WTO, *US—Measures Affecting the Production and Sale of Clove Cigarettes—Recourse to Article 22.6 of the DSU by the United States, Communication from the Arbitrator* (9 October 2014) WT/DS406/18, 2 pp

WTO, *Dominican Republic—Safeguard Measures on Imports of Polypropylene Bags and Tubular Fabric—Report of the Panel* (31 January 2012) WT/DS415-DS416-DS417-DS418, 117, 146 pp

WTO, *India—Measures Concerning the Importation of Certain Agricultural Products—Report of the Panel* (14 October 2014) WT/DS430/R, 212 pp

WTO, *India—Measures Concerning the Importation of Certain Agricultural Products—Notification of an Appeal by India under Article 16.4 and Article 17 of the Understanding on Rules and Procedures Governing the Settlement of Disputes (DSU) and under Rule 20(1) of the Working Procedures for Appellate Review* (2 February 2015) WT/DS430/8, 6 pp

WTO, *India—Measures Concerning the Importation of Certain Agricultural Products—Appellate Body Report* (4 June 2015) WT/DS430/AB/R, 135 pp

WTO, *China—Measures Related to the Exportation of Rare Earths, Tungsten and Molybdenum—Reports of the Panel* (26 March 2014) WT/DS431-DS432-DS433/R, 261 pp

WTO, *China—Measures Related to the Exportation of Rare Earths, Tungsten and Molybdenum—Reports of the Panel, Addendum* (26 March 2014) WT/DS431-DS432-DS433/R/Add.1, 123 pp

WTO, *China—Measures Relating to the Production and Exportation of Apparel and Textile Products—Request for Consultations by Mexico* (18 October 2012) WT/DS451/1, 12 pp

WTO, *Argentina—Measures Relating to Trade in Goods and Services—Report of the Panel* (30 September 2015) WT/DS453/R, 266 pp

WTO, *Argentina —Measures Relating to Trade in Goods and Services—Report of the Panel, Addendum* (30 September 2015) WT/DS453/R/Add. 1, 84 pp

WTO, *Australia—Certain Measures Concerning Trademarks, Geographical Indications and other Plain Packaging Requirements applicable to Tobacco Products and Packaging—Request for consultations by Indonesia* (25 September 2013) WT/DS467/1, 3 pp

WTO, DSB, Minutes of the Meeting, WT/DSB/M/62, 2 July 1999, 4 pp

WTO, DSB, Minutes of the Meeting, WT/DSB/M/80, 26 June 2000, 13 pp

WTO, DSB, Minutes of the Meeting, WT/DSB/M/157, 18 December 2003, 8 pp

WTO, DSB, Minutes of the Meeting, WT/DSB/M/159, 15 January 2004, 5 pp

WTO, DSB, Minutes of the Meeting, WT/DSB/M/174, 1 September 2004, 3 pp

WTO, DSB, Minutes of the Meeting, WT/DSB/M/159, 15 January 2005, 9 pp

WTO, DSB, Minutes of the Meeting, WT/DSB/M/189, 17 June 2005, 23 pp

WTO, DSB, Minutes of the Meeting, WT/DSB/M/205, 31 March 2006, 21 pp

WTO, DSB, Minutes of the Meeting, WT/DSB/M/210, 30 May 2006, 24 pp

WTO, DSB, Minutes of the Meeting, WT/DSB/M/222, 12 January 2007, 19 pp

WTO, DSB, Minutes of the Meeting, WT/DSB/M/261, 6 March 2009, 19 pp

WTO, DSB, Minutes of the Meeting, WT/DSB/M/273, 6 November 2009, 21 pp

WTO, DSB, Minutes of the Meeting, WT/DSB/M/276, 29 January 2010, 17 pp

WTO, DSB, Minutes of the Meeting, WT/DSB/M/302, 28 October 2011, 15 pp
WTO, DSB, Minutes of the Meeting, WT/DSB/M/294, 9 June 2011, 30 pp
WTO, DSB, Minutes of the Meeting, WT/DSB/M/332, 31 July 2013, 23 pp
WTO, DSB, Minutes of the Meeting, WT/DSB/M/352, 30 January 2015, 15 pp

e) Miscellaneous

WTO, Communication from the Working Group on the Interaction between Trade and Competition Policy, WT/WGTCP/W/243, 28 July 2003, 33 pp
WTO, Communication from the Working Group on the Interaction between Trade and Competition Policy, WT/WGTCP/W/244, 28 July 2003, 19 pp
WTO, Recommendations of the Task Force on Aid for Trade, WT/AFT/1, 27 July 2006, 25 pp
WTO, Transparency Mechanism for Regional Trade Agreements, Decision of 14 December 2006, WT/L/671, 18 December 2006, 6 pp
WTO, Monitoring Mechanism on Special and Differential Treatment, Ministerial Decision of 7 December 2013, Ministerial Conference, Ninth Session, Bali, 3–6 December 2013, WT/MIN(13)/45, WT/L/920, 11 December 2013, 2 pp
Deborah K. Elms and Patrick Low (eds) *Global Value Chains in a Changing World* (Fung Global Institute (FGI) Nayang Technological University (NTU) and WTO 2013) 436 pp
WTO, *World Trade Statistical Review* (WTO, 2016) 163 pp

2. Secondary sources related to the WTO

a) Books

Boorman, A and Koopmann, G, *Adapting the WTO Trade Policy Reviews to the Needs of Developing Countries: Starting Points and Options* (Hamburg Institute of International Economics 2002) 110 pp
Chayes, A and Chayes, AH, *The New Sovereignty—Compliance with International Regulatory Agreements* (Harvard University Press 1995) 404 pp
Cline, WR (ed) *Trade Policy in the 1980s* (The Institute for International Economics 1983) 796 pp
Fabri, HL, Sicilianos, LA, and Sorel, JM, *L'effectivité des Organisations Internationales, Mécanismes de suivi et de contrôle* (Paris 2000) 338 pp
Ghosh, A, *See No Evil, Speak No Evil, The WTO, The Trade Policy Review Mechanism, And Developing Countries* (DPhil thesis, University of Oxford 2008) 431 pp
Jackson, JH, *Restructuring the GATT System* (The Royal Institute of International Affairs 1990) 121 pp
Jackson, JH, *The World Trade Organization, Constitution and Jurisprudence* (The Royal Institute of International Affairs 1998) 193 pp
Kessing, D, *Improving Trade Policy Reviews in the World Trade Organization* (Institute for International Economics 1998) 80 pp
Lamy, P, *The Geneva Consensus—Making Trade Work for All* (Cambridge University Press 2013) 202 pp
Mei, CY, *WTO Trade Policy Review Mechanism, Legal Issues* (1991)
Qureshi, AH, *The World Trade Organization: Implementing Trade Norms* (Manchester University Press 1996) 272 pp
Ratnesh K, *WTO (World Trade Organization): Structure, Functions, Tasks and Challenges* (Deep & Deep 2002) 249 pp
Shatz, D, *Peer Review—A Critical Inquiry* (Rowman & Littlefield Publishers 2004) 249 pp

Steward, TP, *The GATT Uruguay Round: A Negotiating History (1986–1992)* vol II (Kluwer Law International 1993–1999) 2921 pp

VanGrasstek, C, *The History and Future of the World Trade Organization* (WTO 2013) 700 pp

Ying, QY, *WTO Trade Policy Review Mechanism* (2009) 199 pp

Ying, QY, *The Principles and Functions of WTO Trade Policy Review Mechanism* (2012) 397 pp

b) Articles and compilations

Abbot, R, 'GATT and the Trade Policy Review Mechanism: Further Reflections on Earlier Reflections' (1993) 27(3) Journal of World Trade 117–19

Ala'I, P, 'From the Periphery to the Center? The Evolving WTO Jurisprudence on Transparency and Good Governance' (2008) 11(4) Journal of International Economic Law 779–802

Ala'I, P, 'Transparency and the Expansion of the WTO Mandate' (2011) 26(4) American University International Law Review 1009–29

Anderson, K, 'The GATT's Review of Australian Trade Policy' [1995] The World Economy: Global Trade Policy 91–105

Ankersmit, LJ and Lawrence, JC, 'The Future of Environmental Labelling: US—Tuna II and the Scope of the TBT' (2012) 39 Legal Issues of Economic Integration 127–47

Armin, S, 'A New Form of Governance? Comparing the Open Method of Coordination to Multilateral Surveillance by the IMF and the OECD' (2006) 13(1) Journal of European Public Policy, 70–88

Appleton, A, 'GATT Article XX's Chapeau: A Disguised 'Necessity' Test? The WTO Appellate Body's Ruling in United States—Standards for Reformulated and Conventional Gasoline' (1997) 6(2) Review of European Community & International Environmental Law 13–138

Athukorala, P, 'Malaysian Trade Policy and the 2001 WTO Trade Policy Review' [2002] The World Economy: Global Trade Policy 1297–317

Athukorala, P, 'Trade Policy Making in a Small Island Economy: The WTO Review of the Maldives' [2004] The World Economy: Global Trade Policy 1401–419

Balasubramanyam, VN, 'India's Trade Policy Review' [1995] The World Economy: Global Trade Policy 79–90

Balasubramanyam, VN, 'India: Trade Policy Review' [2002] The World Economy: Global Trade Policy 1368

Ballet, L, 'Losing Flavour: Indonesia's WTO Complaint Against the US Ban on Clove Cigarettes' (2011) 26(2) American University International Law Review 515–41

Berlinski, J, 'The WTO Trade Policy Review of Argentina' [2000] The World Economy: Global Trade Policy 1195–213

Biagioli, M, 'From Book Censorship to Academic Peer Review' (2002) 12(1) Emergences: Journal for the Study of Media & Composite Cultures 11–45

Blackhurst, R, 'Strengthening GATT Surveillance of Trade-Related Policies' in M Hilf and E-U Petersman (eds) *The New GATT Round of Multilateral Trade Negotiations: Legal and Economic Aspects* (Kluwer Law and Taxation Publishers 1988) 124–55

Bourgeois, HJ, 'GATT Surveillance of Trade Related Policies: A Comment' in M Hilf and E-U Petersman, *The New GATT Round of Multilateral Trade Negotiations: Legal and Economic Aspects* (Kluwer Law and Taxation Publishers 1988) 157–61

Canada Challenges Korean Beef Ban at the WTO (2009) 13(14) Bridges 8–9

South Korea Lifts Ban on Canadian Beef Imports (2012) 16(3) Bridges 11–12

WTO Panel Grants US Victory in India Poultry Ban Dispute (2014) 18(34) Bridges, 16–17

WTO Affirms US Victory in India Poultry Ban Case (2015) 19(21) Bridges 15–17

Chaisse J and Chakraborty, D, 'Implementing WTO Rules Through Negotiations and Sanctions: The Role of Trade Policy Review Mechanism and Dispute Settlement System' (2007) 28(1) Pennsylvania Journal of International Economic Law 153–86

Chaisse, J and Matsushita, M, 'Maintaining the WTO's Supremacy in the International Trade Order: A Proposal to Refine and Revise the Role of the Trade Policy Review Mechanism' (2013) 16(1) Journal of International Economic Law 9–36

Charnovitz, S, 'Transparency and Participation in the World Trade Organization' (2004) 56 Rutgers Law Review 1–31

Collier, P, 'The Trade Policy Review of Uganda' [1997] The World Economy: Global Trade Policy 649–64

Cottier, T, 'Preparing for structural reform in the WTO' (2007) 10(3) Journal of International Economic Law 497–508

Cottier, T, 'The Common Law of International Trade and the Future of the World Trade Organization' (2015) 18 Journal of International Economic Law 3–20

Cuthbertson, AG (Sandy) 'The Trade Policy Review of Sri Lanka' [1997] The World Economy: Global Trade Policy 633–48

Damijan, JP and Majcen, B, 'Trade Policy in a Small Advanced Transition Economy: Trade Policy Review of Slovenia, 2002' [2002] The World Economy: Global Trade Policy 1369–394

Delimatsis, P, 'Institutional Transparency in the WTO', in A Bianchi and A Peters (eds) *Transparency in International Law* (Cambridge University Press 2014) 112–42

Downs, GW, Rocke, DM, and Barsoom, PN, 'Is the Goods News about Compliance Good News about Co-operation?' (1996) 50(3) International Organization 379–406

'After Kennedy and Tokyo, the Leutwiler Round', *The Economist* (London, 30 March 1985) 73–4

'Trouble at the Lab—Scientists like to Think of Science as Self-correcting. To an Alarming Degree, it is not', *The Economist* (London, 19 October 2013) 21–4

Fane, G, 'The Trade Policy Review of Indonesia' [1996] The World Economy: Global Trade Policy 101–17

Flores, RG, 'Brazilian Trade Policy and the WTO' [1997] The World Economy: Global Trade Policy 615–31

Footer, M and Zia-Zarifi, S, 'Case Notes—European Communities—Measures Affecting Asbestos and Asbestos-Containing Products, The World Trade Organization on Trial for its Handling of Occupational Health and Safety Issues' (2002) 3(1) Melbourne Journal of International Law 120–42

Francois, JF, 'Trade Policy Transparency and Investor Confidence: Some Implications for an Effective Trade Policy Review Mechanism' (2001) 9 (2) Review of International Economics 303–16

Froese, MD, 'Trade Policy Review and Dispute Settlement at the WTO', in DA. Deese (eds) *Handbook of the International Political Economy of Trade* (Edward Elgar Publishing 2012) 349–97

Gangjee, D, 'Quibbling Siblings: Conflicts between Trademarks and Geographical Indications' (2007) 82(3) Chicago-Kent Law Review 1253–291

Goh, G, 'Tipping the Apple Cart: The Limits of Science and Law in the SPS Agreement after Japan—Apples' (2006) 40(4) Journal of World Trade 655–86

Ghosh, A, 'Developing Countries in the WTO Trade Policy Review Mechanism' (2010) 9(3) World Trade Review 419–55

Ghosh, A, 'Strengthening WTO surveillance: Making Transparency Work for Developing Countries', in CD Birbeck (ed) *Making Global Trade Governance Work for*

Development: Perspectives and Priorities from Developing Countries (Cambridge University Press 2011) 394–441

Gunning, JW, 'The Trade Policy Review of Zimbabwe' [1996] The World Economy: Global Trade Policy 157–66

Hare, PG, 'Trade Policy Review of Poland, 2000' [2001] The World Economy: Global Trade Policy 1179–204

Hauser, H and Straw, R, 'Swiss Trade Policy and the 1996 WTO Review' [1997] The World Economy: Global Trade Policy 665–79

Head, K and Ries, J, 'Regionalism Within Multilateralism: The WTO Trade Policy Review of Canada' [2004] The World Economy: Global Trade Policy 1377–399

Henry, H, 'Formulating Trade Policy in a Small Hydrocarbon-dependent Economy: The Case of Trinidad and Tobago' [2007] The World Economy: Global Trade Policy 1222–251

Holden, M, 'GATT Trade Policy Review—South Africa: 1993' [1995] The World Economy: Global Trade Policy 121–33

Howse, R, 'The Sardines Panel and AB Rulings – Some Preliminary Reactions' (2002) 29(3) Legal Issues of Economic Integration 247–54

Howse, R, Langille, J, and Sykes, K, 'Sealing the Deal: The WTO's Appellate Body Report in EC—Seal Products' (2014) 18(12) American Society of International Law, Insights, 2 pp

Kehoe, TJ, 'A Review of Mexico's Trade Policy from 1982 to 1994' [1995] The World Economy: Global Trade Policy 135–51

Kende, M, 'Monetary Affairs in the WTO Trade Policy Review Mechanism' in T Cottier, RM Lastra, C Tietje, and L Satragno (eds) *The Rule of Law in Monetary Affairs* (Cambridge University Press 2014) 384–408

Kolsky Lewis, M, 'Australians Get Their First Taste of New Zealand Apples in Ninety Years,' (2011) 25(25) American Society of International Law, Insights, 6 pp

Kreinin, ME, 'Israel's Trade Policy Review' [1996] The World Economy: Global Trade Policy 119–32

Krueger, AO, 'US Trade Policy and the GATT Review' [1995] The World Economy: Global Trade Policy 65–77

Laird, S, 'The WTO's Trade Policy Review Mechanism—From Through the Looking Glass' (1999) 22(6) The World Economy 741–64

Laird, S and Messerlin, P, 'Institutional Reform for Trade Liberalization' (1990) 13(2) The World Economy 230–49

Laird, S and Valdés, R, 'The Trade Policy Review Mechanism', in A Narlikar, M Daunton, and RM Stern (eds) *The Oxford Handbook on The World Trade Organization* (Oxford University Press 2012) 463–84

Lee, J-E, 'Identifying Trade Structure and Macroeconomic Caveats: The Post-crisis of Korea' [2006] The World Economy: Global Trade Policy 1311–327

Ludema, RD, 'Allies and Friends: The Trade Policy Review of the United States, 2006' [2007] The World Economy: Global Trade Policy 1209–221

Marceau G and Hurley M, 'Transparency and Public Participation in the WTO: A Report Card on WTO Transparency Mechanisms' (2012) 4(1) Trade Law and Development 19–44

Marotti, M, 'Primum non nocere: Authors or Reviewers' (2011) 57(5) Revista Da Associacao Medica Brasileira 477–87

Matsushita, M, 'A View on Future Roles of the WTO: Should there be More Soft Law in the WTO' (2014) 17 Journal of International Economic Law 701–15

Mavroidis, P, 'Surveillance Schemes: The GATT's New Trade Policy Review Mechanism' (1992) 13(2) Michigan Journal of International Law 399–414

McKay, A, 'Trade Policy Issues in a Small African Economy: The Trade Policy Review of the Gambia 2004' [2005] The World Economy: Global Trade Policy 1197–209

Melchior, A, 'The Most and Least Favoured Nations: Norway's Trade Policy in Perspective' [2006] The World Economy: Global Trade Policy 1329–346

Milner, C, 'Trade Policy in Burundi: Reform Without Political Stability' [2004] The World Economy: Global Trade Policy 1363–376

Ostry, S, 'China and the WTO: Transparency Issue' (1998) 3(1) UCLA Journal of International Law and Foreign Affairs 1–22

Panagariya, A, 'The WTO Trade Policy Review of India, 1998' [1999] The World Economy: Global Trade Policy 799–824

Patterson, G and Patterson, E, 'Importance of a GATT Review in the New Negotiations' (1986) 9(2) The World Economy 153–69

Pauwelyn, J, 'The WTO Agreement on Sanitary and Phytosanitary (SPS) Measures as Applied in the First Three SPS Disputes: EC—Hormones, Australia—Salmon and Japan—Varietals' (1999) 2(4) Journal of International Economic Law 641–64

Pauwelyn, J, 'Rules-Based Trade 2.0? The Rise of Informal Rules and International Standards and How They May Outcompete WTO Treaties' (2014) 17 Journal of International Economic Law 739–51

Pelkmans, J and Carzaniga, AG, 'The Trade Policy Review of the European Union' [1996] The World Economy: Global Trade Policy 81–100

Prévost, D, 'Opening Pandora's Box: The Panel's Findings in the EC–Biotech Products Dispute' (2007) 34 Legal Issues of Economic Integration 67–101

Price, VC, 'GATT's New Trade Policy Review Mechanism' (1991) 14(2) The World Economy 227–38

Price, VC, 'New Institutional Developments in GATT' (1992) 1(1) Minnesota Journal of Global Trade 87–110

Prusa, TJ, '2004 Trade Policy Review—The United States' [2005] The World Economy: Global Trade Policy, 1263–275

Qureshi, AH, 'The New GATT Trade Policy Review Mechanism: An Exercise in Transparency or 'Enforcement'' (1990) June, Journal of World Trade 149–60

Qureshi, AH, 'Some Reflections on the GATT TPRM, in the Light of the Trade Policy Review of the European Communities—A Legal Perspective' (1992) 26(6) Journal of World Trade 103–20

Qureshi, AH, 'Some Lessons from "Developing Countries" Trade Policy Reviews in the GATT Framework: An Enforcement Perspective' (1995) 18(3) The World Economy 489–503

Rajapatirana, S, 'Columbian Trade Policies and the 1996 WTO Trade Policy Review' [1998] The World Economy: Global Trade Policy 515–27

Ramasamy, B and Yeung, M, 'Malaysia—Trade Policy Review 2006' [2007] The World Economy: Global Trade Policy 1193–208

Regan, DH, 'United States—Certain Measures Affecting Imports of Poultry from China: The Fascinating Case that Wasn't' (2012) 11(2) World Trade Review 273–305

Richardson, M, 'New Zealand Trade Policy and the 1996 WTO Review' [1998] The World Economy: Global Trade Policy 529–47

Roberts, D, 'Preliminary Assessment of the Effects of the WTO Agreement on Sanitary and Phytosanitary Trade Regulations' (1998) 1(3) Journal of International Economic Law 377–405

Stern, RM, 'The Trade Policy Review of Japan' [1996] The World Economy: Global Trade Policy 133–55

Stern, RM, 'The WTO Trade Policy Review of the United States' [1998] The World Economy: Global Trade Policy 483–514

Taylor, MD, 'The WTO Panel Decision on Australia's Salmon Import Guidelines: Evidence that the SPS Agreement can Effectively Protect Human Health Interests' (2000) 9(2) Pacific Rim Law & Policy Journal Association 473–506

Teal, F, 'Export Growth and Trade Policy in Ghana in the Twentieth Century' [2002] The World Economy: Global Trade Policy 1319–337

Thangavelu, SM and Toh, M-H, 'Bilateral WTO-Plus Free Trade Agreements: The WTO Trade Policy Review of Singapore 2004' [2005] The World Economy: Global Trade Policy 1211–228

Tharakan, PKM, 'Beyond Transparency: An Analysis of the Trade Policy Review of the European Union' [1999] The World Economy: Global Trade Policy 825–36

Tharakan, PKM, 'Storm Signals: An Analysis of the Trade Policy Review of the European Communities' [2006] The World Economy: Global Trade Policy 1301–310

Togan, S, 'Trade Policy Review of the Republic of Turkey' [1995] The World Economy: Global Trade Policy, 107–20

Togan, S, 'Turkey: Trade Policy Review' [2005] The World Economy: Global Trade Policy 1229–262

Van Damme, I, 'Seventh Annual WTO Conference: An Overview' (2007) 11(1) Journal of International Economic Law 155–65

Warr, PG, 'Thailand's Post-crisis Trade Policies, The 1999 WTO Review' [2000] The World Economy: Global Trade Policy 1215–236

Wiers, J, 'Responsible Decision-makers, Do It Yourself: The Panel Report in the Asbestos Case' (2001) 28(1) 117–26

Wirth, D, 'The World Trade Organization Dispute Over Genetically Modified Organisms: The Precautionary Principle Meets International Trade Law' (2013) 4, Vermont Law Review 1153–188

Wolfe, R, 'Regulatory Transparency, Developing Countries and the WTO' (2003) 2(2) World Trade Review 157–82

Wonnacott, RJ, 'Canadian Trade Policy: The GATT's 1995 Review' [1996] The World Economy: Global Trade Policy 67–80

Wouters, J and Odermatt, J, 'Comparing the "Four Pillars" of Global Economic Governance: A Critical Analysis of the Institutional Design of the FSB, IMF, World Bank, and WTO' (2014) 17 Journal of International Economic Law 49–76

c) Conference, research, and working papers and reports

Ala'I, P, 'From the Periphery to the Center? The Evolving Jurisprudence on Transparency and Good Governance' (4th Global Administrative Law Seminar: From Fragmentation to Unity? Viterbo, 2008) 32 pp. <https://prd-idrc.azureedge.net/sites/default/files/open-ebooks/455-0/index.html#page_165> accessed 6 May 2017

Baracat, E and Nogués, JJ, 'WTO Safeguards and Trade Liberalization – Lessons from the Argentina Footwear Case' (2005) World Bank Policy Research Working Paper No 3614, 35 pp. <http://elibrary.worldbank.org/doi/abs/10.1596/1813-9450-3614> accessed 6 May 2017

Brown, T, *Peer Review and the Acceptance of New Scientific Ideas* (November 2004–May 2004) Sense About Science, Discussion paper from a Working Party on equipping the public with an understanding of peer review, 49 pp. <http://archive.senseaboutscience.org/data/files/resources/17/peerReview.pdf> accessed 13 May 2017

Carmichael, B, 'Trade Policy at the Cross-Roads' (2005) Australian National University, Pacific Economic Papers, No 351, 24 pp. <https://crawford.anu.edu.au/pdf/pep/pep-351.pdf> accessed 17 June 2017

Conzelmann, T, 'Beyond the Carrot and the Stick'—(How) Do State Reporting Procedures Matter?' (ECPR Uppsala Joint Sessions, 2004) 23 pp. <https://ecpr.eu/Filestore/PaperProposal/8e9b4d5a-1ba2-4933-af69-c2c59f40f368.pdf> accessed 6 May 2017

Conzelmann, T, 'Beyond the Carrot and the Stick: The Authority of Peer Reviews in the WTO and the OECD' (Paper for presentation at the ECPR Standing Group for International Relations, 2010) 27 pp

Dimitropoulos, G, 'Compliance Through Collegiality—Peer Review in International Law' (2014) Max Planck Institute Luxembourg Working Paper 3, 72 pp. <http://www.mpi.lu/fileadmin/mpi/medien/research/Dimitropoulos_Compliance_through_Collegiality_2014_8_18_WPS.pdf> accessed 6 May 2017

Evenett, SJ and Jara, A, 'Building on Bali—A Work Programme for the WTO' (Centre for Economic Policy Research, A VoxEU.org eBook, 2013) 203 pp. <http://voxeu.org/content/building-bali-work-programme-wto> accessed 25 May 2017

Francois, JF, 'Maximizing the Benefits of the Trade Policy Review Mechanism for Developing Countries' [1999] Tinbergen Institute and CEPR, 13 pp. <https://www.iatp.org/sites/default/files/Maximizing_the_Benefits_of_the_Trade_Policy_5.htm> accessed 6 May 2017

Greene, JL, 'Country-of-Origin Labelling for Food and the WTO Trade Dispute on Meat Labelling' (Report 7-5700, US Congressional Research Service, 5 November 2014) 51 pp

Greven, T, 'Social Standards in Bilateral and Regional Trade and Investment Agreements—Instruments, Enforcement and Policy Options for Trade Unions' (Friedrich Ebert Stiftung, No 16, March 2005) 55 pp

Johnson, R, 'The U.S.–EU Beef Hormones Dispute' (Report 40449, US Congressional Research Service, 14 January 2015) 34 pp

Jurenas, R and Manyin, ME, 'US–South Korea Beef Dispute: Issues and Status' (Report RL34528, Congressional Research Service, 23 September 2010) 15 pp

Levy, PI and Regan, DH, 'EC—Seal Products: Seals and Sensibilities (TBT Aspects of the Panel and Appellate Body Reports)' (2014) European University Institute, Working Papers, RSCAS 2014/108, 39 pp. <http://cadmus.eui.eu/bitstream/handle/1814/33774/RSCAS_2014_108.pdf;sequence=1> accessed 17 June 2017

Opromolla, A, 'Enhancing Labour Rights in a Globalised World: A Comparative Transatlantic Perspective' (2007) CRIDHO Working Paper No 4, 28 pp

Santarius, T, Dalkmann, H, Steigenberger, M, and Vogelpohl, K, 'Balancing Trade and Environment—An Ecological Reform of the WTO as a Challenge in Sustainable Global Governance' (Wuppertal Institute for Climate, Environment and Energy, 2004) 62 pp

Shaffer, G, Mosoti, V, and Qureshi, A, 'Towards A Development–Supportive Dispute Settlement System in the WTO' (2003) No 5, ICTSD Resource Paper, 113 pp

Zahrnt, V, 'The WTO's Trade Policy Review Mechanism: How to Create Political Will for Liberalization' (2009) 11 ECIPE Working Paper, 29 pp. <http://www.ecipe.org/app/uploads/2014/12/the-wto2019s-trade-policy-review-mechanism-how-to-create-political-will-for-liberalization-1.pdf> accessed 6 May 2017

d) Written and oral interviews

Answers from Dr Richard Eglin to a questionnaire of the author, fourth director of the Trade Policy Review Division (Geneva, 15 January 2013)

Answers from Mr Peter Tulloch to a questionnaire of the author, second director of the Trade Policy Review Division (Geneva, 18 January 2014)

Interview with a diplomat of the Delegation of the Russian Federation (Geneva, 20 January 2014)

Interview with a diplomat of the Delegation of Canada (Geneva, 20 January 2014)

Interview with a diplomat of the Delegation of the European Union (Geneva, 27 January 2014)

Answers from Mr Frank Wolter to a questionnaire of the author, first director of the Trade Policy Review Division (Geneva, 2 April 2014)

Interview with a diplomat of the Delegation of the Republic of Argentina (Geneva, 6 August 2014)

Interview with a former WTO expert, April 2015, 5 pp

Interview with a diplomat of the Delegation of the Republic of Peru (Geneva, 6 May 2015)

Interview with Dr Clemens Boonekamp, third director of the Trade Policy Review Department (Geneva, July 2015)

Interview with Mr Willy Alfaro, fifth director of the Trade Policy Review Department (Geneva, July 2015)

Answers from the Budgetary Department of the WTO to questions of the author (23 July 2015 and 24 January 2016)

Interview with a diplomat of the Delegation of the Republic of Israel (Geneva, 7 September 2015)

Answers from the Human Resources Department of the WTO to questions of the author (4 December 2015)

Answers from the Budgetary Department of the WTO to questions of the author (29 January 2016)

B. NON-WTO-RELATED SOURCES

1. Primary sources

African Union (Assembly of Heads of State and Government) 'Declaration on Democracy, Political, Economic and Corporate Governance' (8 July 2002) AHG/235 (XXXVIII) Annex I (hereafter African Union, Declaration on Democracy, Political, Economic and Corporate Governance) 10 pp

New Partnership for Africa's Development (6th Summit of the NEPAD Heads of State and Government Implementation Committee) 'African Peer Review Mechanism (APRM): Base Document' (9 March 2003) NEPAD/HSGIC/03-2003/APRM/MOU/Annex II, 7 pp

New Partnership for Africa's Development (6th Summit of the NEPAD Heads of State and Government Implementation Committee) 'African Peer Review Mechanism Organisation and Process' (9 March 2003) NEPAD/HSGIC/03-2003/APRM/Guideline/O & P, 16 pp

Benelux BTWC peer review 2014–2015, Concept Paper (30 September 2014) 3 pp (Document on file with the author)

Financial Stability Board, 'FSB Framework for Strengthening Adherence to International Standards' (FSB 9 January 2010) 8 pp. <http://www.fsb.org/wp-content/uploads/r_100109a.pdf> accessed 13 May 2017

Financial Stability Board—Standing Committee on Standards Implementation, 'Handbook for FSB Peer Reviews' (FSB 7 January 2014) 14 pp. <http://www.fsb.org/wp-content/uploads/r_140106.pdf> accessed 13 May 2017

Financial Stability Board—Standing Committee on Standards Implementation, 'Handbook for FSB Peer Reviews' (FSB 12 March 2015) 14 pp. <http://www.fsb.org/wp-content/uploads/FSB-Peer-Review-Handbook-12-March-2015.pdf> accessed 13 May 2017

UNGA Res 60/251 UN Doc A/RES/60/251, 4 pp

UNHRC Res 5/1 UN Doc A/HRC/RES/5/1, 27 pp

UNHRC Decision 6/102 UN Doc A/HRC/DEC/6/102, 5 pp

UNHRC Res 16/21 UN Doc A/HRC/RES/16/21, 10 pp

UNHRC Decision 17/119 UN Doc A/HRC/DEC/17/119, 7 pp

International Monetary Fund, 'Managing Director's Statement on Strengthening Surveillance—2011 Triennial Surveillance Review' (27 October 2011) 6 pp. <http://www.imf.org/en/Publications/Policy-Papers/Issues/2016/12/31/Managing-Director-s-Statement-on-Strengthening-Surveillance-2011-Triennial-Surveillance-PP4607> assessed 13 May 2017

International Monetary Fund, 'Managing Director's Action Plan for Strengthening Surveillance—2014 Triennial Surveillance Review' (December 2014) 9 pp. <https://www.imf.org/external/np/pp/eng/2014/112114.pdf> accessed 26 May 2017

International Monetary Fund, 'Guidance Note for Surveillance Under Article IV Consultations' (May 2015) 55 pp. <http://www.imf.org/external/np/pp/eng/2015/031915.pdf> accessed 13 May 2017

Organisation for Economic Co-operation and Development, *Trade, Employment and Labour Standards, A Study of Core Workers' Rights and International Trade* (OECD, 9 September 1996) 248 pp

Organisation for Economic Co-operation and Development, *Mapping Global Value Chains, Policy Dialogue on Aid for Trade* (TAD/TC/WP/RD(2012)9, OECD, 3 December 2012) 44 pp

Organisation for Economic Co-operation and Development, *Export Restrictions: Benefits of Transparency and Good Practices* (TAD/TC/WP(2012)22/FINAL, OECD, 20 March 2013) 38 pp

Organisation for Economic Co-operation and Development, 'Information Note on the DAC Peer Review Process' (DCD(2013)6, OECD, 27 October 2014) 7 pp

Organisation for Economic Co-operation and Development, 'DAC Peer Review Reference Guide' (DCD/DAC(2014)52, OECD, 2014) 19 pp

2. Secondary sources (articles, books, compilations, and working papers)

Adisa, J, 'Making the Mechanism Work' (2002) 11(4) African Security Review, 110–14

Ashoff, G, '50 Years of Peer Reviews by the OECD's Development Assistance Committee: An Instrument of Quality Assurance and Mutual Learning' (2013) 12, German Development Institute, Briefing Paper, 2 <https://www.die-gdi.de/en/briefing-paper/article/50-years-of-peer-reviews-by-the-oecds-development-assistance-committee-an-instrument-of-quality-assurance-and-mutual-learning/> accessed 6 May 2017

Backer, LC, 'Private Actors and Public Governance Beyond the State: The Multinational Corporation, the Financial Stability Board, and the Global Governance Order' (2011) 18(2) Indiana Journal of Global Legal Studies 752–802

Bassiouni, MC and Schabas, WA (eds) *New Challenges for the UN Human Rights Machinery—What Future for the UN Treaty Body System and the Human Rights Council Procedure* (Intersentia Publishing 2011) 480 pp

Chukwumerije, O, 'Peer Review and the Promotion of Good Governance in Africa' [2006–2007] North Carolina Journal of International Law and Commercial Regulation 49–114

Cowan, JK and Billaud, J, 'Between Learning and Schooling: The Politics of Human Rights Monitoring at the Universal Periodic Review' (2015) 36(6) Third World Quarterly 1175–190

Curtis, JM, 'Intellectual Property Rights and International Trade: An Overview' (2012) The Centre for International Governance Innovation CIGI Papers No 3, 20 pp

Freedman, R, *The United Nations Human Rights Council—A Critique and Early Assessment* (Routledge 2013) 319 pp

Gadinis, S, 'The Financial Stability Board: The New Politics of International Financial Regulation' (2013) 48(2) Texas International Law Journal 157–76

Gruzd, S, 'The African Peer Review Mechanism: Assessing Origins, Institutional Relations and Achievements' (2009) No 29, Governance and APRM Programme, Occasional Paper, 19 pp. <http://dspace.africaportal.org/jspui/bitstream/123456789/29715/1/SAIIA%20Occasional%20Paper%20no%2029.pdf?1> accessed 6 May 2017

Herbert, R, 'The Survival of NEPAD and the African Peer Review Mechanism: A Critical Analysis' (2004) 11(1) South African Journal of International Affairs 21–38

International Monetary Fund, *Report by a Group of Independent Experts, External Evaluation of IMF Surveillance* (IMF 1999) 121 pp

International Monetary Fund—Independent Evaluation Office, *The Historical Development of IMF Governance* (IMF 2008) 23 pp

International Monetary Fund—Independent Evaluation Office, *Involvement in International Trade Policy Issues, Evaluation Report* (IMF 2009) 213 pp

International Monetary Fund—Independent Evaluation Office, *Studies of IMF Governance—A Compendium* (IMF 2009) 378 pp

International Monetary Fund—Strategy, Policy and Review Department, *Changing Patterns of Global Trade* (IMF 2012) 77 pp. <https://www.imf.org/external/pubs/ft/dp/2012/dp1201.pdf> accessed 17 June 2017

International Monetary Fund—Independent Evaluation Office, *The Role of the IMF as Trusted Advisor* (IMF 2013) 51 pp. <http://www.ieo-imf.org/ieo/files/completedevaluations/RITA_-_Main_Report.pdf> accessed 20 May 2017

International Monetary Fund, *From Stabilization to Sustainable Growth—Annual Report 2014* (IMF 2014) 78 pp

International Monetary Fund, *Tackling Challenges Together—Annual Report 2015* (IMF 2015) 112 pp

Kanbur, R, 'The African Peer Review Mechanism—An Assessment of Concept and Design' (2004) January, Cornell University, Working Paper, 15 pp. <http://www.arts.cornell.edu/poverty/kanbur/APRM.pdf > accessed 6 May 2017

Kebonang, Z and Fombad, CM, 'The African Peer Review Mechanism: Challenges and Prospects' in Henning Melber (ed), *AU, NEPAD and the APRM—Democratisation Efforts Explored* (2006) Current African Issues No 32, 39–54 <http://www.diva-portal.org/smash/get/diva2:240536/FULLTEXT02.pdf> accessed 13 May 2017

Killander, M, 'The African Peer Review Mechanism and Human Rights: The First Reviews and the Way Forward' (2008) 30(1) Human Rights Quarterly 41–75

Kishore, A and Mohanty, D, 'How Effective Will the IMF's New Surveillance Framework Be?' (2008) 43(18) Economic and Political Weekly 31–36

Lavigne, R and Schembri, L, *Strengthening IMF Surveillance: An Assessment of Recent Reforms* (2009–2010) Bank of Canada, Discussion Paper, 19 pp. <https://www.econstor.eu/handle/10419/66936> accessed 6 May 2017

Lombardi, D and Woods, N, 'The Politics of Influence: An Analysis of IMF Surveillance' (2008) 15(5) Review of International Political Economy 711–39

Mangu, AM, 'The African Union and the Promotion of Democracy and Good Political Governance under the African Peer-Review Mechanism: 10 Years On' (2014) No 1 Africa Review 59–72

McMahon, E and Ascherio, M, 'A Step Ahead in Promoting Human Rights? The Universal Periodic Review of the UN Human Rights Council' (2012) 18 Global Governance 231–48

McMahon, ER, Busia, K, and Ascherio, M, 'Comparing Peer Reviews: The Universal Periodic Review of the UN Human Rights Council and the African Peer Review Mechanism' (2013) 12 African and Asian Studies 266–89

Momani, B, 'Assessing the Utility of, and Measuring Learning from, Canada's IMF Article IV Consultations' (2006) 39(2) Canadian Journal of Political Science 249–69

Momani, B, 'IMF Staff: Missing Link in Fund Reform Proposals' (2007) 2 Review of International Organizations 39–57

Moschella, M, 'IMF Surveillance in Crisis: The Past, Present and Future of the Reform Process' (2012) 26(1) Global Society 43–60

Mussa, M, 'IMF Surveillance' (1997) 87(2) The American Economic Review 28–31

Pagani, F, 'Peer Review, a Tool for Global Co-Operation and Change' (2002) No 235 The OECD Observer 55–56, <http://oecdobserver.org/news/archivestory.php/aid/881/Peer_review.html> accessed 13 May 2017

Redondo, ED, 'The Universal Periodic Review of the UN Human Rights Council: An Assessment of the First Session' (2008) 7(3) Chinese Journal of International Law 721–34

Redondo, ED, 'The Universal Periodic Review—Is There Life Beyond Naming and Shaming in Human Rights Implementation' (2012) 4 New Zealand Law Review 673–706

Revill, J, 'A Peer-Review Mechanism for the Biological and Toxin Weapons Convention' (UNIDIR, 2013) 96 pp. <http://sro.sussex.ac.uk/43353/9/UNPeer_Review.pdf> accessed 13 May 2017

Rivera, HC (ed) *The Special Procedures of the Human Rights Council—A Brief Look from the Inside and Perspectives from Outside* (Intersentia Publishing 2015) 160 pp

Schäfer, A, 'A New Form of Governance? Comparing the Open Method of Coordination to Multilateral Surveillance by the IMF and the OECD' (2004), MPIFG Working Paper No 04/5, 21 pp. <https://www.econstor.eu/bitstream/10419/41651/1/639580173.pdf> accessed 6 May 2017

Spier, R, 'The History of the Peer-Review Process' (2002) 20(8) Trends in Biotechnology 357–58

Svensson, NL, 'The Universal Periodic Review—A Study on the Effectiveness of the United Nations Human Rights Council's Monitoring Mechanism' (2015) 9(5) Vienna Journal on International Constitutional Law <https://www.icl-journal>

Svensson, NL, 'The Universal Periodic Review—A Study on the Effectiveness of the United Nations Human Rights Council's Monitoring Mechanism' (Stockholm University, Faculty of Law, 2014) 87. <http://www.pcom/download/4fe235aea328fcc9974200b4d47660a5/ICL_Thesis_Vol_9_5_15.pdf> accessed 13 May 2017

United Nations Conference on Trade and Development, *World Investment Report 2011—Non-Equity Modes of International Production and Development* (UNCTAD/WIR/2011, UNCTAD, 26 July 2011) 226 pp

United Nations Conference on Trade and Development, *Feed for Improving the Efficiency of the Application of UNCTAD Voluntary Peer Reviews* (TD/RBP/CONF.8/10, UNCTAD, 27 April 2015) 17 pp

United Nations System Task Team on the Post-2015 UN Development Agenda, Science, Technology and Innovation and Intellectual Property Rights: The Vision for Development, 2012, 14 pp

University of Oxford, *The Report of the Oxford Martin Commission for Future Generations* (Oxford Martin School, October 2013) 85 pp

World Economic Forum, *Mega-Regional Trade Agreements—Game Changers or Costly Distractions for the World Trading System*, 49 pp. <http://www3.weforum.org/docs/GAC/2014/WEF_GAC_TradeFDI_MegaRegionalTradeAgreements_Report_2014.pdf> accessed 25 May 2017 (hereafter World Economic Forum, *Mega-Regional Trade Agreements—Game Changers or Costly Distractions for the World Trading System*)

Index

www.ingramcontent.com/pod-product-compliance
Lightning Source LLC
LaVergne TN
LVHW020056220926
848484LV00002BB/550

* 9 7 8 0 1 9 8 8 1 7 6 1 1 *